ST/ESA/STAT/SER.F/113

Department of Economic and Social Affairs
Statistics Division

Studies in Methods
Handbook on National Accounting
Series F No. 113

Financial Production, Flows and Stocks in the System of National Accounts

United Nations

EUROPEAN CENTRAL BANK
EUROSYSTEM

New York, 2015

Department of Economic and Social Affairs

The Department of Economic and Social Affairs of the United Nations Secretariat is a vital interface between global policies in the economic, social and environmental spheres and national action. The Department works in three main interlinked areas: (i) it compiles, generates and analyses a wide range of economic, social and environmental data and information on which States Members of the United Nations draw to review common problems and to take stock of policy options; (ii) it facilitates the negotiations of Member States in many intergovernmental bodies on joint courses of action to address ongoing or emerging global challenges; and (iii) it advises interested Governments on the ways and means of translating policy frameworks developed in United Nations conferences and summits into programmes at the country level and, through technical assistance, helps build national capacities.

Note

The designations used and the presentation of material in this publication do not imply the expression of any opinion whatsoever on the part of the Secretariat of the United Nations concerning the legal status of any country, territory, city or area, or of its authorities, or concerning the delimitation of its frontiers or boundaries.

The term "country" as used in this publication also refers, as appropriate, to territories or areas.

The designations "developed regions" and "developing regions" are intended for statistical convenience and do not necessarily express a judgment about the stage reached by a particular country or area in the development process.

Symbols of United Nations documents are composed of letters combined with figures. Mention of such a symbol indicates a reference to a United Nations document.

ST/ESA/STAT/SER.F/113

UNITED NATIONS PUBLICATION
Sales No.: 14.XVII.7

ISBN: 978-92-1-161577-7
eISBN: 978-92-1-054153-4

Acknowledgements

The *Handbook of National Accounting: Financial Production, Flows and Stocks in the System of National Accounts* (the Handbook) has been jointly prepared by the Statistics Division of the Department of Economic and Social Affairs of the United Nations Secretariat and the European Central Bank Directorate General Statistics as part of a series of handbooks on national accounting being developed to assist countries and international organizations in the implementation of the *System of National Accounts 2008* (2008 SNA).

Throughout the process of developing the Handbook, helpful guidance was provided by a review group comprising experts in national accounts and monetary and financial statistics from national statistical offices, central banks and international organizations during meetings and consultations from 2011 to 2013. Members of the review group included (in alphabetical order of countries followed by international organizations) Derick Cullen (Australia), Michael Andreasch (Austria), Patrick O'Hagan (Canada), Feng Lu (China), Chihiro Sakuraba and Yoshiko Sato (Japan), Vetle Hvidsten (Norway), Filipa Lima (Portugal), Karen Kuhn (South Africa), Susan Hume McIntosh and Marshall Reinsdorf (United States of America), Artak Harutyunyan and Kimberly Zieschang (International Monetary Fund), and Nadim Ahmad, Michèle Chavoix-Mannato and Satoru Hagino (Organisation for Economic Co-operation and Development).

The *Handbook* has also benefited greatly from the numerous useful comments and suggestions made by national statistical offices, central banks, regional commissions, international organizations and colleagues from the Statistics Division and European Central Bank, as well as individual experts, during global consultations in May and June 2011 and in June and July 2013.

Vetle Hvidsten and Herman Smith (Statistics Division) developed earlier drafts of the first three chapters under the general supervision and guidance of Viet Vu. Benson Sim completed these chapters under the general supervision and guidance of Herman Smith. He also introduced a number of illustrative worked examples, with step-by-step guidance, on the compilation and allocation of the production of financial services with assistance from Feng Lu and Qiong Qiu (National Bureau of Statistics of China), as well as Nathan Menton and Leonardo Souza (Statistics Division).

Reimund Mink (European Central Bank) prepared the remaining seven chapters of the Handbook, working in close collaboration with colleagues in the Directorate General Statistics of the European Central Bank. These chapters deal with the design, compilation and use of an integrated system of sectoral financial accounts, other flow accounts and balance sheets—also in the context of from-whom-to-whom relationships. During this drafting process he got broad assistance and support from Remigio Echeverría. Andreas Hertkorn and Jorge Diz Dias (European Central Bank) contributed to the drafts by providing substantial comments. The members of the European System of Central Banks Statistics Committee also gave useful comments based on regular written consultations.

Ivo Havinga (Statistics Division) and Werner Bier (European Central Bank) provided overall supervision of the work.

Contents

Worked Examples

Tables

Boxes

Figures

Abbreviations

ABCP	Asset-backed commercial paper
ABO	Accrued benefit obligation
ABS	Asset-backed securities
BEA	Bureau of Economic Analysis
BIS	Bank for International Settlements
BOP	Balance of payments
BPM	Balance of Payments and International Investment Position Manual
CCD	Certificates of capital development
CDO	Collateralized debt obligations
CDR	Credit default risk
CMBS	Commercial mortgage-backed securities
CMO	Collateralized mortgage obligations
CPI	Consumer price index
ECB	European Central Bank
EDP	Excessive debt procedure
ELN	Equity-linked note
ESA	European System of National and Regional Accounts
ESO	Employee stock option
ETF	Exchange-traded fund
EU	European Union
FDI	Foreign direct investment
FISIM	Financial intermediation services indirectly measured
FRA	Forward rate agreement
FSI	Financial soundness indicator
GAAP	Generally Accepted Accounting Principles
GAB	General Arrangements to Borrow
GDP	Gross domestic product
GFSM	Government Finance Statistics Manual
GNI	Gross national income
HSS	Handbook on Securities Statistics
IASB	International Accounting Standards Board
ICPF	Insurance corporations and pension funds
IFRS	International Financial Reporting Standards
IIP	International investment position
IMF	International Monetary Fund
IPO	Initial public offering
ISIC	International Standard Industrial Classification of All Economic Activities
ISIN	International securities identification number
ISO	International Organization for Standardization

ISWGNA	Intersecretariat Working Group on National Accounts
ITRS	International transactions reporting system
LIBOR	London Interbank Offered Rate
MFI	Monetary financial institution
MFSMCG	Monetary and Financial Statistics Manual and Compilation Guide
MMF	Money market fund
MNE	Multinational enterprise
NAB	New Arrangements to Borrow
NACE	European Classification of Economic Activities
NAV	Net asset value
n.e.c.	Not elsewhere classified
NFA	Net financial assets
NPISH	Non-profit institution serving households
NPV	Net present value
OECD	Organisation for Economic Cooperation and Development
OTC	Over-the-counter
PBO	Projected benefit obligation
PIM	Perpetual inventory method
PPI	Producer price index
PSDSG	Public Sector Debt Securities: Guide for Compilers and Users
REIT	Real estate investment trust
RMBS	Residential mortgage-backed securities
RMSPE	Root mean square prediction error
SBS	Security-by-security (database)
SDMX	Statistical Data and Metadata Exchange
SDR	Special Drawing Rights
SNA	System of National Accounts
SPE	Special purpose entity
STRIPS	Separate trading of registered interest and principal securities
TFI	Table on financing and investment
VAT	Value added tax
VRN	Variable-rate note

Introduction

Background

At its thirty-ninth and fortieth sessions in February 2008 and February 2009, the United Nations Statistical Commission adopted the *System of National Accounts 2008* (2008 SNA) as the international statistical standard for national accounts and encouraged Member States, regional and subregional organizations to implement the standard and support all aspects of the implementation of the updated SNA. Countries are encouraged to use the 2008 SNA as the framework for compiling and integrating economic and related statistics, as well as in the national and international reporting of national accounts statistics. At its fortieth session, the Statistical Commission also requested a coordinated effort by the Intersecretariat Working Group on National Accounts (ISWGNA) on the development of manuals, implementation guides, data collection tools and standardized training material, and in use of modern and innovative tools, such as distance learning and knowledge bases, to provide easy access on a range of information, including best practices, to facilitate the implementation of the SNA. The ISWGNA subsequently also formulated a global strategy for the implementation of the 2008 SNA and supporting statistics, taking into account the different levels of implementation of existing international standards and the statistical capacity in the various countries.

Context and purpose

The *Handbook of National Accounting: Financial Production, Flows and Stocks in the System of National Accounts* (the Handbook) is one of a number of manuals, handbooks and guidance notes initiated by the ISWGNA to strengthen the statistical capacity for compiling national accounts, in accordance with the implementation programme for the 2008 SNA and supporting statistics, and in line with the request of the Statistical Commission. The Handbook has been jointly prepared by the Statistics Division of the Department of Economic and Social Affairs of the United Nations Secretariat and the European Central Bank Directorate General Statistics. The Handbook complements the 2008 SNA and related manuals, handbooks and guides. The concepts are described and defined in line with the 2008 SNA. Manuals and handbooks which have been developed in recent years, or are being developed to be consistent with the 2008 SNA, include the *Balance of Payments and International Investment Position Manual, Sixth Edition* (BPM6), the *Monetary and Financial Statistics Manual and Compilation Guide* (MFSMCG), the *Government Finance Statistics Manual 2014* (GFSM 2014), the *Handbook on Securities Statistics* (HSS) and the *Public Sector Debt Statistics: Guide for Compilers and Users* (PSDSG). In particular, the Handbook and the MFSMCG are complementary, as the former focuses on the financial corporations sector in relation to the other sectors of an economy and the rest of the world from an SNA perspective, while the latter focuses on monetary and financial statistics as a building block for policy purposes.

There are instances in which special considerations may need to be applied to the compilation of monetary and financial statistics in certain countries. One example is countries with financial systems that are governed by Islamic rules and principles (sharī'ah), which, among other things, prohibit usurious payment (riba), including predetermined returns on borrowed funds for specific terms. The Handbook will not discuss the main features of Islamic financial institutions or the primary types of Islamic financial instruments and their treatment in monetary and financial statistics, as they are already covered in the MFSMCG and the HSS (Part 1, Debt securities issues).

Structure of the Handbook

The Handbook comprises 10 chapters. Chapter 1 provides an overview of the 2008 SNA accounting framework and its sequence of accounts, the institutional sectors in the 2008 SNA, and valuation and recording principles. Chapter 2 describes each subsector of the financial corporations sector within the 2008 SNA framework. In addition to the breakdown of the subsectors in the 2008 SNA, which basically follows that in the International Standard Industrial Classification of All Economic Activities (ISIC), this chapter also provides guidance on other ways to group these subsectors. Chapter 3 goes on to discuss the ways in which financial services are provided and charged for, as well as provides guidance on how to compute and allocate the charges and output. The chapter also discusses how to compute and allocate the output and related transactions associated with social insurance schemes, including social security schemes. It also discusses the supplementary table for pensions which was introduced in the 2008 SNA to show the extent of pension schemes included in, and excluded from, the 2008 SNA sequence of accounts. In a number of sections, the chapter also describes how to compute volume measures of the output of financial services and social security funds. This chapter concludes by describing the types of property income which are payable and receivable by financial corporations and the possible data sources from which to derive and allocate the property income.

Chapter 4 deals with how the 2008 SNA classifies financial assets and liabilities. It also provides guidance on other ways to group these financial instruments. Chapter 5 deals with how to value financial assets and liabilities in the 2008 SNA and how to handle revaluations in these instruments. As will be observed, even with an explanation of subsectors and financial instruments, the framework is still not fully articulated. It shows which sectors and subsectors incur loans and make deposits, but it does not allow an in-depth examination of the intermediation process whereby a financial institution draws in funds, repackages them and issues them as other instruments to other units. In order to explore this, a three-dimensional "from-whom-to-whom" style of presentation is needed. The basics of the from-whom-to-whom framework are dealt with in Chapter 6.

Chapter 7 looks at how to collect monetary and other statistics for such a framework. Chapter 8 deals with tables and charts to present the accounts under this framework. Chapter 9 looks at the use of these accounts for policy and other purposes. Chapter 10, the last chapter, goes beyond the confines of an economic territory and deals with how to compile such accounts for financial corporations within an economic or monetary union.

Where appropriate, illustrative worked examples are provided in the Handbook, especially in chapter 3, to give compilers and users a better picture of how to apply and interpret the various concepts.

Conventions for references

Given the nature of the Handbook and its strong linkages with the 2008 SNA framework, it is inevitable that the Handbook will make many references to the 2008 SNA. In particular, the text in the Handbook directly follows the text in the 2008 SNA in numerous instances to avoid any inference that a different meaning is intended. Owing to this, references to specific paragraphs of the 2008 SNA are not included in the text of the Handbook. Instead, where appropriate, references to particular chapters of the 2008 SNA are usually specified at the start of a section in each chapter. In addition, the Handbook does not provide a thorough explanation of the definitions and methods of national accounts, as it is assumed that the reader will have a copy of the 2008 SNA available for cross reference. However, the Handbook does provide detailed explanations of classifications and concepts if:

(a) The 2008 SNA is not detailed enough for the accounting of financial services, flows and balance sheets;

(b) The demands of compilers and users require more explanation than is given in the 2008 SNA, such as for the vertical and horizontal balancing, as well as balancing between flows and stocks, or more detailed breakdowns of financial instruments, for example by maturity, currency, interest rate, counterpart sector, country, or type of activity.

Chapter 1
System of National Accounts 2008 architecture

A. Introduction

1.1. This chapter provides an overview of the central framework of the 2008 SNA. First, the conceptual elements of the central framework which reflect its accounting structure are presented. This is followed by a description of the coverage and accounting principles of the central framework. The chapter then describes the integrated economic accounts, which comprise a set of accounts that is central to understanding the economic process. It concludes with an overview of the three-dimensional (from-whom-to-whom) accounts showing financial transactions and stocks of financial assets which fully articulate the intermediation process whereby a financial institution draws in funds, repackages them and issues them as other instruments to other units.

B. The central framework

Reference:
2008 SNA, Chapter 2, Overview

1.2. The central framework of the 2008 SNA consists of the following five conceptual elements which reflect its accounting structure:

(a) Integrated economic accounts by institutional sector which trace production and income through to wealth accumulation for each institutional sector;

(b) Supply and use framework, which traces the production of products by industries through their use as intermediate inputs or final demand by institutional sectors;

(c) Sociodemographic and employment tables which are consistent with the accounting structure of the 2008 SNA for per capita and productivity analysis;

(d) Three-dimensional (from-whom-to-whom) accounts of financial transactions and stocks of financial assets showing the relationship between sectors;

(e) Functional accounts whereby certain transactions of institutional sectors are presented according to the purpose they serve, for example expenditure by general government (health, education, defence, etc.), households (accommodation, food, transportation, health, etc.) and corporations (intermediate use and investment).

1.3. The accounting structure of the central framework can be used to create a macroeconomic database which is suitable for analysing and evaluating the performance of an economy. Some specific uses of the accounting structure include monitoring the behaviour of the economy through key aggregates such as gross domestic product (GDP) and GDP per capita, macroeconomic analysis such as the econometric analysis of the causal mechanisms at work within an economy, and international comparisons such as cross-country comparisons of GDP and GDP per head and structural statistics such as ratios of investment, taxes or government expenditure to GDP.

1.4. The central framework also offers flexibility in that attention paid to various aspects of it may vary according to analytical requirements and data availability. Thus, given the objectives of this Handbook, the integrated economic accounts and three-dimensional accounts of flows and stocks will be explained in the publication.

C. Coverage of the central framework

References:
2008 SNA, Chapter 2, Overview
2008 SNA, Chapter 4, Institutional units and sectors
2008 SNA, Chapter 26, The rest of the world accounts and links to the balance of payments

1. Institutional units and sectors

1.5. The institutional sectors and units within each institutional sector are the building blocks of the integrated sequence of accounts. An institutional sector groups institutional units on the basis of their principal functions, behaviour and objectives. An institutional unit is an economic entity that is capable, in its own right, of owning assets, incurring liabilities and engaging in economic activities and in transactions with other entities. There are two main types of units that may qualify as institutional units, namely persons or groups of persons in the form of households, and legal or social entities.

1.6. To describe production, income, expenditure or financial flows, and balance sheets, institutional units are grouped into five mutually exclusive institutional sectors based on their principal functions, behaviour and objectives: (*a*) non-financial corporations; (*b*) financial corporations; (*c*) general government; (*d*) households; and (*e*) non-profit institutions serving households (NPISHs) (table 1.1). The five institutional sectors together make up the total economy. The system allows for a complete set of accounts and balance sheets to be compiled for each institutional sector, for the total economy and for the rest of the world. Each institutional sector may also contain a number of subsectors which are split according to hierarchical classification. The division of sectors into subsectors depends upon the type of analysis to be undertaken, the needs of policymakers, the availability of data and the economic circumstances and institutional arrangements within a country.

Table 1.1
Institutional sectors

Total economy
◆ Non-financial corporations
◆ Financial corporations
◆ General government
◆ Households
◆ Non-profit institutions serving households (NPISHs)
Rest of the world

1.7. The institutional units in the economy may also engage in economic activities with units outside the economy. Units which are outside the economy are referred to as the "rest of the world". Thus, whenever accounts are drawn up for institutional sectors, as well as an account for the total economy, a further account is shown showing the relationship with the rest of the world. In effect, therefore, transactions with the rest of the world are recorded as if the rest of the world is a de facto sixth sector. The rest of the world sector plays a role in the accounting structure similar to that of an institutional sector. A resource or a change in liabilities for the rest of the world is a use or a change in assets for the total economy and vice versa. In the rest of the world account, if a balancing item is positive, it means a surplus for the rest of the world and a deficit for the total economy, and vice versa if the balancing item is negative.

2. Residence

1.8. The residence of each institutional unit is the economic territory with which it has the strongest connection, expressed as its centre of predominant economic interest. An institutional unit is resident in an economic territory when there exists, within the economic territory, some location, dwelling, place of production, or other premises on which or from which the unit engages and intends to continue engaging, either indefinitely or over a finite but long period of time, in economic activities and transactions on a significant scale. The location need not be fixed so long as it remains within the economic territory. Actual or intended location for one year or more is used as an operational definition; while the choice of one year as a specific period is somewhat arbitrary, it is adopted to avoid uncertainty and facilitate international consistency. Most units have strong connections to only one economy but with globalization, a growing number have strong links to two or more economies. For highly mobile individuals who have close connections with two or more economies, the residence is determined on the basis of the territory in which the predominant amount of time is spent in the year. In addition, those studying overseas; patients seeking medical treatment overseas; diplomats, military personnel and civil servants employed in government enclaves abroad and their households; and crews of ships, aircraft, oil rigs, space stations or other similar equipment that operate outside a territory or across several territories are considered to be residents of their home economic territory, even if the length of stay from their home economic territory is more than one year.

1.9. As a general principle, an enterprise is resident in an economic territory when the enterprise is engaged in a significant amount of production of goods and/or services from a location in the territory. In contrast to individuals and households, which may have connections to two or more economies, enterprises are almost always connected to a single economy. Taxation and other legal requirements tend to result in the use of a separate legal entity for operations in each legal jurisdiction. In addition, a separate institutional unit is identified for statistical purposes where a single legal entity has substantial operations in two or more territories (for example, for branches, land ownership and multiterritory enterprises). As a result of splitting such legal entities, the residence of each of the subsequently identified enterprises is usually clear. In some cases, the physical location of an enterprise is not sufficient to identify its residence because the enterprise has little or no physical presence, for example, its administration is entirely contracted out to other entities. Banking, insurance, investment funds, securitization vehicles and some special purpose entities may operate in this way. Many trusts, corporations, or foundations that hold private wealth also have little or no physical presence. In the absence of any significant physical dimension to an enterprise, its residence is determined according to the economic territory under whose laws the enterprise is incorporated or registered. The incorporation and registration represent a substantial degree of connection to the economy, associated with jurisdiction over the enterprise's existence and operations. In contrast, other connections such as ownership, location of assets, or location of its managers or administrators may be less clear-cut.[1]

[1] As an example, if a financial corporation is incorporated in a tax haven but has all its employees in another economy, it is classified as a resident institutional unit of the tax haven. Transactions between the financial corporation and its employees will be recorded in international transactions in the rest of the world account. As another example, a hedge fund might have feeder funds in, say, the United States, but register its main investment fund in the Cayman Islands. In this instance, the hedge fund is classified as a resident institutional unit of the Cayman Islands, while the feeder funds are classified as resident institutional units of the United States.

3. Corporations and non-profit institutions

1.10. In the SNA, the term "corporation" is used more broadly than in just the legal sense. In general, all entities that are (a) capable of generating a profit or other financial gain for their owners; (b) recognized at law as separate legal entities from their owners who enjoy limited liability; and (c) set up for purposes of engaging in market production, are treated as corporations in the SNA, however they may describe themselves or whatever they may be called. As well as legally constituted corporations, the term "corporations" is used to include cooperatives, limited liability partnerships, notional resident units and quasi-corporations. Whenever the term "corporation" is used, the broader coverage rather than the narrow legal definition is intended unless otherwise stated. By definition, corporations are market producers. They can be split between non-financial and financial corporations. This Handbook focuses on financial corporations and their economic interactions with the other institutional units.

1.11. Financial corporations consist of all resident corporations that are principally engaged in providing financial services, including insurance and pension funding services, to other institutional units. The production of financial services is the result of financial intermediation, financial risk management, liquidity transformation or auxiliary financial activities.

1.12. Financial services are also provided by non-profit institutions which are market producers. Non-profit institutions (NPIs) are legal or social entities created for the purpose of producing or distributing goods and services, whose status does not permit them to be a source of income, profit or other financial gain for the institutional units that establish, control or finance them. In practice, their productive activities are bound to generate either surpluses or deficits, but any surpluses they make cannot be appropriated by other institutional units. The articles of association by which they are established are drawn up in such a way that the institutional units that control or manage them are not entitled to a share in any profits or other income they generate.

D. Accounting principles of the central framework

References:
2008 SNA, Chapter 2, Overview
2008 SNA, Chapter 3, Stocks, flows and accounting rules
2008 SNA, Chapter 6, The production account
2008 SNA, Chapter 11, The financial account
BPM6, Chapter 3, Accounting principles
MFSMCG, Chapter 5, Stocks, flows and accounting rules

1. Principle of double and quadruple entry accounting

1.13. For an institutional unit, national accounting is based on the principle of double entry, as in business accounting. Each transaction must be recorded twice, once as a resource (or a change in liabilities) and once as a use (or a change in assets). The total of transactions recorded as resources or changes in liabilities and the total of transactions recorded as uses or changes in assets must be equal, thus permitting a check of the consistency of the accounts. Economic flows that are not transactions have their counterpart directly as changes in net worth.

1.14. In principle, the recording of the consequences of an action as it affects all units and all sectors is based on a principle of quadruple entry accounting, because most transactions involve two institutional units. Each transaction of this type must be recorded twice by each of the two transactors involved. On the other hand, internal transactions or transactions within a single unit (such as consumption of fixed capital and own-account consumption of output by the producing unit) require only two entries, whose values have to be estimated, as it is not necessary to enter counterpart entries to show how these transactions are financed.

1.15. The transactions can be split between financial and non-financial transactions. A financial transaction always has a counterpart entry in the 2008 SNA, which is recorded in a non-financial account or the financial account itself. When a transaction and its counterpart are both financial transactions, they change the distribution of the portfolio of financial assets and liabilities and may change the totals of both financial assets and liabilities of the financial corporations involved, but they do not change the difference between total financial assets and liabilities.

1.16. An example of the counterpart to a financial transaction being another financial transaction is the issue or redemption of a debt security. This should result in the recording of four entries—two for each institutional unit involved in the transaction (the debtor and the creditor). As an illustration, debt securities are issued by a financial corporation (the debtor) and acquired by a household (the creditor) in exchange for currency or a transferable deposit. In the financial account for the financial corporation, an increase is recorded in liabilities (debt securities) and in financial assets (currency or transferable deposits). In the financial account of the household, an increase in financial assets (debt securities) is offset by a decrease in financial assets (currency or transferable deposits), with no change recorded in liabilities.

1.17. Transactions can involve the exchange of one financial instrument for another without an exchange of currency or transferable deposits. Such operations include, for example, the conversion of debt securities into equity securities. Within a framework of "from-whom-to-whom" accounts, such conversions should be treated as two financial transactions, that is, as a redemption of debt securities and an issue of equity securities.

1.18. Examples where the counterpart entry of a financial transaction is a non-financial transaction include transactions in products, distributive transactions, or transactions in non-financial non-produced assets. If the counterpart entry of a financial transaction is not a financial transaction, the net lending/net borrowing of the resident or non-resident institutional units involved will change.

1.19. The counterpart entry of a financial transaction may also be a transfer (current or capital). In this case, the financial transaction involves a change in ownership of a financial asset, an assumption of a liability as debtor (debt assumption) or the simultaneous liquidation of a financial asset and the counterpart liability (debt cancellation or debt forgiveness). Debt assumptions and debt cancellations are distributive transactions classified in the capital transfers (D9) category and recorded in the capital account.

1.20. The counterpart entry of a financial transaction may also be property income in the form of interest (D41), distributed income of corporations (dividends (D421) and withdrawals of income from quasi-corporations (D422)), reinvested earnings on foreign direct investment (FDI) (D43), other investment income (investment income attributable to insurance policyholders (D441), investment income payable on pension entitlements (D442) and investment income attributable to holders of investment fund shares or units (D443)) or rent (D45). For example, dividends paid in cash by a corporation to a household are recorded in the allocation of primary income account of the corporation as a use under property income and as a negative acquisition of financial assets under currency and deposits in the financial account. In the households sector, it is recorded as a resource under property income in the allocation of primary income account and as an acquisition of financial assets under currency and deposits in the financial account.

1.21. Quadruple-entry accounting aims to ensure symmetry of the reporting by the institutional units involved, thus permitting complete consistency within the accounts in measuring variables across sectors and accounts. It guarantees that the closing balance on the balance sheet of each sector also reflects the transfer of income from one sector to another, thereby imposing stock-flow consistency on the system as well. This is very important for analysing and understanding the economic process. This feature is key to ensuring that many of the types of analyses provide consistent results.

2. Time of recording

1.22. One implication of the quadruple-entry accounting principle is that transactions and other flows have to be recorded at the same point in time for both institutional units involved.

1.23. The general principle in national accounting is that transactions between institutional units should be recorded when claims and obligations arise, are transformed or are cancelled. This form of recording is called an accrual basis. In many cases, there is a delay between the actual transaction and the corresponding payment or receipt, so transactions are recorded on a cash basis. These two different accounting approaches can result in transactions being recorded at different times.

1.24. The change of economic ownership determines the time of recording for transactions in goods, non-produced non-financial assets, and financial assets. Transactions in services are recorded when services are provided.

1.25. Distributive transactions (income and transfers) are recorded at the moment the related claims arise. This means that interest payable or receivable by a financial corporation is recorded on a continuous basis, dividends are recorded at the moment the shares go ex dividend, distributed profits are recorded when they actually take place, and reinvested earnings are recorded in the period in which the retained earnings accrue.

3. Valuation principles

1.26. Market valuation is the key principle for valuing transactions, as well as positions of assets and liabilities. The market value is that at which financial assets are acquired or disposed of, between willing parties, on the basis of commercial considerations only, excluding commissions, fees and taxes, whether charged explicitly, included in the purchaser's price or deducted from the seller's proceeds. This is because both debtors and creditors should record the same amount for the transaction in the same financial instrument. The commissions, fees and taxes should be recorded separately from the transaction in the financial asset and liability, under appropriate categories. In determining market values, trading parties also take account of accrued interest.

1.27. Market prices are usually available for tradable financial assets and liabilities, existing real estate (buildings and other structures plus the underlying land), existing transport equipment, crops and livestock, as well as for newly produced fixed assets and inventories. When there are no observable market prices available—which may be the case if there is a market but no assets have recently been sold on it, or if no market exists—estimates should be made of what the price would be if the assets were acquired on the market on the date to which the balance sheet relates.

1.28. Market prices are also applied to valuing goods and services—inclusive of appropriate taxes and subsidies and after taking into account any rebates or refunds. Unlike financial instruments, taxes are included in market prices, as it is not necessary to ensure that buyers and sellers of goods and services record the same amount for the same transaction.

1.29. Nominal valuation reflects the sum of funds originally advanced, plus any subsequent advances, less any repayments, plus any accrued interest. Nominal value refers to the outstanding amount the debtor owes to the creditor, which is composed of the outstanding principal amount including any accrued interest. It is usually applied to financial instruments such as loans and deposits. It refers to the outstanding amount the debtor owes to the creditor, which is composed of the outstanding principal amount including any accrued interest.

1.30. Nominal value is often mistakenly considered to be the same as face value. However, the two concepts are different: face value is defined as the amount of principal to be repaid. It is equivalent to the redemption price of a debt security excluding accrued interest.

1.31. At any specific point in time, the market value of a financial instrument may deviate from its nominal value due to revaluations arising from market price changes. Movements in market prices arise from general market conditions, such as changes in the market rate of interest; specific circumstances, such as changes in the perceived creditworthiness of the issuer of a financial instrument and changes in general market liquidity and in that specific to the financial instrument.

1.32. Thus, the following basic equations apply to positions in financial instruments:

Market value = Nominal value + Accumulated revaluations arising from market price changes

Face value = Nominal value − Accrued interest

Market value − Accumulation revaluations = Face value + Accrued interest

4. Aggregation and gross and net recording

1.33. Aggregation is the summation of all gross positions, transactions, revaluations and other changes in the volume of assets of institutional units belonging to a subsector, sector or an economy.

1.34. Netting is a process whereby accounting entries on the two sides of the account for the same transaction item and same institutional unit are offset against each another. This process is also known as net recording. In contrast, combinations in which all elementary items are shown for their full values are called gross recordings. The process of gross recording meets the legal requirements for presentation (showing actual payments of coupon, etc.) and preserves the consistency of the presentation with market statistics.

1.35. The 2008 SNA recommends gross recording apart from the degree of netting that is inherent in the classifications themselves. In fact, netting is already a feature of many of the recommendations of the 2008 SNA. It mostly serves to highlight an economically important property that is not apparent from gross data.

1.36. Netting is implicit in various transaction categories, the most outstanding example being "changes in inventories", which underlines the analytically significant aspect of overall capital formation rather than tracking daily additions and withdrawals. Similarly, with few exceptions, the financial account and other changes in assets accounts record increases in assets and in liabilities on a net basis, bringing out the final consequences of these types of flows at the end of the accounting period. All balancing items also involve netting. To avoid confusion, the SNA uses the words "gross" and "net" in a very restrictive sense. Apart from a few headings ("net premiums", "net worth" and "net lending or net borrowing"), the SNA classifications employ the word "net" exclusively to indicate the value of variables after deduction of consumption of fixed capital.

1.37. In the case of flows of financial assets and liabilities, the terms "net changes in assets" and "net changes in liabilities" are used to reflect the nature of the financial flows.. Financial flows reflect changes due to all credit and debit entries during an accounting period. That is, financial transactions are recorded on a net basis separately for each financial asset and liability. The use of the terms "net changes in assets" and "net changes in liabilities" brings the financial account into line with the convention used in the accumulation accounts. These are general terms that apply to both the financial account and the other changes in financial assets and liabilities account. The use of these terms also simplifies the interpretation of data. For both assets and liabilities, a positive change indicates an increase in stocks and a negative change indicates a decrease in stocks. The interpretation of increase or decrease under the credit or debit notion, however, depends on whether the increase or decrease refers to assets or liabilities (a debit for an asset is an increase while a debit for a liability is a decrease). While the debit and credit presentation is not emphasized for financial transactions, it is important to recognize and maintain the accounting identities; for example, a credit is always conceptually matched with a corresponding debit, the latter relating to either an increase in an asset, or a reduction in a liability.

5. Consolidation

1.38. Consolidation must be distinguished from netting. Consolidation refers to the elimination from both uses and resources of transactions which occur between units that are grouped together and to the elimination of financial assets and the counterpart liabilities. Consolidation can arise at various levels of grouping. Consolidation is the approach used by supervisors to present data, as opposed to aggregation, which is the approach used in the compilation of the financial account.

1.39. As a matter of principle, transactions between institutional units within subsectors or sectors are not consolidated. The 2008 SNA focuses on the unconsolidated presentation of accounting entries, which is recommended for monetary and macroeconomic analysis. Such a presentation sums up all gross positions, transactions, revaluations and other changes in the volume of assets of institutional units belonging to a sector or subsector vis-à-vis all institutional units belonging to the same sector or subsector, to other sectors of the economy and to other economies. In practice, data limitations often make a consolidated presentation necessary. For example, the transactions of the households sector may be derived as a residual, so flows or claims within the sector cannot be shown on a gross basis. Also, corporations typically consolidate their subsidiaries in corporate tax data. In addition, globalization has resulted in the increasing presence of multinational enterprises (MNEs). This means that statisticians have to ensure that the national and financial accounts are compiled with a domestic consolidation of MNEs so that the transactions of overseas units of these MNEs are excluded. This can be done by surveying domestically consolidated enterprises directly.

1.40. However, consolidated accounts may be compiled for complementary presentations and analyses. In the 2008 SNA, institutional units are grouped together and consolidated at a subsectoral or sectoral level. Consolidation at a subsectoral or sectoral level eliminates intra-subsectoral or sectoral positions and flows.

1.41. Consolidation should not be seen as a sheer loss of information; it entails an elementary specification by the transaction partner. In some cases, it may be useful for analytical purposes to present consolidated data. One example of the analytical enrichment of information is the consolidation of the intrasectoral position of domestic nonfinancial corporations showing the "external need" (by other economic sectors) of this sector when comparing non-consolidated and consolidated figures.

1.42. A second form of consolidation, namely consolidation at a (corporate) group level, is common practice, although it is not recommended in the SNA. There are large groups of financial or non-financial corporations or conglomerates whereby a parent corporation controls several subsidiaries, some of which may control subsidiaries of their own. Therefore, the concept of a group of corporations deviates from the grouping or aggregation of institutional units to an institutional sector, as it groups institutional units based on the concept of control.

1.43. Consolidation at a group level eliminates the positions and flows of liabilities that have been incurred by institutional units within the same group of financial or non-financial corporations as the financial asset holders. If related institutional units are grouped together to form one corporate group (for example, foreign branches of domestic banks are grouped with their parent bank), then all intra-group positions and flows of financial instruments within that reporting entity are eliminated from the information reported—that is, all positions and flows among the branches and with their parent are eliminated. This approach can involve both residence-based and non-residence-based data and is relevant for financial stability and globalization analysis.

1.44. For financial stability purposes, it is important to have information on financial assets consolidated at the level of groups of corporations, such as conglomerates, with a breakdown by debtor, currency, maturity and type of interest rate. The stability of a financial system can only be assessed by analysing the broad financial interlink information given by group consolidated data. Nevertheless, strong intra-sector linkages may be a source of financial instability. A comparison of consolidated and unconsolidated accounts may help to provide information on these links. The strengths and vulnerabilities of a financial system can also be assessed using the financial soundness indicators (FSIs) developed by the International Monetary Fund (IMF). As described by IMF (2006), FSIs are indicators of the current financial health and soundness of the financial institutions in a country, and of their corporate and household counterparts. They include both aggregated individual institution data and indicators that are representative of the markets in which the financial institutions operate. FSIs are calculated and disseminated for the purpose of supporting macroprudential analysis. This is the assessment and surveillance of the strengths and vulnerabilities of financial systems, with the objective of enhancing financial stability and, in particular, limiting the likelihood of failure of the financial system.

E. The integrated economic accounts

References:
2008 SNA, Chapter 2, Overview
2008 SNA, Chapter 4, Institutional units and sectors
2008 SNA, Chapter 13, The balance sheet
BPM6, Chapter 3, Accounting principles

1.45. The accounting model of the 2008 SNA traces the transmission of income to wealth using the "sequence of accounts." The building blocks of the sequence of accounts are the five resident institutional sectors and the rest of the world. The whole economic process from production, income, consumption and saving through the accumulation of assets to the position of net worth is recorded for each resident institutional sector and the rest of the world.

1.46. Table 1.2 illustrates how transactions, revaluations, other changes in the volume of assets and liabilities, and stocks are recorded in the 2008 SNA. Transactions are presented in the current account, which covers the production account and the various income accounts, as well as in the capital and financial accounts. Other flows cover revaluations and other changes in the volume of assets and liabilities; they are recorded in the revaluation account and in the other changes in the volume of assets account. Stocks of assets and liabilities are recorded on the balance sheet.

Table 1.2
Transactions, other flows and stocks as presented in the 2008 SNA

		Transactions	Other flows	Stocks
Current accounts	Production account	Production of goods and services, as well as the generation, distribution, redistribution and use of income		
	Generation of income account			
	Allocation of primary income account			
	Secondary distribution of income account			
	Use of income account			
Accumulation accounts	Capital account	Net acquisition of non-financial assets, saving and capital transfers		
	Financial account	Net acquisition of financial assets and net incurrence of liabilities		
	Other changes in the volume of assets account		Other changes in the volume of non-financial assets, financial assets and liabilities	
	Revaluation account		Holding gains and losses in non-financial assets, financial assets and liabilities	
Balance sheet				Non-financial assets, financial assets, liabilities and net worth as a balancing item

1.47. Two sequences of accounts are discussed in this section: the (vertical) sequence of transaction accounts (table 1.2 area framed in grey) and the (horizontal) sequence of accumulation accounts and balance sheets (table 1.2 area shaded in grey). An account is a means of recording, for a given aspect of economic life, the uses and resources or changes in assets and liabilities during the accounting period, as well as serving as a balance sheet covering the assets and liabilities at the beginning or end of a given period in time.

1. An integrated presentation of the sequence of accounts

1.48. Table 1.3 shows an integrated presentation of the sequence of accounts by institutional sector. It covers the production account and the generation, distribution, redistribution and use of income accounts (which are collectively known as the current accounts); as well as the capital, financial, other changes in the volume of assets, and revaluation accounts (which are collectively known as the accumulation accounts); and the balance sheet.

1.49. The term "resources" is used for transactions which add to the amount of the economic value of a unit or a sector. By convention, resources are shown on the right-hand side of the current accounts (i.e. I and II). As an example, wages and salaries are a resource for the unit or sector receiving them. The left-hand side of the accounts shows "uses". It relates to transactions recorded in the current accounts that reduce the amount of economic value of a unit or sector.

1.50. To continue the example, wages and salaries are a use for the unit or sector paying them. The term "changes in assets" is used for transactions or other flows which change the amount of assets held by a unit or a sector. By convention, changes in assets are shown on the left-hand side of the capital, financial, other changes in the volume of

Table 1.3
Integrated presentation of the sequence of accounts

	Total	Goods and services	Rest of the world	Total economy	NPISHs	Households	General government	Financial corporations	Non-financial corporations	Transactions and balancing items	Non-financial corporations	Financial corporations	General government	Households	NPISHs	Total economy	Rest of the world	Goods and services	Total
Uses																			**Resources**
I. Production account/External account of goods and services																			
II.1. Generation of income account																			
II.2. Allocation of primary income account																			
II.3. Secondary distribution of income account																			
II.4. Use of income account																			
Changes in assets																			**Changes in liabilities and net worth**
III.1. Capital account																			
III.2. Financial account																			
III.3. Other changes in the volume of assets account																			
III.4. Revaluation account																			
Assets																			**Liabilities and net worth**
IV.1. Balance sheet																			

assets, and revaluation accounts. The right-hand side refers to "changes in liabilities and net worth". This is used for transactions or other flows which change the amount of liabilities held by a unit or a sector. In the case of transactions in financial instruments, changes in liabilities are often referred to as the (net) incurrence of liabilities and the changes in assets as (net) acquisition of financial assets. In the case of the balance sheet, the term "assets" is used to describe the left-hand side of the account, while the term "liabilities and net worth" is used to describe the right-hand side of the account.

1.51. The integrated presentation of the accounts includes a column on each side labelled "total economy". Entries in these columns represent the sum of all the five sectors of the total economy (non-financial corporations, financial corporations, general government, non-profit institutions serving households (NPISHs) and households).

1.52. Next to the column for total economy is a column for the rest of the world. The column covers transactions between resident and non-resident institutional units and the related stocks of assets and liabilities where relevant. The entries for exports and imports of goods and services are recorded in the external account of goods and services, which is shown at the same level as the production account for institutional sectors. As the rest of the world plays a role in the accounting structure similar to that of an institutional sector, the rest of the world account is established from the point of view of the rest of the world. A resource for the rest of the world is a use for the total economy and vice versa.

1.53. The integrated presentation of the accounts also includes a column on each side labelled "goods and services". Entries in these columns reflect the various transactions in goods and services that appear in the accounts of the institutional sectors. Uses of goods and services in these accounts are reflected in the right-hand column for goods and services, while resources of goods and services are reflected in the left-hand column for goods and services. On the resources side of the table, the figures appearing in the column for goods and services are the counterparts of the uses made by the various sectors and the rest of the world. On the uses side of the table, the figures in the column for goods and services are the counterparts of the resources of the various sectors and the rest of the world.

1.54. The last column is a column representing the sum of the previous three (total economy, rest of the world, and goods and services). This column has little economic meaning, but is a critical way of ensuring that the tables are complete and consistent, since the totals on the left-hand side and right-hand side of the accounts must be equal line by line.

1.55. Many macroeconomic variables are calculated as balancing items in the sequence of transaction accounts as shown in tables 1.4 to 1.7. The sequence of the transaction accounts for financial corporations is shown using a thicker border in the tables. The balancing items are presented on a gross basis, indicating that the consumption of fixed capital has not been deducted.

2. The production account

1.56. The production account in gross terms shows output plus taxes less subsidies on products as resources and intermediate consumption as a use (see table 1.4). The 2008 SNA recommends that output be valued at basic prices. The basic price is the amount receivable by the producer from the purchaser for a unit of a good or service produced as output minus any tax payable, and plus any subsidy receivable, by the producer as a consequence of its production or sale. It excludes any transport charges invoiced separately by the producer. Taxes on products (less subsidies) are included on the resource side of the accounts. The part (possibly the total) of taxes on products (less subsidies on products) that is not included in the value of output does not originate in any specific sector or industry; it is a resource of the total economy. In the numerical example, taxes less

Table 1.4
Production account

Uses | Resources

Total	Goods and services	Rest of the world	Total economy	NPISHs	Households	General government	Financial corporations	Non-financial corporations	Transactions and balancing items	Non-financial corporations	Financial corporations	General government	Households	NPISHs	Total economy	Rest of the world	Goods and services	Total
I. Production Account/External Account of Goods and Services																		
499.0	499.0								Imports of goods and services							499.0		499.0
540.0		540.0							Exports of goods and services								540.0	540.0
3604.0	3604.0								Output	2808.0	146.0	348.0	270.0	32.0	3604.0			3604.0
1883.0			1883.0	17.0	115.0	222.0	52.0	1477.0	Intermediate consumption								1883.0	1883.0
133.0	133.0								Taxes less subsidies on products						133.0			133.0
1854.0			**1854.0**	**15.0**	**155.0**	**126.0**	**94.0**	**1331.0**	**Value added, gross/Gross domestic product**									
-41.0		**-41.0**							**External balance of goods and services**									

subsidies on products are shown directly in the column for goods and services. They are a component of the value of the supply of goods and services which has no counterpart in the value of the output of any institutional sector. The balancing item in the production account is value added. The value of taxes less subsidies on products plus the sum of value added of resident units results in the value of gross domestic product (GDP). Of specific importance are the calculation of financial services provided by deposit-taking corporations and other financial corporations (calculation and allocation of financial intermediation services indirectly measured (FISIM), and the measurement of the production of life and non-life insurance and pension schemes). Chapter 3 of the Handbook will elaborate on the methods used to compute the output of financial corporations.

1.57. The external account of goods and services is shown at the same level as the production account for institutional sectors. Imports of goods and services are a resource for the rest of the world, while exports are a use. The external balance of goods and services is negative, indicating that the economy has a surplus with the rest of the world.

3. The income accounts

1.58. The 2008 SNA has the following income accounts: the generation of income, the allocation of primary income, the secondary distribution of income and the use of disposable income (see table 1.5). They are used to derive the various types of income. The balancing item of the production account, value added, is the starting point of the first account (i.e. the generation of income account).

1.59. The generation of income account shows how value added is distributed to labour (compensation of employees), capital and government (taxes on production and imports less subsidies as far as they are included in the valuation of output). The distribution to capital appears in the balancing item in this account, operating surplus or mixed income.

1.60. The allocation of primary income account records, for each sector, property income receivable and payable, and compensation of employees and taxes, less subsidies, on production and imports receivable by households and government, respectively. Since transactions of this kind may appear in the rest of the world account, these must be included also. The balancing item of the allocation of primary income account is the balance of primary income.

1.61. The secondary distribution of income account covers redistribution of income through current transfers other than social transfers in kind made by government and NPISHs to households. Social transfers in kind are recorded in the redistribution of income in kind account. The secondary distribution of income account records as resources, in addition to balance of primary incomes, current taxes on income, wealth, etc. and other current transfers except social transfers in kind. On the uses side, the same types of transfers are also recorded. Since these transfers are resources for some sectors and uses for others also, their precise content varies from one sector to another. The balancing item of the secondary distribution of income account is disposable income.

1.62. The use of disposable income account shows how, for those sectors that undertake final consumption (i.e. general government, NPISHs and households), disposable income is allocated between final consumption and saving. In addition, the account includes, for households and for pension funds, an adjustment item for the change in pension entitlements which relates to the way transactions between households and pension funds are recorded in the SNA. This adjustment item will be explained in chapter 3 of the Handbook. The balancing items of the use of disposable income account are

Table 1.5

Income accounts

Uses																		Resources
Total	**Goods and services**	**Rest of the world**	**Total economy**	**NPISHs**	**Households**	**General government**	**Financial corporations**	**Non-financial corporations**	**Transactions and balancing items**	**Non-financial corporations**	**Financial corporations**	**General government**	**Households**	**NPISHs**	**Total economy**	**Rest of the world**	**Goods and services**	**Total**
II.1. Generation of income account																		
									Value added, gross/ Gross domestic product	1331.0	94.0	126.0	155.0	15.0	1854.0			**1854.0**
1150.0			1150.0	11.0	11.0	98.0	44.0	986.0	Compensation of employees									
133.0			133.0						Taxes less subsidies on products									
58.0			58.0	1.0	-1.0	1.0	4.0	53.0	Other taxes less subsidies on production and imports									
513.0			513.0	3.0	145.0	27.0	46.0	292.0	Operating surplus, gross/Mixed income, gross									
II.2. Allocation of primary income account																		
									Operating surplus, gross/Mixed income, gross	292.0	46.0	27.0	145.0	**3.0**	**513.0**			**513.0**
6.0		6.0							Compensation of employees				1154.0		1154.0	2.0		1156.0
									Taxes less subsidies on products			133.0			133.0			133.0
									Other taxes less subsidies on production			58.0			58.0			58.0
435.0		44.0	391.0	6.0	41.0	42.0	168.0	134.0	Property income	96.0	149.0	22.0	123.0	7.0	397.0	38.0		435.0
1864.0			**1864.0**	**4.0**	**1381.0**	**198.0**	**27.0**	**254.0**	Balance of primary income, gross/ National income, gross									
II.3. Secondary distribution of income account																		
									Balance of primary income, gross/ National income, gross	**254.0**	**27.0**	**198.0**	**1381.0**	**4.0**	**1864.0**			**1864.0**
213.0		1.0	212.0	0.0	178.0	0.0	10.0	24.0	Current taxes on income and wealth			213.0			213.0	0.0		213.0
333.0		0.0	333.0		333.0				Net social contributions	66.0	213.0	50.0	0.0	4.0	333.0	0.0		333.0
384.0		0.0	384.0	5.0	0.0	112.0	205.0	62.0	Social benefits other than social transfers in kind				384.0		384.0	0.0		384.0
299.0		16.0	283.0	2.0	71.0	136.0	62.0	12.0	Other current transfers	6.0	62.0	104.0	36.0	36.0	244.0	55.0		299.0
1826.0			**1826.0**	**37.0**	**1219.0**	**317.0**	**25.0**	**228.0**	Disposable income, gross									
II.4. Use of disposable income account																		
									Disposable income, gross	**228.0**	**25.0**	**317.0**	**1219.0**	**37.0**	**1826.0**			**1826.0**
1399.0			1399.0	32.0	1015.0	352.0			Final consumption expenditure									
11.0		0.0	11.0	0.0		0.0	11.0	0.0	Adjustment for the change in pension entitlements				11.0		11.0	0.0		11.0
427.0			427.0	5.0	215.0	-35.0	14.0	228.0	Saving, gross									
-13.0		**-13.0**							Current external balance									

saving for the total economy and current external balance. The current external balance is negative, indicating a deficit for the rest of the world, but a surplus for the total economy. These two balancing items end the subsequence of current accounts.

4. The capital account

1.63. The capital account shows how saving and capital transfers are available to finance net capital formation and capital consumption. Table 1.6 shows the capital account for broad categories of assets. Gross saving from the use of income account is the starting point of the capital account as a source of funds for capital accumulation. Gross saving represents the resources at the institutional units' disposal to fund the replacement of worn-out capital assets, net additions to the stock of capital assets and net payments of capital transfers without the need for borrowing. The balancing item of the capital account is called net lending/net borrowing. When positive, it is referred to as net lending and measures the net amount a unit or a sector has available to finance, directly or indirectly, other units or sectors. When negative, it is referred to as net borrowing and corresponds to the amount a unit or a sector is obliged to borrow from others. The sum of net lending/net borrowing across all sectors (including the rest of the world) is zero, as the net lending/net borrowing of the total economy must match the net borrowing/net lending of the rest of the world.

1.64. The major part of the net acquisition of non-financial assets is gross fixed capital formation, which equals the acquisition less disposal of fixed assets, including certain improvements to the value of non-produced assets like land. "Gross" means before the deduction of consumption of fixed capital, but after the deduction of sales of capital assets.

1.65. Net acquisition of other non-financial assets comprises changes in inventories, net acquisition of valuables and net acquisition of non-financial non-produced as-

Table 1.6
Capital account

Changes in assets | **Changes in liabilities and net worth**

Total	Goods and services	Rest of the world	Total economy	NPISHs	Households	General government	Financial corporations	Non-financial corporations	Transactions and balancing items	Non-financial corporations	Financial corporations	General government	Households	NPISHs	Total economy	Rest of the world	Goods and services	Total
									Saving, gross	**228.0**	**14.0**	**-35.0**	**215.0**	**5.0**	**427.0**			**427.0**
									Current external balance							-13.0		-13.0
376.0			376.0	5.0	48.0	35.0	8.0	280.0	Gross fixed capital formation									
28.0			28.0	0.0	2.0	0.0	0.0	26.0	Changes in inventories									
10.0			10.0	0.0	5.0	3.0	0.0	2.0	Acquisitions less disposals of valuables									
0.0			0.0	1.0	4.0	2.0	0.0	-7.0	Acquisitions less disposals of non-produced assets									
									Capital transfers, receivable	33.0	0.0	6.0	23.0	0.0	62.0	4.0		66.0
									Capital transfers, payable	-16.0	-7.0	-34.0	-5.0	-3.0	-65.0	-1.0		-66.0
									Changes in net worth due to saving and capital transfers	245.0	7.0	-63.0	233.0	2.0	424.0	-10.0		414.0
0.0		**-10.0**	**10.0**	**-4.0**	**174.0**	**-103.0**	**-1.0**	**-56.0**	**Net lending (+)/ net borrowing (-)**									

sets. "Net" means net of the sale of assets. Changes in inventories include the acquisition of products to be held in stock for subsequent use as intermediate consumption, less the sale or consumption of products that had been held in stock, and changes in inventories of work-in-progress and finished goods. Net acquisition of valuables is the acquisition of non-financial goods that are not used primarily for production or consumption, but are held primarily as stores of value, such as precious metals and art objects. Net acquisition of non-financial non-produced assets consists of the net acquisition of non-produced assets that may be used in the production of goods and services, and includes three distinct types of assets: natural resources, contracts, leases and licences, and goodwill and marketing assets.

1.66. Capital transfers payable and receivable consist of investment grants paid or received by other units and other capital transfers, such as those recorded as the counterpart to an assumption of debt by mutual consent. In national accounts, capital transfers payable are shown with a negative sign.

5. The financial account

1.67. The financial account is the final account in the full sequence of accounts that records transactions between institutional units. It shows changes caused by transactions in financial assets and liabilities classified by type of financial instrument. The balancing item of the financial account is also net lending (+)/net borrowing (-), which is conceptually the same as in the capital account. As a result, this provides a numerical check on the consistency of the set of accounts as a whole. However, in practice, as the measure is derived independently, it could differ significantly from the measure in the capital account because of errors and omissions. In practice, achieving this identity is one of the most difficult tasks in compiling national accounts.

1.68. Looking at the financial corporations sector, net lending (+)/net borrowing (-) is the net acquisition of financial assets over the net incurrence of liabilities or, vice versa, the excess of the financial corporations' saving, including net capital transfers, over their non-financial investment (see table 1.7).

6. The other changes in the volume of assets account

1.69. The other changes in the volume of assets account records the effect of exceptional events that cause not only the value but also the volume of assets and liabilities to vary. In addition to events such as the consequences of war or earthquakes, this account also includes some adjustment elements, such as changes in classification and structure,

Table. 1.7
Financial account

Changes in assets | Changes in liabilities and net worth

Total	Goods and services	Rest of the world	Total economy	NPISHs	Households	General government	Financial corporations	Non-financial corporations	Transactions and balancing items	Non-financial corporations	Financial corporations	General government	Households	NPISHs	Total economy	Rest of the world	Goods and services	Total
									Net lending (+)/ net borrowing (-)	-56.0	-1.0	-103.0	174.0	-4.0	10.0	-10.0		0.0
483.0		47.0	436.0	2.0	189.0	-10.0	172.0	83.0	Net acquisition of financial assets									
									Net incurrence of liabilities	139.0	173.0	93.0	15.0	6.0	426.0	57.0		483.0

Table 1.8
The other changes in the volume of assets account

Changes in assets | **Changes in liabilities and net worth**

Total	Goods and services	Rest of the world	Total economy	NPISHs	Households	General government	Financial corporations	Non-financial corporations	Transactions and balancing items	Non-financial corporations	Financial corporations	General government	Households	NPISHs	Total economy	Rest of the world	Goods and services	Total
33.0			33.0	0.0	0.0	7.0	0.0	26.0	Economic appearance of assets									
-11.0			-11.0	0.0	0.0	-2.0	0.0	-9.0	Economic disappearance of assets									
-11.0			-11.0	0.0	0.0	-6.0	0.0	-5.0	Catastrophic losses									
0.0			0.0	0.0	0.0	5.0	0.0	-5.0	Uncompensated seizures									
2.0			2.0	0.0	0.0	0.0	1.0	1.0	Other changes in volume n.e.c.	0.0	0.0	0.0	1.0	0.0	1.0			1.0
0.0			0.0	0.0	0.0	-4.0	-2.0	6.0	Changes in classification	0.0	0.0	2.0	0.0	0.0	2.0			2.0
13.0			13.0	0.0	0.0	0.0	-1.0	14.0	Total other changes in volume	0.0	0.0	2.0	1.0	0.0	3.0			3.0
-7.0			-7.0	0.0	0.0	-3.0	-2.0	-2.0	Produced non-financial assets									
17.0			17.0	0.0	0.0	3.0	0.0	14.0	Non-produced non-financial assets									
3.0			3.0	0.0	0.0	0.0	1.0	2.0	Financial assets	0.0	0.0	2.0	1.0	0.0	3.0			3.0
									Changes in net worth due to other changes in volume of assets	**14.0**	**-1.0**	**-2.0**	**-1.0**	**0.0**	**10.0**			

which may or may not have an influence on net worth. The balancing item, changes in net worth due to other changes in the volume of assets, is recorded on the right-hand side. Table 1.8 shows an example of an other changes in the volume of assets account. As this account does not record transactions, the starting point of the account is not a balancing item from a previous transaction account.

7. The revaluation account

1.70. The revaluation account records holding gains or losses. It starts with nominal holding gains and losses. This item records the full change in the value of the various assets or liabilities due to the change in the prices of those assets and liabilities since the beginning of the accounting period or the time of entry into stock and the time of exit from stock or the end of the accounting period.

1.71. Just as transactions and other flows in assets appear on the left of the account and transactions in liabilities on the right, so nominal gains or losses on assets appear on the left-hand side of the revaluation account, while nominal gains and losses on financial liabilities are recorded on the right-hand side. A positive revaluation of financial liabilities is equivalent to a nominal holding loss; a negative revaluation of liabilities is equivalent to a nominal holding gain.

1.72. The balancing item of the revaluation account is changes in net worth due to nominal holding gains and losses.

1.73. Nominal holding gains and losses are subdivided between two components. The first shows the revaluation in proportion to the general price level which is obtained by applying, during the same periods of time, an index of the change in general price level to the initial value of all assets or liabilities, even to those that are fixed in monetary terms. The results of this operation are called neutral holding gains and losses because all assets and liabilities are revalued so as to preserve exactly their purchasing power.

Table 1.9
Revaluation account

Changes in assets										Changes in liabilities and net worth								
Total	Goods and services	Rest of the world	Total economy	NPISHs	Households	General government	Financial corporations	Non-financial corporations	**Transactions and balancing items**	Non-financial corporations	Financial corporations	General government	Households	NPISHs	Total economy	Rest of the world	Goods and services	Total
Nominal holding gains and losses																		
280.0			280.0	8.0	80.0	44.0	4.0	144.0	Non-financial assets									
91.0		7.0	84.0	2.0	16.0	1.0	57.0	8.0	Financial assets/ liabilities	18.0	51.0	7.0	0.0	0.0	76.0	15.0		91.0
									Changes in net worth due to nominal holding gains/losses	134.0	10.0	38.0	96.0	10.0	288.0	-8.0		280.0
Neutral holding gains and losses																		
198.0			198.0	6.0	56.0	32.0	3.0	101.0	Non-financial assets									
148.0		12.0	136.0	3.0	36.0	8.0	71.0	18.0	Financial assets/ liabilities	37.0	68.0	13.0	5.0	3.0	126.0	22.0		148.0
									Changes in net worth due to neutral holding gains/losses	82.0	6.0	27.0	87.0	6.0	208.0	-10.0		198.0
Real holding gains and losses																		
82.0			82.0	2.0	24.0	12.0	1.0	43.0	Non-financial assets									
-57.0		-5.0	-52.0	-1.0	-20.0	-7.0	-14.0	-10.0	Financial assets/ liabilities	-19.0	-17.0	-6.0	-5.0	-3.0	-50.0	-7.0		-57.0
									Changes in net worth due to real holding gains/losses	52.0	4.0	11.0	9.0	4.0	80.0	2.0		82.0

1.74. The second component of holding gains and losses shows the difference between nominal holding gains and losses and neutral holding gains and losses. This difference is called real holding gains and losses. If the nominal holding gains and losses are higher than the neutral holding gains and losses, there is a real holding gain, to the fact that, on average, the actual prices of the assets in question have increased more (or decreased less) than the general price level. In other words, the relative prices of its assets have increased. Similarly, a decrease in relative prices of assets leads to a real holding loss.

1.75. Each of the three types of holding gains or losses are subdivided according to the main groups of assets and liabilities, a decomposition which is necessary even in a simplified accounting presentation. Changes in net worth due to nominal holding gains and losses can be subdivided into changes due to neutral holding gains and losses and changes due to real holding gains and losses. Table 1.9 shows an example of a revaluation account for non-financial assets and financial assets/liabilities by institutional sector.

8. The balance sheet

1.76. A balance sheet is a statement, drawn up in respect of a particular point in time, of the values of assets owned and of the liabilities owed by an institutional unit or group of units. The opening and closing balance sheets display assets on the left-hand side, liabilities and net worth on the right-hand side. Assets and liabilities are valued at the prices of the date a balance sheet is established.

1.77. A balance sheet displays the opening and closing stocks of non-financial assets and financial assets and liabilities at a particular point in time. The stock of financial assets and liabilities comprises the financial balance sheet.

1.78. The balancing item of a balance sheet is net worth, the difference between assets and liabilities. Net worth is equivalent to the present value of the stock of economic value a unit or a sector holds. For the economy as a whole, the balance sheet shows the sum of non-financial assets and net claims on the rest of the world. This sum is often referred to as national wealth.

1.79. The changes in the balance sheet recapitulate the content of the accumulation accounts, that is, the entry for each asset or liability is the sum of the entries in the four accumulation accounts corresponding to that asset or liability. The changes in net worth can be calculated from these entries, but must, by definition, be equal to the changes in net worth due to saving and capital transfers from the capital account plus changes in net worth due to other changes in the volume of assets from the other changes in the volume of assets account plus nominal holding gains and losses from the revaluation account.

1.80. Conceptually, the entries for the closing balance sheet are equal, asset by asset and liability by liability, to the entries in the opening balance sheet plus the changes recorded in the four accumulation accounts. The relationship between stocks and flows for assets and liabilities is shown in table 1.10 and can be summarized as follows:

$$Stock_t - Stock_{t-1} = Flows_t.$$

Table 1.10.
Relationship between stocks and flows

Stocks of assets and liabilities at the beginning of accounting period *t* (= stocks at the end of period *t*–1)
+ Flows (changes in assets and liabilities during the accounting period *t* due to:
transactions;
other changes in the volume of assets and liabilities;
revaluations)
= Stocks of assets and liabilities at the end of accounting period *t* (= stocks at the beginning of period *t*+1)

1.81. The term $Stock_t$ is an institutional unit's (or economy's, sector's or subsector's) holding (of assets) or incurrence (of liabilities) at the end of the accounting period *t* and the term $Stock_{t-1}$ is an institutional unit's (or economy's, sector's or subsector's) holding (of assets) or incurrence (of liabilities) at the end of the accounting period *t–1*.

1.82. The term $Flows_t$ refers to the changes in outstanding positions between two consecutive points in time. It is the sum of the flows in assets or liabilities during the accounting period *t*. It comprises transactions, other changes in the volume of assets and liabilities, and revaluations:

$$Flows_t = Transactions_t + Other\ changes\ in\ the\ volume\ of\ assets\ and\ liabilities_t + Revaluations_t$$

1.83. The term $Transactions_t$ refers to net acquisitions (gross acquisitions less disposals) of assets or net incurrences (gross incurrences less repayments) of liabilities during the accounting period *t*. Net acquisitions of financial assets or net incurrences of liabilities also include accrued interest receivable or accrued interest payable:[2]

$$Transactions\ in\ assets_t = Net\ acquisitions_t = Gross\ acquisitions_t - Disposals_t\ or$$
$$Transactions\ in\ liabilities_t = Net\ incurrences_t = Gross\ incurrences_t - Repayments_t$$

[2] Further explanations on the creditor and debtor approaches to recording accrued interest are provided in chapter 5.

1.84. The term *Revaluations*$_t$ refers to the changes in stocks due to changes in the level of prices of assets and liabilities during the accounting period *t*. Revaluations on assets or liabilities arise from changes in their prices and/or from changes in exchange rates. In the BPM6, revaluations are classified into those that are due to exchange rate changes and those that are due to other price changes.

1.85. The term *Other changes in the volume of assets and liabilities*$_t$ refers to all changes in positions between the end of accounting period *t-1* and the end of accounting period *t* that are due neither to transactions nor to revaluations.

1.86. Table 1.11 shows the 2008 SNA classification of non-financial assets and financial assets and liabilities in the balance sheet. Non-financial assets are broken down by produced and non-produced assets and further subcategories. Financial assets are shown, together with liabilities, as the components of the financial balance sheet. They are classified according to their legal characteristics, liquidity and economic purpose. While financial innovation leads to the need for new types of financial assets, the classification is intended to provide broad definitions that allow for international comparability and the inclusion of new instruments within the existing categories. Provision is made for further subdividing, in particular according to original maturity and type of instrument. Equity, for instance, is broken down into listed and unlisted shares and other equity.

1.87. An example of a balance sheet for non-financial assets and financial assets and liabilities by institutional sector is shown in table 1.12.

Table 1.11
The balance sheet as a means to show assets, liabilities and net worth

Assets	Liabilities and net worth
Non-financial assets	
Produced assets	
Fixed assets	
Inventories	
Valuables	
Non-produced assets	
Natural resources	
Contracts, leases and licences	
Goodwill and marketing assets	
Financial assets	
Monetary gold and special drawing rights (SDRs)	Monetary gold and SDRs
Currency and deposits	Currency and deposits
Debt securities	Debt securities
Loans	Loans
Equity and investment fund shares or units	Equity and investment fund shares or units
Insurance, pension and standardized guarantee schemes	Insurance, pension and standardized guarantee schemes
Financial derivatives and employee stock options	Financial derivatives and employee stock options
Other accounts receivable/payable	Other accounts receivable/payable
	Net worth

Table 1.12
Balance sheet

Stocks and changes in assets																		Stocks and changes in liabilities and net worth
Total	**Goods and services**	**Rest of the world**	**Total economy**	**NPISHs**	**Households**	**General government**	**Financial corporations**	**Non-financial corporations**	**Transactions and balancing items**	**Non-financial corporations**	**Financial corporations**	**General government**	**Households**	**NPISHs**	**Total economy**	**Rest of the world**	**Goods and services**	**Total**
Opening balance sheet																		
4621.0			4621.0	159.0	1429.0	789.0	93.0	2151.0	Non-financial assets									
9036.0		805.0	8231.0	172.0	3260.0	396.0	3421.0	982.0	Financial assets/ liabilities	3221.0	3544.0	687.0	189.0	121.0	7762.0	1274.0		9036.0
									Net worth	-88.0	-30.0	498.0	4500.0	210.0	5090.0	-469.0		4621.0
Total changes in assets																		**Total changes in liabilities and net worth**
482.0			482.0	11.0	116.0	57.0	-2.0	300.0	Non-financial assets									
577.0		54.0	523.0	4.0	205.0	-9.0	230.0	93.0	Financial assets/ liabilities	157.0	224.0	102.0	16.0	6.0	505.0	72.0		577.0
									Changes in net worth, total	236.0	4.0	-54.0	305.0	9.0	500.0	-18.0		482.0
Closing balance sheet																		
5103.0			5103.0	170.0	1545.0	846.0	91.0	2451.0	Non-financial assets									
9613.0		859.0	8754.0	176.0	3465.0	387.0	3651.0	1075.0	Financial assets/ liabilities	3378.0	3768.0	789.0	205.0	127.0	8267.0	1346.0		9613.0
									Net worth	148.0	-26.0	444.0	4805.0	219.0	5590.0	-487.0		5103.0

F. Three-dimensional accounts of financial transactions and stock of financial assets

References:
2008 SNA, Chapter 2, Overview
2008 SNA, Chapter 27, Links to monetary statistics and flow of funds
MFSMCG, Chapter 8, Financial statistics

1.88. The system of accumulation accounts and balance sheets, as described above, is two-dimensional. They are limited in that they do not reveal counterpart sectors to the transactions, other changes in assets or balance sheet positions. In other words, although they show which sectors are acquiring financial assets and what financial assets they are holding, they do not identify the sectors issuing the assets. Similarly, while they make it possible to identify net borrowing sectors and show how they incur liabilities, the financial accounts and balance sheets do not show which sectors made acquisitions and are holding the financial claims as assets. The same applies to other changes in assets. Thus, a complete picture of the financial flows and positions in the economy is not furnished.

1.89. To obtain a complete picture of the financial flows and positions in the economy, a three-dimensional system of accumulation accounts and balance sheets, with a breakdown of the financial corporations sector and financial assets and liabilities, as well as a breakdown by counterpart, is needed. This "from-whom-to-whom" style of presentation, which follows the underlying principles and framework of the 2008 SNA, is sometimes referred to as a flow of funds matrix. The three-dimensional table of financial transactions is usually presented as a series of matrices, with one matrix for each kind of financial instrument showing the flows from one sector to another.

1.90. The SNA provides an integrated framework for developing financial flows and positions on a from-whom-to-whom basis, as its underlying principles ensure that the linkages of the economic and financial actions of an economy are captured. However, the SNA standard presentation is not explicitly designed to show the intersectoral linkages, as it has traditionally focused primarily on answering the question of who does what, but not who does what with whom. As the SNA is the internationally accepted methodology for the compilation of the national accounts, the lack of prominence it gives to the from-whom-to-whom principle for data compilation and presentation may be one of the main reasons this approach for compiling data has not yet received a wider application.

1.91. The availability of from-whom-to-whom accounts permits the debtor/creditor relationships between institutional sectors to be fully articulated, i.e. they can be used to show transactions, revaluations, other changes in the volume of financial assets and liabilities, and balance sheet positions cross-classified by debtor sector and creditor sector. Thus, the integrated framework on a from-whom-to-whom basis allows questions to be answered such as, "Who is financing whom, in what amount and with which type of financial instrument?"

1.92. Detailed from-whom-to-whom accounting information is necessary to understand how financing is being carried out, how it is changing over time and how it is affecting the long-term development of financial markets and institutions. In particular, the from-whom-to-whom accounts and balance sheets can be useful in relating financial transactions to the behaviour of the non-financial economy. The joint presentation of the capital and financial accounts (showing a complete record of transactions contributing to the net acquisition of assets and the net incurrence of liabilities) provides a tool to combine financial and non-financial investment with the various sources of financing through net saving, net capital transfers and net incurrence of liabilities, thus establishing a link between financial activity and the "real" economy.

1.93. A three-dimensional system of accumulation accounts and balance sheets, with a breakdown of the financial corporations sector and the financial asset and liability categories, as well as a breakdown by counterpart, opens up the possibility of identifying economic aggregates in a matrix. This will allow analysis of economic developments in the broadest possible financial framework in a way that makes it easier to relate them to the economic developments recorded in the production and income accounts. As regards the allocation of income, the accounts also permit whoever is paying/receiving income (such as interest) to/from whom to be traced.

1.94. From a statistical point of view, setting up the accounts on a from-whom-to-whom basis is an important way of enhancing the quality and consistency of the data. It allows for the cross-checking of information from the sides of both the debtor and the creditor, thus allowing for full consistency in terms of values and timing for recording transactions, other flows and positions.

1.95. Table 1.13 shows the integrated framework of accounts on a from-whom-to-whom basis by institutional sector and the rest of the world for one financial instrument in a matrix format. For an economy, it shows transactions, revaluations, other changes in the volume of assets and liabilities, and positions for a financial instrument acquired/held by residents, grouped into sectors or subsectors, and non-residents vis-à-vis institutional units as debtors, broken down by residency and by institutional sector (cells of table 1.13 shaded grey).

1.96. For residents, the presentation of unconsolidated data is recommended. This means that intrasectoral positions, transactions, revaluations and other changes in the volume of assets and liabilities are not eliminated (cells shaded grey with diagonal lines).

The financial assets of non-residents issued by non-residents are not covered (black cell). These are not relevant from a national economy's perspective.

1.97. Holdings of financial instruments by non-residents (vis-à-vis resident sectors as debtors) are shown as positions on the rest of the world balance sheet, while acquisitions by non-residents of financial instruments issued by residents are recorded as financial transactions in the rest of the world financial account. Revaluations or other changes in the volume of assets and liabilities are reflected in the rest of the world accumulation accounts (cross-hatched cells in the non-residents column of table 1.13). For economies in which the role of the global financial markets is important, information on counterparty economies and non-residents becomes highly desirable.

Table 1.13
From-whom-to-whom transactions between five resident sectors and the rest of the world for one financial instrument, unconsolidated

Creditor by residency and by resident sector / Debtor by residency and by resident sector		Residents					Non-residents	All creditors
		Non-financial corporations	Financial corporations	General government	Households	Non-profit institutions serving households		
Residents	Non-financial corporations							
	Financial corporations							
	General government							
	Households							
	Non-profit institutions serving households							
Non-residents								
All debtors								

Source: Shrestha and Mink (2011).

Chapter 2
Financial corporations within the *System of National Accounts 2008* framework

A. Introduction

2.1. This chapter provides an overview of the financial corporations sector and its subsectors within the framework of the 2008 SNA. It defines and describes financial corporations, as well as the subsectors of the financial corporations sector. The chapter also describes the various ways in which financial corporations can be grouped for various purposes.

B. The financial corporations sector and its subsectors

References:
2008 SNA, Chapter 4, Institutional units and sectors
2008 SNA, Chapter 11, The financial account
BPM6, Chapter 4, Economic territory, units, institutional sectors, and residence
ESA 2010, Chapter 2, Units and groupings of units
MFSMCG, Chapter 3, Institutional units and sectors

2.2. Financial corporations consist of all resident corporations that are principally engaged in providing financial services, including insurance and pension funding services, to other institutional units. Financial services are the result of financial intermediation, financial risk management, liquidity transformation or auxiliary financial activities. As the provision of financial services is typically subject to strict regulation, it is usually the case that units providing financial services do not produce other goods and services and financial services are not provided as secondary production.

2.3. The financial corporations sector is composed of the following set of resident institutional units:

(a) All resident financial corporations (as understood in the SNA and not just restricted to legally constituted corporations), regardless of the residence of their shareholders;

(b) The branches of non-resident enterprises that are engaged in financial activity on the economic territory on a long-term basis;

(c) All resident non-profit institutions that are market producers of financial services.

2.4. Financial corporations can be divided into three broad classes, namely, financial intermediaries, financial auxiliaries and other financial corporations. Financial intermediaries are institutional units that incur liabilities on their own account for the purpose of acquiring financial assets by engaging in financial transactions on the market. They include insurance corporations and pension funds. Financial auxiliaries are institutional units principally engaged in serving financial markets, but do not take ownership of the financial assets and liabilities they handle. Other financial corporations are institutional units providing financial services, where most of their assets or liabilities are not available on open financial markets. The later parts of this chapter will provide examples of these classes of financial corporations.

2.5. According to their activity in the market and the liquidity of their liabilities, the financial corporations sector can be divided into nine subsectors as shown in table 2.1.[3] Depending on the type of control, each subsector can also be further divided into the following subsectors:

(a) Public financial corporations;

(b) National private financial corporations;

(c) Foreign-controlled financial corporations.

2.6. A corporation is controlled by another unit if the other unit owns more than 50 per cent of the equity of the corporation. However, control may also be possible with a holding of less than half the equity if the unit can exercise some powers that indicate possible control. These include control of the board or other governing body, control of the appointment and removal of key personnel, control of key committees of the corporations, control through a dominant customer, and ownership of golden shares and options. In the case of public corporations, the government can also assert control through regulations and conditions attached to lending to these corporations.

2.7. The public financial corporations can also be merged with public non-financial corporations and the general government sector to form the public sector.

2.8. Table 2.1 also shows the 2008 SNA codes for the subsectors. The subsequent paragraphs in this section provide a list of financial corporations under each subsector. However, the nature of the financial corporations sector may vary from country to country and financial corporations may have various names, depending on their principal activities and the national naming conventions. Thus, the list is neither exhaustive or prescriptive. The compiling agency may need to investigate the characteristics of a financial corporation which is not listed to determine to which subsector to allocate it.

2.9. Owing to the substantial variations among countries in defining money, the 2008 SNA does not include a definition of money. However, the MFSMCG includes a definition of money which is intended to help compilers determine the scope of broad money, taking into account their own national circumstances. The classification of fi-

Table 2.1
Financial corporations sector and its subsectors

Sector and subsectors	Total economy	Publicly controlled	National private	Foreign controlled
Financial corporations	S12			
Central bank	S121			
Deposit-taking corporations except the central bank	S122	S12201	S12202	S12203
Money market funds (MMFs)	S123	S12301	S12302	S12303
Non-MMF investment funds	S124	S12401	S12402	S12403
Other financial intermediaries except insurance corporations and pension funds	S125	S12501	S12502	S12503
Financial auxiliaries	S126	S12601	S12602	S12603
Captive financial institutions and moneylenders	S127	S12701	S12702	S12703
Insurance corporations	S128	S12801	S12802	S12803
Pension funds	S129	S12901	S12902	S12903

[3] However, depending on the historical development of the financial system, some countries may have more or less than the nine subsectors and somewhat different classifications below the subsector level.

nancial corporations and instruments is designed to be compatible with the definition of broad money in the MFSMCG.

1. Central bank (S121)

2.10. The central bank is the national financial institution that exercises control over key aspects of the financial system. In general, the following financial intermediaries are classified in this subsector:

(a) The national central bank, including where it is part of a system of central banks;

(b) Currency boards or independent currency authorities that issue national currency that is fully backed by foreign exchange reserves;

(c) Central monetary agencies of essentially public origin (for example, agencies managing foreign exchange or issuing bank notes and coins) that keep a complete set of accounts, but are not classified as part of central government. Supervisory authorities that are separate institutional units are not included with the central bank, but are included with financial auxiliaries.

2.11. As long as the central bank is a separate institutional unit, it is always allocated to the financial corporations sector, even if it is primarily a non-market producer.

2.12. A few economies do not have central banks. Typical central banking activities that are performed by general government and cannot be separated into specific institutional units are treated as part of general government and are not allocated to the central bank subsector.

2. Deposit-taking corporations except the central bank (S122)

2.13. Deposit-taking corporations except the central bank have financial intermediation as their principal activity. To this end, they have liabilities in the form of deposits or financial instruments (such as short-term certificates of deposits) that are close substitutes for deposits. The liabilities of deposit-taking corporations are typically included in measures of money broadly defined.

2.14. In general, this subsector comprises:

(a) Commercial banks, universal banks and all-purpose banks;

(b) Savings banks (including trustee savings banks, and savings and loan associations);

(c) Post office giro institutions, post banks and giro banks;

(d) Rural credit banks and agricultural credit banks;

(e) Cooperative credit banks and credit unions;

(f) Specialized banks or other financial corporations if they take deposits or issue close substitutes for deposits (for example, corporations engaged in granting mortgages, including building societies and mortgage banks, merchant banks, and municipal credit institutions, including regional or provincial credit institutions which accept deposits).[4]

2.15. The following institutional units are not deposit-taking corporations:

[4] In paragraph 2.77 of the ESA 2010, corporations engaged in granting mortgages, including building societies and mortgage banks, and municipal credit institutions are allocated to the deposit-taking corporations except the central bank subsector where it is their business to receive repayable funds from the public, whether in the form of deposits or in other forms such as the continuing issue of long-term debt securities. In addition, in paragraph 4.71 of BPM6, traveller's cheque companies that mainly engage in financial activities are allocated to the deposit-taking corporations except the central bank subsector.

(a) Head offices which oversee and manage other units of a group consisting predominantly of deposit-taking corporations except the central bank, but which are not deposit-taking corporations themselves. They are classified as financial auxiliaries (S126);

(b) Non-profit institutions recognized as independent legal entities serving deposit-taking corporations, but not engaged in financial intermediation. They are classified as financial auxiliaries (S126);

(c) Holding corporations, which are allocated to the captive financial institutions and moneylenders subsector (S127), even if all their subsidiary corporations are deposit-taking corporations.

3. Money market funds (S123)

2.16. Money market funds (MMFs) are collective investment schemes that raise funds by issuing shares or units to the public. The proceeds are invested primarily in money market instruments, MMF shares or units, transferable debt instruments with a residual maturity of not more than one year, bank deposits and instruments that provide a rate of return that approaches the interest rates of money market instruments. MMF shares or units can be transferred by cheque or other means of direct third-party payment. Because of the nature of the instruments the schemes invest in, their shares or units may be regarded as close substitutes for deposits.

2.17. In general, investment funds, including investment trusts, unit trusts and other collective investment schemes whose shares or units are seen as close substitutes for deposits, are classified as MMFs.

2.18. MMFs do not include the following:

(a) Head offices which oversee and manage a group consisting predominantly of MMFs, but which are not MMFs themselves. These are classified as financial auxiliaries (S126);

(b) Non-profit institutions serving MMFs that are not engaged in financial intermediation. They are classified as financial auxiliaries (S126).

4. Non-money market fund investment funds (S124)

2.19. Non-MMF investment funds are collective investment schemes that raise funds by issuing shares or units to the public. The proceeds are invested primarily in financial assets, other than short-term assets, and in non-financial assets (usually real estate). Non-MMF investment fund shares or units are generally not close substitutes for deposits. They are not transferable by means of cheque or direct third-party payments.

2.20. Non-MMF investment funds can be divided into open-ended and closed-ended non-MMF investment funds. Open-ended investment funds issue and redeem shares on a continuous basis: each time a new investment is performed, new shares or units are created; when shares are redeemed, an investment must be sold to match such redemption. Close-ended investment funds are open for subscription only during a specified period at the launch of the scheme; thereafter, investors can acquire shares only by buying them on a secondary market from other investors.

2.21. Non-MMF investment funds cover investment trusts, unit trusts and other collective investment schemes whose investment fund shares or units are not seen as close substitutes for deposits.

2.22. They may be constituted under: (*a*) the contract law (as common funds managed by management companies); (*b*) the trust law (as unit trusts); (*c*) the statute (as investment companies); or (*d*) otherwise with similar effect.

2.23. In general, the following financial intermediaries are classified as non-MMF investment funds:

(a) Equity based investment funds;

(b) Security based investment funds;

(c) Real estate investment trusts, which invest in debt and equity securities of companies that purchase real estate;

(d) Mortgage real estate investment trusts (REITs),[5] which provide money to real estate owners and operators either directly in the form of mortgages or other types of real estate loans, or indirectly through the acquisition of mortgage-backed securities;

(e) Investment funds investing in other funds ("funds of funds");

(f) Hedge funds covering a heterogeneous range of collective investment schemes, typically involving high minimum investments, light regulation and a wide range of investment strategies;

(g) Private equity funds, which are collective investment schemes used for making investments in companies, many of which are not listed on a stock exchange;

(h) Exchange-traded funds (ETFs).

2.24. Non-MMF investment funds do not include:

(a) Pension funds which are part of the pension funds subsector (S129);

(b) Special purpose government funds, usually called sovereign wealth funds, which are classified as captive financial institutions (S127), given the nature of their liabilities, if classified as a financial corporation;

(c) Head offices that oversee and manage a group consisting predominantly of non-MMF investment funds, but which are not investment funds themselves. These are classified as financial auxiliaries (S126);

(d) Non-profit institutions serving non-MMF investment funds, but not engaged in financial intermediation. They are classified as financial auxiliaries (S126).

5. Other financial intermediaries, except insurance corporations and pension funds (S125)

2.25. Other financial intermediaries, except insurance corporations and pension funds consist of financial corporations that are engaged in providing financial services by incurring liabilities in forms other than currency, deposits or close substitutes for deposits on their own account for the purpose of acquiring financial assets by engaging in financial transactions on the market. It is a feature of a financial intermediary that transactions on both sides of the balance sheet are carried out in open markets.

2.26. This subsector includes financial intermediaries predominantly engaged in long-term financing. This predominant maturity distinguishes this subsector from deposit-taking corporations except the central bank (S122) and money market funds (S123) subsectors. Based on the non-existence of liabilities in the form of investment fund shares or units which are not seen as close substitutes for deposits or insurance, pension and standardized guarantee schemes, the borderline with the non-MMF investment funds (S124), insurance corporations (S128) and pension funds (S129) subsectors can be determined.

[5] Mortgage REITs are different from equity REITs which directly own and manage real estate properties. The latter are not considered as financial intermediaries and, thus, are not part of the financial corporations sector.

2.27. In particular, this subsector may be further subdivided into:

(a) Financial corporations engaged in the securitization of assets;[6]

(b) Security and derivative[7] dealers (operating on own account);

(c) Financial corporations engaged in lending,[8] including financial leasing,[9] hire purchase and the provision of personal or commercial finance;

(d) Central clearing counterparties. These organizations provide clearing and settlement transactions in securities and derivatives. Clearing relates to identifying the obligations of both parties to the transaction, while settlement is the exchange of the securities or derivatives and the corresponding payment. The central clearing counterparties involve themselves in the transaction and mitigate counterparty risk;

(e) Specialized financial corporations that assist other corporations in raising funds in equity and debt markets and provide strategic advisory services for mergers, acquisitions and other types of financial transactions. These corporations are sometimes known as "investment banks". In addition to assisting with the raising of funds for their corporate clients, such corporations invest

Box 2.1

Defining and classifying head offices and holding companies

The 2008 SNA and the BPM6 classify head offices according to their main activity either as a non-financial corporation (S11) or, by convention, as a financial auxiliary (S126). Holding companies are always included in the financial corporations subsector "captive financial institutions and moneylenders" (S127), irrespective of whether all their subsidiary corporations are financial or non-financial corporations.

	Head offices	**Holding companies**
Description in ISIC Rev.4 and NACE Rev.2	ISIC Rev.4 Class 7010 (NACE Rev. 2, class 70.10): This class includes the overseeing and managing of other units of the company or enterprise; undertaking the strategic or organizational planning and decision-making role of the company or enterprise; exercising operational control and managing the day-to-day operations of their related units	ISIC Rev.4 Class 6420 (NACE Rev. 2 class 64.20): This class includes the activities of holding companies, i.e. units that hold the assets (owning controlling-levels of equity) of a group of subsidiary corporations and whose principal activity is owning the group. The holding companies in this class do not provide any other service to the businesses in which the equity is held, i.e. they do not administer or manage other units
Sector/subsector classification	Head offices are allocated to the **non-financial corporations sector (S11)** unless all or most of their subsidiaries are financial corporations, in which case they are treated, by convention, as **financial auxiliaries (S126)**. Other entities that hold and manage subsidiaries may have substantial operations in their own right, in which case the holding company functions may be secondary, so they would be classified according to their predominant operations	Holding companies are always allocated to the **captive financial institutions and moneylenders subsector (S127)**, even if all their subsidiary corporations are non-financial corporations.

[6] Paragraph 2.90 of the ESA 2010 describes these corporations as financial vehicle corporations.

[7] Derivatives are financial instruments that are linked to a specific financial instrument, indicator or commodity, through which specific financial risks can be traded in financial markets in their own right.

[8] Specific examples of these financial corporations include property companies, as well as aircraft and other transport leasing companies which specialize in financial leasing, and the finance associates of retailers.

[9] A financial lease is one where the lessor as legal owner of an asset passes the economic ownership to the lessee who then accepts the operating risks and receives the economic benefits from using the asset in a productive activity.

Box 2.2

The delineation of head offices, holding corporations and special purpose entities

Head offices, holding companies and similar entities, which often have characteristics typical of special purpose entities (SPEs), tend to have large financial balance sheets, as a consequence of which their recognition as institutional units and their sector classification can have a significant impact on the measurement of non-consolidated debt and equity measures by institutional sector. The classification of these units, usually being important receivers and payers of property income, may also have a significant impact on the allocation of primary income in the non-financial sector accounts.

To ensure the analytical usefulness and the interpretability of the resulting national accounts data by sector and other data, such as the statistics on foreign direct investment, the following recommendations on the internationally comparable recording of head offices and holding companies and typology and classification of SPEs were established in accordance with the SNA update procedures:

(a) For head offices, holding companies and similar SPE-type entities, the standard SNA criteria for an institutional unit should always be applied;

(b) Entities owned by non-residents are always to be considered as institutional units, and, in this respect, "downstream consolidation" of a holding with its subsidiary/subsidiaries should not be done;

(c) For entities wholly owned by a single resident unit, "no employees and no compensation of employees" is not a sufficient criterion to determine the lack of institutional independence; however, it can be used as an indicator to consider units for further investigation into its lack of independence;

(d) Having multiple parents/shareholders is a sufficient qualification for a unit to be considered an institutional unit;

(e) Head offices are always to be considered as separate institutional units;

(f) The kind of economic activity is the determining factor for identifying head offices and holding companies, and, in this respect, an entity having at least 50 per cent of its assets consisting of equity vis-à-vis its subsidiaries can be considered as a practical indicator for identifying entities as being either head offices or holding companies;

(g) In the case of employment thresholds being used as a practical indicator for the delineation between head offices and holding companies, this indicator should be applied taking into account national circumstances. In particular, national legislative requirements for the number of employees of holding companies should be considered. In general, employment of three or more persons could be considered as a first indicator for a unit being a head office;

(h) In arriving at a clear definition of SPEs, such units could have non-financial assets on their balance sheets;

(i) As a general rule, the ownership of assets of SPEs should not be rerouted. Further clarification is needed on the (economic) ownership and the subsequent recording of certain assets of SPEs;

(j) For SPE-type entities engaged in financial activities on the market, following commonly applied approaches for the measurement of output and value added seems to be feasible. In relation to captive SPEs, measurement of output and value added following the sum of costs approach is considered a practical alternative. For SPEs engaged in holding non-financial assets that provide services in the form of rents, royalties and licences, this issue is related to the question of (economic) ownership, and that further reflection is needed.

their own funds, including in private equity, in hedge funds dedicated to venture capital, and in collateralized lending. However, if such corporations take deposits or close substitutes for deposits, they are classified as deposit-taking corporations;

(f) Specialized financial corporations that provide the following:

- Short-term financing for corporate mergers and takeovers.
- Export/import finance.
- Factoring services.
- Venture capital and development capital firms.
- Loans against mortgage on real estate by issuing mortgage bonds.[10]

[10] These are known as mortgage credit institutions.

2.28. This subsector does not include:

(a) Head offices which oversee and manage a group of subsidiaries principally engaged in financial intermediation and/or in auxiliary financial activities—these are classified as financial auxiliaries (S126);

(b) Non-profit institutions serving other financial intermediaries, but not engaged in financial intermediation—these are classified as financial auxiliaries (S126).

6. Financial auxiliaries (S126)

2.29. Financial auxiliaries consist of financial corporations that are principally engaged in activities associated with transactions in financial assets and liabilities or with providing the regulatory context for these transactions, but in circumstances that do not involve the auxiliary taking ownership of the financial assets and liabilities being transacted.

2.30. The most common types of financial auxiliaries are the following:

(a) Insurance brokers, salvage and claims adjusters (whether employed by the insurance corporation, an independent adjuster or a public adjuster employed by the policyholder), and insurance and pension consultants;

(b) Loan brokers, securities brokers who arrange trades between security buyers and sellers but do not purchase and hold securities on their own account, investment advisers, etc.;

(c) Flotation corporations that manage the issue of securities;

(d) Corporations whose principal function is to guarantee, by endorsement, bills and similar instruments;

(e) Corporations that arrange derivative and hedging instruments, such as swaps, options and futures (without issuing them);

(f) Corporations providing infrastructure for financial markets, including those providing transaction processing and settlement activities, such as for credit card transactions, as well as securities depository companies, custodians, clearing offices[11] and nominee companies;

(g) Managers of pension funds,[12] mutual funds, etc. (but not the funds they manage);

(h) Corporations providing stock exchange, insurance exchange, and commodity and derivative exchange;

(i) Foreign exchange bureaux;[13]

(j) Non-profit institutions recognized as independent legal entities serving financial corporations, but that do not themselves provide financial services;

(k) Head offices of financial corporations that are principally engaged in controlling financial corporations or groups of financial corporations, but that do not themselves conduct the business of financial corporations;

(l) Central supervisory authorities of financial intermediaries and financial markets when they are separate institutional units.

[11] Clearing offices are classified as financial auxiliaries when they facilitate transactions without acting as the counterparty; in contrast, central clearing counterparties are counterparties and are thus classified as intermediaries rather than auxiliaries.

[12] As these units only manage the activities of the pension funds without taking ownership of their assets and liabilities, they are also known as pension administrators.

[13] In some countries, they are also known as money changers.

7. Captive financial institutions and moneylenders (S127)

2.31. Captive financial institutions and moneylenders consists of institutional units providing financial services, where most of either their assets or liabilities are not transacted on open financial markets. It includes entities transacting within only a limited group of units (such as with subsidiaries) or subsidiaries of the same holding corporation or entities that provide loans from own funds provided by only one sponsor. In general, the following financial corporations are classified under this subsector:[14]

(a) Units which are legal entities, such as trusts, estates, agencies' accounts or brass plate companies;

(b) Holding corporations that hold only the assets (owning controlling-levels of equity) of a group of subsidiary corporations and whose principal activity is owning the group without providing any other service to the enterprises in which the equity is held, that is, they do not administer or manage other units;

(c) SPEs or conduits that qualify as institutional units and raise funds in open markets to be used by their parent corporation;

(d) Special purpose government funds, usually called sovereign wealth funds, if they are institutional units and provide financial services on a market basis to the government;

(e) Units which provide financial services exclusively with own funds or funds provided by a sponsor to a range of clients, and incur the financial risk of the debtor defaulting, including:

- Moneylenders.[15]
- Corporations engaged in lending (for example providing student loans or import/export loans) from funds received from a sponsor, such as a government unit or non-profit institution.
- Pawnshops that predominantly engage in lending.

2.32. Captive financial institutions which are simply passive holders of assets and liabilities and which are always related to another corporation, often as a subsidiary, are not treated as separate institutional units, but as integral parts of the parent corporation, as they cannot act independently of their parent corporation. If such institutions are set up outside the country where the parent corporation resides, they are treated as separate units and residents of the economic territory where they are incorporated or registered. SPEs set up by general government with characteristics and functions similar to captive financial institutions are also treated as an integral part of general government if they are resident, but as separate institutional units if they are non-resident units.

2.33. Captive financial institutions and moneylenders do not include SPEs whose principal activity is the provision of goods or non-financial services. If they are resident in an economy different from that of their parents, they are classified according to their main activity as non-financial corporations.

---

[14] This subsector excludes financial corporations engaged in the securitization of assets, which are classified under the other financial intermediaries, except insurance corporations and pension funds subsector.

[15] Moneylenders which are unincorporated enterprises owned by households are excluded, as they are allocated to the households sector.

8. Insurance corporations (S128)

2.34. Insurance corporations consist of incorporated, mutual and other entities whose principal function is to provide life, accident, sickness, fire or other forms of insurance to individual institutional units or groups of units, or reinsurance services to other insurance corporations. Insurance corporations are mostly incorporated or mutual entities. Incorporated entities are owned by shareholders and many are listed on stock exchanges. Mutuals are owned by their policyholders and return their profits to the "with profits" or "participating" policyholders through dividends or bonuses. Captive insurance corporations, that is, those that serve only their owners, are included in this subsector. Deposit insurers,[16] issuers of deposit guarantees and other issuers of standardized guarantees that are separate entities and act like insurers by charging premiums and have reserves are classified as insurance corporations.

2.35. Insurance corporations provide services of the following:

(a) Life and non-life insurance to individual units or groups of units;

(b) Reinsurance to other insurance corporations.

2.36. Services of non-life insurance corporations may be provided in the following forms of insurance:

(a) Fire (including commercial and private property);

(b) Liability (casualty);

(c) Motor (own damage and third party liability);

(d) Marine, aviation and transport (including energy risks);

(e) Accident and health;

(f) Flood;

(g) Crop;

(h) Hurricane;

(i) Financial (provision of guarantees or surety bonds).

Flood, crop and hurricane insurance are typically provided by the government. Thus, only those government units which provide these types of insurance on a market basis should be included in insurance corporations. On the other hand, those government units which provide these types of insurance on a non-market basis are included in the general government sector.

2.37. Insurance corporations do not include the following:

(a) Institutional units whose principal activity is to provide social benefits and which fulfil each of the following two criteria: (i) by law or by regulation, certain groups of the population are obliged to participate in the scheme or to pay contributions; and (ii) general government is responsible for the management of the institution in respect of the settlement or approval of the contributions and benefits independently from its role as supervisory body or employer. These are classified as social security funds (S1314);

[16] These should only include those units to which the fees paid represent payments for an insurance-type of transaction rather than taxes. The criterion of proportionality between payments and the provision of an insurance-type of services (including payments for the risk element) should be examined on a case-by-case basis. The existence of a fund functioning under insurance rules and with a full set of accounts may indicate proportionality. On the contrary, if the payments are not put aside or can be used for other purposes, this would be an indication to treat the payments as a tax.

Box 2.3
Types of insurance

Three types of insurance are distinguished: direct insurance, reinsurance and social insurance. Direct insurance covers (individual) life insurance and non-life insurance, while social insurance covers social security and employment-related social insurance.

Type of insurance	Direct insurance		Reinsurance	Social insurance			
			Insurance bought by an insurer to protect itself against an unexpectedly large number of claims or exceptionally large claims	Policyholder/beneficiary is obliged or encouraged to insure against contingencies by intervention of a third party. Participation is obligatory, the scheme is collective and the employer makes contributions, whether or not the employees make contributions			
	Life insurance	Non-life insurance		Social security		Employment-related social insurance	
	Policyholder makes regular payments to an insurer, in return for which the insurer guarantees to provide the policyholder with an agreed sum, or an annuity, at a given date or earlier	Insurance to cover risks like accidents, sickness, fire, etc.		Organized by general government via social security schemes		Organized by employers on behalf of their employees and their dependents or by others on behalf of a specified group	
				Social security pensions	Other social security	Employment-related pensions	Other employment-related social insurance
Sector/ subsector	Insurance corporations	Insurance corporations		General government Social security		Sector of employer (in the case of non-autonomous funds) or insurance corporations and pension funds	

(b) Head offices which oversee and manage a group consisting predominantly of insurance corporations, but which are not insurance corporations themselves. These are classified as financial auxiliaries (S126);

(c) Non-profit institutions serving insurance corporations, but not engaged in financial intermediation. These are classified as financial auxiliaries (S126).

9. Pension funds (S129)

2.38. Employers (or unions in collaboration with employers) set up pension schemes to provide retirement benefits for specific groups of employees (and self-employed persons). Governments sometimes organize pension schemes for their employees that are independent of the social security system. The pension fund subsector consists of only those social insurance pension funds that are institutional units separate from the units that create them. Excluded from this subsector are non-autonomous pension schemes managed by employers, government-sponsored pension schemes funded through wage taxes (pay-as-you-go schemes), social security funds and arrangements organized by non-government employers, when the reserves of the fund are simply included among the employer's own reserves or invested in securities issued by that employer.

2.39. The typical groups of participants in such schemes include employees of a single enterprise or a group of enterprises, employees of a branch or industry, and persons having the same profession. The benefits included in the insurance contract might encompass survivor benefits which are paid after death of the insured to the widow(er) and children (mainly death in service), benefits which are paid after retirement and benefits which are paid after the insured becomes disabled.

2.40. In some countries, all these types of risks could be insured equally well by life insurance corporations as by pension funds. In other countries, some of these classes of risks have to be insured through life insurance corporations. In contrast to life insurance corporations, pension funds are restricted (by law) to specified groups of employees and self-employed persons.

2.41. Such schemes may be organized by employers or by general government; they may also be organized by insurance corporations on behalf of employees; or separate institutional units may be established to hold and manage the assets to be used to meet the pension entitlements and to distribute the pensions.

2.42. The pension funds included in this financial corporations subsector are those which are autonomous. These funds operate as separate institutional units from the units (such as corporations) which create them. They are set up to provide benefits on retirement for specific groups of employees and have their own assets and liabilities. They also make their own transactions in financial assets in the market. These funds are organized, and directed, by individual private or government employers, or jointly by individual employers and their employees. The employers and/or employees make regular contributions to these funds. The separately constituted pension funds of international organizations are regarded as financial corporations and are classified under this subsector.

2.43. Pensions funds classified in the financial corporations sector do not include the following:

(a) Non-autonomous pension funds. Such pension funds refer to the pension arrangements for the employees of government or private sector entities which do not include a separately organized fund, but do include arrangements by a non-government employer in which the reserves of the fund are simply added to that employer's own reserves or invested in securities issued by that employer. These funds are not considered as separate bodies, so they are classified under the sector of the employer. The main non-autonomous pension schemes in many countries are for government sector employees (such as the civil service pension scheme);

(b) Institutional units whose principal activity is to provide social benefits and which fulfil each of the following two criteria: (i) by law or by regulation, certain groups of the population are obliged to participate in the scheme or to pay contributions; and (ii) general government is responsible for the management of the institution in respect of the settlement or approval of the contributions and benefits independently from its role as supervisory body or employer; they are classified as social security funds (S1314). In the case of social security funds, the benefits already accrued under the fund's benefit formula can be taken away by the government, whereas employees have property rights to benefits that they have already accrued in a pension scheme, that is, entitlements may be changed by law on social security schemes, but cannot be altered without previous agreement if they derive from past contributions for employment-related pension schemes;

(c) Head offices which only control and direct a group consisting predominantly of pension funds, but which are not pension funds themselves. These are classified as financial auxiliaries (S126);

(d) Non-profit institutions recognized as independent legal entities serving pension funds, but not engaged in financial intermediation. These are classified as financial auxiliaries (S126).

C. Grouping of subsectors of the financial corporations sector

Reference:
2008 SNA, Chapter 27, Links to monetary statistics and the flow of funds
BPM6, Chapter 4, Economic territory, units, institutional sectors, and residence
MFSMCG, Chapter 3, Institutional units and sectors

1. Grouping of subsectors of the financial corporations sector for monetary policy purposes

2.44. It is not always useful for all the nine subsectors to be distinguished at the same time in a system of institutional sector accounts. However, they represent a flexible set of building blocks for alternative aggregations to be compiled according to different needs and possibilities. At the same time, further disaggregation within one of the subsectors may be desirable on occasion, for example to separate different types of deposit-taking corporations or insurance corporations.

2.45. There are various useful ways in which the subsectors of the financial corporations sector may be combined, one of which may be adopted for monetary policy purposes following demand from users, analysts and policymakers. It distinguishes between monetary financial institutions (MFIs), insurance corporations and pension funds (ICPFs) and other financial corporations. The groups are presented in table 2.2. MFIs comprise the central bank (S121), deposit-taking corporations except the central bank (S122) and MMFs (S123). MMFs are included in monetary financial institutions if the liabilities they issue are considered to be part of broad money. ICPFs comprise insurance corporations (S128) and pension funds (S129). Other financial corporations comprise non-MMF investment funds (S124), other financial intermediaries except insurance corporations and pension funds (S125), financial auxiliaries (S126) and captive financial institutions and moneylenders (S127). These groups correspond to the groups for the subsectors of the financial corporations sector in the templates for the minimum and encouraged data sets for internationally comparable sectoral national accounts and balance sheets. These templates have been developed to fulfil recommendation 15 of the 20 recommendations endorsed by the Group of 20 finance ministers and central bank governors to address data gaps which were identified after the 2008 global financial cri-

Table 2.2
Grouping of subsectors of the financial corporations sector for monetary policy purposes

Financial corporations (S12)									
Monetary financial institutions			Insurance corporations and pension funds		Other financial corporations				*Of which*: Public financial corporations (S12001)
Central bank (S121)	Deposit-taking corporations except the central bank (S122)	Money market funds (S123)	Insurance corporations (S128)	Pension funds (S129)	Non-MMF investment funds (S124)	Other financial intermediaries except insurance corporations and pension funds (S125)	Financial auxiliaries (S126)	Captive financial institutions and moneylenders (S127)	

= Minimum
= Encouraged

sis.[17] Recommendation 15 calls for the development of a strategy to promote the compilation and dissemination of the balance sheet approach, flow of funds, and sectoral data more generally, starting with the Group of 20 economies.[18]

2.46. The business of MFIs is to receive deposits and/or close substitutes for deposits from institutional units other than MFIs and, for their own account, to grant loans and make investments in securities. Deposits and close substitutes for deposits from institutional units other than MFIs are considered to be part of broad money.

2.47. Other monetary financial institutions (deposit-taking corporations except the central bank and MMFs) cover those financial intermediaries through which the main effects of the monetary policy of the central bank are transmitted to the other entities of the economy.

2.48. This combination of subsectors has the advantage of clearly specifying the two main groups of financial intermediaries covered by the subsectors MFIs and ICPFs. It also allows the compilation of from-whom-to-whom financial accounts and balance sheets based on a reasonable number of combinations. Depending on national peculiarities, non-MMF investment funds might be combined with MMFs if money market fund shares/units are not seen as broad money.

2. Grouping of subsectors of the financial corporations sector in the Monetary and Financial Statistics Manual and Compilation Guide

2.49. The MFSMCG groups the subsectors of the financial corporations sector in a slightly different way from that described above. The central bank (S121), deposit-taking corporations except the central bank (S122) and MMFs (S123), if the liabilities they issue are considered to be part of broad money, are grouped together to form the "depository corporations subsector". This subsector is, in turn, split into the central bank subsector and the other depository corporations subsector (comprising deposit-taking corporations except the central bank and MMFs if the liabilities they issue are considered to be part of broad money). Furthermore, the remaining subsectors of the financial corporations sector are grouped to form the "other financial corporations" subsector.

3. Financial intermediaries, financial auxiliaries and other financial institutions

2.50. Another way combines the various subsectors to group all financial intermediaries separately. Financial intermediation is carried out by the majority of the financial corporations, for example, the central bank, deposit-taking corporations except the central bank, investment funds (MMFs and non-MMF investment funds), ICPFs, and other financial intermediaries, while no financial intermediation is provided by financial auxiliaries (S126) or captive financial institutions and moneylenders (S127).

2.51. Accordingly, financial corporations are divided into three broad classes, namely financial intermediaries, financial auxiliaries and other financial corporations. Financial intermediaries as institutional units incur liabilities on their own account for the purpose of acquiring financial assets by engaging in financial transactions on the market. They comprise all the subsectors of the financial corporations sector in table 2.1, except financial auxiliaries (S126) and captive financial institutions and moneylenders (S127). Financial auxiliary units (which belong to S126) mainly serve financial markets without taking ownership of the financial assets and liabilities they handle. Other finan-

[17] The 20 recommendations are described in Financial Stability Board and International Monetary Fund (2009).

[18] Shrestha (2012) provides more information on the templates.

cial corporations comprise captive financial institutions and moneylenders (S127). Such corporations provide financial services, whereby most of their assets or liabilities are not available on open financial markets.

4. Grouping of financial corporations based on control

2.52. As with non-financial corporations, financial corporations might, on the basis of the criterion of control, be split into: (a) public financial corporations; (b) national private financial corporations; and (c) foreign-controlled financial corporations. The corresponding subsectoring of financial corporations is shown in table 2.1.

5. Grouping of subsectors of the financial corporations sector in the Balance of Payments and International Investment Position Manual, Sixth Edition

2.53. Compared with the 2008 SNA, the subsectoring of financial corporations in the BPM6 is somewhat different. The standard components in the BPM6 classify financial corporations into the following three subsectors: the central bank,[19] deposit-taking corporations except the central bank, and other financial corporations (which comprises the other seven subsectors of the financial corporations sector in the 2008 SNA). Additional details can be compiled according to circumstances.

[19] An additional subsector may be identified for monetary authorities, where needed, as discussed in paragraph 4.70 of the BPM6.

Chapter 3
Financial production and income

A. Introduction

3.1. This chapter describes the nature of financial services produced by enterprises in the financial corporations sector and how the output of these services is calculated. An overview of the source data to calculate the output is provided in the chapter. In many instances, the source data to compute the output of financial services can be obtained from the returns of the financial institutions to the relevant government agency, such as the central bank, or from surveys conducted by the compiling agency or other government agencies responsible for the financial sector. Chapter 7 of the Handbook provides a more detailed description of how to collect the source data. This chapter will also provide an overview of social security schemes, as well as the methods and data sources which are used to calculate the output and other transactions associated with these schemes. It will also describe the supplementary table which was introduced in the 2008 SNA to show the extent of pension schemes included in, and excluded from, the 2008 SNA sequence of accounts and non-core accounts.

3.2. The output of financial services, which is computed using the source data, is measured at current prices, which are prices prevailing in the current period. Changes over time in the current-price value of an economic variable such as the output of financial services are caused by a combination of price and volume changes. This means that it is not meaningful to compare the changes in the value of these services at current prices over time, as they may reflect the full impact of changing prices. Thus, there is a need to isolate the price element from the current-price output of financial services so that the corresponding volume measures can be produced. This chapter will also provide guidance on how to compute the volume measures of the output of financial services. In principle, these volume measures should take changes in quality into account.

3.3. A number of illustrative worked examples are provided in this chapter to show how the output of the various types of financial services at current prices and the corresponding volume measures are calculated, as well as how the output and related transactions of financial corporations are recorded in the SNA. For convenience and where appropriate, some of the worked examples use the same figures from the relevant tables in the 2008 SNA. Given that the nature of the financial corporations sector may vary from country to country, the compiling agency may need to adapt the worked examples according to the circumstances of the country concerned. For easy reference, each item in the tables in the worked examples is assigned a line number. In addition, where appropriate, each item in the tables in the worked examples which is entered in the 2008 SNA sequence of accounts is also assigned an appropriate 2008 SNA code. The line numbers in the tables start afresh in each worked example. In addition, many of the worked examples show how to record in the financial account the counterpart entries to show the means of payment for some of the transactions between the institutional units. For simplicity, it is assumed that these transactions are settled in currency or transferable deposits, which are part of "currency and deposits" in the financial account. In these worked examples, the net lending/net borrowing which is recorded in the capital account and financial account is identical. In practice, differences in data sources and in the timing of the recording of transactions may result in a discrepancy between the estimates of net lending/net borrowing in the capital account and the financial account. Furthermore, the worked examples describe annual transactions. Nevertheless, they are generally applicable to quarterly transactions. The chapter concludes by describing the various types of property income which are payable and receivable by financial corporations and the possible data sources to compute and allocate the property income.

B. Nature of financial services and measurement of output

References:
2008 SNA, Chapter 4, Institutional units and sectors
2008 SNA, Chapter 6, The production account
2008 SNA, Chapter 17, Cross-cutting and other special issues

3.4. Corporations are divided between those resident institutional units mainly providing financial services and those mainly providing goods and other services. The principal activity of financial corporations is to provide financial services. The production of financial services is the result of financial intermediation, financial risk management, liquidity transformation or auxiliary financial activities.

3.5. Financial intermediation services are provided by financial intermediaries and typically comprise a major part of the services provided by the financial corporations sector. Financial intermediation services also involve financial risk management and liquidity transformation. Corporations engaged in these activities obtain funds, not only by taking deposits but also by issuing bills, bonds or other securities. They use these funds as well as their own funds to acquire mainly financial assets, not only by making advances or loans to others but also by purchasing bills, bonds or other securities.

3.6. Auxiliary financial activities facilitate financial intermediation, risk management and liquidity transformation activities. Financial auxiliaries typically act on behalf of other units and do not put themselves at risk by incurring financial liabilities or by acquiring financial assets as part of an intermediation service.

3.7. Other financial services comprise services provided by institutional units where most of their assets or liabilities are not available on open financial markets. Such services tend to take place between entities transacting within only a limited group of units (such as with subsidiaries) or subsidiaries of the same holding corporation, or are undertaken by entities providing loans from own funds provided by only one sponsor.

3.8. Besides the types of financial services above, there are also financial services associated with insurance and pension schemes. These institutional units provide financial services by redistributing funds between different units in the same period or between different periods for a single client. These services also involve risk management and liquidity transformation.

3.9. On the basis of the classification of the financial corporations sector into nine subsectors (see table 2.1 in chapter 2), financial intermediation services are mainly provided by the central bank (S121), deposit-taking corporations except the central bank (S122), money market funds (MMFs) (S123), non-MMF investment funds (S124), other financial intermediaries except insurance corporations and pension funds (S125), insurance corporations (S128) and pension funds (S129); financial auxiliary services are mainly provided by financial auxiliaries (S126); other financial services are mainly provided by captive financial institutions and moneylenders (S127).

3.10. Financial services may be paid for explicitly or implicitly. Some transactions in financial assets may involve both explicit and implicit charges. Four main ways in which financial services are provided and charged for may be considered:

(a) Financial services provided in return for explicit charges;

(b) Financial services provided in association with interest charges on loans and deposits;

(c) Financial services associated with the acquisition and disposal of financial assets and liabilities in financial markets;

(d) Financial services associated with insurance and pension schemes.

Examples of explicit charges include fees paid for getting a bank draft, the annual fees for credit cards, and commissions paid to brokers for the sales and purchases of stocks and shares. Examples of implicit charges arise from the financial services provided in association with interest charges on loans and deposits, the acquisition and disposal of financial assets and liabilities in financial markets, and insurance and pension schemes. The financial services provided in association with interest charges on loans and deposits are described in the SNA as FISIM.

3.11. The service charges are paid when financial corporations sell their output to other institutional units. Given the close linkage between service charges and output, there is a need to understand how the output of financial corporations is computed in the SNA. Since financial services may be paid for explicitly or implicitly, this implies that the output of financial corporations is also computed explicitly or implicitly. As a preview, table 3.1 summarizes the methods used in the SNA to compute the output of the institutional units in these subsectors based on the discussion in the previous paragraph. As can be observed, a number of methods are used to calculate the output of the institutional units in the subsectors of the financial corporations sector. Some of these methods are peculiar to the financial corporations sector. Furthermore, for many of these institutional units, there is more than one method to compute their output. In general, the method used depends on a number of factors, including whether the output is market or non-market output, whether the output is for own final use, as well as the type of subsector the institutional unit is in and data availability. The output associated with explicit service charges can be directly obtained from household surveys, enterprise surveys or the returns of financial institutions to the monetary authorities in many countries. In contrast, the output associated with implicit service charges is not directly reflected in the above-mentioned data sources. Instead, it will have to be computed by the compiling agency by putting together information from these sources.

3.12. As can be observed in table 3.1, explicit fees are charged by most of the financial corporations. These explicit fees can be in the form of flat rate fees or fees based on the value of a transaction stock or flow (i.e. an ad valorem charge). An example of a flat rate fee is the annual fee for the provision of a credit or charge card. An example of an ad valorem charge is the commission paid to brokers for the transaction in stocks and shares. The fee paid may be computed as a percentage of the transaction value of the stocks and shares. In many instances, however, explicit fees may comprise only a minor portion of the output of many financial corporations. For instance, financial corporations which are engaged in lending, including the finance associates of retailers, who may be responsible for financial leasing and both personal or commercial finance, are mainly involved in the provision of financial intermediation services. As indicated in table 3.1, the output associated with these services will have to be implicitly computed. However, these corporations may also charge miscellaneous explicit fees which may not comprise a substantial portion of their output. Nevertheless, the compiling agency should account for these fees when computing the output of these corporations.

3.13. Table 3.1 also shows that the output of financial services associated with a number of financial corporations can be calculated as the sum of costs. These include the central bank, head offices of financial corporations that are principally engaged in controlling financial corporations or groups of financial corporations but that do not themselves conduct the business of financial corporations, units which are legal entities (such as trusts, estates, agencies accounts or brass plate companies), holding corporations that hold only the assets of a group of subsidiary corporations and whose principal activity is owning the group without any other service to the enterprises in which the equity is held, non-life insurance, life insurance, and pension funds. However, it can also be observed that there are differences in the composition of the items which are used to compute the output of these financial corporations. Effectively, these result in three methods to compute output using the sum of costs. In the first method, the output is computed as the sum of intermediate consumption, compensation of employees, consumption of fixed capital and other taxes less subsidies on production. This applies to the non-market output of monetary policy and supervisory services of the central bank. In the second method, the output is computed as the sum of intermediate consumption, compensation of employees, capital costs and other taxes less subsidies on production. Capital costs are the sum of consumption of fixed capital and return to fixed capital. This applies to the output of head offices of financial corporations that are principally engaged in controlling financial corporations or groups of financial corporations but that do not themselves conduct the business of financial corporations, units which are legal entities (such as trusts, estates, agencies accounts or brass plate companies), holding corporations that hold only the assets of a group of subsidiary corporations and whose principal activity is owning the group without any other service to the enterprises in which the equity is held, and pension funds. The output is typically produced for own final use by related institutional units. It is computed using the sum of costs, mainly because of the difficulty in finding a genuine market price to value the output. The difference between the first and second methods is that the former excludes the return to fixed capital because, by convention, national accounting does not include this item in the computation of non-market output. In the third method, the output is computed as the sum of intermediate consumption, compensation of employees, capital costs and other taxes less subsidies on production, plus an allowance for "normal profit". This applies in the case of non-life and life insurance. The output has to be computed using the sum of costs owing to the lack of data to compute it using other methods. The difference between the second and third methods is that the latter includes an allowance for "normal profit". This is because the non-life and life insurance output is very likely to be purchased by non-related institutional units. Thus, there is a need to include an allowance for "normal profit", which is estimated by smoothing past profits and is not deducted for taxes.

3.14. The rest of this chapter will elaborate on the methods described in table 3.1 and, where appropriate, provide illustrative worked examples to give a better picture of how to compute the output of the various financial corporations. Given that the nature of financial corporations may differ from country to country, the methods as described in table 3.1 are neither exhaustive or prescriptive. The compiling agency may need to investigate the nature of the financial services provided by a financial corporation before deciding how to compute its output.

Table 3.1
Summary of methods to calculate the output of corporations in the financial corporations sector

Subsector	Method to compute output
Central bank (S121)[a]	
Monetary policy services	The services are non-market output, which is estimated as the sum of costs (i.e. intermediate consumption, compensation of employees, consumption of fixed capital and other taxes (less subsidies) on production)
Financial intermediation services	The services are market output, which is described as financial intermediation services indirectly measured (FISIM) and calculated as: $FISIM = (r_L - rr) \times Y_L + (rr - r_D) \times Y_D$, where r_L, r_D, rr, Y_L and Y_D represent the lending rate, deposit rate, reference rate, average stock of loans and average stock of deposits respectively
Borderline cases, such as supervisory services	The services may be market or non-market output, depending on whether explicit fees are sufficient to cover the costs of providing such services. Market output is the value of the explicit fees. Non-market output is estimated as the sum of costs (i.e. intermediate consumption, compensation of employees, consumption of fixed capital and other taxes (less subsidies) on production)
Deposit-taking corporations except the central bank (S122)	Output comprises a combination of the following: (a) Explicit fees charged in lieu of providing services; (b) Financial intermediation services indirectly measured (FISIM), which is calculated as $(r_L - rr) \times Y_L + (rr - r_D) \times Y_D$, where r_L, r_D, rr, Y_L and Y_D represent the lending rate, deposit rate, reference rate, average stock of loans and average stock of deposits respectively; (c) Transactions in foreign currencies, which are calculated as the difference between the buying price (or ask price) and mid-price, and the mid-price and selling price (or bid price) of the foreign currency that is exchanged
Money market funds (MMFs) (S123)	Output comprises a combination of the following fees: (a) Purchase and redemption fees, which are calculated as a percentage of the purchase and redemption values of the units/shares; (b) Exchange fees; (c) Account fees; (d) Annual recurring fees, such as management fees, distribution and/or service fees and other fees based on a percentage of a fund's asset value
Non-MMF investment funds (S124)	Output comprises a combination of the following fees: (a) Purchase and redemption fees which are calculated as a percentage of the purchase value and redemption value of the units/shares; (b) Exchange fees; (c) Account fees; (d) Annual recurring fees, such as management fees, distribution and/or service fees and other fees based on a percentage of a fund's asset value; (e) Performance fees (likely to be more applicable to hedge funds), which are calculated as a percentage of the profits earned by the funds

[a] If it is not possible to separate the market output from the non-market output, the whole of the output of the central bank should be treated as non-market and valued as the sum of costs.

Subsector	Method to compute output
Other financial intermediaries, except insurance corporations and pension funds (S125)	
Financial corporations engaged in the securitization of assets	Output is the value of the explicit fees
Security and derivative dealers (operating on own account)	Output is the difference between the buying price (or ask price) and mid-price, and the mid-price and selling price (or bid price) of the financial instrument that is exchanged
Financial corporations engaged in lending, including financial leasing, hire purchase and the provision of personal or commercial finance	Output comprises a combination of the following: (a) Explicit fees; (b) Implicit financial services provided, which are calculated as $(r_L - rr) \times Y_L$, where r_L, rr and Y_L represent the lending rate, reference rate and average stock of loans respectively
Central clearing counterparties	Output is the value of the explicit fees
Specialized financial corporations that assist other corporations in raising funds in equity and debt markets and provide strategic advisory services for mergers, acquisitions and other types of financial transactions	Output is the value of the explicit fees
Specialized financial corporations that provide short-term financing for corporate mergers and takeovers; export/import finance; factoring services; venture capital and development capital firms; loans against mortgage on real property by issuing mortgage bonds	Output comprises a combination of the following: (a) Explicit fees; (b) Implicit financial services provided, which are calculated as $(r_L - rr) \times Y_L$, where r_L, rr and Y_L represent the lending rate, reference rate and average stock of loans respectively
Financial auxiliaries (S126)	
Insurance brokers, salvage and claims adjusters (whether employed by the insurance corporation, an independent adjuster or a public adjuster employed by the policyholder), and insurance and pension consultants	Output is the value of the explicit fees
Loan brokers, securities brokers who arrange trades between security buyers and sellers but do not purchase and hold securities on their own account, investment advisers, etc	Output is the value of the explicit fees
Flotation corporations that manage the issue of securities	Output is the value of the explicit fees
Corporations whose principal function is to guarantee, by endorsement, bills and similar instruments	Output is the value of the explicit fees
Corporations that arrange derivative and hedging instruments (without issuing them)	Output is the value of the explicit fees
Corporations providing infrastructure for financial markets, including those providing transaction processing and settlement activities, such as for credit card transactions, as well as securities depository companies, custodians, clearing offices and nominee companies	Output is the value of the explicit fees
Managers of pension funds, mutual funds, etc. (but not the funds they manage)	Output is computed as follows: (a) For managers of pension funds (i.e. pension administrators), output is the value of the explicit fees; (b) For managers of mutual funds, output is the value of fees such as management fees and distribution and/or service fees, performance fees (for hedge funds), which are calculated as a percentage of the value of the funds, and performance fees (typically for hedge funds), which are calculated as a percentage of the profits earned by the funds

Subsector	Method to compute output
Corporations providing stock exchange, insurance exchange, and commodity and derivative exchange	Output is the value of the explicit fees
Foreign exchange bureaux	Output is the difference between the buying price (or ask price) and mid-price, and the mid-price and selling price (or bid price) of the foreign currency that is exchanged
Non-profit institutions recognized as independent legal entities serving financial corporations, but that do not themselves provide financial services	Output is the value of the explicit fees
Head offices of financial corporations that are principally engaged in controlling financial corporations or groups of financial corporations, but that do not themselves conduct the business of financial corporations	Output is calculated as the value of explicit fees or the sum of costs (i.e. intermediate consumption, compensation of employees, capital costs and other taxes (less subsidies) on production)
Central supervisory authorities of financial intermediaries and financial markets when they are separate institutional units	Output is the value of the explicit fees
Captive financial institutions and moneylenders (S127)	
Units which are legal entities, such as trusts, estates, agencies' accounts or brass plate companies	Output is estimated as the sum of costs (i.e. intermediate consumption, compensation of employees, capital costs and other taxes (less subsidies) on production)
Holding corporations that hold only the assets (owning controlling-levels of equity) of a group of subsidiary corporations and whose principal activity is owning the group without providing any other service to the enterprises in which the equity is held, i.e. they do not administer or manage other units	Output is calculated as the value of explicit fees or the sum of costs (i.e. intermediate consumption, compensation of employees, capital costs and other taxes (less subsidies) on production)
Special purpose entities (SPEs) or conduits that qualify as institutional units and raise funds in open markets to be used by their parent corporation	Output is calculated as the value of explicit fees or the sum of costs (i.e. intermediate consumption, compensation of employees, capital costs and other taxes (less subsidies) on production)
Units which provide financial services exclusively with own funds or funds provided by a sponsor to a range of clients and incur the financial risk of the debtor defaulting. They include moneylenders, corporations engaged in lending (providing student and import/export loans, for example) from funds received from a sponsor, such as a government unit or non-profit institution, as well as pawnshops that predominantly engage in lending	Output comprises a combination of the following: (a) Implicit financial services provided, which are calculated as $(r_L - rr) \times Y_L$, where r_L, rr and Y_L represent the lending rate, reference rate and average stock of loans respectively; (b) Explicit fees
Insurance corporations (S128)	
Non-life insurance	Besides (d), output is computed using either (a), (b) or (c): (a) Output is calculated as actual premiums earned plus expected premium supplements minus expected claims incurred, where expected claims and premium supplements are estimated from past experience (expectations approach); (b) Output is calculated as actual premiums earned plus premium supplements minus adjusted claims incurred, where adjusted claims are determined by using claims due plus the changes in equalization provisions and, if necessary, changes to own funds (accounting approach); (c) Output is calculated as the sum of costs (i.e. intermediate consumption, compensation of employees, capital costs and other taxes (less subsidies) on production) plus an allowance for "normal profit"; (d) Explicit fees

Subsector	Method to compute output
Life insurance	Besides (c), output is computed using either (a) or (b): (a) Output is calculated as actual premiums earned plus premium supplements minus benefits due minus increases (plus decreases) in actuarial reserves and reserves for with-profits insurance; (b) Output is calculated as the sum of costs (i.e. intermediate consumption, compensation of employees, capital costs and other taxes (less subsidies) on production) plus an allowance for "normal profit"; (c) Explicit fees
Reinsurance	Output includes a combination of the following: (a) Output is calculated as actual premiums earned less commissions payable plus premium supplements minus both adjusted claims incurred and profit sharing; (b) Explicit fees
Pension funds (S129)	Output is estimated as the sum of costs (i.e. intermediate consumption, compensation of employees, capital costs and other taxes (less subsidies) on production)

1. Financial services provided in return for explicit charges

References:
2008 SNA, Chapter 6, The production account
2008 SNA, Chapter 17, Cross-cutting and other special issues, Part 4, The recording of flows associated with financial assets and liabilities
BPM6 Compilation Guide, Chapter 12, Services

3.15. As table 3.1 shows, financial services provided in return for explicit charges are provided by many categories of financial institutions. Deposit-taking corporations may charge households to arrange a mortgage, manage an investment portfolio, give taxation advice, administer an estate, and so on. Specialized financial institutions may charge non-financial corporations to arrange a flotation of shares or to administer a restructuring of a group of corporations.

3.16. The most pervasive and probably largest direct fee is likely to be that charged by credit card issuers to the units that accept credit cards as a means of payment for the goods and services they provide. The charge is usually calculated as a percentage of the sale; in the case of retailers, the sale value corresponds to turnover and not output. Although the percentage is usually small, maybe 1-2 per cent, the fact that it is applied to such large totals means that the total value of the charge is very significant. The charge represents output of the credit card companies and intermediate consumption of the corporations that accept credit cards as means of payment. Ignoring the role of the credit card company does not affect the measurement of the expenditure (usually final consumption or exports) on the goods and services concerned, but does underestimate the costs of the provider of goods and services and the output of the credit card company. This, in turn, leads to a misallocation of value added from the credit card company to the provider of the goods and services paid for by credit card.

3.17. The example of the credit card company is one that clearly demonstrates that a financial corporation may provide services that are paid for by different means by different customers or in different circumstances. In addition to the fee charged to the corporations accepting a credit card as means of payment, the card holder may also be charged an explicit fee, usually each year, for holding the card. In addition, if a card holder uses the credit facilities offered by the card, he will pay indirect charges associated with interest payable on the outstanding credit (which is treated as a loan in the SNA).

3.18. Both resident and non-resident financial institutions can provide financial services in return for explicit fees. Explicit fees should always be recorded as payable by the unit to whom the services are rendered to the institution performing the service. If the services are rendered to a corporation, government or NPISHs, the costs will form part of intermediate consumption. If they are rendered to households, they will be treated as final consumption unless the financial service is performed in relation to an unincorporated enterprise, including the owning and occupying of a dwelling. If they are rendered to non-residents, they will be treated as exports of goods and services. The estimates of explicit fees for financial services which are provided by resident financial institutions can be obtained in a relatively straightforward manner from various sources, including surveys of resident financial institutions and the returns of resident financial institutions to the monetary authorities. If possible, the compiling agency should request respondents to provide a sectoral breakdown of these explicit fees in their survey returns or returns to the monetary authorities. If such a breakdown is unavailable, the compiling agency should consider breaking down the data by sector using data from various sources such as household surveys, enterprise surveys and government financial statements.

3.19. The explicit fees payable by resident institutional units to non-resident financial institutions for the financial services they provide are included in total imports of goods and services. The estimates of these explicit fees can be obtained directly from balance of payments statistics. However, if the balance of payments statistics do not report estimates of these items, the compiling agency may need to estimate them using a combination of sources, including an international transactions reporting system (ITRS), international trade in services enterprise surveys, household surveys or partner country data. An ITRS measures individual balance of payments cash transactions passing through the domestic banks and foreign bank accounts of enterprises, as well as non-cash transactions and stock positions. Statistics are compiled from forms submitted by domestic banks to the compilers and from forms submitted by enterprises to the compiler. The compiling agency should estimate the explicit charges in consultation with the compilers of the balance of payments to ensure that there is consistency in the recording of these transactions in the national accounts and balance of payments statistics. After obtaining the required data either directly from the balance of payments statistics or through the other sources mentioned above, the compiling agency will still need to allocate the data on total imports of these explicit charges to the resident institutional sectors. The allocation can be carried out using data from the ITRS if it is able to provide a reliable breakdown of the data by user sector. Alternatively, the compiling agency can consider allocating the data in proportion to the consumption of corresponding domestically produced explicit charges by the resident user sectors.

Volume measures of financial services provided in return for explicit charges

2008 SNA, Chapter 15, Price and volume measures
Handbook on Price and Volume measures in National Accounts, Chapter 4, A/B/C methods for output by product

3.20. The estimates of the explicit fees for financial services which are discussed in the previous section are expressed in current prices, which are prices prevailing in the accounting period. Changes over time in the current-price value of an economic variable such as explicit fees are caused by a combination of price and volume changes. Thus, there is a need to isolate the price element from current-price explicit fees so as to obtain a measure of explicit fees which is free of price changes. Measures of inflation-free explicit fees are known in the SNA as the volume measures of explicit fees.

3.21. The methods used to construct volume measures of financial services provided in return for explicit fees may depend on whether these services are provided by resident or non-resident financial institutions. The ideal method of obtaining volume measures of explicit fees payable to resident financial institutions is to deflate the current-price value of each type of explicit fee by an appropriate price index, which should be adjusted for quality changes as far as possible. In this instance, the appropriate price index will be a sub-index of the producer price index (PPI), as this price index is associated with price changes in the output of a product. Thus, to obtain the volume measures of annual card fees, the compiling agency should, in principle, use the PPI for annual credit fees as a deflator. In instances where this sub-index of the PPI is not available, it can consider alternative price indices, such as a PPI with a broader coverage for financial services. Alternatively, if the financial service in question is used only or mostly by households, an appropriate sub-index of the consumer price index can be used as a deflator. However, it may be the case that price indices for many financial services do not exist and are potentially difficult to collect because of the wide range of services involved. As a result, the compiling agency may need to consider the use of appropriate volume indicators to construct volume measures of explicit fees. For example, one volume indicator that can be used to construct volume measures of annual credit card fees is the number of credit cards in circulation.

3.22. Current-price estimates of the financial services provided by non-resident financial institutions in return for explicit fees may not be disaggregated enough to allow the compiling agency to construct the corresponding volume measures using the appropriate sub-indices of the import price index. Thus, the compiling agency can consider using an import price index with a broader coverage for financial services. If the appropriate import price indices are not available, the compiling agency may consider constructing a composite price index comprising the appropriate price indices for the entire category of explicit charges for financial services from partner countries which are adjusted for changes in exchange rates. The compiling agency can also consider constructing a composite volume index comprising the volume measures of the exports of the relevant explicit fees or volume measures of the relevant explicit fees from partner countries. The composite volume index can then be used to extrapolate base-period imports of the explicit fees to obtain the corresponding volume measures. If data from partner countries are not available, the compiling agency may consider using the price indices which are used to deflate domestically produced current-price explicit fees.

2. Financial services provided in association with interest charges on loans and deposits

(a) Financial intermediation services indirectly measured

References:
2008 SNA, Chapter 6, The production account
2008 SNA, Chapter 7, The distribution of income accounts
2008 SNA, Chapter 11, The financial account
2008 SNA, Annex 3, Changes from the 1993 System of National Accounts
BPM6 Compilation Guide, Appendix 3, Financial intermediation services indirectly measured

3.23. One traditional way in which financial services are provided is by means of financial intermediation. This is understood to refer to the process whereby a financial institution, such as a deposit-taking corporation, accepts deposits from units wishing to receive interest on funds for which the unit has no immediate use and lends them to other units whose funds are insufficient to meet their needs at higher interest rates. The deposit-taking corporation thus provides an implicit financial service by allowing the first unit to lend to the second and relies on these net interest receipts generated by a positive spread between the interest rate paid to deposits and the rate received from borrowers to finance a large part of its operating costs. In principle, interest receipts are not normally included in the computation of output and value added in the SNA, as they are classified as property income. In the case of deposit-taking corporations, however, not to include net interest receipts would result in a measure of output that fails to capture much of the value of the services that they provide to their clients because interest rate spreads are substitutes for explicit fees for services. Hence, if the value added for deposit-taking corporations were to be computed in the same way as for other corporations, their value added and operating surplus would be very low or even negative. To avoid this paradoxical outcome, there is a need to incorporate the value of the implicit financial services produced by deposit-taking corporations into the SNA. These implicit financial services are known in the SNA as financial intermediation services indirectly measured, or FISIM.

3.24. FISIM is computed by splitting the interest transactions with financial corporations into two transaction categories, one showing interest as understood in the SNA and the other representing the implicit payment for financial intermediation services. The actual interest payable to, or receivable from, financial corporations is known as "bank interest". Bank interest payable to financial corporations can be divided into two components: interest as understood in the SNA known as "SNA interest" and the implicit payment for financial intermediation services known as FISIM. SNA interest receivable from financial corporations can be divided into actual bank interest and FISIM. As noted in the 2008 SNA, FISIM applies "only to loans and deposits and only when those loans and deposits are provided by, or deposited with, financial institutions."

3.25. The types of loans to be included in the calculation of FISIM include the amount overdrawn on overdrafts, instalment loans, hire-purchase credit, revolving credit, loans to finance trade credit and mortgage loans. Securities repurchase agreements, gold swaps and financing by means of a financial lease may also be classified as loans. Even if such loans are given out using the financial institution's own funds, they should still be included in the calculation of FISIM.

3.26. The types of deposits to be included in FISIM include transferable deposits and other deposits, which typically include savings deposits, fixed-term deposits, non-negotiable certificates of deposit, deposits of limited transferability, and overnight and very short-term repurchase agreements if they are considered part of the definition of broad money. Shares or similar evidence of deposit issued by savings and loan associations, building societies, credit unions and the like, as well as repayable margin payments in cash related to financial derivative contracts, are also included.

3.27. Furthermore, the financial institution does not necessarily have to offer both deposit-taking and loan facilities to produce FISIM. The financial subsidiaries of retailers and financial corporations that specialize in leasing (for example, property companies or aircraft leasing companies) are examples of financial institutions that make loans without accepting deposits. A moneylender who has sufficiently detailed accounts to be treated as an actual or quasi-corporation may receive this sort of charge; indeed, since moneylenders usually charge especially high rates of interest, their service charges may exceed the SNA interest payments by significant amounts.

3.28. Figure 3.1 shows the relationship between actual bank interest, SNA interest and FISIM for loans and deposits. It highlights the key role of SNA interest in the calculation of FISIM. The computation of SNA interest requires the application of an

Figure 3.1
Relationship between actual bank interest, SNA interest and FISIM

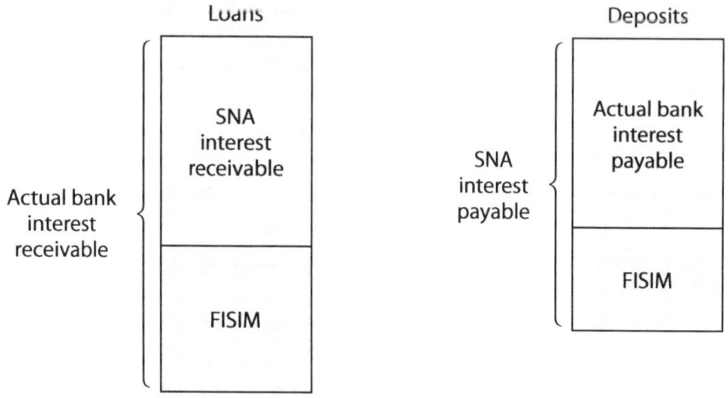

appropriate interest rate to loans and deposits. This interest rate is described in the 2008 SNA as a "reference" rate of interest. The reference rate is a rate of interest at which lending and borrowing take place without including any service charges. This reference rate is used to calculate SNA interest for deposits and loans. After the SNA interest is calculated, FISIM is calculated as shown in figure 3.1 as the difference between the actual bank interest receivable and the SNA interest receivable by financial corporations on the loans they issue, and the difference between SNA interest payable and the actual bank interest payable by financial corporations on the deposits of their customers. FISIM is a component of the bank interest receivable by financial corporations on the loans they issue, partly because borrowers are willing to pay more than the SNA interest in order to utilize the services provided by financial corporations. Likewise, FISIM is one component of the SNA interest payable by financial corporations on the deposits of their customers because the latter are willing to accept lower bank interest payments on their deposits in order to receive the services provided by financial corporations.

3.29. Mathematically, FISIM can be written as:

$$FISIM = FISIM_L + FISIM_D = \left(\frac{r_L - rr}{100.0}\right)Y_L + \left(\frac{rr - r_D}{100.0}\right)Y_D \qquad (3.1)$$

where $FISIM_L$, $FISIM_D$, r_L, r_D, rr, Y_L and Y_D represent FISIM on loans made by financial institutions, FISIM on deposits held by financial institutions, the lending and deposit rates of interest, the reference rate of interest, the average stock of loans and average stock of deposits respectively. The various interest rates are expressed as a percentage.

3.30. It is seldom the case that the amount of funds lent by a financial institution exactly matches the amount deposited with them. Some money may have been deposited but not yet loaned; some loans may be financed by the bank's own funds and not from borrowed funds. However, the depositor of funds receives the same amount of interest and service whether or not his funds are lent by the bank to another customer, and the borrower pays the same rate of interest and receives the same service whether his funds are provided by intermediated funds or from the bank's own funds. For this reason, FISIM is to be imputed in respect of all loans and deposits offered by a financial institution, irrespective of the source of the funds.

3.31. The financial institutions in question need not be resident; nor need the clients of the financial institution be resident. Thus, imports and exports of financial intermediation services are possible.

3.32. The 2008 SNA recommends that the output and supply of FISIM should be distributed to users across the institutional sectors. This includes the rest of the world, given that the financial institutions which provide FISIM need not be resident. Allocation to resident institutional units will allow the use of FISIM to be classified as intermediate or final consumption, while allocation to the rest of the world is included in exports of services. The distinction between intermediate and final consumption will depend on the purpose for which the institutional sector is consuming the service. Intermediate consumption is incurred by corporations, general government, households (in their role as owners of dwellings and unincorporated enterprises) and NPISHs. Allocation of FISIM to intermediate consumption of institutional sectors will also need to be broken down into the respective industries so as to properly account for their value added. Final consumption expenditure is incurred by general government, households (in their role as consumers) and NPISHs. The output of FISIM is allocated to the intermediate and final consumption of general government and NPISHs because these sectors comprise non-market producers whose output is valued as the sum of costs. The output of FISIM which is allocated to the intermediate consumption of the institutional units in these two sectors increases the value of their output and also the value of their final consumption expenditure.

3.33. The reference rate to be used in the calculation of SNA interest is a rate between bank interest rates on deposits and loans. The reference rate should contain no service element and reflect the risk and maturity structure of deposits and loans. If the absolute value of the effect on the average rate payable to depositors of the FISIM provided to depositors equals the effect on the average rate receivable from borrowers of the FISIM provided to borrowers,[20] then a simple way to obtain a reference rate that reflects the maturity structure of the financial assets and liabilities is to calculate the simple average of the ratio of interest receivable on loans to the stock of loans and ratio of interest payable on deposits to the stock of deposits as shown in equation (3.2):

$$rr_s = 0.5\left(\frac{R_L}{Y_L} + \frac{R_D}{Y_D}\right) \times 100.0 \tag{3.2}$$

where rr_s is the simple average reference rate expressed as a percentage, R_L is the interest receivable on loans made by financial institutions, R_D is the interest payable on deposits held with financial institutions, Y_L is the average stock of loans and Y_D is the average stock of deposits.

3.34. The approach above is known as the endogenous reference rate approach and is probably more suitable for countries with less detailed data. It should be evaluated carefully to ensure that the result is appropriate. Ideally, only intermediated loans (such as loans provided by banks) should be used in the calculation to avoid questionable results. The compiling agency may also consider calculating the reference rate as a weighted average of the interest rates on loans and deposits using the following formula:

$$rr_w = \frac{R_L + R_D}{Y_L + Y_D} \times 100.0 \tag{3.3}$$

where rr_w is the weighted average reference rate expressed as a percentage and the terms on the right-hand side are as defined in equation (3.2).

If the service element in the rate on loans differs from that in the rate on deposits, half the difference will either be added to, or subtracted from, the weighted reference rate if the mid-point method is used. If the difference is significant, the weighted average reference rate may be preferable to the simple average reference rate.

3.35. Instead of using endogenous interest rates on loans and deposits, the compiling agency can also consider calculating the reference rate as the weighted average of

[20] This implies that the margins for loans and deposits are equal.

observable exogenous rates of maturities with different terms (weighted by the stock of loans and deposits in each maturity).

3.36. The rate prevailing for interbank borrowing and lending may be another suitable choice as a reference rate, although this may not exactly reflect the risk and maturity structure of deposits and loans, since the rate only reflects short-term lending and borrowing. Other potential reference rate candidates include the rate on service-free financial instruments such as government bonds. However, different reference rates may be needed for each currency in which loans and deposits are denominated, especially when a non-resident financial institution is involved. Thus, the compiling agency may need to compute reference rates for international trade in FISIM in addition to reference rates for domestically produced FISIM. For exports of FISIM, the reference rate can follow the reference rate which is used to calculate the output of domestically produced FISIM. For imports of FISIM, the reference rates can follow the respective reference rates which are used to calculate the domestically produced FISIM of the supplying countries. This is to ensure global consistency in international trade statistics. As noted in box 3.1, countries will need to select the reference rate according to national circumstances. For banks within the same economy, there is often little if any service provided in association with banks lending to and borrowing from other banks.

3.37. Banks may offer loans that they describe as being fixed interest loans. This is to be interpreted as a situation where the level of bank interest is fixed, but, as the reference rate changes, the level of SNA interest and the service charge will vary. Effectively, this means that the fixed interest rate is set so that, on average over the life of the loan, the gap between the loan interest rate and the reference rate will cover the service charge.

Box 3.1

The System of National Accounts 2008 research agenda on financial intermediation services indirectly measured

It has been long recognized since at least the 1953 version of the SNA that the current-price value of financial services has a significant indirectly measured component whose value is covered wholly or in part in the spread between financial institutions' return on financial assets and expense on liabilities. Measuring the economy's output and use of FISIM has been the subject of refinements in every revision of the SNA since 1968, including the preparation of the 2008 SNA.[a] Although the 2008 SNA notes that the production of financial services is the result of financial intermediation, financial risk management, liquidity transformation or auxiliary financial activities, there remained a broad international consensus that the following aspects of the international recommendations on FISIM should be clarified or investigated further:

(a) How the composition of the services that FISIM covers – particularly risk management and liquidity transformation – affects the selection of the reference rate and the price and volume breakdown of FISIM;

(b) The financial instrument and unit scope of FISIM;

(c) The connection between the recommendations on the implementation of FISIM and the definition of income.

Aspect (a) is a short-term issue for clarification on how the existing 2008 SNA text should be understood and applied in the compilation of national accounts. Aspects (b) and (c) are two research issues which will be dealt with at a later stage. Aspect (b) reflects a medium-term need for answers to research questions concerning how the 2008 SNA handles the role of financial capital in production in the context of the analysis and recommendations of, for example, the OECD Manual on Measuring Capital. Aspect (c) concerns, among other things, how the findings under (a) and (b) shed light on another 2008 SNA research agenda topic, namely the definition of income.

[a] OECD (1998) provides a broad overview of the treatment of FISIM in the 1953, 1968 and 1993 SNA.

There are four clarification questions related to aspect (a):

- How should financial institutions' risk management/mitigation activities be characterized and reflected in FISIM?
- How should this liquidity transformation element be represented in FISIM? Should the differences in maturities be reflected in FISIM calculations? If so, how?
- How can FISIM be made consistent in international trade?
- What are the implications for the price and volume measures of FISIM that follow from the clarification of the issues raised above?

In accordance with the SNA update procedures, the following key recommendations were subsequently made:

(a) For estimating imports and exports of FISIM, FISIM should be calculated by at least two groups of currencies (national and foreign currency);

(b) The reference rate for a specific currency need not be the same for FISIM providers resident in different economies. However, they should be expected, under normal circumstances, to be relatively close, so national statistics agencies are encouraged to use partner country information where national estimates are not available;

(c) Liquidity transformation services should remain part of FISIM and a single reference rate should be used to determine FISIM;

(d) The calculation (definition) of the reference rate should be determined according to national circumstances, using preferably any of the following approaches:

(i) A reference rate based on a single observable exogenous rate for a specific instrument, such as interbank lending rates;

(ii) A reference rate based on a weighted average of observable exogenous rates of maturities with different terms (weighted by the stock of loans and deposits in each maturity);

(iii) A weighted average of the endogenous interest rates on loans and deposits;

(e) Considerable care should be taken in determining FISIM estimates during periods of volatile movements in reference rates and when liquidity markets begin to dysfunction. These periods may be characterized by inducing to negative FISIM estimates, particularly for depositors, but also for borrowers. When such incidences occur, countries are encouraged to review the applicability of the underlying reference rate for that period to calculate FISIM;

(f) Volume measures for FISIM should be calculated as follows:

(i) Using a deflated stocks approach (with weights based on types of loans and deposits) in view of its simplicity;

(ii) Deflating stocks of loans and deposits using a general price, which should itself exclude FISIM;

(iii) Using domestic price indices for exports, while for imports the appropriate country price indices should be used;

(iv) Output indicators could also be used to calculate volume measures of FISIM. Double counting for explicitly charged services should be avoided.

Topics for further research in FISIM include:

(a) Developing more clarity regarding FISIM (-related) references in the 2008 SNA, especially in relation to treatment of risk and definition of financial services;

(b) Further develop the conceptual arguments to either include or exclude credit default risk (CDR) in the calculation of FISIM, and in the case of excluding CDR, to develop methods and data that could support a possible exclusion of CDR in the future;

(c) Consider possible hybrid approaches to price and volume measurement;

(d) Further develop the "costs of funds" approach to determine the reference rate, and further develop possible alternative approaches (vintage reference rate);

(e) Consider the financial instruments and unit scope of FISIM;

(f) The connection between the recommendations on implementing FISIM and the definition of income.

The first three items, i.e. (a), (b) and (c), can be considered as clarifications of the 2008 SNA.

3.38. When an enterprise acquires a fixed asset under the terms of a financial lease, a loan is imputed between the lessor and the lessee. Regular payments under the lease are treated as being payments of interest and repayment of capital. When the lessor is a financial institution, the interest payable under the terms of a financial lease corresponds to bank interest and should be separated into SNA interest and financial service charge, as for any other loan.

3.39. Even when a loan is described as non-performing, interest and the associated service charge continue to be recorded in the SNA.

3.40. The calculated value of FISIM may be negative. This gives rise to interpretation problems, as it is not possible for output to be negative. There are some reasons for this result. First, persistent negative FISIM may be due to the use of inappropriate reference rates. For example, a compiling agency may select, say, a short-term interbank lending rate as the reference rate. However, this reference rate may not be aligned with the maturity structure of loans and deposits. Thus, when interest rates offered to depositors are higher than the reference rate, negative FISIM to depositors will occur. To mitigate this, the compiling agency will need to re-examine the reference rate it is using. Second, even if the selected reference rate is appropriate, sporadic episodes of negative FISIM, particularly for depositors, but also for borrowers, may be observed during periods of volatile movements in reference rates when liquidity markets begin to dysfunction. This could occur in times of financial crisis. Considerable care should be taken in determining FISIM estimates during these periods. The compiling agency may need to review the applicability of the underlying reference rate for that period to calculate FISIM when such incidences occur.

Allocation of financial intermediation services indirectly measured to user sectors

Reference:
BPM6 Compilation Guide, Appendix 3, Financial intermediation services indirectly measured
ESA 2010, Chapter 14, Financial intermediation services indirectly measured (FISIM)

3.41. The input data to compute FISIM, SNA interest and bank interest should be available in the reports provided by deposit-taking corporations to the monetary authority. If not, the compiling agency should discuss with the monetary authority how to obtain the data. Some examples of other possible data sources include surveys or censuses conducted by other government agencies, surveys conducted by private enterprises and industry groups, or proprietary data, such as data sets from credit reporting agencies.

3.42. Depending on the nature of the source data, the compiling agency can consider two approaches to allocate FISIM and related transactions to sectors. The first approach can be described as the "bottom-up" approach. This approach assumes that the compiling agency is able to obtain data on the interest receivable on loans, interest payable on deposits and stocks of loans and deposits by institutional sector (including the rest of the world). Thus, it can directly compute the FISIM and SNA interest on loans and deposits to be allocated to each sector. These transactions are then summed up to obtain the economy-wide estimates. During the process, the compiling agency will also need to break down the FISIM allocated to households into the following categories:

- Intermediate consumption of households in their capacity as owners of dwellings.
- Intermediate consumption of households in their capacity as owners of unincorporated enterprises.
- Final consumption of households.

This breakdown corresponds to the following breakdown of loans to households (stocks and interest):

- Dwelling loans.[21]
- Loans to households as owners of unincorporated enterprises.
- Other loans to households.

If dwelling loans and loans to households as owners of unincorporated enterprises are available from, say, monetary and financial statistics, the compiling agency can directly compute the FISIM and SNA interest for these two categories. The FISIM, SNA interest and bank interest for other loans can then be obtained by subtracting the two previously mentioned categories of loans from the total.

Household deposits are broken down into:

- Deposits of households as owners of unincorporated enterprises.
- Deposits of households as consumers.

If the source data according to this breakdown are available, the compiling agency can directly compute the FISIM, SNA interest and bank interest for these categories.

3.43. Even if the source data are available by sector, adjustments may need to be made if the definition of sector in the source data does not match the definition used in national accounting.

3.44. However, it is likely that the input data may only be available without a sectoral breakdown. Consequently, the compiling agency may need to consider the use of the second approach, which can be described as the "top-down" approach. In this approach, the compiling agency can use the available source data to compute the total FISIM, SNA interest and bank interest on loans and deposits. After that, it will use various indicators such as loan/deposit balances or interest receivable/payable from other sources to allocate the computed data to user sectors.[22]

3.45. The compiling agency will also need to distribute the estimates of FISIM, SNA interest and bank interest which are allocated to households to the respective categories, as described earlier. The compiling agency can consider using the same indicators which are described above to carry out the allocation. However, if these indicators are not available, the compiling agency can consider other methods. For example, if data on deposits of households as owners of unincorporated enterprises are unavailable, they can be estimated by assuming that the ratio of stocks of deposits to value added or turnover observed for the smallest corporations applies to unincorporated enterprises. The estimated data on deposits can then be used to allocate the estimates of FISIM, SNA interest and bank interest on deposits for households.

3.46. Resident institutional units are also likely to be clients of non-resident deposit-taking corporations. Estimates of the total imports of FISIM, SNA interest and bank interest on loans and deposits can be obtained directly from balance of payments statistics. However, if the balance of payments statistics do not report estimates of these items, the compiling agency may need to estimate them using a combination of sources. It can consider conducting enterprise and household surveys to collect data on the stock

[21] Dwelling loans obtained by households can be used to purchase homes for owner-occupancy or tenant-occupancy. Revolving lines of credit and business loans secured by dwelling loans should not be included in dwelling loans.

[22] This method can be improved upon if the indicators can be broken down by subcategory of loan/deposit. For example, if FISIM can be computed separately for mortgages, credit cards and other instalment loans, and a separate indicator exists for each of these types of loans, then each type of loan can be allocated to sectors separately and FISIM may be added up across loan subcategories within each sector to yield total FISIM by sector. Similarly, if indicators exist for the different subcategories of deposits, such as demand, time and savings deposits, then this can be done for depositor FISIM.

of loans and deposits, as well as on the associated interest transactions with non-resident deposit-taking corporations. The input data to calculate imports of FISIM by general government can be obtained from general government accounts. Alternatively, it can consider using partner country data. In addition, it can explore the use of Bank for International Settlements (BIS) data on deposits and loans of banks around the world by country of counterpart. The compiling agency should estimate the imports of FISIM, SNA interest and bank interest in consultation with the compilers of the balance of payments to ensure that there is consistency in the recording of these transactions in the national accounts and balance of payments statistics.[23]

3.47. After obtaining the required data either directly from the balance of payments statistics or through estimation techniques, the compiling agency will still need to allocate the data on total imports of FISIM, SNA interest and bank interest to the resident institutional sectors. If the compiling agency is able to obtain the breakdown of the input data by resident institutional sector from various sources such as sample surveys and administrative data such as government financial accounts, then it will be able to directly calculate the consumption of imported FISIM, SNA interest payable and bank interest payable for each sector. The total value of imported FISIM can then be obtained as the sum of the corresponding sectoral estimates. On the other hand, if the compiling agency is only able to calculate the total value of imported FISIM from the input data, it will need to allocate this estimate to the resident institutional sectors using various assumptions. For example, it can consider allocating the data in proportion to the sectoral data on stocks of loans and deposits of resident deposit-taking corporations.

Worked example 3.1. Computation of financial intermediation services indirectly measured and SNA interest by institutional sector

3.48. This worked example shows how to compute the current-price output of FISIM and SNA interest using the "bottom-up" approach.[24] The estimate of FISIM depends on the frequency of computation. FISIM calculated using annual input data may be different from the corresponding estimates of FISIM which are calculated using quarterly input data. The latter estimates may be more accurate and precise. For illustration purposes, annual rather than quarterly data are used to compute FISIM in this worked example, so the compiling agency may need to adapt the worked example to incorporate the use of quarterly data. In addition, the worked example will show how to record in the financial account the counterpart entries to show the means of payment for some of the transactions between the institutional units. For simplicity, it is assumed that these transactions are settled in currency or transferable deposits, which are part of "currency and deposits" in the financial account.

3.49. Table 3.2 shows the information on the breakdown of interest receivable on loans and interest payable on deposits of resident deposit-taking corporations by sector in an economy. The interest receivable on loans and interest payable on deposits are described in the SNA as "bank interest". The interest payable by households for loans provided to them also includes a separate amount for dwelling loans. As mentioned before, the FISIM on dwelling loans is counted as intermediate consumption of the households sector, since it is used as an input to produce dwelling services. For simplicity, it is assumed that households do not own unincorporated enterprises. Thus, the FISIM on loans to households is split between intermediate consumption

---

[23] In general, the data available to calculate imports and exports of FISIM, especially with separate reference rates, and with respect to individual (sub) sectors and industries is low, so there is a need to initiate a form of international coordination such that information on FISIM imports/exports by country could be made available to facilitate consistency across countries.

[24] An example to show how to allocate FISIM using the "top-down" approach to industries is provided in worked example 3.2.

of households in their capacity as owners of dwellings and household final consumption, while the FISIM on deposits to households is entirely allocated to household final consumption.

3.50. The balance sheet showing the breakdown of the loans (assets) and deposits (liabilities) of the deposit-taking corporations by institutional sector is presented in

Table 3.2

Data on the interest receivable on loans and interest payable on deposits offered by resident deposit-taking corporations

Line number	Item	Value
(1)	Interest receivable on loans	150.1
(1a)	Non-financial corporations	80.0
(1b)	Other financial corporations	7.5
(1c)	General government	10.0
(1d)	Households	36.1
(1e)	of which: dwelling loans	20.0
(1f)	NPISHs	7.5
(1g)	Rest of the world	9.0
(2)	Interest payable on deposits	62.9
(2a)	Non-financial corporations	36.0
(2b)	Other financial corporations	6.6
(2c)	General government	5.0
(2d)	Households	8.0
(2e)	NPISHs	4.3
(2f)	Rest of the world	3.0

Table 3.3

Data on the stock of loans and deposits of resident deposit-taking corporations

Line number	Financial assets and liabilities	Value
(3)	Stock of loans granted on 1 January	1809.0
(3a)	Non-financial corporations	982.0
(3b)	Other financial corporations	102.0
(3c)	General government	110.0
(3d)	Households	430.0
(3e)	of which: dwelling loans	230.0
(3f)	NPISHs	90.0
(3g)	Rest of the world	95.0
(4)	Stock of deposits held on 1 January	1127.0
(4a)	Non-financial corporations	650.0
(4b)	Other financial corporations	99.0
(4c)	General government	98.0
(4d)	Households	150.0
(4e)	NPISHs	80.0
(4f)	Rest of the world	50.0
(5)	Stock of loans granted on 31 December	1893.0
(5a)	Non-financial corporations	1022.0
(5b)	Other financial corporations	104.0
(5c)	General government	116.0
(5d)	Households	440.0
(5e)	of which: dwelling loans	240.0
(5f)	NPISHs	96.0
(5g)	Rest of the world	115.0
(6)	Stock of deposits held on 31 December	1155.0
(6a)	Non-financial corporations	660.0
(6b)	Other financial corporations	101.0
(6c)	General government	92.0
(6d)	Households	152.0
(6e)	NPISHs	84.0
(6f)	Rest of the world	66.0

table 3.3. The balance sheet data in table 3.3 are used to derive the average levels of these loans and deposits, as well as their changes for each sector in table 3.4. The average level is obtained by taking the simple average of the level of loans or deposits as at 1 January and 31 December, while the change is obtained by taking the difference between the level of loans and deposits as at 1 January and 31 December.

3.51. Table 3.5 shows how to derive the average interest rate for the loans and deposits for each sector using the data in tables 3.2 and 3.4. Each average interest rate is computed by dividing the interest flow for the year by the average stock of loan or deposit and then multiplying the result by 100.0. Table 3.5 also shows the domestic reference rate (rr_{DOM}), which is derived using the endogenous method, as described earlier in equation (3.2). The endogenous reference rate is computed as follows:

- Calculate the average interest rate on all loans (r_L) by dividing the total interest income receivable on all loans made by resident deposit-taking corporations by the average stock of all loans and then multiply the result by 100.0.
- Calculate the average interest rate on all deposits (r_D) by dividing the total interest payable on all deposits with resident deposit-taking corporations by the average stock of all deposits and then multiply the result by 100.0.
- Obtain the domestic reference rate (rr_{DOM}) by taking the simple average of the two values.

Table 3.4
Average stock of, and changes in, loans and deposits of resident deposit-taking corporations

Line number	Financial assets and liabilities	Description	Value
(7)	Average stock of loans granted ($Y_{L,av}$)	[(3)+(5)]/2	1851.0
(7a)	Non-financial corporations	[(3a)+(5a)]/2	1002.0
(7b)	Other financial corporations	[(3b)+(5b)]/2	103.0
(7c)	General government	[(3c)+(5c)]/2	113.0
(7d)	Households	[(3d)+(5d)]/2	435.0
(7e)	of which: dwelling loans	[(3e)+(5e)]/2	235.0
(7f)	NPISHs	[(3f)+(5f)]/2	93.0
(7g)	Rest of the world	[(3g)+(5g)]/2	105.0
(8)	Average stock of deposits held ($Y_{D,av}$)	[(4)+(6)]/2	1141.0
(8a)	Non-financial corporations	[(4a)+(6a)]/2	655.0
(8b)	Other financial corporations	[(4b)+(6b)]/2	100.0
(8c)	General government	[(4c)+(6c)]/2	95.0
(8d)	Households	[(4d)+(6d)]/2	151.0
(8e)	NPISHs	[(4e)+(6e)]/2	82.0
(8f)	Rest of the world	[(4f)+(6f)]/2	58.0
(9)	Change in loans granted	(5)–(3)	84.0
(9a)	Non-financial corporations	(5a)–(3a)	40.0
(9b)	Other financial corporations	(5b)–(3b)	2.0
(9c)	General government	(5c)–(3c)	6.0
(9d)	Households	(5d)–(3d)	10.0
(9e)	of which: dwelling loans	(5e)–(3e)	10.0
(9f)	NPISHs	(5f)–(3f)	6.0
(9g)	Rest of the world	(5g)–(3g)	20.0
(10)	Change in deposits held	(6)–(4)	28.0
(10a)	Non-financial corporations	(6a)–(4a)	10.0
(10b)	Other financial corporations	(6b)–(4b)	2.0
(10c)	General government	(6c)–(4c)	-6.0
(10d)	Households	(6d)–(4d)	2.0
(10e)	NPISHs	(6e)–(4e)	4.0
(10f)	Rest of the world	(6f)–(4f)	16.0

Table 3.5

Calculation of average interest rates on loans and deposits offered by resident deposit-taking corporations and of the reference rate

Line number	Item	Description	Value
(11)	Average interest rate on loans (r_L)	(1)/(7)×100.0	8.11
(11a)	Non-financial corporations	(1a)/(7a)×100.0	7.98
(11b)	Other financial corporations	(1b)/(7b)×100.0	7.28
(11c)	General government	(1c)/(7c)×100.0	8.85
(11d)	Households	(1d)/(7d)×100.0	8.30
(11e)	of which: dwelling loans	(1e)/(7e)×100.0	8.51
(11f)	NPISHs	(1f)/(7f)×100.0	8.06
(11g)	Rest of the world	(1g)/(7g)×100.0	8.57
(12)	Average interest rate on deposits (r_D)	(2)/(8)×100.0	5.51
(12a)	Non-financial corporations	(2a)/(8a)×100.0	5.50
(12b)	Other financial corporations	(2b)/(8b)×100.0	6.60
(12c)	General government	(2c)/(8c)×100.0	5.26
(12d)	Households	(2d)/(8d)×100.0	5.30
(12e)	NPISHs	(2e)/(8e)×100.0	5.24
(12f)	Rest of the world	(2f)/(8f)×100.0	5.17
(13)	Reference rate domestic (rr_{DOM})	[(11)+(12)]/2	6.81

3.52. Table 3.6 shows the data on the loans provided by non-resident deposit-taking corporations to the economy and interest receivable on loans granted by these corporations. For simplicity, it is assumed that these loans originate from the non-resident deposit-taking corporations in only one foreign country and are denominated in the currency of that foreign country. It is also assumed that these loans are granted only to resident non-financial corporations.

3.53. As the data on the loans provided by non-resident deposit-taking corporations and the interest receivable by them are denominated in foreign currency, there is a need to convert these data into local currency before they can be recorded in the SNA. Assuming, for simplicity, that the exchange rate between the local currency and foreign currency is constant throughout the accounting period, this is done as follows in table 3.6:

- Multiply the average stock of loans and interest receivable on loans granted by non-resident financial corporations which are denominated in foreign currency by the exchange rate to get the equivalent in local currency terms.

Table 3.6

Loans granted by non-resident deposit-taking corporations to resident non-financial corporations

Line number	Item	Description	Value
(14)	Stock of loans granted in foreign currency on 1 January		80.0
(15)	Stock of loans granted in foreign currency on 31 December		86.0
(16)	Average stock of loans in foreign currency ($Y_{L,F,av}$)	(14)/(15)×100.0	83.0
(17)	Change in loans in foreign currency	(15)–(14)	6.0
(18)	Interest payable in foreign currency		5.8
(19)	Average interest rate ($r_{L,F}$)	(18)/(16)×100.0	7.00
(20)	Reference rate in foreign country (rr_F)	Interbank rate	5.00
(21)	Exchange rate	1.3 local currency units for 1 foreign currency unit	1.3
(22)	Average stock of loans in local currency	(16)×(21)	107.9
(23)	Change in loans in local currency	(17)×(21)	7.8
(24)	Interest payable in local currency on loans	(18)×(21)	7.5

In addition, the table also computes the average interest rate in foreign currency terms which will be used to compute FISIM. This is done as follows:

- Divide interest receivable by the average stock of loans in foreign currency terms and multiply the result by 100.0.

To compute FISIM, there is also a need to determine what foreign reference rate should be used. In this example, it is assumed that the value of FISIM in the foreign country which provides the loans is calculated using the interbank rate in that country, so this interbank rate will be used as the foreign reference rate.

If loans from non-resident financial corporations are also available in other foreign currencies, the aforementioned steps will need to be repeated for each currency to obtain the loans and interest receivable in local currency terms. In addition, the worked example assumes that resident institutional units do not have deposits with non-resident deposit-taking corporations. If resident institutional units do have deposits with non-resident deposit-taking corporations, the aforementioned steps will need to be repeated to obtain the deposits and interest payable by the latter in local currency terms.

3.54. Using data from the tables above, FISIM is computed separately for loans and deposits for each sector in table 3.7. For each sector, the FISIM on loans provided by resident deposit-taking corporations is calculated as follows:

- Compute the difference between the average interest rate on loans and the domestic reference rate (rr_{DOM}) in table 3.5.
- Multiply this difference by the average level of loans to get the FISIM on loans.

For example, the FISIM on loans which are provided by resident deposit-taking corporations to non-financial corporations is $\left(\frac{7.98-6.81}{100.0}\right)\times 1002.0 = 11.8$ units.

For each sector, the FISIM on deposits with resident deposit-taking corporations is obtained as follows:

- Compute the difference between the domestic reference rate (rr_{DOM}) and the average interest rate on deposits in table 3.5.
- Multiply this difference by the average level of deposits to get the FISIM on deposits.

For example, the FISIM on deposits of non-financial corporations with resident deposit-taking corporations is $\left(\frac{6.81-5.50}{100.0}\right)\times 665.0 = 8.6$ units.

In the case of loans from non-resident deposit-taking corporations, FISIM is computed as follows:

- Compute the difference between the average interest rate on loans ($r_{L,F}$) and the foreign reference rate (rr_F), both of which are denominated in foreign currency terms, in table 3.6.
- Multiply this difference by the average level of loans ($Y_{L,F,av}$) to get the FISIM on loans in foreign currency terms.
- Convert the FISIM on loans in foreign currency units to local currency units using the given exchange rate (1.3 local currency units to 1 foreign currency unit).

In the case of this worked example, the FISIM on loans provided by non-resident deposit-taking corporations is $\left(\frac{r_{L,F}-rr_F}{100.0}\right)\times Y_{L,F,av}\times 1.3 = \left(\frac{7.00-5.00}{100.0}\right)\times 83.0\times 1.3 = 2.2$ units.

Table 3.7
Calculation of financial intermediation services indirectly measured

Line number	Item	Description	Value	2008 SNA code
(25)	Total supply of FISIM	(27)+(28)+(29)	41.0	
(26)	Output of domestically produced FISIM	(27)+(28)	38.8	P1
(27)	Domestic FISIM on loans	(27a)+(27b)+(27c)+(27d)+(27f)+(27g)	24.0	
(27a)	Non-financial corporations	[(11a)–(13)]/100.0×(7a)	11.8	
(27b)	Other financial corporations	[(11b)–(13)]/100.0×(7b)	0.5	
(27c)	General government	[(11c)–(13)]/100.0×(7c)	2.3	
(27d)	Households	[(11d)–(13)]/100.0×(7d)	6.5	
(27e)	of which: dwelling loans	[(11e)–(13)]/100.0×(7e)	4.0	
(27f)	NPISHs	[(11f)–(13)]/100.0×(7f)	1.2	
(27g)	Rest of the world	[(11g)–(13)]/100.0×(7g)	1.8	
(28)	Domestic FISIM on deposits	(28a)+(28b)+(28c)+(28d)+(28e)+(28f)	14.8	
(28a)	Non-financial corporations	[(13)–(12a)]/100.0×(8a)	8.6	
(28b)	Other financial corporations	[(13)–(12b)]/100.0×(8b)	0.2	
(28c)	General government	[(13)–(12c)]/100.0×(8c)	1.5	
(28d)	Households	[(13)–(12d)]/100.0×(8d)	2.3	
(28e)	NPISHs	[(13)–(12e)]/100.0×(8e)	1.3	
(28f)	Rest of the world	[(13)–(12f)]/100.0×(8f)	1.0	
(29)	Imports of FISIM	[(19)–(20)]/100.0×(22)	2.2	P7
(30)	Total use of FISIM	(31)+(32)+(33)	41.0	
(31)	Intermediate consumption	(31a)+(31b)+(31c)+(31d)+(31e)	33.4	P2
(31a)	Non-financial corporations	(27a)+(28a)+(29)	22.5	P2
(31b)	Other financial corporations	(27b)+(28b)	0.7	P2
(31c)	General government	(27c)+(28c)	3.8	P2
(31d)	Households (dwelling services)	(27e)	4.0	P2
(31e)	NPISHs	(27f)+(28e)	2.5	P2
(32)	Household consumption expenditure	(27d)–(27e)+(28d)	4.8	P3
(33)	Exports of FISIM	(27g)+(28f)	2.8	P6

The FISIM on loans provided by resident deposit-taking corporations to each sector is then summed up to obtain total domestic FISIM on loans (24.0 units). Similarly, the FISIM on deposits provided by resident deposit-taking corporations to each sector is then summed up to obtain total domestic FISIM on deposits (14.8 units). Total FISIM on foreign currency loans is 2.2 units. The lower part of the table also shows how FISIM is allocated to final and intermediate uses.[25] In the case of households, there is a need to distinguish between FISIM for final consumption and FISIM for intermediate consumption in the case of dwelling loans.

3.55. Table 3.8 shows how to derive SNA interest for the loans and deposits of each institutional sector. In the case of loans, SNA interest is derived as the difference between bank interest receivable by deposit-taking corporations and FISIM for each sector. In the case of deposits, SNA interest is derived as the sum of bank interest payable by deposit-taking corporations and FISIM for each sector. The SNA interest receivable/payable on loans/deposits from/to each sector is then summed up to obtain the corresponding economy-wide estimates. As mentioned before, SNA interest, and not bank interest, is recorded in the allocation of primary income account.[26]

3.56. Table 3.9 shows how to calculate the changes in financial assets and liabilities arising from the transactions between resident deposit-taking corporations and the other institutional units. In general, the changes in financial assets and liabilities are computed using the following principles: for resident deposit-taking corporations, interest received on loans during the accounting period represents an increase

[25] For simplicity, the effects of FISIM on the output and final consumption expenditure of general government and NPISHs are not shown.

[26] SNA interest on loans and deposits can also be obtained by multiplying the reference rate by the average stock of loans and deposits respectively.

Table 3.8
Calculation of SNA interest

Line number	Item	Description	Value	2008 SNA code
	SNA interest of resident deposit-taking corporations			
(34)	SNA interest receivable on loans	(34a)+(34b)+(34c)+(34d)+(34e)+(34f)	126.1	D4, D41
(34a)	Non-financial corporations	(1a)–(27a)	68.2	
(34b)	Other financial corporations	(1b)–(27b)	7.0	
(34c)	General government	(1c)–(27c)	7.7	
(34d)	Households	(1d)–(27d)	29.6	
(34e)	NPISHs	(1f)–(27f)	6.3	
(34f)	Rest of the world	(1g)–(27g)	7.2	
(35)	SNA interest payable on deposits	(35a)+(35b)+(35c)+(35d)+(35e)+(35f)	77.7	D4,D41
(35a)	Non-financial corporations	(2a)+(28a)	44.6	
(35b)	Other financial corporations	(2b)+(28b)	6.8	
(35c)	General government	(2c)+(28c)	6.5	
(35d)	Households	(2d)+(28d)	10.3	
(35e)	NPISHs	(2e)+(28e)	5.6	
(35f)	Rest of the world	(2f)+(28f)	4.0	
	SNA interest of non-resident deposit-taking corporations			
(36)	SNA interest receivable on loans	(24)–(29)	5.4	
	SNA interest of non-financial corporations			
(37)	SNA interest receivable on deposits	(35a)	44.6	D4, D41
(38)	SNA interest payable on loans	(34a)+(36)	73.6	D4, D41
	SNA interest of other financial corporations			
(39)	SNA interest receivable on deposits	(35b)	6.8	D4, D41
(40)	SNA interest payable on loans	(34b)	7.0	D4, D41
	SNA interest of general government			
(41)	SNA interest receivable on deposits	(35c)	6.5	D4, D41
(42)	SNA interest payable on loans	(34c)	7.7	D4, D41
	SNA interest of households			
(43)	SNA interest receivable on deposits	(35d)	10.3	D4, D41
(44)	SNA interest payable on loans	(34d)	29.6	D4, D41
	SNA interest of NPISHs			
(45)	SNA interest receivable on deposits	(35e)	5.6	D4, D41
(46)	SNA interest payable on loans	(34e)	6.3	D4, D41
	SNA interest of non-residents			
(47)	SNA interest receivable on deposits and loans	(35f)+[(24)–(29)]	9.3	D4, D41
(48)	SNA interest payable on loans	(34f)	7.2	D4, D41

in currency and deposits in the financial account, while interest paid on deposits and loans granted during the accounting period represent a decrease in these financial assets in the financial account. The converse applies to the counterpart institutional units. As an example, resident deposit-taking corporations have a net decrease of 3.2 units in their assets of currency and deposits during the accounting period. This is the result of the following:

- Interest received on loans (150.1 units).
- Interest paid on deposits (-62.9 units).
- Loans granted (-84.0 units).

In addition, resident deposit-taking corporations have a net increase of 84.0 units in their assets of loans during the accounting period.

3.57. Table 3.10 shows how to record FISIM and other transactions. To simplify the presentation and analysis, transactions which are not related to the worked example are ignored. Also ignored are the impact of FISIM on the output and final consumption expenditure of non-market producers (i. e. general government and NPISHs). To ensure clarity, the transactions of deposit-taking corporations and other financial corporations

Table 3.9
Calculation of changes in financial assets and liabilities related to financial intermediation services indirectly measured

Line number	Item	Description	Value	2008 SNA code
	Changes in financial assets (currency and deposits)			
(49)	Non-financial corporations	-(1a)+(2a)+(9a)+(23)–(24)	-3.7	F2
(50)	Deposit-taking corporations	(1)–(2)–(9)	3.2	F2
(51)	Other financial corporations	-(1b)+(2b)+(9b)	1.1	F2
(52)	General government	-(1c)+(2c)+(9c)	1.0	F2
(53)	Households	-(1d)+(2d)+(9d)	-18.1	F2
(54)	NPISHs	-(1f)+(2e)+(9f)	2.8	F2
(55)	Rest of the world	-(1g)+(2f)+(9g)+(23)-(24)	13.7	F2
	Changes in financial assets (loans)			
(56)	Deposit-taking corporations	(9)	84.0	F4
(57)	Rest of the world	(23)	7.8	F4
	Changes in liabilities (loans)			
(57)	Non-financial corporations	(9a)+(24)	47.8	F4
(58)	Other financial corporations	(9b)	2.0	F4
(59)	General government	(9c)	6.0	F4
(60)	Households	(9d)	10.0	F4
(61)	NPISHs	(9f)	6.0	F4
(62)	Rest of the world	(9g)	20.0	F4

are shown separately rather than combined to show the transactions of the financial corporations sector. The transactions are described as follows:

(a) The output of deposit-taking corporations is 38.8 units. This comprises FISIM on loans (24.0 units) and on deposits (14.8 units). The output is recorded in the production account of the deposit-taking corporations. FISIM on loans from non-resident deposit-taking corporations (2.2 units) is recorded as imports of goods and services. The FISIM on loans and deposits of non-financial corporations (22.5 units), other financial corporations (0.7 units), general government (3.8 units), NPISHs (2.5 units) and households (4.0 units) is recorded as intermediate consumption in the production account. As mentioned before, the intermediate consumption of FISIM by households represents the FISIM on dwelling loans. Table 3.10 also disaggregates the intermediate consumption of FISIM by these sectors into FISIM on loans and on deposits. Owing to the assumptions made, the FISIM on loans consumed by non-financial corporations (13.9 units) also includes the 2.2 units of imports of FISIM;

(b) The interest recorded in the allocation of primary income account represents SNA interest rather than bank interest;

(c) The FISIM consumed by households as final consumption (4.8 units) is recorded in the use of disposable income account. This account also shows the gross saving of each sector and the total economy plus the current external balance;

(d) Since there are no capital account transactions, net lending/net borrowing in the capital account is the same as gross saving and the current external balance in the use of disposable income account;

(e) The financial account records the changes in currency and deposits and loans of the institutional units. Since these entries are the counterparts to entries in the other accounts or only reflect the exchange in financial assets and liabilities, net lending/net borrowing is identical to net lending/net borrowing in the capital account. However, in practice, differences in data sources

Table 3.10

Recording financial intermediation services indirectly measured and related transactions

Uses																					Resources
Total	Goods and services	Rest of the world	Total economy	NPISHs	Households	General government	Other financial corporations	Deposit-taking corporations	Non-financial corporations	2008 SNA code	Transactions and balancing items	Non-financial corporations	Deposit-taking corporations	Other financial corporations	General government	Households	NPISHs	Total economy	Rest of the world	Goods and services	Total
Production account																					
2.2	2.2									P7	Imports of goods and services								2.2		2.2
2.2	2.2										FISIM on loans								2.2		2.2
											FISIM on deposits										
2.8		2.8								P6	Exports of goods and services									2.8	2.8
1.8		1.8									FISIM on loans									1.8	1.8
1.0		1.0									FISIM on deposits									1.0	1.0
38.8	38.8									P1	Output		38.8					38.8			38.8
24.0	24.0										FISIM on loans		24.0					24.0			24.0
14.8	14.8										FISIM on deposits		14.8					14.8			14.8
33.4			33.4	2.5	4.0	3.8	0.7		22.5	P2	Intermediate consumption									33.4	33.4
21.9			21.9	1.2	4.0	2.3	0.5		13.9		FISIM on loans									21.9	21.9
11.6			11.6	1.3		1.5	0.2		8.6		FISIM on deposits									11.6	11.6
5.4			5.4	-2.5	-4.0	-3.8	-0.7	38.8	-22.5	B1g	Value added, gross/ Gross domestic product										
-0.6		-0.6								B11	External balance of goods and services										
Allocation of primary income account																					
209.2		7.2	202.0	6.3	29.6	7.7	7.0	77.7	73.6	D4	Property income	44.6	126.1	6.8	6.5	10.3	5.6	199.8	9.3		209.2
209.2		7.2	202.0	6.3	29.6	7.7	7.0	77.7	73.6	D41	Interest (SNA interest)	44.6	126.1	6.8	6.5	10.3	5.6	199.8	9.3		209.2
3.2			3.2	-3.2	-23.3	-5.0	-0.9	87.2	-51.5	B5g	Balance of primary income, gross/ National income, gross										
Use of disposable income account																					
4.8			4.8		4.8					P3	Final consumption expenditure									4.8	4.8
2.5			2.5		2.5						FISIM on loans									2.5	2.5
2.3			2.3		2.3						FISIM on deposits									2.3	2.3
-1.5			-1.5	-3.2	-28.1	-5.0	-0.9	87.2	-51.5	B8g	Saving, gross										
1.5		1.5								B12	Current external balance										
Changes in assets																					**Changes in liabilities and net worth**
Capital account																					
0.0		1.5	-1.5	-3.2	-28.1	-5.0	-0.9	87.2	-51.5	B9	Net lending (+)/ net borrowing (-)										
Financial account																					
										B9	Net lending (+)/ net borrowing (-)	-51.5	87.2	-0.9	-5.0	-28.1	-3.2	-1.5	1.5		0.0
0.0		13.7	-13.7	2.8	-18.1	1.0	1.1	3.2	-3.7	F2	Currency and deposits										
91.8		7.8	84.0					84.0		F4	Loans	47.8		2.0	6.0	10.0	6.0	71.8	20.0		91.8

and the timing of the recording of transactions may result in a discrepancy between the estimates of net lending/net borrowing in these two accounts.

Allocation of financial intermediation services indirectly measured by industry

3.58. The previous section discussed how to allocate FISIM to user sectors. The allocation of FISIM to corporations, general government, households in their role as owners of dwellings and unincorporated enterprises, and NPISHs is classified as the intermediate consumption expenditure of these institutional units. The allocation of FISIM to the intermediate consumption expenditure of these institutional units will also need to be broken down into the respective industries so as to properly account for their value added.

3.59. It is unlikely that the input data to calculate FISIM and SNA interest by industry will be available at the industry level. Thus, it may not be possible for the compiling agency to directly compute the FISIM and SNA interest for each industry using the "bottom-up" approach. Instead, the compiling agency will need to allocate the intermediate consumption of domestically produced FISIM to industries using the "top-down" approach using indicators such as the shares of the stocks of loans and deposits, gross value added, or the output of each industry. The compiling agency will need to assess which method or combination of methods to use for allocating the intermediate consumption of domestically produced FISIM to industries. This will depend on the type of data available and which method or combination of methods are considered to be the most reliable.

3.60. Some of the imports of FISIM provided by non-resident deposit-taking corporations will also need to be allocated to the intermediate consumption expenditure of industries. Again, it is unlikely that the compiling agency will be able to obtain detailed source data on the breakdown of the stocks of loans and deposits and interest receivable on loans and interest payable on deposits of non-resident deposit-taking corporations by industry. Thus, the value of imports of the intermediate consumption of FISIM will need to be allocated to each industry using the methods described in the previous paragraph. Again, the compiling agency will need to assess which method or combination of methods are the most reliable.

3.61. The allocation of the intermediate consumption of FISIM to households in their role as owners of dwellings, which are treated in the SNA as producers of housing services, will also need to be considered. For these households, the FISIM payable on dwelling loans is counted as the intermediate consumption of real estate activities.

Worked example 3.2. Allocation of the intermediate consumption of financial intermediation services indirectly measured by industry

3.62. This worked example shows how to allocate the intermediate consumption of FISIM to industries using the "top-down" approach by making use of the FISIM computed in worked example 3.1.

3.63. Table 3.11 reproduces the total supply of FISIM in the economy which was calculated in worked example 3.1. The total supply of FISIM is measured at current prices and comprises FISIM produced by resident deposit-taking corporations and imports of FISIM. The FISIM produced by resident deposit-taking corporations is further split into FISIM on loans and FISIM on deposits. The table also shows the allocation of FISIM to intermediate and final consumption as well as exports. The intermediate consumption of FISIM (41.0 units) is further disaggregated by sector. As shown in the table, imports of

Table 3.11
Data on output and imports of FISIM

Line number	Item	Description	Value
(1)	Total supply of FISIM	(2)+(3)+(4)	41.0
(2)	Domestic FISIM on loans	(2a)+(2b)+(2c)+(2d)+(2f)+(2g)	24.0
(2a)	Non-financial corporations		11.8
(2b)	Other financial corporations		0.5
(2c)	General government		2.3
(2d)	Households		6.5
(2e)	of which: dwelling loans		4.0
(2f)	NPISHs		1.2
(2g)	Rest of the world		1.8
(3)	Domestic FISIM on deposits	(3a)+(3b)+(3c)+(3d)+(3e)+(3f)	14.8
(3a)	Non-financial corporations		8.6
(3b)	Other financial corporations		0.2
(3c)	General government		1.5
(3d)	Households		2.3
(3e)	NPISHs		1.3
(3f)	Rest of the world		1.0
(4)	Imports of FISIM		2.2
(5)	Total use of FISIM	(6)+(7)+(8)	41.0
(6)	Intermediate consumption	(6a)+(6b)+(6c)+(6d)+(6e)	33.4
(6a)	Non-financial corporations	(2a)+(3a)+(4)	22.5
(6b)	Other financial corporations	(2b)+(3b)	0.7
(6c)	General government	(2c)+(3c)	3.8
(6d)	Households (dwelling services)	(2e)	4.0
(6e)	NPISHs	(2f)+(3e)	2.5
(7)	Household consumption expenditure	(2d)–(2e)+(3d)	4.8
(8)	Exports of FISIM	(2g)+(3f)	2.8

FISIM are allocated to the non-financial corporations sector based on the assumption in worked example 3.1. The question now is how to allocate the intermediate consumption of FISIM to the respective industries.

3.64. Assume that the economy in question comprises the following broad industry groups:

- Agriculture, forestry and fishing.
- Mining and quarrying.
- Manufacturing.
- Electricity, gas, steam and air conditioning supply.
- Water supply; sewerage, waste management and remediation activities.
- Construction.
- Wholesale and retail trade; repair of motor vehicles and motorcycles.
- Transportation and storage.
- Accommodation and food service activities.
- Information and communication.
- Real estate activities.
- Professional, scientific and technical activities.
- Administrative and support service activities.
- Education.
- Human health and social work activities.
- Arts, entertainment and recreation.

- Other service activities.
- Financial and insurance activities.
- Public administration and defence; compulsory social security.

The non-financial corporations sector comprises all enterprises engaged in the broad industry groups above except those associated with financial and insurance activities and with public administration and defence; compulsory social security. Real estate activities also include ownership of dwellings. Assume that NPISHs are only located in the broad industry groups associated with education and with human health and social work activities. The intermediate consumption of the FISIM of financial and insurance activities corresponds to the intermediate consumption of the FISIM of other financial corporations, while the intermediate consumption of the FISIM of public administration and defence; compulsory social security can be taken to correspond to the intermediate consumption of the FISIM of general government. Thus, the intermediate consumption of the FISIM of the other financial corporations and general government sectors can be directly allocated to these two broad industry groups. On the other hand, there is a need to allocate the FISIM of non-financial corporations and NPISHs into the respective broad industry groups.

3.65. Table 3.12 shows the data on the stock of loans and deposits for those broad industry groups which belong to the non-financial corporations and NPISHs sectors as at 1 January and 31 December. Assume that the compiling agency is able to collect data on the stock of loans and deposits for these broad industry groups from surveys. The average stock of loans and deposits for these broad industry groups is computed in table 3.13. Given the assumptions in the previous paragraph, the data in these tables contain a mixture of the stocks of loans and deposits of non-financial corporations and NPISHs. However, the data do not have any breakdown for market producers and NPISHs for education or human health and social work activities. Thus, when allocating the intermediate consumption of FISIM to these units, some more assumptions will need to be made, which will be described in the next paragraph. Note that data on the total stock of loans and deposits in table 3.12 are different from the corresponding data for non-financial corporations and NPISHs in table 3.13, as the data in these two tables are assumed to be obtained from different sources.

3.66. Table 3.14 shows how to allocate the intermediate consumption of FISIM to the respective broad industry groups using the data in the tables above. For each broad industry group associated with the non-financial corporations sector, the allocation of FISIM is calculated separately for loans and deposits as follows:

- Calculate the share of the average stock of loans/deposits of the broad industry group in the total average stock of loans/deposits provided to/held by the broad industry groups.
- Multiply the intermediate consumption of FISIM on loans/deposits which is allocated to the non-financial corporations sector by this share to obtain the intermediate consumption of FISIM on loans/deposits by the broad industry group.

As an example, the share of manufacturing in the intermediate consumption of FISIM on loans for the non-financial corporations sector is calculated as

$$13.9 \times \left(\frac{229.9}{1189.9} \right) = 2.7 \text{ units.}$$

As mentioned earlier, the FISIM on loans for the non-financial corporations sector includes FISIM on loans granted by non-resident deposit-taking corporations. Furthermore, as mentioned earlier, the education and the human health and social work ac-

Table 3.12
Date on the stock of loans and deposits by broad industry group

Line Number	Broad industry group	Value
(9)	Loans granted to broad industry groups on 1 January	1138.0
(9a)	Agriculture, forestry and fishing	55.0
(9b)	Mining and quarrying	8.0
(9c)	Manufacturing	220.0
(9d)	Electricity, gas, steam and air conditioning supply	18.0
(9e)	Water supply; sewerage, waste management and remediation activities	12.0
(9f)	Construction	66.0
(9g)	Wholesale and retail trade; repair of motor vehicles and motorcycles	100.0
(9h)	Transportation and storage	78.0
(9i)	Accommodation and food service activities	110.0
(9j)	Information and communication	22.0
(9k)	Real estate activities	60.0
(9l)	Professional, scientific and technical activities	45.0
(9m)	Administrative and support service activities	32.0
(9n)	Education	120.0
(9o)	Human health and social work activities	150.0
(9p)	Arts, entertainment and recreation	17.0
(9q)	Other service activities	25.0
(10)	Deposits held by broad industry groups on 1 January	924.0
(10a)	Agriculture, forestry and fishing	48.0
(10b)	Mining and quarrying	9.0
(10c)	Manufacturing	160.0
(10d)	Electricity, gas, steam and air conditioning supply	13.0
(10e)	Water supply; sewerage, waste management and remediation activities	9.0
(10f)	Construction	56.0
(10g)	Wholesale and retail trade; repair of motor vehicles and motorcycles	78.0
(10h)	Transportation and storage	65.0
(10i)	Accommodation and food service activities	70.0
(10j)	Information and communication	15.0
(10k)	Real estate activities	48.0
(10l)	Professional, scientific and technical activities	37.0
(10m)	Administrative and support service activities	22.0
(10n)	Education	106.0
(10o)	Human health and social work activities	150.0
(10p)	Arts, entertainment and recreation	20.0
(10q)	Other service activities	18.0
(11)	Loans granted to broad industry groups on 31 December	1241.7
(11a)	Agriculture, forestry and fishing	56.1
(11b)	Mining and quarrying	8.8
(11c)	Manufacturing	239.8
(11d)	Electricity, gas, steam and air conditioning supply	19.8
(11e)	Water supply; sewerage, waste management and remediation activities	13.2
(11f)	Construction	73.3
(11g)	Wholesale and retail trade; repair of motor vehicles and motorcycles	110.0
(11h)	Transportation and storage	79.6
(11i)	Accommodation and food service activities	113.3
(11j)	Information and communication	23.1
(11k)	Real estate activities	67.2
(11l)	Professional, scientific and technical activities	48.6
(11m)	Administrative and support service activities	32.6
(11n)	Education	138.0
(11o)	Human health and social work activities	174.0
(11p)	Arts, entertainment and recreation	17.9
(11q)	Other service activities	26.5
(12)	Deposits held by broad industry groups on 31 December	948.9
(12a)	Agriculture, forestry and fishing	49.0

Line Number	Broad industry group	Value
(12b)	Mining and quarrying	9.2
(12c)	Manufacturing	164.8
(12d)	Electricity, gas, steam and air conditioning supply	13.1
(12e)	Water supply; sewerage, waste management and remediation activities	9.7
(12f)	Construction	57.7
(12g)	Wholesale and retail trade; repair of motor vehicles and motorcycles	79.6
(12h)	Transportation and storage	66.3
(12i)	Accommodation and food service activities	71.4
(12j)	Information and communication	15.5
(12k)	Real estate activities	49.9
(12l)	Professional, scientific and technical activities	37.7
(12m)	Administrative and support service activities	22.7
(12n)	Education	109.2
(12o)	Human health and social work activities	153.0
(12p)	Arts, entertainment and recreation	21.0
(12q)	Other service activities	19.3

Table 3.13
Average stock of loans and deposits by broad industry group

Line Number	Broad industry group	Description	Value
(13)	Average stock of loans by broad industry group	[(9)+(11)]/2	1189.9
(13a)	Agriculture, forestry and fishing	[(9a)+(11a)]/2	55.6
(13b)	Mining and quarrying	[(9b)+(11b)]/2	8.4
(13c)	Manufacturing	[(9c)+(11c)]/2	229.9
(13d)	Electricity, gas, steam and air conditioning supply	[(9d)+(11d)]/2	18.9
(13e)	Water supply; sewerage, waste management and remediation activities	[(9e)+(11e)]/2	12.6
(13f)	Construction	[(9f)+(11f)]/2	69.6
(13g)	Wholesale and retail trade; repair of motor vehicles and motorcycles	[(9g)+(11g)]/2	105.0
(13h)	Transportation and storage	[(9h)+(11h)]/2	78.8
(13i)	Accommodation and food service activities	[(9i)+(11i)]/2	111.7
(13j)	Information and communication	[(9j)+(11j)]/2	22.6
(13k)	Real estate activities	[(9k)+(11k)]/2	63.6
(13l)	Professional, scientific and technical activities	[(9l)+(11l)]/2	46.8
(13m)	Administrative and support service activities	[(9m)+(11m)]/2	32.3
(13n)	Education	[(9n)+(11n)]/2	129.0
(13o)	Human health and social work activities	[(9o)+(11o)]/2	162.0
(13p)	Arts, entertainment and recreation	[(9p)+(11p)]/2	17.4
(13q)	Other service activities	[(9q)+(11q)]/2	25.8
(14)	Average stock of deposits by broad industry group	[(10)+(12)]/2	936.5
(14a)	Agriculture, forestry and fishing	[(10a)+(12a)]/2	48.5
(14b)	Mining and quarrying	[(10b)+(12b)]/2	9.1
(14c)	Manufacturing	[(10c)+(12c)]/2	162.4
(14d)	Electricity, gas, steam and air conditioning supply	[(10d)+(12d)]/2	13.1
(14e)	Water supply; sewerage, waste management and remediation activities	[(10e)+(12e)]/2	9.4
(14f)	Construction	[(10f)+(12f)]/2	56.8
(14g)	Wholesale and retail trade; repair of motor vehicles and motorcycles	[(10g)+(12g)]/2	78.8
(14h)	Transportation and storage	[(10h)+(12h)]/2	65.7
(14i)	Accommodation and food service activities	[(10i)+(12i)]/2	70.7
(14j)	Information and communication	[(10j)+(12j)]/2	15.2
(14k)	Real estate activities	[(10k)+(12k)]/2	49.0
(14l)	Professional, scientific and technical activities	[(10l)+(12l)]/2	37.4
(14m)	Administrative and support service activities	[(10m)+(12m)]/2	22.3
(14n)	Education	[(10n)+(12n)]/2	107.6
(14o)	Human health and social work activities	[(10o)+(12o)]/2	151.5
(14p)	Arts, entertainment and recreation	[(10p)+(12p)]/2	20.5
(14q)	Other service activities	[(10q)+(12q)]/2	18.6

Table 3.14
Allocation of intermediate consumption of financial intermediation services indirectly measured by broad industry group

Line Number	FISIM allocation	Description	Value
(15)	Intermediate consumption of FISIM on loans	(16)+(18)+(19)+(20)	21.9
(16)	Broad industry groups in the non-financial corporations sector (including ownership of dwellings)	17+(17l)	17.9
(17)	Broad industry groups in the non-financial corporations sector (excluding ownership of dwellings)	(2a)+4	13.9
(17a)	Agriculture, forestry and fishing	(17)×(13a)/(13)	0.6
(17b)	Mining and quarrying	(17)×(13b)/(13)	0.1
(17c)	Manufacturing	(17)×(13c)/(13)	2.7
(17d)	Electricity, gas, steam and air conditioning supply	(17)×(13d)/(13)	0.2
(17e)	Water supply; sewerage, waste management and remediation activities	(17)×(13e)/(13)	0.1
(17f)	Construction	(17)×(13f)/(13)	0.8
(17g)	Wholesale and retail trade; repair of motor vehicles and motorcycles	(17)×(13g)/(13)	1.2
(17h)	Transportation and storage	(17)×(13h)/(13)	0.9
(17i)	Accommodation and food service activities	(17)×(13i)/(13)	1.3
(17j)	Information and communication	(17)×(13j)/(13)	0.3
(17k)	Real estate activities	(17)×(13k)/(13)	0.7
(17l)	Including ownership of dwellings	(2e)	4.0
(17m)	Professional, scientific and technical activities	(17)×(13l)/(13)	0.5
(17n)	Administrative and support service activities	(17)×(13m)/(13)	0.4
(17o)	Education	(17)×(13n)/(13)	1.5
(17p)	Human health and social work activities	(17)×(13o)/(13)	1.9
(17q)	Arts, entertainment and recreation	(17)×(13p)/(13)	0.2
(17r)	Other service activities	(17)×(13q)/(13)	0.3
(18)	Broad industry groups in the NPISHs sector	(2f)	1.2
(18a)	Education	(18)×(13n)/[(13n)+(13o)]	0.5
(18b)	Human health and social work activities	(18)×(13o)/[(13n)+(13o)]	0.6
(19)	Financial and insurance activities	(2b)	0.5
(20)	Public administration and defence; compulsory social security	(2c)	2.3
(21)	Intermediate consumption of FISIM on deposits	(22)+(23)+(24)+(25)	11.6
(22)	Broad industry groups in the non-financial corporations sector	(3a)	8.6
(22a)	Agriculture, forestry and fishing	(22)×(14a)/(14)	0.4
(22b)	Mining and quarrying	(22)×(14b)/(14)	0.1
(22c)	Manufacturing	(22)×(14c)/(14)	1.5
(22d)	Electricity, gas, steam and air conditioning supply	(22)×(14d)/(14)	0.1
(22e)	Water supply; sewerage, waste management and remediation activities	(22)×(14e)/(14)	0.1
(22f)	Construction	(22)×(14f)/(14)	0.5
(22g)	Wholesale and retail trade; repair of motor vehicles and motorcycles	(22)×(14g)/(14)	0.7
(22h)	Transportation and storage	(22)×(14h)/(14)	0.6
(22i)	Accommodation and food service activities	(22)×(14i)/(14)	0.7
(22j)	Information and communication	(22)×(14j)/(14)	0.1
(22k)	Real estate activities	(22)×(14k)/(14)	0.5
(22l)	Professional, scientific and technical activities	(22)×(14l)/(14)	0.3
(22m)	Administrative and support service activities	(22)×(14m)/(14)	0.2
(22n)	Education	(22)×(14n)/(14)	1.0
(22o)	Human health and social work activities	(22)×(14o)/(14)	1.4
(22p)	Arts, entertainment and recreation	(22)×(14p)/(14)	0.2
(22q)	Other service activities	(22)×(14q)/(14)	0.2
(23)	Broad industry groups in the NPISHs sector	(3e)	1.3
(23a)	Education	(23)×(14n)/[(14n)+(14o)]	0.5
(23b)	Human health and social work activities	(23)×(14o)/[(14n)+(14o)]	0.8
(24)	Financial and insurance activities	(3b)	0.2
(25)	Public administration and defence; compulsory social security	(3c)	1.5
(26)	Intermediate consumption of FISIM on loans and deposits	(26a)+(26b)+(26c)+(26d)+(26e)+(26f)+(26g)+(26h)+(26i)+(26j)+(26k)+(26l)+(26m)+(26n)+(26o)+(26p)+(26q)+(26r)+(26s)	33.4
(26a)	Agriculture, forestry and fishing	(17a)+(22a)	1.1
(26b)	Mining and quarrying	(17b)+(22b)	0.2

Line Number	FISIM allocation	Description	Value
(26c)	Manufacturing	(17c)+(22c)	4.2
(26d)	Electricity, gas, steam and air conditioning supply	(17d)+(22d)	0.3
(26e)	Water supply; sewerage, waste management and remediation activities	(17e)+(22e)	0.2
(26f)	Construction	(17f)+(22f)	1.3
(26g)	Wholesale and retail trade; repair of motor vehicles and motorcycles	(17g)+(22g)	2.0
(26h)	Transportation and storage	(17h)+(22h)	1.5
(26i)	Accommodation and food service activities	(17i)+(22i)	2.0
(26j)	Information and communication	(17j)+(22j)	0.4
(26k)	Real estate activities	(17k)+(17l)+(22k)	5.2
(26l)	Professional, scientific and technical activities	(17m)+(22l)	0.9
(26m)	Administrative and support service activities	(17n)+(22m)	0.6
(26n)	Education	(17o)+(18a)+(22n)+(23a)	3.5
(26o)	Human health and social work activities	(17p)+(18b)+(22o)+(23b)	4.7
(26p)	Arts, entertainment and recreation	(17q)+(22p)	0.4
(26q)	Other service activities	(17r)+(22q)	0.5
(26r)	Financial and insurance activities	(19)+(24)	0.7
(26s)	Public administration and defence; compulsory social security	(20)+(25)	3.8

tivities industry groups contain a mixture of market producers and NPISHs. Thus, the calculations for these two industry groups assume that the inclusion of the loans and deposits of NPISHs will not significantly affect the shares of market producers belonging to these two broad groups in the total loans and deposits of non-financial corporations.

For the broad industry groups associated with education and with human health and social work activities which are operating in the NPISHs sector, the allocation of the intermediate consumption of FISIM is calculated separately for loans and deposits for each industry group as follows:

- Calculate the share of the stock of loans/deposits of each industry group in the total stock of loans/deposits provided to/held by the broad industry groups associated with education and with human health and social work activities which are operating in the non-financial corporations sector.
- Multiply the intermediate consumption of FISIM on loans/deposits which is allocated to the NPISHs sector by this share to obtain the intermediate consumption of FISIM on loans/deposits by the broad industry group.

As an example, the share of education in the intermediate consumption of FISIM on loans for the NPISHs sector is calculated as $1.2\times\left(\frac{129.0}{129.0+162.0}\right)=0.5$ units.

Thus, the calculations above assume that the loans/deposits of the broad industry groups associated with education and with human health and social work activities which are operating in the NPISHs sector are distributed in the same proportion as those of their counterparts in the non-financial corporations sector.

3.67. This worked example has shown how to allocate the intermediate consumption of FISIM to industries. The allocation of the intermediate consumption of FISIM was carried out using data on the breakdown of the stock of loans and deposits by broad industry group. Alternatively, the compiling agency can consider using other methods, such as the shares of gross value added or the output of each industry group to carry out the allocation if it assesses that these methods will provide more reliable results. The compiling agency can use the steps above to distribute the intermediate consumption of FISIM to the sub-industries in each broad industry group. Again, the choice of which method to use to perform the allocation will depend on data availability and on which indicators the compiling agency considers to be reliable. Further, the compiling agency can consider using the methods described to allocate the SNA interest to the broad industry groups.

Volume measures of financial intermediation services indirectly measured

3.68. The worked examples on FISIM above involved calculating the output of FISIM at current prices or at the prices prevailing in the accounting period. Changes over time in the current-price value of an economic variable such as the output of FISIM are caused by a combination of price and quantity changes. This means that changes in the output of FISIM over time measured using current-price data may reflect changing prices. Thus, to obtain measures of volume change, there is a need to isolate the price element from the current-price output of FISIM so as to obtain a measure of FISIM output which is free of price changes. Measures of inflation-free FISIM output are known in the SNA as the volume measures of FISIM.

3.69. The ideal method to obtain volume measures of FISIM would be to deflate each detailed component of FISIM by an appropriate price index for that component. However, this method may not be feasible in practice because it is difficult to find directly observable prices that are truly representative of the output of FISIM. Thus, there is a need to consider other methods to compute volume measures of FISIM.

3.70. The first method is known as the output indicator method. This method constructs a volume indicator for each type of loan and deposit using output indicators that are representative of the activities that generate FISIM on the loan or deposit concerned. This should also apply to imports of FISIM. Examples of possible output indicators include the number of bank accounts, numbers of loans and deposits, numbers of cheques processed, number of transfers, number of new consumer loans granted, number of credit cards issued, number of new dwelling loans granted, etc. The output indicators are then weighted according to cost compositions or the value of FISIM for each activity to produce the volume indicator for the loan or deposit, which can be used to produce its volume measures. Separate volume indicators should be constructed for businesses and consumers if there are important differences between both markets. The volume measures of each type of loan or deposits can then be aggregated to produce the volume measures of FISIM for the total economy. As recommended in the SNA, the aggregate volume measures of FISIM should be chain-linked. In principle, given its linkages to the activities of deposit-taking corporations, the output indicator method may offer an insight into the operations of these corporations. However, one problem with this method is that it is very data-demanding and input data to construct these indicators may not be readily available to identify for each type of loan and deposit the appropriate activities that generate FISIM. Another problem is that each type of loan and deposit may be associated with a number of activities, so a single indicator may not be appropriate for a particular type of loan or deposit. For example, the services associated with a single demand deposit account may include cheque clearing, ATM services, bill payment services, bookkeeping services, safe keeping, etc. Since these services are offered in a bundle at a single price, weights for these indicators will be unavailable. If the levels of these indicators do not grow at the same rate, then equal weighting is likely to generate bias. The indicator method will only be valid if a single indicator serves as a good proxy for all the activities carried out by a deposit-taking corporation that are associated with a particular type of loan or deposit.

3.71. The second method is known as the deflation method. This method applies base-period interest margins on loans and deposits to the stocks of loans and deposits which are deflated to base-period prices. The base-period interest margin on loans is the difference between the interest rate on loans and the reference rate. The base-period interest margin on deposits is the difference between the reference rate and interest rate on deposits. Base-period margins should be applied to each type of loan and deposit, since different kinds of loans and deposits have different margins between their interest rates and reference rate. Thus, they should be treated as having different prices.[27] The resultant volume measures for each type of loan and deposit should then be aggregated to produce chain-linked volume measures of FISIM. It is not advisable to apply base-period margins to the total stocks of loans and deposits, since this would be equivalent to using a unit measure of price change which will be affected by changes in the composition of loans or deposits and changes in the structure of interest rates. An ideal deflator for the stocks of loans and deposits should measure the actual change in the price of money. However, this is not possible in practice, so deflation by a general price index seems to provide the best approximation for providing a measure of the change in the purchasing power of money. Examples of general price indices that can be used include the GDP deflator, the deflator for final domestic demand and the all-items CPI. The first two indices should exclude FISIM. In principle, the deflation method should be applied to imports of FISIM, provided data on base-period interest margins on loans from, and deposits with, non-resident deposit-taking corporations are available. If such information is not available, the compiling agency can consider using appropriate price indices for FISIM from partner economies. Although the available price indices for deflating the stocks of loans and deposits may not be directly related to the change in the price of money, this method offers an operationally simple way of calculating volume measures of FISIM. Given its less demanding data requirements, this method may, in general, be preferable to the output indicator method.

3.72. The third method is a hybrid method combining the indicator and deflation methods. This method can be used if the compiling agency is able to find appropriate indicators for some types of loans or deposits. For other types of loans and deposits for which appropriate indicators are not available, the compiling agency can use the deflation method.

Worked example 3.3. Calculating volume measures of FISIM

3.73. This worked example shows how to compute annually chain-linked volume measures of FISIM using the deflation method. For simplicity, the chain-linked volume measures of FISIM are computed using the prices of the previous year. This means that these volume measures are computed using the Laspeyres index number formula.

3.74. Table 3.15 shows the data on the breakdown of interest receivable by type of loan and interest payable by type of deposit for five years. It is assumed that the data belong to the same resident deposit-taking corporations which were covered in worked example 3.1 and that these corporations have three types of loans and three types of

Table 3.15
Data on interest receivable on loans and interest payable on deposits offered by resident deposit-taking corporations

Line number	Item	*t*	*t*+1	*t*+2	*t*+3	*t*+4
(1)	Interest receivable on loans	150.1	156.2	162.3	174.9	181.9
(1a)	Mortgage loans	20.0	20.5	21.3	23.2	23.9
(1b)	Automobile loans	13.5	13.7	14.0	15.7	16.0
(1c)	Commercial loans	116.6	122.0	127.0	136.0	142.0
(2)	Interest payable on deposits	62.9	63.3	63.5	64.3	65.7
(2a)	Demand deposits	2.5	2.2	1.7	1.5	1.2
(2b)	Time deposits	46.0	46.6	47.1	48.0	49.0
(2c)	Saving deposits	14.4	14.5	14.7	14.8	15.5

[27] The base-period interest margins on loans and deposits can also be obtained by dividing the base-period value of FISIM on loans and deposits by the corresponding base-period average stocks of loans and deposits.

Table 3.16
Data on the average stock of loans and deposits of resident deposit-taking corporations

Line number	Item	t	t+1	t+2	t+3	t+4
(3)	Average stock of loans	1851.0	2013.3	2184.9	2304.4	2488.2
(3a)	Mortgage loans	235.0	259.8	288.2	305.2	337.6
(3b)	Automobile loans	182.0	199.3	218.1	231.1	250.5
(3c)	Commercial loans	1434.0	1554.2	1678.6	1768.1	1900.1
(4)	Average stock of deposits	1141.0	1254.9	1373.2	1445.1	1552.2
(4a)	Demand deposits	233.0	255.3	284.0	297.1	322.9
(4b)	Time deposits	678.0	746.0	810.0	850.0	911.3
(4c)	Saving deposits	230.0	253.6	279.2	298.0	318.0

deposits. It is also assumed that the total interest receivable on loans and total interest payable on deposits for year *t* are the same as those in worked example 3.1.

3.75. Table 3.16 shows the data on the average stock of the three types of loans and deposits and total loans and deposits of the resident deposit-taking corporations for the same time period. The data are calculated using the same method as outlined in worked example 3.1. Given the assumptions, the data for year *t* are the same as those in worked example 3.1.

3.76. Table 3.17 shows the data on the average interest rates for the three types of loans and deposits and total loans and deposits for the resident deposit-taking corporations for the same period. Data on the endogenous reference rates and GDP deflator excluding FISIM are also shown. The average interest rates and reference rates are calculated using the same method as described in worked example 3.1. The GDP deflator excluding FISIM is calculated at the prices of the previous year. As mentioned earlier, other general price indices that can be considered include the deflator for final domestic demand (excluding FISIM) and the all-items CPI. The choice of which price index to use will depend on the assessment of the compiling agency.

3.77. Table 3.18 shows how to calculate FISIM at current prices for each type of loan and deposit. The data are calculated using the same method as described in worked example 3.1.

3.78. Table 3.19 shows how to calculate the deflated average stock of loans and deposits for each type of loan and deposit at the prices of the previous year. The deflated stock of each type of loan and deposit is calculated by dividing its current-price stock by the GDP deflator excluding FISIM and then multiplying the result by 100.0. It is not necessary to calculate the data for year *t*, since it is the starting year of the series.

3.79. Table 3.20 shows how to calculate the unchained Laspeyres volume measure of FISIM for each type of loan and deposit at the prices of the previous year. For each type of loan starting from year *t*+1, the volume measures of FISIM are obtained as follows:

- Compute the difference between the average interest rate on the loan and the reference rate for the previous year and divide the result by 100.0 (this is known as the base-period interest margin for loans).
- Multiply the deflated stock of loans in the current year by this difference to obtain the volume measure of FISIM at the price of the previous year.

For example, the volume measure of FISIM on mortgage loans for year *t*+1 is obtained as $256.2 \times \left(\frac{8.51 - 6.81}{100} \right) = 4.35$ units.

Table 3.17
Data on average interest rates, the reference rate and the gross domestic product deflator (excluding financial intermediation services indirectly measured)

Line number	Item	Description	t	t+1	t+2	t+3	t+4
(5)	Average interest rate on loans	[(1)/(3)]×100.0	8.11	7.76	7.43	7.59	7.31
(5a)	Mortgage loans	[(1a)/(3a)]×100.0	8.51	7.89	7.39	7.60	7.08
(5b)	Automobile loans	[(1b)/(3b)]×100.0	7.42	6.87	6.42	6.79	6.39
(5c)	Commercial loans	[(1c)/(3c)]×100.0	8.13	7.85	7.57	7.69	7.47
(6)	Average interest rate on deposits	[(2)/(4)]×100.0	5.51	5.04	4.62	4.45	4.23
(6a)	Demand deposits	[(2a)/(4a)]×100.0	1.07	0.86	0.60	0.50	0.37
(6b)	Time deposits	[(2b)/(4b)]×100.0	6.78	6.25	5.81	5.65	5.38
(6c)	Saving deposits	[(2c)/(4c)]×100.0	6.26	5.72	5.27	4.97	4.87
(7)	Reference rate domestic (rr_{DOM})	[(5)+(6)]/2	6.81	6.40	6.03	6.02	5.77
(8)	GDP deflator (excluding FISIM) (previous year = 100.0)			101.4	103.5	103.5	102.8

Table 3.18
Calculation of financial intermediation services indirectly measured at current prices

Line number	Item	Description	t	t+1	t+2	t+3	t+4
(9)	FISIM on loans	(9a)+(9b)+(9c)	24.03	27.32	30.63	36.18	38.29
(9a)	Mortgage loans	[(5a)–(7)]/100.0×(3a)	3.99	3.87	3.93	4.83	4.42
(9b)	Automobile loans	[(5b)–(7)]/100.0×(3b)	1.10	0.94	0.86	1.79	1.54
(9c)	Commercial loans	[(5c)–(7)]/100.0×(3c)	18.93	22.51	25.84	29.57	32.33
(10)	FISIM on deposits	(10a)+(10b)+(10c)	14.81	17.03	19.25	22.69	23.89
(10a)	Demand deposits	[(7)–(6a)]/100.0×(4a)	13.37	14.14	15.41	16.38	17.44
(10b)	Time deposits	[(7)–(6b)]/100.0×(4b)	0.18	1.15	1.71	3.17	3.60
(10c)	Saving deposits	[(7)–(6c)]/100.0×(4c)	1.27	1.73	2.13	3.14	2.85
(11)	Total domestic FISIM	(9)+(10)	38.84	44.35	49.88	58.87	62.18

Table 3.19
Calculation of the deflated average stock of loans and deposits at the prices of the previous year

Line number	Item	Description	t+1	t+2	t+3	t+4
(12)	Deflated average stock of loans	(12a)+(12b)+(12c)	1985.3	2112.0	2225.8	2419.7
(12a)	Mortgage loans	(3a)/(8)×100.0	256.2	278.6	294.8	328.3
(12b)	Automobile loans	(3b)/(8)×100.0	196.5	210.8	223.2	243.6
(12c)	Commercial loans	(3c)/(8)×100.0	1532.6	1622.6	1707.8	1847.8
(13)	Deflated average stock of deposits	(13a)+(13b)+(13c)	1237.5	1327.4	1395.8	1509.5
(13a)	Demand deposits	(4a)/(8)×100.0	251.8	274.5	287.0	314.0
(13b)	Time deposits	(4b)/(8)×100.0	735.6	783.0	821.0	886.2
(13c)	Saving deposits	(4c)/(8)×100.0	250.1	269.9	287.8	309.2

Table 3.20
Calculation of unchained Laspeyres volume measures of financial intermediation services indirectly measured at the prices of the previous year

Line number	Item	Description	t+1	t+2	t+3	t+4
(14)	FISIM on loans	(14a)+(14b)+(14c)	25.78	28.65	31.19	37.98
(14a)	Mortgage loans	(12a)_t×[(5a)_t–1–(7)_t–1]/100.0	4.35	4.15	4.02	5.19
(14b)	Automobile loans	(12b)_t×[(5b)_t–1–(7)_t–1]/100.0	1.19	1.00	0.88	1.89
(14c)	Commercial loans	(12c)_t×[(5c)_t–1–(7)_t–1]/100.0	20.23	23.50	26.29	30.90
(15)	FISIM on deposits	(15a)+(15b)+(15c)	16.01	18.26	19.50	23.88
(15a)	Demand deposits	(13a)_t ×[(7)_t–1–(6a)_t–1]/100.0	14.45	15.21	15.58	17.32
(15b)	Time deposits	(13b)_t ×[(7)_t–1–(6b)_t–1]/100.0	0.19	1.21	1.74	3.30
(15c)	Saving deposits	(13c)_t ×[(7)_t–1–(6c)_t–1]/100.0	1.38	1.85	2.19	3.26
(16)	Total domestic FISIM	(14)+(15)	41.79	46.91	50.69	61.85

The resultant volume measures of FISIM are then summed up to get the total unchained volume measures of FISIM on loans at the prices of the previous year.

For each type of deposit starting from year *t*+1, the volume measures of FISIM are obtained as follows:

- Compute the difference between the reference rate and average interest rate on the deposit for the previous year and divide the result by 100.0 (this is known as the base-period margin for deposits).
- Multiply the deflated stock of deposits in the current year by this difference to obtain the volume measure of FISIM at the price of the previous year.

For example, the volume measure of FISIM on demand deposits for year *t*+1 is obtained as $251.8\times\left(\frac{6.81-1.07}{100.0}\right)=14.45$ units.

The resultant volume measures of FISIM are then summed up to get the total unchained volume measures of FISIM on deposits at the prices of the previous year. The total unchained volume measures of FISIM on loans and deposits are then summed up to get the unchained volume measures of FISIM at the prices of the previous year.

3.80. Table 3.21 shows how to calculate the growth rates of the Laspeyres volume of FISIM at the prices of the previous year. For each item in the table, the growth rate is calculated by dividing the value at the prices of the previous year in table 3.20 by the corresponding current-price value in table 3.18.

Table 3.21

Growth rate of unchained Laspeyres volume measures of financial intermediation services indirectly measured at the prices of the previous year

Line number	Item	Description	*t*+1	*t*+2	*t*+3	*t*+4
(17)	Growth rate of volume measures of FISIM on loans	[(14)_*t*]/[(9)_*t*−1]	1.073	1.048	1.018	1.050
(17a)	Mortgage loans	[(14a)_*t*]/[(9a)_*t*−1]	1.090	1.072	1.023	1.076
(17b)	Automobile loans	[(14b)_*t*]/[(9b)_*t*−1]	1.080	1.058	1.023	1.054
(17c)	Commercial loans	[(14c)_*t*]/[(9c)_*t*−1]	1.069	1.044	1.017	1.045
(18)	Growth rate of volume measures of FISIM on deposits	[15_*t*]/[10_*t*−1]	1.081	1.072	1.013	1.052
(18a)	Demand deposits	[(15a)_*t*]/[(10a)_*t*−1]	1.080	1.075	1.010	1.057
(18b)	Time deposits	[(15b)_*t*]/[(10b)_*t*−1]	1.085	1.050	1.014	1.043
(18c)	Saving deposits	[(15c)_*t*]/[(10c)_*t*−1]	1.087	1.064	1.031	1.038
(19)	Growth rate of total volume measures of domestic FISIM	[16_*t*]/[11_*t*−1]	1.076	1.058	1.016	1.051

Table 3.22

Annually chained Laspeyres volume measures of financial intermediation services indirectly measured (reference year = *t*)

Line number	Item	Description[a]	*t*	*t*+1	*t*+2	*t*+3	*t*+4
(20)	FISIM on loans	[20_*t*−1]×[17_*t*]	24.03	25.78	27.03	27.52	28.89
(20a)	Mortgage loans	[(20a)_*t*−1]×[(17a)_*t*]	3.99	4.35	4.67	4.78	5.14
(20b)	Automobile loans	[(20b)_*t*−1]×[(17b)_*t*]	1.10	1.19	1.26	1.29	1.36
(20c)	Commercial loans	[(20c)_*t*−1]×[(17c)_*t*]	18.93	20.23	21.12	21.49	22.46
(21)	FISIM on deposits	[21_*t*−1]×[18_*t*]	14.81	16.01	17.17	17.40	18.31
(21a)	Demand deposits	[(21a)_*t*−1]×[(18a)_*t*]	13.37	14.45	15.53	15.69	16.59
(21b)	Time deposits	[(21b)_*t*−1]×[(18b)_*t*]	0.18	0.19	0.20	0.21	0.21
(21c)	Saving deposits	[(21c)_*t*−1]×[(18c)_*t*]	1.27	1.38	1.46	1.51	1.57
(22)	Total domestic FISIM	[22_*t*−1]×[19_*t*]	38.84	41.79	44.20	44.92	47.20

[a] Applies to data from year *t*+1.

3.81. Table 3.22 shows how to chain the Laspeyres volume measures of FISIM which were calculated earlier so that they are expressed at the prices of a specific reference year. Since the Laspeyres volume measures are chained using annual prices, they are known as annually chained Laspeyres volume measures. In this example, it is assumed that the reference year is year *t*. For each item in the table, the annually chained volume measures from year *t*+1 are obtained by multiplying the annually chained volume measure for the previous year by its growth rate. It is not necessary to calculate the annually chained volume measures of FISIM for year *t*, since it is the reference year. In addition, except for years *t* and *t*+1 , the annually chained volume measures of FISIM are not additive. The loss of additivity is the natural outcome of chaining.

3.82. This worked example has shown how to compute annually chained Laspeyres volume measures of FISIM using the deflation method. Base-period interest margins were applied to deflated stocks of loans and deposits before the resultant volume measures for each type of loan and deposit were aggregated to produce annually chained Laspeyres volume measures of FISIM. Applying base-period interest margins to each type of loan and deposit is better than applying base-period margins to the total stocks of loans and deposits, as the latter is equivalent to the use of a unit measure of price change which will be affected by changes in the composition of loans or deposits and changes in the structure of interest rates.

(b) Financial services associated with institutional units which engage in lending using own funds or funds provided by a sponsor

References:
2008 SNA, Chapter 4, Institutional units and sectors
2008 SNA, Chapter 6, The production account

3.83. It is also possible for financial institutions to make loans without accepting deposits. The loans granted by these financial institutions are made using their own funds or funds provided by a sponsor. Examples of such financial institutions include moneylenders, credit card issuers, finance associates of retailers who may be responsible for financial leasing, pawnshops and corporations involved in lending (for example, in providing student loans and import/export loans). Like deposit-taking corporations, these financial institutions provide implicit financial services on the loans they grant. However, no financial services are provided on deposits, since they do not accept deposits. Mathematically, the output of the implicit financial services produced by these financial institutions is calculated by modifying the formula to compute FISIM in equation (3.4) and can be written as:

$$F_L = \left(\frac{r_L - rr}{100.0}\right) Y_L \qquad (3.4)$$

where F_L, r_L, rr and Y_L represent the output of financial services on loans, the lending interest rate, the reference rate and the average stock of loans respectively. The interest rates are expressed in per cent.

Like FISIM, the output should be allocated to the institutional sectors and industries.[28] The lending interest rate will vary among the financial institutions, while the reference rate is taken to be the same as the reference rate which is used to compute the FISIM provided by deposit-taking corporations operating in the same economy. This is on the basis that the key recommendations on FISIM which were made in accordance with the SNA update procedures in box 3.1 imply that within an economy, only one reference rate

[28] The allocation can be carried out using the methods to allocate FISIM which were described earlier.

should be calculated for each currency. Since moneylenders usually charge especially high rates of interest, their service charges may exceed the SNA interest payments by significant amounts.

3.84. Moneylenders are a major source of credit in many countries. In addition, in many developing countries, money lending is provided by unincorporated enterprises owned by households. These units are allocated to the households sector rather than the captive financial institutions and moneylenders subsector of the financial corporations subsector. These unincorporated financial enterprises are not usually registered with the authorities and operate in the informal sector.[29] They thrive where collateral is scarce and legal enforcement of debt contracts is difficult, especially in rural areas. The advantages that allow them to make loans that banks could not make include better knowledge about the creditworthiness of their clients, greater ability to enforce repayment and the ability to overcome the lack of economies of scale by charging high rates.

3.85. The activities of moneylenders and other financial institutions which are engaged in lending using their own funds are very likely to be captured in formal enterprise surveys or by the monetary authority if they are actual corporations or quasi-corporations. However, this may not be so in the case of unincorporated financial enterprises owned by households. Furthermore, given the relatively undeveloped state of the formal banking system in many developing countries, they are likely to comprise a significant share of the lending activity in these countries. Thus, the failure to account for their activities will result in the understatement of their contribution to the economy. Hence, there is a need to capture and measure the extent of the financial services provided by these unincorporated enterprises. This can be done through either household or enterprise surveys. In the case of household surveys, relevant questions to collect information on, say, the level of loans, purpose, duration and interest payable can be included in household expenditure surveys, which are regularly conducted in many developing countries. In addition, resources permitting, these questions can also be included in special surveys to collect information on the financial status of households.[30] However, pure household-based surveys may not be able to capture the portion of the financial services which is consumed by enterprises. Hence, there may be a need to compute financial services of informal moneylenders through specially conducted establishment surveys. Alternatively, mixed household enterprise surveys may be conducted to collect data on the money lending activities undertaken by households in their role as unincorporated enterprises. Regardless of the method used, the survey should be able to divide the services provided into those provided to businesses and households in their roles as consumers and owners of unincorporated enterprises. Ultimately, the choice of the appropriate method to capture the activities of unincorporated moneylenders depends upon how adequately established data collection methods cover their activities. The choice will also depend upon what information is missing from existing collections, the organization of statistical systems, the resources available and user needs.

Worked example 3.4. Computing the output of financial services provided by moneylenders

3.86. This worked example shows how to calculate the output of the financial services provided by moneylenders at current prices. It is assumed that the compiling agency is able to collect the input data to calculate the output from surveys and has grossed up the data to obtain the estimates for the total economy. In addition, transactions be-

---

[29] Kulshreshtha (2006) notes that, in many Asian and African countries, the size of these informal financial activities is not insignificant.

[30] Examples of these surveys are available in Coleman and Williams (2006) and India, Ministry of Statistics and Programme Implementation (2001).

tween two institutional units are recorded using the quadruple principle of accounting. For many of these transactions, the counterpart entries are recorded in the financial account to show the means of payment to settle these transactions. The worked example will also show how to record the counterpart entries for these transactions in the financial account. For simplicity, it is assumed these transactions are settled in currency or transferable deposits, which are part of "currency and deposits" in the financial account.

3.87. Table 3.23 shows the data on the interest receivable by moneylenders on the loans they grant. It is assumed that the survey data show that moneylenders lend only to institutional units in the non-financial corporations and households sector. It is also assumed that all moneylenders in the economy are corporations or quasi-corporations. Furthermore, it is assumed the loans to households are only for final consumption. There are no data on the interest payable on deposits held by moneylenders, as they do not accept deposits.

3.88. Table 3.24 shows the data on the stock of loans granted by the moneylenders to non-financial corporations and households as at 1 January and 31 December plus the average stock of loans for these sectors. For each sector, the average stock of loans is obtained by taking the simple average of the stock of loans at the start and end of the year. No data on the stock of deposits are shown, as moneylenders make loans using their own funds and, thus, do not accept deposits.

3.89. Table 3.25 shows how to calculate the average interest rate for the loans granted by moneylenders to non-financial corporations and households using the data in tables 3.23 and 3.24. Each average interest rate is computed by dividing the interest flow for the year by the average stock of loans and then multiplying the result by 100.0. Table 3.25 also shows the domestic reference rate to be used to compute the output of financial services of the moneylenders. It is assumed in this worked example that moneylenders belong to the same economy as the other institutional units in worked example 3.1, so the reference rate in the earlier worked example is used here.

Table 3.23
Data on interest receivable on loans granted by moneylenders

Line number	Item	Value
(1)	Interest receivable on loans from	62.0
(1a)	Non-financial corporations	12.0
(1b)	Households	50.0

Table 3.24
Data on the stock of, and changes in, loans granted by moneylenders

Line number	Item	1 January	31 December	Average	Change
(2)	Loans	468.0	474.0	471.0	6.0
(2a)	Non-financial corporations	94.0	96.0	95.0	2.0
(2b)	Households	374.0	378.0	376.0	4.0

Table 3.25
Calculation of average interest rates on loans granted by moneylenders

Line number	Item	Description	Value
(3)	Average interest rate on loans	$(1)/(2)_{av}\times 100.0$	13.16
(3a)	Non-financial corporations	$(1a)/(2a)_{av}\times 100.0$	12.63
(3b)	Households	$(1b)/(2b)_{av}\times 100.0$	13.30
(4)	Reference rate	rr_{DOM}	6.81

3.90. Table 3.26 shows how to calculate the output of financial services provided by moneylenders using the data in the earlier tables. For each sector, the output of financial services is computed as follows:

- Compute the difference between average interest rate on loans and the reference rate and divide the result by 100.0.
- Multiply the difference by the average stock of loans to obtain the output.

3.91. Table 3.27 shows how to calculate the SNA interest arising from transactions with moneylenders using the data in tables 3.23 and 3.24. For each sector, SNA interest is computed as the difference between the actual interest receivable by moneylenders and the output of financial services.[31] The SNA interest should be recorded in the allocation of primary income account.

3.92. Table 3.28 shows how to calculate the changes in financial assets and liabilities arising from the transactions between moneylenders and the other institutional units, and, where appropriate, the means of payment for these transactions. In general, the changes in financial assets and liabilities are computed using the following principles: for moneylenders, the interest received on loans during the accounting period

Table 3.26
Calculation of the output of financial services provided by moneylenders

Line number	Item	Description	Value	2008 SNA code
(5)	Output of financial services on loans	(5a)+(5b)	29.9	P1
(5a)	Non-financial corporations	$[(3a)-(4)]/100.0\times(2a)_{av}$	5.5	P2
(5b)	Households	$[(3b)-(4)]/100.0\times(2b)_{av}$	24.4	P3

Table 3.27
Calculation of SNA interest receivable by moneylenders

Line number	Item	Description	Value	2008 SNA code
(6)	SNA interest receivable by moneylenders	(6a)+(6b)	32.1	D4, D41
(6a)	SNA interest receivable from non-financial corporations	(1a)–(5a)	6.5	D4, D41
(6b)	SNA interest receivable from households	(1b)–(5b)	25.6	D4, D41

Table 3.28
Calculation of changes in the financial assets and liabilities of moneylenders and other institutional units

Line number	Item	Description	Value	2008 SNA code
	Changes in financial assets (currency and deposits)			
(7)	Moneylenders	$(1)-(2)_{ch}$	56.0	F2
(8)	Non-financial corporations	$-(1a)+(2a)_{ch}$	-10.0	F2
(9)	Households	$-(1b)+(2b)_{ch}$	-46.0	F2
	Changes in financial assets (loans)			
(10)	Moneylenders	$(2)_{ch}$	6.0	F4
	Changes in liabilities (loans)			
(11)	Non-financial corporations	$(2a)_{ch}$	2.0	F4
(12)	Households	$(2b)_{ch}$	4.0	F4

[31] SNA interest on loans can also be obtained by multiplying the reference rate by the average stock of loans.

represents an increase in their currency and deposits in the financial account. On the other hand, the value of loans granted represents a decrease in these assets in the financial account. The converse applies to the counterpart institutional units. As an example, moneylenders have a net increase of 56.0 units in their assets of currency and deposits during the accounting period. This is the result of:

- Interest received on loans (62.0 units).
- Loans granted (-6.0 units).

In addition, they have a net increase of 6.0 units in their assets of loans during the accounting period.

3.93. Table 3.29 shows how to record the output of the financial services provided by moneylenders and other transactions. To simplify the presentation and analysis, transactions which are not related to the worked example are ignored. The transactions are described as follows:

(a) The output of moneylenders is 29.9 units. This output is recorded in the production account of the moneylenders. Part of this output (5.5 units) is

Table 3.29

Recording the output of financial services provided by moneylenders, SNA interest and other related transactions

Uses													Resources
Total	Goods and services	Total economy	Households	Moneylenders	Non-financial corporations	2008 SNA code	Transactions and balancing items	Non-financial corporations	Moneylenders	Households	Total economy	Goods and services	Total
Production account													
29.9	29.9					P1	Output		29.9		29.9		29.9
5.5		5.5			5.5	P2	Intermediate consumption					5.5	5.5
24.4		24.4		29.9	-5.5	B1g	Value added, gross/ Gross domestic product						
Allocation of primary income account													
32.1		32.1	25.6		6.5	D4	Property income		32.1		32.1		32.1
32.1		32.1	25.6		6.5	D41	Interest (SNA interest)		32.1		32.1		32.1
24.4		24.4	-25.6	62.0	-12.0	B5g	Balance of primary income, gross/ National income, gross						
Use of disposable income account													
24.4		24.4	24.4			P3	Final consumption expenditure					24.4	24.4
0.0		0.0	-50.0	62.0	-12.0	B8g	Saving, gross						
Changes in assets													**Changes in liabilities and net worth**
Capital account													
0.0		0.0	-50.0	62.0	-12.0	B9	Net lending (+)/ net borrowing (-)						
Financial account													
						B9	Net lending (+)/ net borrowing (-)	-12.0	62.0	-50.0	0.0		0.0
0.0		0.0	-46.0	56.0	-10.0	F2	Currency and deposits						
6.0		6.0		6.0		F4	Loans	2.0		4.0	6.0		6.0

consumed by non-financial corporations. This amount is recorded as their intermediate consumption in the production account;

(b) The interest recorded in the allocation of primary income account represents SNA interest rather than bank interest;

(c) The remaining part of the output of financial services produced by moneylenders (24.4 units) is consumed by households as final consumption expenditure. This amount is recorded in the use of disposable income account as a use by households. The use of disposable income account also shows the gross saving of each sector and the total economy;

(d) Since there are no capital account transactions, net lending/net borrowing in the capital account is the same as gross saving in the use of disposable income account;

(e) The financial account records the changes in currency and deposits and loans of the institutional units. Since these entries are the counterparts to entries in the other accounts or reflect the exchange in financial assets and liabilities only, net lending/net borrowing is identical to net lending/net borrowing in the capital account, although, in practice, differences in data sources and the timing of the recording of transactions may result in a discrepancy between the estimates of net lending/net borrowing in these two accounts.

3.94. The method to calculate the output of financial services provided by moneylenders in this worked example can also be used to calculate the output of financial services provided by other institutional units which make loans using their own funds, such as credit card issuers, finance associates of retailers who may be responsible for financial leasing, pawnshops and corporations involved in lending (for example, in providing student loans and import/export loans).

Volume measures of the output of financial services associated with institutional units which engage in lending using own funds or funds provided by a sponsor

3.95. The worked example above involved calculating the output of financial services provided by moneylenders at current prices. Time series data on the output will need to be adjusted to remove the effects of price changes. In principle, volume measures of the output can be obtained using the deflation method to compute volume measures of FISIM, as described earlier. This method is also applicable to the output of financial services provided by other institutional units which make loans using their own funds, such as credit card issuers, finance associates of retailers who may be responsible for financial leasing, pawnshops and corporations involved in lending (for example, in providing student loans and import/export loans).

(c) Financial services produced by the central bank

References:
2008 SNA, Chapter 6, The production account
2008 SNA, Chapter 8, The redistribution of income account

3.96. Services produced by the central bank can be broadly classified into three groups:

- Monetary policy services.
- Financial intermediation services.
- Borderline cases, such as supervisory services.

Monetary policy refers to measures or actions taken by the central bank to influence the general price level and the level of liquidity in the economy. These could include setting interest rates and determining the level of money supply in the economy through various tools, such as increasing/decreasing the reserve requirements. Monetary policy services are collective in nature, serving the community as a whole, and thus represent non-market output of the central bank. Financial intermediation services are individual in nature and, in the absence of policy intervention in the interest rates charged by the central banks, would be treated as market production. The method to calculate the output of these financial intermediation services is the same as the method to calculate FISIM. The borderline cases, such as supervisory services, may be classified as market or non-market services, depending on whether explicit fees are charged that are sufficient to cover the costs of providing these services.

3.97. In principle, a distinction should be made between market and non-market output, but, in practice, the possible resource intensiveness of the exercise and the relative importance of making the distinction should be considered before implementing the conceptual recommendations. In cases where it is not possible to separate market output from non-market output, the whole of the output of the central bank should be treated as non-market and valued at the sum of costs. Since the output is non-market, it should be measured as the sum of intermediate consumption, compensation of employees, consumption of fixed capital and other taxes less subsidies on production.

3.98. The non-market output of the central bank should be recorded as collective consumption expenditure by general government. However, the general government does not actually make outlays on the non-market output of the central bank. Therefore, a current transfer equivalent to the value of the non-market output should be recorded as payable by the central bank and receivable by the general government to cover the purchase of the non-market output of the central bank by government. In the SNA, the current transfer is included in miscellaneous current transfers (D75).[32]

3.99. Central banks frequently provide supervisory services overseeing the financial corporations. One could argue that this is for the benefit of society in general and the national accounts should record them as government final consumption. In support of this view, one could draw a parallel with government performing market regulation policies, which it also may entrust to a specialized agency, or to government providing for roads, dams and bridges. From this point of view, surveillance services are collective services and should be recorded as government consumption expenditure.

[32] In contrast, paragraph 14.16 of the ESA 2010 states that, by convention, only the part of the total central bank output (sum of costs less commissions and fees) which is not sold has to be allocated to the intermediate consumption of other financial intermediaries – the subsectors deposit-taking corporations except the central bank (S122) and other financial intermediaries except insurance corporations and pension funds (S125) – in proportion to the respective value added of each of these subsectors.

3.100. However, one could also argue that government's regulatory services are to the benefit of the financial intermediaries, because these services contribute to the functioning and financial performance of these institutions. From this perspective, they are comparable to regulatory services of government such as quality control on food and drugs, which the national accounts record as intermediate consumption of producers. The fact that financial intermediaries pay a fee for these services in some countries (for example in a number of countries in Latin America) supports this view. Following this reasoning, surveillance services are not collective services, but should be recorded as intermediate consumption of financial intermediaries. The central bank should be able to provide information on the explicit charges receivable for providing these surveillance services. However, even if the view is taken that supervisory services are market output because a fee is charged, if the fees are not sufficient to cover the costs incurred by the bank in providing such services, then the services should be treated as non-market output of the central bank and part of government consumption expenditure.

3.101. If the financial intermediation services provided by the central bank are significant, and if it is possible and worthwhile to compile data for a separate establishment providing them, these services should be shown as payable by the units to whom they are delivered. Supervisory services treated as market output are recorded similarly.

Worked example 3.5. Calculating and recording the non-market output of the central bank[33]

3.102. This worked example shows how to compute the non-market output of the central bank at current prices and record the output and other transactions between the central bank and general government. As mentioned above, non-market output can comprise monetary policy services and/or the non-market component of supervisory services. In addition, transactions between two institutional units are recorded in the SNA using the quadruple principle of accounting. For many of these transactions, the counterpart entries are recorded in the financial account to show the means of payment to settle these transactions. The worked example also shows how to record the counterpart entries for these transactions in the financial account. For simplicity, it is assumed that these transactions are settled in currency or transferable deposits, which are part of "currency and deposits" in the financial account.

3.103. Table 3.30 shows the costs associated with the production of the non-market output of the central bank. These costs will need to be estimated by the compiling agency in consultation with the central bank if the latter is not the compiling agency. For simplicity, we assume that these costs comprise only intermediate consumption and compensation of employees, and that there is no consumption of fixed capital and other taxes less subsidies on production. All the goods and services for intermediate consumption are purchased from the non-financial and financial sectors in the economy. Since we are measuring non-market output, it is not necessary to obtain an estimate of the return to fixed capital. The non-market output of the central bank is computed as the sum of its intermediate consumption and compensation of employees.

3.104. Table 3.31 shows how to calculate the changes in financial assets and liabilities arising from the transactions between the central bank and the other institutional units. In general, the changes in financial assets and liabilities are computed using the following principles: for the central bank, its intermediate consumption and the compensation of its employees represent an increase in the liabilities of currency and deposits in the financial account. This is because the central bank is the is-

[33] The worked example is adapted from Bloem, Gorter and Rivas (2006).

Table 3.30
Costs incurred by the central bank in producing non-market output

Line number	Item	Description	Value	2008 SNA code
(1)	Intermediate consumption		90.0	P1, P2
(2)	Compensation of employees		360.0	D1
(3)	Non-market output of the central bank	(1)+(2)	450.0	P1, P3, P32, D7, D75

Table 3.31
Calculation of changes in financial assets and liabilities of central bank and other institutional units

Line number	Item	Description	Value	2008 SNA code
	Changes in financial assets (currency and deposits)			
(4)	Households	(2)	360.0	F2
(5)	Non-financial and financial corporations	(1)	90.0	F2
	Changes in liabilities (currency and deposits)			
(6)	Central bank	(3)	450.0	F2

suer of currency, so it does not hold currency and deposits as financial assets. For the institutional units which provide goods and services and labour inputs to the central bank, the counterpart of these transactions represent an increase in their assets of currency and deposits. For example, the central bank has an increase in liabilities of currency and deposits of 450.0 units during the accounting period. This is the result of the following:

- Payment for intermediate consumption (90.0 units).
- Payment for compensation of employees (360.0 units).

3.105. Table 3.32 shows how to record the non-market output of the central bank and other transactions. To ensure clarity, the transactions of the central bank are shown separately rather than combined with those of the other financial corporations. Furthermore, to simplify the presentation and analysis, other transactions, such as the intermediate consumption of goods and services of the other institutional units, are ignored, while the transactions of the non-financial and other financial corporations are combined. The transactions are described as follows:

(a) The non-market output of the central bank (450.0 units) is recorded in the production account. The intermediate consumption of the central bank (90.0 units) is also recorded in this account. This amount is also recorded as the output of the non-financial and other financial corporations sector, since it is assumed that all the intermediate consumption of the central bank is sourced from these corporations;

(b) The compensation paid by the central bank to its employees to produce the non-market output (360.0 units) is entered in the "uses" column in the generation of income account;

(c) This amount is then recorded as the resources of households in the allocation of primary income account;

(d) The collective consumption expenditure represented by the non-market output of the central bank (450.0 units) is consumed by the general government. Hence, it is recorded as part of the collective consumption expenditure of the general government in the use of disposable income account. However, this output is not produced by the general government.

Table 3.32
Recording transactions related to the non-market output of the central bank

Uses | **Resources**

Total	Goods and services	Total economy	Households	General government	Central bank	Non-financial and financial corporations	2008 SNA code	Transactions and balancing items	Non-financial and financial corporations	Central bank	General government	Households	Total economy	Goods and services	Total
Production account															
540.0	540.0						P1	Output	90.0	450.0			540.0		540.0
90.0		90.0			90.0		P2	Intermediate consumption						90.0	90.0
450.0		450.0			360.0	90.0	B1g	Value added, gross/Gross domestic product							
Generation of income account															
360.0		360.0			360.0		D1	Compensation of employees							
90.0		90.0			0.0	90.0	B2g	Operating surplus, gross							
Allocation of primary income account															
							D1	Compensation of employees				360.0	360.0		360.0
450.0		450.0	360.0		0.0	90.0	B5g	Balance of primary income, gross/National income, gross					450.0		450.0
Secondary distribution of income account															
450.0		450.0			450.0		D7	Other current transfers			450.0		450.0		450.0
450.0		450.0			450.0		D75	Miscellaneous current transfers			450.0		450.0		450.0
450.0		450.0	360.0	450.0	-450.0	90.0	B6g	Disposable income, gross							
Use of disposable income account															
450.0		450.0		450.0			P3	Final consumption expenditure						450.0	450.0
450.0		450.0		450.0			P32	Collective consumption expenditure						450.0	450.0
0.0		0.0	360.0	0.0	-450.0	90.0	B8g	Saving, gross							
Changes in assets															**Changes in liabilities and net worth**
Capital account															
0.0		0.0	360.0	0.0	-450.0	90.0	B9	Net lending (+)/ net borrowing (-)							
Financial account															
							B9	Net lending (+)/ net borrowing (-)	90.0	-450.0	0.0	360.0	0.0		0.0
450.0		450.0	360.0			90.0	F2	Currency and deposits		450.0	0.0		450.0		450.0

As a result, there is a fall in government saving and, hence, net lending/ net borrowing. For the central bank, the opposite effects are observed. To remove these effects, a current transfer (450.0 units) is also recorded as payable by the central bank to the general government to cover its purchase of the non-market output of the central bank. The current transfer is recorded as part of miscellaneous current transfers in the secondary distribution of income account;

(e) Since there are no capital account transactions, net lending/net borrowing in the capital account is the same as gross saving and the current external balance in the use of disposable income account;

(f) The financial account records the changes in currency and deposits as the means of payment for most of the transactions in the earlier accounts. Since these entries are the counterparts to entries in the other accounts, net lending/net borrowing is identical to net lending/net borrowing in the capital account, although, in practice, differences in data sources and the timing of the recording of transactions may result in a discrepancy between the estimates of net lending/net borrowing in these two accounts.

Volume measures of the output of the central bank

References:
2008 SNA, Chapter 15, Price and volume measures
Handbook on Price and Volume Measures in National Accounts, Chapter 4, A/B/C methods for output by product

3.106. The market and non-market output of the central bank which are calculated from source data are measured at current prices. There is a need to remove the price effects to derive the corresponding volume measures. How the volume measures are computed depends on the nature of the output. In the case of explicit charges – supervisory services, say – volume measures can be obtained by deflating the current-price output using an appropriate sub-index of the PPI (adjusted for quality changes). Given that such a sub-index is likely to be unavailable, the compiling agency can consider using a PPI with a broader coverage. Alternatively, it can consider the use of volume indicators. In the case of output related to financial intermediation, volume measures can be obtained using the method to compute volume measures of FISIM which was described earlier. In the case of the non-market output of collective services, no market prices exist. Thus, it is not possible to deflate the output using an output price index such as the PPI. This means that other methods will have to be considered. For collective services, two methods are discussed below.

3.107. The first method is to derive a pseudo-output price index such that, when it is compared to the aggregate input price index, the difference reflects the productivity growth thought to be occurring in the production process. Pseudo-output price indices can be derived in various ways, such as by adjusting the input price index according to the observed productivity growth of a related production process or by basing the growth of the pseudo-output price index on the output price indices observed for similar products. However, this method is unlikely to apply to the output of collective services of the central bank, as it will be difficult to find products similar to these services.

3.108. The second method is called the "input method". This method may be more appropriate for collective services. The "input method" consists of measuring changes in output by changes in the weighted sum of volume measures of all the inputs. The latter should fully reflect both changes in quantity and quality. They are generally best derived by deflating the various input costs by corresponding constant-quality price indices, or, when such price indices are unavailable, using volume indicators that reflect input volume change (for example, the number of hours worked by employees).

3.109. Measuring changes in the volume of collective services is generally more difficult than measuring the volume changes in individual services because the former are hard to define and observe. This is an area where further research is needed. The compiling agency should also consider providing explanatory information that draws users' attention to the method of measurement used.

(d) Interest rates set by the central bank and financial intermediation

Reference:
2008 SNA, Chapter 7, The distribution of income accounts

3.110. The central bank's main responsibility is to formulate and carry out part of economic policy of the government. It therefore often acts differently from other financial corporations and generally has the authority of the government to enforce it. In cases where the central bank uses its special powers to obligate market participants to pay transfers without a direct quid pro quo, it is appropriate to record the proceeds as implicit taxes. Conversely, in cases when the central bank makes payments that are clearly for policy rather than commercial purposes, it may be argued that implicit subsidies are paid. Three cases are considered:

- The central bank is able to dictate below market rates for reserve deposits.
- The central bank pays above market rates in a situation where the external value of the currency is under pressure.
- The central bank acts as a development bank offering loans at below market rates to priority industries.

3.111. If central bank interest rates are out of line with those of commercial banks, they will distort the estimates of FISIM output and thus should be removed from the calculations. The difference between flows calculated using the reference rate and the actual rate set by the central bank should be recorded not as market output, specifically FISIM, but as implicit taxes and subsidies. FISIM output should be calculated using market interest rates. This procedure is analogous to, and consistent with, the practice of treating the difference between the market exchange rate and an alternative exchange rate imposed by the central bank as an implicit tax or subsidy. Specifically, the implicit taxes and subsidies are classified as other taxes on production (D29) and other subsidies on production (D39), since they do not influence the level of production of the producers affected. In addition, compensating transfers between the government and the central bank should be recorded in the SNA to avoid any imbalance between the current and financial accounts. These transfers are classified as miscellaneous current transfers (D75).

3.112. Given that deviations from market rates may be relatively small in practice, it may not be worthwhile to try to remove them from the calculation of FISIM output in all cases. However, when deviations are considerable, the compiling agency should be encouraged to identify them and remove them from the calculations of FISIM output to avoid significant overestimation or underestimation of the output of the central bank.

Worked example 3.6. Recording transactions where the central bank dictates interest rates below the market rates for reserve deposits[34]

3.113. This worked example shows how to record transactions in the case of the central bank dictating interest rates below the market rates for reserve deposits. The recording of changes in financial assets and liabilities due to these transactions is also presented.

3.114. Table 3.33 shows the average stock of reserve deposits that commercial banks maintain with the central bank, the interbank interest rate and actual interest

[34] The worked example is adapted from Bloem, Gorter and Rivas (2006).

Table 3.33
Data on the average stock of reserve deposits, the interbank interest rate and the actual interest rate

Line number	Item	Description	Value
(1)	Average stock of reserve deposits from commercial banks		50000.0
(2)	Interbank interest rate (reference rate) (per cent)		4.5
(3)	Actual interest rate (payable to commercial banks) (per cent)		3.0
(4)	FISIM using the actual and interbank interest rates	(1)×[(2)–(3)]/100.0	750.0

Table 3.34
Calculation of interest income, other taxes on production, FISIM and changes in financial assets and liabilities

Line number	Item	Description	Value	2008 SNA code
(5)	SNA interest income payable by the central bank to commercial banks	(1)×(2)/100.0	2250.0	D4, D41
(6)	Actual interest income payable by the central bank to commercial banks	(1)×(3)/100.0	1500.0	
(7)	Other taxes on production payable by commercial banks	(1)×[(2)–(3)]/100.0	750.0	D2, D29, D7, D75
(8)	FISIM of the central bank using market interest rates	(1)×[(2)–(2)]/100.0	0.0	P1, P2
	Changes in financial assets (currency and deposits)			
(9)	Commercial banks	(6)	1500.0	F2
	Changes in liabilities (currency and deposits)			
(10)	Central bank	(6)	1500.0	F2

rate payable by the central bank to these banks on their reserve deposits during an accounting period. Such data should be available with the central bank. The reference rate is taken to be the interbank interest rate. Reserve deposits serve among other things to protect financial intermediaries from runs on deposits that might cause a banking crisis. The actual interest rate paid by the central bank to banks (3.0 per cent) is lower than the reference rate (4.5 per cent). Table 3.33 also shows the FISIM output which is calculated using the actual interest rate payable by the central bank on the reserve deposits of the commercial banks and the interbank interest rate as the reference rate. The use of the below market interest rate causes the output of FISIM of the central bank to be unusually high. Thus, FISIM should be calculated using market interest rates, while the difference between flows calculated using the reference rate and actual interest rate set by the central bank should be recorded as other taxes on production.

3.115. Table 3.34 shows how to calculate the various types of income payable by the central bank to commercial banks, the output of FISIM of the central bank and the other taxes on production. The method to calculate the SNA interest and actual interest payable by the central bank and the output of FISIM of the central bank is the same as the corresponding method used in worked example 3.1, except that, in this worked example, loans are not taken into account. FISIM is calculated using market interest rates and is zero. The other taxes on production payable by commercial banks are calculated as follows:

- Find the difference between the interbank and actual interest rates on reserve deposits.
- Multiply this difference by the average stock of reserve deposits to obtain other taxes on production.

Table 3.34 also shows the changes in financial assets and liabilities arising from the transactions between the central bank and commercial banks. The central bank has an increase in liabilities of currency and deposits due to the interest payable to banks on the reserve deposits (1500.0 units). The converse applies to commercial banks for changes in their assets of currency and deposits.

Table 3.35

Recording transactions for which the central bank dictates interest rates below the market rates for reserve deposits

Uses								Resources					
Total	**Goods and services**	**Total economy**	**General government**	**Central bank**	**Other financial corporations**	**2008 SNA code**	**Transactions and balancing items**	**Other financial corporations**	**Central bank**	**General government**	**Total economy**	**Goods and services**	**Total**
Production account													
0.0	0.0					P1	Output		0.0		0.0		0.0
0.0		0.0			0.0	P2	Intermediate consumption					0.0	0.0
0.0		0.0		0.0	0.0	B1g	Value added, gross/Gross domestic product						
Generation of income account													
750.0		750.0			750.0	D2	Taxes on production and imports						
750.0		750.0			750.0	D29	Other taxes on production						
-750.0		-750.0		0.0	-750.0	B2g	Operating surplus, gross						
Allocation of primary income account													
						D2	Taxes on production and imports			750.0	750.0		750.0
						D29	Other taxes on production			750.0	750.0		750.0
2250.0		2250.0		2250.0		D4	Property income	2250.0			2250.0		2250.0
2250.0		2250.0		2250.0		D41	Interest	2250.0			2250.0		2250.0
0.0		0.0	750.0	-2250.0	1500.0	B5g	Balance of primary income, gross/National income, gross						
Secondary distribution of income account													
750.0		750.0	750.0			D7	Other current transfers		750.0		750.0		750.0
750.0		750.0	750.0			D75	Miscellaneous current transfers		750.0		750.0		750.0
0.0		0.0	0.0	-1500.0	1500.0	B6g	Disposable income, gross						
Use of disposable income account													
0.0		0.0	0.0	-1500.0	1500.0	B8g	Saving, gross						
Changes in assets								**Changes in liabilities and net worth**					
Capital account													
0.0		0.0	0.0	-1500.0	1500.0	B9	Net lending (+)/ net borrowing (-)						
Financial account													
						B9	Net lending (+)/ net borrowing (-)	1500.0	-1500.0	0.0	0.0		0.0
1500.0		1500.0			1500.0	F2	Currency and deposits		1500.0		1500.0		1500.0

3.116. Table 3.35 shows how to record the various transactions. To ensure clarity, the transactions of the central bank and commercial banks are recorded separately rather than combined under the financial corporations sector. The transactions of commercial banks are recorded under the other financial corporations sector. To simplify the presentation and analysis, other transactions, such as wages and salaries, are ignored. The transactions are described as follows:

(a) The output of FISIM produced by the central bank is zero and it is recorded in the production account. This output is also recorded as the intermediate consumption of the commercial banks;

(b) Commercial banks actually receive only 1500.0 units (i.e. 3.0 per cent times 50000.0) as "interest" on their reserve deposits. This amount is recorded in the financial account. However, they are recorded as receiving 2250.0 units (i.e. 4.5 per cent times 50000.0) as SNA interest in the allocation of primary income account and paying 750.0 units (i.e. 1.5 per cent times 50000.0) to government as other taxes on production in the generation of income account;

(c) The general government is recorded as receiving 750.0 units from commercial banks as other taxes on production, which are recorded in the allocation of primary income account, and as making a miscellaneous current transfer of 750.0 units to the central bank, which is recorded in the secondary distribution of income account. Both these flows are notional;

(d) The central bank actually pays 1500.0 units in interest on the reserve deposits maintained by commercial banks with it. This amount is recorded in the financial account. However, it is recorded as paying 2250.0 units to the commercial banks in the allocation of primary income account and receiving a miscellaneous current transfer of 750.0 units from the general government in the secondary distribution of income account;

(e) Gross saving in the use of disposable income account is the same as net lending/net borrowing in the financial account, as there are no transactions in the capital account. The equality between net lending/net borrowing in the capital account and financial account has been maintained due to the inclusion of a compensating current transfer from the general government to the central bank, although, in practice, differences in data sources and the timing of the recording of transactions may result in a discrepancy between the estimates of net lending/net borrowing in these two accounts.

Worked example 3.7. Recording transactions for which the central bank pays above market rates in a situation in which the external value of the currency is under pressure

3.117. This worked example shows how to record the transactions in the SNA in the case of the central bank setting interest rates above the market rates for a limited period in a situation in which the external value of the currency is under pressure. The changes in financial assets and liabilities due to these transactions are also recorded.

3.118. Table 3.36 shows the average stock of deposits commercial banks maintain with the central bank, the interbank interest rate and the actual interest rate payable by the central bank to these banks on their deposits during an accounting period. These data should be available with the central bank. The reference rate is taken

Table 3.36
Data on average stock deposits, the interbank interest rate and the actual interest rate

Line number	Item	Description	Value
(1)	Average stock of deposits from commercial banks		50000.0
(2)	Interbank interest rate (reference rate) (per cent)		4.5
(3)	Actual interest rate (payable to commercial banks) (per cent)		7.0
(4)	FISIM using the actual interest rate and the interbank interest rate	(1)×[(2)–(3)]/100.0	-1250.0

Table 3.37

Calculation of interest income, other subsidies on production, financial intermediation services indirectly measured and changes in financial assets and liabilities

Line number	Item	Description	Value	2008 SNA code
(5)	SNA interest income payable by the central bank to commercial banks	(1)×(2)/100.0	2250.0	D4, D41
(6)	Actual interest income payable by the central bank to commercial banks	(1)×(3)/100.0	3500.0	
(7)	Other subsidies on production receivable by commercial banks	(1)×[(3)–(2)]/100.0	1250.0	D3, D39, D7, D75
(8)	FISIM of the central bank using market interest rates	(1)×[(2)–(2)]/100.0	0.0	P1, P2
	Changes in financial assets (currency and deposits)			
(9)	Commercial banks	(6)	3500.0	F2
	Changes in liabilities (currency and deposits)			
(10)	Central bank	(6)	3500.0	F2

to be the interbank interest rate. The actual interest rate paid by the central bank to commercial banks (7.0 per cent) is higher than the market interest rate, which is the interbank interest rate (4.5 per cent). Table 3.36 also shows the FISIM output which is calculated using the actual interest rate payable by the central bank on the deposits of the commercial banks and the interbank interest rate as the reference rate. The use of the above market interest rate causes the output of FISIM of the central bank to be negative. Thus, FISIM should be calculated using market interest rates, while the difference in flows calculated using the reference rate and the interest rate set by the central bank should be recorded as other subsidies on production.

3.119. Table 3.37 shows how to calculate the various types of interest income payable by the central bank to commercial banks, the output of FISIM of the central bank and other subsidies on production. The method to calculate the SNA interest and actual interest payable by the central bank and the output of FISIM of the central bank is the same as the corresponding method in worked example 3.1, except that, in this worked example, loans are not taken into account. FISIM is calculated using market interest rates and is zero. The other subsidies on production payable to commercial banks are calculated as follows:

- Find the difference between the actual interest rate and the interbank interest rate on deposits.
- Multiply this difference by the average stock of deposits to obtain other subsidies on production.

Table 3.37 also shows the changes in financial assets and liabilities arising from the transactions between the central bank and commercial banks. The central bank has an increase in liabilities of currency and deposits due to the interest payable to commercial banks on their deposits (3500.0 units). The converse applies to commercial banks for changes in their assets of currency and deposits.

3.120. Table 3.38 shows how to record the various transactions in the SNA. To ensure clarity, the transactions of the central bank and commercial banks are recorded separately rather than combined under the financial corporations sector. The transactions of commercial banks are recorded under the other financial corporations sector. To simplify the presentation and analysis, other transactions, such as wages and salaries, are ignored. The transactions are described as follows:

(a) The output of FISIM produced by the central bank is zero and it is recorded in the production account. This output is also recorded as the intermediate consumption of the commercial banks;

(b) Commercial banks actually receive 3500.0 units (i.e. 7.0 per cent times 50000.0 units) as "interest" on their deposits. This amount is recorded in

Table 3.38

Recording transactions for which the central bank pays above market rates in a situation in which the external value of the currency is under pressure

Uses													Resources
Total	**Goods and services**	**Total economy**	**General government**	**Central bank**	**Other financial corporations**	**2008 SNA code**	**Transactions and balancing items**	**Other financial corporations**	**Central bank**	**General government**	**Total economy**	**Goods and services**	**Total**
Production account													
0.0	0.0					P1	Output		0.0		0.0		0.0
0.0		0.0			0.0	P2	Intermediate consumption					0.0	0.0
0.0		0.0		0.0	0.0	B1g	Value added, gross/ Gross domestic product						
Generation of income account													
-1250.0		-1250.0			-1250.0	D3	Subsidies (-)						
-1250.0		-1250.0			-1250.0	D39	Other subsidies on production (-)						
1250.0		1250.0			1250.0	B2g	Operating surplus, gross						
Allocation of primary income account													
						D3	Subsidies (-)			-1250.0	-1250.0		-1250.0
						D39	Other subsidies on production (-)			-1250.0	-1250.0		-1250.0
2250.0		2250.0		2250.0		D4	Property income	2250.0			2250.0		2250.0
2250.0		2250.0		2250.0		D41	Interest	2250.0			2250.0		2250.0
0.0		0.0	-1250.0	-2250.0	3500.0	B5g	Balance of primary income, gross/National income, gross						
Secondary distribution of income account													
1250.0		1250.0		1250.0		D7	Other current transfers			1250.0	1250.0		1250.0
1250.0		1250.0		1250.0		D75	Miscellaneous current transfers			1250.0	1250.0		1250.0
0.0		0.0	0.0	-3500.0	3500.0	B6g	Disposable income, gross						
Use of disposable income account													
0.0		0.0	0.0	-3500.0	3500.0	B8g	Saving, gross						
Changes in assets													**Changes in liabilities and net worth**
Capital account													
0.0		0.0	0.0	-3500.0	3500.0	B9	Net lending (+)/ net borrowing (-)						
Financial account													
						B9	Net lending (+)/ net borrowing (-)	3500.0	-3500.0	0.0	0.0		0.0
3500.0		3500.0			3500.0	F2	Currency and deposits		3500.0		3500.0		3500.0

the financial account. However, they are recorded as receiving 2250.0 units (i.e. 4.5 per cent times 50000.0 units) as SNA interest, which are recorded in the allocation of primary income account, and receiving another 1250.0 units (i.e. 2.5 per cent times 50000.0 units) from the general government as other subsidies on production, which are recorded in the generation of income account;

(c) The general government is recorded as paying 1250.0 units to commercial banks as other subsidies on production, which are recorded in the allocation of primary income account, and as receiving a miscellaneous current transfer of 1250.0 units from the central bank, which is recorded in the secondary distribution of income account. Both these flows are notional;

(d) The central bank actually pays 3500.0 units in interest on the deposits maintained by commercial banks with it. This amount is recorded in the financial account. However, it is recorded as paying 2250.0 units to the commercial banks, which are recorded in the allocation of primary income account, and providing a miscellaneous current transfer of 1250.0 units to the general government, which is recorded in the secondary distribution of income account;

(e) Gross saving in the use of disposable income account is the same as net lending/net borrowing in the financial account, as there are no transactions in the capital account. The equality between net lending/net borrowing in the capital account and financial account has been maintained due to the inclusion of a compensating current transfer from the central bank to the general government, although, in practice, differences in data sources and the timing of the recording of transactions may result in a discrepancy between the estimates of net lending/net borrowing in these two accounts.

Worked example 3.8. Recording transactions for which the central bank acts as a development bank by offering loans at below market rates to priority industries[35]

3.121. This worked example shows how to record the transactions in the SNA in the case of the central bank acting as a development bank and offering loans at below market interest rates to priority industries. The changes in financial assets and liabilities due to these transactions are also recorded.

Table 3.39
Data on the average stock of loans, the interbank interest rate and the actual interest rate

Line number	Item	Description	Value
(1)	Average stock of loans to priority industries (non-financial corporations)		100000.0
(2)	Interbank interest rate (reference rate) (per cent)		4.5
(3)	Actual interest rate (receivable on loans by the central bank to priority industries) (per cent)		3.0
(4)	Market interest rate for loans (per cent)		5.0
(5)	FISIM using the actual interest rate and the interbank interest rate	(1)×[(3)–(2)]/100.0	-1500.0

Table 3.40
Calculation of interest income, other subsidies on production, financial intermediation services indirectly measured and changes in financial assets and liabilities

Line number	Item	Description	Value	2008 SNA code
(6)	SNA interest receivable by the central bank from priority industries	(1)×(2)/100.0	4500.0	D4, D41
(7)	Actual interest receivable by the central bank from priority industries	(1)×(3)/100.0	3000.0	
(8)	Other subsidies on production receivable by priority industries	(1)×[(4)–(3)]/100.0	2000.0	D3, D39, D7, D75
(9)	FISIM of the central bank	(1)×[(4)–(2)]/100.0	500.0	P1, P2
	Changes in financial assets (loans)			
(10)	Central bank	(7)	3000.0	F4
	Changes in liabilities (loans)			
(11)	Priority industries	(7)	3000.0	F4

[35] The worked example is adapted from Bloem, Gorter and Rivas (2006).

3.122. Table 3.39 shows the average stock of loans granted by the central bank to priority industries, the interbank interest rate, the actual interest rate payable by the priority industries on the loans granted by the central bank and market interest rates for such loans during an accounting period. These data should be available with the central bank. The reference rate is taken to be the interbank interest rate. The actual interest rate payable by priority industries on loans granted by the central bank is 3.0 per cent, while the actual market interest rate for such loans is 5.0 per cent. For simplicity, priority industries are assumed to be from the non-financial corporations sector. Table 3.39 also shows the output of FISIM of the central bank which is calculated using the reference rate and the interest rate set by the central bank on loans granted to priority industries. The use of an interest rate below the reference rate causes the output of FISIM of the central bank to be negative. Thus, FISIM should be calculated using market interest rates, while the difference in flows calculated using the market interest rate for loans and the interest rate set by the central bank on such loans should be recorded as other subsidies on production.

3.123. Table 3.40 shows how to calculate the various types of interest income receivable by the central bank on its loans to priority industries, the output of FISIM of the central bank and other subsidies on production. The method to calculate the SNA interest and actual interest payable by the central bank and the output of FISIM of the central bank is the same as the corresponding method in worked example 3.1, except that, in this worked example, deposits are not taken into account. FISIM is calculated using market interest rates and is 500.0 units. The other subsidies on production receivable by priority industries are calculated as follows:

- Find the difference between the market interest rate for loans and the actual interest rate set by the central bank on such loans to priority industries.
- Multiply this difference by the average stock of loans to obtain other subsidies on production.

Table 3.40 also shows the changes in financial assets and liabilities arising from the transactions between the central bank and priority industries. The central bank has an increase in assets of loans due to the interest receivable on the loans granted to priority industries (3000.0 units). This amount also represents the increase in liabilities of loans of the priority industries.

3.124. Table 3.41 shows how to record the various transactions. The transactions of priority industries are recorded under the non-financial corporations sector, since it is assumed that all these industries belong to this sector. To simplify the presentation and analysis, other transactions, such as wages and salaries, are ignored. The transactions are described as follows:

(a) The output of FISIM produced by the central bank is 500.0 units and is recorded in the production account. This output is also recorded as the intermediate consumption of the priority industries under the non-financial corporations sector in the production account;

(b) Non-financial corporations actually pay 3000.0 units (i.e. 3.0 per cent of 100000.0 units) as "interest" on the loans from the central bank. This amount is recorded in the financial account. However, they are recorded as paying 5000.0 units (i.e. 5.0 per cent of 100000.0 units) as interest which is split into SNA interest in the allocation of primary income account (4500.0 units) and FISIM (500.0 units), and as receiving 2000.0 units (i.e. 2.0 per cent of 100000.0 units) from the general government as other subsidies on production, which are recorded in the generation of income account;

Table 3.41

Recording transactions for which the central bank acts as a development bank by offering loans at below market rates to priority industries

Uses													Resources
Total	**Goods and services**	**Total economy**	**General government**	**Central bank**	**Non-financial corporations**	**2008 SNA code**	**Transactions and balancing items**	**Non-financial corporations**	**Central bank**	**General government**	**Total economy**	**Goods and services**	**Total**
Production account													
500.0	500.0					P1	Output		500.0		500.0		500.0
500.0		500.0			500.0	P2	Intermediate consumption					500.0	500.0
0.0		0.0		500.0	-500.0	B1g	Value added, gross/ Gross domestic product						
Generation of income account													
-2000.0		-2000.0			-2000.0	D3	Subsidies (-)						
-2000.0		-2000.0			-2000.0	D39	Other subsidies on production (-)						
2000.0		2000.0		500.0	1500.0	B2g	Operating surplus, gross						
Allocation of primary income account													
						D3	Subsidies on production and import (-)			-2000.0	-2000.0		-2000.0
						D39	Other subsidies on production (-)			-2000.0	-2000.0		-2000.0
4500.0		4500.0			4500.0	D4	Property income		4500.0		4500.0		4500.0
4500.0		4500.0			4500.0	D41	Interest		4500.0		4500.0		4500.0
0.0		0.0	-2000.0	5000.0	-3000.0	B5g	Balance of primary income, gross/National income, gross						
Secondary distribution of income account													
2000.0		2000.0		2000.0		D7	Other current transfers			2000.0	2000.0		2000.0
2000.0		2000.0		2000.0		D75	Miscellaneous current transfers			2000.0	2000.0		2000.0
0.0		0.0	0.0	3000.0	-3000.0	B6g	Disposable income, gross						
Use of disposable income account													
0.0		0.0	0.0	3000.0	-3000.0	B8g	Saving, gross						
Changes in assets													**Changes in liabilities and net worth**
Capital account													
0.0		0.0	0.0	3000.0	-3000.0	B9	Net lending (+)/ net borrowing (-)						
Financial account													
						B9	Net lending (+)/ net borrowing (-)	-3000.0	3000.0	0.0	0.0		0.0
3000.0		3000.0		3000.0		F4	Loans	3000.0			3000.0		3000.0

(c) The general government is recorded as paying 2000.0 units to non-financial corporations as other subsidies on production, which are recorded in the allocation of income account, and as receiving a miscellaneous current transfer of 2000.0 units from the central bank, which is recorded in the secondary distribution of income account. Both these flows are notional;

(d) The central bank actually receives 3000.0 units from the non-financial corporations as "interest" on the loans it provides to them. This amount is recorded in the financial account. However, it is recorded as receiving 5000.0 units from the non-financial corporations as interest which is split into SNA interest in the allocation of primary account (4500.0 units) and FISIM (500.0 units), and as paying a miscellaneous current transfer of 2000.0 units to the general government, which is recorded in the secondary distribution of income account;

(e) Gross saving in the use of disposable income account is the same as net lending/net borrowing in the financial account, as there are no transactions in the capital account. The equality between net lending/net borrowing in the capital and financial accounts has been maintained owing to the inclusion of a compensating current transfer from the central bank to the general government, although, in practice, differences in data sources and the timing of the recording of transactions may result in a discrepancy between the estimates of net lending/net borrowing in these two accounts.

3. Financial services associated with the acquisition and disposal of financial assets and liabilities

References:
2008 SNA, Chapter 6, The production account
2008 SNA, Chapter 17, Cross-cutting and other special issues, Part 4, The recording of flows associated with financial assets and liabilities
BPM6, Chapter 10, Goods and services account
BPM6, Chapter 11, Primary income account
BPM6 Compilation Guide, Chapter 12, Services

3.125. Many financial corporations may charge in full or in part for their services provided for the acquisition and disposal of financial assets by having a spread between the buying and selling price. This spread is known as the buy-sell spread. The current-price output or margin arising from the financial service provided to the buyer is calculated as the difference between the selling (ask or offer) price and mid-price at the time of purchase of the financial asset. The purchase price thus represents the market value of the financial asset plus the margin. The current-price output or margin arising from the financial service provided to the seller is the difference between the mid-price and buying (bid) price at the time of sale of the financial asset. The selling price, thus, represents the market value of the financial asset less the margin. The bid and offer prices should be those applicable to the individual buyer and seller, since these may vary according to the quantity being transacted or other factors. The mid-price of the financial asset is the average at a given point in time between the bid and ask prices. By using the mid-price at the time of purchase or sale, any holding gains or losses on the financial asset are excluded from the financial service provided. To ignore the margins would understate the value of output of financial services arising from these transactions.

3.126. As indicated in table 3.1, financial corporations whose output is calculated this way include security and derivative dealers, foreign exchange bureaux and deposit-taking corporations. The existence of a buy-sell spread shows that these financial corporations serve the market in a somewhat similar way to a wholesaler by providing liquidity and inventory. Financial assets which are bought and sold this way by these financial corporations include foreign exchange, shares, debt securities – such as bills and bonds – financial derivatives and investment fund shares.

3.127. Given that the bid and offer prices to be used to compute the margins should be those applicable to the individual buyer and seller, the compiling agency will need to develop a securities database capturing each transaction in the financial asset together with the bid and offer prices so that it can calculate the margin for each transaction. However, in many countries, such a database may not be readily available or may be too costly to develop and maintain. Thus, as a proxy, the compiling agency can collect data on the value of transactions in the financial assets which are traded using buy-sell spreads and then apply the average margin as a percentage to the value of these transactions. The average margin can be determined by consulting those financial corporations which earn service charges through buy-sell spreads.

3.128. The margins should be recorded as the intermediate consumption of corporations, general government or NPISHs if the financial services are provided to these sectors. If they are provided to households, these should be recorded as their final consumption expenditure unless the financial service is provided to an unincorporated enterprise. The margins which are recorded as the intermediate consumption of general government and NPISHs are also recorded in their output and final consumption expenditure, since the institutional units in these two sectors are non-market producers whose output is calculated as the sum of costs. On the other hand, the margins should be recorded in exports of goods and services if the financial services are provided to the rest of the world. Where possible, the compiling agency should try to use a "bottom-up" approach to compute the economy-wide value of the margins. This can be done by computing the value of the margins consumed by each sector by applying an average sectoral margin as a percentage of the sectoral value of transactions in the financial assets which are traded using buy-sell spreads. After that, the value of the sectoral margins can be summed up to obtain the economy-wide value. In many instances, it may not be possible for the compiling agency to directly calculate the value of the margins consumed by each sector from the input data. Thus, the compiling agency can consider using a "top-down" approach. This is done by first applying an economy-wide average margin as a percentage of the total value of transactions in the financial assets which are traded using buy-sell spreads. The economy-wide value of the margin can then be allocated to the user sectors using various indicators, such as the sectoral value of the transactions.

3.129. Resident institutional units may also incur these margins when they buy and sell foreign exchange, debt securities, shares, financial derivatives and investment fund shares through non-resident financial institutions. Estimates of the imports of these margins can be obtained directly from balance of payments statistics. However, if the balance of payments statistics do not report estimates of these margins, the compiling agency may need to estimate them. One way is to estimate the share of the country concerned in partner country data on exports of these implicit service charges. Another way is to estimate the share of the country concerned in the world turnover data for cross-border transactions in financial instruments such as foreign exchange and financial derivatives, and then apply an average margin to the share. The average margin can be determined in consultation with industry experts. The compiling agency should estimate the average margin in consultation with the compilers of the balance of payments to ensure that there is consistency in the recording of these transactions in the national accounts and balance of payments statistics. After obtaining the required data either directly from the balance of payments statistics or through estimation techniques, the compiling agency will still need to allocate the data on the imports of these margins to the resident institutional sectors. This can be done directly if the compiling agency is able to obtain the input data for each institutional sector. If not, the compiling agency will need to consider the use of various techniques to allocate the total value of the imported margins. For example, the compiling agency can consider allocating the imported margins in proportion to the consumption of domestically produced margins by the resident user sectors.

3.130. Debt securities, such as bills and bonds, give rise to interest payments, interest being payable to the owner of the securities by the issuer. Some of these interest charges may themselves be imputed from changes in the value of securities as they approach maturity. Interest on debt securities arises when they are issued at a discount to their face value. Interest is equal to the amount the issuers of the securities will have to pay to their holders over and above the repayment of the amount advanced by the initial holders. Interest accrual on a debt instrument is determined for the entire life by the conditions set at the inception of the instrument. Interest accrued is determined using the original yield-to-maturity. A single effective yield, established at the time of security issuance, is used to calculate the amount of accrued interest in each period to maturity. This approach is also known as the debtor approach. In addition, interest is recorded as accruing continuously to the holders in the allocation of primary income account. The interest accruing is then "reinvested" in the debt security by the holders, and this is recorded in the financial account as the acquisition of more debt securities by the holders and a further issue of more debt securities by the issuers.

3.131. In addition, besides being issued at a discount to face value, long-term debt securities, such as bonds and debentures, may be issued at a price which is equal or at a premium to the face value. In all of these instances, they may also pay a fixed or contractually determined variable money income in the form of coupon payments periodically throughout the life of the debt security. Thus, the interest receivable by the holders of these securities includes the interest accruing that is due to the difference between the redemption price and issue price and the coupon payments. Both the interest accruing and coupon payments should be recorded in the allocation of primary income account.

3.132. It is important when measuring interest as the increase in value of a debt security between the date it is purchased and the date it matures (or is subsequently sold) to measure from one midpoint value to another and to treat the differences between midpoint price and bid or ask price at the time of purchase, sale or redemption as a service margin. Ignoring the margins understates the value of output of financial institutions and may understate interest payments also.

3.133. Equities and investment fund shares or units also give rise to property income other than interest. In the case of equities, the property income is known as dividends and is recorded in the allocation of primary income account. In the case of investment fund shares, the property income comprises two items. The first item is dividends distributed to investment fund shareholders. The second item is retained earnings attributed to investment fund shareholders. Dividends are recorded in the allocation of primary income account. Retained earnings are recorded in the allocation of primary income account and are then "reinvested" by the holders of the investment fund shares. The reinvestment is recorded in the financial account together with the associated financial instrument.

3.134. Data on the interest accruing for debt securities can be obtained by the compiling agency from a securities database if one is available. If such a database is not available, the compiling agency will need to conduct a survey to collect the information required. Likewise, the compiling agency can conduct surveys to collect the data on the property income associated with equities and investment fund shares.

3.135. There is no property income associated with foreign exchange and financial derivatives.

Worked example 3.9. Recording transactions in financial services associated with the acquisition and disposal of financial assets and liabilities

3.136. This worked example shows how to calculate and record the current-price output of financial services associated with the purchase and sale of debt securities and other related transactions. In addition, transactions between two institutional units are recorded in the SNA using the quadruple principle of recording. For many of these transactions, the counterpart entries are recorded in the financial account to show the means of payment to settle these transactions. The worked example also shows how to record the counterpart entries for these transactions in the financial account. For simplicity, it is assumed that these transactions are settled in currency or transferable deposits, which are part of "currency and deposits" in the financial account.

3.137. Table 3.42 presents the information on the transactions in a treasury bill. Assume that the compiling agency is able to collect the information from a database capturing individual transactions in financial assets. Assume that household I is holding an existing treasury bill issued by the general government and that the market interest rate on the treasury bill is unchanged during the accounting period, so there is no change in its value due to holding gains/losses. The treasury bill does not pay a coupon payment. Household I decides to sell the treasury bill to household II through a dealer. For simplicity, assume that household II then decides to sell the same security to household III through the same dealer. Assume that the three households do not acquire or dispose of the treasury bill as owners of unincorporated enterprises. The mid-price of the transaction between the first two households is 100.0 units, while the midpoint of the transaction between the second and third households is 120.0 units.

3.138. Table 3.43 shows how to use the information in table 3.42 to calculate the output of the dealer from transactions to acquire and dispose of the treasury bill, as well as the accrued interest on the bill which is payable by the securities issuer to the holder of the bill. The output represents the margin earned by the dealer from the acquisitions and disposals of the security. From the viewpoint of the dealer, its output is calculated as follows:

Table 3.42
Data on transactions in the treasury bill

Line number	Item	Value
	Prices for the sale of the treasury bill from household I to household II through a dealer	
(1)	Ask price	102.0
(2)	Bid price	98.0
(3)	Mid-price	100.0
	Prices for the sale of the treasury bill from household II to household III through the same dealer	
(4)	Ask price	122.0
(5)	Bid price	118.0
(6)	Mid-price	120.0

Table 3.43
Calculation of the output of the dealer and the accrued interest receivable by households on the treasury bill

Line number	Item	Description	Value	2008 SNA code
(7)	Output of the dealer	(7a)+(7b)+(7c)	8.0	P1
(7a)	Household I – Sale of the treasury bill to household II	(3)–(2)	2.0	P3
(7b)	Household II	(7b.i)+(7b.ii)	4.0	P3
(7b.i)	Purchase of the treasury bill from household I	(1)–(3)	2.0	
(7b.ii)	Sale of the treasury bill to household III	(6)–(5)	2.0	
(7c)	Household III – purchase of the treasury bill from household II	(4)–(6)	2.0	P3
	Accrued interest receivable by households			
(8)	Household II	(6)–(3)	20.0	D4, D41

- For a disposal, compute output as the difference between the mid-price and the bid price.
- For an acquisition, compute output as the difference between the ask price and the mid-price.

As can be seen, there are four transactions involving the acquisitions and disposals of the security, and this results in the dealer producing an output of 8.0 units for the service it provides.

The accrued interest (20.0 units) is receivable by household II, since this value accrued during the period it held the treasury bill before selling it to household III. The accrued interest is computed as the difference between the mid-prices of the two transactions.

3.139. Table 3.44 shows how to calculate the changes in financial assets and liabilities arising from the transactions between the dealer and the other institutional units, as well as the means of payment for these transactions. In general, the changes in financial assets and liabilities are computed using the following principles: the changes in currency and deposits of the dealer and households are the result of payments for the purchases and sales of the treasury bill. These changes are obtained using the bid and ask prices. For the dealer and households, a disposal represents an increase in its assets of currency and deposits, while an acquisition represents a decrease in its assets of currency and deposits. For example, consider the case of the dealer. It has an increase in its assets of currency and deposits of eight units during the accounting period. This is the result of the following:

- An increase in assets of currency and deposits arising from disposals of the treasury bill (102.0+122.0=224.0 units).
- A decrease in assets of currency and deposits arising from acquisitions of the treasury bill (98.0+118.0= 216.0 units).

The changes in assets of debt securities of households are the result of the acquisitions and disposals of the treasury bill by households, as well as the reinvestment of the accrued interest payable on the security. For example, consider the case of household III. It has an increase in assets of debt securities of 120.0 units. This is the result of the following:

- The acquisition of the treasury bill for 122.0 units.
- The removal of the margin of 2.0 units, since financial transitions should be valued excluding the service charges payable for their acquisitions and disposals.

Table 3.44
Calculation of changes in financial assets and liabilities related to acquisitions and disposals of the treasury bill

Line number	Item	Description	Value	2008 SNA code
	Changes in financial assets (currency and deposits)			
(9)	Dealer	[(1)–(2)]+[(4)–(5)]	8.0	F2
(10)	Household I	(2)	98.0	F2
(11)	Household II	(5)–(1)	16.0	F2
(12)	Household III	–(4)	-122.0	F2
	Changes in financial assets (debt securities)			
(13)	Household I	(2)–(7a)	-100.0	F3
(14)	Household II	[(1)–(7b.i)]+[(–5)–(7b.ii)]+(8)	0.0	F3
(15)	Household III	(4)–(7c)	120.0	F3
	Changes in liabilities (debt securities)			
(16)	Securities issuer	(8)	20.0	F3

Table 3.45
Recording transactions in the treasury bill

Uses																	Resources
Total	Goods and services	Total economy	Household III	Household II	Household I	General government	Financial corporations	2008 SNA code	Transactions and balancing items	Financial corporations	General government	Household I	Household II	Household III	Total economy	Goods and services	Total
Production account																	
8.0	8.0							P1	Output	8.0					8.0		8.0
8.0		8.0					8.0	B1g	Value added, gross/ Gross domestic product								
Allocation of primary income account																	
20.0		20.0				20.0		D4	Property income				20.0		20.0		20.0
20.0		20.0				20.0		D41	Interest				20.0		20.0		20.0
8.0		8.0		20.0		-20.0	8.0	B5g	Balance of primary income, gross/National income, gross								
Use of disposable income account																	
8.0		8.0	2.0	4.0	2.0			P3	Final consumption expenditure							8.0	8.0
0.0		0.0	-2.0	16.0	-2.0	-20.0	8.0	B8g	Saving, gross								
Changes in assets										**Changes in liabilities and net worth**							
Capital account																	
0.0		0.0	-2.0	16.0	-2.0	-20.0	8.0	B9	Net lending (+)/ net borrowing (-)								
Financial account																	
								B9	Net lending (+)/ net borrowing (-)	8.0	-20.0	-2.0	16.0	-2.0	0.0		0.0
0.0		0.0	-122.0	16.0	98.0		8.0	F2	Currency and deposits								
20.0		20.0	120.0	0.0	-100.0			F3	Debt securities		20.0				20.0		20.0

In the case of the securities issuer, it has an increase in its liabilities of debt securities of 20.0 units. This is due to the reinvestment of the accrued interest payable to household II.

3.140. Table 3.45 shows how to record the various transactions. The transactions of the dealer are recorded under the financial corporations sector, while the transactions of the securities issuer are recorded under the general government sector. To ensure clarity, the transactions of the three households are recorded separately rather than combined under the households sector. The transactions are described as follows:

(a) The output of the dealer (8.0 units) is recorded in the production account for the financial corporations sector;

(b) The accrued interest payable (20.0 units) by the securities issuer on the treasury bill is recorded as a use of general government in the allocation of primary income account. It is also recorded as a resource of household II in the same account;

(c) The output of the dealer is consumed by the three households and is recorded as their final consumption expenditure in the use of disposable income account, since it is assumed that they do not buy or sell the security as owners of unincorporated enterprises;

(d) Since there are no capital account transactions, net lending/net borrowing in the capital account is the same as gross saving in the use of disposable income account;

(e) In the financial account, the financial corporations sector has a net increase of 8.0 units in currency and deposits on account of the dealer's role in the acquisitions and disposals of the treasury bill. The general government sector has an increase in its liabilities of debt securities due to the reinvestment of the accrued interest payable on the treasury bill. Household I has an increase in its assets of currency and deposits (98.0 units) arising from its disposal of the treasury bill. This is offset by a decrease in its assets of debt securities (100.0 units) due to the disposal. Household II has an increase in its assets of currency and deposits (16.0 units) due to its acquisition (102.0 units) and disposal (118.0 units) of the treasury bill. It does not have any change in its assets of debt securities because its acquisition (100.0 units) less disposal (120.0 units) of the security is completely offset by the reinvestment of the accrued interest receivable on the security (20.0 units). Household III has a decrease in its assets of currency and deposits (122.0 units) due to its acquisition of the treasury bill. It also has an increase in assets of debt securities (120.0 units) due to the acquisition of the security.[36] Since these entries are the counterparts to entries in the other accounts or only reflect the exchange in financial assets and liabilities, net lending/net borrowing is identical to net lending/net borrowing in the capital account, although, in practice, differences in data sources and the timing of the recording of transactions may result in a discrepancy between the estimates of net lending/net borrowing in these two accounts.

3.141. The method explained in the worked example above is also applicable to situations in which financial corporations charge for the services they provide in acquiring and disposing of other financial assets, such as bonds, financial derivatives, equities and investment funds and foreign currencies through a buy-sell spread, except that, in the case of financial derivatives and foreign currencies, there is no property income associated with these financial instruments.

Volume measures of the output of financial services associated with transactions in financial assets and liabilities

References:
2008 SNA, Chapter 15, Price and volume measures
Handbook on Price and Volume Measures in National Accounts, Chapter 4, A/B/C methods for output by product

3.142. The previous section explains the calculation of the output (margins) arising from financial services associated with transactions in financial assets and liabilities at current prices. In order to derive the volume measure of this output, the time series data on the margins will need to be adjusted to remove the effects of price changes. In principle, volume measures of the output can be obtained by deflating the current price output by an appropriate sub-index of the PPI adjusted for quality changes. Thus, to obtain the volume measures of the output of financial services provided by dealers for transactions in debt securities, a PPI for transactions in such securities made by dealers should be used as the deflator. In instances in which such a price index is not available, the compiling agency can consider using alternative price indices, such as a PPI with a broader coverage, say, for financial services. However, if the compiling agency is unable to find a suitable price index for deflation, it can consider using appropriate volume indicators to construct volume measures of the margins. For example, volume measures of the margins arising

[36] In all the transactions involving the acquisitions and disposals of the treasury bill by the households, the changes in the assets of currency and deposits are different from the corresponding changes in the assets of debt securities because service charges are excluded from the value of transactions in the latter.

from transactions in debt securities can be obtained by extrapolating base-period margins by the change in the number of units of debt securities which are traded.

3.143. To obtain volume measures of the imports of these margins, the compiling agency can consider deflating the current-price estimates by an appropriate sub-index of the import price index adjusted for quality changes. In instances in which such a price index is not available, the compiling agency can consider using alternative price indices, such as an import price index with a broader coverage, say, for financial services. If no suitable import price indices are available, the compiling agency can consider constructing a composite price index comprising appropriate price indices from partner countries which are adjusted for changes in exchange rates. Alternatively, the compiling agency can consider constructing a composite volume index comprising the volume measures of total exports or output of these margins from partner countries. The composite volume index can then be used to extrapolate base-period imports of the margins to obtain the corresponding volume measures. If data from partner countries are not available, the compiling agency may consider using the price indices which are used to deflate the domestically produced current-price margins.

4. Financial services associated with insurance and pension schemes

References:
2008 SNA, Chapter 6, The production account
2008 SNA, Chapter 17, Cross-cutting and other special issues, Part 1, The treatment of insurance
BPM6, Appendix 6c, Topical summary – Insurance, pension schemes, and standardized guarantees

3.144. Five types of activities are covered under insurance and pension schemes:

- Non-life insurance.
- Standardized guarantee schemes.
- Life insurance and annuities.
- Reinsurance.
- Social insurance schemes.

3.145. Insurance schemes cover non-life insurance, life insurance and annuities, and reinsurance. It provides individual institutional units exposed to certain risks with financial protection against the consequences of the occurrence of specified events. Financial protection is provided by insurance corporations in the form of an insurance policy. At its simplest, an insurance policy is an agreement between an insurance corporation and another institutional unit, called the policyholder. Under the agreement, the policyholder makes a payment (a premium) to the insurance corporation and, if or when a specified event occurs, the insurance corporation makes a payment (claim) to the policyholder. In this way, the policyholder protects itself against certain forms of risk; by pooling the risks, the insurance corporation aims to receive more from the receipt of premiums than it has to pay out as claims. In addition, insurers often act as financial intermediaries who invest funds collected from policyholders in financial or other assets to meet future claims.

3.146. The most common form of insurance is called direct insurance, whereby the policy is issued by an insurance corporation to another type of institutional unit other than an insurance corporation. There are two types of direct insurance: life and non-life insurance. Life insurance is an activity whereby a policyholder makes regular payments to an insurer in return for which the insurer guarantees to provide the policyholder (or, in some cases, another nominated person) with an agreed sum, or an annuity, at a given date or earlier if the policyholder dies beforehand. Non-life insurance is an activity similar to life insurance, except that it covers all other risks, accidents, sickness, fire, etc. Another form of insurance is provided by one insurance corporation to another. This sort of insurance is called reinsurance.

3.147. Standardized guarantee schemes cover the provisions for guarantees that are provided for certain standardized types of liabilities, such as export credit and student loans. They are issued in large numbers, usually for fairly small amounts, along identical lines. Guarantees of payments of principal and interest to holders of insured bonds, deposit insurance and insurance of pension benefits are also included here. Issuers of standardized guarantees include insurance corporations, government agencies and commercial banks. As will be described later in this chapter, the recording of the transactions of standardized guarantee schemes is similar to that for non-life insurance.

3.148. Social insurance schemes comprise both pension and social security schemes. Pension schemes are established for the purpose of providing benefits for retirement or for the invalidity of specific groups of employees. Pension schemes may be operated by a separately constituted fund or by a fund that is part of the employer or be unfunded. Pension funds are similar to insurance in that they act as intermediaries for investing the funds for their beneficiaries and redistribute some risks. Social security schemes cover the community as a whole or large sections of the community and are imposed and controlled by government units. The schemes cover a wide variety of programmes, providing benefits in cash or in kind for old age, invalidity or death, survivors, sickness and maternity, work injury, unemployment, family allowance, health care, etc. There is not necessarily a direct link between the amount of the contribution paid by an individual and the benefits he or she may receive.

3.149. Insurance and pension fund operations have common features but can be distinguished in that life insurance and pension funds include a large saving component, whereas the objective of non-life insurance is largely to pool risk.

3.150. All these schemes lead to redistribution of funds, which are recorded in either the secondary distribution of income account or the financial account. For non-life insurance and standardized guarantee schemes, most of the redistribution takes place between different units in the same period and is recorded in the secondary distribution of income account. Many clients pay relatively small policy premiums or fees and a small number of them receive relatively large claims or payments. For life insurance, annuities and pension schemes, the redistribution is primarily, though not entirely, between different periods for a single client and is recorded in the financial account. In fulfilling their responsibilities as managers of these funds, insurance corporations and pension funds are involved in risk management and liquidity transformation, the prime functions of financial corporations.

(a) Non-life insurance

References:
2008 SNA, Chapter 6, The production account
2008 SNA, Chapter 17, Cross-cutting and other special issues, Part 1, The treatment of insurance
BPM6, Chapter 5, Classification of financial assets and liabilities

3.151. Under a non-life insurance policy, the insurance company accepts a premium from a client and holds it until a claim is made or the period of the insurance expires. In the meantime, the insurance company invests the premium and the property income earned is an extra source of funds from which to meet any claim due. The property income represents income foregone by the policyholder and so is treated as an implicit supplement to the actual premium. The insurance company sets the level of the actual premiums to be such that the sum of the actual premiums plus the property income earned on them less the expected claim will leave a margin that the insurance company can retain; this margin represents the output of the insurance company. Within the SNA, the output of the insurance industry is determined in a manner intended to mimic the premium setting policies of the insurance corporations.

3.152. The basic method for measuring non-life insurance output is as follows:

Premiums earned[37]
plus adjusted premium supplements (3.5)
minus adjusted claims incurred.

The use of adjusted premium supplements and adjusted claims incurred in the calculation of non-life insurance output is due to the fact that, in cases of catastrophic losses, the output of the insurance activity estimated using the basic algorithm of the 1993 SNA, depending on the balance of premiums and claims (on an accrual basis), could be extremely volatile (even negative). The next section will provide more information on how to compute the adjusted claims incurred and when premium supplements should be adjusted in the calculation of non-life insurance output.

There are various types of non-life insurance. Examples include motor vehicle insurance, personal accident insurance, travel insurance, workmen's compensation insurance, home insurance, cargo insurance, health and medical care insurance, flood insurance, crop insurance and hurricane insurance. Non-life insurance output should be computed for each line of insurance, before they are summed up to obtain the economy-wide estimate.

3.153. The actual premium is the amount payable to the direct insurer to secure insurance cover for a specific event over a stated time period. Actual premiums are measured by the amounts payable after all allowances, discounts or bonuses are taken into account. Cover is frequently provided for one year at a time with the premium due to be paid at the outset, though cover may be provided for shorter (or longer) periods and the premium may be payable in instalments, for example monthly. Insurance corporations may purchase reinsurance to protect themselves against the risks of claims above certain thresholds. If a risk is reinsured, the insurance corporation will cede to a reinsurer a part of the premiums in proportion to the risk assumed. The other part is used by the insurance corporation to finance the risk that remains. On the other hand, insurance corporations may act as reinsurer and accept indirect business from another insurance corporation in the form of assumed premiums. Actual premiums receivable by the direct insurer should not be netted for any premiums ceded to reinsurers and should exclude premiums assumed from other insurance corporations. The rationale is that the direct insurance corporation is fully liable vis-à-vis the policyholder, regardless of whether or not part of the risks is reinsured.

3.154. The premium earned is the part of the actual premium that relates to cover provided in the accounting period. This item, rather than actual premiums, is one of the components used to calculate non-life insurance output, since it corresponds to the output associated with the cover provided in the accounting period. For example, if an annual policy with a premium of 120 units comes into force on 1 April and accounts are being prepared for a calendar year, the premium earned in the calendar year is 90. The unearned premium is the amount of the actual premium received that relates to the period past the accounting point. In the example just given, at the end of the accounting

[37] In the 2008 SNA, the term "actual premiums earned" is used in the formula to calculate non-life insurance output. The Handbook uses the term "premiums earned" so as to avoid confusion with the term "actual premiums". The terms "actual premiums" and "premiums earned" are defined in paragraphs 3.153 and 3.154, respectively.

period there will be an unearned premium of 30, intended to provide cover for the first three months of the next year. Thus, the sum of premiums earned and unearned premiums is the actual premiums.[38] Both items should not be netted for any premiums ceded to reinsurers and should exclude premiums assumed from other insurance corporations.

3.155. A claim (benefit) is the amount payable to the policyholder by the direct insurer or reinsurer in respect of an event covered by the policy occurring in the period for which the policy is valid. Claims become due when the event occurs, even if the payment is made sometime later. Claims that become due are described as claims incurred.[39] In some contested cases, the delay between the occurrence of the event giving rise to the claim and the settlement of the claim may be several years. Claims outstanding cover claims that have not been reported, have been reported but are not yet settled or have been both reported and settled but not yet paid. Paid claims occur when actual payments of cash have been made to claimants for insured events of the current or previous periods. Claims incurred are the sum of claims paid and the changes in claims outstanding during the accounting period. Claim-associated expenses are generally considered part of the claim cost for an insurance corporation.

3.156. The insurance corporation has at its disposal reserves consisting of unearned premiums, unexpired risks and claims outstanding to invest until claims are later reported and settled. These reserves are called technical reserves.[40] In the SNA, the income earned from the investment of the technical reserves, regardless of the source, is recorded as investment income attributable to the policyholders in the allocation of primary income account, since the technical reserves are a liability of the insurance corporation to the policyholders. However, this income remains with the insurance corporation and is, in effect, a hidden supplement to the apparent premium. This income is therefore recorded as a premium supplement payable by the policyholder to the insurance corporation in the secondary distribution of income account.

3.157. The data on total estimates of premiums earned, unearned premiums, claims paid, changes in outstanding claims, and investment income attributable to policyholders are typically available from the monetary authority or an agency which is responsible for supervising or regulating the insurance industry, such as an insurance regulatory commission.

3.158. On occasion, the levels of technical reserves and of equalization provisions (which give a guide to the funds insurance corporations set aside to meet unexpectedly large claims) may be altered in response to financial regulation and not because of changes in the expected patterns of premiums and claims. Such changes should be recorded in the other changes in the volume of assets account and excluded from the formula to determine output.

Measuring non-life insurance output

References:
2008 SNA, Chapter 6, The production account
2008 SNA, Chapter 17, Cross-cutting and other special issues, Part 1, The treatment of insurance
2008 SNA, Annex 3, Changes from the 1993 System of National Accounts

---

38 In the accounts of insurance corporations, actual premiums are also known as written premiums.

39 Claims incurred are also known as losses incurred in insurance accounting.

40 In addition, paragraph 5.64b of the BPM6 and paragraph 5.173 of the ESA 2010 state that other reserves, such as equalization reserves (which are provisions in the accounts of insurance corporations that give a guide to the funds the insurance corporations set aside to meet unexpectedly large claims), may be identified by insurers. However, these are recognized as liabilities and corresponding assets only when there is an event that gives rise to a liability. Otherwise, equalization reserves are internal accounting entries by the insurer that represent saving to cover irregularly occurring catastrophes, and thus do not represent any existing corresponding claims for policyholders.

3.159. The output of a non-life insurance corporation represents the service provided to policyholders. This output is based on the principle of adding premiums and premium supplements (which may need to be adjusted depending on the method used to compute the output) and deducting adjusted claims incurred. The input data to calculate the output of non-life insurance can be obtained from the returns of insurers to the government agency responsible for the insurance sector, for example, the insurance regulatory commission. If such information is not available, the compiling agency may need to conduct surveys to collect the information. Typically, the financial statements of insurers should contain the input data needed to calculate the output of non-life insurance.

3.160. The output of non-life insurance services should be distributed to users across the institutional sectors, including the rest of the world. The allocation to resident institutional sectors will allow the output consumed to be classified as intermediate or final consumption, while the allocation to the rest of the world is included in exports of services. The distinction between intermediate and final consumption will depend on which sector is consuming the service. Intermediate consumption is incurred by corporations, general government, households in their role as owners of dwellings and unincorporated enterprises, and NPISHs. The allocation of the service charge to intermediate consumption of institutional sectors will also need to be broken down into the respective industries so as to properly account for their value added. Final consumption expenditure is incurred by general government, households in their role as consumers and NPISHs. The output of non-life insurance is allocated to the intermediate and final consumption of general government and NPISHs because these sectors comprise non-market producers whose output is valued as the sum of costs. The output of non-life insurance which is allocated to the intermediate consumption of the institutional units in these two sectors increases the value of their output and also the value of their final consumption expenditure.

3.161. As described below, the 2008 SNA recommends three methods to measure the output of non-life insurance corporations.

Expectations approach

3.162. The first method is known as the expectations approach, which consists of replicating the ex ante model used by insurance corporations to set their premiums. In this approach, the formula to calculate the output takes the following form:

Premiums earned
plus expected premium supplements (3.6)
minus expected claims incurred.

3.163. As mentioned earlier, actual premiums earned should not be netted for any premiums ceded to reinsurers and should exclude premiums assumed from other insurance corporations.

3.164. In accepting risk and setting premiums, insurers consider both their expectation of loss (claims) and of income (premiums and premium supplements). The expected margin (premiums plus expected premium supplements minus expected claims) provides a measure of the non-life insurance service.

3.165. Two techniques can be considered to calculate expected claims and expected premium supplements. The first technique is known as the n-point moving average technique. This technique calculates the moving average of the n most recent observations to estimate the current value of the mean, and this mean is taken to be the forecast for the next period. The averaging technique is meant to smooth out the volatility in the original series. The choice for the n-point average is between a lagged moving average or a centred moving average.[41] Computationally, both procedures are simple to implement. However, there are some disadvantages with the n-point moving average technique. First, the choice of n largely depends on subjective judgement because the method is not based on any statistical modelling. Second, the forecasts generated from this technique will lag as the trend of the actual data increases or decreases. Third, the technique places equal weight on the n observations and ignores all the past observations which are not used in the computation. Finally, the centred moving average procedure does not replicate the theoretical notion of expectation, as it uses ex post data. Thus, the output of non-life insurance will have to be recalculated upon the availability of actual data.

3.166. The second technique is known as the geometrically weighted moving average technique. This technique can be viewed as estimating the value of α (a smoothing parameter between 0 and 1) that best fits the following regression model:

$$Z = w_1 Z_{t-1} + w_2 Z_{t-2} + \ldots + e_t \qquad (3.7)$$

where $w_i = \alpha(1-\alpha)^{i-1}$ for $i=1, \ldots,$ and e_1 is a white noise disturbance term.

This formula is identical to that derived from the adaptive expectations model developed by Cagan (1956). The geometrically weighted moving average technique is superior to the n-point moving average technique because it places relatively more weight on the most recent observations. In addition, the technique depends on a smoothing parameter that is estimated from the entire time series. For these reasons, it is preferred to the n-point moving average technique.

3.167. The geometrically weighted moving average technique is used by the United States Bureau of Economic Analysis (BEA) to calculate the output of non-life insurance.[42]

3.168. For each type of non-life insurance, a geometrically weighted moving average of past claims incurred ratios ($l_{t+1|t}$) is multiplied by the premiums earned (P_{t+1}) during the accounting period t+1 to obtain the expected claims incurred.[43] Mathematically, the expected claims incurred[44] in period t+1, can be written as $L_{t+1|t}$,

$$L_{t+1|t} = l_{t+1|t} \times P_{t+1} \qquad (3.8)$$

where

$l_{t+1|t}$ is the geometrically weighted expected claims incurred ratio in time period $t+1$, given the information available in time period t and

P_{t+1} is the premiums earned.

3.169. The term $l_{t+1|t}$ is computed as $l_{t+1|t} = E(l_{t+1} \mid l_t,\ l_{t-1}, \ldots)$, so the geometrically weighted moving average model takes the form:

$$\begin{aligned} E(l_{t+1} \mid l_t, l_{t-1}, \ldots) &= \alpha l_t + (1-\alpha) E(l_t \mid l_{t-1}, l_{t-2}, \ldots) = \alpha \sum_{i=0}^{\infty} (1-\alpha)^i l_{t-i} \\ &= \alpha l_t + \alpha(1-\alpha) l_{t-1} + \alpha(1-\alpha)^2 l_{t-2} + \ldots \end{aligned} \qquad (3.9)$$

where

l_t is the claims incurred ratio $(\frac{L_t}{P_t})$,

L_t is the actual claims incurred in period t and

P_t is the premiums earned.

The same interpretation applies to terms l_{t-1}, l_{t-2} and so on.

[41] For example, the Australian Bureau of Statistics calculates expected claims using a centred five-year moving average of claims incurred in the measurement of non-life insurance output. For more information, see Australian Bureau of Statistics (1999).

[42] Details of the technique used by the BEA are found in Moulton and Seskin (2003), Chen and Fixler (2003), and Seskin and Smith (2009).

[43] Smoothing using claims incurred to premiums earned ratios is preferable to direct smoothing using claims incurred data, as the former is better at handling inflation than the latter.

[44] The BEA describes these expected claims incurred as normal losses.

3.170. In the formula above, more weight is given to the most recent claims incurred ratios in the calculation of expected claims incurred on the basis that the most recent observations would be a better predictor of expected claims incurred. α is the smoothing constant in the interval (0,1) and needs to be estimated first. If a data series has at least 30 observations and is free of serial correlation,[45] α can be estimated fairly well using regression techniques. The estimated value of α is then used to calculate $l_{t+1|t}$ and $L_{t-1|t}$.

3.171. However, if the data series is not long enough or if it exhibits serial correlation, then setting α to a reasonable value produces more reliable results than relying on imprecise estimates. According to the statistical and engineering literature, the value of α is often chosen between 0.1 and 0.3. The chosen α is the one with the minimum root mean square prediction error (RMSPE).[46] Typically, it is sufficient to choose α to be 0.1, 0.2 or 0.3. Some studies point out that an estimated value of α greater than 0.3 may suggest serial correlation in the data series. In the case of the BEA, α is assigned a value of 0.3 based on evidence that it provides the best prediction of future values. This means that, for every deviation in the loss ratio from its previously expected value, the normal, or expected, value for the subsequent period is adjusted by 30 per cent.

3.172. Similarly, for each type of non-life insurance, a geometrically weighted moving average of past investment gain/loss ratios ($i_{t+1|t}$) is multiplied by the premiums earned (P_{t+1}) during the accounting period t+1 to obtain expected premium supplements. Mathematically, the expected premium supplement in period t+1, $I_{t+1|t}$, can be written as

$$I_{t+1|t} = i_{t+1|t} \times P_{t+1} \tag{3.10}$$

where

$i_{t+1|t}$ is the geometrically weighted expected investment gain/loss ratio in time period $t+1$, given the information available in time period t and

P_{t+1} is the premiums earned.

3.173. Again, the term $i_{t+1|t}$ is computed as $i_{t+1|t} = E(i_{t+1} \mid i_t, i_{t-1}, \ldots)$, so the geometrically weighted moving average model takes the form:

$$\begin{aligned} E(i_{t+1} \mid i_t, i_{t-1}, \ldots) &= \beta i_t + (1-\beta) E(i_t \mid i_{t-1}, i_{t-2}, \ldots) = \beta \sum_{i=0}^{\infty} (1-\beta)^i i_{t-i} \\ &= \beta i_t + \beta(1-\beta) i_{t-1} + \beta(1-\beta)^2 i_{t-2} + \ldots \end{aligned} \tag{3.11}$$

where

i_t is the net investment gain/loss ratio $(\frac{I_t}{P_t})$,

I_t is the net investment gain/loss in period t and

P_t is the premiums earned.

The same interpretation applies to terms i_{t-1}, i_{t-2} and so on.

3.174. The smoothing constant β has a similar interpretation as α. It is also chosen using the same method as α. Again, in the case of the BEA, it is assigned a value of 0.3 based on evidence that it provides the best prediction of future values.

3.175. As circumstances vary from country to country, the compiling agency may need to determine how frequently to estimate the smoothing constants (α and β). How-

[45] Serial correlation refers to the existence of a relationship between the error terms of time series data.

[46] The root mean square prediction error is the square root of the average of the squared differences between the actual values and the predicted values for the sample period. A value of zero means that the predicted values match the actual values with perfect accuracy.

ever, it may not be necessary for the compiling agency to estimate these parameters every year, as they tend to be relatively stable over the short term.

3.176. The expected claims incurred and expected premium supplements are then used with the actual premiums earned data to compute the output of insurance services provided by each type of non-life insurance.

3.177. However, any normal smoothing method will still encounter a significant increase in claims incurred when exceptional events such as catastrophic losses enter in the smoothing formula. To moderate the effect of catastrophic losses which will result in exceptionally large claims payable, the method is adjusted as follows.[47] First, the expected claims incurred ratios are computed and the data for the year with the catastrophe are treated as missing observations. Second, the catastrophic claim ratio is computed as the difference between the actual claims incurred ratio and the estimated claims incurred ratio. Third, the catastrophic claim ratio is spread forward equally for 20 years, starting from the year with the catastrophe.[48] The adjustment for the catastrophic claims ratio is then added back to the forecast of claims incurred ratios for the subsequent years.

3.178. The application of the weighted moving average method requires the availability of relatively long time series data on premiums earned, investment income attributable to policyholders and claims incurred so as to ensure that the weights in the geometrically weighted expected claims incurred ratio ($l_{t+1|t}$) and investment gain/loss ratio ($i_{t+1|t}$) sum up or are close to one. Typically, at least 30 observations are needed to ensure that the weights are sufficiently close to one. Such time series data may not be readily available in many countries. Thus, if the available time series data are too short, the compiling agency may need to modify the geometrically weighted ratios by standardizing the parameters to ensure that the weights sum up to one. For instance, if the compiling agency currently has only five years of data on premiums earned, investment income attributable to policyholders and claims incurred, it will need to modify the computation of the expected claims incurred ratio in year five by dividing each α-related term by the standardizing parameter $\alpha\sum_{i=0}^{3}(1-\alpha)^{i}$.

3.179. The expected claims incurred ratio will need to be modified to include more terms as more observations become available. A similar adjustment will also need to be made to the expected investment gain/loss ratio.

3.180. Besides requiring a number of intermediate steps to derive the output of non-life insurance, this method is also rather data-intensive. Thus, it may be more suitable for compiling agencies with technically competent staff who are able to obtain consistent and reliable time series input data to implement the approach.

Accounting approach

3.181. The second approach is known as the accounting approach, whereby output is calculated as:

Premiums earned
plus premium supplements (3.12)
minus adjusted claims incurred.

[47] The 2008 SNA recommends that claims arising from catastrophic losses should be classified as capital rather than current transfers. However, it does not specify a threshold for determining when a single event should be classified as a catastrophe. As described in Seskin and Smith (2009), in the United States national accounts, the threshold for determining whether any single event is treated as a catastrophe will be if either the associated property losses or the insurance payouts exceed 0.1 per cent of GDP.

[48] The rationale behind using 20 years to spread catastrophic claims forward in the expectations approach of calculating output may be related to the depreciation rate of the underlying assets, which is usually 5 per cent (meaning that the value of the assets is recovered after 20 years).

This approach differs from the expectations approach in the following ways. First, actual rather than expected premium supplements are used in the calculation of non-life insurance output. Second, adjusted claims incurred are determined ex post as the sum of actual claims incurred plus the changes in equalization provisions (i.e. additions to less withdrawals from equalization provisions) and, if necessary, changes to own funds (i.e. additions to less withdrawals from own funds). The item "changes in equalization provisions" is an entry in the accounts of insurance corporations that gives a guide to the funds the insurance corporations set aside to meet unexpectedly large claims. In circumstances where the equalization provisions are insufficient to bring adjusted claims back to a normal level, some contribution from own funds must be added also. Provided the required data are available, this method may be more suitable for compiling agencies that may not be in a position to implement the expectations method for various reasons, such as the lack of staff with the required skills and/or lack of consistent and reliable time series input data.

Sum of costs plus "normal profit" approach

3.182. The third method is the sum of costs plus "normal profit" approach. If the necessary accounting data are not available and the historical statistical data are not sufficient to allow reasonable average estimates of output to be made, the output of non-life insurance may be estimated as the sum of costs (including intermediate costs, labour and capital costs, and other taxes less other subsidies on production) plus an allowance for "normal profit". Capital costs are the sum of consumption of fixed capital and return to fixed capital. They represent the value of the flow of productive services that are provided by fixed assets in the production process. The consumption of fixed capital is the decline, during the course of the accounting period, in the current value of the stock of fixed assets owned and used by a producer as a result of physical deterioration, normal obsolescence or normal accidental damage. The return to fixed capital represents the income earned by the owners of fixed assets from the use of these assets in the production process. Like other institutional units which are involved in production, insurance corporations usually own the fixed assets they use in producing insurance services. Thus, the value of capital costs cannot be directly observed and will need to be imputed. To do so, the compiling agency will need to construct estimates of productive capital stock and user costs of capital services. The product of these two items will provide an estimate of capital costs. The productive capital stock measures the stock of fixed assets which is corrected for efficiency loss and retirement. The user costs of capital services are the price the owner-user of a fixed asset pays to himself for the service of using his own fixed assets. User costs of capital are derived from data on the rate of return to fixed capital, the depreciation rate and changes in asset prices.[49]

3.183. The allowance for normal profit can be obtained by smoothing past actual profits. The compiling agency will have to decide on the length of past profits to be used for smoothing. This will depend on the reliability and consistency of historical data on profits. The past profits for smoothing should be gross profits (i.e. profits before the deduction of any income taxes payable). However, since any reasonable estimate for "normal profit" is likely to involve expected claims, this option is hardly different from the expectations approach (see box 3.2).

---

[49] More information on how to compute capital costs can be obtained from OECD (2009).

Box 3.2
Relationship between the sum of costs plus the "normal profit" and expectations approaches[a]

The output of non-life insurance can be measured by $o = p + ie - ce$, where o is output, p is premiums earned, ie is expected premium supplements, and ce is expected claims. However, premiums can also be written as $p - ce + a + w - ie$, where o is split into the costs of handling the insurance service charge (a) and the profit margin (w). Output can then be obtained as $o = a - w$. Costs can be obtained easily, but this is not the case for the profit margin, which can be volatile. One way to moderate the volatility of the profit margin is to develop an estimate of "normal" profit, so we can rewrite the previous equation as $o = a + we$, where we is a measure of "normal" profit. "Normal" profit can be obtained by directly smoothing past profits. Rearranging the equations above, we have $we = p + ie - ce - a$, which shows the relationship between expected profit and expected claims and expected premium supplements. Thus, implicitly, the sum of costs plus "normal profit" approach is equivalent to the expectations approach.

[a] This box is based on Lequiller (2004).

Transactions other than output of non-life insurance corporations

3.184. This section describes the transactions other than output of non-life insurance corporations so that the full implications of a non-life insurance policy can be understood.

3.185. The premiums earned and the premium supplements are shown in the SNA divided between two types of transactions. The first is the value of the output of insurance, which, as mentioned before, is shown as either consumption or exports of insurance services. The second is net premiums earned by the insurance corporations. Net premiums are defined as actual premiums earned plus premium supplements less the insurance service charge payable by the policyholders. Because of the way in which the value of the service output is defined, net premiums for non-life insurance are equal in total to adjusted, and not actual, claims. Any variation between adjusted and actual claims represents a transfer between the policyholders and the insurance corporation. Over time, a transfer in one direction is offset by one in the other.

3.186. The time of recording claims incurred is generally in the period in which the event to which the claim relates took place. This principle is applied even when, in the case of disputed claims, the settlement may take place years after the event concerned. An exception is made in cases where the possibility of making a claim is recognized only long after the event has happened. For example, an important series of claims were recognized only when exposure to asbestos was established as a cause of serious illness and was judged to give rise to claims under an insurance policy valid at the time of the exposure. In such cases, the claim is recorded at the time that the insurance company accepts the liability. This may not be the same time as when the size of the claim is agreed on or when the claim is paid.

3.187. Because the formula for output uses adjusted claims and not actual claims, only when the actual claims happen to be the same value as expected claims will net premiums and claims be equal in a given period. They should, however, be approximately equal over a period of years excluding a year in which a disaster is recorded.

3.188. Claims incurred are normally recorded as current transfers payable by the insurance corporation to the policyholder. In some circumstances, an insurance corporation may set the level of premiums so low that they are not expected to cover costs and the predicted level of claims. This may happen when the surplus from one line of business, for example home insurance, is being used to cross-subsidize another line of business, for example, vehicle insurance.

3.189. There is one case where claims may be recorded as capital transfers rather than current transfers, and that is in the wake of a major catastrophe. The criteria for when the effects of a disaster should be treated like this must be determined according to national circumstances, but these may involve the number of policyholders affected and the amount of the damage done. The rationale for recording the claims as capital transfers in this case comes from the fact that many of the claims will relate to destruction or serious damage to assets such as dwellings, buildings and structures. Damage corresponding to a normal level of claims is covered by, for example, consumption of fixed capital or losses from inventories. These losses are thus captured as current expenditure elsewhere in the system. However, major losses in the wake of a disaster are recorded as the result of unforeseen events in the other changes in the volume of assets account and omitted from current expenditures. The recommendation is thus to record claims as current or capital transfers analogously.

3.190. It is recommended that, following a catastrophe, the total value of the claims in excess of the premiums should be recorded as a capital transfer from the insurance corporation to the policyholder. This implies that within the accounts of the insurance corporations, they are met not from insurance technical reserves but from own funds. Overall, however, the net worth of the insurance corporation is not affected by the alternative recording.

3.191. A consequence of recording such claims as capital transfers means that the disposable income of households and other policyholders does not increase counter-intuitively as would be the case if the claims were recorded as current transfers. The net worth of the policyholders will show the effects of both the destruction of assets (as an other volume change) and an increase (initially) in financial assets from the capital transfers. This recording is consistent with the recording of assistance by government or an NPISH to cover some or all of the costs of repairing or replacing the assets of those affected by the catastrophe who are not covered by an insurance policy.

Worked examples on recording transactions in non-life insurance

3.192. This section presents worked examples to calculate the current-price output of non-life insurance and other related transactions of a particular line of non-life insurance. The examples assume that the compiling agency is able to obtain the input data on earned premiums, unearned premiums, investment income attributable to policyholders, claims paid and changes in claims outstanding from insurance corporations. Earned and unearned premiums should not be netted for any premiums ceded to reinsurers and should exclude premiums assumed from other insurance corporations. Changes in claims outstanding are obtained as the difference between the level of claims outstanding between the start and end of the accounting period.

3.193. In worked example 3.10, the expectations approach used by the United States BEA is used to calculate output in the case of no large claims being incurred as a result of catastrophes. Expected claims incurred are different from actual claims incurred, and expected premium supplements differ from actual premium supplements. This means that net non-life insurance premiums will not be equal to non-life insurance claims in the secondary distribution of income account. This decoupling has the advantage of volatile claims and premium supplements being reflected in disposable income rather than output. In worked example 3.11, the expectations approach is repeated, but we assume that there are large claims incurred as a result of catastrophes. Hence, the approach is modified to exclude these large claims incurred in the calculation of output. In addition, some of the claims are recorded as capital transfers in the capital account in order not to unduly affect gross disposable income and gross saving. Worked example 3.12 is based on the accounting approach. In the example, claims incurred are not the result of catastrophes. For simplicity, these worked examples assume that the only policyholders are resident households in their capacity as final consumers.[50] In addition, the worked examples will show how to record in the financial account the counterpart entries to show the means of payment for some of the transactions between the institutional units. For simplicity, it is assumed that these transactions are settled in currency or transferable deposits, which are part of "currency and deposits" in the financial account. Worked example 3.13 assumes that insufficient data are available to allow reasonable estimates of output to be computed using the approaches above. Hence, output is computed using the sum of costs plus "normal profit" approach.

Worked example 3.10. Calculation of non-life insurance output using the expectations approach if there are no catastrophic claims

3.194. This worked example uses the expectations approach used by the United States BEA to calculate the output of non-life insurance.

3.195. Table 3.46 presents the relevant information for a particular line of non-life insurance which can be used to compute its output and other transactions for the years *t*–4 to *t*. Assume that the compiling agency is only able to collect the input data for these five years. Investment income refers to the property income receivable by insurance corporations from investing the technical reserves. For simplicity, it is assumed that this property income is payable by other resident sectors and that all the investment income attributable to policyholders comprises this property income.

Table 3.46
Data from insurance corporations on non-life insurance transactions

Line number	Item	*t*–4	*t*–3	*t*–2	*t*–1	*t*	2008 SNA code
(1)	Earned premiums (P_t)	510.0	564.0	624.0	693.0	750.0	
(2)	Unearned premiums	89.0	116.0	140.0	165.0	195.0	
(3)	Claims paid	137.0	148.0	167.0	176.0	195.0	
(4)	Changes in claims outstanding	131.0	139.0	156.0	161.0	166.0	
(5)	Investment income (I_t)	57.0	69.0	61.0	68.0	63.0	D4, D441

3.196. Since the data series is relatively short, it will not be possible to use regression techniques to estimate the values of α and β (the smoothing constants) for calculating the expected claims incurred and expected investment gains/losses ratios. Instead, α and β are first assigned the values of 0.1, 0.2 and 0.3. Next, the values of α and β with the minimum RMSPE are chosen to calculate the expected claims incurred and expected investment gain/loss ratios.

3.197. Table 3.47 shows how to derive the expected claims incurred ratios, investment gain/loss ratios, expected claims incurred and expected premium supplements using a value of 0.3 for α and β. The claims incurred ratios and expected claims incurred are obtained as follows:

[50] In practice, it is likely for non-life insurance output to be consumed by more than one resident institutional sector, as well as exported. A worked example on how to allocate the output of non-life insurance and other related transactions to institutional sectors and the rest of the world using data on actual premiums will be presented in a subsequent section.

Table 3.47
Deriving claims incurred ratios, investment gain/loss ratios, expected claims and expected premium supplements using α, β=0.3

Line number	Item	Description	t–4	t–3	t–2	t–1	t
(6)	α		...	0.300	0.300	0.300	0.300
(7)	$1-\alpha$	1–(6)	...	0.700	0.700	0.700	0.700
(8)	$\alpha(1-\alpha)$	(6)×(7)	...	...	0.210	0.210	0.210
(9)	$\alpha(1-\alpha)$^2	(6)×(7)^2	...	...	...	0.147	0.147
(10)	$\alpha(1-\alpha)$^3	(6)×(7)^3	...	...	...	...	0.103
(11)	Sum of parameters	(6)+(8)+(9)+(10)	...	0.300	0.510	0.657	0.760
(12)	Actual claims incurred (L_t)	(3)+(4)	268.0	287.0	323.0	337.0	361.0
(13)	Actual claims incurred ratio (l_t)	(12)/(1)	0.525	0.509	0.518	0.486	0.481
(14)	Expected claims incurred ratio ($l_{t\|t-1}$)	$\alpha\sum_{i=0}(1-\alpha)^i l_{t-i-1}/(11)_t$	...	0.525	0.516	0.517	0.505
(15)	Expected claims incurred ($L_{t\|t-1}$)	(14)×(1)	...	296.4	321.8	358.0	378.5
(16)	β		...	0.300	0.300	0.300	0.300
(17)	$1-\beta$	1–(16)	...	0.700	0.700	0.700	0.700
(18)	$\beta(1-\beta)$	(16)×(17)	...	...	0.210	0.210	0.210
(19)	$\beta(1-\beta)$^2	(16)×(17)^2	...	...	...	0.147	0.147
(20)	$\beta(1-\beta)$^3	(16)×(17)^3	...	...	...	...	0.103
(21)	Sum of parameters	(16)+(18)+(19)+(20)	...	0.300	0.510	0.657	0.760
(22)	Investment gain/loss ratio (i_t)	(5)/(1)	0.112	0.122	0.098	0.098	0.084
(23)	Expected investment gain/loss ratio ($i_{t\|t-1}$)	$\beta\sum_{i=0}(1-\beta)^i i_{t-i-1}/(21)_t$	...	0.112	0.118	0.109	0.105
(24)	Expected premium supplements ($I_{t\|t-1}$)	(23)×(1)	...	63.0	73.6	75.4	78.4

- Multiply the value of α (0.3) by its complement $(1-\alpha)$ which is raised to the appropriate exponent to derive the various geometric weights.
- Compute the actual claims incurred (L_t) for each year as the sum of claims paid and changes in reserves for outstanding claims.
- Compute the claims incurred ratio (l_t) for each year by dividing the actual claims incurred (L_t) by the premiums earned (P_t).
- Multiply the claims incurred ratios (l_t) by the appropriate α terms for each year to obtain the geometrically weighted claims incurred ratios.
- Sum up these ratios to obtain the expected claims incurred ratio ($l_{t|t-1}$).
- Since the time series of the data is relatively short, there is a need to modify the geometrically weighted claims incurred ratios by standardizing the parameters to ensure that the weights sum up to one. This is done by dividing each α-related term in the formula to calculate the expected claims incurred ratio by the sum of all the α-related terms. Thus, if the compiling agency has only five years of input data, the formula for year five given the information available in year four will become

$$l_{5|4} = \frac{\alpha}{\alpha+\alpha(1-\alpha)^3} l_4 + \frac{\alpha(1-\alpha)}{\alpha+\alpha(1-\alpha)+\ldots+\alpha(1-\alpha)^3} l_3 + $$
$$+ \frac{\alpha(1-\alpha)^2}{\alpha+\alpha(1-\alpha)+\ldots+\alpha(1-\alpha)^3} l_2 + \frac{\alpha(1-\alpha)^3}{\alpha+\alpha(1-\alpha)+\ldots+\alpha(1-\alpha)^3} l_1$$

- Multiply the expected claims incurred ratio by premiums earned (P_t) to obtain expected claims incurred ($L_{t|t-1}$).

The same steps are also used to calculate the investment gain/loss ratios (i_t), expected investment gain/loss ratios ($i_{t|t-1}$) and expected premium supplements ($I_{t|t-1}$).

3.198. The whole procedure is repeated to calculate the expected claims incurred ratios, expected claims incurred, expected investment gain/loss ratios and expected premium supplements using the values of 0.1 and 0.2 for α and β. The detailed computations are not shown, as they are the same as those in table 3.47.

3.199. Table 3.48 shows the RMSPE using the values of 0.1, 0.2 and 0.3 for α and β. In the case of α, the RMSPE is calculated as the square root of the average of the squared differences between the actual claims incurred (L_t) and the expected claims incurred (NL_T) for the sample period. In the case of β, the actual (I_t) and expected investment incomes (PS_t) are used. As an example, in the case where α=0.3, the RMSPE is calculated as:

$$\sqrt{\frac{(361.0-378.5)^2+(337.0-358.0)^2+(323.0-321.8)^2+(287.0-296.4)^2}{4}}=14.451.$$

Table 3.48
Root mean square prediction errors (RMSPE) using α, β=(0.10, 0.20, 0.30)

	α			β		
	0.1	**0.2**	**0.3**	**0.1**	**0.2**	**0.3**
RMSPE	15.960	15.047	14.451	11.852	11.353	11.031

3.200. From the table, it can be observed that α=0.3 and β=0.3 have the least RMSPE. Thus, these values are chosen for the calculation of non-life insurance output.

3.201. Table 3.49 shows how to use the information in the tables above to compute non-life insurance output and net non-life insurance premiums in year *t* using the chosen values of 0.3 for α and β. The table also shows the claims incurred data in year *t*. The output of non-life insurance is computed as follows:

Premiums earned
plus expected premium supplements
minus expected claims incurred.

Net non-life insurance premiums are computed as follows:

Premiums earned
plus actual premium supplements
minus non-life insurance output.

Table 3.49
Calculation of non-life insurance output, net non-life insurance premiums and claims incurred in year *t* using α, β=0.3

Line number	Item	Description	Value	2008 SNA code
(25)	Output of insurance corporations (insurance service charge)	(1)+(25)–(15)	449.9	P1, P3
(26)	Net non-life insurance premiums	(1)+(5)–(26)	363.1	D71, D711
(27)	Claims incurred	(12)	361.0	D72, D721

3.202. Table 3.50 shows how to calculate the changes in financial assets and liabilities arising from the transactions between insurance corporations and the other institutional units, as well as the means of payments for these transactions in year *t*. In general, the changes in financial assets and liabilities are computed using the fol-

Table 3.50
Calculation of changes in financial assets and liabilities related to non-life insurance transactions under the expectations approach with no catastrophic claims in year *t*

Line number	Item	Description	Value	2008 SNA code
	Changes in financial assets (currency and deposits)			
(28)	Insurance corporations	(1)+(2)–(3)+(5)	813.0	F2
(29)	Households	(3)–(1)–(2)	-750.0	F2
(30)	Other sectors	–(5)	-63.0	F2
	Changes in financial assets (non-life insurance technical reserves)			
(31)	Households	(2)+(4)	361.0	F61
	Changes in liabilities (non-life insurance technical reserves)			
(32)	Insurance corporations	(2)+(4)	361.0	F61

lowing principles: the changes in currency and deposits are the result of the premiums paid by the other institutional units to the insurance corporations and the claims paid by the latter to the former. For insurance corporations, premiums received represent an increase in currency and deposits, while claims paid represent a decrease. The converse applies to the counterpart institutional units. On the other hand, the changes in non-life insurance technical reserves are the result of unearned premiums and changes in reserves against outstanding claims. For insurance corporations, these items represent an increase in liabilities, while for the other institutional units they represent an increase in financial assets. As an example, insurance corporations have an increase in assets of currency and deposits of 813.0 units during the accounting period. This is the result of:

- An increase in assets of currency and deposits arising from premiums received (945.0 units), which are made up of earned (750.0 units) and unearned premiums (195.0 units); and investment income receivable (63.0 units).
- A decrease in assets of currency and deposits arising from claims paid (195.0 units).

In addition, insurance corporations have an increase in liabilities of technical reserves of 361.0 units, which are accrual adjustments. This is the result of an increase in:

- Unearned premiums (195.0 units).
- Reserves in outstanding claims (166.0 units).

3.203. Table 3.51 makes use of the relevant information in previous tables to record the various transactions for non-life insurance. To simplify the presentation and analysis, other transactions, such as the other intermediate consumption of goods and services of the institutional units, are ignored. The following pairs of transactions need to be recorded: two pairs relate to the measurement of the production and consumption of the insurance service, three pairs relate to redistribution and two to the financial account. The transactions are described as follows:

(a) The output of non-life insurance (449.9 units) is recorded in the production account of insurance corporations;

(b) The allocation of primary income account records the property income receivable by insurance corporations from other sectors (63.0 units) from investing the technical reserves. This amount is then recorded as investment income attributable to policyholders in respect of non-life insurance (in this instance, households) by the insurance corporations;

Table 3.51

Recording non-life insurance transactions using the expectations approach with no catastrophic claims in year *t*

Uses													Resources
Total	**Goods and services**	**Total economy**	**Other Sectors**	**Households**	**Insurance corporations**	**2008 SNA code**	**Transactions and balancing items**	**Insurance corporations**	**Households**	**Other Sectors**	**Total economy**	**Goods and services**	**Total**
Production account													
449.9	449.9					P1	Output	449.9			449.9		449.9
449.9		449.9			449.9	B1g	Value added, gross/ Gross domestic product						
Allocation of primary income account													
63.0		63.0	63.0			D4	Property income	63.0			63.0		63.0
63.0		63.0			63.0	D441	Investment income attributable to insurance policyholders		63.0		63.0		63.0
449.9		449.9	-63.0	63.0	449.9	B5g	Balance of primary income, gross/ National income, gross						
Secondary distribution of income account													
363.1		363.1		363.1		D71	Net non-life insurance premiums	363.1			363.1		363.1
363.1		363.1		363.1		D711	Net non-life direct insurance premiums	363.1			363.1		363.1
361.0		361.0			361.0	D72	Non-life insurance claims		361.0		361.0		361.0
361.0		361.0			361.0	D721	Non-life direct insurance claims		361.0		361.0		361.0
449.9		449.9	-63.0	60.9	452.0	B6g	Disposable income, gross						
Use of disposable income account													
449.9		449.9		449.9		P3	Final consumption expenditure					449.9	449.9
0.0		0.0	-63.0	-389.0	452.0	B8g	Saving, gross						
Changes in assets													**Changes in liabilities and net worth**
Capital account													
0.0		0.0	-63.0	-389.0	452.0	B9	Net lending (+)/ net borrowing (-)						
Financial account													
						B9	Net lending (+)/ net borrowing (-)	452.0	-389.0	-63.0	0.0		0.0
0.0		0.0	-63.0	-750.0	813.0	F2	Currency and deposits						
361.0		361.0		361.0		F61	Non-life insurance technical reserves	361.0			361.0		361.0
195.0		195.0		195.0			Unearned premiums	195.0			195.0		195.0
166.0		166.0		166.0			Claims outstanding	166.0			166.0		166.0

(c) In the secondary distribution of income account, net non-life insurance premiums receivable by the insurance corporations from households amount to 363.1 units. In contrast, non-life direct insurance claims payable by the insurance corporations to households are estimated to be 361.0 units. Thus, there is a decoupling of net non-life direct insurance premiums (D711) and non-life direct insurance claims (D721);

(d) The output of non-life insurance (449.9 units) is recorded as the final consumption expenditure of households in the use of disposable income account;

(e) Since there are no capital account transactions, net lending/net borrowing in the capital account is the same as gross saving in the use of disposable income account;

(f) The financial account records the changes in currency and deposits, as well as in technical reserves (comprising unearned premiums and outstanding claims), of the institutional units. Insurance corporations have an increase in liabilities of unearned premiums (195.0 units) and outstanding claims (166.0 units). Households have a corresponding increase in these financial assets. Insurance corporations have a net increase in currency and deposits of 813.0 units, which is offset by the net decrease in the same financial assets of the other institutional units. Net lending/net borrowing is the same as net lending/net borrowing in the capital account, since the financial account transactions are the counterparts to entries in the other accounts or only reflect the exchange in financial assets and liabilities, although, in practice, differences in data sources and the timing of the recording of transactions may result in a discrepancy between the estimates of net lending/net borrowing in the capital and financial accounts.

3.204. The compiling agency can repeat the steps above for other classes of non-life insurance to obtain the economy-estimates of non-life insurance output and other related transactions.

Worked example 3.11. Calculating non-life insurance output using the expectations approach, whereby catastrophic claims are recorded as capital transfers

3.205. This worked example uses the method in worked example 3.10 to compute non-life insurance output, but assumes that there are catastrophic claims. The impact of these claims on the SNA can be assessed as follows. First, assume that these catastrophic claims are not moderated, so their impact on the output of non-life insurance, and gross disposable income and gross saving can be assessed. Next, we recompute the output of non-life insurance by adjusting the expectations approach to dampen the effects of these catastrophic claims. Furthermore, adjustments are also made to record some of the catastrophic claims incurred as capital transfers to avoid a sharp increase in the gross disposable income and gross saving of policyholders.

3.206. Table 3.52 presents the relevant information from insurance corporations for the same type of non-life insurance as in the previous worked example for the years $t-4$ to $t+2$. Assume that the compiling agency has continued to collect input data for two more years after year t. Thus, the data in table 3.52 for the years $t-4$ to t are identical to those in table 3.46. Assume also that there are exceptionally large claims arising from an event which is classified as a catastrophe in year $t+1$. Investment income refers to the property income receivable by insurance corporations from investing the technical reserves. For simplicity, it is assumed that this property income is payable by other resident sectors and that all the investment income attributable to policyholders comprises this property income.

Table 3.52
Data from insurance corporations on non-life insurance transactions

Line number	Item	$t-4$	$t-3$	$t-2$	$t-1$	t	$t+1$	$t+2$	2008 SNA code
(1)	Earned premiums (P_t)	510.0	564.0	624.0	693.0	750.0	825.0	870.0	
(2)	Unearned premiums	89.0	116.0	140.0	165.0	195.0	236.0	281.0	
(3)	Claims paid	137.0	148.0	167.0	176.0	195.0	1670.0	200.0	
(4)	Changes in claims outstanding	131.0	139.0	156.0	161.0	166.0	197.0	222.0	
(5)	Investment income (I_t)	57.0	69.0	61.0	68.0	63.0	70.0	65.0	D4, D441

Table 3.53
Deriving claims incurred ratios, investment gain/loss ratios, expected claims and expected premium supplements without moderating the effects of catastrophic claims using α, β=0.3

Line number	Item	Description	t–4	t–3	t–2	t–1	t	t+1	t+2
(6)	α		...	0.300	0.300	0.300	0.300	0.300	0.300
(7)	1–α	1–(6)	...	0.700	0.700	0.700	0.700	0.700	0.700
(8)	α(1–α)	(6)×(7)	...	...	0.210	0.210	0.210	0.210	0.210
(9)	α(1–α)^2	(6)×(7)^2	...	...	...	0.147	0.147	0.147	0.147
(10)	α(1–α)^3	(6)×(7)^3	...	...	...	...	0.103	0.103	0.103
(11)	α(1–α)^4	(6)×(7)^4	...	...	...	...	...	0.072	0.072
(12)	α(1–α)^5	(6)×(7)^5	...	...	...	...	...	...	0.050
(13)	Sum of parameters	(6)+(8)+(9)+(10)+(11)+(12)	...	0.300	0.510	0.657	0.760	0.832	0.882
(14)	Actual claims incurred (L_t)	(3)+(4)	268.0	287.0	323.0	337.0	361.0	1867.0	422.0
(15)	Actual claims incurred ratio (l_t)	(14)/(1)	0.525	0.509	0.518	0.486	0.481	2.263	0.485
(16)	Expected claims incurred ratio ($l_{t\|t-1}$)	$\alpha\sum_{i=0}^{i}(1-\alpha)^{i} l_{t-i-1} / (13)_t$	...	0.525	0.516	0.517	0.505	0.496	1.097
(17)	Expected claims incurred ($L_{t\|t-1}$)	(16)×(1)	...	296.4	321.8	358.0	378.5	409.4	954.3
(18)	β		...	0.300	0.300	0.300	0.300	0.300	0.300
(19)	1–β	1–(18)	...	0.700	0.700	0.700	0.700	0.700	0.700
(20)	β(1–β)	(18)×(19)	...	...	0.210	0.210	0.210	0.210	0.210
(21)	β(1–β)^2	(18)×(19)^2	...	...	...	0.147	0.147	0.147	0.147
(22)	β(1–β)^3	(18)×(19)^3	...	...	...	...	0.103	0.103	0.103
(23)	β(1–β)^4	(18)×(19)^4	...	...	...	...	...	0.072	0.072
(24)	β(1–β)^5	(18)×(19)^5	...	...	...	...	...	...	0.050
(25)	Sum of parameters	(18)+(20)+(21)+(22)+(23)+(24)	...	0.300	0.510	0.657	0.760	0.832	0.882
(26)	Investment gain/loss ratio (i_t)	(5)/(1)	0.112	0.122	0.098	0.098	0.084	0.085	0.075
(27)	Expected investment gain/loss ratio ($i_{t\|t-1}$)	$\beta\sum_{i=0}^{i}(1-\beta)^{i} i_{t-i-1} / (25)_t$	...	0.112	0.118	0.109	0.105	0.097	0.093
(28)	Expected premium supplements ($I_{t\|t-1}$)	(27)×(1)	...	63.0	73.6	75.4	78.4	80.1	80.9

3.207. Table 3.53 shows how to derive claims incurred ratios, investment gain/loss ratios, expected claims and expected premium supplements using the chosen values of $\alpha=0.3$ and $\beta=0.3$ if no attempt is made to moderate the effects of the catastrophic claims. The steps to derive these items are basically the same as those in worked example 3.10. One immediately noticeable result is that the claims incurred ratio in year t+2 is significantly higher than those in the previous years because of the exceptionally large claims payable. Consequently, the expected claims incurred are also much higher.

3.208. Table 3.54 uses the information in tables 3.52 and 3.53 to compute non-life insurance output, net non-life insurance premiums, claims incurred and gross disposable income for the most recent three years. The strict application of the expectations method will result in the output of non-life insurance becoming negative in year t+2 owing to the very large expected claims in year t+1.[51] Furthermore, the table shows that the exceptionally large claims in year t+1 will result in a very large increase in the gross disposable income (and, by extension, gross saving) of policyholders in the same year. Thus, there is a need to adjust the expectations method by moderating the effects of catastrophic claims so that a more reasonable estimate of

[51] In addition, if the compiling agency were to calculate non-life insurance output in year t+1 using the 1993 SNA method as premiums earned plus premium supplements minus actual claims incurred, this will turn out to be 825.0 plus 70.0 minus 1867.0, which will equal -972.0 units. Thus, the exceptionally large claims in year t+1 will cause the output for that year to be negative.

Table 3.54
Calculation of non-life insurance output, net non-life insurance premiums and claims incurred in year *t* without moderating the effects of catastrophic claims

Line number	Item	Description	Value
(29)	Output of insurance corporations (insurance service charge) in year *t*	(1)+(28)–(17)	449.9
(30)	Output of insurance corporations (insurance service charge) in year *t*+1	(1)+(28)–(17)	495.8
(31)	Output of insurance corporations (insurance service charge) in year *t*+2	(1)+(28)–(17)	-3.5
(32)	Net non-life insurance premiums in year *t*	(1)+(5)–(31)	363.1
(33)	Net non-life insurance premiums in year *t*+1	(1)+(5)–(31)	399.2
(34)	Claims incurred in year *t*	(14)	361.0
(35)	Claims incurred in year *t*+1	(14)	1867.0
(36)	Gross disposable income of households in year *t*	(5)+(34)–(32)	60.9
(37)	Gross disposable income of households in year *t*+1	(5)+(35)–(33)	1537.8

non-life insurance output can be calculated. Also, there is a need to reclassify some of the exceptionally large claims as capital transfers to avoid the counter-intuitive outcome of a sharp increase in the gross disposable income and gross saving of policyholders.

3.209. Table 3.55 shows the derivation of claims incurred ratios, investment gain/loss ratios, expected claims and expected premium supplements in year *t* using the information in table 3.52 after adjustments are made to the expectations approach to moderate the effects of the catastrophic claims. The adjustments are made as follows:

- First, remove the year with the catastrophe from the calculation of the expected claims incurred ratio. In this example, this means that actual claims data for year *t*+1 are not included in the computation of the expected claims incurred ratio for year *t*+2.
- After that, compute the catastrophic claims ratio as the difference between the actual claims incurred ratio and the computed expected claims incurred ratio.
- Spread the computed catastrophic claims ratio equally over 20 years, starting from the year with the catastrophe.
- Add the adjustment for the catastrophic claims ratio to the expected claims incurred ratio for each year of the 20-year period.[52]

One immediately noticeable result is that the claims incurred ratios are now much lower than those in table 3.53. Consequently, the expected claims incurred in year *t*+2 have become much lower as well.

3.210. Table 3.56 uses the information in tables 3.52 and 3.55 to compute non-life insurance output and net non-life insurance premiums for the latest two years in the case of adjustments being made to dampen the effects of catastrophic claims. The output of non-life insurance is now non-negative owing to the use of claims incurred ratios without data from the year with the catastrophe.

3.211. The actual claims incurred will need to be adjusted to classify some of these claims as capital rather than current transfers in order to avoid the counter-intuitive outcome of the disposable income of policyholders increasing substantially in the event of catastrophes. The compiling agency can request insurance corporations to provide estimates of the claims payable for catastrophes and classify these claims as capital transfers. If these data are not available, the compiling agency will need to estimate these

[52] As in worked example 3.10, there is a need to standardize the parameters to ensure that the weights sum up to one, since the data series is relatively short.

Table 3.55

Deriving claims ratios and expected claims by moderating the effects of catastrophic claims using *α, β*=0.3

Line number	Item	Description	*t*-4	*t*-3	*t*-2	*t*-1	*t*	*t*+1	*t*+2
(38)	α		...	0.300	0.300	0.300	0.300	0.300	0.300
(39)	1-α	1–(38)	...	0.700	0.700	0.700	0.700	0.700	0.700
(40)	α(1-α)	(38)×(39)	...	...	0.210	0.210	0.210	0.210	0.210
(41)	α(1-α)^2	(38)×(39)^2	...	...	...	0.147	0.147	0.147	0.147
(42)	α(1-α)^3	(38)×(39)^3	...	...	...	...	0.103	0.103	0.103
(43)	α(1α)^4	(38)×(39)^4	...	...	...	...	...	0.072	0.072
(44)	α(1-α)^5	(6)×(7)^5					...	...	0.050
(45)	Sum of parameters	(38)+(40)+(41)+(42)+(43)+(44)	...	...	...	...	0.760	0.832	0.832
(46)	Actual claims incurred (L_t)	(3)+(4)	268.0	287.0	323.0	337.0	361.0	1867.0	422.0
(47)	Actual claims incurred ratio (l_t)	(46)/(1)	0.525	0.509	0.518	0.486	0.481	2.263	0.485
(48)	Expected claims incurred ratio ($l_{t\mid t-1}$) excluding year with catastrophe	$\alpha\sum_{i=0}(1-\alpha)^i l_{t-i-1} / (45)_t$	...	...	...	...	0.505	0.496	0.496
(49)	Difference between actual claims incurred ratio (l_t) and expected claims incurred ratio ($l_{t\mid t-1}$) excluding year with catastrophe	(47)–(48)	...	...	...	...	...	1.767	...
(50)	Difference between actual claims incurred ratio (l_t) and expected claims incurred ratio ($l_{t\mid t-1}$) excluding year with catastrophe spread over 20 years	(49)/20	...	...	...	...	...	0.088	0.088
(51)	Expected claims incurred ($l_{t\mid t-1}$) plus smoothed catastrophic claims ratios	(48)+(50)	...	...	...	...	...	0.585	0.585
(52)	Expected claims incurred ($l_{t\mid t-1}$) plus smoothed catastrophic claims	(51)×(1)	...	...	...	...	...	482.3	508.6
(53)	Total catastrophic claims	(49)×(1)	...	...	...	...	...	1457.6	...

Table 3.56

Calculation of non-life insurance output, net non-life insurance premiums and claims incurred in year *t* by moderating the effects of catastrophic claims using *α, β*=0.3

Line number	Item	Description	Value	2008 SNA code
(54)	Output of insurance corporations (insurance service charge) in year *t*+1	(1)+(28)–(52)	422.9	P1, P3
(55)	Output of insurance corporations (insurance service charge) in year *t*+2	(1)+(28)–(52)	442.3	
(56)	Net non-life insurance premiums in year *t*+1	(1)+(5)–(54)	472.1	D71, D711

Table 3.57

Derivation of catastrophic claims which are classified as capital transfers and gross disposable income in year *t*+1

Line number	Item	Description	Value	2008 SNA code
(57)	Claims incurred	(46)	1867.0	
(58)	Claims incurred classified as capital transfers	(53)	1457.6	D9r, D99r, D9p, D99p
(59)	Claims incurred classified as current transfers	(57)–(58)	409.4	D72, D721
(60)	Gross disposable income of households	(5)+(59)–(56)	7.3	B6g

Table 3.58
Calculation of changes in financial assets and liabilities related to non-life insurance transactions under the expectations approach, whereby catastrophic claims are treated as capital transfers in year *t*+1

Line number	Item	Description	Value	2008 SNA code
	Changes in financial assets (currency and deposits)			
(61)	Insurance corporations	(1)+(2)–(3)+(5)	-539.0	F2
(62)	Households	(3)–(1)–(2)	609.0	F2
(63)	Other sectors	–(5)	-70.0	F2
	Changes in financial assets (non-life insurance technical reserves)			
(64)	Households	(2)+(4)	433.0	F61
	Changes in liabilities (non-life insurance technical reserves)			
(65)	Insurance corporations	(2)+(4)	433.0	F61

claims itself. One way to do so is shown in table 3.57. Let the catastrophic claims which have been estimated in table 3.55 be the capital transfers. The current transfers are then calculated as the difference between the claims incurred and capital transfers. The table also shows the gross disposable income for the policyholders after some of the claims have been classified as capital transfers. Compared with the previous estimate in table 3.54, the estimate of gross disposable income (and, by extension, gross saving) has not increased sharply.

3.212. Table 3.58 shows how to calculate the changes in financial assets and liabilities arising from the transactions between insurance corporations and the other institutional units, as well as the means of payment for these transactions in year *t*. The steps to compute these changes are similar to those in table 3.50.

3.213. Table 3.59 shows how to record the relevant transactions. The analysis of these transactions is basically the same as that for worked example 3.10. The estimated amount of catastrophic claims is recorded as capital transfers in the capital account. This will help to moderate volatility in gross disposable income and gross saving.

Worked example 3.12. Calculating non-life insurance output using the accounting approach

3.214. This worked example uses the accounting approach to calculate the output of non-life insurance. The method involves adding changes in equalization provisions to claims incurred to obtain adjusted claims to compute the output.

3.215. Table 3.60 presents the relevant information from insurance corporations for a particular line of non-life insurance. The table essentially has the same data as those for year *t* in table 3.46, except that it also includes data on changes in equalization provisions. It is assumed that the changes in equalization provisions do not give rise to a liability, so they are not recorded in the financial account. Investment income refers to the property income receivable by insurance corporations from investing the technical reserves. For simplicity, it is assumed that this property income is payable by other resident sectors and that all the investment income attributable to policyholders comprises this property income.

3.216. Table 3.61 shows how to use the information in table 3.60 to compute claims incurred, adjusted claims incurred, non-life insurance output and net non-life insurance premiums. Claims incurred are derived as follows:

Table 3.59

Recording non-life insurance transactions using the expectations approach, whereby catastrophic claims are treated as capital transfers in year *t*+1

Uses								Resources					
Total	Goods and services	Total economy	Other sectors	Households	Insurance corporations	2008 SNA code	Transactions and balancing items	Insurance corporations	Households	Other sectors	Total economy	Goods and services	Total
Production account													
422.9	422.9					P1	Output	422.9			422.9		422.9
422.9		422.9			422.9	B1g	Value added, gross/ Gross domestic product						
Allocation of primary income account													
70.0		70.0	70.0			D4	Property income	70.0			70.0		70.0
70.0		70.0			70.0	D441	Investment income attributable to insurance policyholders		70.0		70.0		70.0
422.9		422.9	-70.0	70.0	422.9	B5g	Balance of primary income, gross/ National income, gross						
Secondary distribution of income account													
472.1		472.1		472.1		D71	Net non-life insurance premiums	472.1			472.1		472.1
472.1		472.1		472.1		D711	Net non-life direct insurance premiums	472.1			472.1		472.1
409.4		409.4			409.4	D72	Non-life insurance claims		409.4		409.4		409.4
409.4		409.4			409.4	D721	Non-life direct insurance claims		409.4		409.4		409.4
422.9		422.9	-70.0	7.3	485.6	B6g	Disposable income, gross						
Use of disposable income account													
422.9		422.9		422.9		P3	Final consumption expenditure					422.9	422.9
0.0		0.0	-70.0	-415.6	485.6	B8g	Saving, gross						
Changes in assets								**Changes in liabilities and net worth**					
Capital account													
1457.6		1457.6		1457.6		D9r	Capital transfers, receivable						
1457.6		1457.6		1457.6		D99r	Other capital transfers, receivable						
						D9p	Capital transfers, payable	1457.6			1457.6		1457.6
						D99p	Other capital transfers, payable	1457.6			1457.6		1457.6
0.0		0.0	-70.0	1042.0	-972.0	B9	Net lending (+)/net borrowing (-)						
Financial account													
						B9	Net lending (+)/net borrowing (-)	-972.0	1042.0	-70.0	0.0		0.0
0.0		0.0	-70.0	609.0	-539.0	F2	Currency and deposits						
433.0		433.0		433.0		F61	Non-life insurance technical reserves	433.0			433.0		433.0
236.0		236.0		236.0			Unearned premiums	236.0			236.0		236.0
197.0		197.0		197.0			Claims outstanding	197.0			197.0		197.0

Table 3.60

Data from insurance corporations on non-life insurance transactions

Line number	Item	Value	2008 SNA code
(1)	Earned premiums	750.0	
(2)	Unearned premiums	195.0	
(3)	Claims paid	195.0	
(4)	Changes in claims outstanding	166.0	
(5)	Changes in equalization provisions	200.0	
(6)	Investment income	63.0	D4, D441

Claims paid
plus changes in reserves against outstanding claims.

Adjusted claims are computed as follows:
Claims incurred
plus changes in equalization provisions.

The output of non-life insurance is computed as follows:
Premiums earned
plus premium supplements
minus adjusted claims.

Net non-life insurance premiums are computed as follows:
Premiums earned
plus premium supplements
minus the non-life insurance output.

3.217. Table 3.62 shows how to calculate the changes in financial assets and liabilities arising from the transactions between insurance corporations and the other institutional units, as well as the means of payment for these transactions. In general, the computations are similar to those in the other worked examples on non-life insurance.

3.218. Table 3.63 shows how to record the relevant transactions. The analysis is essentially the same as that for the earlier worked examples on non-life insurance. As in the earlier worked examples, there is a decoupling between net non-life direct insurance premiums and non-life direct insurance claims. This is due to the use of adjusted rather than actual claims incurred in the formula. The entries in the financial account are the same as those in worked example 3.10, since they are not affected by the use of the adjusted items to compute the output of non-life insurance.

3.219. The compiling agency can repeat the steps above for other classes of non-life insurance to obtain the economy-estimates of non-life insurance output and other related transactions.

Table 3.61

Calculation of claims and adjusted claims incurred, non-life insurance output and net non-life insurance premiums

Line number	Item	Description	Value	2008 SNA code
(7)	Claims incurred	(3)+(4)	361.0	D72, D721
(8)	Adjusted claims incurred	(7)+(5)	561.0	
(9)	Output of insurance corporations (insurance service charge)	(1)+(6)–(8)	252.0	P1, P3
(10)	Net non-life insurance premiums	(1)+(6)–(9)	561.0	D71, D711

Table 3.62

Calculation of changes in financial assets and liabilities related to non-life insurance transactions under the accounting approach

Line number	Item	Description	Value	2008 SNA code
	Changes in financial assets (currency and deposits)			
(11)	Insurance corporations	(1)+(2)–(3)+(6)	813.0	F2
(12)	Households	(3)–(1)–(2)	-750.0	F2
(13)	Other sectors	-(6)	-63.0	F2
	Changes in financial assets (non-life insurance technical reserves)			
(14)	Households	(2)+(4)	361.0	F61
	Changes in liabilities (non-life insurance technical reserves)			
(15)	Insurance corporations	(2)+(4)	361.0	F61

Table 3.63

Recording non-life insurance transactions using the accounting approach

Uses													Resources
Total	Goods and services	Total economy	Other sectors	Households	Insurance corporations	2008 SNA code	Transactions and balancing items	Insurance corporations	Households	Other sectors	Total economy	Goods and services	Total
Production account													
252.0	252.0					P1	Output	252.0			252.0		252.0
252.0		252.0			252.0	B1g	Value added, gross/Gross domestic product						
Allocation of primary income account													
63.0		63.0	63.0			D4	Property income	63.0			63.0		63.0
63.0		63.0			63.0	D441	Investment income attributable to insurance policyholders		63.0		63.0		63.0
252.0		252.0	-63.0	63.0	252.0	B5g	Balance of primary income, gross/National income, gross						
Secondary distribution of income account													
561.0		561.0		561.0		D71	Net non-life insurance premiums	561.0			561.0		561.0
561.0		561.0		561.0		D711	Net non-life direct insurance premiums	561.0			561.0		561.0
361.0		361.0			361.0	D72	Non-life insurance claims		361.0		361.0		361.0
361.0		361.0			361.0	D721	Non-life direct insurance claims		361.0		361.0		361.0
252.0		252.0	-63.0	-137.0	452.0	B6g	Disposable income, gross						
Use of disposable income account													
252.0		252.0		252.0		P3	Final consumption expenditure					252.0	252.0
0.0		0.0	-63.0	-389.0	452.0	B8g	Saving, gross						
Changes in assets													**Changes in liabilities and net worth**
Capital account													
0.0		0.0	-63.0	-389.0	452.0	B9	Net lending (+)/ net borrowing (-)						
Financial account													
						B9	Net lending (+)/ net borrowing (-)	452.0	-389.0	-63.0	0.0		0.0
0.0		0.0	-63.0	-750.0	813.0	F2	Currency and deposits						
361.0		361.0		361.0		F61	Non-life insurance technical reserves	361.0			361.0		361.0
195.0		195.0		195.0			Unearned premiums	195.0			195.0		195.0
166.0		166.0		166.0			Claims outstanding	166.0			166.0		166.0

Worked example 3.13. Calculating non-life insurance output using the sum of costs plus "normal profit" approach

3.220. There could be instances of the necessary historical statistical data and the accounting data either being insufficient or unavailable to allow reasonable estimates of the output of non-life insurance to be calculated using the expectations and accounting approaches. In such situations, the output of non-life insurance will need to be estimated using the sum of costs approach. This basically involves computing the output by summing up the costs involved (including intermediate costs, capital and labour costs, and other taxes less other subsidies on production) plus an allowance for normal profit. This worked example uses this approach to calculate the output of non-life insurance.

3.221. Table 3.64 presents the relevant information which is needed to compute the output of non-life insurance using the sum of costs approach. The data on compensation of employees, intermediate consumption, other taxes and other subsidies on production can be obtained from insurance corporations. Normal profit is obtained by smoothing past actual profits. The past profits for smoothing should be gross profits (i. e. they should not be deducted for any income taxes payable). The information on past actual profits can be obtained from insurance corporations. The compiling agency will have to decide on the length of past profits to be used for smoothing.

Table 3.64
Data for computing the output of non-life insurance using the sum of costs plus "normal profit" approach

Line number	Item	Description	Value
(1)	Compensation of employees		100.0
(2)	Intermediate consumption		20.0
(3)	Capital costs		15.0
(4)	Other taxes on production		8.0
(5)	Other subsidies on production		3.0
(6)	Normal profit		20.0
(7)	Output of insurance corporations (insurance service charge)	(1)+(2)+(3)+(4)–(5)+(6)	160.0

3.222. Assume that insurance corporations own all the fixed assets they use in producing non-life insurance services. Thus, capital costs or the rental values of these fixed assets are not directly observable from rental transactions. Capital costs will need to be imputed as the sum of consumption of fixed capital and return to capital. Insurance corporations will most likely be unable to provide information on the consumption of fixed capital and return to capital, as these two items are computed according to national rather than commercial accounting principles.

3.223. Using the information in the table, the output of non-life insurance is computed as follows:

Compensation of employees
plus intermediate consumption
plus capital costs
plus other taxes on production
less other subsidies on production
plus normal profit.

Allocation of non-life insurance output to user sectors

References:
2008 SNA, Chapter 9, The use of income account
2008 SNA, Chapter 17, Cross-cutting and other special issues, Part 1, The treatment of insurance
BPM6 Compilation Guide, Appendix 2, Insurance transactions and positions, and pension schemes

3.224. The worked examples in the previous section on describing the expectations and accounting approaches to compute non-life insurance output assume that, for simplicity, all the output is allocated to households in their capacity as final consumers.

However, various types of non-life insurance are likely to have policyholders across the five resident institutional sectors, including unincorporated enterprises. It is also likely for non-residents to be policyholders of certain types of non-life insurance.[53] Given this, it will not be possible for the compiling agency to merely assign all the non-life insurance output to one particular user sector. Instead, the compiling agency will need to assess how to allocate the non-life insurance output to more than one user sector. Depending on the nature of the source data, two approaches can be considered. The first approach can be described as the "bottom-up" approach. This approach assumes that, for each line of non-life insurance, the compiling agency is able to obtain data from insurance corporations on the breakdown of each of the items to calculate non-life insurance output and other related transactions by institutional sector (including the rest of the world). Thus, it can directly compute the non-life insurance output and related transactions, such as net non-life insurance premiums, to be allocated to each sector for each line of non-life insurance. These transactions are then summed up to obtain the economy-wide estimates. However, it is very likely that the input data according to this breakdown may not be readily available. For example, it may not be possible for insurance corporations to provide the sectoral breakdown of the investment income receivable by them from investing technical reserves. Thus, some of the source data may only be available without any sectoral breakdown. Consequently, the compiling agency may need to consider the use of the second approach, which can be described as the "top-down" approach. In this approach, the compiling agency can use the source data available to compute the total non-life insurance output for each line of non-life insurance. After that, it will use various assumptions to allocate the output to user sectors based on the data available. For instance, if insurance corporations have data on the breakdown of actual premiums by sector, this information can be used to allocate the total output of non-life insurance in proportion to the actual premiums data.[54] The investment income attributable to policyholders (i.e. premium supplements) should, in principle, be allocated to the user sectors in proportion to the reserves attributed to the different classes of insurance and policyholders. In practice, the usual method is to carry out the allocation in proportion to actual premiums data. This is to ensure consistency with the method used to allocate the total output of non-life insurance. Estimates of net non-life insurance premiums payable by each sector are then directly computed by deducting the output allocated to each user sector from the corresponding data on premiums earned and premium supplements. The sectoral estimates are then summed up to obtain the estimates receivable by the insurance corporations.

3.225. Resident institutional units are also likely to purchase non-life insurance from non-resident insurance corporations. Estimates of the total imports of non-life insurance service charge, as well as transactions in investment income attributable to policyholders, unearned premiums, claims incurred and net non-life insurance premiums between residents and non-resident non-life insurance corporations can be obtained directly from balance of payments statistics. However, if the balance of payments statistics do not report estimates of these items, the compiling agency may need to estimate them using a combination of sources, including ratios available from the domestic non-life insurance sector, information from the ITRS (which captures information on the destinations of premiums paid by residents and sources of claims received by residents on a cash basis), partner country data or a survey that can be used to collect premiums paid and claims recovered from the domestic policyholder. If an economy

[53] An example is motor vehicle insurance, the policyholders of which can include all five resident institutional sectors, as well as overseas students who are studying in the host economy and are thus classified as non-residents.

[54] Another option is to use claims data to allocate the output of non-life insurance. However, this is not recommended, as claims depend on the insured events occurring to trigger payments. Besides, claims also tend to fluctuate more than premiums. The allocation of the output of non-life insurance to industries should also be made in proportion to the actual premiums payable by these industries.

has a non-life insurance sector, the compiling agency can apply the service charge to the premiums paid ratio derived from this sector to the premiums paid by residents to non-resident non-life insurers to obtain an estimate of the imported non-life insurance service charge. Appropriate ratios can be also be applied to the premiums paid by residents to non-resident non-life insurers to obtain estimates of transactions in unearned premiums, investment income attributable to policyholders, claims incurred and net non-life insurance premiums between resident policyholders and non-resident non-life insurance corporations. On the other hand, if the economy does not have a non-life insurance sector, the compiling agency can consider contacting partner countries to obtain these ratios. Information on which countries to contact can be obtained from the ITRS. The compiling agency should estimate the non-life insurance transactions between residents and non-resident non-life insurance corporations in consultation with the compilers of the balance of payments to ensure that there is consistency in the recording of these transactions in the national accounts and balance of payments statistics. After obtaining the required data either directly from the balance of payments statistics or through estimation techniques, the compiling agency will still need to allocate the data on the total imports of non-life insurance service charge, as well as transactions in investment income attributable to policyholders, unearned premiums, claims incurred and net non-life insurance premiums, to the resident institutional sectors. The allocation can be carried out using data on premiums from the ITRS. Alternatively, the compiling agency can consider allocating the data in proportion to the consumption of the domestically produced non-life insurance service charge by the resident user sectors.

Worked example 3.14. Allocating the output of non-life insurance to user sectors

3.226. This worked example shows how to allocate the output of non-life insurance and other related transactions to institutional sectors (including the rest of the world) in a situation in which there is incomplete information to directly compute the output consumed by each sector. For simplicity, it is assumed that the output which is allocated to the households sector is meant for final consumption. In addition, the worked example will show how to record the counterpart entries in the financial account to show the means of payment for some of the transactions between the institutional units. For simplicity, it is assumed that these transactions are settled in currency or transferable deposits, which are part of "currency and deposits" in the financial account.

3.227. Table 3.65 shows data from insurance corporations for a particular line of non-life insurance. The data on total earned premiums, unearned premiums, claims paid, changes in outstanding claims, changes in equalization provisions and investment income earned from investing technical reserves are the same as those in table 3.60. For simplicity, it is assumed that the investment income is payable by other resident sectors and that all the investment income attributable to policyholders comprises this property income. Insurance corporations are able to provide a breakdown of the data for earned premiums, unearned premiums, claims paid and changes in outstanding claims by institutional sector. However, they are unable to provide any breakdown of the data for changes in equalization provisions and investment income attributable to policyholders. Given the partial data set, a "top-down" approach is needed to allocate the output of non-life insurance. Thus, total non-life insurance output is computed first. After that, the total output together with the investment income attributable to policyholders can be allocated to each institutional sector using the data on actual premiums as weights. Estimates of non-life insurance premiums payable by each sector are then directly calculated before the sectoral estimates are aggregated to obtain the estimates receivable by the insurance corporations.

Table 3.65
Data from insurance corporations on non-life insurance transactions

Line number	Item	Value
(1)	Earned premiums	750.0
(1a)	Non-financial corporations	240.0
(1b)	Financial corporations	210.0
(1c)	General government	120.0
(1d)	Households	90.0
(1e)	NPISHs	60.0
(1f)	Rest of the world	30.0
(2)	Unearned premiums	195.0
(2a)	Non-financial corporations	60.0
(2b)	Financial corporations	52.5
(2c)	General government	37.5
(2d)	Households	22.5
(2e)	NPISHs	15.0
(2f)	Rest of the world	7.5
(3)	Claims paid	195.0
(3a)	Non-financial corporations	60.0
(3b)	Financial corporations	45.0
(3c)	General government	35.0
(3d)	Households	26.0
(3e)	NPISHs	21.0
(3f)	Rest of the world	8.0
(4)	Changes in claims outstanding	166.0
(4a)	Non-financial corporations	45.0
(4b)	Financial corporations	39.0
(4c)	General government	32.0
(4d)	Households	22.0
(4e)	NPISHs	17.0
(4f)	Rest of the world	11.0
(5)	Changes in equalization provisions	200.0
(6)	Investment income	63.0

3.228. Table 3.66 shows how to compute the actual premiums payable by each sector. The actual premiums payable by each sector are computed as the sum of the corresponding earned and unearned premiums. The total actual premiums payable by all sectors is computed as the sum of the corresponding data on earned and unearned premiums.

Table 3.66
Computation of actual premiums by sector

Line number	Item	Description	Value
(7)	Actual premiums	(1)+(2)	945.0
(7a)	Non-financial corporations	(1a)+(2a)	300.0
(7b)	Financial corporations	(1b)+(2b)	262.5
(7c)	General government	(1c)+(2c)	157.5
(7d)	Households	(1d)+(2d)	112.5
(7e)	NPISHs	(1e)+(2e)	75.0
(7f)	Rest of the world	(1f)+(2f)	37.5

3.229. Table 3.67 uses the data in table 3.66 to derive the share of each sector in total actual premiums. The share of each sector in total actual premiums is obtained by dividing the actual premiums payable by each sector by the total actual premiums payable by all sectors and then multiplying the result by 100.0. These data will be used to break down total non-life insurance output and investment income attributable to policyholders.

Table 3.67
Breakdown of actual premiums by sector (as a percentage)

Line number	Item	Description	Per cent
(8)	Actual premiums	(8a)+(8b)+(8c)+(8d)+(8e)+(8f)	100.0
(8a)	Non-financial corporations	[(7a)/(7)]×100.0	31.7
(8b)	Financial corporations	[(7b)/(7)]×100.0	27.8
(8c)	General government	[(7c)/(7)]×100.0	16.7
(8d)	Households	[(7d)/(7)]×100.0	11.9
(8e)	NPISHs	[(7e)/(7)]×100.0	7.9
(8f)	Rest of the world	[(7f)/(7)]×100.0	4.0

3.230. Table 3.68 shows how to calculate the total output of non-life insurance using the accounting approach and then allocate the total output to each sector. The table also shows how to allocate the investment income attributable to policyholders and how to compute the net non-life insurance premiums payable by each sector. The total output (252.0 units) is allocated to each sector by multiplying the share of each sector in total actual premiums in table 3.67 by the total output and then dividing the result by 100.0. The investment income attributable to policyholders (63.0 units) is also allocated to each sector using the same procedure. Net non-life insurance premiums payable by each sector are then directly calculated before the sectoral estimates are aggregated to compute the estimates receivable by the insurance corporations.

3.231. Table 3.69 shows how to calculate the changes in financial assets and liabilities arising from the transactions between insurance corporations and the other institutional units, as well as the means of payment for these transactions. In general, the computations are similar to those in the other worked examples on non-life insurance.

3.232. Table 3.70 shows how to record the relevant transactions. The analysis is essentially the same as that for the earlier worked examples on non-life insurance, except that some of the non-life insurance output is now recorded as the intermediate consumption of the other corporations, general government and NPISHs. To simplify the presentation and analysis, the impact of allocating non-life insurance output to the output and final consumption expenditure of non-market producers (i.e. general government and NPISHs) is ignored. In addition, since non-residents are also policyholders, some of the output is also recorded as exports of goods and services. As in the earlier worked examples, there is a decoupling between net non-life direct insurance premiums and non-life direct insurance claims. This is due to the use of adjusted claims rather than actual claims incurred in the formula. Given that the policyholders include all the resident sectors and non-residents, these two items are also recorded in the secondary distribution of income account of these sectors and the rest of the world. Unlike the earlier worked examples on non-life insurance, net lending/net borrowing for the total economy is no longer zero. The estimate of -9.0 units for net lending/net borrowing for the total economy implies that there is an increase of 9.0 units in net borrowing from the rest of the world.

3.233. The compiling agency can repeat the steps above for other classes of non-life insurance to obtain the sectoral estimates of non-life insurance output and other related transactions.

Table 3.68

Calculation and allocation of non-life insurance output, investment income attributable to policyholders and net non-life insurance premiums

Line number	Item	Description	Value	2008 SNA code
(9)	Claims incurred	(3)+(4)	361.0	D72, D721
(9a)	Non-financial corporations	(3a)+(4a)	105.0	D72, D721
(9b)	Financial corporations	(3b)+(4b)	84.0	D72, D721
(9c)	General government	(3c)+(4c)	67.0	D72, D721
(9d)	Households	(3d)+(4d)	48.0	D72, D721
(9e)	NPISHs	(3e)+(4e)	38.0	D72, D721
(9f)	Rest of the world	(3f)+(4f)	19.0	D72, D721
(10)	Adjusted claims	(9)+(5)	561.0	
(11)	Output of non-life insurance corporation (insurance service charge)	(1)+(6)–(10)	252.0	P1
(11a)	Non-financial corporations	[(8a)/100.0]×(11)	80.0	P2
(11b)	Financial corporations	[(8b)/100.0]×(11)	70.0	P2
(11c)	General government	[(8c)/100.0]×(11)	42.0	P2
(11d)	Households	[(8d)/100.0]×(11)	30.0	P3
(11e)	NPISHs	[(8e)/100.0]×(11)	20.0	P2
(11f)	Rest of the world	[(8f)/100.0]×(11)	10.0	P6
(12)	Investment income attributable to policyholders	(6)	63.0	D4, D441
(12a)	Non-financial corporations	[(8a)/100.0]×(12)	20.0	D441
(12b)	Financial corporations	[(8b)/100.0]×(12)	17.5	D441
(12c)	General government	[(8c)/100.0]×(12)	10.5	D441
(12d)	Households	[(8d)/100.0]×(12)	7.5	D441
(12e)	NPISHs	[(8e)/100.0]×(12)	5.0	D441
(12f)	Rest of the world	[(8f)/100.0]×(12)	2.5	D441
(13)	Net non-life insurance premiums	(13a)+(13b)+(13c)+(13d)+(13e)+(13f)	561.0	D71, D711
(13a)	Non-financial corporations	(1a)+(12a)–(11a)	180.0	D71, D711
(13b)	Financial corporations	(1b)+(12b)–(11b)	157.5	D71, D711
(13c)	General government	(1c)+(12c)–(11c)	88.5	D71, D711
(13d)	Households	(1d)+(12d)–(11d)	67.5	D71, D711
(13e)	NPISHs	(1e)+(12e)–(11e)	45.0	D71, D711
(13f)	Rest of the world	(1f)+(12f)–(11f)	22.5	D71, D711

Table 3.69

Calculation of changes in financial assets and liabilities related to the allocation of non-life insurance output

Line number	Item	Description	Value	2008 SNA code
	Changes in financial assets (currency and deposits)			
(14)	Non-financial corporations	(3a)–(1a)–(2a)	-240.0	F2
(15)	Insurance corporations	(1)+(2)+(6)–(3)	813.0	F2
(16)	Financial corporations	(3b)–(1b)–(2b)–(6)	-280.5	F2
(17)	General government	(3c)–(1c)–(2c)	-122.5	F2
(18)	Households	(3d)–(1d)–(2d)	-86.5	F2
(19)	NPISHs	(3e)–(1e)–(2e)	-54.0	F2
(20)	Rest of the world	(3f)–(1f)–(2f)	-29.5	F2
	Changes in financial assets (non-life insurance technical reserves)			
(21)	Non-financial corporations	(2a)+(4a)	105.0	F61
(22)	Financial corporations	(2b)+(4b)	91.5	F61
(23)	General government	(2c)+(4c)	69.5	F61
(24)	Households	(2d)+(4d)	44.5	F61
(25)	NPISHs	(2e)+(4e)	32.0	F61
(26)	Rest of the world	(2f)+(4f)	18.5	F61
	Changes in liabilities (non-life insurance technical reserves)			
(27)	Insurance corporations	(2)+(4)	361.0	F61

Table 3.70

Recording non-life insurance transactions for which output is allocated using the "top-down" approach

Uses																					Resources
Total	Goods and services	Rest of the world	Total economy	NPISHs	Households	General government	Other financial corporations	Insurance corporations	Non-financial corporations	2008 SNA code	Transactions and balancing items	Non-financial corporations	Insurance corporations	Other financial corporations	General government	Households	NPISHs	Total economy	Rest of the world	Goods and services	Total
Production account																					
10.0		10.0								P6	Exports of goods and services									10.0	10.0
252.0	252.0									P1	Output		252.0					252.0			252.0
212.0			212.0	20.0		42.0	70.0		80.0	P2	Intermediate consumption (service charge)									212.0	212.0
40.0			40.0	-20.0		-42.0	-70.0	252.0	-80.0	B1g	Value added, gross/Gross domestic product										
-10.0		-10.0								B11	External balance of goods and services										
Allocation of primary income account																					
63.0			63.0				63.0			D4	Property income		63.0					63.0			63.0
63.0			63.0					63.0		D441	Investment income attributable to insurance policyholders	20.0		17.5	10.5	7.5	5.0	60.5	2.5		63.0
37.5			37.5	-15.0	7.5	-31.5	-115.5	252.0	-60.0	B5g	Balance of primary income, gross/National income, gross										
Secondary distribution of income account																					
561.0		22.5	538.5	45.0	67.5	88.5	157.5		180.0	D71	Net non-life insurance premiums		561.0					561.0			561.0
561.0		22.5	538.5	45.0	67.5	88.5	157.5		180.0	D711	Net non-life direct insurance premiums		561.0					561.0			561.0
361.0			361.0					361.0		D72	Non-life insurance claims	105.0		84.0	67.0	48.0	38.0	342.0	19.0		361.0
361.0			361.0					361.0		D721	Non-life direct insurance claims	105.0		84.0	67.0	48.0	38.0	342.0	19.0		361.0
41.0			41.0	-22.0	-12.0	-53.0	-189.0	452.0	-135.0	B6g	Disposable income, gross										
Use of disposable income account																					
30.0			30.0		30.0					P3	Final consumption (service charge)									30.0	30.0
11.0			11.0	-22.0	-42.0	-53.0	-189.0	452.0	-135.0	B8g	Saving, gross										
-11.0		-11.0								B12	Current external balance										
Changes in assets																					**Changes in liabilities and net worth**
Capital account																					
0.0		-11.0	11.0	-22.0	-42.0	-53.0	-189.0	452.0	-135.0	B9	Net lending (+)/ net borrowing (-)										
Financial account																					
										B9	Net lending (+)/ net borrowing (-)	-135.0	452.0	-189.0	-53.0	-42.0	-22.0	11.0	-11.0		0.0
0.0		-29.5	29.5	-54.0	-86.5	-122.5	-280.5	813.0	-240.0	F2	Currency and deposits										

Total	Goods and services	Rest of the world	Total economy	NPISHs	Households	General government	Other financial corporations	Insurance corporations	Non-financial corporations	2008 SNA code	Transactions and balancing items	Non-financial corporations	Insurance corporations	Other financial corporations	General government	Households	NPISHs	Total economy	Rest of the world	Goods and services	Total
361.0		18.5	342.5	32.0	44.5	69.5	91.5		105.0	F61	Non-life insurance technical reserves		361.0					361.0			361.0
195.0		7.5	187.5	15.0	22.5	37.5	52.5		60.0		Unearned premiums		195.0					195.0			195.0
166.0		11.0	155.0	17.0	22.0	32.0	39.0		45.0		Claims outstanding		166.0					166.0			166.0

Volume measures of non-life insurance output

References:
2008 SNA, Chapter 15, Price and volume measures
Handbook on Price and Volume Measures in National Accounts, Chapter 4, A/B/C methods for output by product

3.234. The worked examples above calculated non-life insurance output at current prices. As in the case of other economic variables, there is a need to compute volume measures of non-life insurance by removing the effects of price changes. The ideal method is to deflate the current-price output of non-life insurance by a corresponding output price index to obtain the volume measure. However, as in many other types of financial services, it is not possible to directly observe prices which represent the true nature of non-life insurance output. Thus, there is a need to resort to other methods.

3.235. One method is known as the deflation method. This method involves deflating current-price measures of premiums earned plus premium supplements for each line of non-life insurance by an appropriate price index and then using the deflated values to extrapolate the level of output of non-life insurance in the base year to obtain the volume measures. The price index for insurance premiums could be available from the CPI or PPI.[55] The resultant volume measures of each line of non-life insurance are then aggregated to produce chain-linked volume measures of non-life insurance output. In the case where the current-price output of non-life insurance is obtained using the sum of costs method, the compiling agency can consider deflating the output by a composite index of input prices to obtain the volume measures.

3.236. Another method is known as the volume indicator method. One variation of this method is to make use of detailed activity-level indicators, such as the acquisition and administration of policies and the administration claims which are weighted according to cost to construct a volume index for each line of non-life insurance. The volume index is then used to extrapolate the base-period output of non-life insurance. The volume measures of each line of insurance are then aggregated to form chain-linked volume measures of insurance output. However, this method requires activity-level detail on the different services produced together with detailed cost information to provide weights. This can be very resource intensive. In addition, it may be difficult to account for quality changes. Another variation is to use the number of policies sold for each line of non-life insurance to extrapolate the corresponding base-period output. However, this approach has conceptual and practical drawbacks. For example, the year-to-year change in the number of policies may be affected by changes in the marketing of policies which would be difficult to interpret as a change in the volume of non-life insurance

[55] Implicitly, this method assumes that premiums earned and premium supplements have the same real growth rates as adjusted claims.

services unless one has in mind only a concept of volume of non-life insurance service as the pure activity of the insurance corporations. The insurance service provided to policyholders does not rely on the number of policies, but on the amount of assets and revenue. Furthermore, unlike the deflation method, this method does not take into account the amount insured. To illustrate this, if two homeowner insurance policies are bundled together, but the amount of premium paid by the policyholder and premium supplements remain unchanged, the deflated method will result in no volume change, while the method based on the number of policies will wrongly decrease. Conversely, suppose a policyholder insures a cheap car in year one and then changes to an expensive car in year two. Assuming there are no changes in the prices of these cars and insurance premiums, the insurance premium of this policyholder is going to increase significantly in year two, as the amount insured is much bigger. Using the volume indicator method, the number of policies remains constant and, thus, the volume of non-life insurance services remains constant. With the deflation method, the volume of non-life insurance services consumed will increase, since the amount of car insurance has increased while its price has remained unchanged. This appears sound, as, for the customer, the volume output of insurance services rises with the real value of assets and income insured. Thus, there is a preference for using the deflation method to construct volume measures of non-life insurance output.[56]

3.237. It may also not be possible to use the volume indicator method to construct volume measures of imports of non-life insurance service charge owing to the difficulty in obtaining the required detailed data. Thus, volume measures of imports of the non-life insurance service charge will need to be produced using the deflation method. This would involve constructing a composite price index comprising the appropriate price indices from partner countries, which are adjusted for changes in exchange rates. The compiling agency can also consider constructing a composite volume index comprising the volume measures of exports or output of non-life insurance from partner countries. The composite volume index can then be used to extrapolate base-period imports of the non-life insurance service charge to obtain the corresponding volume measures. If data from partner countries are not available, the compiling agency may consider using the price indices which are used to deflate domestically produced current-price output of non-life insurance.

Worked example 3.15. Calculating volume measures of non-life insurance output

3.238. This worked example shows how to calculate chain-linked volume measures of non-life insurance using the deflation method. It is assumed that current-price output of non-life insurance is computed using the accounting approach. For simplicity, the chain-linked volume measures of non-life insurance are computed using the prices of the previous year, which means that the Laspeyres index number formula is used in the exercise.

3.239. Table 3.71 shows the input data from insurance corporations to compute current-price non-life insurance output using the accounting approach for five years. It is assumed that insurance corporations provide three classes of non-life insurance. The data for motor vehicle insurance for year *t* are the same as those in table 3.60.

3.240. Table 3.72 shows how to compute the current-price output of each line of non-life insurance using the accounting approach. The total current-price output of non-life insurance is obtained by summing up the corresponding output of each line of non-life insurance.

[56] A more detailed discussion of the advantages of the deflation method over the volume indicator method is available in Nordin (2006).

Table 3.71
Data from insurance corporations on non-life insurance transactions

Line number	Item	*t*	*t*+1	*t*+2	*t*+3	*t*+4
(1)	Earned premiums	2055.0	2226.0	2640.0	2910.0	3135.0
(1a)	Motor vehicle insurance	750.0	771.0	876.0	945.0	990.0
(1b)	Medical and health insurance	765.0	900.0	1134.0	1260.0	1380.0
(1c)	Home insurance	540.0	555.0	630.0	705.0	765.0
(2)	Unearned premiums	537.0	583.5	675.5	717.5	774.0
(2a)	Motor vehicle insurance	195.0	202.5	220.5	232.5	249.0
(2b)	Medical and health insurance	207.0	240.0	263.0	270.0	285.0
(2c)	Home insurance	135.0	141.0	192.0	215.0	240.0
(3)	Claims paid	560.0	612.0	612.0	633.0	616.0
(3a)	Motor vehicle insurance	195.0	222.0	200.0	210.0	198.0
(3b)	Medical and health insurance	210.0	230.0	245.0	255.0	260.0
(3c)	Home insurance	155.0	160.0	167.0	168.0	158.0
(4)	Changes in claims outstanding	447.0	450.0	450.0	465.0	487.0
(4a)	Motor vehicle insurance	166.0	155.0	152.0	160.0	167.0
(4b)	Medical and health insurance	170.0	180.0	186.0	187.0	200.0
(4c)	Home insurance	111.0	115.0	112.0	118.0	120.0
(5)	Changes in equalization provisions	567.0	521.6	525.2	494.3	488.9
(5a)	Motor vehicle insurance	180.0	163.6	178.2	165.5	172.7
(5b)	Medical and health insurance	167.0	154.3	148.8	141.6	132.5
(5c)	Home insurance	220.0	203.6	198.2	187.3	183.6
(6)	Investment income	173.0	179.3	174.6	173.9	179.9
(6a)	Motor vehicle insurance	63.0	65.3	63.6	63.3	65.6
(6b)	Medical and health insurance	65.0	67.4	65.6	65.3	67.5
(6c)	Home insurance	45.0	46.7	45.5	45.3	46.8

Table 3.72
Calculation of the current-price output of non-life insurance

Line number	Item	Description	*t*	*t*+1	*t*+2	*t*+3	*t*+4
(7)	Output of insurance corporations	(7a)+(7b)+(7c)	654.0	821.7	1227.4	1491.6	1723.0
(7a)	Motor vehicle insurance	(1a)+(6a)–(3a)–(4a)–(5a)	272.0	295.6	409.4	472.8	517.8
(7b)	Medical and health insurance	(1b)+(6b)–(3b)–(4b)–(5b)	283.0	403.1	619.7	741.7	855.0
(7c)	Home insurance	(1c)+(6c)–(3c)–(4c)–(5c)	99.0	123.0	198.3	277.0	350.2

Table 3.73
Price indices for constructing volume measures of non-life insurance output

Line number	Item	*t*+1	*t*+2	*t*+3	*t*+4
(8)	Price index for insurance premiums (year *t*–1 = 100.0)				
(8a)	Motor vehicle insurance	103.5	102.1	103.0	103.8
(8b)	Medical and health insurance	106.0	105.0	105.6	104.0
(8c)	Home insurance	104.0	103.2	104.8	105.4

3.241. Table 3.73 shows the price indices which are needed to construct volume measures of non-life insurance output. It is assumed that, for each line of non-life insurance, a price index is available for the corresponding premiums. The price indices are scaled so that the index value of the previous year is 100.0.

3.242. Table 3.74 shows how to compute unchained volume measures of non-life insurance output:

- For each year from year t+1, deflate the data on current-price premiums earned plus premium supplements by the price index for each line of non-life insurance to obtain the corresponding unchained volume measures at the prices of the previous year.
- Compute the growth rate of the unchained volume measures of premiums earned plus premium supplements for each line of non-life insurance. As indicated in the table, this growth rate represents the growth rate of the unchained volume measures of each line of non-life insurance.
- For each line of non-life insurance, use its growth rate to extrapolate its current-price output for the previous year to compute the corresponding unchained volume measure. Sum up the unchained volume measures to obtain the corresponding unchained volume measures of non-life insurance output at the prices of the previous year. Compute the growth rate of the unchained volume measures of total non-life insurance output.

3.243. Table 3.75 shows how to chain the unchained Laspeyres volume measures of non-life insurance output in table 3.74 so that they are expressed at the prices of a specific reference year. In this example, it is assumed that the reference year is year t. The annually chained Laspeyres volume measures of non-life insurance output and its three components are obtained by extrapolating their current-price output by their real growth rates, which were calculated in table 3.74. It is not necessary to calculate the annually chained Laspeyres volume measures of non-life insurance output for year t, since it is the reference year. In addition, except for years t and t+1, the annually chained

Table 3.74
Calculation of unchained Laspeyres volume measures of non-life insurance output at the prices of the previous year

Line number	Item	Description	t+1	t+2	t+3	t+4
(9)	Volume measures of earned premiums plus premium supplements					
(9a)	Motor vehicle insurance	[(1a)+(6a)]/(8a)	808.0	920.3	978.9	1016.9
(9b)	Medical and health insurance	[(1b)+(6b)]/(8b)	912.6	1142.5	1255.0	1391.9
(9c)	Home insurance	[(1c)+(6c)]/(8c)	578.5	654.5	715.9	770.2
(10)	Growth rate of volume measures of earned premiums plus premium supplements[a]					
(10a)	Motor vehicle insurance[a]	[(9a)_t]/[(1a)_t−1+(6a)_t−1]	0.994	1.100	1.042	1.009
(10b)	Medical and health insurance[a]	[(9b)_t]/[(1b)_t−1+(6b)_t−1]	1.100	1.181	1.046	1.050
(10c)	Home insurance[a]	[(9c)_t]/[(1c)_t−1+(6c)_t−1]	0.989	1.088	1.060	1.027
(11)	Volume measures of non-life insurance output	(11a)+(11b)+(11c)	679.4	935.2	1285.1	1540.2
(11a)	Motor vehicle insurance	[(7a)_t−1]×[(10a)_t]	270.3	325.3	426.6	476.9
(11b)	Medical and health insurance	[(7b)_t−1]×[(10b)_t]	311.2	476.1	648.4	779.0
(11c)	Home insurance	[(7c)_t−1]×[(10c)_t]	97.9	133.8	210.2	284.4
(12)	Growth rate of volume measure of non-life insurance output	[11_t]/[7_t−1]	1.039	1.138	1.047	1.033

[a] Represents the growth rate of unchained Laspeyres volume measures of non-life insurance output.

Table 3.75
Calculation of annually chained Laspeyres volumes measures of non-life insurance output (reference year= t)

Line number	Item	Description[a]	t	t+1	t+2	t+3	t+4
(13)	Non-life insurance output	[(13)_t−1]×[(12)_t]	654.0	679.4	773.2	809.5	835.9
(13a)	Motor vehicle insurance	[(13a)_t−1]×[(10a)_t]	272.0	270.3	297.5	309.9	312.6
(13b)	Medical and health insurance	[(13b)_t−1]×[(10b)_t]	283.0	311.2	367.5	384.5	403.8
(13c)	Home insurance	[(13c)_t−1]×[(10c)_t]	99.0	97.9	106.5	112.9	115.9

[a] Applies to data from year t+1.

Laspeyres volume measures of non-life insurance output are not additive. The loss of additivity is due to chaining.

(b) Standardized guarantee schemes[57]

References:
2008 SNA, Chapter 6, The production account
2008 SNA, Chapter 17, Cross-cutting and other special issues, Part 3, The treatment of standardized guarantees in the SNA

Types of guarantees

3.244. A loan guarantee is normally an arrangement whereby one party, the guarantor, undertakes to a lender that, if a borrower defaults, the guarantor will make good the loss the lender would otherwise suffer. Often, a fee is payable for the provision of a guarantee, though the form of this varies. Sometimes, the guarantor will acquire some rights over the defaulting borrower. Similar guarantees may be offered in respect of other financial instruments, including deposits. This section refers to similar guarantees of all financial instruments.

3.245. Guarantees have a significant impact on the behaviour of economic agents, both by influencing their decisions on production, income, investment or saving and by modifying the lending and borrowing conditions on financial markets. Some borrowers might have no access to loans or be willing to make deposits in the absence of guarantees, while others might not benefit from comparatively low interest rates. Guarantees are particularly significant for the general government sector and for the public sector, as government activities are often linked to the issuance or activation of guarantees.

3.246. Three classes of guarantees are recognized. No special treatment is proposed for guarantees in the form of manufacturers' warranties or other forms of guarantee. (The cost of replacing defective merchandise is an intermediate cost of the manufacturer.)

3.247. The first class of guarantees is composed of those guarantees provided by means of a financial derivative, such as a credit default swap. These derivatives are actively traded on financial markets. The derivative is based on the risk of default of a reference instrument and so is not actually linked to an individual loan or bond.

3.248. The second class of guarantees, standardized guarantees, is composed of the sorts of guarantees that are issued in large numbers, usually for fairly small amounts, along identical lines. There are three parties involved in these arrangements: the debtor, the creditor and the guarantor. Either the debtor or creditor may contract with the guarantor to repay the creditor if the debtor defaults. The classic examples are export credit guarantees and student loan guarantees. Government guarantees of other financial instruments, such as loans and some other debt securities, in return for a fee are other examples. Here, although it is not possible to establish the likelihood of any one debtor defaulting, it is not only possible but standard practice to estimate how many out of a batch of similar debts will default. If the guarantor is working on purely commercial lines, he will expect all the fees paid, plus the investment income earned on the fees and any reserves, to cover the expected defaults, along with the costs, and leave a profit. This is exactly the same paradigm as operates for non-life insurance and a similar treatment is adopted for these guarantees, described as "standardized guarantees". This involves including transactions and balance sheet items parallel to those for non-life insurance, including the generation of output and payments of a fee supplement and a service fee by those taking out the guarantees.

---

[57] This section discusses the output and related transactions for standardized guarantee schemes. Chapter 4 of the Handbook discusses standardized guarantee schemes as one of the categories of financial assets in the 2008 SNA.

3.249. The third class of guarantees, described as one-off guarantees, consists of those where the loan or the security is so particular that it is not possible for the degree of risk associated with the debt to be calculated with any degree of accuracy. In most cases, the granting of a one-off guarantee is considered a contingency and is not recorded as a financial asset/liability. (As an exception, one-off guarantees granted by governments to corporations in certain well-defined financially distressed situations and with a very high likelihood to be called are treated as if these guarantees are called when the financial distress is recognized.) If a fee is charged, this is recorded as a payment for a service at the time of payment. If a call is made under a guarantee, a capital transfer is recorded from the guarantor to the guarantee holder at the time of default or, in cases where the guarantor obtains an effective claim on the guarantee holder, a financial transaction (including increases in equity participation) is recorded.

3.250. Standardized guarantees are to be distinguished from one-off guarantees based on two criteria:

(a) They are characterized by often repeated transactions with similar features and pooling of risks;

(b) Guarantors are able to estimate the average loss based on available statistics by using a probability-weighted concept.

One-off guarantees are, on the contrary, individual, and guarantors are not able to make a reliable estimate of the risk of calls.

Transactions associated with standardized guarantee schemes

3.251. Standardized guarantees may be provided by a financial institution, including, but not confined to, insurance corporations. They may also be provided by government units. It is possible, but unlikely, that non-financial corporations may provide these sorts of guarantees; it is most unlikely that they would be provided by any unit to a non-resident unit. As indicated above, standardized guarantee schemes have much in common with non-life insurance. In the general case, similar recording is recommended, as described below.

3.252. When a unit offers standardized guarantees, it accepts fees and incurs liabilities to meet the call on the guarantee. The value of the liabilities in the accounts of the guarantor is equal to the present value of the expected calls under existing guarantees, net of any recoveries the guarantor expects to receive from the defaulting borrowers. The liability is entitled provisions for calls under standardized guarantees.

3.253. A guarantee may cover a multiyear period. A fee may be payable annually or upfront. In principle, the fee should represent charges earned in each year the guarantee holds with the liability decreasing as the period gets shorter, and so the same sort of recording should be followed here as for annuities with the fee paid earned as the future liability decreases. In practice, some units operating guarantees may have data only on a cash basis. This is inaccurate for an individual guarantee but the nature of the standardized guarantee scheme is that there are many guarantees of the same type, though not all for exactly the same time period, nor all starting and finishing on the same dates. Unless there is reason to suppose that there is a major change in the nature of the guarantee holders over time, using cash based data should not introduce significant error.

3.254. Altogether, six sets of transactions need to be recorded in respect of standardized guarantee schemes: two relating to the measurement of the production and consumption of the guarantee service, three relating to redistribution and one in the financial account. The value of the output of the activity, the investment income to be attributed to the guarantee holder (whether creditor or debtor) and the value of the service charge are calculated in the manner described above for non-life insurance, with the concepts of fees replacing premiums and calls under a standardized guarantee scheme replacing claims.

3.255. The production and consumption transactions are as follows:

(a) The output is recorded in the production account of the sector or subsector to which the guarantor belongs;

(b) The service may be paid for by either the borrower or the lender of the debt being guaranteed. When non-financial corporations, financial corporations, general government or non-profit institutions pay fees to obtain this sort of guarantee, the fees constitute intermediate consumption, recorded in their production account. Any fees for such guarantees payable by households are part of final consumption expenditure, recorded in the use of income accounts.

3.256. The redistributive transactions cover investment income attributed to guarantee holders in respect of standardized guarantee schemes, net fees, and calls under standardized guarantee schemes:

(a) Investment income attributed to guarantee holders in respect of standardized guarantee schemes is recorded as payable by the guarantor. It is recorded as receivable by the unit paying the fee. Both payables and receivables are recorded in the allocation of primary income account;

(b) Net fees are calculated as fees receivable plus fee supplements (equal to the investment income attributed to the unit paying the fee for the guarantee) less the value of the services consumed. These net fees are payable by all sectors of the economy and receivable by the sector of the guarantor;

(c) Calls under standardized guarantee schemes are payable by the guarantor and receivable by the lender of the debt under guarantee, regardless of whether the fee was paid by the lender or the borrower. Both net fees and calls are recorded in the secondary distribution of income account.

3.257. In the financial account, an entry shows the difference between payment of fees for new guarantees and calls made under existing guarantees.

3.258. The input data to compute the output of standardized schemes and other related transactions should be available from the central bank or a supervisory authority responsible for the financial sector. However, the compiling agency may not be able to obtain the breakdown of the input data by sector to compute these transactions. Thus, it will need to compute the total output of these schemes and other related transactions first before allocating them to the respective institutional sectors using indicators, such as fees.

Guarantees provided by government

3.259. Governments often offer guarantees for specific policy purposes. Export credit guarantees are one example. The guarantees may be issued by a government unit that can be treated as a separate institutional unit. When this is so, the normal rules for the allocation of government units to either publicly controlled corporations or as part of general government apply. If a guarantee unit charges fees that are economically significant (in this case this may be equivalent to saying that most of the calls plus the administrative costs are covered by the fees charged), then this is a market activity. It should be treated as a financial corporation and transactions should be recorded as described above. If the fees cover most but not all the costs, the recording is still as above. The loss made by the agency offering the guarantees may be covered by government on a regular or intermittent basis but this is not passed on to those seeking the guarantees as a subsidy. Regular payments are recorded as a subsidy to the agency and intermittent payments, covering cumulated losses, are recorded as capital transfers only when such payments are made.

3.260. In general, when a government unit provides standardized guarantees without fees or at such low rates that the fees are significantly less than the calls and administrative costs, the unit should be treated as a non-market producer within general government. The output of the scheme should be computed as the sum of costs. However, if government recognizes the probability of having to finance some of the calls under the guarantee scheme to the extent of including a provision in its accounts, a transfer of this size from government to the units concerned and a liability of this amount (under provisions for calls under standardized guarantees) should be recorded.

3.261. The input data to compute the output of standardized schemes and other related transactions should be available from the general government or public financial corporations. Again, if the compiling agency is unable to obtain the breakdown of the input data by sector to compute these transactions, it will need to compute the total output of these schemes and other related transactions first before allocating them to the respective institutional sectors using indicators, such as fees.

Volume measures of the output of standardized guarantee schemes

3.262. The output of standardized guarantee schemes which is computed from input data is measured at current prices. Volume measures of the output need to be computed by removing the effects of price changes. The method used to compute the volume measures will depend on the method used to compute the current-price output. For output which is computed as the sum of costs, the compiling agency can consider deflating this output by a composite index of input prices to obtain the volume measures. In the case of output being computed using the non-life insurance output formula, the volume measures can be estimated using the method used to compute volume measures of non-life insurance output.

(c) Life insurance and annuities

Life insurance

References:
2008 SNA, Chapter 6, The production account
2008 SNA, Chapter 17, Cross-cutting and other special issues, Part 1, The treatment of insurance
BPM6, Appendix 6c, Topical summary – Insurance, pension schemes, and standardized guarantees

3.263. Life insurance is an activity whereby a policyholder makes regular payments to an insurer in return for which the insurer guarantees to provide the policyholder (or, in some cases, another nominated person) with an agreed sum, or an annuity, at a given date or earlier if the policyholder dies beforehand. The agreed sum of money that the insurer guarantees to provide the policyholder is known as a benefit. A life insurance policy is a sort of saving scheme. For a number of years, the policyholder pays premiums to the insurance corporation against a promise of benefits at some future date. The benefits are paid to the policyholder or, in some cases, another nominated person. These benefits may be expressed in terms of a formula related to the premiums paid or may be dependent on the level of success the insurance corporation has in investing the funds. For the latter, the terms "with-profits" life insurance or endowment policy are generally used.[58] Although the date and sum may be variable, a claim is always paid in the case of a life policy.

3.264. A policy that provides a benefit in the case of death within a given period but in no other circumstances, usually called term insurance,[59] is regarded as non-life insurance because, as with other non-life insurance, a claim is payable only if a specified contingency occurs and not otherwise. In practice, because of the way in which insurance corporations keep their accounts, it may not always be possible to separate term insurance from other life insurance. In these circumstances, term insurance may have to be treated in the same way as life insurance for purely practical reasons. Box 3.3 summarizes the key similarities and differences between non-life and life insurance policies.

3.265. The insurance corporation cumulates premiums paid until the promised date when benefits become payable and, in the meantime, uses the reserves to produce investment income (interest and dividends). This income is recorded in the SNA as investment income attributable to policyholders. It is also possible that the insurance corporation may own properties, such as real estate, and generate a net operating surplus on these properties, which is also included in the investment income attributable to policyholders. Some of the investment income is added to the life insurance reserves belonging to the policyholders to meet benefits in future. This allocation is an asset of the policyholders, but is retained by the insurance corporation, which continues to invest

Box 3.3
Comparing non-life and life insurance

What life and non-life insurance have in common is that they both involve spreading risk. Insurers receive many (relatively) small regular payments of premiums from policyholders and pay much larger sums to claimants when the contingencies covered by the policy occur. For non-life insurance, the risks are spread over the whole population that takes out the insurance policies. For example, an insurance corporation determines the premiums charged for vehicle insurance in a year by relating them to the amount of claims it expects to pay on vehicle insurance in the same year. Typically, the number of claimants is much smaller than the number of policyholders. For an individual non-life policyholder, there is no relationship between the premiums paid and the claims received, even in the long run, but the insurance corporation establishes such a relationship for every line of non-life insurance on a yearly basis. For life insurance, a relationship between premiums and claims over time is important both to the policyholders and to the insurance corporation. For someone taking out a life policy, the benefits to be received are expected to be at least as great as the premiums paid up until the benefit is due and can be seen as a form of saving. The insurance corporation must combine this aspect of a single policy with the actuarial calculations about the insured population concerning life expectancy (including the risks of fatal accidents) when determining the relationship between the levels of premiums and benefits. Further, in the interval between the receipt of premiums and the payment of benefits, the insurance corporation earns income from investing the premiums received. This income also affects the levels of premiums and benefits set by the insurance corporations.

Despite the similarity of the activity of life and non-life insurance, there are significant differences between them that lead to different types of entries in the accounts of the SNA. Non-life insurance consists of redistribution in the current period between all policyholders and a few claimants. Life insurance mainly redistributes premiums paid over a period of time as benefits paid later to the same policyholder. Essentially, life insurance premiums and benefits are financial transactions and not current transactions.

[58] With-profit policies also include unit-linked life insurance policies, which are fund-linked products whereby policyholders can determine the type of investment by choosing a particular fund and thus carrying the investment risk. The claims in these policies vary according to the value of the chosen fund.

[59] This includes insurance policies which companies take out on the life of employees.

the amounts until benefits become payable. The remainder of the investment income not allocated to the policyholders is retained by the insurance corporation as its fee for the service it provides.

3.266. It is common with life insurance policies for amounts to be explicitly attributable by the insurance corporation to the policyholders in each year. These sums are often described as bonuses.[60] The sums involved are not actually paid to the policyholders, but the liabilities of the insurance corporation towards the policyholders increase by this amount. This amount is shown as investment income attributable to the policyholders. The fact that some of it may derive from holding gains does not change this designation; as far as the policyholders are concerned, it is the return for making the financial asset available to the insurance corporation. In addition, any excess of income from the investment of life reserves over any amounts explicitly attributable to the policyholders is shown as investment income attributable to policyholders, regardless of the source of the income. All investment income attributable to policyholders, whether explicitly by the insurance corporation or implicitly within the SNA, is shown as payable to the policyholders in the allocation of primary income account. In the case of life insurance, this amount is then recorded as premium supplements in the financial account. For direct life insurance, all policyholders are individuals and so the investment income is attributable to households (possibly including some non-resident households).

Measuring life insurance output and other related transactions

References:
2008 SNA, Chapter 6, The production account
2008 SNA, Chapter 17, Cross-cutting and other special issues, Part 1, The treatment of insurance
BPM6, Appendix 6c, Topical summary – Insurance, pension schemes, and standardized guarantees
BPM6 Compilation Guide, Appendix 2, Insurance transactions and positions, and pension schemes

3.267. The output of life insurance is derived as

Premiums earned
plus premium supplements (3.13)
minus benefits due
minus increases (*plus* decreases) in actuarial reserves and reserves for with-profits insurance.

3.268. The method for calculating output for life insurance follows the same general principles as for non-life insurance, but, because of the time interval between when premiums are received and when benefits are paid, special allowances must be made for changes in the technical reserves.

3.269. Premiums are defined in exactly the same way for life insurance as for non-life insurance.

3.270. Premium supplements are more significant for life insurance than for non-life insurance. They consist of all the investment income (including holding gains/losses) earned on the reserves of the policyholders. As mentioned earlier, this includes the bonuses declared by the insurance corporations to policyholders each year. The amount involved is earnings forgone by the policyholders by putting the funds at the disposal of

60 Bonuses are payable to holders of participating or "with-profits" policies. They are not payable to holders of non-participating or "without-profits" policies, such as unit-linked policies.

the insurance corporation and is thus recorded as property income in the distribution of primary income account.

3.271. Benefits are recorded as they are awarded or paid. There is no need under life insurance to derive an adjusted figure, since there is not the same unexpected volatility in the payment due under a life policy. It is possible for the insurance corporation to make robust estimates of the benefits due to be paid even years in advance. A policyholder who cancels a life insurance policy before the agreed expiration date is generally entitled to partial benefits from the insurer. Benefits are thus always paid to the policyholder or to the beneficiary. For these reasons, part of the premiums paid by the policyholders may be regarded as savings and part of the benefits received by the beneficiaries as withdrawals from savings. The recording, therefore, of net premiums (the savings portion) and payment of benefits takes place in the financial account rather than the distribution of secondary income account, as in the case of non-life insurance. Net premiums are derived by deducting the output of life insurance from the sum of actual premiums and premium supplements.

3.272. Actuarial reserves for life insurance and reserves for with-profits insurance represent the amounts set aside for the payment of benefits in the future. They are part of life insurance technical reserves, which also include unearned premiums and reserves against outstanding benefits. Life insurance technical reserves increase each year because of transactions including new premiums paid, new investment income allocated to the policyholders (but not withdrawn by them) and decrease because of transactions including benefits paid and payments due on policies that are surrendered before maturity. Life insurance technical reserves can also decrease owing to the forfeiture of life insurance policies. However, these flows are not considered as transactions and are thus recorded in the other changes in the volume of assets account.

3.273. The input data to calculate the output of life insurance using equation (3.13) can be obtained from the returns of insurers to the government agency responsible for the insurance sector, for example the insurance regulatory commission. If such information is not available, the compiling agency may need to conduct surveys to collect it. Typically, the financial statements of insurers should contain the input data needed to calculate the output of life insurance. If adequate data are not available for the calculation of life insurance according to this formula, an approach based on the sum of costs, similar to that described for non-life insurance, may be used. As for non-life insurance, an allowance for normal profits must be included.

3.274. The holder of a life insurance policy is always an individual, so life insurance transactions take place only between insurance corporations and households, resident and non-resident.[61] The output which is allocated to resident households is recorded as their final consumption expenditure, while the output which is allocated to non-residents is recorded as exports of goods and services. Very often, insurance corporations may not be able to provide the input data on the breakdown of each of the items (premium supplements, for example) to compute life insurance output by sector (i.e. resident households and the rest of the world). Rather, insurance corporations may only be able to provide the input data to enable the compiling agency to calculate total life

[61] Nevertheless, corporations in some countries can purchase life insurance policies, such as whole life policies, on the lives of their top executives to hedge against the financial cost of losing these key employees to unexpected death and the risk of recruiting and training replacements. This type of life insurance is known as corporate-owned life insurance. When the employer is a bank, the insurance is known as bank-owned life insurance. Since the corporations own the policies, they also pay the premiums. These policies can also be used for tax advantages if the death benefits that accrue to corporations are not subject to income tax. Since a significant component of the funding for the tax-free death benefits is accumulated property income on their premiums, buying life insurance on their key executives is a way for corporations to reap property income without having to pay any taxes on it. In the case of corporate-owned or bank-owned life insurance, transactions will take place between insurance corporations and corporations.

insurance output. In such instances, the compiling agency will need to make assumptions to allocate the input data using available data before computing total output and other related transactions. For example, it may be possible for the compiling agency to derive the breakdown of actual premiums payable by resident and non-resident households using the input data from insurance corporations. If insurance corporations are unable to provide a breakdown of the investment income attributable to policyholders (i.e. premium supplements), the compiling agency can allocate this item in proportion to the actual premiums payable by resident households and the rest of the world, after which the life insurance output which is allocated to resident households and the rest of the world is calculated directly. Total life insurance output can then be obtained as the sum of the sectoral output.

3.275. It is also possible for resident households to purchase life insurance from non-resident insurance corporations. In such instances, estimates of imports of the life insurance service charge, investment income attributable to policyholders, benefits due and net premiums can be obtained from balance of payments statistics. However, if balance of payments statistics do not report these data, the compiling agency may need to estimate these items using data from a combination of various sources, including ratios available from the domestic insurance sector, information from the ITRS (which captures information on the destinations of premiums paid by residents and sources of claims received by residents on a cash basis), partner country data or a survey that can be used to collect premiums paid and benefits paid from the domestic policyholder. If an economy has a life insurance sector, the compiling agency can apply the service charge to the premiums paid ratio derived from this sector to the premiums paid by residents to non-resident life insurers to obtain an estimate of the imported life insurance service charge. Appropriate ratios can also be applied to the premiums paid by residents to non-resident life insurers to obtain imported estimates of the investment income attributable to policyholders (premium supplements), benefits due and net premiums. On the other hand, if the economy does not have a life insurance sector, the compiling agency can consider contacting partner countries to obtain these ratios. Information on which countries to contact can be obtained from the ITRS. The estimation of life insurance transactions between resident households and non-resident life insurers will need to be done in consultation with the compilers of the balance of payments so as to ensure the consistent recording of these transactions in the national accounts and balance of payments.

Worked example 3.16. Computation of life insurance output and related transactions

3.276. This worked example computes the output of life insurance and other related transactions. The output of life insurance and other transactions are measured at current prices. In addition, the worked example will show how to record in the financial account the counterpart entries to show the means of payment for some of the transactions between the institutional units. For simplicity, it is assumed that these transactions are settled in currency or transferable deposits, which are part of "currency and deposits" in the financial account.[62]

3.277. The information obtained from life insurance corporations to compute life insurance output and other related transactions is presented in table 3.76. It is assumed that the compiling agency is able to obtain separate data on earned premiums, unearned premiums, benefits due and changes in life insurance technical reserves for resident households and the rest of the world. The item "investment income" refers to the investment income receivable by the insurance corporations from investing the life insurance reserves. For simplicity, it is assumed that the investment income is payable by other

[62] No worked example to calculate the output of life insurance using the sum of costs approach will be provided, since it is similar to the earlier worked example to compute the output of non-life insurance.

Table 3.76
Data from insurance corporations on life insurance transactions

Line number	Item	Value
(1)	Earned premiums	750.0
(1a)	Households	720.0
(1b)	Rest of the world	30.0
(2)	Unearned premiums	195.0
(2a)	Households	187.5
(2b)	Rest of the world	7.5
(3)	Benefits due	195.0
(3a)	Households	187.0
(3b)	Rest of the world	8.0
(4)	Increase in actuarial reserves	240.0
(4a)	Households	225.0
(4b)	Rest of the world	15.0
(5)	Investment income	63.0

resident sectors. In addition, it is assumed that the insurance corporations do not use the life insurance reserves to invest in property. Thus, the investment income represents all the property income receivable by the insurance corporations from investing the insurance reserves, and it is assumed that all the investment income attributable to policyholders comprises this property income. This income is returned to insurance corporations as premium supplements. Insurance corporations are unable to provide any breakdown for this item. Thus, the compiling agency will need to estimate the sectoral breakdown of the investment income attributable to policyholders using data on actual premiums before computing output and other related transactions.

3.278. Table 3.77 shows how to compute the actual premiums payable by each sector. The actual premiums payable by each sector are computed as the sum of the corresponding earned premiums and unearned premiums. The total actual premiums are computed as the sum of the corresponding data on earned premiums and unearned premiums.

3.279. Table 3.78 uses the data on actual premiums in table 3.77 to derive the percentage share of each sector in total actual premiums payable by each sector. The share of each sector in total actual premiums is obtained by dividing the actual premiums payable by each sector by the total actual premiums payable and then multiplying the result by 100.0. These data will be used to break down the investment income attributable to policyholders.

Table 3.77
Computation of actual premiums by sector

Line number	Item	Description	Value
(6)	Actual premiums	(1)+(2)	945.0
(6a)	Households	(1a)+(2a)	907.5
(6b)	Rest of the world	(1b)+(2b)	37.5

Table 3.78
Breakdown of actual premiums by sector (as a percentage)

Line number	Item	Description	Percentage
(7)	Actual premiums	(7a)+(7b)	100.0
(7a)	Households	[(6a)/6]×100.0	96.0
(7b)	Rest of the world	[(6b)/6]×100.0	4.0

3.280. Table 3.79 shows how to allocate the investment income attributable to policyholders to each sector before calculating the output of life insurance and net premiums. This item is allocated to each sector by multiplying the share of each sector in total actual premiums in table 3.78 by the total investment income attributable to policyholders (63.0 units) and then dividing the result by 100.0.

3.281. The output of life insurance which is allocated to each sector is then directly computed as follows:

Premiums earned
plus premium supplements
minus benefits due
minus the increase in life insurance actuarial reserves.

Net premiums allocated to each sector are directly computed as follows:

Actual premiums (i. e. the sum of earned and unearned premiums)
plus premium supplements
minus allocated output of life insurance.[63]

The national-level estimates of life insurance output and net premiums are obtained by summing up the corresponding items for each sector.

3.282. Table 3.80 shows how to calculate the changes in financial assets and liabilities arising from the transactions among insurance corporations and the other institutional units, as well as the means of payment for these transactions. In general,

Table 3.79
Calculation and allocation of investment income attributable to policyholders, life insurance output and net premiums

Line number	Item	Description	Value	2008 SNA code
(8)	Investment income attributable to policyholders	(5)	63.0	D4, D441
(8a)	Households	[(7a)/100.0]×(8)	60.5	D441
(8b)	Rest of the world	[(7b)/100.0]×(8)	2.5	D441
(9)	Output of insurance corporations (insurance service charge)	(9a)+(9b)	378.0	P1
(9a)	Households	(1a)+(8a)–(3a)–(4a)	368.5	P3
(9b)	Rest of the world	(1b)+(8b)–(3b)–(4b)	9.5	P6
(10)	Net premiums	(10a)+(10b)	630.0	
(10a)	Households	(1a)+(2a)+(8a)–(9a)	599.5	
(10b)	Rest of the world	(1b)+(2b)+(8b)–(9b)	30.5	

Table 3.80
Calculation of changes in financial assets and liabilities related to life insurance transactions

Line number	Item	Description	Value	2008 SNA code
	Changes in financial assets (currency and deposits)			
(11)	Insurance corporations	(1)+(2)+(5)–(3)	813.0	F2
(12)	Households	(3a)–(1a)–(2a)	-720.5	F2
(13)	Other sectors	-(5)	-63.0	F2
(14)	Rest of the world	(3b)–(1b)–(2b)	-29.5	F2
	Changes in financial assets (life insurance and annuity entitlements)			
(15)	Households	(10a)–(3a)	412.5	F62
(16)	Rest of the world	(10b)–(3b)	22.5	F62
	Changes in liabilities (life insurance and annuity entitlements)			
(17)	Insurance corporations	(10)–(3)	435.0	F62

[63] Net premiums are also equivalent to the sum of unearned premiums and the increase in actuarial reserves.

the changes in financial assets and liabilities are computed using the following principles: the changes in currency and deposits are the result of the premiums paid by policyholders and investment income paid by other resident units to the insurance corporations, and the benefits paid by the insurance corporations to policyholders. For insurance corporations, premiums and investment income receivable represent an increase in currency and deposits, while benefits paid represent a decrease. The converse applies to the counterpart institutional units. On the other hand, the changes in life insurance technical reserves are the result of changes in net premiums and benefits due. For insurance corporations, these changes represent changes in liabilities, while for the other institutional units they represent increases in financial assets. For example, insurance corporations have a net increase in assets of currency and deposits of 813.0 units during the accounting period. This is the result of:

- An increase in assets of currency and deposits arising from premiums received (945.0 units), which are made up of earned (750.0 units) and unearned premiums (195.0 units); and investment income receivable from other sectors (63.0 units)
- A decrease in assets of currency and deposits arising from benefits paid (195.0 units).

In addition, insurance corporations have a net increase in liabilities of technical reserves of 435.0 units. This is the result of an increase in net premiums (630.0 units), which is offset by benefits due (195.0 units).

3.283. Table 3.81 makes use of the information in the tables above to record the various transactions for life insurance. The transactions are described as follows:

(a) The output of life insurance is 378.0 units. This output is recorded in the production account for insurance corporations;

(b) The investment income receivable by the insurance corporations from investing the insurance technical reserves (63.0 units) is recorded as property income receivable in the allocation of primary income account. This income is payable by other sectors. The income is then recorded as investment income attributable to insurance policyholders in respect of life insurance and is recorded in the allocation of primary income account. Of these 63.0 units, 60.5 units are receivable by households and 2.5 units by the rest of the world;

(c) Of thc output of 378.0 units, 368.5 units are consumed by households as final consumers. This amount is recorded as their final consumption expenditure in the use of disposable income account. The remaining 9.5 units are recorded as exports of goods and services in the rest of the world account;

(d) Since there are no capital account transactions, net lending/net borrowing in the capital account is the same as gross saving and the current external balance in the use of disposable income account;

(e) The financial account records the changes in currency and deposits and in the life insurance and annuity entitlements of the institutional sectors. Insurance corporations have a net increase in liabilities of technical reserves (435.0 units). This amount is recorded in life insurance and annuity entitlements and is equal to net premiums (630.0 units) less benefits due (195.0 units). The net increase in liabilities is offset by the net increase in the corresponding financial assets of the other sectors. Insurance corporations also have a net increase in currency and deposits of 813.0 units, which is offset by the net decrease in the currency and deposits of the other institutional sectors. Since these entries are the counterparts to entries in the other accounts or only reflect the exchange in financial assets and liabilities, net lending/net borrowing is identical to net lending/net borrowing in the capi-

Table 3.81
Recording life insurance transactions

Uses									Resources							
Total	Goods and services	Rest of the world	Total economy	Other sectors	Households	Insurance corporations	2008 SNA code	Transactions and balancing items	Insurance corporations	Households	Other sectors	Total economy	Rest of the world	Goods and services	Total
Production account																
9.5		9.5					P6	Exports of goods and services						9.5	9.5
378.0	378.0						P1	Output	378.0			378.0			378.0
378.0			378.0			378.0	B1g	Value added, gross/Gross domestic product							
-9.5		-9.5					B11	External balance of goods and services							
Allocation of primary income account																
63.0			63.0	63.0			D4	Property income	63.0			63.0			63.0
63.0			63.0			63.0	D441	Investment income attributable to insurance policyholders		60.5		60.5	2.5		63.0
375.5			375.5	-63.0	60.5	378.0	B5g	Balance of primary income, gross/National income, gross							
Use of disposable income account																
368.5			368.5		368.5		P3	Final consumption expenditure						368.5	368.5
7.0			7.0	-63.0	-308.0	378.0	B8g	Saving, gross							
-7.0		-7.0					B12	Current external balance							
Changes in assets									**Changes in liabilities and net worth**							
Capital account																
0.0		-7.0	7.0	-63.0	-308.0	378.0	B9	Net lending (+)/net borrowing (-)							
Financial account																
							B9	Net lending (+)/net borrowing (-)	378.0	-308.0	-63.0	7.0	-7.0		0.0
0.0		-29.5	29.5	-63.0	-720.5	813.0	F2	Currency and deposits							
435.0		22.5	412.5		412.5		F62	Life insurance and annuity entitlements	435.0			435.0			435.0
630.0		30.5	599.5		599.5			Net premiums	630.0			630.0			630.0
-195.0		-8.0	-187.0		-187.0			Benefits due	-195.0			-195.0			-195.0

tal account, although, in practice, differences in data sources and the timing of the recording of transactions may result in a discrepancy between the estimates of net lending/net borrowing in these two accounts.

Volume measures of life insurance output

3.284. The worked example above computes life insurance output at current prices. As in the case of other economic variables, there is a need to compute volume measures of life insurance output by removing the effects of price changes. The ideal method is to deflate the current-price output of life insurance by a corresponding output price index to obtain the volume measure. However, like many other types of financial services, it is not possible to directly observe prices which represent the true nature of life insurance output. Thus, there is a need to resort to other methods.

3.285. As with non-life insurance, there are two methods to obtain volume measures of life insurance: the deflation method and the volume indicator method. As explained in the section on computing volume measures of non-life insurance, there are deficiencies in the volume indicator method. Thus, there is a preference for using the deflated premiums approach to construct volume measures of life insurance output.

3.286. It may also not be possible to use the volume indicator method to construct volume measures of imports of life insurance owing `to the difficulty in obtaining the required detailed data. Thus, volume measures of imports of life insurance will need to be produced using the deflation method. This would involve using a composite price index comprising appropriate price indices from partner countries which are adjusted for changes in exchange rates. Alternatively, the compiling agency can consider using a composite volume index comprising the volume measures of the output or exports of life insurance from partner countries to extrapolate the base-period imports of life insurance service charge to obtain the volume measures. If overseas data are not available, the compiling agency can consider using the price indices which are used to deflate the domestically produced current-price output of life insurance. Alternatively, it can consider producing volume measures of the imports of life insurance service charge by extrapolating the base-period value using the volume growth of domestically produced life insurance output.

Worked example 3.17. Computing volume measures of life insurance output

3.287. This worked example shows how to compute volume measures of life insurance output using the deflation method. The worked example assumes that life insurance is an elementary aggregate, so it is not necessary to chain the volume measures of its output.

3.288. Table 3.82 shows the data from insurance corporations to compute current-price life insurance output for five years. The table also presents the price index to deflate earned premiums and premium supplements (i.e. investment income attributable to policyholders). The price index value for year *t* is given a value of 100.0, as we assume that this period will be the base year of the volume estimates of life insurance. If a price index for insurance premiums is not available, an alternative index to consider could be the overall CPI. The output of life insurance at current prices is also computed.

3.289. Table 3.83 shows how to compute volume measures of life insurance output using the data in table 3.82. The steps are as follows:

- For each year, deflate the data on premiums earned plus premium supplements by the price index for life insurance premiums to obtain the corresponding volume measures.
- Compute the growth in the volume measures of premiums earned plus premium supplements.
- Use this growth to extrapolate the output of the life insurance from year *t* to compute its volume measures.

Table 3.82
Data on life insurance and the consumer price index

Line number	Item	Description	*t*	*t*+1	*t*+2	*t*+3	*t*+4
(1)	Earned premiums		750.0	771.0	810.0	864.0	900.0
(2)	Unearned premiums		195.0	203.0	212.0	226.0	243.0
(3)	Benefits due		195.0	222.0	200.0	210.0	198.0
(4)	Increase in actuarial reserves		240.0	262.0	146.0	85.0	117.0
(5)	Investment income		63.0	68.0	69.0	69.0	70.0
(6)	Output of life insurance at current prices	(1)+(5)−(3)−(4)	378.0	355.0	533.0	638.0	655.0
(7)	Price index for life insurance premiums (year *t*=100.0)		100.0	103.0	104.1	104.7	103.8

Table 3.83
Calculating volume measures of life insurance output

Line number	Item	Description	t	$t+1$	$t+2$	$t+3$	$t+4$
(8)	Volume measures of premiums plus premium supplements	[(1)+(5)]/(7)×100.0	813.0	814.6	844.4	891.5	934.5
(9)	Growth rate of premiums plus premium supplements[a]	[(8)_t]/[(8)_t−1]		1.002	1.037	1.056	1.048
(10)	Volume measures of life insurance output	[(10)_t−1]×[(9)_t][b]	378.0	378.7	392.6	414.5	434.5

[a] Represents the growth rate of volume measures of life insurance output.
[b] Applies to data from year $t+1$.

Annuities

Reference:
2008 SNA, Chapter 17, Cross-cutting and other special issues, Part 1, The treatment of insurance

3.290. An annuity is a contract between a policyholder (known as the annuitant) and an insurance corporation, which promises to pay the annuitant a certain amount of money, on a periodic basis, for a specified period. With the simplest form of annuity, the annuitant pays a single lump sum to the insurance corporation and, in return, receives a stream of payments either for a nominated period or for the rest of the annuitant's life (or possibly for the rest of the life of both the annuitant and a nominated other person). Depending on the timing of the payout, annuities can be classified as immediate annuities and deferred annuities. In an immediate annuity, an annuitant begins to receive payments immediately upon purchasing an annuity. In a deferred annuity, an annuitant typically receives payments starting at some future date, usually at retirement. Deferred annuities are purchased for their income tax advantages. In a deferred annuity, property income accumulates over a period of years before payments to the annuitant begin. The property income is not taxed until it is distributed to the annuitant. Delaying taxation allows a larger amount to accumulate than would have been possible if taxes were payable in the year the property income was received. Deferred annuities can also be inherited by the annuitant's survivors if the payout period has not yet begun when the annuitant dies or include a death benefit for the annuitant's survivors. In addition, immediate and deferred annuities can be split into fixed or variable annuities. In a fixed annuity, an annuitant receives a fixed payout at regular intervals. In a variable annuity, the annuitant is guaranteed a minimum income stream and an excess payment amount that fluctuates with the performance of the annuity's investments. Thus, the annuitant bears some of the investment risks of the annuity and receives some of the gains if the investments perform well.

3.291. Annuities are organized by insurance corporations and are a means of risk management. The annuitant avoids risk by agreeing to accept a known payment stream (known either in absolute terms or subject to a formula, such as being index-linked) in return for parting with a considerable sum. The insurance corporation takes the risk of making more from investing the sum than is due to the annuitant. The rates of annuities are determined taking life expectancy into account. The insurance corporation has to pay more than originally planned to long-lived annuitants, who may receive more than their original payment and the income earned on it. Those who die early receive less, possibly considerably less, and the insurance corporation receives more than expected.

Worked example 3.18. How does an annuity work?

3.292. This worked example explains the working of an annuity.

3.293. Suppose that, in year t, an insurance corporation offers an individual payments of 600.0 units a year for life in return for a lump sum payment of 10000.0 units. Suppose that each payment is made in the middle of the year, starting from year t. Furthermore, suppose that the insurance corporation expects the individual concerned to live for 25 years and that the discount rate being used is 5.0 per cent. The information is presented in table 3.84.

Table 3.84
Data on annuity

Line number	Item	Value
(1)	Purchase price of annuity	10000.0
(2)	Annual payment to annuitant	600.0
(3)	Life expectancy of annuitant (years)	25.0
(4)	Discount rate (percentage)	5.0

3.294. Table 3.85 shows how to compute the annual service charge (output) associated with the annuity, the investment income attributable to the annuitant and other transactions. The annualized service charge associated with the annuity is derived as follows:

- Since the annual payments to the annuitant are constant (600.0 units) and the annuitant is expected to live for 25 years, the series of payments represents a finite geometric progression, with the first payment in the middle of the first year. Thus, the net present value of the annual payments to the annuitant (*NFV*) can be computed using the formula for a finite geometric progression $FV\left[\frac{1-(1+i)^{-n}}{i}\right]$ which is corrected by a factor $\sqrt{1+i}$ as follows:

$$NFV = \left(\sqrt{1+i}\right)\left\{FV\left[\frac{1-(1+i)^{-n}}{i}\right]\right\} = \left(\sqrt{1+0.05}\right)(600.0)\left[\frac{1-(1+0.05)^{-25}}{0.05}\right] = 8665.2 \text{ units},$$

where

FV = annual payment

i = discount rate (in decimals)

n = number of years

- The net present value of the annual payments to the annuitant is only 8665.2 units. Since the purchase price of the annuity is 10000.0 units, this implies that the remaining 1334.8 units represent the net present value of the annual service charges the insurance corporation expects to receive.

- The net present value of the annual service charges (*NSC*) can be expressed as $\left(\sqrt{1+i}\right)\left\{ASC\left[\frac{1-(1+i)^{-n}}{i}\right]\right\}$, where *ASC* represents the annualized service charge. Combining this expression with the expression to derive the net present value of the annual payments ($NFV = \left(\sqrt{1+i}\right)\left\{FV\left[\frac{1-(1+i)^{-n}}{i}\right]\right\}$) implies that the net present value of the annual service charges can be simplified to $NSC = (ASC)\left(\frac{NFV}{FV}\right)$, which can be rearranged to $ASC = (FV)\left(\frac{NSC}{NFV}\right)$. Thus, the annualized service charge (*ASC*=92.4 units) is obtained by multiplying the annual payment to the annuitant (*FV*–600.0 units) by the net present value of the annual service charges (*NSC*=1334.8 units) and then dividing the result by the net present value of the annual payments to the annuitant (*NFV*= 8665.2 units). The annualized service charge is the output of the insurance corporation for administering the annuity.

Table 3.85

Calculation of the service charge (output) associated with annuity, investment income attributable to annuitant and other transactions assuming mid-year payments starting in year *t*

Line number	Item	Description	Value
(5)	Total net present value of annual payments of 600 for 25 years	sqrt(1+(4)/100.0)×(2)×{[1–(1+(4)/100.0)^–(3)]/[(4)/100.0]}	8665.2
(6)	Total net present value of annual service charges for 25 years	(1)–(5)	1334.8
(7)	Annualized service charges	(2)×(6)/(5)	92.4
	Year *t*		
(8)	Investment income in respect of:		
(8a)	Annuity	(1)×[(4)/100.0]	500.0
(8b)	Annual payment	(5)×[(4)/100.0]	433.3
(8c)	Annualized service charge	(6)×[(4)/100.0]	66.7
(9)	Payments due		
(9a)	Annuity	(2)+(7)	692.4
(9b)	Annual payment	(2)	600.0
(9c)	Annualized service charge	(7)	92.4
(10)	Change in value of stocks		
(10a)	Annuity	(8a)–(9a)	-192.4
(10b)	Annual payment	(8b)–(9b)	-166.7
(10c)	Annualized service charge	(8c)–(9c)	-25.7
(11)	End of year stocks		
(11a)	Annuity	(1)+(10a)	9807.6
(11b)	Annual payment	(5)+(10b)	8498.5
(11c)	Annualized service charge	(6)+(10c)	1309.1
	Year *t*+1		
(12)	Investment income in respect of:		
(12a)	Annuity	(11a)×[(4)/100.0]	490.4
(12b)	Annual payment	(11b)×[(4)/100.0]	424.9
(12c)	Annualized service charge	(11c)×[(4)/100.0]	65.5
(13)	Payments due		
(13a)	Annuity	(2)+(7)	692.4
(13b)	Annual payment	(2)	600.0
(13c)	Annualized service charge	(7)	92.4
(14)	Change in value of stocks		
(14a)	Annuity	(12a)–(13a)	-202.0
(14b)	Annual payment	(12b)–(13b)	-175.1
(14c)	Annualized service charge	(12c)–(13c)	-27.0
(15)	End of year stocks		
(15a)	Annuity	(11a)+(14a)	9605.5
(15b)	Annual payment	(11b)+(14b)	8323.4
(15c)	Annualized service charge	(11c)+(14c)	1282.1

3.295. Thus, whether the annuitant recognizes it or not, the insurance corporation's offer of 600 units a year is a net figure. The annuitant will actually be entitled to 692.4 units a year, but 92.4 units are retained by the insurance corporation as a fee for its services.

3.296. Each year, there is investment income payable to the annuitant equal to the unwinding of the discount factor of 5.0 per cent on the remaining amount held by the insurance corporation. In year *t*, the investment income amounts to 500.0 units, of which 66.7 units[64] are used to finance the annualized service charge. The remaining 25.7

[64] This amount is the investment income from "investing" the net present value of the total annual service charge at the discount rate of 5.0 per cent.

units of the service charge are met from a drawdown of the net present value of the annual service charges of 1334.8 units to 1309.1 units. The remaining investment income (433.3 units) adds to the value of the net annuity reserve of 8665.2 units. At the end of the first year, therefore, the net present value of annual payments is 8498.5 units; the original sum of 8665.2 units plus the interest of 433.3 units and less the payment of 600 units. The drawdown on the start of year amount of the net present value of annual payments is, thus, 166.7 units and the drawdown on the net present value of the annual service charges is 25.7 units. The drawdown on the total annuity reserves is, thus, 192.4 units.

3.297. This process continues year by year. As time progresses, the drawdown of the remaining reserves becomes an increasingly larger part of the payments due and the investment income payable a smaller part. In principle, every year the insurance corporation can review its assumptions about the remaining life expectancy of the annuitant and recalculate the amount available as a service charge. (In practice, this is likely to be done at intervals and by cohort of annuitants.)

3.298. The detailed numerical example is intended to demonstrate the way an annuity functions, but in fact it is not necessary to undertake all these calculations to determine the output of the insurance corporation. Based on the presentation in the preceding paragraphs, the value of output can be determined more simply as the total investment income due to the annuitant (500 units) less the amount payable to him (600 units) less the change in the value of the annuity reserves (a reduction of 192.4 units), or 92.4 units (500-600-(-192.4) units). This result can be seen to be parallel to the measurement of life insurance, except that there is no actual premium element.

Output associated with annuities

3.299. The worked example above shows the detailed steps to compute the output associated with one annuity. However, insurance corporations are very likely to sell multiple annuities in one accounting period. These annuities will also have different assumed lifespans for annuitants, as well as different initial and annual payments. Given this, it will be difficult for the compiling agency to compute the output associated with annuities using the method above. Instead, the output of an insurance corporation associated with administering annuities can be calculated as:

The investment income attributable to the annuitants
minus the amount payable to the annuitants (or surviving beneficiaries) under the terms of the annuity (3.14)
minus the change in the annuity reserves, but excluding the initial payments for new annuities.

3.300. The amount of the investment income attributable to the annuitants is equal to the discount factor times the start of year reserves and is independent of actual investment income earned by the insurance corporation. The item is parallel to the concept of premium supplement in the life insurance context.

3.301. The compiling agency will thus need to collect aggregated information on each of the items in the formula in equation (3.14) to compute the output associated with annuities.

3.302. When an annuity is initiated, there is a transfer of funds from the household to the insurance corporation. In many cases, however, this may simply be a "rollover" from a lump sum payable by that or another insurance corporation from the maturing of a normal life insurance policy immediately into an annuity. In such a case, there is no need to record the payment of the lump sum and the acquisition of the annuity; there will simply be a change from life insurance reserves to annuity reserves in the insurance corporation and pension fund subsector. If an annuity is purchased independently of the maturing of a life insurance policy, this is recorded as a pair of financial transactions between the household and the insurance corporation. The household makes a payment to the insurance corporation and receives in return an asset arising from the terms of the annuity. The insurance corporation receives a financial asset from the household and incurs a liability towards it.

3.303. Annuities are normally terminated by death, at which point any remaining reserves for that annuitant are transferred to the insurance corporation or inherited in the case of deferred annuities. However, assuming the insurance corporation has predicted life expectancy accurately, for the group of annuitants as a whole, the average funds remaining at death will be zero. If life expectancies change, revisions to the reserves must be made. For annuities in operation, an extension of life expectancies will reduce the amount available to the insurance corporation as a service charge, possibly making this negative. In such a case, the insurance corporation will have to draw on its own funds and hope to build these up again in future by associating higher service charges with new annuities.

3.304. As with life insurance, the holder of an annuity is always an individual, so transactions in annuities take place only between insurance corporations and households, resident and non-resident. The output which is allocated to resident households is recorded as their final consumption expenditure, while the output which is allocated to non-residents is recorded as exports of goods and services. Very often, insurance corporations may not be able to provide the input data on the breakdown of each of the items (premium supplements, for example) to compute the output associated with annuities by sector (i.e. resident households and the rest of the world). Rather, insurance corporations may only be able to provide the input data to enable the compiling agency to calculate total output. In such instances, the compiling agency will need to make assumptions to allocate the input data using available data before computing the total output and other related transactions. For example, it may be possible for insurance corporations to provide separate data on the initial payments made by resident households and the rest of the world. If insurance corporations are unable to provide a breakdown of the investment income attributable to annuitants, the compiling agency can allocate this item in proportion to the initial payments made by resident households and the rest of the world before the output associated with annuities which is allocated to each sector is directly calculated. The total output associated with annuities can then be obtained as the sum of the sectoral output.

3.305. It is also possible for resident households to purchase annuities from non-resident insurance corporations. In such instances, estimates of imports of the service charges, investment income attributable to annuitants, the amount payable to annuitants and changes in annuity reserves can be obtained from balance of payments statistics. If these data are not available from the balance of payments statistics, the compiling agency can consider using the methods to derive the transactions related to imported life insurance that were described earlier to estimate the data.

Worked example 3.19. Worked example to record transactions related to annuities

3.306. This worked example shows how to compute the current-price output associated with annuities and other related transactions using aggregated information from insurance corporations. In addition, the worked example will show how to record in the financial account the counterpart entries to show the means of payment for some of the transactions between the institutional units. For simplicity, it is assumed that these transactions are settled in currency or transferable deposits, which are part of "currency and deposits" in the financial account.

3.307. The information obtained from insurance corporations to compute the transactions related to annuities is presented in table 3.86. It is assumed that insurance corporations are able to provide data on change in annuity reserves excluding the initial payments for new annuities. If such data are not provided by insurance corporations, the compiling agency can derive the value by taking the difference between the change in annuity reserves and the initial payments for new annuities. It is assumed that all annuities are purchased by resident households, so it is not necessary to break down the data to show separate transactions between insurance corporations and resident households and the rest of the world. In addition, is it assumed that property income receivable by insurance corporations from investing the annuity reserves is payable by other resident sectors. This amount is different from the investment income attributable to annuitants as the latter is calculated actuarially.

3.308. Table 3.87 shows how to use the information in table 3.86 to compute the output associated with annuities, as well as changes in financial assets and liabilities. The output associated with annuities (462.1 units) is derived as follows:

Investment income attributable to annuitants (2480.8 units)

minus the amount payable to the annuitants (or surviving beneficiaries) under the terms of the annuity (3000.0 units)

minus the change in the annuity reserves, but excluding the initial payments for new annuities (-981.4 units).

Changes in currency and deposits are computed to reflect the actual initial payments for the new annuities and annual payments from the insurance corporations to the annuitants. As an example, consider the case of insurance corporations. They have a net increase in assets of currency and deposits of 29018.6 units. This is the result of the following:

Table 3.86
Data on annuities from insurance corporations

Line number	Item	Value	2008 SNA code
(1)	Initial payments for new annuities	30000.0	
(2)	Investment income attributable to annuitants	2480.8	D441
(3)	Property income receivable by insurance corporations	2587.2	D4
(4)	Annual payment to annuitants	3000.0	
(5)	Change in annuity reserves excluding initial payments for new annuities	-981.4	

Table 3.87
Calculation of output associated with annuities and changes in financial assets and liabilities

Line number	Item	Description	Value	2008 SNA code
(6)	Output associated with annuities	(2)–(4)–(5)	462.1	P1, P3
	Changes in financial assets (currency and deposits)			
(7)	Insurance corporations	(1)+(3)–(4)	29587.2	F2
(8)	Households	(4)–(1)	-27000.0	F2
(9)	Other sectors	–(3)	2587.2	F2
	Changes in financial assets (life insurance and annuity entitlements)			
(10)	Households	(1)+(5)	29018.6	F62
	Changes in liabilities (life insurance and annuity entitlements)			
(11)	Insurance corporations	(1)+(5)	29018.6	F62

- An increase arising from initial payments for new annuities (30000.0 units).
- An increase arising from property income receivable (2587.2 units).
- A decrease arising from the annual payment to annuitants (3000.0 units).

Changes in life insurance and annuity entitlements are computed to reflect the acquisition of financial assets (annuities) by households and the incurrence of liabilities by insurance corporations.

3.309. Table 3.88 shows how to record the entries in the tables above. The recording of the entries is similar to those for the worked example on life insurance.

Volume measures of the output associated with annuities

3.310. The worked example above computes the output associated with annuities at current prices. As in the case of other economic variables, there is a need to compute volume measures of this output by removing the effects of price changes. The ideal method is to deflate current-price output associated with annuities by a corresponding output price index to obtain the volume measure. However, like many other types of financial services, it is not possible to directly observe prices which represent the true nature of life insurance output. Thus, there is a need to resort to other methods.

Table 3.88
Recording transactions related to annuities

Uses													Resources
Total	Goods and services	Total economy	Other sectors	Households	Insurance corporations	2008 SNA code	Transactions and balancing items	Insurance corporations	Households	Other sectors	Total economy	Goods and services	Total
Production account													
462.1	462.1					P1	Output	462.1			462.1		462.1
462.1		462.1			462.1	B1g	Value added, gross/ Gross domestic product						
Allocation of primary income account													
2587.2		2587.2	2587.2			D4	Property income	2587.2			2587.2		2587.2
2480.8		2480.8			2480.8	D441	Investment income attributable to insurance policyholders		2480.8		2480.8		2480.8
462.1		462.1	-2587.2	2480.8	568.6	B5g	Balance of primary income, gross/National income, gross						
Use of disposable income account													
462.1		462.1		462.1		P3	Final consumption expenditure					462.1	462.1
0.0		0.0	-2587.2	2018.6	568.6	B8g	Saving, gross						
Changes in assets								**Changes in liabilities and net worth**					
Capital account													
0.0		0.0	-2587.2	2018.6	568.6	B9	Net lending (+)/net borrowing (-)						
Financial account													
						B9	Net lending (+)/net borrowing (-)	568.6	2018.6	-2587.2	0.0		0.0
0.0		0.0	-2587.2	-27000.0	29587.2	F2	Currency and deposits						
29018.6		29018.6		29018.6		F62	Life insurance and annuity entitlements	29018.6			29018.6		29018.6

3.311. As with other types of insurance, there are two methods to obtain volume measures of the output associated with annuities: the deflation method and the volume indicator method. As explained in the section on computing volume measures of non-life insurance, there are deficiencies in the volume indicator method. Thus, there is a preference for using the deflation method to construct volume measures of the output associated with annuities using appropriate price indices which capture the change in annuity premiums. However, unlike the case of non-life and life insurance, the formula to compute the output associated with annuities excludes the initial payments for new annuities. Thus, the price index for annuity premiums can only be used to deflate the investment income attributable to annuitants, after which the deflated values are used to extrapolate the current-price output in the base year.

3.312. It may also not be possible to use the volume indicator method to construct volume measures of imports of the service charge for annuities owing to the difficulty in obtaining the required detailed data. Thus, the compiling agency can consider producing volume measures of imports of the service charge for annuities using the methods to produce volume measures of imports of the service charge for life insurance that were described earlier.

(d) Reinsurance

References:
2008 SNA, Chapter 17, Cross-cutting and other special issues, Part 1, The treatment of insurance
BPM6, Appendix 6c, Topical summary – Insurance, pension schemes, and standardized guarantees

3.313. Just as an individual institutional unit may limit its exposure by taking out an insurance policy, so may insurance corporations themselves. Insurance between one insurance corporation and another is called reinsurance.[65] All insurance corporations may take out some form of reinsurance, but there tend to be a few large corporations that specialize in issuing reinsurance policies. Because these corporations are concentrated in a few financial centres, many of the flows associated with reinsurance involve transactions with the rest of the world. It is common for reinsurers to take out reinsurance policies with other insurance corporations to spread their risks further. This sort of reinsurance is called retrocession.

3.314. Reinsurance policies are most common for non-life policies, but may also apply to life insurance policies. There are two types of reinsurance: proportionate reinsurance and excess of loss reinsurance. Under a proportionate reinsurance contract, the reinsurer accepts an agreed proportion of the risks; this proportion of the premiums is “ceded” to the reinsurer, who then meets the same proportion of the claims. In this case, any reinsurance commission paid by the reinsurer to the policyholder (either a direct insurer or another reinsurer) is treated as a reduction in reinsurance premiums payable. The reinsurance commission is meant to defray the direct insurer’s operating costs.[66] In excess of loss reinsurance, the reinsurer undertakes to pay all losses over a given threshold. If there are no or few claims above the threshold, the reinsurer may pass a share of his profits to the direct insurer. By convention, profit-sharing is treated as a current transfer from the reinsurer to the direct insurer in a way similar to the payment of claims.

[65] On the other hand, insurance provided by insurance corporations to institutional units which are not insurance corporations is known as direct insurance.

[66] The reinsurance commission is usually expressed as a percentage of the written reinsurance premiums.

Measuring output of reinsurance and other transactions

References:

2008 SNA, Chapter 17, Cross-cutting and other special issues, Part 1, The treatment of insurance

BPM6 Compilation Guide, Appendix 2, Insurance transactions and positions, and pension schemes

3.315. The output of reinsurance is measured in a way similar to that for direct non-life insurance. However, there are some payments peculiar to reinsurance. These are commissions payable to the direct insurer under proportionate reinsurance and profit sharing in excess of loss reinsurance. Once these are taken into account, the output of reinsurance can be calculated as:

Premiums earned less commissions payable
plus premium supplements (3.15)
minus both adjusted claims incurred and profit sharing.

3.316. Premiums earned are defined in the same way as those for life and non-life insurance.

3.317. Adjusted claims incurred can be derived using the expectations or accounting approaches, as described in the section on non-life insurance. In addition, when using the expectations approach, the compiling agency will also need to derive expected premium supplements.

3.318. The direct policyholder does not know, or need to know, whether the direct insurance corporation involves a reinsurance corporation to protect it against loss on the policy. The direct insurance corporation receives actual premiums from its policyholders. Some of these are ceded to a reinsurance corporation. The premiums are shown as being first payable to the direct insurance corporation and then a lesser premium is payable to the reinsurance corporation. In other words, the transactions between the direct insurance and the reinsurance corporations are recorded as an entirely separate set of transactions and no consolidation takes place between the transactions of the direct insurance corporation as issuer of policies to its clients on the one hand and the holder of a policy with the reinsurance corporation on the other. This non-consolidation is known as gross recording on the part of the direct insurance corporation. The alternative (net recording) would be to show part of the direct policyholders' premiums being paid to the direct insurance corporation and part to the reinsurance corporation, but this option is not recommended either in commercial accounting or in the SNA.

3.319. The actual premium payable by the direct insurance corporation to the reinsurance corporation is used by the latter to earn investment income. This investment income is treated as investment income payable to the direct insurance corporation and returned to the reinsurance corporation as a premium supplement. Thus, a direct insurance corporation pays investment income to its policyholders based on the whole of the premiums earned (or, by approximation, payable), but also receives investment income from the reinsurance corporation corresponding to the amount of the premiums it has ceded to the reinsurance corporation. The investment income receivable by the direct insurance corporation from the reinsurer may be used to offset some of the investment income payable by the direct insurance corporation to its policyholders, but is not recorded explicitly as such. Figure 3.2 summarizes the flows between policyholders, direct insurance corporations and reinsurance corporations. The thicker arrows indicate that the flows between policyholders and direct insurance corporations include the corresponding amounts of flows between the direct insurance and reinsurance corporations. The dotted arrows indicate that flows from the direct insurance corporations to the poli-

Figure 3.2
Flows between policyholders, direct insurance corporations and reinsurance corporations

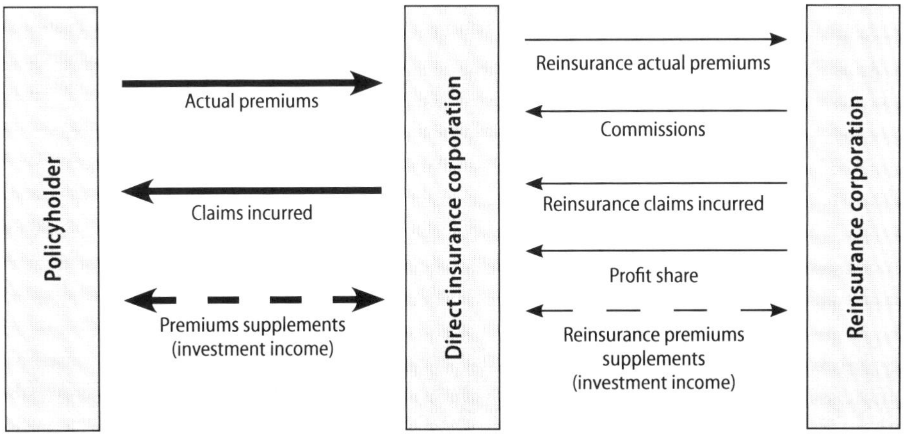

cyholders are returned to the former, and flows from the reinsurance corporations to the direct insurance corporations are returned to the former. It is common for ceding direct insurance corporations to retain a proportion of reinsurance premiums payable to the reinsurance corporation. The motivation is normally that this deposit should serve as a guarantee against the failure of the reinsurance corporation to meet its future liabilities. The reinsurance premiums payable by the ceding direct insurance corporations to the reinsurance corporation should also include these deposit guarantees, since these premiums are recorded on an accrual basis. In the financial account, these deposit guarantees are recorded as the liabilities (financial assets) of the direct insurance corporations (reinsurance corporation) in "loans".

3.320. Reinsurance is a major way for direct insurance corporations to deal with exceptional claims. In the case of catastrophes, a large part of the financing of the claims due by direct insurance corporations comes from reinsurance corporations. Some part of the reinsurance claims may be recorded as capital transfers rather than current transfers. However, because the primary motivation of reinsurance is to limit the direct insurance corporation's exposure to risk, a reinsurance corporation deals with exceptionally large claims as a matter of normal business. For this reason, and because the market for reinsurance is concentrated in relatively few large firms worldwide, it is less likely that the reinsurer will experience an unexpectedly larger loss than a direct insurance corporation does, especially in the case of excess of loss insurance.

3.321. The whole of the output of the reinsurance corporation represents the intermediate consumption of the direct insurance corporation holding the reinsurance policy. As mentioned before, many reinsurance policies are between insurance corporations resident in different economies. Thus, the value of the output in these cases represents imports by the insurance corporation taking out the reinsurance policy and exports by the reinsurance corporation.

3.322. Very often, reinsurance corporations may not be able to provide the input data which will enable the compiling agency to directly calculate the reinsurance output to be allocated to each user sector (i.e. resident direct insurance corporations and the rest of the world). For example, it may not be possible for reinsurance corporations to provide the sectoral breakdown of the investment income receivable by them from investing technical reserves. Thus, in a similar way to non-life insurance, the compiling agency can use the available source data to compute total reinsurance output. After that, it can use various assumptions to allocate the output to user sectors based on available data. For example, it may be possible for reinsurance corporations to provide separate data to allow the compiling agency to compute data on the actual premiums payable by resident direct insurance corporations and the rest of the world. This information can be used to allocate total reinsurance output and the investment income attributable to policyholders (i.e. premium supplements). Estimates of net reinsurance premiums payable by each sector are then directly computed. The sectoral estimates are then summed up to obtain the estimates receivable by the reinsurance corporations.

3.323. Estimates of imports of reinsurance services by resident direct insurance corporations together with other related transactions, such as investment income attributable to policyholders, claims incurred and net reinsurance premiums, can be obtained from balance of payments statistics. However, if the balance of payments statistics do not report these data, the compiling agency may need to estimate these items using a variety of techniques. First, the compiling agency can consider surveying the domestic recipient insurance corporations to obtain data on premiums payable, claims, reinsurance commissions and profits receivable by these corporations. Alternatively, these data may also be available with the agency responsible for supervising the insurance sector. However, the domestic recipient insurance corporations will not be able to provide data on the investment income attributable to them and the equalization provisions of the non-resident reinsurance corporations. The compiling agency will thus need to supplement the data from the domestic recipient insurance corporations by contacting partner countries to obtain data on the two remaining items. After that, appropriate ratios may need to be applied to these two missing items before the compiling agency can estimate the imports of reinsurance service charges, investment income attributable to policyholders, claims incurred and net reinsurance premiums. Second, the compiling agency can consider contacting partner countries to obtain all the input data. This task may be relatively more straightforward than obtaining partner country data on other types of insurance, given that reinsurance corporations are concentrated in a few countries. After that, appropriate ratios can be applied to the input data to obtain estimates of the import of reinsurance service charges, investment income attributable to policyholders, claims incurred and net reinsurance premiums. The compiling agency may need to consult the compilers of balance of payments when estimating the reinsurance transactions. This is to ensure that these transactions are recorded consistently in the national accounts and balance of payments.

3.324. Insurance corporations may set up affiliated reinsurance entities (usually to meet capital requirements) either locally or overseas and purchase reinsurance from these affiliates. As with transactions between multinational enterprises and their affiliates, these transactions may take place at prices which are not representative of market prices. This practice is known as transfer pricing and may distort the measurement of the value of domestically produced and imported reinsurance services. Compiling agencies which are aware of such a practice should consider replacing the transfer prices with market-value equivalents, especially when the distortions are large and when the availability of data (such as adjustments by tax officials or from partner economies) makes it feasible to do so. Nevertheless, the selection of the best market-value equivalents to replace book values is an exercise that calls for cautious and informed judgment. At the same time, when such adjustments are made, compiling agencies should also make corresponding adjustments in other accounts, such as the income and/or financial accounts. This is to ensure the consistent recording of these transactions in all the accounts. In many instances, however, the determination of values comparable to market values may be difficult, and compiling agencies may have no choice other than to accept valuations based on explicit costs incurred in production and any other values assigned by the enterprise.

3.325. The recording of transactions associated with reinsurance resembles the recording for non-life insurance, except that the policyholder of a reinsurance policy is always another insurance corporation.

Worked examples on how to record transactions in reinsurance

3.326. This section presents two worked examples to show how to compute current-price reinsurance output and other related transactions, as well as how to record these transactions. The worked examples assume that reinsurance corporations are unable to provide the compiling agency with the input data necessary to directly calculate the reinsurance output which is to be allocated to resident and non-resident policyholders (direct insurance corporations). Thus, the compiling agency will need to calculate the total reinsurance output first before using the available input data to allocate the output to these two user sectors. In both examples, we assume that the output of reinsurance is computed using the accounting approach. In both examples, all claims are recorded as current transfers, that is, we assume no catastrophic claims. In addition, the worked examples will show how to record in the financial account the counterpart entries to show the means of payment for some of the transactions between the institutional units. For simplicity, it is assumed that these transactions are settled in currency or transferable deposits, which are part of "currency and deposits" in the financial account.

3.327. Worked example 3.20 assumes proportionate reinsurance. It assumes that reinsurance corporations apply the same proportion of risks to be covered by them and the same commission rates to all their policyholders, so the compiling agency is able to calculate the amount of premiums ceded by direct insurance corporations to reinsurance corporations, reinsurance commissions payable by reinsurance corporations to direct insurance corporations and claims incurred by direct insurance corporations which are payable by reinsurance corporations. Worked example 3.21 assumes excess of loss reinsurance. In order to illustrate the concept of excess of loss reinsurance clearly, the worked example assumes that there is only one resident reinsurance corporation, resident direct insurance corporation and non-resident direct insurance corporation. It also assumes that all policyholders have the same proportional share of the profit of the reinsurance corporation, so the compiling agency is able to calculate the amount of profit which will be shared.

3.328. In practice, reinsurance corporations are likely to offer a combination of proportionate and excess of loss reinsurance. In addition, they may not apply the same risk and commission rates (in the case of proportionate reinsurance) or the same profit rates (in the case of excess of loss reinsurance) to all policyholders. An economy is also likely to comprise multiple insurance corporations. Thus, instead of the compiling agency itself directly calculating the amount of premiums ceded, claims incurred by direct insurance corporations which are covered by reinsurance corporations, reinsurance commissions and profits of reinsurance corporations which are payable to their policyholders, the agency can consider obtaining the aggregated data on these items from reinsurance corporations. Alternatively, these input data may be available from a supervisory agency responsible for overseeing the insurance sector.

Worked example 3.20. Computing reinsurance output using proportionate reinsurance

3.329. Table 3.89 shows the data for resident and non-resident direct insurance corporations which are needed to compute the premiums ceded to reinsurance corporations, their share of claims incurred and reinsurance commissions payable by reinsurance corporations.

3.330. Table 3.90 shows the input data from reinsurance corporations. Assume that the direct insurance corporations cover three quarters of the risk and the reinsurance corporations one quarter. The reinsurance corporations also pay a reinsurance commission amounting to 10.0 per cent of the gross reinsurance written premiums to help the direct insurance corporations defray their operating costs. As mentioned earlier, it may not be necessary for the compiling agency to directly calculate the risks ceded and reinsurance commissions, as such data should be available from reinsurance corporations. The investment income receivable by reinsurance corporations from investing the reserves of policyholders is assumed to be payable by other resident sectors. It is assumed that all the investment income attributable to policyholders comprises this property income. Reinsurance corporations are unable to provide any breakdown for the data on this investment income and the changes in equalization provisions. Thus, the compiling agency will need to calculate the total reinsurance out-

Table 3.89
Data from direct insurance corporations

Line number	Item	Value
(1)	Earned premiums	735.0
(1a)	Resident direct insurance corporations	685.0
(1b)	Non-resident direct insurance corporations	50.0
(2)	Unearned premiums	365.0
(2a)	Resident direct insurance corporations	330.0
(2b)	Non-resident direct insurance corporations	35.0
(3)	Claims paid	630.0
(3a)	Resident direct insurance corporations	530.0
(3b)	Non-resident direct insurance corporations	100.0
(4)	Changes in claims outstanding	514.0
(4a)	Resident direct insurance corporations	424.0
(4b)	Non-resident direct insurance corporations	90.0

Table 3.90
Data from reinsurance corporations

Line number	Item	Description	Value
(5)	Earned premiums	(5a)+(5b)	183.8
(5a)	Resident direct insurance corporations	0.25×(1a)	171.3
(5b)	Non-resident direct insurance corporations	0.25×(1b)	12.5
(6)	Unearned premiums	(6a)+(6b)	91.3
(6a)	Resident direct insurance corporations	0.25×(2a)	82.5
(6b)	Non-resident direct insurance corporations	0.25×(2b)	8.8
(7)	Claims paid	(7a)+(7b)	157.5
(7a)	Resident direct insurance corporations	0.25×(3a)	132.5
(7b)	Non-resident direct insurance corporations	0.25×(3b)	25.0
(8)	Changes in claims outstanding	(8a)+(8b)	128.5
(8a)	Resident direct insurance corporations	0.25×(4a)	106.0
(8b)	Non-resident direct insurance corporations	0.25×(4b)	22.5
(9)	Changes in equalization provisions		140.0
(10)	Investment income from insurance reserves		380.0
(11)	Reinsurance commissions	(11a)+(11b)	27.5
(11a)	Resident direct insurance corporations	0.1×[(5a)+(6a)]	25.4
(11b)	Non-resident direct insurance corporations	0.1×[(5b)+(6b)]	2.1

Table 3.91
Computation of actual premiums minus reinsurance commissions receivable by sector

Line number	Item	Description	Value
(12)	Actual premiums minus reinsurance commissions	(5)+(6)–(11)	247.5
(12a)	Resident direct insurance corporations	(5a)+(6a)–(11a)	228.4
(12b)	Non-resident direct insurance corporations	(5b)+(6b)–(11b)	19.1

put first before allocating this output to the user sectors using derived data on the actual premiums payable minus reinsurance commissions receivable by each user sector.

3.331. Table 3.91 shows how to compute the actual premiums payable minus reinsurance commissions receivable by each sector. The actual premiums payable by each sector are computed as the sum of the corresponding earned and unearned premiums. The total actual premiums payable minus reinsurance commissions receivable by all sectors is computed as the sum of the corresponding sectoral data.

3.332. Table 3.92 uses the data in table 3.91 to derive the percentage share of each sector in total actual premiums payable minus reinsurance commissions receivable. The share of each sector in total actual premiums payable minus reinsurance commissions receivable is obtained by dividing the actual premiums payable minus reinsurance commissions receivable by each sector by the total actual premiums payable minus reinsurance commissions receivable by all sectors and then multiplying the result by 100.0. These data will be used to break down the total reinsurance output and investment income attributable to policyholders.

3.333. Table 3.93 shows how to calculate the total output of reinsurance using the accounting approach and then allocate the total output to each sector. The table also shows how to allocate the investment income attributable to policyholders and how to compute the net reinsurance premiums payable by each sector. The total output (110.3 units) is allocated to each sector by multiplying the share of each sector in total actual premiums in table 3.92 by total output and then dividing the result by 100.0. The investment income attributable to policyholders (380.0 units) is also allocated to each sector using the same procedure. Net non-life insurance premiums payable by each sector are then directly calculated before the sectoral estimates are aggregated to compute the estimates receivable by the insurance corporations.

Table 3.92
Breakdown of actual premiums minus reinsurance commissions receivable by sector (as a percentage)

Line number	Item	Description	Percentage
(13)	Actual premiums minus reinsurance commissions	(13a)+(13b)	100.0
(13a)	Resident direct insurance corporations	[(12a)/(12)]×100.0	92.3
(13b)	Non-resident direct insurance corporations	[(12b)/(12)]×100.0	7.7

Table 3.93
Calculation and allocation of reinsurance output, investment income attributable to policyholders and net reinsurance premiums

Line number	Item	Description	Value	2008 SNA code
(14)	Claims incurred	(14a)+(14b)	286.0	D72, D722
(14a)	Resident direct insurance corporations	(7a)+(8a)	238.5	D72, D722
(14b)	Non-resident direct insurance corporations	(7b)+(8b)	47.5	D72, D722
(15)	Adjusted claims incurred	(14)+(9)	426.0	
(16)	Output of reinsurance (insurance service charge)	(5)–(11)+(10)–(15)	110.3	P1
(16a)	Resident direct insurance corporations	[(13a)/100.0]×(16)	101.7	P2
(16b)	Non-resident direct insurance corporations	[(13b)/100.0]×(16)	8.5	P6
(17)	Investment income attributable to policyholders	(17a)+(17b)	380.0	D4, D441
(17a)	Resident direct insurance corporations	[(13a)/100.0]×(17)	350.6	D441
(17b)	Non-resident direct insurance corporations	[(13b)/100.0]×(17)	29.4	D441
(18)	Net reinsurance premiums	(18a)+(18b)	426.0	D71, D712
(18a)	Resident direct insurance corporations	(5a)–(11a)+(17a)–(16a)	394.8	D71, D712
(18b)	Non-resident direct insurance corporations	(5b)–(11b)+(17b)–(16b)	31.2	D71, D712

Table 3.94
Calculation of changes in financial assets and liabilities related to proportionate reinsurance

Line number	Item	Description	Value	2008 SNA code
	Changes in financial assets (currency and deposits)			
(19)	Resident direct insurance corporations	(7a)–(5a)–(6a)+(11a)	-95.9	F2
(20)	Non-resident direct insurance corporations	(7b)–(5b)–(6b)+(11b)	5.9	F2
(21)	Reinsurance corporations	(5)+(6)+(10)–(11)–(7)	470.0	F2
(22)	Other sectors	–(10)	-380.0	F2
	Changes in financial assets (insurance technical reserves)			
(22)	Resident direct insurance corporations	(6a)+(8a)	188.5	F61
(23)	Non-resident direct insurance corporations	(6b)+(8b)	31.3	F61
	Changes in liabilities (insurance technical reserves)			
(24)	Reinsurance corporations	(6)+(8)	219.8	F61

3.334. Table 3.94 shows how to calculate the changes in the financial assets and liabilities of the institutional units. In general, the changes in financial assets and liabilities are computed using the following principles: the changes in currency and deposits are the result of the premiums and investment income paid by the other institutional units to the reinsurance corporations, and the claims and reinsurance commissions paid by the latter to the former. For reinsurance corporations, premiums and investment income receivable represent an increase in currency and deposits, while claims and reinsurance commissions paid represent a decrease. The converse applies to the counterpart institutional units. On the other hand, the changes in non-life insurance technical reserves are the result of unearned premiums and changes in reserves against outstanding claims. For reinsurance corporations, these items represent a change in liabilities, while for the other institutional units they represent a change in financial assets. For example, reinsurance corporations have a net increase in currency and deposits of 470.0 units during the accounting period. This is the result of the following:

- An increase in assets of currency and deposits arising from premiums received (275.1 units), which are made up of earned (183.8 units) and unearned premiums (91.3 units); and investment income receivable from other resident sectors (380.0 units).
- A decrease in assets of currency and deposits arising from claims paid (157.5 units) and reinsurance commissions paid (27.5 units).

In addition, reinsurance corporations have a net increase in liabilities of technical reserves of 219.8 units. This is the result of an increase in the following:

- Unearned premiums (91.3 units).
- Reserves in outstanding claims (128.5 units).

3.335. Table 3.95 records the transactions in the tables above. The recording of reinsurance resembles the recording for non-life insurance, except that the policyholder of a reinsurance policy is always another insurance corporation. To simplify the presentation and analysis, only the transactions between the reinsurance and direct insurance corporations are recorded. To ensure clarity, the transactions of reinsurance and resident direct insurance corporations are shown separately rather than combined to show the transactions of the financial corporations sector. The transactions with non-resident direct insurance corporations are recorded under the rest of the world. The transactions are described as follows:

Table 3.95

Recording transactions related to the proportionate reinsurance approach

Uses: Total	Goods and services	Rest of the world	Total economy	Other sectors	Reinsurance corporations	Resident direct insurance corporations	2008 SNA code	Transactions and balancing items	Resident direct insurance corporations	Reinsurance corporations	Other sectors	Total economy	Rest of the world	Goods and services	Resources: Total
Production account															
8.5		8.5					P6	Exports of goods and services						8.5	8.5
110.3	110.3						P1	Output		110.3		110.3			110.3
101.7			101.7			101.7	P2	Intermediate consumption						101.7	101.7
8.5			8.5		110.3	-101.7	B1g	Value added, gross/Gross domestic product							
-8.5		-8.5					B11	External balance of goods and services							
Allocation of primary income account															
380.0			380.0	380.0			D4	Property income		380.0		380.0			380.0
380.0			380.0		380.0		D441	Investment income attributable to insurance policyholders	350.6			350.6		29.4	380.0
-20.8			-20.8	-380.0	110.3	248.9	B5g	Balance of primary income, gross/National income, gross							
Secondary distribution of income account															
426.0		31.2	394.8			394.8	D71	Net non-life insurance premiums		426.0		426.0			426.0
426.0		31.2	394.8			394.8	D712	Net non-life reinsurance premiums		426.0		426.0			426.0
286.0		286.0			286.0		D72	Non-life insurance claims	238.5			238.5	47.5		286.0
286.0		286.0			286.0		D722	Non-life reinsurance claims	238.5			238.5	47.5		286.0
-37.1			-37.1	-380.0	250.3	92.6	B6g	Disposable income, gross							
Use of disposable income account															
							P3	Final consumption expenditure							
-37.1			-37.1	-380.0	250.3	92.6	B8g	Saving, gross							
37.1		37.1					B12	Current external balance							
Changes in assets															**Changes in liabilities and net worth**
Capital account															
0.0		37.1	-37.1	-380.0	250.3	92.6	B9	Net lending (+)/ net borrowing (-)							
Financial account															
							B9	Net lending (+)/ net borrowing (-)	92.6	250.3	-380.0	-37.1	37.1		0.0
0.0		5.9	-5.9	-380.0	470.0	-95.9	F2	Currency and deposits							
219.8		31.3	188.5			188.5	F61	Non-life insurance technical reserves		219.8		219.8			219.8
91.3		8.8	82.5			82.5		Unearned premiums		91.3		91.3			91.3
128.5		22.5	106.0			106.0		Changes in claims outstanding		128.5		128.5			128.5

(a) The output of reinsurance corporations is 110.3 units. This amount is recorded in the production account of reinsurance corporations. 101.7 units of the output are consumed by resident direct insurance corporations. This amount is recorded as their intermediate consumption in the production account. The other 8.5 units are recorded in exports of goods and services, since they are consumed by non-resident direct insurance corporations;

(b) Investment income receivable by the reinsurance corporations from investing the insurance reserves (380.0 units) is recorded as the property income receivable by them in the allocation of primary income account. This amount is payable by other sectors. The property income is, in turn, recorded as investment income attributable to policyholders (380.0 units). Of this amount, 350.6 units are receivable by resident direct insurance corporations and 29.4 units by the rest of the world. These entries are recorded in the allocation of primary income account;

(c) Both net reinsurance premiums and claims are recorded in the secondary distribution of income account. Net reinsurance premiums of 426.0 units are receivable by reinsurance corporations. Of this amount, 394.8 units are payable by resident direct reinsurance corporations and 31.2 units by the rest of the world. Reinsurance claims of 286.0 units are payable by reinsurance corporations. Of this amount, 238.5 units are receivable by resident direct insurance corporations and 47.5 units by the rest of the world;

(d) Since there are no capital account transactions, net lending/net borrowing in the capital account is the same as gross saving and the current external balance in the use of disposable income account;

(e) In the financial account, reinsurance corporations have a net increase of 219.8 units in their liabilities of insurance technical reserves. This is offset by the net increase in the corresponding assets of resident direct insurance corporations and the rest of the world. Reinsurance corporations also have a net increase of 470.0 units in their currency and deposits. This is offset by the net decrease in the corresponding assets of resident direct insurance corporations and the rest of the world. Since these entries are the counterparts to entries in the other accounts or only reflect the exchange in financial assets and liabilities, net lending/net borrowing is identical to net lending/net borrowing in the capital account.

Worked example 3.21. Computing reinsurance output using excess of loss reinsurance

3.336. Table 3.96 shows the claims data for the resident and non-resident direct insurance corporations, which are needed to determine the extent of their claims payable that will be covered by reinsurance. For each corporation, the claims incurred are computed as the sum of claims paid and the change in outstanding claims. The claims incurred for the resident direct insurance corporation amount to 954.0 units, while the claims incurred for the non-resident direct insurance corporation amount to 190.0 units.

Table 3.96
Data on claims from direct insurance corporations

Line number	Item	Description	Value
(1)	Claims paid	(1a)+(1b)	630.0
(1a)	Resident direct insurance corporation		530.0
(1b)	Non-resident direct insurance corporation		100.0
(2)	Changes in claims outstanding	(2a)+(2b)	514.0
(2a)	Resident direct insurance corporation		424.0
(2b)	Non-resident direct insurance corporation		90.0
(3)	Claims incurred	(3a)+(3b)	1144.0
(3a)	Resident direct insurance corporation	(1a)+(2a)	954.0
(3b)	Non-resident direct insurance corporation	(1b)+(2b)	190.0

3.337. Table 3.97 shows the data from the reinsurance corporation to compute reinsurance output and related transactions under the assumption of excess of loss reinsurance. Under the assumption of excess of loss reinsurance, the reinsurance corporation does not bear a predetermined proportion of the risk incurred by its policyholders and the reinsurance premiums are not a fixed proportion of the premiums of its policyholders. Assume that the reinsurance corporation agrees to pay for all the claims incurred by the resident and non-resident direct insurance corporations which are above 800.0 and 150.0 units respectively. Assume, too, that the reinsurance corporation will pass 15.0 per cent and 10.0 per cent of its profit to the resident and non-resident direct insurance corporations. Since the claims incurred by the resident direct insurance corporation amount to 954.0 units, the reinsurance corporation will cover 154.0 units of the claims. In addition, since the claims incurred by the non-resident direct insurance corporation amount to 190.0 units, the reinsurance corporation will cover 40.0 units of these claims. The amount covered by the reinsurance corporation is assumed to be split equally between claims paid and changes in reserves against outstanding claims. In addition, table 3.97 shows that the reinsurer reports a profit of 207.0 units. Thus, the profit share of the resident direct insurance corporation is 31.1 units, while that of the non-resident direct insurance corporation is 20.7 units. As mentioned earlier, in practice, it may not be necessary for the compiling agency to calculate the profit payable by reinsurance corporations to their policyholders, as such data are available from reinsurance corporations. The investment income receivable by reinsurance corporations from investing the reserves of policyholders is assumed to be payable by other resident sectors. It is assumed that all the investment income attributable to policyholders comprises this property income. The table shows that the reinsurance corporation is unable to provide any breakdown of this investment income and changes in equalization provisions. Thus, total reinsurance output will need to be computed first before it is allocated to the user sectors in proportion to derived data on actual premiums payable by them.

Table 3.97
Data from the reinsurance corporation

Line number	Item	Description	Value
(4)	Earned premiums	(4a)+(4b)	210.0
(4a)	Resident direct insurance corporation		150.0
(4b)	Non-resident direct insurance corporation		60.0
(5)	Unearned premiums	(5a)+(5b)	104.0
(5a)	Resident direct insurance corporation		84.0
(5b)	Non-resident direct insurance corporation		20.0
(6)	Claims paid	(6a)+(6b)	97.0
(6a)	Resident direct insurance corporation	[(3a)–800]/2	77.0
(6b)	Non-resident direct insurance corporation	[(3b)–150]/2	20.0
(7)	Changes in claims outstanding	(7a)+(7b)	97.0
(7a)	Resident direct insurance corporation	[(3a)–800]/2	77.0
(7b)	Non-resident direct insurance corporation	[(3b)–150]/2	20.0
(8)	Changes in equalization provisions		131.0
(9)	Investment income from insurance reserves		388.0
(10)	Profit		207.0
(11)	Profit share payable to policyholders	(11a)+(11b)	51.8
(11a)	Resident direct insurance corporation	0.15×(10)	31.1
(11b)	Non-resident direct insurance corporation	0.10×(10)	20.7

3.338. Table 3.98 shows how to compute the actual premiums payable by each sector. The steps to derive the data are similar to those in table 3.91, except that it is not necessary to adjust the data to remove reinsurance commissions.

Table 3.98
Computation of actual premiums by sector

Line number	Item	Description	Value
(12)	Actual premiums	(12a)+(12b)	314.0
(12a)	Resident direct insurance corporation	(4a)+(5a)	234.0
(12b)	Non-resident direct insurance corporation	(4b)+(5b)	80.0

3.339. Table 3.99 uses the data in table 3.98 to derive the percentage share of each sector in total actual premiums payable. The steps to derive the shares are similar to those in table 3.92. These data will be used to break down the total reinsurance output and investment income attributable to policyholders.

3.340. Table 3.100 shows how to calculate the claims incurred and profit payable to each user sector. For each user sector, claims incurred are obtained as the sum of claims paid and changes in outstanding claims before they are added to profit payable to obtain the required result. The sectoral estimates are then summed up to obtain the amount payable by the reinsurance corporation. In addition, the table also shows how to calculate the total output of reinsurance using the accounting approach and then allocate the total output to each sector. The table also shows how to allocate the investment income attributable to policyholders and how to compute the net reinsurance premiums payable by each sector. The steps to do this are similar to those in worked example 3.20.

Table 3.99
Breakdown of actual premiums by sector (as a percentage)

Line number	Item	Description	Percentage
(13)	Actual premiums	(14a)+(14b)	100.0
(13a)	Resident direct insurance corporation	[(13a)/(13)]×100.0	74.5
(13b)	Non-resident direct insurance corporation	[(13b)/(13)]×100.0	25.5

Table 3.100
Calculation and allocation of claims incurred plus profit share, reinsurance output, investment income attributable to policyholders and net reinsurance premiums

Line number	Item	Description	Value	2008 SNA code
(14)	Claims incurred	(15a)+(15b)	194.0	
(14a)	Resident direct insurance corporation	(6a)+(7a)	154.0	
(14b)	Non-resident direct insurance corporation	(6b)+(7b)	40.0	
(15)	Claims incurred and profit payable	(16a)+(16b)	245.8	D72, D722
(15a)	Resident direct insurance corporation	(6a)+(7a)+(12a)	185.1	D72, D722
(15b)	Non-resident direct insurance corporation	(6b)+(7b)+(12b)	60.7	D72, D722
(16)	Adjusted claims incurred	(8)+(15)	325.0	
(17)	Adjusted claims incurred and profit payable	(17)+(12)	376.8	
(18)	Output of reinsurance corporation (insurance service charge)	(4)+(9)–(18)	221.3	P1
(18a)	Resident direct insurance corporation	[(14a)/100.0]×(19)	164.9	P2
(18b)	Non-resident direct insurance corporation	[(14b)/100.0]×(19)	56.4	P6
(19)	Investment income attributable to policyholders	(9)	388.0	D4, D441
(19a)	Resident direct insurance corporation	[(14a)/100.0]×(20)	289.1	D441
(19b)	Non-resident direct insurance corporation	[(14b)/100.0]×(20)	98.9	D441
(20)	Net reinsurance premiums	(21a)+(21b)	376.8	D71, D712
(20a)	Resident direct insurance corporation	(4a)+(20a)–(19a)	274.3	D71, D712
(20b)	Non-resident direct insurance corporation	(4b)+(20b)–(19b)	102.5	D71, D712

Table 3.101
Calculation of changes in financial assets and liabilities related to excess of loss reinsurance

Line number	Item	Description	Value	2008 SNA code
	Changes in financial assets (currency and deposits)			
(21)	Resident direct insurance corporation	(6a)+(11a)–(4a)–(5a)	-126.0	F2
(22)	Non-resident direct insurance corporation	(6b)+(11b)–(4b)–(5b)	-39.3	F2
(23)	Reinsurance corporations	(4)+(5)–(6)+(9)–(11)	553.3	F2
(24)	Other sectors	–(9)	-388.0	F2
	Changes in financial assets (non-life insurance technical reserves)			
(25)	Resident direct insurance corporation	(5a)+(7a)	161.0	F61
(26)	Non-resident direct insurance corporation	(5b)+(7b)	40.0	F61
	Changes in liabilities (non-life insurance technical reserves)			
(27)	Reinsurance corporations	(5)+(7)	201.0	F61

3.341. Table 3.101 shows how to calculate the changes in financial assets and liabilities of the institutional units. In general, the computations are similar to those in table 3.94, except that additional entries are needed to record the transactions in currency and deposits arising from the profit payable by the reinsurance corporation to the direct insurance corporations and the purchases of goods and services for intermediate consumption by the reinsurance corporation for intermediate consumption by the reinsurance corporation from non-financial corporations.

3.342. Table 3.102 records the relevant transactions. The analysis is essentially the same as that for the worked example on proportionate reinsurance, except that reinsurance claims also include the profit share payable by the reinsurance corporation to the direct insurance corporations.

Volume measures of reinsurance output

3.343. The worked examples above compute reinsurance output at current prices. As in the case of other economic variables, there is a need to compute volume measures of this output by removing the effects of price changes. The ideal method is to deflate current-price output associated with reinsurance by a corresponding output price index to obtain the volume measure. However, like many other types of financial services, it is not possible to directly observe prices which represent the true nature of reinsurance output. Thus, there is a need to resort to other methods.

3.344. As with other types of insurance, there are two methods to obtain volume measures of reinsurance output: the deflation method and the volume indicator method. As explained in the section on computing volume measures of non-life insurance, there are deficiencies in the volume indicator method. Thus, there is a preference for using the deflation method to construct volume measures of reinsurance output. However, given that reinsurance activity may not be as prevalent in many economies as non-life or life insurance, it is quite likely that price indices for reinsurance premiums may not be available. In such instances, given the linkages between reinsurance and life and non-life reinsurance, the compiling agency can consider constructing a composite index based on the price indices for life and non-life insurance premiums using the output of these two types of insurance as weights.

3.345. It may also not be possible to use the volume indicator method to construct volume measures of imports of the service charge for reinsurance owing to the difficulty in obtaining the required detailed data. Thus, the compiling agency can consider producing volume measures of imports of the service charge for reinsurance using the methods to produce volume measures of imports of the service charge for other types of insurance which were described earlier.

Table 3.102

Recording transactions related to the excess of loss reinsurance approach

Uses															Resources
Total	Goods and services	Rest of the world	Total economy	Other sectors	Reinsurance corporations	Resident direct insurance corporations	2008 SNA code	Transactions and balancing items	Resident direct insurance corporations	Reinsurance corporations	Other sectors	Total economy	Rest of the world	Goods and services	Total
Production account															
56.4		56.4					P6	Exports of goods and services						56.4	56.4
221.3	221.3						P1	Output		221.3		221.3			221.3
164.9			164.9			164.9	P2	Intermediate consumption						164.9	164.9
56.4			56.4		221.3	-164.9	B1g	Value added, gross/Gross domestic product							
-56.4		-56.4					B11	External balance of goods and services							
Allocation of primary income account															
388.0			388.0	388.0			D4	Property income		388.0		388.0			388.0
388.0			388.0		388.0		D441	Investment income attributable to insurance policyholders	289.1			289.1	98.9		388.0
-42.5			-42.5	-388.0	221.3	124.3	B5g	Balance of primary income, gross/National income, gross							
Secondary distribution of income account															
376.8		102.5	274.3			274.3	D71	Net non-life insurance premiums		376.8		376.8			376.8
376.8		102.5	274.3			274.3	D712	Net non-life reinsurance premiums		376.8		376.8			376.8
245.8		245.8			245.8		D72	Non-life insurance claims	185.1			185.1	60.7		245.8
245.8		245.8			245.8		D722	Non-life reinsurance claims	185.1			185.1	60.7		245.8
-0.7			-0.7	-388.0	352.3	35.1	B6g	Disposable income, gross							
Use of disposable income account															
-0.7			-0.7	-388.0	352.3	35.1	B8g	Saving, gross							
0.7		0.7					B12	Current external balance							
Changes in assets															**Changes in liabilities and net worth**
Capital account															
0.0		0.7	-0.7	-388.0	352.3	35.1	B9	Net lending (+)/net borrowing (-)							
Financial account															
							B9	Net lending (+)/net borrowing (-)	35.1	352.3	-388.0	-0.7	0.7		0.0
0.0		-39.3	39.3	-388.0	553.3	-126.0	F2	Currency and deposits							
201.0		40.0	161.0			161.0	F61	Non-life insurance technical reserves		201.0		201.0			201.0
104.0		20.0	84.0			84.0		Unearned premiums		104.0		104.0			104.0
97.0		20.0	77.0			77.0		Changes in claims outstanding		97.0		97.0			97.0

(e) Social insurance schemes

References:
2008 SNA, Chapter 8, The redistribution of income account
2008 SNA, Chapter 17, Cross-cutting and other special issues, Part 2, Social insurance schemes

3.346. A social insurance scheme is a form of contractual insurance scheme where the policyholder is obliged or encouraged to insure against certain contingencies by the intervention of a third party. For example, government may oblige all employees to participate in a social security scheme; employers may make it a condition of employment that employees participate in an insurance scheme specified by the employer; an employer may encourage employees to join a scheme by making contributions on behalf of the employee; or a trades union may arrange advantageous insurance cover available only to the members of the trades union. Contributions to social insurance schemes are usually paid by, or on behalf of, employees, though under certain conditions non-employed or self-employed persons may also be covered.

3.347. A social insurance scheme is an insurance scheme where the following two conditions are satisfied:

(a) The benefits received are conditional on participation in the scheme and constitute social benefits as this term is used in the SNA;

(b) At least one of the three conditions following is met:

  (i) Participation in the scheme is obligatory, either by law or under the terms and conditions of employment of an employee, or group of employees;

  (ii) The scheme is a collective one operated for the benefit of a designated group of workers, whether employed or non-employed, participation being restricted to members of that group;

  (iii) An employer makes a contribution (actual or imputed) to the scheme on behalf of an employee, whether or not the employee also makes a contribution.

3.348. Those participating in social insurance schemes make contributions to the schemes (or have contributions made on their behalf) and receive benefits. Contributions and benefits are defined in similar ways to insurance premiums and claims. A social insurance contribution is the amount payable to a social insurance scheme in order for a designated beneficiary to be entitled to receive the social benefits covered by the scheme. A social insurance benefit is a social benefit payable because the beneficiary participates in a social insurance scheme and the social risk insured against has occurred.

Breakdown of social insurance schemes

3.349. Social insurance schemes in the 2008 SNA can be broken down into various attributes, such as type of scheme, institutional sector allocation, type of benefit, autonomy and funding.

3.350. Two main types of social insurance schemes and the respective sectors operating the schemes may be distinguished:

(a) The first consists of social security schemes covering the entire community, or large sections of the community, that are imposed, controlled and financed by government units. Pensions payable under these schemes may or may not be related to levels of salary of the beneficiary or history of employment. Non-pension benefits are less frequently linked to salary levels.

The relative importance of social security relative to other social insurance schemes varies considerably from one country to another depending on institutional arrangements. In some countries, social security may be restricted to basic pension provision of the social safety net variety. In such cases, even the pension provision of general government employees may be dealt with other than via social security. At the other extreme, almost all pension provision, including that accruing to employees in private enterprises, may be routed through social security;

(b) The second type consists of employment-related social insurance schemes other than social security. These schemes derive from an employer-employee relationship in the provision of pension entitlement that is part of the conditions of employment and where responsibility for the provision of benefits does not devolve to general government under social security provisions. These schemes can be operated by the general government for its employees or by employers in the non-government sectors. In addition, it is also possible for an insurance corporation to manage these schemes on the behalf of employers.

3.351. The benefits of social insurance schemes are split between pensions and non-pensions. Accordingly, social insurance contributions are also split into those for pensions and those for non-pensions. The most important pension benefit covered by social insurance schemes is income in retirement, but a number of other contingencies may be covered also. For example, pensions may be payable to widows and widowers or to people who suffer an industrial injury and are no longer able to work. All of these sorts of contingencies that give rise to payments because the main income earner is no longer able, through death or incapacity, to provide an income for himself or herself and dependants are treated as pensions. All other benefits are grouped together as non-pension benefits. These cover, for example, payments due in respect of sickness, unemployment, housing, education or family circumstances. The distinction between the two is important because the SNA recognizes liabilities for some pensions whether there are actually assets set aside to meet the entitlements or not, but recognizes reserves for non-pension benefits only when these actually exist.

3.352. Employment-related social insurance pension schemes other than social security can also be split into defined contribution pension schemes and defined benefit pension schemes. A defined contribution pension scheme (sometimes referred to as a money purchase scheme) is one where the benefits payable to an employee on retirement are defined exclusively in terms of the level of the fund built up from the contributions made over the employee's working life and the increases in value that result from the investment of these funds by the manager of the scheme. The entire risk of the scheme to provide an adequate income in retirement is thus borne by the employee. By definition, the net worth of a pension fund in a defined contribution scheme is always zero, since the value of its liabilities is equal to the value of its assets. A defined benefit scheme is one where the benefits payable to an employee on retirement are determined by the use of a formula, either alone or as a minimum amount payable. In this case, the risk of the scheme to provide an adequate income in retirement is borne either by the employer or is shared between the employer and employee. In certain cases, the employer's risk may be borne by the multiemployer scheme that operates the defined benefit pension scheme on behalf of the employer. A scheme that may be defined in terms similar to a defined contribution scheme but with a guaranteed minimum, say, or other such hybrid schemes, are grouped with defined benefit pension schemes in the SNA.

3.353. Social insurance schemes can also be classified in terms of their degree of autonomy. Autonomous social insurance schemes are those schemes with funds which operate as separate and independent institutional units from the units (such as corporations) that create them. They are set up to provide benefits on retirement for specific groups of employees and have their own assets and liabilities. They also make their own transactions in financial assets in the market. These funds are organized and directed by individual private or government employers, or jointly by individual employers and their employees. The employers and/or employees make regular contributions to these funds. Such funds are also known as pension funds (which are allocated to the financial corporations sector) or social security funds if they are operated by government (which are allocated to the general government sector).[67] In contrast, non-autonomous pension funds refer to the pension arrangements for the employees of government or private sector entities which do not include a separately organized fund. They also include arrangements organized by a non-government employer in which the reserves of the fund are simply added to that employer's own reserves or invested in securities issued by that employer. These funds are allocated to the sector of the employer.

3.354. Social insurance schemes are also classified in terms of whether they are funded or unfunded. A funded scheme is one where identifiable reserves have been accumulated to meet the obligation to pay future benefits accrued to the present. An unfunded scheme is one where there are no identifiable reserves assigned for the payment of benefits. In such cases, benefits are paid from the receipts of contributions with any surplus or deficit going into, or being drawn from, the scheme manager's other resources. Funded social insurance schemes can be autonomous or non-autonomous, while unfunded social insurance schemes are non-autonomous. Defined contribution pension schemes are, by definition, funded, while defined benefit pension schemes can be funded or unfunded.

Individual insurance policies qualifying as social insurance

3.355. Some social insurance schemes may permit, or even require, participants to take out policies in their own names. In order for an individual policy to be treated as part of a social insurance scheme, the benefits payable to the participants must be of the social benefit type and, in addition, one or more of the conditions in paragraph 3.347 (b) b must be satisfied.

3.356. The premiums payable and claims receivable under individual policies taken out under a social insurance scheme are recorded as social contributions and social insurance benefits. Contributions to social insurance schemes are frequently paid on a monthly or even more frequent basis as they are often made directly when wages and salaries are payable.

3.357. Most individual policies that qualify as social insurance schemes are likely to be for pension provision, but it is possible that they may cover other eventualities, for example to provide income if the policyholder is unable to work for a prolonged period because of ill health.

Overview of social benefits

References:
2008 SNA, Chapter 8, The redistribution of income account
2008 SNA, Chapter 17, Cross-cutting and other special issues, Part 2, Social insurance schemes

3.358. Social insurance schemes are an important way in which individuals who participate in the scheme are paid benefits, described as social benefits, when certain

[67] As explained in Dippelsman (2009), the term "pension scheme" should be contrasted with "pension fund". A pension scheme is a set of rules and arrangements for paying pensions, while a pension fund is a designated pool of assets that is used to pay benefits.

conditions exist that would adversely affect their welfare. Some social benefits, however, are payable independently of participation in a social insurance scheme. It is the conditions under which the benefits are payable that identify a social insurance scheme, not the nature of the benefits in themselves. This section provides an overview of social benefits, while an overview of social contributions is provided in the next section.

3.359. Social benefits are current transfers received by households intended to provide for the needs that arise from certain events or circumstances, for example, sickness, unemployment, retirement, housing, education or family circumstances.

3.360. Social benefits become payable when certain events occur, or certain conditions exist, that may adversely affect the welfare of the households concerned, either by imposing additional demands on their resources or reducing their incomes. Social benefits may be provided in cash or in kind. There are a number of circumstances in which social benefits may be payable:

(a) The beneficiaries, or their dependants, require medical, dental or other treatment, or hospital, convalescent or long-term care, as a result of sickness, injuries, maternity, chronic invalidity, old age, etc. The social benefits may be provided in kind in the form of treatments or care provided free or at prices that are not economically significant, or by reimbursing expenditures made by households. Social benefits in cash may also be payable to beneficiaries needing health care;

(b) The beneficiaries have to support dependants of various kinds: spouses, children, elderly relatives, invalids, etc. The social benefits are usually paid in cash in the form of regular dependants' or family allowances;

(c) The beneficiaries suffer a reduction in income as a result of not being able to work, or to work full-time. The social benefits are usually paid in cash regularly for the duration of the condition. In some instances, a lump sum may be provided additionally or instead of the regular payment. People may be prevented from working because of:

  (i) Voluntary or compulsory retirement;

  (ii) Involuntary unemployment, including temporary lay-offs and short-time working;

  (iii) Sickness, accidental injury, the birth of a child, etc., that prevents a person from working, or working full time;

(d) The beneficiaries receive payments to compensate for suffering a reduction in income because of the death of the main income earner;

(e) The beneficiaries are provided with housing, either free or at prices that are not economically significant or by reimbursing expenditure made by households. These are social benefits in kind;

(f) The beneficiaries are provided with allowances to cover education expenses incurred on behalf of themselves or their dependants. Occasionally, education services may be provided in kind.

3.361. The circumstances above are typical of those in which social benefits are payable. However, the list is illustrative rather than exhaustive. It is possible, for example, that under some social insurance schemes other benefits may be payable. Conversely, by no means do all schemes provide benefits in all the circumstances listed above. In practice, the scope of social insurance schemes is liable to vary significantly from country to country, or from scheme to scheme within the same country.

3.362. Social benefits may be provided under social insurance schemes or by social assistance. Social benefits provided under both arrangements may be split into pension and non-pension benefits. Pension benefits are always paid in cash, while non-pension benefits may be payable in cash or in kind. Social insurance benefits may be provided by the general government, by employers to the employees and their dependents or by other units such as a trades union under a social insurance scheme. The benefits received are conditional on participation in the social insurance scheme. Social insurance benefits provided by social security schemes may comprise pensions and/or non-pensions in cash. Social insurance benefits payable by employment-related schemes other than social security may comprise pensions and non-pensions in cash and in kind.[68]

3.363. In contrast, social assistance benefits in cash or in kind which are payable by the general government or NPISHs to households are not considered as social insurance benefits because social assistance is not a scheme and does not require participation, as demonstrated by the payment of social contributions. Social assistance is frequently restricted to individuals with low incomes, disabilities or other particular characteristics. Usually, all members of resident households are entitled to apply for social assistance, but the conditions under which it is granted are often restrictive. Frequently, there is an assessment of available income in relation to the perceived needs of a household, and only those households falling below a given threshold may be entitled to this type of social assistance. (This process is often described as "means testing".) In some countries, though, a universal pension may be paid without any need for participation, in which case it is part of social assistance also.

3.364. Social benefits paid in cash allow households to use this cash indistinguishably from income coming from other sources. When social benefits are payable in kind, the household has no discretion over the use of the benefit; the benefits simply relieve the household from having to meet these expenses out of income from other sources. However, governments and NPISHs all over the world take on responsibility to provide households with services they can make use of but not trade for other services or exchange them with other households. These are the individual services provided by government and NPISHs to households, either free or at prices that are not economically significant. These benefits are described as social transfers in kind. Examples include health and education services. Social transfers in kind consist of social security benefits payable in kind and social assistance benefits payable in kind.

Overview of social contributions

References:
2008 SNA, Chapter 7, The distribution of income account
2008 SNA, Chapter 8, The redistribution of income account

3.365. Social contributions are actual or imputed payments to social insurance schemes to make provision for social insurance benefits to be paid. Social contributions may be made by employers on behalf of their employees. As such, they form part of compensation of employees and are included in the balance of primary income of households. In the secondary distribution of income account, these contributions, together with payments made by households themselves in their capacity as employed, self-employed or unemployed persons, are recorded as payable by households and receivable by the units responsible for the social insurance schemes. Social contributions may be receivable by a unit in any sector in their capacity as providing a social insurance scheme to their employees (even exceptionally households, if in their capacity as unincorporated enterprises they run a social insurance scheme for their employees) or by a third-party unit designated as the institution responsible for administering the scheme.

[68] The benefits which are payable in kind are treated as if they are paid in cash.

Most contributions, however, are likely to be recorded under resources for the general government sector, including social security funds, and insurance corporations and pension funds in the financial corporations sector. Social contributions are recorded under uses only for households, either resident or non-resident.

3.366. Employers' social contributions are social contributions payable by employers to social security funds or other employment-related social insurance schemes to secure social benefits for their employees.

3.367. As employers' social contributions are made for the benefit of their employees, their value is recorded as one of the components of compensation of employees together with wages and salaries in cash and in kind. The social contributions are then recorded as being paid by the employees as current transfers to the social security schemes or other employment-related social insurance schemes. Although it is administratively more efficient for employers to pay the contributions on behalf of their employees, this must not be allowed to obscure the underlying economic reality. The payment made by the employer to the social security scheme or other employment-related social insurance schemes is not, in fact, a current transfer to the fund on the part of the employer. The transfer takes place between the employee and the social security scheme or other employment-related social insurance schemes out of remuneration provided by the employer. The situation is parallel to one in which income taxes payable by employees are deducted by employers from the wages or salaries and paid directly to the tax authorities. In this case, it is evident that the taxes are not current transfers payable by the employers. It is customary to describe the employers' social contributions as being re-routed in the accounts via the employees' primary and secondary distribution of income accounts. However, the accounts depict the various payables and receivables correctly. The direct payment of social contributions, or income taxes, by employers to social security schemes, other employment-related social insurance schemes or tax authorities is merely a short cut taken on grounds of administrative convenience and efficiency.

3.368. The contributions paid to social security schemes may be fixed amounts per employee or may vary with the levels of wages or salaries paid. The amounts paid under other employment-related social insurance schemes depend on the arrangements agreed between employers and employees.

3.369. Social insurance schemes in respect of pensions are of two types, described as defined contribution schemes or defined benefit schemes.

3.370. The contributions made by employers to social insurance schemes are divided into actual and imputed contributions.

3.371. For both actual and imputed contributions, the components relating to pensions and non-pensions are shown separately.

3.372. The actual contributions by employers to social insurance schemes consist of actual contributions made to both social security and other employment-related schemes. The contributions relating to pensions and other benefits are shown separately.

3.373. There are no imputed contributions to social security schemes.

3.374. For a defined contribution pension scheme, there are no imputed contributions unless the employer operates the scheme himself. In that case, the value of the costs of operating the scheme is treated as an imputed contribution payable to the employee as part of compensation of employees. This amount is also recorded as final consumption expenditure by households on financial services.

3.375. For a defined benefit pension scheme, there is an imputed contribution by the employer calculated as a residual. It must be such that the sum of the employer's actual contribution plus the sum of any contribution by the employee plus the imputed contribution by the employer is equal to the increase in benefit due to current period employment plus the costs of operating the scheme.[69]

3.376. Some defined benefit pension schemes may be so well run that the funds available to the scheme exceed the liabilities of the scheme to present and past employees. It is possible that, in this case, the employer may take a "contribution holiday" and not make actual contributions for one or more periods. Nonetheless, an imputed contribution by the employer should be calculated and recorded.

3.377. Some schemes may be expressed as non-contributory because no actual contributions are ever made by the employee. Nevertheless, an imputed contribution by the employer is calculated and imputed.

3.378. Some employers provide non-pension benefits themselves directly to their employees, former employees or dependants without involving an insurance enterprise or autonomous pension fund, and without creating a special fund or segregated reserve for the purpose. In this situation, existing employees may be considered as being protected against various specified needs or circumstances, even though no reserves are built up to provide future entitlement. Remuneration should therefore be imputed for such employees equal in value to the amount of social contributions that would be needed to secure the de facto entitlements to the social benefits they accumulate. These amounts take into account any actual contributions made by the employer or employee and depend not only on the levels of the benefits currently payable but also on the ways in which employers' liabilities under such schemes are likely to evolve in the future as a result of factors such as expected changes in the numbers, age distribution and life expectancies of their present and previous employees. Thus, the values that should be imputed for the contributions ought, in principle, to be based on the same kind of actuarial considerations that determine the levels of premiums charged by insurance enterprises.

3.379. In practice, however, it may be difficult to decide how large such imputed contributions should be. The enterprise may make estimates itself, perhaps on the basis of the contributions paid into similar funded schemes, in order to calculate its likely liabilities in the future, and such estimates may be used when available. Another acceptable method is to use a reasonable percentage of wages and salaries paid to current employees. Otherwise, the only practical alternative may be to use the unfunded non-pension benefits payable by the enterprise during the same accounting period as an estimate of the imputed remuneration that would be needed to cover the imputed contributions. While there are obviously many reasons why the value of the imputed contributions that would be needed may diverge from the unfunded non-pension benefits actually paid in the same period, such as the changing composition and age structure of the enterprise's labour force, the benefits actually paid in the current period may nevertheless provide the best available estimates of the contributions and associated imputed remuneration.

3.380. The fact that, failing other information, the value of contributions for a non-contributory scheme may be set equal to the value of benefits does not mean that the benefits themselves are treated as part of compensation of employees.

[69] The methods to compute the costs or service charges involved in operating social insurance schemes are described in a later section.

Administration and management of defined benefit pension schemes

References:
2008 SNA, Chapter 11, The financial account
2008 SNA, Chapter 17, Cross-cutting and other special issues, Part 2, Social insurance schemes

3.381. An employer may contract with a third party to administer the pension funds for his employees. If the employer continues to determine the terms of the pension schemes and retains the responsibility for any deficit in funding, as well as the right to retain any excess funding, the employer is described as the pension manager[70] and the unit working under the direction of the pension manager is described as the pension administrator.[71] If the agreement between the employer and the third party is such that the employer passes the risks and responsibilities for any deficit in funding to the third party in return for the right of the third party to retain any excess, the third party becomes the pension manager as well as the administrator. When the pension manager is a unit different from the administrator, with the consequence that responsibility for any deficit, or claims on any excess, rests with the pension manager, the claim of the pension fund on the pension manager is shown under this heading. (The entry is negative if the pension fund makes more investment income from the pension entitlements it holds than is necessary to cover the increase in entitlements and the difference is payable to the pension manager of the scheme.)

3.382. However, it is not uncommon for a single unit to contract with several employers to manage their pension funds as a multiemployer pension fund. The arrangements are such that the multiemployer pension fund accepts the responsibility for any shortfall in the funds to meet the liabilities in return for the right to keep any excess funds. By pooling the risks over a number of employers, the multiemployer fund expects to balance under- and over-funding so as to emerge with an excess over all the funds taken as whole in a similar way that an insurance corporation pools risk for many clients. In such a case, the unit assuming responsibility for meeting the pension obligations becomes the pension manager in place of the employer. However, in such cases, if employers' and employees' actual pension contributions are insufficient to match the increase in pension entitlements due to current period employment, employers may still be responsible for this shortfall.

Overview of the measurement of the output of social insurance schemes and other transactions

References:
2008 SNA, Chapter 6, The production account
BPM6, Appendix 6c, Topical summary – Insurance, pension schemes, and standardized guarantees
BPM6 Compilation Guide, Appendix 2, Insurance transactions and positions, and pension schemes

3.383. This section provides an overview of how to calculate the output and related transactions of social insurance schemes. A more thorough description of the transactions will be provided in the subsequent sections on the different pension and non-pension schemes.

3.384. There are four different ways in which social insurance may be organized:

[70] The pension manager is also known as the pension plan sponsor.

[71] The pension administrator is responsible for the day-to-day running of the pension fund.

(a) Some social insurance is provided by government under a social security scheme;

(b) An employer may organize a social insurance scheme for his employees;

(c) An employer may have an insurance corporation run the scheme for the employer in return for a fee;

(d) An insurance corporation may offer to run a scheme for several employers or one employer in return for any property income and holding gains they may make in excess of what is owed to the participants in the scheme. The resulting arrangement is called a multiemployer scheme.

The output for each of these modes of running a social insurance scheme is calculated in a different manner. The entire output of social insurance schemes is consumed by households because they are the ultimate beneficiaries of social insurance benefits.

3.385. Social security schemes are run as part of the operation of general government. If separate units are distinguished, their output is determined in the same way as all non-market output as the sum of costs. If separate units are not distinguished, the output of social security is included with the output of the level of government at which it operates.

3.386. When an employer operates his own social insurance scheme, the value of the output is also determined as the sum of costs including an estimate for a return to any fixed capital used in the operation of the scheme. Even if the employer establishes a segregated pension fund to manage the scheme, the value of output is still measured in the same way.

3.387. When an employer uses an insurance corporation to manage the scheme on his behalf, the value of the output is the fee charged by the insurance corporation. In this instance, the employer is acting as the pension manager, while the insurance corporation is acting as the pension administrator. The explicit fee charged by the insurance corporation is recorded as the intermediate consumption of the pension fund. This amount is also recorded as the output of the pension fund.

3.388. In the case of a multiemployer scheme, the insurance corporation is acting as both the pension manager and pension administrator. The value of output needs to be implicitly measured and is measured as for life insurance policies; it is the excess of the investment income receivable by the schemes less the amount added to the reserves to meet present and future pension entitlements. The output is written as:

Social contributions
plus contribution supplements (3.16)
minus benefits payable
minus increases (*plus* decreases) in pension entitlements.[72]

3.389. Social contributions are defined as earlier. In the case of defined contribution pension funds, they are the sum of employers' and employees' actual pension contributions. In the case of defined benefit pension funds, they are the sum of employers' and employees' actual pension contributions and employers' imputed pension contributions.

3.390. Pension funds hold reserves in the form of pension entitlements to meet obligations to beneficiaries. The pension entitlements represent a liability of the pension fund and an asset of the beneficiaries. Some schemes may also have other liabilities, such as those for non-pension benefits. To meet their liabilities, pension funds make

[72] However, this is equivalent to calculating the output using the sum of costs including a return to fixed capital (see box 3.4).

Box 3.4
Calculating the output of managers of multiemployer pension funds

In the absence of explicit fees, the output (y) of a manager of a multiemployer defined benefit pension fund can be calculated using the formula to calculate life insurance output as shown below:

$$y=e+i+h+cs-p-pe \qquad (3.4.1)$$

where e is employers' actual pension contributions, i is employers' imputed pension contributions, h is employees' actual pension contributions, cs is contribution supplements, p is pensions payable and pe is changes in pension entitlements.

The value of i must be such that the employer's actual contribution plus any contribution by the employee plus the imputed contribution by the employer are equal to the increase in benefit due to current period employment plus the costs incurred by the pension manager in operating the fund. In the case of multiemployer defined benefit pension funds, the costs include an estimate of the return to fixed capital used in managing the funds.

If the costs of operating the defined benefit pension fund are o and the current service increase in the employee's pension entitlement is ce, then i can be related to the other terms as follows:

$$e\text{-}i+h=o+ce \qquad (3.4.2)$$

Substituting (3.4.2) into (3.4.1) results in the following:

$$y=o+ce+cs-p-pe \qquad (3.4.3)$$

However, $pe=ce-cs-p$. Substituting this expression into equation (3.4.3) results in:

$$y=o+ce+cs-p-(ce+cs-p)=o$$

This implies that using the life insurance formula to calculate the output of managers of multiemployer defined benefit pension funds may be equivalent to calculating the output as the sum of costs, including a return to fixed capital used in operating the funds.

The output (y) of a manager of a multi-employer defined contribution pension fund can be calculated using the formula to calculate life insurance output as shown below:

$$y=e+h+cs-p-pe \qquad (3.4.4)$$

The terms in (3.4.4) are as defined in (3.4.1).

If the costs of operating the defined contribution pension fund are o, then the contribution supplements must be such that the employer's actual contribution plus any contribution by the employee plus the contribution supplements are equal to the change in pension entitlements plus the pension benefits payable plus the costs incurred by the pension manager in operating the fund. Thus, we have:

$$o+pe+p=e+h+cs \qquad (3.4.5)$$

Substituting (3.4.5) into (3.4.4) results in:

$$y=o+pe+p-p-pe=o$$

This implies that using the life insurance formula to calculate the output of managers of multiemployer defined contribution pension funds may be equivalent to calculating the output as the sum of costs, including a return to fixed capital used in operating the funds.

investments in various assets, such as financial assets, land or buildings. The income earned from these investments is used to fund the investment income payable on pension entitlements. This income is receivable by households, but, in practice, it is retained by the pension fund. Thus, households are treated as paying an equal amount back to the pension fund in the secondary distribution of income account in the form of contribution supplements.

3.391. The investment income payable on pension entitlements for defined contribution schemes is equal to the investment income on the funds plus any net operating surplus earned by renting land or buildings owned by the fund.

3.392. The investment income payable on pension entitlements for defined benefit schemes is equal to the increase in benefits payable because the date when the entitlements become payable is closer. This is actuarially determined, since the liability of a pension fund under a defined benefit scheme is actuarially calculated. The amount of the increase is not affected by whether the pension scheme has actually earned sufficient income from its assets to meet this obligation. Thus, the investment income payable on pension entitlements (i.e. contribution supplements) will need to include an imputed component in addition to an actual component. The actual component represents the investment income receivable from the actual assets held by the pension funds. The imputed component represents the imputed property income payable by the pension fund manager on the difference between the pension fund's reserves and its actuarial liability. This imputed component is needed when the assets of the pension fund are less than its actuarial liability, resulting in an imputed claim of the pension fund on the pension fund manager. By including the imputed property income receivable from the pension fund manager, equality is maintained between the investment income payable by the pension fund on its pension entitlements and the investment income receivable by the pension fund. This will ensure that the net worth of the pension fund is zero.

3.393. Benefits payable refer to the social insurance benefits, as described earlier. However, it should be noted that the payments of social contributions into the pension schemes and the receipts of pensions by beneficiaries constitute the acquisition and disposal of financial assets. In addition, they are recorded as current transfers in the secondary distribution of income account as social contributions and social benefits respectively so that disposable incomes of households reflect these flows. However, this dual treatment of pension contributions and benefits has an impact on household saving if the contributions and benefits are not exactly the same. In order to reconcile the treatment of pensions as current transfers with the treatment of pension entitlements as financial assets, it is necessary to introduce an adjustment item. This adjustment item adds social contributions back to, and subtracts pension receipts from, the balance on secondary income. After the adjustment, the saving of households is the same as what it would have been if social contributions and pension receipts were not recorded as current transfers. This item is called "adjustment for change in pension entitlements" and is equal to:

The total value of the actual social contributions payable into pension schemes

plus the total value of contribution supplements payable out of the property income attributable to pension fund beneficiaries

minus the value of the associated service charges

minus the total value of the pensions paid out as social benefits by pension schemes.

3.394. The increases/decreases in pension entitlements should include transactions only, that is, changes which are due to service to the employer or investment income on previously accumulated pension entitlements less the pension benefits payable. Changes in pension entitlements due to actuarial gains and losses (surprises), assumption changes and a pension fund's rules should not be included.

3.395. The methods to compute output above generally also apply to social insurance schemes which pay non-pension benefits. However, in instances of a funded social insurance scheme providing non-pension benefits, the output is computed in the same way as the output for non-life insurance rather than life insurance.

3.396. The social contributions and contribution supplements are divided between two types of transactions. The first is the value of the output of social insurance, which constitutes the service fee charged by the unit operating the scheme. Depending on the nature of the scheme, the service fee is included in either the contribution by the employer or the contribution supplements. The second type of transaction is net social contributions. These are the actual or imputed contributions made by households to social insurance schemes to make provision for social benefits to be paid. Net social contributions are computed as follows:

Employers' actual social contributions

plus employers' imputed social contributions

plus employees' actual social contributions

plus contribution supplements corresponding to investment income payable by pension schemes on pension entitlements

minus service charges payable to pension schemes.

3.397. Employers' imputed social contributions are only applicable to unfunded employer-related non-pension schemes, defined contribution pension schemes operated by employers and defined benefit pension schemes. In addition, net social contributions may not be relevant in the case of social security schemes for the following reasons: first, there are no contribution supplements, since pension entitlements are not recorded in the core accounts in the case of these schemes. Second, the service fee is not included in the social contributions by the employer. Instead, the service fee represents the consumption expenditure undertaken by general government for the benefit of individual households. This fee is included in household actual final consumption expenditure and is financed by a social transfer in kind from the general government to households.

3.398. The data sources to compute the output of social insurance schemes and other related transactions depend on the type of scheme in question and whether the fund under the scheme is a resident or non-resident institutional unit. The input data to compute the output and other related transactions associated with resident social security schemes and employment-related schemes other than social security which are operated by the general government for its employees should be available from the accounts of the general government. On the other hand, the input data to compute the output and other related transactions associated with resident employment-related schemes other than social security which are not operated by the general government can be obtained from a variety of sources. One option is for the compiling agency to conduct a survey of resident funds. In addition, in some countries, central registrars have been established to collect data on the resident pension industry. These registrars may constitute another source of input data. Furthermore, pension funds in some countries may be obliged to send their reports on assets, liabilities and expenses to government agencies for auditing or tax calculations. The compiling agencies in these countries may consider using these returns for their own calculations of the output and other related transactions associated with resident social insurance schemes. In all cases, since the input data are measured at current prices, the output derived is also measured at current prices.

3.399. Since the ultimate beneficiaries of social insurance schemes are households, social insurance transactions will only be allocated to households, both resident and non-resident. The output which is allocated to resident households is recorded as their actual final consumption expenditure, while the output which is allocated to non-resident households is recorded as exports of goods and services. Very often, the breakdown of the output and other related transactions, including investment income payable on pension entitlements by sector (i.e. resident households and the rest of the world), may not be available. Rather, the compiling agency may only be able to obtain input data to compute the total output and other related transactions. In such instances, the compiling agency will need to make assumptions to allocate these transactions based on available data. For example, it may be possible for respondents to provide a breakdown of data on actual social contributions by sector. This information can be used to allocate the output associated with social insurance schemes and other related transactions.

3.400. It is also possible for resident households to participate in social insurance schemes which are operated by non-residents. In such instances, the estimates of the imports of the service charge and other related transactions can be obtained from the balance of payments statistics. If the data are not reported in the balance of payments statistics, the compiling agency can, in general, consider using the guidance in the previous sections to estimate imports and related transactions of insurance to estimate the missing transactions. The estimation of these transactions should be done in consultation with the compilers of balance of payments statistics to ensure their consistent recording in the national accounts and balance of payments.

Accounting for pension contributions and benefits

Reference:
2008 SNA, Chapter 17, Cross-cutting and other special issues, Part 2, Social insurance schemes

3.401. Pensions are provided to individuals in an economy under one of three mechanisms: via social security, via employment-related schemes other than social security or via social assistance. Together, social security and employment-related pension schemes other than social security constitute social insurance schemes. Although the benefits provided under social assistance and some social insurance schemes may be very similar, the key distinction is that social insurance benefits are only paid if the beneficiary participates in the social insurance scheme, participation being normally evidenced by the beneficiary or another on his behalf having made qualifying contributions. Social assistance is paid without qualifying contributions having been made, though means-testing may be applied to applicants.

3.402. The means by which pensions are provided to persons in retirement varies considerably from one country to another. This section describes the most common forms of pension provision made under social insurance schemes, though not all aspects may apply to all countries.

3.403. Social insurance pensions in all countries are provided, if at all, in part by general government and in part by employers. The part provided by general government is called social security and the part by employers is called employment-related schemes other than social security. The division between which pensions are provided by social security and which by other employment-related schemes varies considerably from country to country, with the consequence that the coverage and, therefore, national perceptions of what the term "social security" designates also vary considerably. In order to make clear the recommendations in the SNA, it is necessary to consider the types of coverage provided in different countries.

3.404. The narrowest form of social security pension is very basic. The level may be fixed independently of the size of contributions (though not of the fact that contributions have been made for a given period of time). An employee's right to a pension under social security is often transferable from one employer to another, which is an advantage not always applying to other pension provisions, but for many people in low-paid jobs, working temporarily or intermittently, it may be the only form of pension provision they can expect to receive.

3.405. By contrast, in some countries, most or all pension provision may be made via social security. In this case, government acts as an intermediary relative to the employer so that once the government has received the contributions to the scheme paid by the employer and the households, the government then takes on the risk of making the eventual payment. Government relieves the employer of the risk that the cost of pensions may be too great for his enterprise to meet and assures the population that pensions will be paid, though it may do so with the qualification that it may alter the amount of pensions payable, even retrospectively, if economic conditions so dictate.

3.406. Pension schemes run by private employers are usually not subject to retrospective adjustments of the amounts payable, but there is a risk that the employer may be unable to pay because he has gone out of business. Increasingly, though, protection for the pension entitlements of individuals is becoming more common. Equally, the pension built up with one employer may not be transferable to a new employer, though this, too, is undergoing change. While social security may be, and very often is, financed on a pay-as-you-go basis, without building up reserves for future liabilities, other employer schemes are increasingly likely to have reserves set aside. Even if there are no reserves, accounting conventions may require them to recognize pension entitlements of present and past employees in their accounts.

3.407. Employment-related pensions, other than the most basic form of social security, are seen as part of the compensation package, and negotiations between employees and employers may focus on pension entitlements as much as on current conditions of service and pay scales. Often, pensions are provided by private employers from funds that the employers control or contract to a third party, such as an insurance corporation. These funds may also provide social benefits other than pensions, for example private medical coverage. It is sometimes possible for a specialized unit to agree to assume responsibility for providing pensions for a number of employers in return for assuming the risk of ensuring adequate funding is available to make the promised pensions. Such an arrangement is called a multiemployer pension scheme.

3.408. Both current employees and former employees who are current or future beneficiaries may make contributions to the scheme and receive investment income from it. This investment income is then treated as contribution supplements by those receiving it.

Social security pensions

3.409. It is common but not essential for both employers and employees to make contributions towards a social security pension. It is also common for the contributions to be compulsory. Social security pensions are frequently funded on a pay-as-you-go basis. The normal assumption in the main accounts of the SNA is that this is how social security pensions are funded, that is, the contributions receivable in a period are used to fund the benefits payable in the same period. There is no saving element involved, either for the government operating the scheme or for the individuals participating in it. No liabilities for the scheme are recognized in the main accounts of the SNA, although concern is often expressed that benefits may exceed contributions and this situation is likely to worsen in an ageing population. For this reason, estimates of the liabilities of social security, as well as any other pension schemes not included in the main accounts, are included in a supplementary table described in a later section in this chapter.

3.410. The costs of operating social security schemes are treated as part of the normal expenditure of general government if the schemes are not separate institutional units, so the accounting for social security operations does not include measures of output. If these schemes are treated as separate institutional units, their output is computed as the sum of costs. This output is non-market in nature and is recorded in the output of the general government sector. The cost of producing this output is also recorded in government final consumption expenditure, since the government is consuming the output to provide goods and services to the population. Final government consumption expenditure has to be split into individual consumption expenditure (i.e. expenditure incurred for the benefit of individual households) and collective consumption expenditure (i.e. expenditure incurred for the benefit of the community as a whole, or large sections of the community). Individual consumption expenditure is recorded as part of household actual final consumption and is financed by an equivalent social transfer in kind from the general government to households. The output associated with social security schemes is considered as individual consumption expenditure in government final consumption expenditure. Thus, it is included in actual household final consumption and a social transfer in kind from the general government to households equivalent to the value of government final consumption expenditure associated with these schemes will need to be imputed in order to finance the consumption of this output by households.

3.411. In the SNA, flows are recorded as follows:

(a) If the social security scheme is treated as a separate institutional unit, its output will be recorded in the production account;

(b) Employers' social security contributions are shown as payable by the sector in which the employer is located and receivable by households. The sector of the employer may be any of non-financial corporations, financial corporations, general government (as an employer), employer households, NPISHs or the rest of the world (when a resident works for a non-resident institutional unit). For resident employers, the payables are shown in the generation of income account; payables by non-resident employers are shown in the primary distribution of income account for the rest of the world. Receivables by resident households are shown in the allocation of primary income account and by non-resident households in the primary distribution of income account for the rest of the world. The same treatment applies to employees' social security contributions;

(c) In the secondary distribution of income account, the sum of employers' social security contributions and social security contributions by households in their capacities as employees is shown as payable by households and receivable by government. Any contributions made by self-employed or non-employed people are also included with the contributions payable by households to government. Further, social security benefits payable to households are shown as payable by government (or the rest of the world if from a foreign government) and receivable by households;

(d) Consumption of the service charge (output) is first recorded as the individual final consumption expenditure of the social security scheme in the use of disposable income account;

(e) The redistribution of income in kind account records a social transfer in kind from the social security scheme to resident or non-resident households to finance the consumption of service charge by the latter;

(f) The consumption of the service charge is recorded as the actual final consumption in the use of adjusted disposable income account for resident households or as exports for non-resident households.

Worked example 3.22. Computing output and other transactions associated with a social security scheme which pays pension benefits

3.412. This worked example computes the current-price output and other related transactions associated with a social security scheme which pays pension benefits. It is assumed that the scheme exists as a separate institutional unit and that all the participants and beneficiaries are residents. In addition, it is assumed that the social security scheme does not maintain any reserves to pay pension benefits. The worked example also assumes that the compiling agency is able to obtain the required input data from the government. In addition, the worked example will show how to record in the financial account the counterpart entries to show the means of payment for some of the transactions between the institutional units. For simplicity, it is assumed that these transactions are settled in currency or transferable deposits, which are part of "currency and deposits" in the financial account.

3.413. Table 3.103 shows the input data on the social security pension contributions and benefits for a social security fund. It is assumed that both employers and employees are contributing to the social security fund. As observed, the sum of employers' and employees' actual social pension contributions is just sufficient to pay the social security pension benefits for the period.

3.414. The social security fund produces non-market output which is computed as the sum of costs. Table 3.104 shows the costs involved in running the social security scheme. It is assumed that the costs involved only include intermediate consumption of goods and services. It is also assumed that all the goods and services for intermediate consumption are purchased from other resident sectors. Table 3.104 also shows how to derive the output of the social security fund. The output of the social security fund (1.0 unit) is computed as the value of the intermediate consumption of goods and services.

3.415. Table 3.105 shows how to calculate the changes in financial assets arising from the transactions among the social security fund and the other institutional units, as well as the means of payment for these transactions. In general, the changes in financial assets and liabilities are computed using the following principles: changes in currency and deposits are the result of the payments made by the institutional units and the receipts they receive. As an example, the social security fund has a net decrease in assets of currency and deposits of 0.7 units during the accounting period. This is the result of:

Table 3.103
Data from a social security fund which pays pension benefits

Line number	Item	Value	2008 SNA code
(1)	Employers' actual social pension contributions	139.0	D1211, D6111
(2)	Employees' actual social pension contributions	87.0	D11, D6131
(3)	Social security pension benefits	226.0	D62, D6211

Table 3.104
Operating costs and output of a social security fund which pays pension benefits

Line number	Item	Description	Value	2008 SNA code
(4)	Intermediate consumption of goods and services		0.7	P1, P2
(5)	Output of social security fund	(4)	0.7	P1, P3, P31, D63, P4, P41

Table 3.105
Calculation of changes in financial assets related to transactions among a social security fund which pays pension benefits and other institutional units

Line number	Item	Description	Value	2008 SNA code
	Changes in financial assets (currency and deposits)			
(6)	Employers	–(1)–(2)	-226.0	F2
(7)	Social security fund	(1)+(2)–(3)–(4)	-0.7	F2
(8)	Households	(3)	226.0	F2
(9)	Other sectors	(4)	0.7	F2

- An increase in assets of currency and deposits arising from employers' actual social pension contributions (139.0 units) and employees' actual social pension contributions (87.0 units) receivable.
- A decrease in assets of currency and deposits arising from intermediate consumption of goods and services purchased from other sectors (0.7 units); and social security pension benefits payable (226.0 units).

3.416. Table 3.106 uses the information in the tables above to record the various transactions. To ensure clarity, the transactions of employers and the social security fund are shown separately rather than combined with those of the institutional sector to which they belong. The transactions are described as follows:

(a) The output of the social security fund is 0.7 units. This output is recorded in the production account of the fund. The intermediate consumption of goods and services of the fund (0.7 units) is also recorded in its production account. The same amount is also recorded in the output of other sectors, since it is assumed that these goods and services are purchased from those sectors;

(b) Employers' actual pension contributions (139.0 units) are treated as part of the compensation of employees and are recorded as payable by employers in the generation of income account. In addition, employees' actual pension contributions (87.0 units) are part of wages and salaries (and, by extension, compensation of employees) and are recorded as payable by employers in the same account;

(c) The entries in the generation of income account are recorded as receivable by households in the allocation of primary income account;

(d) Employers' (139.0 units) and households' actual pension contributions (87.0 units) are recorded in the secondary distribution of income account as payable by households and receivable by the social security fund. Social security benefits payable by the social security fund and receivable by households (226.0 units) are also recorded in the secondary distribution of income account;

(e) The output of the social security fund (0.7 units) is recorded as the individual final consumption expenditure of the fund in the use of disposable income account;

(f) The redistribution of income in kind account records a social transfer in kind (0.7 units) from the social security fund to households to finance households' consumption of the output of the fund;

(g) The use of adjusted disposable income account then records households' actual final individual consumption of the service provided by the social security fund (0.7 units);

(h) Since there are no capital account transactions, net lending/net borrowing in the capital account is the same as gross saving in the use of disposable income account;

(i) The financial account records the changes in currency and deposits as the counterpart entries to the above transactions. Thus, net lending/net borrowing is identical to net lending/net borrowing in the capital account, although, in practice, differences in data sources and the timing of the recording of transactions may result in a discrepancy between the estimates of net lending/net borrowing in these two accounts. No other transactions are recorded in the financial account, since pension entitlements for social security are not recorded in the core accounts.

Table 3.106

Recording transactions related to a social security fund which pays pension benefits

Uses															Resources
Total	**Goods and services**	**Total economy**	**Other sectors**	**Households**	**Social security fund**	**Employers**	**2008 SNA code**	**Transactions and balancing items**	**Employers**	**Social security fund**	**Households**	**Other sectors**	**Total economy**	**Goods and services**	**Total**
Production account															
1.4	1.4						P1	Output		0.7		0.7	1.4		1.4
0.7		0.7			0.7		P2	Intermediate consumption							
0.7		0.7	0.7		0.0		B1g	Value added, gross/Gross domestic product							
Generation of income account															
226.0		226.0				226.0	D1	Compensation of employees							
87.0		87.0				87.0	D11	Wages and salaries							
139.0		139.0				139.0	D1211	Employers' actual pension contributions							
-225.3		-225.3	0.7		0.0	-226.0	B2g	Operating surplus, gross							
Allocation of primary income account															
							D1	Compensation of employees			226.0		226.0		226.0
							D11	Wages and salaries			87.0		87.0		87.0
							D1211	Employers' actual pension contributions			139.0		139.0		139.0
0.7		0.7	0.7	226.0	0.0	-226.0	B5g	Balance of primary income, gross/ National income, gross							
Secondary distribution of income account															
139.0		139.0		139.0			D6111	Employers' actual pension contributions		139.0			139.0		139.0
87.0		87.0		87.0			D6131	Households' actual pension contributions		87.0			87.0		87.0
226.0		226.0			226.0		D62	Social benefits other than social transfers in kind			226.0		226.0		226.0
226.0		226.0			226.0		D6211	Social security pension benefits			226.0		226.0		226.0
0.7		0.7	0.7	226.0	0.0	-226.0	B6g	Disposable income, gross							
Use of disposable income account															
0.7		0.7			0.7		P3	Final consumption expenditure						0.7	0.7
0.7		0.7			0.7		P31	Individual consumption expenditure						0.7	0.7
0.0		0.0	0.7	226.0	-0.7	-226.0	B8g	Saving, gross							
Redistribution of income in kind account															
0.7		0.7			0.7		D63	Social transfers in kind			0.7		0.7		0.7
0.7		0.7	0.7	226.7	-0.7	-226.0	B7g	Adjusted disposable income, gross							
Use of adjusted disposable income account															
0.7		0.7		0.7	0.0		P4	Actual final consumption						0.7	0.7
				0.7	0.0		P41	Actual individual consumption						0.7	0.7
0.0		0.0	0.7	226.0	-0.7	-226.0	B8g	Saving, gross							
Changes in assets															**Changes in liabilities and net worth**
Capital account															
0.0		0.0	0.7	226.0	-0.7	-226.0	B9	Net lending (+)/net borrowing (-)							
Financial account															
							B9	Net lending (+)/net borrowing (-)	-226.0	-0.7	226.0	0.7	0.0		0.0
0.0		0.0	0.7	226.0	-0.7	-226.0	F2	Currency and deposits							

Employment-related pension schemes other than social security

3.417. There are two forms of employment-related pension schemes other than social security. One is called a defined contribution scheme, sometimes referred to as a money purchase scheme. (The expression "defined contribution pension scheme" is not intuitive, but is widely used in the pension industry.) The other is a defined benefit scheme, sometimes referred to as a final salary scheme, though this term does not accurately describe all defined benefit schemes. Typically, both schemes are contributory, often by both the employer and the employee. Both schemes have been defined in the section on the breakdown of social insurance schemes.

3.418. For both types of schemes, pension entitlements of the participants are recorded as they build up. In both cases, there is investment income earned on existing entitlements, and this is recorded as being distributed to the beneficiaries and reinvested by them in the pension scheme. There are, though, a number of different features of the two schemes, so the transactions relating to each are described in detail separately before turning to other changes in the levels of pension entitlements. The recording of transactions for a defined contribution scheme is less complicated than the defined benefit scheme and is described first.

3.419. For both types of schemes, a pension fund is assumed to exist. For a defined contribution pension scheme, a fund must exist. For a defined benefit pension scheme, a fund may exist in reality or it may be a notional fund. If it exists, it may be part of the same institutional unit as the employer, it may be a separate institutional unit (an autonomous pension scheme) or it may be part of another financial institution, either an insurance corporation or a multiemployer pension scheme. In describing the recording of transactions, transactions with the pension fund must be attributed to the sector where the fund is located. This could be the sector in which the employer is located if the fund is part of the employer or the financial corporations sector if the fund is a separate institutional unit or part of another financial institution.

3.420. The method to measure the output of pension funds depends on how they are organized. When an employer operates its own social insurance scheme, the output is measured as the sum of costs including an estimate for the return to fixed capital, regardless of whether the employer establishes a segregated pension fund to manage the scheme. When an employer uses an insurance corporation to manage the scheme on its behalf, the value of output is the fee charged by the insurance corporation. In the case of a multi-employer scheme which is administered and managed by an insurance corporation, the output of the pension fund is implicitly measured using the formula to compute the output of life insurance.

Defined contribution pension schemes

3.421. Recording the transactions related to a defined contribution pension scheme presents no conceptual problems. There are no associated imputations, either for the flows concerned or for the values appearing in balance sheets for the pension entitlements of the beneficiaries, nor any doubt as to which unit has a liability and which an asset.

Transactions recorded for a defined contribution pension scheme

3.422. The contribution made by an employer to a defined contribution pension scheme on behalf of his employee is treated as part of compensation of employees. It is recorded as payable by the employer in the generation of income account and receivable by the employee in the allocation of primary income account. The same treatment applies to the contribution of employees.

3.423. The investment income on the cumulated pension entitlements is also recorded as being distributed to (receivable by) households in the allocation of primary income account and is shown as payable by the pension fund. The investment income includes interest and dividends payable plus the distributed income of collective investment schemes if the pension fund holds shares in them. It is possible that the pension fund may own property and generate net operating surplus on this which is also included, along with the investment income, as being distributed to the pension beneficiaries. In this case, the term investment income is to be interpreted as being elastic enough to include this source of income if it exists. Holding gains and losses generated by the investment of the cumulated pension entitlements are not included in investment income.

3.424. Part of the income distributed to households is used to meet the costs of operating the pension fund. This cost is shown as the output of the pension fund in the production account and as an element of consumption expenditure by households in the use of income account. The remaining part of the distributed income is treated as pension contribution supplements paid back by households to the pension funds.

3.425. In the secondary distribution of income account, social contributions are shown as payable by households and receivable by the pension fund. The total amount of the social contributions payable is made up of the actual contributions payable by the employers as part of compensation of employees, actual contributions by employees and possibly by other individuals (individuals formerly participating in a scheme, self-employed and non-employed persons, as well as retirees) plus the contribution supplements just specified. For clarity, and to enhance the comparison with defined benefit schemes, the supplements are shown at full value in both the allocation of primary income account, where they appear as investment income, and in the secondary distribution of income account, where they appear as contribution supplements. However, the service charge is shown as an offsetting negative element to total household contributions in the secondary distribution of income account so that net social contributions can be derived. The net social contributions made by households to the pensions scheme are net in the same way that insurance premiums are net, that is to say they are the total of all contributions made less the service charge appearing in the use of income account.

3.426. Those other than employees who contribute to a defined contribution pension scheme may be self-employed persons participating in a defined contribution pension scheme or may be persons not employed who participate in a defined contribution pension scheme by virtue of their profession or former employment status, for example.

3.427. Also in the secondary distribution of income account, the pension benefits payable to households by the pension fund are shown. However, the benefits payable under a defined contribution pension scheme take the form of a lump sum payable at the moment of retirement. It may be a requirement of the scheme that these sums are to be immediately converted to an annuity with the same or another financial institution, but this is not a universal requirement. The appropriate recording of the benefits is not to show the benefit as payable immediately on retirement and then, where appropriate, reinvested in terms of an annuity or other forms of financial assets, but notionally as a reclassification from life insurance entitlements to annuities entitlements. However, since no distinction is normally made between these two sets of entitlements, no actual classification change will show in the accounts.

3.428. In the use of income account, there is an entry for the payment of the service provided by the pension fund (equal to the value of the pension fund's output)[73] payable by households to the pension fund.

[73] The output of a defined contribution pension fund is conceptually different from the pension expense for the fund reported in company accounts. Pension expense is the amount of the employers' social contributions.

3.429. In the same account, there is an entry showing the increase (or decrease) in pension entitlements caused by the excess (or deficit) of contributions payable less benefits receivable in the secondary distribution of income account. This amount is shown as payable to households by the pension fund. The rationale for this is that, since this increase (or decrease) in pension entitlements directly affects the net worth of households, it should be included in the saving of the households sector. Because much of the increase in the pension entitlement of participants in a defined contribution pension scheme, and, thus, ultimately the funding for the benefits, comes from holding gains that are not included in the contribution supplements of participants in defined contribution pension schemes, the adjustment for the change in pension entitlements for these individuals will frequently be negative.

3.430. The adjustment for the change in pension entitlements that is included in the use of income account as payable by the pension fund to households is shown in the financial account as payable by households to the pension fund. The effect of any transfer of the obligations to meet pension entitlements from a unit in one sector to another is also reflected in the financial account item.

3.431. If the defined contribution pension schemes are managed by a pension fund manager, the transactions will be recorded between the pension fund manager and the other institutional units, such as the pension fund participants and beneficiaries.

3.432. The other factors affecting the change in the balance sheet entry for the change in pension entitlements are shown in the other changes in assets accounts. In particular, the liabilities of the scheme to the beneficiaries show holding gains or losses in the revaluation account corresponding exactly to those on the assets held by the scheme to meet these obligations. When payments under a defined contribution scheme are made via annuities, other volume changes may need to be recorded.

Worked example 3.23. Computing output and other transactions associated with defined contribution pension schemes

3.433. This worked example computes the current-price output and other related transactions associated with defined contribution pension schemes. It is assumed that the schemes comprise funds which are operated by pension fund managers. The pension fund managers do not charge explicit fees, so their output will have to be derived implicitly using the formula to compute life insurance output. The worked example also assumes that the compiling agency is able to obtain the required input data to compute the output and other related transactions and that all participants and beneficiaries are residents. In addition, the worked example will show how to record in the financial account the counterpart entries to show the means of payment for some of the transactions between the institutional units. For simplicity, it is assumed that these transactions are settled in currency or transferable deposits, which are part of "currency and deposits" in the financial account.

3.434. Table 3.107 shows the input data on defined contribution pension funds. Both employers and employees are contributing to the funds. The funds report that investment income earned on pension entitlements amounts to 16.2 units. It is assumed that this investment income is payable by other resident sectors. It is also assumed that the pension fund manager does not use the pension entitlements to invest in properties, so the investment income represents the investment income which is payable on pension entitlements.

3.435. Table 3.108 shows how to calculate the output of the pension fund managers and the net social contributions. The output of the pension fund managers (1.4 units) is computed as follows:

Employers' actual pension contributions (11.0 units)

plus employees' actual pension contributions (11.5 units)

plus contribution supplements (equivalent to investment income on pension entitlements) (16.2 units)

minus pension benefits (26.0 units)

minus the increase in pension entitlements (11.3 units).

Net social contributions (37.3 units) are computed as follows:

Employers' actual pension contributions (11.0 units)

plus employees' actual pension contributions (11.5 units)

plus contribution supplements (equivalent to investment income on pension entitlements) (16.2 units)

less output of defined contribution pension funds (service charge) (1.4 units).

3.436. Table 3.109 shows how to calculate the changes in financial assets related to the transactions among the pension fund managers and the other institutional units, as well as the means of payment for these transactions. In general, the changes in financial assets and liabilities are computed using the following principles: changes in currency and deposits are the result of the payments made by the institutional units and the receipts they receive. On the other hand, the defined contribution pen-

Table 3.107
Data on defined contribution pension funds

Line number	Item	Value	2008 SNA code
(1)	Employers' actual pension contributions	11.0	D1211, D6111
(2)	Employees' actual pension contributions	11.5	D11, D6131
(3)	Investment income on pension entitlements	16.2	D4, D442, D6141
(4)	Pension benefits	26.0	D62, D6221
(5)	Increase in pension entitlements	11.3	

Table 3.108
Calculation of output and net social contributions for pension fund managers of defined contribution pension funds

Line number	Item	Description	Value	2008 SNA code
(6)	Output of pension fund managers	(1)+(2)+(3)–(4)–(5)	1.4	P1, P3
(7)	Net social contributions	(1)+(2)+(3)–(6)	37.3	D61

Table 3.109
Calculation of changes in financial assets and liabilities related to transactions among pension fund managers of defined contribution pension funds and other institutional units

Line number	Item	Description	Value	2008 SNA code
	Changes in financial assets (currency and deposits)			
(8)	Employers	-(1)–(2)	-22.5	F2
(9)	Pension fund managers	(1)+(2)+(3)–(4)	12.7	F2
(10)	Households	(4)	26.0	F2
(11)	Other sectors	-(3)	-16.2	F2
	Changes in financial assets (pension entitlements)			
(12)	Households	(5)	11.3	D8, F63
	Changes in liabilities (pension entitlements)			
(13)	Pension fund managers	(5)	11.3	D8, F63

sion funds also incur an increase in liabilities of pension entitlements to beneficiaries. These changes in liabilities are recorded as the corresponding changes in the financial assets of households. For example, pension fund managers have a net increase in assets of currency and deposits of 12.7 units during the accounting period. This is the result of the following:

- An increase in assets of currency and deposits arising from employers' actual pension contributions (11.0 units) and employees' actual pension contributions (11.5 units) receivable; and investment income on pension entitlements receivable from other sectors (16.2 units).
- A decrease in assets of currency and deposits arising from pension benefits payable (26.0 units).

In addition, they have a net increase in liabilities of pension entitlements of 11.3 units.

3.437. Table 3.110 uses the information in the tables above to record the various transactions. To simplify the presentation and analysis, transactions which are not related to the worked example are ignored. To ensure clarity, the transactions of employers and the defined contribution pension funds are shown separately rather than combined with those of the institutional sectors to which they belong. The transactions are described as follows:

(a) The output of the pension fund managers is 1.4 units. This output is recorded in the production account of the managers;

(b) Employers' actual pension contributions (11.0 units) are treated as part of the compensation of employees and are recorded as payable by employers in the generation of income account. Employees' actual pension contributions (11.5 units) are part of wages and salaries (and, by extension, compensation of employees) and are recorded as payable by employers in the same account;

(c) The entries in the generation of income account are recorded as receivable by households in the allocation of primary income account. Investment income earned on the assets of the pension funds (16.2 units) is first recorded as property income payable by other sectors and receivable by the pension fund managers in this account. The same amount is then recorded as investment income payable on pension entitlements by the pension fund managers and receivable by households in the same account;

(d) Net social contributions (37.3 units) are recorded in the secondary distribution of income account as payable by households and receivable by the pension fund managers. Net social contributions payable by households include employers' actual pension contributions (11.0 units), since all social insurance contributions are to be recorded as being paid by households to social insurance schemes. The pension benefits payable (26.0 units) are recorded as other social pension benefits payable by the pension fund managers and receivable by households in this account;

(e) The output of the pension fund managers (1.4 units) is recorded as the final consumption expenditure of households in the use of disposable income account. This account also records an adjustment for change in pension entitlements (11.3 units) in order to ensure that gross saving is invariant to the dual treatment of pensions as current transfers and pension entitlements as financial assets;

(f) Since there are no capital account transactions, net lending/net borrowing in the capital account is the same as gross saving in the use of disposable income account;

Table 3.110

Recording transactions related to pension fund managers of defined contribution pension funds

Uses															Resources
Total	Goods and services	Total economy	Other sectors	Households	Pension fund managers	Employers	2008 SNA code	Transactions and balancing items	Employers	Pension fund managers	Households	Other sectors	Total economy	Goods and services	Total
Production account															
1.4	1.4						P1	Output		1.4			1.4		1.4
1.4		1.4			1.4		B1g	Value added, gross/ Gross domestic product							
Generation of income account															
22.5		22.5				22.5	D1	Compensation of employees							
11.5		11.5				11.5	D11	Wages and salaries							
11.0		11.0				11.0	D1211	Employers' actual pension contributions							
-21.1		-21.1			1.4	-22.5	B2g	Operating surplus, gross							
Allocation of primary income account															
							D1	Compensation of employees			22.5		22.5		22.5
							D11	Wages and salaries			11.5		11.5		11.5
							D1211	Employers' actual pension contributions			11.0		11.0		11.0
16.2		16.2	16.2				D4	Property income		16.2			16.2		16.2
16.2		16.2			16.2		D442	Investment income payable on pension entitlements			16.2		16.2		16.2
1.4		1.4	-16.2	38.7	1.4	-22.5	B5g	Balance of primary income, gross/ National income, gross							
Secondary distribution of income account															
37.3		37.3		37.3			D61	Net social contributions		37.3			37.3		37.3
11.0		11.0		11.0			D6111	Employers' actual pension contributions		11.0			11.0		11.0
11.5		11.5		11.5			D6131	Households' actual pension contributions		11.5			11.5		11.5
16.2		16.2		16.2			D6141	Household pension contribution supplements		16.2			16.2		16.2
-1.4		-1.4		-1.4				Pension scheme service charges (-)		-1.4			-1.4		-1.4
26.0		26.0			26.0		D62	Social benefits other than social transfers in kind			26.0		26.0		26.0
26.0		26.0			26.0		D6221	Other social insurance pension benefits			26.0		26.0		26.0
1.4		1.4	-16.2	27.4	12.7	-22.5	B6g	Disposable income, gross							
Use of disposable income account															
1.4		1.4		1.4			P3	Final consumption (service charge)						1.4	1.4
11.3		11.3			11.3		D8	Adjustment for the change in pension entitlements			11.3		11.3		11.3
0.0		0.0	-16.2	37.3	1.4	-22.5	B8g	Saving, gross							
Changes in assets															**Changes in liabilities and net worth**
Capital account															
0.0		0.0	-16.2	37.3	1.4	-22.5	B9	Net lending (+)/ net borrowing (-)							
Financial account															
							B9	Net lending (+)/ net borrowing (-)	-22.5	1.4	37.3	-16.2	0.0		0.0
0.0		0.0	-16.2	26.0	12.7	-22.5	F2	Currency and deposits							
11.3		11.3		11.3			F63	Pension entitlements		11.3			11.3		11.3

(g) The financial account records the changes in currency and deposits and the changes in pension entitlements of the various sectors. Since the entries in the financial account are the counterparts to entries in the other accounts or only reflect the exchange of financial assets and liabilities, net lending/net borrowing is identical to net lending/net borrowing in the capital account.

3.438. Employers can also use pension fund managers to manage the pension funds on their behalf for an explicit fee. This fee is recorded as the output of the pension fund managers and the intermediate consumption of the pension funds. It is then recorded as the output of the pension funds which is consumed by the households sector.

Defined benefit pension schemes

Differences between a defined benefit and a defined contribution pension scheme

3.439. The fundamental difference in accounting for a defined benefit pension scheme as compared with a defined contribution pension scheme is that, for the defined benefit pension scheme, the benefit to the employee in the current period is determined in terms of the undertakings made by the employer about the level of pension ultimately receivable, whereas for the defined contribution pension scheme the benefit to the employee in the current period is determined entirely by the contributions made to the scheme and the investment income and holding gains and losses earned on these and previous contributions. Thus, while there is (in principle) exact information available on the benefits for the participant in the defined contribution pension scheme, the benefits for the participants in a defined benefit pension scheme must be estimated. The source of these estimates is the actuarial estimates the employer is faced with in drawing up his own accounts.

3.440. There are four sources of changes in pension entitlements in a defined benefit pension scheme:

- The current service increase, which is the increase in entitlement associated with the wages and salaries earned in the current period.
- The past service increase, which is the increase in the value of the entitlement due to the fact that, for all participants in the scheme, retirement (and death) are one year nearer.
- The decrease in the level of entitlement due to the payment of benefits to retirees of the scheme.
- Other factors, which are reflected in the other changes in assets account.

3.441. As with a defined contribution pension scheme, both employer and employee may make actual contributions to the scheme in the current period. However, these payments may not be sufficient to meet the increase in the benefits accruing from the current year's employment. Therefore, an additional contribution from the employer is imputed to bring equality between the contributions and the increase in current service entitlements. These imputed contributions are usually positive, but it is possible for them to be negative if the sum of the contributions received exceeds the increase in current service entitlements. The implications of this case are discussed below when examining the relationship between the employer and the fund.

3.442. At the end of an accounting period, the level of the pension entitlements due to past and present employees can be calculated by estimating the present value of the amounts due to be paid in retirement using actuarial estimates of the expected life length of the beneficiaries.[74] This is the amount that appears in the balance sheet as the

[74] Detailed information on how to compute actuarial estimates of pension entitlements is available in Eurostat and European Central Bank (2011).

liability towards the employees. One element in the increase of this amount year by year is the fact that the present value of the entitlements existing at the beginning of the year and still due at the end of the year have increased because the future is one year nearer and so one fewer discount factor must be used to calculate the present value. It is this unwinding of the discount that accounts for the past service increase in entitlements.

3.443. A further basic difference between a defined benefit pension scheme and a defined contribution pension scheme concerns the payment for the cost of operating the pension scheme. As already noted, under a defined contribution pension scheme, all the risk is borne by the beneficiaries. The pension scheme is operated on their behalf and they pay for the cost of it. Since the fund may be operated by a unit other than the employer, it is appropriate to treat the operating cost as part of the investment income that is retained by the fund to meet its costs (and generate a profit). In keeping with accounting for insurance, the investment income is treated as being attributed in full to the beneficiaries, part being used to meet the cost and the remainder being reinvested with the fund.

3.444. For a defined benefit pension scheme, the situation is somewhat different. The risk that the fund may be insufficient to meet the promises of entitlement is met in part or in whole by the pension manager (either the employer or a unit that has assumed the risk of meeting the pension obligations) and not by the beneficiaries alone. The fund may be directly controlled by the employer and be part of the same institutional unit, or may be purely notional. Even in this case, there are costs associated with operating the scheme. Although these are initially borne by the employer, it is appropriate to regard this as a form of income in kind provided to the employees and, for convenience, it may be included with the employers' contributions. There is an element of pragmatism in this, since this assumes all the costs are borne by current employees and none by retirees. It also assumes that the attribution that must be made in the case of notional schemes can be applied in other circumstances also.

3.445. For a defined benefit scheme, it is unlikely that self- and non-employed persons currently contribute, though it is possible if they were previously in employment giving rise to a defined benefit pension and have the right to continue to participate. Those previously in employment (whether currently in receipt of a pension or not) receive investment income and pay contribution supplements.

Transactions recorded for a defined benefit pension scheme

3.446. The initial discussion assumes that the employer retains the whole responsibility for meeting the pension payments.

3.447. The total contribution made by an employer to a defined benefit pension scheme on behalf of his employee must be sufficient that, together with any actual contribution by the employee and excluding the cost of operating the scheme, it exactly matches the current service increase in the employee's pension entitlements. The contribution by the employer is divided into an actual and an imputed part, the latter being calculated so as to meet the need of an exact match between all contributions to the fund adding to the entitlements of the employee and the current service cost of these entitlements.

3.448. The contribution by the employer should be calculated in relation to the pension entitlement earned in the period regardless of any investment income earned by the scheme in the same period or any overfunding of the scheme. The current period entitlement is part of compensation of employees, and not to include the full value of the employer's contribution understates compensation of employees and therefore overstates operating surplus. An extreme case has occurred in the past when the investment of the pension entitlements has done so well that the employer has taken a "contribution holiday", that is he has not made an actual contribution towards new entitlements. It is important that contributions continue to be recorded even in the event of a contributions holiday, the benefit to the employer being regarded as a change in liabilities between the pension fund and the employer. This leaves the net worth of both the same as when contributions are not recorded under a contributions holiday without reducing compensation of employees artificially.

3.449. Under many defined benefit schemes, there is a qualifying period before an employee does in fact become eligible to receive a pension in retirement. Despite this qualifying period, both contributions and entitlements should be recorded from the start of employment, adjusted by a factor reflecting the probability that the employee will in fact satisfy the qualifying period.

3.450. The sum of employers' actual and imputed pension contributions is treated as part of compensation of employees. It is recorded as payable by the employer in the generation of income account and receivable by the employee in the allocation of primary income account. The same treatment applies to employees' actual pension contributions.

3.451. The increase in the present value of the entitlements of continuing employees and those who no longer contribute but remain eligible for pensions in future (the past service increase) represents the investment income distributed to the employees. No deduction is made for any amount that may be funded from holding gains or that is not actually matched by existing funds. It matches the amount that is unequivocally due to the employee under the prevailing agreements; the means by which the employer may ultimately match this obligation is not relevant for the recording of this as investment income any more than the means by which interest or dividends are actually financed affect their recording as investment income. The investment income is recorded as payable by the pension fund and receivable by households in the allocation of primary income account. It is immediately reinvested by the households in the fund and, in this guise, is described as pension contribution supplements. The allocation of primary income account also records the actual property income earned by the pension fund on the funds it manages. The actual property income is used to fund the investment income payable on pension entitlements. However, the employer is generally responsible for covering shortfalls between the investment income payable on pension entitlements and the actual property income earned by the pension fund on the funds it manages. The shortfall is computed as the difference between the investment income payable on pension entitlements and the actual property income earned by the pension fund on the funds it manages, and is recorded as an imputed property income payable by the employer and receivable by the pension fund in the same account.

3.452. In the secondary distribution of income account, social contributions are shown as payable by households and receivable by the pension fund. The total amount of the social contributions payable is made up of the actual and imputed contributions payable by the employers as part of compensation of employees (excluding the amount of the costs of running the pension scheme), plus actual contributions by employees plus the contribution supplements just specified. As explained in the discussion under defined contribution schemes, the accounts show the full value of the contributions and contribution supplements with an offsetting item representing the service charge payable. The amount actually payable is, thus, a net contributions figure.

3.453. Also in the secondary distribution of income account, the pension benefits payable to households by the pension fund are shown. When the benefits are taken in terms of an annuity, it is the annuity payments that are shown here, not the lump sums payable at the time of retirement. (Unless the demographics of the retirees change dramatically, the two figures will be very similar in any case.)

3.454. In the use of income account, there is an entry for the payment of the service provided by the pension fund (equal to the value of the pension fund's output[75] plus the output of the enterprises operating annuities bought with pension entitlements) payable by households to the pension fund and recorded as final consumption expenditure.

3.455. Also in the use of income account, there is an entry showing the increase (or decrease) in pension entitlements caused by the excess of contributions payable less benefits receivable in the secondary distribution of income account. This amount is shown as payable to households by the pension fund. The rationale for this is that, since this increase (or decrease) in pension entitlements directly affects the net worth of households, it should be included in the saving of the households sector. In the case of a defined benefit pension scheme, the amount is unlikely to be negative unless it is a scheme for a defunct employer and it is only paying benefits and not receiving new contributions.

3.456. The same amount that is included in the use of income account as the adjustment for the change in pension entitlements is included in the financial account as a claim by households on the pension fund. The financial account also records entries for a claim of the pension fund on the pension manager to show the liability of the employer for any underfunding or the benefit receivable by it from any overfunding. (The other part of this item reflects any change in responsibility for pension entitlements recorded as part of capital transfers.) The claim of the pension fund on the employer (the pension manager) is equal to the increase in pension entitlements arising from service to the employer and investment income payable on the opening value of the benefit entitlement, plus the fee charged by the pension administrator, less the sum of the actual contributions and actual contribution supplements.[76] When the amount accruing to the pension fund exceeds the increase in entitlements, there is an amount payable by the pension fund to the employer as pension manager. In this way, the net worth of the pension fund remains exactly zero at all times.

3.457. The amount due from the pension fund manager to the pension fund will reflect the impact of a contribution holiday, since this amount due equals the difference between the employer's actual contributions and the contribution needed to cover benefits accrued in the current period and interest on the cumulative amount due from prior periods.

3.458. The other factors affecting the change in the balance sheet entry for the change in pension entitlements are shown in the other changes in assets accounts.

Defined benefit pension schemes operated by those other than employers

3.459. It is possible that some other organization, such as a trades union, may operate a defined benefit pension scheme for its members that is in all respects parallel to an employer's defined benefit pension scheme. Exactly the same recording is followed as just described except that references to the employer should be understood to refer to the scheme organizer and references to the employee should be understood to refer to the participant in the scheme. The output of the defined benefit fund should also be calculated as the sum of costs.

[75] The output of a defined benefit pension fund is conceptually different from the pension expense for the fund reported in company accounts. The pension expense is a direct composite of periodic changes that occur in both the pension entitlements and fund assets. It is the sum of the current service increase plus the past service increase minus the actual return on the fund assets plus the amortized portion of prior service cost attributed to employee service before an amendment to the pension fund plus/minus the amortized portion of losses/gains from revisions in the pension entitlement or from investing fund assets.

[76] The claim of the pension fund on the pension manager can also be derived as the sum of the employers' imputed social contributions and imputed property income arising from past service increase.

Worked example 3.24. Computing output and other transactions associated with defined benefit schemes[77]

3.460. This worked example computes the current-price output and other related transactions associated with defined benefit pension schemes. It is assumed that these schemes are operated by employers, so the output of the funds will have to be derived using the sum of costs. Employers are also assumed to retain the liability for any underfunding or the benefit for any overfunding. Thus, employers are also acting as pension managers. The worked example also assumes that the compiling agency is able to obtain the required input data to compute the output and other related transactions, and that the participants and beneficiaries are all residents. In addition, the worked example will show how to record in the financial account the counterpart entries to show the means of payment for some of the transactions between the institutional units. For simplicity, it is assumed that these transactions are settled in currency or transferable deposits, which are part of "currency and deposits" in the financial account.

3.461. Table 3.111 shows the data on defined benefit pension funds. It is assumed that both employers and employees are contributing to the funds. The funds also report that actual property income earned on the funds they manage amounts to 2.2 units. For simplicity, it is assumed that this property income is payable by other resident sectors. In addition, actuarial calculations show that the increase in pension entitlements is 19.0 units, which comprise the current service increase (15.0 units) and investment income payable on pension entitlements (4.0 units). The investment income payable on pension entitlements represents the increase in pension entitlements coming from the past service increase due to the unwinding of the discount factor because retirement is one year nearer. Since the actual property income earned by the pension funds is less than the investment income payable on pension entitlements, there is a shortfall which will need to be covered by employers. The table also shows the operating costs associated with operating the defined benefit pension funds. It is assumed that the costs involved only include intermediate consumption of goods and services. It is also assumed that all the goods and services for intermediate consumption are purchased from other resident sectors.

Table 3.111
Data on defined benefit pension funds

Line number	Item	Value	2008 SNA code
	From observed transactions		
(1)	Employers' actual pension contributions	10.0	D1211, D6111
(2)	Employees' actual pension contributions	1.5	D11, D6131
(3)	Property income	2.2	D4
(4)	Pension benefits	16.0	D62, D6221
(5)	Intermediate consumption of goods and services	0.6	P1, P2
	From actuarial estimates		
(6)	Increase in pension entitlements	19.0	
(6a)	Current service increase	15.0	
(6b)	Investment income payable on pension entitlements	4.0	D4, D442, D6141

3.462. Table 3.112 shows how to derive the output of the pension funds, employers' imputed social contributions, imputed property income, and net social contributions. The output of the pension funds (0.6 units) is computed as the value of interme-

[77] This worked example is adapted from Reinsdorf (2011).

Table 3.112

Calculating output, employers' imputed social contributions, imputed property income, and net social contributions for defined benefit pension funds

Line number	Item	Description	Value	2008 SNA code
(7)	Output of defined benefit pension funds	(5)	0.6	P1, P3
(8)	Employers' imputed pension contributions	(6a)–(1)–(2)+(7)	4.1	D1221, D6121
(9)	Imputed property income	(6b)–(3)	1.8	D4
(10)	Net social contributions	(1)+(2)+(6b)+(8)–(7)	19.0	D61

diate consumption of goods and services. Employers' imputed social contributions (4.1 units) are computed as follows:

Increase in pension entitlements from current service (15.0 units)
minus employers' actual pension contributions (10.0 units)
minus households' (employees') actual pension contributions (1.5 units)
plus the service charge (output) of pension funds (0.6 units).

Imputed property income (1.8 units) is computed as follows:

Investment income payable on pension entitlements (4.0 units)
minus actual investment income (2.2 units).

Net social contributions payable to the pension funds (19.0 units) are obtained as follows:

Employers' actual pension contributions (10.0 units)
plus employers' imputed pension contributions (4.1 units)
plus households' (employees') actual pension contributions (1.5 units)
plus household pension contribution supplements (equivalent to investment income payable on pension supplements) (4.0 units)
less the service charge (output) of pension funds (0.6 units).

3.463. Table 3.113 shows how to calculate the changes in financial assets arising from the transactions among the defined benefit pension funds and the other institutional units, as well as the means of payment for these transactions. In general, the changes in financial assets and liabilities are computed using the following principles: changes in currency and deposits are the result of the payments made by the institutional units and the receipts they receive. On the other hand, the defined benefit pension funds also incur an increase in liabilities of pension entitlements to beneficiaries. These changes in liabilities are recorded as the corresponding changes in the financial assets of households. Furthermore, since employers are responsible for any shortfall in the funds, the pension funds also have a claim on the employers (pension managers). As an example, the defined benefit pension funds have a net decrease in assets of currency and deposits of 2.9 units during the accounting period. This is the result of the following:

- An increase in assets of currency and deposits arising from employers' actual pension contributions (10.0 units) and employees' actual pension contributions (1.5 units) receivable; and actual investment income receivable from other resident sectors (2.2 units).
- A decrease in assets of currency and deposits arising from pension benefits payable (16.0 units); and purchases of goods and services for intermediate consumption from other sectors (0.6 units).

These funds also have a net increase in liabilities of pension entitlements of 3.0 units. Furthermore, they have a claim on employers (pension managers) of 5.9 units, which

Table 3.113
Calculation of changes in financial assets and liabilities related to transactions among defined benefit pension funds and other institutional units

Line number	Item	Description	Value	2008 SNA code
	Changes in financial assets (currency and deposits)			
(11)	Employers	-(1)–(2)	-11.5	F2
(12)	Defined benefit pension funds	(1)+(2)+(3)–(4)–(5)	-2.9	F2
(13)	Households	(4)	16.0	F2
(14)	Other sectors	(5)–(3)	-1.6	F2
	Changes in financial assets (pension entitlements)			
(15)	Households	(6)–(4)	3.0	D8, F63
	Changes in liabilities (pension entitlements)			
(16)	Defined benefit pension funds	(6)–(4)	3.0	D8, F63
	Changes in financial assets (claim of the pension fund on pension managers)			
(17)	Defined benefit pension funds	(8)+(9)	5.9	F64
(17a)	From current service increase	(8)	4.1	
(17b)	From past service increase	(9)	1.8	
	Changes in liabilities (claim of the pension fund on pension managers)			
(18)	Employers	(8)+(9)	5.9	F64
(18a)	From current service increase	(8)	4.1	
(18b)	From past service increase	(9)	1.8	

comprise the claim from the current service increase (4.1 units) and the claim from past service increase (1.8 units).

3.464. Table 3.114 uses the information in the tables above to record the various transactions. To simplify the presentation and analysis, transactions which are not related to the worked example are ignored. To ensure clarity, the transactions of employers and the defined contribution pension funds are shown separately rather than combined with those of the institutional sectors to which they belong. Figures which are imputed are in bold, while those which result from re-routing are in italics. The transactions are described as follows:

(a) The output of the defined benefit pension funds is 0.6 units. This output is recorded in the production account of the funds. The intermediate consumption of goods and services of the funds (0.6 units) is also recorded in their production account. The same amount is also recorded in the output of the other sectors, since it is assumed that these goods and services are purchased from resident producers;

(b) Employers' actual (10.0 units) and imputed pension contributions (4.1 units) are treated as part of the compensation of employees and are recorded as payable by employers in the generation of income account. Employees' actual pension contributions (1.5 units) are treated as part of wages and salaries (and, by extension, compensation of employees) and are recorded as payable by employers in the same account;

(c) The entries in the generation of income account are recorded as receivable by households in the allocation of primary income account. The actuarial investment income earned on the cumulated pension entitlements (4.0 units) is also recorded as payable by the funds and receivable by households in the allocation of primary income account. The actual investment income earned by the funds (2.2 units) is also recorded as property income receivable by the funds and payable by other sectors in the allocation of pri-

Table 3.114
Recording transactions related to defined benefit pension funds

Uses															Resources
Total	Goods and services	Total economy	Other sectors	Households	Defined benefit pension funds	Employers	2008 SNA code	Transactions and balancing items	Employers	Defined benefit pension funds	Households	Other sectors	Total economy	Goods and services	Total
Production account															
1.2	1.2						P1	Output		**0.6**		0.6	1.2		1.2
0.6		0.6			0.6		P2	Intermediate consumption							
0.6		0.6	0.6		0.0		B1g	Value added, gross/Gross domestic product							
Generation of income account															
15.6		15.6				15.6	D1	Compensation of employees							
1.5		1.5				1.5	D11	Wages and salaries							
10.0		10.0				10.0	D1211	Employers' actual pension contributions							
4.1		**4.1**				**4.1**	D1221	Employers' imputed pension contributions							
-15.0		-15.0	0.6		0.0	-15.6	B2g	Operating surplus, gross							
Allocation of primary income account															
							D1	Compensation of employees			15.6		15.6		15.6
							D11	Wages and salaries			1.5		1.5		1.5
							D1211	Employers' actual pension contributions			*10.0*		*10.0*		*10.0*
							D1221	Employers' imputed pension contributions			***4.1***		***4.1***		***4.1***
4.0		4.0	2.2			**1.8**	D4	Property income		4.0			4.0		4.0
4.0		**4.0**			**4.0**		D442	Investment income payable on pension entitlements			***4.0***		***4.0***		***4.0***
0.6		0.6	-1.6	19.6	0.0	-17.4	B5g	Balance of primary income, gross/ National income, gross							
Secondary distribution of income account															
19.0		19.0		19.0			D61	Net social contributions		19.0			19.0		19.0
10.0		*10.0*		*10.0*			D6111	Employers' actual pension contributions		10.0			10.0		10.0
4.1		***4.1***		***4.1***			D6121	Employers' imputed pension contributions		**4.1**			**4.1**		**4.1**
1.5		1.5		1.5			D6131	Households' actual pension contributions		1.5			1.5		1.5
4.0		***4.0***		***4.0***			D6141	Household pension contribution supplements		**4.0**			**4.0**		**4.0**
-0.6		***-0.6***		***-0.6***				Pension scheme service charges (-)		**-0.6**			**-0.6**		**-0.6**
16.0		16.0			16.0		D62	Social benefits other than social transfers in kind			16.0		16.0		16.0
16.0		16.0			16.0		D6221	Other social insurance pension benefits			16.0		16.0		16.0
0.6		0.6	-1.6	16.6	3.0	-17.4	B6g	Disposable income, gross							
Use of disposable income account															
0.6		**0.6**		**0.6**			P3	Final consumption (service charge)						**0.6**	**0.6**
3.0		3.0			3.0		D8	Adjustment for change in pension entitlements			3.0		3.0		3.0
0.0		0.0	-1.6	19.0	0.0	-17.4	B8g	Saving, gross							
0.0		0.0	-1.6	19.0	-5.9	-11.5	B8g	Saving, gross (actual)							
0.0		**0.0**			**5.9**	**-5.9**	B8g	Saving, gross (imputed)							
Changes in assets															**Changes in liabilities and net worth**
Capital account															
0.0		0.0	-1.6	19.0	0.0	-17.4	B9	Net lending (+)/net borrowing (-)							
0.0		0.0	-1.6	19.0	-5.9	-11.5	B9	Net lending (+)/net borrowing (-) (actual)							
0.0		**0.0**			**5.9**	**-5.9**	B9	Net lending (+)/net borrowing (-) (imputed)							

Total	Goods and services	Total economy	Other sectors	Households	Defined benefit pension funds	Employers	2008 SNA code	Transactions and balancing items	Employers	Defined benefit pension funds	Households	Other sectors	Total economy	Goods and services	Total
Financial account															
							B9	Net lending (+)/net borrowing (-)	-17.4	0.0	19.0	-1.6	0.0		0.0
							B9	Net lending (+)/net borrowing (-) (actual)	-11.5	-5.9	19.0	-1.6	0.0		0.0
							B9	Net lending (+)/net borrowing (-) (imputed)	**-5.9**	**5.9**			**0.0**		**0.0**
0.0		0.0	-1.6	16.0	-2.9	-11.5	F2	Currency and deposits							
3.0		3.0		3.0			F63	Pension entitlements		3.0			3.0		3.0
5.9		**5.9**			**5.9**		F64	Claim of the pension fund on pension managers	**5.9**				**5.9**		**5.9**
4.1		**4.1**			**4.1**			From current service increase	**4.1**				**4.1**		**4.1**
1.8		**1.8**			**1.8**			From past service increase	**1.8**				**1.8**		**1.8**

mary income account. The shortfall of 1.8 units (i.e. the difference between actuarial investment income on pension entitlements and actual property income) is recorded as imputed property income payable by employers and receivable by the funds in the same account;

(d) Net social contributions (19.0 units) are recorded in the secondary distribution of income account as payable by households and receivable by the pension funds. Net social contributions payable by households include employers' actual pension contributions (10.0 units) and employers' imputed social contributions (4.1 units), since all social insurance contributions are to be recorded as being paid by households to social insurance schemes. The pension benefits paid by the pension funds (16.0 units) are recorded as other social pension benefits payable by the pension funds and receivable by households in this account;

(e) The output of the defined benefit pension funds (0.6 units) is recorded as the final consumption expenditure of households in the use of disposable income account. This account also records an adjustment for the change in pension entitlements (3.0 units) in order to ensure that gross saving is invariant to the dual treatment of pensions as current transfers and pension entitlements as financial assets;

(f) Since there are no capital account transactions, net lending/net borrowing in the capital account is the same as gross saving in the use of disposable income account;

(g) The financial account records the changes in currency and deposits and the changes in pension entitlements of the various sectors. As employers undertake to be responsible for any underfunding of the pension funds, the financial account also records the amount of underfunding of the pension funds (5.9 units) as a claim by the pension funds on the employers. This claim comprises the claim from the current service increase (4.1 units) and the claim from the past service increase (1.8 units). Since the entries in the financial account are the counterparts to entries in the other accounts or only reflect the exchange of financial assets and liabilities, net lending/net borrowing is identical to net lending/net borrowing in the capital account, although, in practice, differences in data sources and the timing of the recording of transactions may result in a discrepancy between the estimates of net lending/net borrowing in these two accounts.

Computation of pension entitlements under defined benefit pension schemes using the accrued and projected benefit obligations

3.465. Many defined benefit pension schemes use a formula[78] to set benefits that involves either the final salary or average salary as a key determinant. This implies that any wage increase means that the total pension entitlements accrued to date are increased to take account of the new salary level. This is a significant benefit for the individual employee concerned, but what are the consequences for the employer's pension liabilities?

3.466. The accounting profession uses two actuarial terms that bear on this discussion: the projected benefit obligation (PBO) and accrued benefit obligation (ABO) approaches. The main difference between these two compilation methods refers to the treatment of future wage increases. In the case of the PBO approach, (expected) future increases in income — either through promotions or through a general increase in wages for various reasons, such as keeping up with inflation, sharing productivity gains with employees, changes in the legal minimum wage and changes in labour market conditions — are fully taken into account. For an individual, the PBO makes assumptions about the expected future increases in income that the person is likely to receive and calculates his final salary accordingly. Then, if he has in fact only worked for 20 out of an expected 40 years, it halves the final salary and calculates the pension entitlement for the individual as if this were his current salary. The ABO approach, on the other hand, considers only the present value of benefits earned to date. Future wage increases are not taken into account. It represents the amount the employee could walk away with if he left the firm tomorrow and may be the basis of assessing a person's net worth in, say, the case of a divorce settlement. If an individual's ABO increases in steps as his wage increases, the PBO increases steadily over time. For the individual employee, the PBO is always higher than the ABO until the moment of retirement, when the ABO catches up with the PBO. From the viewpoint of the pension manager, a PBO approach is a more prudent measure of what the eventual level of entitlement is likely to be. Conversely, from the viewpoint of the individual, the ABO approach is more prudent in the context where the risk of losing the opportunity to benefit from future wage increases is high.

3.467. It would seem at first sight that the level of pension entitlements for a corporation should be the sum of all the pension entitlements of each of the employees and that therefore the sum of the PBO estimates would be considerably higher than that of the sum of the ABO estimates and would evolve more smoothly over time. However, what is true for the individual is not necessarily true for the cohort of employees. Suppose the employer has five classes of people for whose pensions he is responsible, four grades of employees and one set of retirees, and for simplicity, there are the same number of each. Consider the situation where in a year, the retirees die; the most senior set of employees retire, the next three sets of employees are all promoted and a new set of employees is recruited at the lowest level. Every current employee is better off after promotion, but the overall liability of the employer has not changed. The effect of aggregating ABOs is to smooth the total entitlement, and, while it will still be lower than the aggregate PBOs, it will not necessarily be more volatile. Indeed, it may be more stable. In contrast, the PBO approach could be volatile when pay increases do not happen as projected or when employees exit a pension scheme because the pension manager or employer goes out of business or terminates the scheme.

3.468. While the profile of the ABO of an individual will show step changes when wage increases occur, for a cohort of employees, the effect is much smoother. For a cohort of the same age remaining with the corporation for the whole of their working lives, the ABO estimates will be considerably lower than PBO estimates in the early years, but

[78] The pension formula might define the retirement benefits as, say, 1.5 per cent times years of service times final year's salary.

the rate of increase of the ABOs will be faster than that of the PBOs so that at the point immediately before retirement, the two sets of estimates will be equal. Merging cohorts of employees with different periods of service with the corporation will bring the ABO estimates for all employees closer to the PBO ones also.

3.469. As long as the grade structure of the corporation stays the same, ABO and PBO will move roughly in step. If the firm expands and takes on many new employees at the lower grades, the PBOs will increase noticeably faster than the ABOs because the PBOs make estimates of how long the new employees will stay and how far they will be promoted, while the ABOs record simply the pension accrued in their first year. If the firm decides to downsize and reduces the number of their managerial staff, this will reduce the promotion prospects of the employees and a downward revision in PBO will be necessary. Because ABOs reflect simply the "locked-in" pension, this estimate is not affected.

3.470. The question arises, though, of how to record the impact of promotion on the employee if an ABO recording is used. Any version of treating the increase as a form of compensation of employees or investment income falls back into the assumption that the aggregate of entitlements is the sum of the individual entitlements but without looking at other individual impacts on the aggregates, such as when someone leaves and loses the pension entitlement because not enough time has been served or when someone dies before retirement age. A simpler and adequate solution is to treat the impact of promotions for the unit as a whole as a price change and record the change in the revaluation account.

3.471. If the PBO method of recording entitlements is chosen as the preferred valuation, an adjustment in the other changes in volume of assets account is needed only if the structure of the enterprise changes so the chances of promotion change. On the other hand, the regular estimates of the employer's contributions to social insurance schemes included in compensation of employees will be systematically higher than those made under an ABO regime because the increase in pension entitlement that determines the size of the contributions will be based on a notional salary calculated on a PBO basis rather than the actual one.

Volume measures of the output associated with social insurance schemes which pay pension benefits

3.472. The output associated with social insurance pension schemes which is computed from input data is measured at current prices. Volume measures of the output need to be computed by removing the effects of price changes. The method used to compute the volume measures will depend on the method used to compute the current-price output. For output which is computed as the sum of costs, the compiling agency can consider deflating this output by a composite index of input prices to obtain the volume measures. For output derived from an explicit fee, the volume measures can be obtained by deflation using an appropriate price index. In the case where output is computed using the life insurance output formula, the volume measures can be estimated by extrapolating the base-period output by the volume growth of social contributions. The volume measures of social contributions can be obtained by deflation using an appropriate wage index.

3.473. Volume measures of the service charges associated with non-resident social insurance schemes which pay pension benefits can be obtained by deflating the current-price imports of the service charges by a composite price index comprising the price indices for these charges from partner countries. The price indices will need to be adjusted for changes in exchange rates first. Alternatively, the compiling agency can consider extrapolating the base-period imports of these service charges by the growth in a composite volume index comprising the volume indices for output or exports of these charges from partner countries. If data from partner countries are not available, the compiling agency can consider using the price indices which are used to deflate domestically produced current-price output of these service charges or extrapolate the base-period value of the imported service charges by the volume growth of the domestically produced service charges.

Supplementary table on pension schemes in social insurance

3.474. As mentioned earlier in this chapter, social insurance is subdivided into social security schemes and employment-related social insurance schemes other than social security.

3.475. The most important schemes under social insurance schemes are pension schemes. However, as social security is normally financed on a pay-as-you-go basis, pension entitlements accruing under social security are not normally shown in the SNA. If all countries had similar benefits provided under social security and under private schemes, international comparisons would be relatively straightforward. However, this is far from being the case and national perceptions of exactly what is covered by social security vary considerably.

3.476. There are two problems with simply suggesting that entitlements from social security should be shown in the SNA. The first is that reliable estimates of the entitlements may not be readily available, whereas it is increasingly the case that such estimates exist for private schemes. Secondly, there is an argument that such estimates are of limited usefulness where government has the possibility of changing the basis on which entitlements are determined in order to keep the entitlements within the bounds of what is budgetarily feasible. However, the consequence of simply accepting that en-

Box 3.5

Comparison of the accrued benefit obligation and project benefit obligation methods[a]

The differences between the ABO and PBO methods can be illustrated using a simple hypothetical pension scheme. Participants in the pension scheme work for three years, retire in the fourth year and spend one year in retirement in the fifth year. Their salary grows by 5 per cent per period from a starting level of 25000.0 units. Vesting is immediate, there are no breaks in service and there is no early retirement. The accrued retirement benefit equals 10.0 per cent of salary times the number of periods worked times final salary. The interest rate is 15.0 per cent. It is standard actuarial practice to require that the current service increase be paid at the start of each period.

Table 3.5.1 follows a single participant through his career and retirement. The steps to calculate the pension liability are as follows:

- Determine the accrued retirement benefits using the pension formula.
- Find the present value of the retirement benefits as of the retirement date.
- Find the present value of the retirement benefits (pension liability) as of the current date.

For example, the accrued retirement benefit in year two under the ABO method (2500.0 units) is calculated using the pension formula as 10.0 per cent times 1 year times 25000.0 units. The amount of 2500.0 units also represents the present value of retirement benefits as at the retirement date, since the retirement period is assumed to be one year. The present value of the retirement benefits in year two (1890.4 units) is obtained as $\frac{2500.0}{(1.15)^2}$. The same steps can be used to obtain the pension liability under the ABO method in years three and four, except that the final salary used is that in years two and three and different discount factors will need to be used.

In the case of the PBO method, the same steps are also used to obtain the pension liability in year two, except that the final salary used is 27562.5 units throughout.

The steps to calculate the current service increase are as follows:

- Determine the increase in pension entitlement using the data on accrued retirement benefits.
- Find the present value of the increase in pension entitlement to get the current service increase as of the current date.

For example, under the ABO method, the increase in pension entitlement in year two is obtained as the difference in accrued retirement benefits for year three (5250.0 units) and year two (2500.0 units). This increase is then discounted to obtain the current service increase in year two. A similar approach can be used to calculate the current service increase under the PBO method.

For each year, the past service increase is calculated by multiplying the interest rate by the sum of the pension liability and the current service increase. For example, under the ABO method, the past service increase in year two is calculated by multiplying the interest rate (15.0 per cent) by the sum of the corresponding pension liability (1890.4 units) and current service increase (2079.4 units). A similar approach can be used to calculate the past service increase under the PBO method. The current service increase is included in the calculation of the past service increase owing to the assumption that the former is paid at the start of the year.

From the table, it can be observed that the PBO liability is initially higher than that of the ABO and that they become equal at retirement. The PBO current service increase is higher than that of the ABO at first, but becomes lower in the last year of the career.

Table 3.5.1
Comparison of the ABO and PBO methods for a hypothetical employee's lifespan

Age	Salary paid	Pension benefit paid	Accrued retirement benefit			Pension liability			Current service increase			Past service increase		
			ABO	PBO	PBO/ ABO	ABO	PBO	PBO/ ABO	ABO	PBO	PBO/ ABO	ABO	PBO	PBO/ ABO
1	25000.0	0.0	0.0	0.0	...	0.0	0.0	...	1643.8	1812.3	1.10	246.6	271.8	1.10
2	26250.0	0.0	2500.0	2756.3	1.10	1890.4	2084.1	1.10	2079.4	2084.1	1.00	595.5	625.2	1.05
3	27562.5	0.0	5250.0	5512.5	1.05	4565.2	4793.5	1.05	2625.0	2396.7	0.91	1078.5	1078.5	1.00
4	0.0	8268.8	8268.8	8268.8	1.00	8268.8	8268.8	1.00	0.0	0.0	...	0.0	0.0	...
5	0.0	0.0	0.0	0.0	...	0.0	0.0	...	0.0	0.0	...	0.0	0.0	...

Table 3.5.2 follows a pension scheme that has the same conditions as those in table 3.5.1. The employer operating the pension scheme starts with 10 newly hired participants and adds 10 more every year until year five. Hiring then ceases and the scheme stops in year nine. As the workforce ages, the ABO measure of service cost as a percentage of payroll rises faster than that of the PBO. If the distribution of ages in the workforce is uniform, the ABO measure of service cost is higher than that of the PBO, so, on the whole, the ABO method tends to attribute the growth of pension entitlement more to compensation in the form of imputed contributions, while the PBO method tends to attribute it more to imputed property income earned on the scheme's benefit liability.

Table 3.5.2
Comparison of ABO and PBO methods for a hypothetical pension scheme from initiation to termination (units, except numbers of participants, ratios and percentages)

Year	Salaries paid	Pension benefits paid	Accrued retirement benefits			Pension liability		
			ABO	PBO	PBO/ABO	ABO	PBO	PBO/ABO
1	250000.0	0.0	0.0	0.0	...	0.0	0.0	...
2	512500.0	0.0	25000.0	27562.5	1.10	18903.6	20841.2	1.10
3	788125.0	0.0	77500.0	82687.5	1.07	64555.8	68776.0	1.07
4	788125.0	82687.5	160187.5	165375.0	1.03	147243.3	151463.5	1.03
5	788125.0	82687.5	160187.5	165375.0	1.03	147243.3	151463.5	1.03
6	538125.0	82687.5	160187.5	165375.0	1.03	147243.3	151463.5	1.03
7	275625.0	82687.5	135187.5	137812.5	1.02	128339.7	130622.3	1.02
8	0.0	82687.5	82687.5	82687.5	1.00	82687.5	82687.5	1.00
9	0.0	0.0	0.0	0.0	...	0.0	0.0	...

Current service increase			Current service increase as a percentage of payroll		Past service increase			Participants	
ABO	PBO	PBO/ABO	ABO	PBO	ABO	PBO	PBO/ABO	Active	Retired
16437.9	18122.8	1.10	6.6	7.2	2465.7	2718.4	1.10	10	0
37231.9	38964.0	1.05	7.3	7.6	8420.3	8970.8	1.07	20	0
63481.9	62931.4	0.99	8.1	8.0	19205.6	19756.1	1.03	30	0
63481.9	62931.4	0.99	8.1	8.0	19205.6	19756.1	1.03	30	10
63481.9	62931.4	0.99	8.1	8.0	19205.6	19756.1	1.03	30	10
47044.0	44808.6	0.95	8.7	8.3	16740.0	17037.7	1.02	20	10
26250.0	23967.4	0.91	9.5	8.7	10785.3	10785.3	1.00	10	10
0.0	0.0	...	...	...	0.0	0.0	...	0	10
0.0	0.0	...	...	...	0.0	0.0	...	0	0

[a] The box is adapted from Reinsdorf (2009) and Reinsdorf and Lenze (2009).

titlements for private schemes are shown and for social security are not is that some countries would include the greater part of pension entitlements in the accounts and some would show almost none.

3.477. In view of the different institutional arrangements on pensions in countries, the 2008 SNA recommends that countries can consider compiling a supplementary table showing the entire range of pension schemes. The supplementary table is shown in table 3.115.[79] It does not cover social assistance schemes.

3.478. One of the main functions of the supplementary table is to provide users with comprehensive information which allows the compilation and comparison of various alternative key macroeconomic variables, such as pension entitlements, household saving rates or general government deficit and debt figures.

3.479. The overall logic of the table is to present the opening and closing stocks of pension entitlements of households vis-à-vis the pension obligations of all pension schemes in social insurance (including social security), and the transactions and other economic flows during the period which account for the difference between the opening and the closing positions, thus showing systematically the pension obligations of all these schemes. In addition to the data on the pension obligations and their accumulation, other related indicators are shown which might be of benefit for the users of the table. These are the output produced, the assets held by pension schemes and the changes of their pension obligations related to the revaluation of assets.

3.480. The columns of the table distinguish pension schemes as follows:

(a) By type of recording: positions and flows of pension schemes recorded in the core accounts (pension schemes in columns A to F), and positions of pension schemes recorded only in the supplementary table (pension schemes in columns G and H);

(b) By type of pension manager: non-general government (columns A to C), and general government pension schemes (columns D to H);

(c) By institutional sector: pension schemes classified in non-government sectors (columns A to E), and pension schemes including social security pension schemes classified in the general government sector (columns F, G and H);

(d) By type of pension scheme: defined contribution scheme (columns A and D), and defined benefit schemes including other non-defined contribution schemes (columns B and E to G).

3.481. Column A includes defined contribution schemes managed by the non-government sector, while column D includes those defined contribution schemes managed by the general government sector. All defined contribution pension schemes should be included in the core accounts.

3.482. Column B includes non-government-managed defined benefit schemes; however, it also contains hybrid pension schemes which have both a defined benefit and defined contribution element. Column C is the total of column A and column B.

3.483. Government schemes for their own employees where separate accounting information, distinct from social security, is shown in the main accounts appear in columns E and F. Column E shows schemes managed by an insurance corporation and column F those managed by government itself. Column F shows that part of all defined benefit schemes of government that are retained within the government accounts as distinct from being moved into separate units or managed for government by another institutional unit.

[79] Detailed information on how to compute the supplementary table is available in Eurostat and European Central Bank (2011).

Table 3.115

A supplementary table showing the extent of pension schemes included in, and excluded from, the System of National Accounts sequence of accounts

Row number	Position/transaction/other flow	Liabilities appear in the core national accounts							Liabilities do not appear in the core national accounts		
	Pension manager	Non-general government			General government						
						General government employee defined benefit schemes					
		Defined contribution schemes	Defined benefit schemes	Total	Defined contribution schemes	In the financial corporations sector	In the general government sector	In the general government sector	Social security pension schemes	Total pension schemes	Pension entitlements of nonresident households
	Column number	A	B	C	D	E	F	G	H	I	J
	Opening balance sheet										
1	Pension entitlements										
	Transactions										
2	Social contributions relating to pension schemes										
2.1	Employers' actual social contributions										
2.2	Employers' imputed social contributions										
2.3	Households' actual social contributions										
2.4	Households' social contribution supplements										
3	Other (actuarial) accumulation of pension entitlements in social security funds										
4	Pension benefits										
5	Adjustment to the change in pension entitlements										
6	Changes in pension entitlements due to transfers of entitlements										
7	Changes in entitlements due to negotiated changes in scheme structure										
	Other economic flows										
8	Revaluations										
9	Other changes in volume										
	Closing balance sheet										
10	Pension entitlements										
	Related indicators										
11	Output										

Notes: Empty cells show where entries appear in the main ("core") accounts. Black cells show where no entry is appropriate. Grey cells show where information is provided in the supplementary table only.

Row 2 is the sum of rows 2.1 to 2.4.

Row 3 is the analogue of employers' imputed contributions in the case where government has assumed the ultimate responsibility for any shortfall in pension provision.

Row 5 is the sum of rows 2 and 3 less 4 less the service charge.

3.484. Columns G and H cover those pension schemes whose stocks, transactions and other flows in pension obligations are not included in the core national accounts. Any government schemes for their own employees distinct from social security that do not appear in the main accounts are shown in column G. The distinction between columns F and G is based on how close the scheme is to the national social security scheme. Column H relates to social security schemes. Columns G and H are the focus of this supplementary table: by adding pension obligations of these columns to those of the core accounts, it will be possible to better compare data by country.

3.485. The sum of columns E, F and G shows the total responsibility of government for pension provision for their own employees. Column I is the total of all schemes including social security. It sums up all the pension entitlements acquired or held by resident households. Column J shows the pension entitlements acquired or held by non-resident households. These pension entitlements acquired or held by non-resident households should be shown if they are significant for a country. However, the data sources for this column may be weak.

3.486. The rows of the table relate to positions, transactions and other economic flows associated with pension obligations of the schemes included in the table. Social contributions of both an actual and imputed nature are recorded. Two related indicators refer to the output and the assets held by the pension scheme to meet pensions.

3.487. Row 1 is the opening stock of pension entitlements, which is equivalent to the closing stock of the previous year. The corresponding closing stock of pension entitlements at the end of the relevant period is shown in row 10.

3.488. Rows 2.1 and 2.3 record the actual social contributions by employers and employees. In Columns G and H, the actual social contributions made by both employers (row 2.1) and employees (row 2.3) appear in the core accounts, while all other entries in these two columns are shown only in the supplementary table (except row 4). Row 2.2 records the imputed social contributions by employers in the case of defined benefit schemes. Employer-imputed social contributions are generally measured as the balancing item. Any changes in pension entitlements over the year not included in the other rows of the table are captured in row 2.2. This row also covers any "experience effects", whereby the observed outcome of pension modelling assumptions (real wage growth rate, discount rate, etc.) differs from the levels assumed.[80] It should be noted that, for social security pension schemes, such "experience effects" are not recorded in row 2.2, but in row 3. By construction, this row is not applicable to defined contribution schemes. Row 2.4 refers to the property income earned, or imputed, on the schemes which are routed via the household or the rest of the world sector. For all defined benefit schemes, including social security, whether funded or unfunded, this property income would be the equivalent to the unwinding of the nominal discount rate.

3.489. Given that the supplementary table provides a complete overview of the changes in pension entitlements over the accounting period, a specific row is needed to show cases where actual social contributions to the social security pension scheme are not actuarially based. Such cases reflect an imputed contribution (which is not the responsibility of any employer). Row 3 shows these imputed transactions of social security pension schemes (as other (actuarial) increases to pension entitlements in social security pension schemes). The entries in this row can be positive or negative. Negative cases arise in a social security pension scheme when the discount rate is higher than the scheme's internal rate of return, for example, if contributions have been increased above the actuarially required level to finance a short-run cash shortfall. By contrast, positive values can occur when the discount rate is lower than the scheme's internal rate of return. Row 3 does not show cash transfers from tax revenues, which are recorded in the core accounts as current transfers between government units, unless they affect pension entitlements. "Experience effects" found in social security pension schemes in which the observed outcome of pension mod-

[80] These "experience effects" are included in row 2.2, as they have an impact on the costs of pension schemes to employers.

elling assumptions (real wage growth rate, discount rate, etc.) differs from the levels assumed in the previous estimation are also recorded in row 3.

3.490. Row 4 records the pension benefits that are payable during the period. Row 5 presents changes in pension entitlements due to contributions and benefits. It is equal to row 2 plus row 3 minus row 4 minus the service charge. This balancing item measured from the non-financial side is conceptually equivalent to that measured from the financial side.

3.491. Row 6 shows possible transfers of pension entitlements between schemes, both domestic and in the rest of the world. Transfer of pension entitlements can occur if there is a change in employers or if a government assumes responsibility for pension obligations for the employees of a non-government unit through an explicit transaction.

3.492. Row 7 shows the impact of negotiated pension reforms on pension entitlements. Negotiated reforms are recorded as transactions in the following manner:

(a) If the entitlements of a pension scheme are included in the core accounts, and the employer/manager agrees to change the terms of pension entitlements via negotiation with the employees concerned, this change should be recorded as a transaction in the supplementary table under row 7;

(b) If the entitlements of a pension scheme are not recorded in the core accounts, and the employer/manager agrees to a change in the terms of pension entitlements via negotiation with the employees concerned, this change should be recorded as a transaction in row 7 of the supplementary table;

(c) Changes agreed in parliament to pension entitlements under social security schemes are recorded as if the changes had been negotiated.

3.493. Rows 8 and 9 show the other economic flows as revaluations and other changes in volume associated with pension schemes in social insurance. Table 3.116 breaks down other economic flows into revaluations and other changes in the volume of assets.

Table 3.116
Other economic flows as revaluations and other changes in the volume of assets

Row number	Other economic flows
8	Revaluations
	Changes in the assumed discount rate
	Changes in assumed real wage developments
	Changes in assumed price developments
9	Other changes in volume
	Other changes in assumptions and model specifications
	Other changes

3.494. Revaluations are due to changes to the key model assumptions in the actuarial calculations and are covered in row 8. These assumptions are the discount rate, the wage rate and, if used in the model, the inflation rate. Other changes in prices, such as write-downs, are also covered in row 8. Experience effects are not to be included here in principle, though in some circumstances it may not be possible to single them out.

3.495. When the demographic assumptions used in the actuarial calculations are changed, they are recorded as other changes to the volume of assets (row 9). Any other changes to assumptions which are not revaluations are covered in row 9. These include presumptions on future retirement behaviour. If these retirement patterns are altered in the model, the resulting changes to the outcomes are recorded in row 9. However, such changes are only covered in row 9 if they are not derived from legislative reform.

3.496. Besides changes to the underlying assumptions, the general framework of the actuarial model applied may also change from one year to the next to improve the accuracy of the results. Row 9 records these changes to the estimation approach which are not due to altered assumptions, but result from a change in the model framework.

3.497. Row 9 also covers a number of other changes in the volume of assets. These include changes to pension entitlements that are imposed without negotiation, and defined contribution pension schemes that hold losses of pension funds.

3.498. Row 11 shows the output of financial services associated with the schemes. The previous sections have already discussed how to calculate this output.

Accounting for non-pension contributions and benefits

Reference:
2008 SNA, Chapter 17, Cross-cutting and other special issues, Part 2, Social insurance schemes

3.499. Non-pension benefits may be payable under social security and under employment-related schemes other than social security. Although in many countries there may in fact be no non-pension benefits, a description is given of how these should be recorded if they exist. For other social insurance schemes, the way of recording varies depending on whether reserves for provision of future benefits are set aside or not. Although in many cases, there may be no such reserves and the benefits are paid on a pay-as-you-go basis, a description of the appropriate recording in each case is given.

Non-pension benefits payable under social security

3.500. As is typical of social security schemes, there may be contributions payable by both the employer and the employee. The costs of operating social security schemes are treated as part of the normal expenditure of general government if the schemes are not separate institutional units, so the accounting for social security operations does not include measures of output. If these schemes are treated as separate institutional units, their output is computed as the sum of costs.

3.501. The recording of the transactions of social security schemes which pay non-pension benefits is similar in content to social security schemes which pay pension benefits. Thus, the Handbook will not provide a worked example to show how to record the transactions of social security schemes which pay non-pension benefits.

Unfunded non-pension benefits other than those from social security

3.502. In the SNA, an employer operating an unfunded scheme is regarded as making an imputed social contribution to the scheme on behalf of the employees. In practice, the value of the employers' and employees' contributions is usually set equal in value to the benefits payable in the period under consideration (plus the cost of operating the scheme as described in the following paragraph). The imputed contribution forms part of the compensation of employees and is also shown as being payable by the employees to the scheme together with any actual payments by the employees. Even though the scheme is unfunded, the employee may still make a contribution; however, it is not uncommon for unfunded schemes to be non-contributory for the employees.

3.503. Even if a scheme is unfunded, there are costs involved in administering it. In principle, output equal to the sum of these costs should be treated as being paid for by the beneficiaries from an imputed element of contributions. The imputed contribution to employees should include these costs, as well as the value of the benefits received by employees. A value equal to the amount of the costs of operating the scheme is then recorded in the use of income account as a purchase of a service by the employees from the employer.

3.504. There are two transactions recorded for the production and consumption of the services provided by the employer. Because the scheme is unfunded, there are no investment income flows and no contribution supplements to be recorded. There are two sets of redistributive transactions recorded.

3.505. The production and consumption transactions are as follows:

(a) Output of services is imputed in the production account of the employer, and the value of the output forms part of the imputed employers' contributions to social insurance incorporated in compensation of employees;

(b) Consumption of the service is recorded as household final consumption expenditure in the use of income account for resident households or as exports for non-resident households.

3.506. The redistributive transactions are as follows:

(a) Employers' imputed contributions to unfunded social insurance schemes are shown as payable by the sector in which the employer is located in the generation of income account and receivable by households in the allocation of primary income account;

(b) In the secondary distribution of income account, employers' imputed contributions and any actual contributions by employees are shown as payable by households and receivable by the employer. The service charge of the unfunded social insurance schemes will need to be deducted from these contributions to obtain net social contributions. Further, benefits payable to households by the employer are shown as payable by the employer and receivable by households.

Worked example 3.25. Computing output and other transactions associated with unfunded employment-related social insurance schemes other than social security which pay non-pension benefits

3.507. This worked example computes the current-price output and other related transactions associated with unfunded employment-related social insurance schemes other than social security which pay non-pension benefits. Since the schemes are unfunded, they are non-autonomous, so their output will be computed using the sum of costs. As the schemes are non-autonomous, the accounts of their social insurance funds are embedded in the accounts of the employers. It is assumed that all the participants and beneficiaries are residents. The worked example also assumes that the compiling agency is able to obtain the required input data for the transactions. In addition, the worked example will show how to record in the financial account the counterpart entries to show the means of payment for some of the transactions between the institutional units. For simplicity, it is assumed that these transactions are settled in currency or transferable deposits, which are part of "currency and deposits" in the financial account.

3.508. Table 3.117 shows the input data from unfunded employment-related social insurance funds which pay non-pension benefits. It is assumed that employees do not make social non-pension contributions to the funds. There are no employers' actual non-pension contributions, since, as mentioned before, an employer operating an unfunded scheme is regarded as making an imputed social contribution to the scheme on behalf of the employees. The table also shows the costs involved in operating the social insurance funds. It is assumed that these costs only include intermediate consumption of goods and services. It is also assumed that all the goods and services for intermediate consumption are purchased from other resident sectors.

Table 3.117
Data from employment-related social insurance funds which pay non-pension benefits

Line number	Item	Value	2008 SNA code
(1)	Non-pension benefits	9.0	D62, D6222
(2)	Intermediate consumption of goods and services	0.7	P1, P2

3.509. Table 3.118 shows how to derive the output of the employment-related social insurance funds, employers' imputed non-pension contributions and net social contributions. The output of the other employment-related social insurance funds (0.7 units) is computed as the value of intermediate consumption of goods and services. Employers' imputed non-pension contributions (9.7 units) are computed as follows:

> Output of the other employment-related social insurance funds (0.7 units)
>
> *plus* other social insurance non-pension benefits (9.0 units).

Net social contributions to the other employment-related social insurance funds (9.0 units) are obtained as follows:

> Employers' imputed non-pension contributions (9.7 units)
>
> *minus* the service charge (output) of employment-related social insurance funds (0.7 units).

Table 3.118
Calculation of output, employers' imputed non-pension contributions and net social contributions for unfunded employment-related social insurance funds which pay non-pension benefits

Line number	Item	Description	Value	2008 SNA code
(3)	Output	(2)	0.7	P1, P3
(4)	Employers' imputed non-pension contributions	(3)+(1)	9.7	D1, D1222, D6122
(5)	Net social contributions	(4)–(3)	9.0	D61

3.510. Table 3.119 shows how to calculate the changes in financial assets arising from the above transactions above, as well as the means of payment for these transactions. In general, the calculations of these changes are similar to those for worked example 3.22, except that, since the employment-related social insurance funds are non-autonomous, their transactions are included in the transactions of employers.

Table 3.119
Calculation of changes in financial assets related to transactions among unfunded employment-related social insurance funds which pay non-pension benefits and other institutional units

Line number	Item	Description	Value	2008 SNA code
	Financial assets (currency and deposits)			
(6)	Employers	–(2)–(1)	-9.7	F2
(7)	Households	(1)	9.0	F2
(8)	Other sectors	(2)	0.7	F2

3.511. Table 3.120 uses the information in the tables above to record the various transactions. To simplify the presentation and analysis, transactions which are not related to the worked example are ignored. The recording of the transactions is similar to that in worked example 3.22, except that this worked example only records employers' imputed rather than actual social non-pension contributions which are partly used to finance the operating costs of the funds. In addition, since the unfunded social insurance funds are non-autonomous, their output, net social contributions and social insurance non-pension benefits payable are recorded in the sector of the employers. Furthermore, since the entries in the financial account are the counterparts to entries in the other

Table 3.120

Recording transactions related to unfunded employment-related social insurance funds which pay non-pension benefits

Uses													Resources
Total	**Goods and services**	**Total economy**	**Other sectors**	**Households**	**Employers**	**2008 SNA code**	**Transactions and balancing items**	**Employers**	**Households**	**Other sectors**	**Total economy**	**Goods and services**	**Total**
Production account													
1.4	1.4					P1	Output	0.7		0.7	1.4		1.4
0.7		0.7			0.7	P2	Intermediate consumption					0.7	0.7
0.7		0.7	0.7		0.0	B1g	Value added, gross/ Gross domestic product						
Generation of income account													
9.7		9.7			9.7	D1	Compensation of employees						
9.7		9.7			9.7	D1222	Employers' imputed non-pension contributions						
-9.0		-9.0	0.7		-9.7	B2g	Operating surplus, gross						
Allocation of primary income account													
						D1	Compensation of employees		9.7		9.7		9.7
						D1222	Employers' imputed non-pension contributions		9.7		9.7		9.7
0.7		0.7	0.7	9.7	-9.7	B5g	Balance of primary income, gross/ National income, gross						
Secondary distribution of income account													
9.0		9.0		9.0		D61	Net social contributions	9.0			9.0		9.0
9.7		9.7		9.7		D6122	Employers' imputed non-pension contributions	9.7			9.7		9.7
-0.7		-0.7		-0.7			Social insurance funds service charges (-)	-0.7			-0.7		-0.7
9.0		9.0			9.0	D62	Social benefits other than social transfers in kind		9.0		9.0		9.0
9.0		9.0			9.0	D6222	Other social insurance non-pension benefits		9.0		9.0		9.0
0.7		0.7	0.7	9.7	-9.7	B6g	Disposable income, gross						
Use of disposable income account													
0.7		0.7		0.7		P3	Final consumption (service charge)					0.7	0.7
0.0		0.0	0.7	9.0	-9.7	B8g	Saving, gross						
Changes in assets													**Changes in liabilities and net worth**
Capital account													
0.0		0.0	0.7	9.0	-9.7	B9	Net lending (+)/net borrowing (-)						
Financial account													
						B9	Net lending (+)/net borrowing (-)	-9.7	9.0	0.7	0.0		0.0
0.0		0.0	0.7	9.0	-9.7	F2	Currency and deposits						

accounts, net lending/net borrowing is identical to net lending/net borrowing in the capital account, although, in practice, differences in data sources and the timing of the recording of transactions may result in a discrepancy between the estimates of net lending/net borrowing in these two accounts.

Funded social insurance other than pensions

3.512. Funded schemes for benefits other than pensions are not very common. They may, however, exist in two circumstances. The first is when an employer has a fund for such benefits and accumulates any underspend in one year to pay for possible overspends in future years. Alternatively, an employer may realize that the commitments to make payments in future are such that it is prudent to build reserves to be able to make such payments. An example of such a scheme might be one that provides health cover to present and past employees. Unlike in the case of pensions, estimates of possible future claims on social insurance benefits other than pensions are not necessarily included in the SNA. Liabilities are recorded only when and to the extent that they exist in the employer's accounts.

3.513. Funded social insurance covering benefits other than pensions may be carried out by insurance corporations or by employers on behalf of their employees. The output of this activity is measured in the same way as the output of non-life insurance,[81] but the matching consumption of the services is payable only by the households of the beneficiaries. These will be resident households except where a resident producer is liable to pay benefits to a present or former employee who is a non-resident or who has a non-resident family member entitled to the benefits. The investment income attributed to the beneficiaries of the social insurance schemes can only be receivable by the same households.

3.514. Employers' contributions relate only to employees. However, both current and former employees who are now or may in future be beneficiaries may make contributions to the scheme and receive investment income from it. This investment income is then treated as contribution supplements payable by those receiving it.

3.515. All contributions to the schemes are recorded as payable by households. These contributions include that part paid by the employer as part of compensation of employees in the generation of income account, as well as contributions paid directly by the employee funded from wages and salaries or by others, including former employees. Further, households receive investment income attributable to policyholders in respect of these contributions and this is treated, in total, as contribution supplements. Two items of contributions appear in the secondary distribution of income account. The first, the employers' actual social contributions, is exactly equal in value to the amount receivable by households from the employer in the generation of income account. The second item, called households' social contributions, includes the direct payment by households plus the contribution supplements less the service charge payable to the social insurance schemes.

3.516. Seven transactions must be recorded, one relating to production and consumption of the insurance service, three relating to contributions and benefits, one to the investment income attributable to policyholders and two relating to the difference between contributions and benefits:

(a) The activity by resident units is undertaken by insurance corporations or by an employer; the output is recorded in the production account of the insurance corporations or in the sector of the employer as appropriate;

[81] The use of the non-life insurance formula to measure output is appropriate, as these social insurance schemes tend to accumulate liabilities by chance rather than systematically based on the intentions of beneficiaries.

(b) Employers' actual social contributions to employment-related social insurance schemes are shown as payable by the sector in which the employer is located in the generation of income account and receivable by households in the allocation of primary income account. The same treatment applies to employees' actual social contributions;

(c) Investment income attributed to policyholders (beneficiaries) in respect of these schemes is payable by insurance corporations and employers, and receivable by households. Both payables and receivables are recorded in the allocation of primary income account;

(d) Net social contributions are shown in the secondary distribution of income account as payable by households and receivable by insurance corporations or the sector of the employer as appropriate;

(e) Employment-related social benefits other than pensions are also shown in the secondary distribution of income account as payable by insurance corporations or the sector of the employer and receivable by households;

(f) The value of the service is payable by households as part of final consumption expenditure and is recorded in the use of income account, except for non-resident employee households, where it is payable by the rest of the world;

(g) The excess of net contributions over benefits represents an increase in the liability of the insurance scheme towards the beneficiaries. This item is shown as an adjustment in the use of income account. As an increase in a liability, it is also shown in the financial account. As noted, the item is likely to occur only rarely and, for pragmatic reasons, changes in such non-pension entitlements may be included with those for pensions.

Worked example 3.26. Computing output and other transactions associated with funded employment-related social insurance schemes which pay non-pension benefits

3.517. This worked example computes the current-price output and other related transactions of funded employment-related social insurance schemes which pay non-pension benefits. It is assumed that the schemes are operated by insurance corporations. Also, it is assumed that there are no explicit charges, so the output of the funds will need to be computed using the formula to compute the output of non-life insurance. It is also assumed that all the participants and beneficiaries are residents. The worked example also assumes that the compiling agency is able to obtain the required input data for the transactions. In addition, the worked example will show how to record in the financial account the counterpart entries to show the means of payment for some of the transactions between the institutional units. For simplicity, it is assumed that these transactions are settled in currency or transferable deposits, which are part of "currency and deposits" in the financial account.

3.518. Table 3.121 shows the input data from insurance corporations operating funded other employment-related social insurance funds which pay non-pension benefits. It is assumed that both employers and employees make social non-pension contributions to the funds. Investment income on non-pension entitlements will be used as contribution supplements to compute the output of the funds. It is assumed this investment income is receivable from the other resident sectors.

3.519. Table 3.122 shows how to derive the output and net social contributions of the insurance corporations. For the purpose of computing the output, it is as-

Table 3.121
Data from insurance corporations operating employment-related social insurance funds which pay non-pension benefits

Line number	Item	Value	2008 SNA code
(1)	Employers' actual non-pension contributions	6.0	D1212, D6112
(2)	Employees' actual non-pension contributions	5.0	D11, D6132
(3)	Investment income on non-pension entitlements	4.0	D4, D442, D6142
(4)	Non-pension benefits	7.0	D62, D6222

Table 3.122
Calculation of output and net social contributions for insurance corporations operating funded other employment-related social insurance funds which pay non-pension benefits

Line number	Item	Description	Value	2008 SNA code
(5)	Adjusted other social insurance non-pension benefits		8.0	
(6)	Output	(1)+(2)+(3)−(5)	7.0	P1, P3
(7)	Net social contributions	(1)+(2)+(3)−(6)	8.0	D61

sumed that the compiling agency has estimated that adjusted other social insurance non-pension benefits are 8.0 units.[82]

3.520. The output of the insurance corporations operating the funded other employment-related social insurance schemes (7.0 units) is computed as follows:

> Employers' actual non-pension contributions (6.0 units)
>
> *plus* employees' actual non-pension contributions (5.0 units)
>
> *plus* contribution supplements (equivalent to investment income on non-pension entitlements) (4.0 units)
>
> *less* adjusted other social insurance non-pension benefits (8.0 units).

Net social contributions (8.0 units) are computed as follows:

> Employers' actual non-pension contributions (6.0 units)
>
> *plus* employees' actual non-pension contributions (5.0 units)
>
> *plus* contribution supplements (equivalent to investment income on non-pension entitlements) (4.0 units)
>
> *minus* output of insurance corporations (service charge) (7.0 units).

3.521. Table 3.123 shows how to calculate the changes in financial assets arising from the transactions among the insurance corporations and other institutional units, as well as the means of payment for these transactions. In general, the changes in financial assets and liabilities are computed using the following principles: changes in currency and deposits are the result of the payments made by the institutional units and the payments they receive. On the other hand, the insurance corporations also incur an increase in liabilities of non-pension entitlements to beneficiaries arising from the excess of net social contributions over other social insurance non-pension benefits. These changes in liabilities are recorded as the corresponding changes in the financial assets of households. As an example, consider the case of the insurance corporations operating the other employment-related social insurance schemes.

[82] The estimation method is the same as the methods used to derive adjusted claims for non-life insurance which were described earlier and is not repeated in this worked example.

Table 3.123
Calculation of changes in financial assets and liabilities related to transactions among insurance corporations operating funded employment-related social insurance schemes which pay non-pension benefits and other institutional units

Line number	Item	Description	Value	2008 SNA code
	Changes in financial assets (currency and deposits)			
(8)	Employers	–(1)–(2)	-11.0	F2
(9)	Insurance corporations	(1)+(2)–(4)+(3)	8.0	F2
(10)	Households	(4)	7.0	F2
(11)	Other sectors	–(3)	-4.0	F2
	Changes in financial assets (entitlements to non-pension benefits)			
(12)	Households	(7)–(4)	1.0	D8, F65
	Changes in liabilities (entitlements to non-pension benefits)			
(13)	Insurance corporations	(7)–(4)	1.0	D8, F65

They have a net increase in assets of currency and deposits of 8.0 units during the accounting period. This is the result of the following:

- An increase in assets of currency and deposits arising from employers' (6.0 units) and employees' (5.0 units) actual non-pension contributions receivable; and investment income receivable on non-pension entitlements from other sectors (4.0 units).
- A decrease in assets of currency and deposits arising from other social non-pension benefits payable (7.0 units).

In addition, these insurance corporations have a net increase in liabilities of entitlements to non-pension benefits of 1.0 unit. This is the result of:

Net social contributions receivable (8.0 units)

minus other social non-pension benefits payable (7.0 units).

3.522. Table 3.124 uses the information in the tables above to record the various transactions. To simplify the presentation and analysis, transactions which are not related to the worked example are ignored. To ensure clarity, the transactions of employers and the employment-related social insurance funds are shown separately rather than combined with those of the institutional sectors to which they belong. The transactions are described as follows:

(a) The output of the insurance corporations operating the other employment-related social insurance schemes is 7.0 units. This output is recorded in the production account of the insurance corporations;

(b) Employers' actual non-pension contributions (6.0 units) are treated as part of the compensation of employees and are recorded as payable by employers in the same generation of income account. Employees' actual non-pension contributions (5.0 units) are treated as part of wages and salaries (and, by extension, compensation of employees) and are recorded as payable by employers in the same account;

(c) The entries in the generation of income account are recorded as receivable by households in the allocation of primary income account. Investment income earned on the assets of the social insurance funds (4.0 units) is first recorded as property income payable by other sectors and receivable by the insurance corporations in this account. The same amount is then recorded as investment income payable on non-pension entitlements by the insurance corporations and receivable by households in the same account;

Table 3.124
Recording transactions related to funded employment-related social insurance funds which pay non-pension benefits

Uses															Resources
Total	Goods and services	Total economy	Other sectors	Households	Insurance corporations	Employers	2008 SNA code	Transactions and balancing items	Employers	Insurance corporations	Households	Other sectors	Total economy	Goods and services	Total
Production account															
7.0	7.0						P1	Output		7.0			7.0		7.0
7.0		7.0			7.0		B1g	Value added, gross/Gross domestic product							
Generation of income account															
11.0		11.0				11.0	D1	Compensation of employees							
5.0		5.0				5.0	D11	Wages and salaries							
6.0		6.0				6.0	D1212	Employers' actual non-pension contributions							
-4.0		-4.0			7.0	-11.0	B2g	Operating surplus, gross							
Allocation of primary income account															
							D1	Compensation of employees			11.0		11.0		11.0
							D11	Wages and salaries			5.0		5.0		5.0
							D1212	Employers' actual non-pension contributions			6.0		6.0		6.0
-4.0		-4.0	-4.0				D4	Property income		4.0			4.0		4.0
4.0		4.0			4.0		D442	Investment income payable on non-pension entitlements			4.0		4.0		4.0
7.0		7.0	-4.0	15.0	7.0	-11.0	B5g	Balance of primary income, gross/ National income, gross							
Secondary distribution of income account															
8.0		8.0		8.0			D61	Net social contributions		8.0			8.0		8.0
6.0		6.0		6.0			D6112	Employers' actual non-pension contributions		6.0			6.0		6.0
5.0		5.0		5.0			D6132	Households' actual non-pension contributions		5.0			5.0		5.0
4.0		4.0		4.0			D6142	Household non-pension contribution supplements		4.0			4.0		4.0
-7.0		-7.0		-7.0				Social insurance scheme service charges (-)		-7.0			-7.0		-7.0
7.0		7.0			7.0		D62	Social benefits other than social transfers in kind			7.0		7.0		7.0
7.0		7.0			7.0		D6222	Other social insurance non-pension benefits			7.0		7.0		7.0
7.0		7.0	-4.0	14.0	8.0	-11.0	B6g	Disposable income, gross							
Use of disposable income account															
7.0		7.0		7.0			P3	Final consumption (service charge)						7.0	7.0
1.0		1.0			1.0		D8	Adjustment for the change in non-pension entitlements			1.0		1.0		1.0
0.0		0.0	-4.0	8.0	7.0	-11.0	B8g	Saving, gross							
Changes in assets															**Changes in liabilities and net worth**
Capital account															
0.0		0.0	-4.0	8.0	7.0	-11.0	B9	Net lending (+)/net borrowing (-)							
Financial account															
							B9	Net lending (+)/net borrowing (-)	-11.0	7.0	8.0	-4.0	0.0		0.0
0.0		0.0	-4.0	7.0	8.0	-11.0	F2	Currency and deposits							
1.0		1.0		1.0			F65	Entitlements to non-pension benefits		1.0			1.0		1.0

(d) Net social contributions (8.0 units) are recorded in the secondary distribution of income account as payable by households and receivable by the insurance corporations. Net social contributions payable by households include employers' actual non-pension contributions (6.0 units), since all social insurance contributions are to be recorded as being paid by households to social insurance schemes. Other social non-pension benefits payable by the insurance corporations and receivable by households (7.0 units) are also recorded in the secondary distribution of income account;

(e) The output of the insurance corporations (7.0 units) is recorded as the final consumption expenditure of households in the use of disposable income account;

(f) Since there are no capital account transactions, net lending/net borrowing in the capital account is the same as gross saving in the use of disposable income account;

(g) The financial account records the changes in currency and deposits and the changes in entitlements to non-pension benefits of the various sectors. The changes in entitlements to non-pension benefits are also recorded as an adjustment in the use of disposable income account. Since the entries in the financial account are the counterparts to entries in the other accounts or only reflect the exchange of financial assets and liabilities, net lending/net borrowing is identical to net lending/net borrowing in the capital account, although, in practice, differences in data sources and the timing of the recording of transactions may result in a discrepancy between the estimates of net lending/net borrowing in these two accounts.

Volume measures of the output associated with social insurance schemes which pay non-pension benefits

3.523. The worked examples above calculated the output associated with social insurance schemes which pay non-pension benefits at current prices. Volume measures of the output need to be computed by removing the effects of price changes. The method used to compute the volume measures of output will depend on the method used to compute the current-price output. For output which is computed as the sum of costs, the compiling agency can consider deflating this output by a composite index of input prices to obtain the volume measures. In the case where output is computed using the non-life insurance output formula, the volume measures can be estimated by extrapolating the base-period output by the composite volume growth rate of the relevant classes of non-life insurance which are also found in social insurance.

3.524. Volume measures of the service charges associated with non-resident social insurance schemes which pay non-pension benefits can be obtained by deflating the current-price imports of the service charges by a composite price index comprising the price indices for these charges from partner countries. The price indices will need to be adjusted for changes in exchange rates first. Alternatively, the compiling agency can consider extrapolating the base-period imports of these service charges by the growth in a composite volume index comprising the volume indices for output or exports of these charges from partner countries. If data from partner countries are not available, the compiling agency can consider using the price indices which are used to deflate domestically produced current-price output of these service charges or extrapolate the base-period value of the imported service charges by the volume growth of the domestically produced service charges.

C. Property income payable and receivable by financial corporations

Reference:
2008 SNA, Chapter 7, The distribution of income accounts

3.525. The transactions of financial corporations give rise to property income. This section describes the property income payable or receivable by financial corporations and the possible data sources for computing and allocating the property income.

1. Property income

3.526. Property income (D4) accrues when the owners of financial assets and natural resources put them at the disposal of other institutional units. The income payable for the use of financial assets is called investment income, while that payable for the use of a natural resource is called rent. Property income is the sum of investment income and rent.

3.527. Property income is classified in the following way in the 2008 SNA:

Investment income

- Interest (D41)
- Distributed income of corporations (D42)
  - Dividends (D421)
  - Withdrawals from income of quasi-corporations (D422)
  - Reinvested earnings on foreign direct investment (D43)
- Other investment income (D44)
  - Investment income attributable to insurance policyholders (D441)
  - Investment income payable on pension entitlements (D442)
  - Investment income attributable to collective investment funds shareholders (D443)

Rent (D45)

2. Investment income

3.528. Investment income comprises the following items:

(a) Interest (D41)

3.529. Interest is a form of income that is receivable by the owners of certain kinds of financial assets, namely: deposits, debt securities, loans and (possibly) other accounts receivable for putting the financial asset at the disposal of another institutional unit. Income on SDR holdings and allocations and on unallocated gold accounts is also treated as interest. The financial assets giving rise to interest are all claims of creditors over debtors. Creditors lend funds to debtors that lead to the creation of one or other of the financial instruments listed above. Interest also includes the coupon payments that are payable by the issuers of debt securities at specified intervals over the life of the financial instruments.

3.530. Interest is recorded on an accrual basis, that is, interest is recorded as accruing continuously over time to the creditor on the amount of principal outstanding. The interest accruing in each accounting period must be recorded, irrespective of whether or not it is actually paid or added to the principal outstanding. When it is not actually paid, the increase in the principal must also be recorded in the financial account as a further acquisition of that kind of financial asset by the creditor and an equal acquisition of a liability by the debtor.

3.531. Interest is to be recorded before the deduction of any taxes levied on it. Interest received and paid is always recorded inclusive of grants for interest relief, even if those grants are paid directly to financial institutions and not to the beneficiaries.

3.532. The actual payments or receipts of interest to or from financial intermediaries need to be adjusted to eliminate the margins that represent the implicit charges made by financial intermediaries. The amounts of interest paid by borrowers to financial intermediaries must be reduced by the estimated values of the charges payable, while the amounts of interest receivable by depositors must be similarly increased. The values of the charges are treated as payments for services rendered by financial intermediaries to their customers and not as payments of interest.

3.533. Certain financial instruments, for example, bills and zero coupon bonds, are such that the debtor is under no obligation to make any payments to the creditor until the asset matures. In effect, no interest becomes due for payment until the end of the asset's life, at which point the debtor's liability is discharged by a single payment covering both the amount of the funds originally provided by the creditor and the interest accumulated over the entire life of the asset. In such cases, the amount of interest payable over the life of the security is derived as the difference between the value at which the instrument is acquired and its value when it matures.

(b) Distributed income of corporations (D42)

3.534. Distributed income of corporations covers dividends (D421), withdrawals from income of quasi-corporations (D422) and reinvested earnings on foreign direct investment (D43).

Dividends (D421)

3.535. Dividends are a form of property income to which owners of shares become entitled as a result of placing funds at the disposal of corporations. Raising equity capital through the issue of shares is an alternative way of raising funds to borrowing. In contrast to loans, however, equity capital does not give rise to a liability that is fixed in monetary terms and it does not entitle the holders of shares of a corporation to a fixed or predetermined income.

3.536. Dividends may occasionally take the form of an issue of shares, but this excludes issues of bonus shares that simply represent a reclassification between own funds, reserves and undistributed profits. If dividends are disproportionately large relative to the recent level of dividends and earnings such that the ratio of these dividends to the distributable income of a corporation is greatly in excess of recent ratios, the excess should be treated as a withdrawal of owner's equity from the corporation and thus be recorded in the financial account.

3.537. Although dividends represent a part of income that has been generated over a period of time, dividends are not to be recorded on a strict accrual basis. For a short period after a dividend is declared, but before it is actually payable, shares may be sold "ex dividend", meaning that the dividend is still payable to the owner at the date the dividend was declared, and not to the owner on the date payable. A share sold "ex dividend" is therefore worth less than one sold without this constraint. The time of recording of dividends is the point in time at which the share price starts to be quoted on an ex dividend basis, rather than at a price that includes the dividend.

Withdrawals from the income of quasi-corporations (D422)

3.538. Withdrawals from the income of quasi-corporations consist of the amounts which entrepreneurs actually withdraw for their own use from the profits earned by the quasi-corporations which belong to them. Withdrawals from the income of quasi-corporations are recorded when they are made by the owners.

Reinvested earnings on foreign direct investment (D43)

3.539. Reinvested earnings on foreign direct investment are the foreign direct investors' share of the retained earnings of the foreign direct investment enterprise. Retained earnings of the foreign direct investment enterprise are equal to the operating surplus of the foreign direct investment enterprise plus any property incomes or current transfers receivable minus any property incomes or current transfers payable, including actual remittances to foreign direct investors and any current taxes payable on the income, wealth, etc., of the foreign direct investment enterprise. Reinvested earnings on foreign direct investment are recorded when they are earned.

(c) Other investment income (D44)

3.540. Other investment income covers investment income attributable to insurance policyholders (D441), investment income payable on pension entitlements (D442) and investment income attributable to collective investment funds shareholders (D443).

Investment income attributable to insurance policyholders (D441)

3.541. Investment income attributable to insurance policyholders corresponds to total primary incomes received from the investment of insurance reserves. The reserves concerned are those whereby insurance corporations recognize corresponding liabilities to the policyholders. The reserves are invested by insurance corporations in financial assets or land (from which net property income, i.e. after deducting any interest paid, is received) or in buildings (which generate net operating surpluses). Investment income attributable to insurance policyholders should be divided between holders of non-life and life policies and annuities. This category may also include investment income attributable to units which purchase standardized guarantees.

Investment income payable on pension entitlements (D442)

3.542. Investment income payable on pension entitlements arises from one of two different types of pension schemes. These are defined contribution and defined benefit schemes. The investment income payable on defined contribution entitlements is equal to the investment income on the funds plus any income earned by renting land or buildings owned by the fund.

3.543. The characteristic of a defined benefit scheme is that a formula is used to determine the level of payments to be made to pensioners. Because of this characteristic, it is possible to determine the level of entitlements as the present value of all future payments, calculated using actuarial assumptions about life lengths and economic assumptions about the interest or discount rate. The present value of the entitlements existing at the start of the year increases because the date when the entitlements become payable has become one year nearer. This increase is regarded as investment income attributable to the pension holders in the case of the defined benefit scheme. The amount of the increase is not affected by whether the pension scheme actually has sufficient funds to meet all the obligations, nor by the type of increase in the funds, whether it is investment income or holding gains, for example.

Investment income attributable to collective investment funds shareholders (D443)

3.544. Investment income attributable to collective investment funds shareholders (including mutual funds and unit trusts) is composed of two separate items. The first of these is the dividends distributed to holders of investment fund shares or units. The second is retained earnings attributable to holders of investment fund shares or units.

3.545. The dividend component is recorded in the same way as dividends for individual corporations, as described above. The retained earnings component is recorded using the same principles as those described for foreign direct investment enterprises but is calculated excluding any reinvested earnings on foreign direct investment. That is to say, the remaining retained earnings are distributed to the shareholders (leaving the investment fund with no saving) and are reinjected into the fund by the shareholders in a transaction recorded in the financial account.

3. Rent (D45)

3.546. Rent is the income receivable by the owner of a natural resource (the lessor or landlord) for putting the natural resource at the disposal of another institutional unit (a lessee or tenant) for use of the natural resource in production. Two particular cases of resource rents are considered: rent on land and rent on subsoil resources. Resource rents on other natural resources, such as radio spectra, follow the same pattern laid out by these two instances. It is quite unlikely that financial corporations will engage in transactions which give rise to rent.

4. Data sources for computing and allocating property income payable and receivable by financial corporations

3.547. The possible data sources to compute and allocate most of the categories of property income payable and receivable by financial corporations have been discussed in the respective sections on the calculation of the various types of financial services earlier in this chapter. Typically, the property income receivable and payable by financial corporations can be obtained from a combination of sources, such as their returns to supervisory authorities, surveys or the ITRS. The compiling agency should try to collect data showing the sectoral breakdown of property income from these sources. If this is not possible, the compiling agency will need to consider various methods to allocate the total value of each type of property income to user sectors using various assumptions. For example, if the compiling agency is unable to obtain the sectoral breakdown of investment income attributable to insurance policyholders from the input data, it can consider allocating the total estimated value of this transaction in proportion to the actual premiums payable by resident institutional units and the rest of the world. There may also be instances of financial corporations being unable to provide the input data. For instance, resident insurance corporations will not be able to provide data on the investment income attributable to them from non-resident reinsurance corporations. In such cases, the compiling agency may need to obtain the missing data from partner countries.

Chapter 4
Financial assets and liabilities

References:
2008 SNA, Chapter 11, The financial account
BPM6, Chapter 5, Classifications of financial assets and liabilities
MFSMCG, Chapter 4, Classification of Financial Assets
GFSM 2014, Chapter 7, The balance sheet, and Chapter 9, Transactions in financial assets and liabilities
HSS

A. Introduction

4.1. This chapter provides an overview of the classifications of financial assets and liabilities within the framework of the 2008 SNA. It defines and describes the various categories of financial assets and liabilities by type of financial instrument, as well as other classification schemes.

4.2. This chapter overlaps somewhat with chapter 5 of BPM6, on Classifications of financial assets and liabilities, chapter 4 of MFSMCG, on Classification of financial assets, chapters 7 and 9 of the GFSM 2014, on the Balance sheet and transactions in financial assets and liabilities, and HSS. Consistency with the 2008 SNA and with these manuals is maintained in this Handbook.

B. Definition of financial assets, financial claims and liabilities

4.3. Financial assets consist of all financial claims, shares or other equity in corporations plus gold bullion held by monetary authorities as a reserve asset.

4.4. A financial claim is the payment or series of payments due to the creditor by the debtor under the terms of a liability. A liability is established when one unit (the debtor) is obliged, under specific circumstances, to provide a payment or series of payments to another unit (the creditor).

4.5. Equity and investment fund shares are treated as financial assets with a corresponding liability even though the financial claim the holder has on the issuer is not a fixed or predetermined monetary amount.

4.6. Gold bullion as a component of monetary gold held by monetary authorities as a reserve asset is treated as a financial asset even though the holder does not have claims on other designated units. There is no matching liability for gold bullion.

C. Classification of financial assets and liabilities

4.7. Financial assets and liabilities may be presented according to different criteria: by type of financial instrument and by functional breakdown, as well as by negotiability, income, maturity, currency, interest and counterparty (the from-whom-to-whom presentation). The functional breakdown is applied in balance of payments and international investment position statistics (see BPM6).

4.8. The classification of financial assets and liabilities by type of financial instrument is described in detail. Because of the symmetry of financial assets and liabilities, the term "instrument" is used to relate to both the asset and the liability aspect of financial transactions, other flows and financial balance sheets. Its use in the 2008 SNA is for convenience only and does not imply an extension of the coverage of financial assets and liabilities by including off-balance-sheet items that are sometimes described as financial instruments in monetary and financial statistics.

D. Classification by type of financial instrument

4.9. Eight categories of financial assets as balance sheet items (AF) are distinguished: monetary gold and special drawing rights (SDRs) (AF1); currency and deposits (AF2); debt securities (AF3); loans (AF4); equity and investment fund shares (AF5); insurance, pension and standardized guarantee schemes (AF6); financial derivatives and employee stock options (AF7); and other accounts receivable/payable (AF8).

4.10. Each financial asset has a counterpart liability, with the exception of gold bullion held by monetary authorities as a reserve asset classified in the category monetary gold and SDRs (AF1). Unallocated gold accounts held with non-residents, the other component of monetary gold, have a counterpart liability. Thus, eight categories of liabilities are distinguished, corresponding to the categories of the counterpart financial assets (with the exception of part of monetary gold).

4.11. The classification of financial transactions (F) corresponds to the classification of financial assets and liabilities as balance sheet items. Eight categories of financial transactions are distinguished: transactions in monetary gold and SDRs (F1); transactions in currency and deposits (F2); transactions in debt securities (F3); transactions in loans (F4); transactions in equity and investment fund shares (F5); transactions in insurance, pension and standardized guarantee schemes (F6); transactions in financial derivatives and employee stock options (F7); and transactions in other accounts receivable/payable (F8).

4.12. The proposed classification of financial transactions is summarized in table 4.1. Financial transactions are listed by category, subcategory and subposition. All maturity breakdowns are by original or initial maturity, because this is an important feature of the financial instrument. The value of residual maturity for some purposes could be recognized in memorandum items.

1. Monetary gold and special drawing rights

4.13. Monetary gold and special drawing rights (SDRs) (AF1 as stocks and F1 as transactions) issued by the International Monetary Fund (IMF) are financial assets that are normally held only by monetary authorities. The category consists of two subcategories: (a) monetary gold (AF11); and (b) SDRs (AF12).

(a) Monetary gold

Coverage of monetary gold

4.14. *Monetary gold* is gold to which the monetary authorities (or others who are subject to the effective control of the monetary authorities) have title and is held as reserve assets as defined in BPM6 (paras. 6.64–6.92). Monetary gold comprises gold

Table 4.1
Classification of transactions in financial assets and liabilities by type of financial instrument

Type of transaction in financial assets and liabilities by category, subcategory and subposition	2008 SNA code		
	Category	Subcategory	Subposition
Monetary gold and SDRs	F1		
Monetary gold		F11	
SDRs		F12	
Currency and deposits	F2		
Currency		F21	
Transferable deposits		F22	
Other deposits		F29	
Debt securities	F3		
Short-term		F31	
Long-term		F32	
Loans	F4		
Short-term		F41	
Long-term		F42	
Equity and investment fund shares	F5		
Equity		F51	
Listed shares			F511
Unlisted shares			F512
Other equity			F519
Investment fund shares/ units		F52	
Money market fund shares/units (MMFs)			F521
Non-MMF investment fund shares/ units			F522
Insurance, pension and standardized guarantee schemes	F6		
Non-life insurance technical reserves		F61	
Life insurance and annuity entitlements		F62	
Pension entitlements		F63	
Claims of pension funds on pension managers		F64	
Entitlements to non-pension benefits		F65	
Provisions for calls under standardized guarantees		F66	
Financial derivatives and employee stock options	F7		
Financial derivatives		F71	
Employee stock options		F72	
Other accounts receivable/payable	F8		
Trade credits and advances		F81	
Other accounts receivable/payable		F89	

bullion (including gold held in allocated gold accounts) and unallocated gold accounts with non-residents that give title to claims on the delivery of gold. All monetary gold is included in reserve assets or is held by international financial organizations. Except in limited institutional circumstances, gold bullion can be a financial asset only for the central bank or central government. Gold bullion holdings that are not part of reserve assets are classified as non-financial assets.

4.15. Gold bullion included in monetary gold is a financial asset for which there is no corresponding liability. Transactions in gold bullion, excluding those among monetary authorities and international financial institutions, are treated as transactions in nonfinancial assets.

Box 4.1
Contingent assets, contingent liabilities and guarantees in the *System of National Accounts 2008*

Contingent assets and contingent liabilities

Contingent assets and contingent liabilities are contractual financial arrangements between resident institutional units, or between a resident institutional unit and a non-resident institutional unit. They involve a legal contract stating that one party is obliged to provide a payment, series of payments or other deliveries (like goods) to another unit only if certain specific conditions prevail. As they do not give rise to unconditional obligations either to make payments or to provide other objects of value, contingent assets and contingent liabilities are not financial assets and liabilities, and are not recorded in the 2008 SNA.

Contingent assets and contingent liabilities include:

(a) One-off guarantees of payment by third parties since payment is only required if the debtor defaults;

(b) Loan commitments providing a guarantee that funds will be made available but no financial asset exists until funds are actually advanced;

(c) Letters of credit constituting promises to make a payment conditional on the presentation of certain documents specified by a contract;

(d) Lines of credit which constitute facilities, i.e. contingent assets and contingent liabilities, and the creation of these facilities give rise to no entry in the financial account;

(e) Underwritten note issuance facilities providing a guarantee that a potential debtor will be able to sell short-term debt securities (notes) that he issues, i.e. the bank(s) granting the facility will take up any notes not sold in the market or will provide equivalent advances.

Pension entitlements under unfunded government-managed defined benefit employer pension schemes (S13 except S1314) are sometimes excluded, and pension entitlements under social security pension funds (S1314) are always excluded from the balance sheet. However, such pension entitlements are not contingent assets and contingent liabilities because there is only uncertainty as to their size and not as to whether they will be paid. Such positions in pension entitlements are recorded only in the supplementary table on pension schemes in social insurance.

Contingent assets and contingent liabilities do not include:

(a) Insurance, pension and standardized guarantee schemes (AF6); which are recorded in the 2008 SNA as financial assets of the institutional units holding the policies;

(b) Financial derivatives and employee stock options (AF7) where the contractual arrangements themselves have a market value because they are tradable or can be offset on the market.

Guarantees

Guarantees are contractual financial arrangements whereby one party, the guarantor, undertakes to a lender that if a borrower defaults, the guarantor will make good the loss the lender would otherwise suffer. Often a fee is payable for the provision of a guarantee although the form of this varies. Three types of guarantees are recognized:

(a) Guarantees that meet the definition of a financial derivative;

(b) Standardized guarantees;

(c) One-off guarantees.

No special treatment is proposed for guarantees in the form of a manufacturer's warranty or other form of guarantee.

The first type of guarantee comprises guarantees provided by means of a financial derivative, such as a credit default swap (CDS). These derivatives are based on the risk of default of reference financial assets and so are not actually linked to individual loans or debt securities. When such a guarantee is initiated, the purchaser makes a payment to the financial institution creating the derivative. This is recorded as a transaction in financial derivatives. Changes to the value of the financial derivative are recorded as revaluations. If the reference instrument defaults, the guarantor pays the purchaser for its theoretical loss on the reference loan or debt security. This is also recorded as a transaction in financial derivatives.

The second type comprises standardized guarantees. They are issued in large numbers, usually for fairly small amounts, along identical lines. Examples are export credit guarantees or student loan guarantees. Even though the probability of any one standardized guarantee being called is uncertain, the fact that there are many similar guarantees means that a reliable estimate of the number of calls under the guarantee can be made. Standardized guarantees are treated as giving rise to financial assets and not contingent assets. This will be explained under the financial instrument category insurance, pension and standardized guarantee schemes.

The third type comprises one-off guarantees, where the loan or the debt security is so particular that it is not possible for the associated risk to be calculated with any degree of accuracy. The granting of a one-off guarantee is considered a contingent asset or a contingent liability and is not recorded as a financial asset or a liability.

As an exception, one-off guarantees granted by governments to corporations in certain financially distressed situations and with a very high likelihood to be called are treated as if these guarantees were called at inception.

4.16. An allocated gold account is equivalent to a custody record of title to gold, whereas an unallocated gold account does not give the holder the title to physical gold but provides a claim against the account provider denominated in gold.

4.17. An unallocated gold account is classified as a foreign currency deposit.[83] If unallocated gold accounts represent claims only on non-residents they are classified under "Other deposits in foreign currency vis-à-vis non-residents".[84] The same principle applies to unallocated accounts for other precious metals (e.g. silver or platinum). Unallocated accounts for all precious metals are included in foreign currency deposits, and allocated accounts for all metals, other than for gold held by monetary authorities,[85] are included in non-financial assets.

4.18. *Transactions in monetary gold* consist of sales and purchases of gold between monetary authorities that hold the gold as foreign assets or international financial organizations. These transactions are recorded as monetary gold in the financial account. The treatment of monetary gold in the 2008 SNA balance sheet is illustrated in table 4.2.

Table 4.2
Treatment of monetary gold in the balance sheet

Monetary authority		**Rest of the world**		**Resident sectors (such as deposit-taking corporations except the central bank)**	
Financial assets	Liabilities	Financial assets	Liabilities	Financial assets	Liabilities
Monetary gold			**Deposits**		
Gold bullion (including gold bullion held in allocated gold accounts)					
Unallocated gold accounts with non-residents			Unallocated gold accounts with resident monetary authority		
Deposits					**Deposits**
Unallocated gold accounts with residents					Unallocated gold accounts with resident monetary authority

Monetization and demonetization of gold

4.19. Purchases (sales) of gold bullion are recorded in the accounts of the monetary authority (the central bank or central government) as increases (decreases) in assets. Transactions in gold bullion, excluding those between monetary authorities and international financial institutions, are treated as transactions in non-financial assets.

4.20. When a monetary authority purchases gold bullion for inclusion in official reserves the gold is *monetized*, resulting in a change in the classification of gold bullion from a non-financial asset to a financial asset. If the monetary authority sells gold that is part of official reserves, the gold is *demonetized*, resulting in a change in the classifica-

[83] Other deposit-taking corporations except the central bank in a few countries offer deposit accounts settled in domestic currency for which the interest return is linked to the market price of gold, but without linkage to physical gold. These deposits are also classified as foreign currency deposits.

[84] Gold-denominated deposit account with a third-party-payment feature would, however, be classified under "Transferable deposits—In foreign currency".

[85] Monetary gold is treated differently because of its role as a means of international payments and store of value for use as a reserve asset.

tion of gold bullion from a financial asset to a non-financial asset before the transaction in non-financial assets is recorded.

4.21. The *monetization* or *demonetization of gold* is recorded as a change in the classification of gold bullion (i.e. between monetary and non-monetary gold) in the other changes in the volume of assets account of the monetary authority.

4.22. *Monetization of gold* occurs when a monetary authority reclassifies gold bullion from stocks of valuables to reserve assets held by the monetary authority. The other changes in the volume of assets account of the monetary authority records then a decrease in its holding of valuables and an increase in its holding of monetary gold. *Demonetization of gold* occurs when a monetary authority transfers gold from reserve assets to valuables. Holdings of monetary gold by the monetary authority then decrease and valuables show an increase.

4.23. Purchases or sales of *monetary gold between monetary authorities* are classified as transactions in monetary gold. All other purchases or sales, including those from or to financial intermediaries or via an organized gold market are recorded as purchases or sales of valuables, followed or preceded by a classification change. Purchases of valuables are followed by a classification change to monetized gold, while sales of valuables are preceded by a classification change to demonetized gold.

4.24. The corresponding accounting entries are shown in tables 4.3 and 4.4.

Table 4.3
Accounting treatment of monetization

			Accounting entries			Accounting entries	
Monetary authority	**Counterparty**	**Acquisition**	**Monetary authority**	**Counterparty**	**Monetization**	**Monetary authority**	**Counterparty**
Purchase of gold bullion	(iii) to non-resident	Transaction in products	Import (+100) Decrease of currency (-100)	Export (-100) Increase of currency (+100)	Monetization recorded as a change in classification of assets	Monetary gold (+100) Valuables (-100)	No entries
	(iv) to resident		Acquisition less disposal of valuables / change in inventories (+100) Decrease of currency (-100)	Acquisition less disposal of valuables / change in inventories (-100) Increase of currency (+100)			

Table 4.4
Accounting treatment of demonetization

			Accounting entries			Accounting entries	
Monetary authority	**Counterparty**	**Demonetization**	**Monetary authority**	**Counterparty**	**Disposal**	**Monetary authority**	**Counterparty**
Sale of gold bullion	(i) to non-resident	Demonetization recorded as a change in classification of assets	Monetary gold (-100) Valuables (+100)	No entries	Transaction in products	Export (-100) Increase of currency (+100)	Import (+100) Decrease of currency (-100)
	(ii) to resident					Acquisition less disposal of valuables / change in inventories (-100) Increase of currency (+100)	Acquisition less disposal of valuables / change in inventories (+100) Decrease of currency (-100)

4.25. Before the monetization an acquisition of non-monetary gold by the monetary authority will be recorded in the capital account as a positive entry under acquisition less disposal of valuables or change in inventories. If the non-monetary gold is acquired from abroad, there is an entry under imports.

4.26. Demonetization is treated symmetrically. After the demonetization a disposal of non-monetary gold by the monetary authority will be recorded in the capital account as a negative entry under acquisition less disposal of valuables or change in inventories. If the non-monetary gold is disposed of abroad, there is an entry under exports.

Non-monetary gold versus monetary gold

4.27. Gold bullion not held as reserve assets is not a financial asset and is included in non-monetary gold (table 4.5). In some cases, a central bank may own gold bullion that is not held as reserves (such as sometimes occurs when it acts as a monopoly reseller of mined gold).

4.28. Non-monetary gold can be in the form of bullion (that is, coins, ingots, or bars with a purity of at least 995 parts per thousand, including such gold that is held in allocated gold accounts), gold powder and gold in other unwrought or semi-manufactured forms. Jewelry, watches, etc. that contain gold are included under general merchandise, not non-monetary gold. Non-monetary gold may be held either as a store of value or for industrial purposes.

4.29. Accordingly, transactions in non-monetary gold are recorded as acquisitions less disposals of valuables (if the sole purpose is to provide a store of wealth) and otherwise as final or intermediate consumption, changes in inventories, exports or imports.

Table 4.5
Monetary gold and non-monetary gold

Monetary gold	Only gold as a component of foreign reserves is treated as monetary gold; essentially only monetary authorities or international financial organizations hold monetary gold as a financial asset
Non-monetary gold	Gold as a non-financial asset, either as a type of inventory or as a valuable; full outright ownership of the gold

Deposits, loans and securities denominated in gold

4.30. Deposits, loans and securities denominated in gold are classified as if they are denominated in a foreign currency.

4.31. Gold swaps are similar to repurchase agreements except that the collateral is gold. A gold swap involves an exchange of gold for foreign exchange deposits with an agreement that the transaction be reversed at an agreed future date at an agreed gold price. The gold taker (cash provider) will not usually record the gold on its balance sheet, while the gold provider (cash taker) will not usually remove the gold from its balance sheet. In this manner, the transaction is analogous to a repurchase agreement and should be recorded as a collateralized loan or deposit. Monetary gold swaps are undertaken between monetary authorities or between a monetary authority and another party, while non-monetary gold swaps are similar transactions without the involvement of monetary authorities.

4.32. Gold loans consist of the delivery of gold for a given time period. As for other reverse transactions, legal ownership of the gold is transferred (the temporary borrower may on-sell the gold to a third party), but the risks and benefits of changes in the gold price remain with the lender. Gold borrowers (usually market dealers or brokers) often use these transactions to cover their sales to third parties in periods of (temporary) gold shortage. A fee, determined by the value of the gold, is paid to the original owner for the use of the gold.

4.33. All fees payable to the owners of gold used for gold loans (whether from allocated or non-allocated gold accounts) should be recorded by convention as interest.

(b) Special drawing rights

4.34. SDRs (AF12) are international reserve assets created by the IMF and allocated to its members to supplement existing reserve assets.[86] The SDR Department of the IMF[87] manages reserve assets by allocating SDRs among member countries of the IMF and certain international agencies (collectively known as the participants).

4.35. SDRs are held only by central banks (or central government) and a limited number of international financial institutions that are authorized holders, and are transferable among participants. SDR holdings represent each holder's assured and unconditional right to obtain foreign exchange or other reserve assets from other IMF members.

4.36. The mechanism by which SDRs are created (referred to as SDR allocation) and extinguished (SDR cancellation) gives rise to transactions. These transactions are recorded at the gross amount of the allocation and are recorded in the financial accounts of the monetary authority of the individual participant on the one hand and the rest of the world representing the participants collectively on the other.

4.37. SDRs are assets with matching liabilities but the assets represent claims on the participants collectively and not on the IMF. A participant may sell some or all of its SDR holdings to another participant and receive in return other reserve assets, most likely foreign exchange.

4.38. SDR holdings and SDR allocations should be recorded as gross assets and liabilities in the balance sheets of monetary authorities. In particular, SDR allocations are classified as long-term debt liability to non-residents.[88] This classification is based on two main debt attributes of SDR allocations: (a) interest is payable on the allocation; and (b) if a member left the membership of the IMF or the SDR scheme was ended, it would be required to repay its obligations including any SDR allocations.

4.39. SDR allocations and cancellations are to be recorded based on the quadruple-entry accounting principle; this means that allocations are always accompanied by an increase in SDR holdings and cancellations by a decrease in SDR holdings (table 4.6).

2. Currency and deposits

4.40. The category currency and deposits (AF2) is divided into three subcategories: (a) currency (AF21); (b) transferable deposits (AF22); and (c) other deposits (AF29).

---

86 See also annex 4.2 to the MFSMCG.

87 The SDR Department of the IMF, relating to administration arrangement of financial resources, was established to conduct all transactions in SDRs, following the creation of the new international reserve asset by the IMF in 1969. The Articles of Agreement require that the General and SDR Departments be kept strictly separate. This separation reflects the fact that the SDR facility is an entirely separate financial mechanism within the IMF (see *Financial Organization and Operations of the IMF*, Pamphlet Series, No. 45, Sixth Edition, 2001).

88 In the 1993 SNA and the BPM5, SDRs were classified as an asset without a corresponding liability. In the *Monetary and Financial Statistics Manual* (IMF, 2000), SDR allocations were classified as shares and other equity.

Table 4.6
Accounting treatment of special drawing rights allocations, cancellations and transfers

(a) **SDR allocation**

Rest of the world (representing the participants)		**Monetary authority**	
Transaction in financial assets	*Transaction in liabilities*	*Transaction in financial assets*	*Transaction in liabilities*
SDR allocated (+100)	SDRs (+100)	SDRs (+100)	SDRs allocated (+100)

(b) **SDR cancellation**

Rest of the world (representing the participants)		**Monetary authority**	
Transaction in financial assets	*Transaction in liabilities*	*Transaction in financial assets*	*Transaction in liabilities*
SDRs allocated (-50)	SDRs (-50)	SDRs (-50)	SDRs allocated (-50)

(c) **SDR transfer from monetary authority A to monetary authority B**

Rest of the world (representing the participants)		**Monetary authority A**		**Monetary authority B**	
Transaction in financial assets	*Transaction in liabilities*	*Transaction in financial assets*	*Transaction in liabilities*	*Transaction in financial assets*	*Transaction in liabilities*
(1) **SDR redemption**					
Currency (-80)	SDRs vis-à-vis monetary authority A (-80)	SDRs (-80) Currency (+80)			
(2) **SDR acquisition**					
Currency (+80)	SDRs vis-à-vis monetary authority B (+80)			SDRs (+80) Currency (-80)	

(a) Currency

4.41. Currency consists of notes and coins that are of fixed face value and are issued or authorized by central banks or general governments.[89]

4.42. A distinction is drawn between domestic currency (that is, currency that is the liability of resident units, such as the central bank and general government) and foreign currency as claims on non-resident central banks or general governments (table 4.7).[90]

Table 4.7
Issues and holdings of currency

	Currency holdings	
Domestic currency in circulation issued by the central bank and general government	**By residents**	By non-residents
Foreign currency issued by non-resident central banks and general governments	**By residents**	

4.43. Currency does not include:

(a) Notes and coins that are not in circulation, for example, a central bank or general government holdings of unissued currency;

(b) Commemorative coins that are not commonly used to make payments. They are classified as valuables (AN13).

[89] In some countries, the central bank or general government may authorize commercial banks to issue currency.

[90] In monetary unions, domestic currency and foreign currencies are treated differently (see chapter 10).

Table 4.8
Issues and holdings of domestic currency and foreign currency by residence

Assets				Liabilities			
Total currency holdings	**Currency holdings of the rest of the world**	**Currency holdings of the national economy**	**Domestic currency holdings**	**Domestic currency issues**	**Currency issues of the national economy**	**Currency issues by the rest of the world**	**Total currency issues**
Domestic currency 100	Domestic currency 10	Domestic currency 90	Domestic currency 90	Domestic currency 100	Domestic currency 100		Domestic currency 100
Foreign currency 15		Foreign currency 15	Foreign currency 15			Foreign currency 15	Foreign currency 15
Domestic currency and foreign currency 115	Domestic currency 10	Domestic currency and foreign currency 105	Domestic currency and foreign currency 105	Domestic currency 100	Domestic currency 100	Foreign currency 15	Domestic currency and foreign currency 115

4.44. Notes and coins are treated as liabilities at face value. The cost of producing notes and coins is recorded as government expenditure and is not netted against the receipts from issuing the currency. The seigniorage (monetary income) from coinage activity is therefore the net margin earned on this zero interest rate debt (on the assumption that the coins are exchanged for interest-bearing assets) minus the costs of production.

4.45. In the example described in table 4.8, the amount of domestic currency in circulation is 100. It is held by residents (90) and by non-residents (10). In addition, residents hold an amount of foreign currencies of 15.

(b) Deposits

4.46. Deposits include all claims on the central bank, deposit-taking corporations except the central bank, government units and, in some cases, other institutional units that are represented by evidence of deposit. The category of deposits comprises transferable deposits (AF22) and other deposits (AF29).

4.47. Deposits are usually standardized, non-negotiable contracts open to the public at large that allow the placement of a variable amount of money. Deposits usually involve the debtor giving back the full principal amount to the creditor.[91]

4.48. They are offered mainly by deposit-taking corporations (the central bank (S121) and deposit-taking corporations except the central bank (S122)) and, in some cases, by central government (S1311) as debtors.

(c) Transferable deposits

4.49. Transferable deposits (AF22) comprise all deposits that are:

(a) Exchangeable for bank notes and coins on demand at par and without penalty or restriction;

(b) Directly usable for making third-party payments by cheque, draft, giro order, direct debit/credit or other direct payment facility.

[91] The relationship between deposits and loans is described in paragraphs 4.120 to 4.125.

4.50. Some types of deposits embody only limited features of transferability. For example, some deposits have restrictions, such as on the number of third-party payments.

4.51. Transferable deposits predominantly represent liabilities of resident deposit-taking corporations (the central bank (S121) and deposit-taking corporations except the central bank (S122)), in some cases of central government (S1311), and of corresponding non-resident institutional units. All resident sectors and the rest of the world may hold transferable deposits.

4.52. Transferable deposits include:

(a) *Interbank positions* other than securities and accounts receivable or payable between deposit-taking corporations except the central bank. The 2008 SNA recommends that interbank positions be shown as a separate component of deposits. The borrowing and lending within the banking subsector, which may be substantial, is of different economic significance from that subsector's intermediation activities involving other sectors. Interbank positions are to be identified and recorded under transferable deposits (2008 SNA, paras. 11.56 and 11.57);[92]

(b) Deposits held with the central bank by deposit-taking corporations except the central bank and which they are able to transfer;

(c) Customers of deposit-taking corporations except the central bank purchase cashier's cheques or similar instruments to use in paying suppliers of goods or services or in settling financial obligations. A cashier's cheque is a cheque drawn on the own account of a deposit-taking corporation. The deposit-taking corporation's cashier signs the cheque and it is made payable to the party specified by the purchaser. Whether purchased with currency or through deposit withdrawal, a cashier's cheque should be included within transferable deposit liabilities of the deposit-taking corporation on which it is written;[93]

(d) Customers of deposit-taking corporations may purchase a bank draft (sometimes called a teller's cheque), that is, a cheque or similar instrument written by a deposit-taking corporation against funds in its deposit account at another deposit-taking corporation. For a bank draft purchased by one of its customers, a deposit-taking corporation should record: (i) a reduction in deposit liabilities, arising from a withdrawal from the customer's deposit holdings (or an increase in the deposit-taking corporation's currency holdings, if the cheque was purchased with cash); and (ii) a reduction in its deposit holdings at the deposit-taking corporation on which the draft was written.[94] A bank draft (or teller's cheque) should be included within transferable deposit liabilities of the deposit-taking corporation on which it is written;[95]

---

[92] There may be cases where the instrument classification of interbank positions is unclear, for example because the parties are uncertain, or because one party considers it as a loan and the other a deposit. Therefore, as a convention to ensure symmetry, all interbank positions other than securities and accounts receivable or payable are classified under deposits.

[93] For deposit classification by sector, the bank cheque should be attributed to the economic sector of the purchaser of the cheque, rather than to the economic sector of the recipient. If purchased by a customer in a money-holding sector, the cashier's cheque should be included in transferable deposits included in broad money. If purchased by central government, a non-resident, or (conceivably) another deposit-taking corporation, the cashier's cheque should be included in transferable deposits excluded from broad money.

[94] The deposit-taking corporation should record a reduction in its deposit holdings at the other deposit-taking corporation, even though the corresponding entry will not be made in the other depository corporation's accounts until the item has been presented for payment through the clearing system.

[95] While the bank draft is being held by the purchaser of the draft or is in transit to the payee, it is not included in broad money.

(e) Depositors in some countries are authorized to obtain credit in the form of an *overdraft* – a cheque or other item in an amount that overdraws a transferable deposit account. All outstanding claims arising from overdrawn deposit accounts should be classified as loans rather than as negative balances in depositors' accounts, regardless of whether the depositor intentionally created the overdraft or inadvertently had insufficient funds in the account;

(f) Traveller's cheques are issued by financial corporations or non-financial corporations to provide a medium of exchange with characteristics of both currency and liquid deposits. They are prepaid paper-based products issued in specific denominations for general purpose use in business and personal travel. Traveller's cheques do not specify any particular payee, are non-transferable once signed and can be converted into cash only by their specified owner.[96] A traveller's cheque should be included within transferable deposit liabilities of the depository corporation on which it is written.

4.53. Transferable deposits may be divided by currency into transferable deposits denominated in domestic currency and in foreign currencies.

(d) Other deposits

4.54. Other deposits (AF29) comprise all claims, other than transferable deposits, that are represented by evidence of deposit.

4.55. Other deposits cannot be used to make third-party payments except on maturity or after an agreed period of notice, and they are not exchangeable for currency or for transferable deposits without some significant restriction or penalty.

4.56. Other deposits include:

(a) Time deposits, which are deposits not immediately disposable, but disposable with an agreed maturity;

(b) Sight deposits that permit immediate cash withdrawals but not direct third-party payments;

(c) Savings deposits;[97]

(d) Fixed-term deposits and non-negotiable certificates of deposit;

(e) Financial corporations' liabilities in the form of shares or similar evidence of deposit that are, legally or in practice, redeemable immediately or at relatively short notice;

(f) Deposits of limited transferability that are excluded from the category of transferable deposits;

(g) Claims on the IMF that are components of international reserves (different from loans to the General Resources Account), including lending under the General Arrangements to Borrow (GAB) and the New Arrangements to Borrow (NAB);

(h) Liquid claims on IMF managed trust funds;

(i) Repayable margin payments in cash related to financial derivatives contracts, which are liabilities of deposit-taking corporations except the central bank;

---

[96] Each cheque is given a unique number, similar to a normal cheque. If a cheque is lost or stolen, the owner can simply cancel it and obtain a new one from the issuer.

[97] Savings deposits with an automatic transfer service facility are transferable deposits.

Box 4.2
Electronic money

Electronic money (e-money) is a payment instrument whereby monetary value is electronically stored on a technical device or remotely at a server in the possession of the customer.[a] The amount of stored monetary value is decreased or increased, as appropriate, whenever the owner of the device uses it to make purchases, sales and transactions. To qualify as electronic money, the payment instrument must represent *general purchasing power*, i.e. it must be usable for purchases of goods and services from a wide range of vendors.[b]

Electronic money includes hardware-based and software-based products.[c] Hardware-based devices (generally a plastic card with an embedded microprocessor chip) are used primarily for face-to-face payments, but can also be used for remote payments by means of a card reader that is linked to an Internet connection. Electronic money may be used as a broad term for a number of more specific "electronic value" products and services. Examples include prepaid cards, electronic purses, web-based e-money services (such as PayPal), network money[d] and mobile money. Network money refers to electronic money transferred through telecommunication channels, by means of either hardware-based or software-based technology. Mobile money (also referring to mobile payment, mobile money transfer and mobile wallet solutions) refers to payment services operated under financial regulations and performed via a mobile phone or a mobile device. The payment instrument in association with mobile payment services has features of electronic money.

Electronic money is stored on a physical device or remotely at a server. The recipients of such payments must forward evidence of ownership of the funds to the card issuer for redemption under the closed circulation of electronic money. Open circulation allows the funds to be transferred through a sequence of buyer-to-buyer transactions without involvement of the issuer of the electronic money.[e]

While most issuers of electronic money are financial corporations, non-financial corporations can be authorized to issue electronic money. Data collection is straightforward for electronic money issued under closed circulation by deposit-taking corporations except the central bank, given that accounting for transactions and balances for electronic money and for regular transferable deposits are similar.[f]

[a] See also the MFSMCG.

[b] Specific cheques are given unique cheque numbers, similar to a normal cheque. When a lost or stolen cheque is identified, it is simply cancelled and the individual is reissued a new cheque.

[c] The two types of technology-based electronic money are also referred to as *card-based e-money schemes* and *software-based e-money schemes*.

[d] Network money refers to electronic money transferred through telecommunication channels, by means of either hardware-based or software-based technology.

[e] Whereas currency has physical features, security for electronic money transactions is provided by electronic cryptograph for authentication, confidentiality and data-processing integrity.

[f] In the loading of funds to the electronic-money card, the deposit-taking corporation acquires "handheld deposits" in exchange for regular deposits (or currency). The deposit-taking corporation's transactions with the recipients of the electronic funds are similar to electronic settlements for other types of transferable items.

(j) Overnight and short-term repurchase agreements that are included in broad money. Repurchase agreements that are not included in broad money should be classified under loans;

(k) Unallocated gold (and other precious metal) deposits are classified as foreign currency deposits.[98] If unallocated gold accounts represent claims only on non-residents they will be classified under "Other deposits in foreign currency vis-à-vis non-residents".[99] The same principle applies to an unallocated account for another precious metal (e.g. silver or platinum). Unallocated accounts for all precious metals are included in foreign currency deposits, and allocated accounts for all metals, other than for gold held by monetary authorities,[100] are included in non-financial assets;[101]

[98] Other depository corporations in a few countries offer deposit accounts settled in domestic currency for which the interest return is linked to the market price of gold, but without linkage to physical gold. These deposits are also classified as "Deposits—in foreign currency".

[99] A gold-denominated deposit account with a third-party payment feature would, however, be classified under "Transferable deposits—in foreign currency".

[100] Monetary gold is treated differently because of its role as a means of international payments and store of value for use in reserve assets.

[101] Conceivably, deposit accounts could arise for financial claims on unallocated commodities other than precious metals.

(l) Restricted deposits, that is, deposits from which withdrawals are restricted on the basis of legal, regulatory or commercial requirements.[102] Examples of restricted deposits are as follows:

(i) Import deposits that are required of importers in advance of importation;

(ii) Transferable deposits that have been posted to depositors' accounts, but that cannot be drawn upon until the deposited items (e.g. cheques or drafts) have been collected by the depository corporations that accepted them;

(iii) Compulsory savings deposits arising from an official requirement that a share of a worker's earnings be placed in a deposit account that can be accessed only after a specified period or from which withdrawals may be made only for specified purposes (such as home purchase or retirement);

(iv) Foreign currency deposits that are blocked (i.e. no withdrawals) because of the rationing of foreign exchange as a matter of national policy;

(v) Deposits in financial corporations that are under liquidation or reorganization;

The nature and the period of such restrictions needs to be considered in deciding which, if any, types of restricted deposits should be included in broad money;[103]

(m) Foreign currency deposits under swap arrangements.[104]

4.57. Fixed-term deposits or time deposits are deposits which are not immediately disposable, but disposable with an agreed maturity. Their availability is subject to a fixed term or they are redeemable at notice of withdrawal. They also include deposits with the central bank (S121) held by deposit-taking corporations except the central bank as compulsory reserves to the extent that the depositors cannot use them without notice or restriction.

4.58. Other deposits do not include negotiable certificates of deposit and negotiable savings certificates. They are classified as debt securities (AF3).

4.59. Other deposits may be divided by currency into other deposits denominated in domestic currency and in foreign currency.

(e) Structured deposits

4.60. A structured deposit typically combines a deposit with a financial derivative or a basket of financial derivatives. The financial derivative or basket of financial derivatives is typically embedded in the deposit. Non-negotiable instruments with embedded financial derivatives are classified as deposits in cases where the investor pays a principal amount at inception.

---

102 Deposit restrictions do not include limitations on early withdrawal of deposits that have agreed maturities. A time deposit withdrawal prior to maturity may not be allowed, or, if allowed, typically carries a penalty for early withdrawal. Such withdrawal conditions are treated as standard maturity provisions of time deposits, rather than as deposit restrictions.

103 Financial corporations' holdings of impaired deposits are restricted deposits.

104 Foreign exchange swaps are contracts between the central bank and deposit-taking corporations except the central bank. The central bank acquires foreign exchange from a deposit-taking corporation in return for a deposit at the central bank and there is a commitment to reverse the transaction at a later date. Even if the deposit account allows for transfers, the deposit holder is not able to make payments for the duration of the swap arrangement. Foreign exchange swaps are not classified in the category loans.

Box 4.3
Margin deposits[a]

Margins are payments of cash or deposits of collateral that cover actual or potential obligations incurred. The required provision of margin reflects counterparty risk and is standard in financial derivatives markets (see also the section on financial derivatives below). The classification of margins depends on whether they are repayable or non-repayable.[b]

Repayable margin consists of cash or other collateral deposited to protect the counterparty against default risk. Ownership of the margin remains with the unit that deposited it. Although its use may be restricted, a margin is classified as repayable if the depositor retains the risks and rewards of ownership, such as the receipt of income or exposure to holding gains and losses. At settlement, a repayable margin (or the amount of repayable margin in excess of any liability owed on the financial contract) is returned to the depositor. In organized markets, repayable margin is sometimes known as *initial margin*.

Repayable margin payments are transactions in *deposits*, not transactions in the associated financial assets (e.g. financial derivatives). Repayable margin payments in cash are classified as deposits if issued by other deposit-taking corporations, or in other accounts receivable/payable if not issued by other deposit-taking corporations. When a repayable margin deposit is made in a non-cash asset (such as securities), no transaction is recorded because no change in economic ownership has occurred.

Non-repayable margin payments are transactions in the associated financial assets (e.g. financial derivatives); the payments reduce the financial liability created through the associated financial asset with, as the contra-entry, a reduction in another financial asset (probably in currency or deposits). The receipt of non-repayable margin is recorded as a reduction in the associated financial asset; the contra-entry is an increase in another financial asset (probably in currency or deposits).

In some countries, repayable and non-repayable margins are recorded in a single account and it may be difficult to distinguish between the two types. The institutional arrangements (such as the identities of units making payments and types of instruments used) must be reviewed. The key test is whether the margin is repayable or whether payment of the margin represents an effective transfer of ownership between counterparties to the financial contract.

[a] See also MFSMCG, paras. 4.39–4.43.

[b] See also the MFSMCG.

3. Debt securities

4.61. Debt securities (AF3) are negotiable financial instruments serving as evidence of debt.[105] A financial asset is *negotiable* if the legal ownership is readily capable of being transferred from one unit to another unit by delivery or endorsement. Debt securities (like equity securities) are negotiable instruments that are designed to be traded usually on an organized exchange or in an over-the-counter (OTC) market. Actual trading is not required for a debt security to be considered negotiable.

4.62. Debt securities include bills, bonds, negotiable certificates of deposit, commercial paper, debentures, asset-backed securities, and similar instruments normally traded in the financial markets.

4.63. Bills are usually short-term debt securities that give the holder the unconditional right to receive a stated fixed sum on a specified date. Bills are issued and usually traded in organized markets at a discount to face value that depends on the rate of interest and the time to maturity. Examples of short-term securities are treasury bills, negotiable certificates of deposit, bankers' acceptances and commercial paper.

4.64. Bonds and debentures are long-term debt securities that give the holder the unconditional right to: (a) a fixed or contractually determined variable money income in the form of coupon payments; or (b) a stated fixed sum on a specific date or dates when the security is redeemed; or (c) both (a) and (b). Most bonds fall into this category.

4.65. Debt securities are issued by resident non-financial and financial corporations, general government and non-residents. They can usually be held by any resident

[105] See also the *HSS* (jointly published by the BIS, ECB and IMF). The HSS deals with the conceptual framework for the compilation and presentation of securities statistics.

institutional sector and subsector and by non-residents as part of their portfolio of financial assets.

(a) Main features of debt securities

4.66. Debt securities as negotiable financial instruments traded on secondary markets display all, or virtually all, of the following characteristics:

(a) An issue date on which the debt security is issued;

(b) An issue price at which investors buy the debt securities when first issued;

(c) A redemption date or maturity date on which the final contractually scheduled repayment of the principal is due;[106]

(d) A redemption price or face value, which is the amount to be paid by the issuer to the holder at maturity;

(e) An original maturity, which is the period from the issue date until the final contractually scheduled payment or maturity date;

(f) A remaining (or residual) maturity, which is the period from the reference date until the final contractually scheduled payment or maturity date;

(g) A coupon rate that the issuer pays to holders of the debt securities; the coupon may be fixed throughout the life of the debt security or vary with inflation, interest rates or asset prices. Bills and zero-coupon debt securities offer no coupon interest;

(h) Coupon dates on which the issuer pays the coupon to the securities' holders;

(i) The issue price, redemption price and coupon rate may be denominated (or settled) in either domestic currency or foreign currencies;

(j) The credit rating of debt securities, which indicates the creditworthiness of individual debt securities issues. Rating categories are assigned by recognized agencies.

4.67. Debt securities include financial assets and liabilities, which may be described according to different classifications – by maturity, holding and issuing sector and subsector, currency and type of interest rate.

(b) Classification by original maturity and currency

4.68. Debt securities may be divided by original maturity into two subcategories: (a) short-term debt securities (AF31); and (ii) long-term debt securities (AF32). Short-term debt securities have an original maturity of one year or less or are repayable on demand, while long-term debt securities have an original maturity of more than one year or have no stated maturity. The breakdown is based on the contractual maturity at the time of issuance.

4.69. Debt securities may be denominated in domestic currency or in foreign currencies. A further breakdown of debt securities denominated in various foreign currencies may be appropriate and may vary depending on the relative importance of the individual foreign currencies for a national economy.

4.70. Debt securities with both their principal and coupon linked to a foreign currency are classified as denominated in that foreign currency. Dual currency bonds are

[106] The maturity date may coincide with the conversion of a debt security into a share. In this context, convertibility means that the holder may exchange a debt security for the issuer's common equity. Exchangeability means that the holder may exchange the debt security for shares of a corporation other than the issuer. Perpetual securities, which have no stated maturity date, are classified as debt securities.

debt securities in which coupon and principal payments are made in a different currency from the denomination of the bond.

(c) Classification by type of interest rate

4.71. Debt securities may be classified by type of interest rate. Three groups of debt securities are distinguished: fixed, variable and mixed interest rate debt securities.

Fixed interest rate debt securities

4.72. Fixed interest rate debt securities cover:

(a) Plain debt securities, which are issued and redeemed at face value;

(b) Debt securities issued at discount or at premium to their face value, apart from zero-coupon bonds (see below). Examples are treasury bills, treasury notes, commercial paper, promissory notes, bill acceptances, bill endorsements and negotiable certificates of deposit;

(c) Deep-discounted bonds having small interest payments and issued at a considerable discount to face value;

(d) Zero-coupon bonds, which are usually single-payment debt securities with no coupon payments. The bond is sold at a discount from face value and the principal is repaid at maturity or sometimes redeemed in tranches. Zero-coupon bonds may be created from fixed rate debt securities by "stripping off" the coupons, that is, by separating the coupons from the final principal payment of the security and trading them independently;

(e) Separate trading of registered interest and principal securities (STRIPS), or stripped debt securities, which are securities whose interest and principal payment portions have been separated, or "stripped", and may then be sold separately;

(f) Perpetual (undated), callable (redeemable), puttable debt securities and debt securities with sinking fund provision;

(g) Convertible bonds, usually classified as fixed-rate debt securities, which may, at the option of the holder, be converted into the equity of the issuer, at which point they are classified as shares;

(h) Exchangeable bonds, which are usually fixed-rate securities with an embedded option to exchange the security for a share in a corporation other than the issuer, usually a subsidiary or company in which the issuer owns a stake, at some future date and under agreed conditions.

4.73. Fixed interest rate debt securities may also include other debt securities like equity warrant bonds, subordinated bonds, non-participating preference shares[107] that pay a fixed income but do not give the holder the right to participate in the distribution of the residual value of a corporation on dissolution, and stapled instruments.

Variable interest rate debt securities

4.74. Variable interest rate debt securities have their interest and/or principal payments linked to:

(a) A general price index for goods and services (such as the CPI);

[107] Preference shares are also known as preferred shares, preferred stocks or participating and non-participating preferred shares.

(b) An interest rate;

(c) An asset price.

4.75. Variable interest rate debt securities are usually classified as long-term debt securities, unless they have an original maturity of one year or less or are repayable on demand.

4.76. Inflation-linked and asset price-linked debt securities include those debt securities issued as inflation-linked bonds and as commodity-linked bonds. The coupons and/or the principal of a commodity-linked bond are linked to the price of a commodity. Debt securities with interest linked to the credit rating of another borrower should be classified as index-linked debt securities, as credit ratings do not change continuously in response to market conditions.

4.77. For interest rate-linked debt securities, the contractual nominal interest and/or the redemption value are variable in terms of domestic currency. At the date of issue, the issuer cannot know the value of interest and principal repayments.

4.78. A specific type of interest rate-linked debt security is a variable-rate note (VRN). Its spread to the reference index varies over time depending on changes in the perceived credit risk of the issuer.

4.79. *Indexed securities* are financial instruments for which either the coupon payments (interest) or the principal or both are linked to an index such as a price index or the price of a commodity. These securities are classified as variable interest rate debt securities.

Mixed interest rate debt securities

4.80. Mixed interest rate debt securities have both a fixed and a variable coupon rate over their life and are classified as variable interest rate debt securities. They cover debt securities that have:

(a) A fixed coupon and a variable coupon at the same time;

(b) A fixed or a variable coupon until a reference point and then a variable or a fixed coupon from that reference point to the maturity date;

(c) Coupon payments that are pre-fixed over the life of the debt securities, but are not constant over time. They are called stepped debt securities.

(d) Bankers' acceptances

4.81. Bankers' acceptances are treated as financial assets from the time of acceptance (even though funds may not be exchanged until a later stage) and are classified under debt securities. A banker's acceptance involves the acceptance by a financial corporation of a draft or bill of exchange and the unconditional promise to pay a specific amount at a specified date. A banker's acceptance must be tradable. The banker's acceptance represents an unconditional claim on the part of the holder and an unconditional liability on the part of the accepting financial corporation; the financial corporation's counterpart asset is a claim on its customer.

(e) Private placements

4.82. Debt securities also include private placements. Private placements involve an issuer selling debt securities directly to a small number of investors. The creditworthiness of the issuers of these debt securities is typically not assessed by credit rating agencies, and the securities are generally not resold or repriced, so the secondary market is shallow. However, most private placements meet the criterion of negotiability and are classified as debt securities.

(f) Depository receipts

4.83. Depository receipts allow a non-resident institutional unit to introduce its equity or debt into another market in a form more readily acceptable to the investors in that market. A resident deposit-taking corporation will purchase the underlying securities and then issue receipts in a currency more acceptable to the investor. After issuance, depository receipts can be traded freely between investors, either on a stock exchange or OTC. Depository receipts are classified according to the underlying financial instrument backing them, that is, as equity securities or debt securities. This is because the "issuer" (the deposit-taking corporation) does not take the underlying securities on to its balance sheet, but rather acts as a facilitator.

(g) Securitization

4.84. Securitization is the issuance of debt securities for which coupon or principal payments are backed by specified assets or by future income streams. A variety of assets or future income streams may be securitized, including:

(a) Financial assets, such as residential and commercial mortgage loans, consumer loans, corporate loans, government loans; insurance contracts; and credit derivatives;

(b) Non-financial assets;

(c) Future revenue.

4.85. Securitization of assets or of future income streams is an important financial innovation that has led to the creation and extensive use of new financial corporations to facilitate the creation, marketing and issuance of debt securities. Securitization has been driven by different considerations. For corporations these include: cheaper funding than is available through banking facilities; the reduction in regulatory capital requirements; the transfer of various types of risk, such as credit risk and insurance risk; and the diversification of funding sources.

4.86. Securitization schemes vary within and across debt securities markets. These schemes can be grouped into two broad types:

(a) A financial corporation engaging in the securitization of assets and a transfer of the assets providing collateral from the original holder, known as a true-sale;

(b) Securitization schemes involving a financial corporation engaged in the securitization of assets and a transfer of credit risk only, using CDS: the original owner retains the assets but passes on the credit risk. This is known as synthetic securitization.[108]

4.87. Referring to securitization scheme (a), a securitization corporation is created to hold securitized assets or other assets that have been securitized by the original holder, and issue debt securities collateralized by those assets.

---

[108] See Regulation (EC) No. 24/2009 of the European Central Bank of 19 December 2008 concerning statistics on the assets and liabilities of financial vehicle corporations engaged in securitization transactions (ECB/2008/30) (OJ L 15, 20.1.2009, p. 1). The work of the OECD Working Party on Financial Statistics on securitization is reflected in Chavoix-Mannato (2011).

4.88. It is essential to establish, in particular, whether the financial corporation engaged in the securitization of assets actively manages its portfolio by issuing debt securities, rather than simply acting as a trust that passively manages assets or holds debt securities. Where the financial corporation is the legal owner of a portfolio of assets, issues debt securities that present an interest in the portfolio, and has a full set of accounts, it is acting as a financial intermediary classified in other financial intermediaries, except insurance corporations and pension funds (S125).

4.89. Financial corporations engaged in the securitization of assets are distinguished from entities that are created solely to hold specific portfolios of financial assets and liabilities. The latter are combined with their parent corporation, if resident in the same country as the parent. However, as non-resident entities they are treated as separate institutional units and are classified as captive financial institutions and moneylenders (S127).

4.90. Referring to securitization scheme (b), the original owner of the assets, or protection buyer, by means of CDS, transfers the credit risk related to a pool of diversified reference assets to a securitization corporation, but retains the assets itself. The proceeds from the issue of debt securities are placed in a deposit or in another safe investment such as AAA bonds, and the interest accrued on the deposit, together with the premium from, the CDS, finances the interest on the debt securities issued. If a default occurs, the principal owed to the holders of the asset-backed securities is reduced, with junior tranches getting the first "hit", etc. Coupon and principal payments may also be redirected to the original collateral owner from investors in the debt securities to cover default losses.

(h) Asset-backed securities

4.91. Asset-backed securities (ABS) are debt securities whose principal and/or interest is payable solely from the cash flows produced by a specified pool of financial or non-financial assets.[109] ABS are typically issued by financial corporations engaged in the securitization of assets and the holders do not have a residual claim on the underlying assets. They are often issued in different tranches of seniority corresponding to a different priority in the right to receive repayment of principal and/or interest out of the cash flows generated by the asset pool. ABS include:

(a) Residential mortgage-backed securities (RMBS) and commercial mortgage-backed securities (CMBS), which typically have long-term original maturities and are backed by pools of mortgage loans;

(b) Collateralized debt obligations (CDO), which are backed by more heterogeneous pools of financial assets, often including tranches of RMBS, CMBS and/or other CDO;

(c) Collateralized loan obligations, which are often actively managed and are backed by a portfolio of investments in medium to large-sized loans, often syndicated and purchased in the secondary market;

(d) Other ABS, backed by other assets such as pools of credit card receivables, trade receivables, student loans or the income streams of a whole business or an entire business division;

(e) Asset-backed commercial paper (ABCP), which are notes issued with a short-term original maturity in the context of an ABCP programme. Such programmes are often sponsored by banks and typically utilize the proceeds of the notes to finance trade receivables, consumer credit, financial and non-

[109] The maturity of the debt usually corresponds to the type of collateral.

financial leases and tranches of long-term asset-backed securities, often from a variety of originators including non-financial firms;

(f) Collateralized mortgage obligations (CMO), which are bonds that represent claims on specific cash flows from large pools of residential mortgages.

(i) Covered bonds

4.92. Covered bonds are debt securities issued or fully guaranteed by a financial corporation. These bonds are, in addition, secured by a pledge on a cover pool of mortgage loans or government debt. Covered bond issuance is governed by special legal frameworks and is subject to prudential supervision.[110] In the event of default of the issuing or guarantor financial corporation, bondholders have a priority claim on the cover pool, in addition to their ordinary claim on the financial corporation.

4.93. Covered bonds are different from ABS in that the issuer/owner of the assets assumes an unconditional obligation to repay principal and interest irrespective of the performance of the assets. The assets function simply as collateral pledged for the benefit of the bondholders in case those obligations are not fulfilled. Thus, the collateral pledged does not serve to reduce credit risk from the perspective of the asset owner in a covered bond issuance.

(j) Perpetual bonds

4.94. Perpetual bonds (or perpetuities) are bonds with no maturity date. They have an infinite life. Issuers pay coupons on perpetual bonds forever and they do not have to redeem the principal.

4.95. A perpetual bond is an annuity in which the periodic payments begin on a fixed date and continue indefinitely. It is sometimes referred to as a perpetual annuity. The value of the perpetuity is finite because receipts that are anticipated far in the future have an extremely low present value (present value of the future cash flows). Unlike a typical bond, because the principal is never repaid, there is no present value for the principal. Assuming that payments begin at the *end* of the current period, the price of a perpetual bond is simply the coupon amount over the appropriate discount rate or yield, that is:

$$PV = A/(1+r)^1 + A/(1+r)^2 + \ldots + A/(1+r)^\infty$$

$$PV = A/r$$

4.96. Where PV = present value of the perpetual bond, A = the amount of the periodic payment, and r=yield, discount rate or interest rate.

4.97. A perpetual bond has a face value of 1,000 and provides an annual coupon interest A of 80. The discount rate r is 10 per cent and the value of the perpetual bond is derived as:

$$PV = A/(1+r)^1 + A/(1+r)^2 + \ldots + A/(1+r)^\infty$$

$$PV = A/r$$

$$= 80/0.1 = 800.$$

[110] For example, Regulation (EU) No. 575/2013 of the European Parliament and of the Council of 26 June 2013 on prudential requirements for credit institutions and investment firms and amending Regulation (EU) No. 648/2012 (OJ L 176, 27.6.2013, p. 1 (part of the so-called CRD IV package replacing the Capital Requirements Directives) establishes rules on the treatment of covered bonds). The cover pool consists mainly of mortgages with a high credit rating or loans provided to general government. Debt securities issued under similar schemes include: *Pfandbriefe*; *obligations foncières*; *obbligazioni bancarie garantite*; *lettres de gage hypothécaires* and *lettres de gage publiques*; *obrigações hipotecárias* and *obrigações hipotecárias sobre a sector público*; and *cédulas hipotecarias* and *cédulas territoriales*.

Box 4.4

Securities lending, repurchase agreements and buy/sell-backs

Securities lending is the temporary transfer of securities by the lender (the seller of the securities or cash receiver) to the borrower. The securities borrower may be required to provide assets as collateral to the securities lender in the form of cash or securities. Legal title passes on both sides of the transaction so that the borrowed securities and collateral can be sold or lent.

A *securities repurchase agreement* is an arrangement involving the provision of securities like debt securities or shares in exchange for cash or other means of payment, with a commitment to repurchase the same or similar securities at a fixed price. The commitment to repurchase may be either on a specified future date or an "open" maturity. Buy/sell-backs are synthetic repurchase agreements involving a combination of a spot transaction and a forward transaction.

Securities lending with cash collateral, repurchase agreements ("repos") and buy/sell-backs are different terms for arrangements having the same economic effects, namely those of a secured loan, as they involve the provision of securities as collateral for a loan or a deposit, where a deposit-taking corporation sells the securities under such an arrangement.

Where securities are provided under securities lending, repurchase agreements and buy/sell-backs, no change in economic ownership occurs because the lender is still the beneficiary of the income yielded by the security (by means of the coupon and dividend pass-on mechanism, the so-called "manufactured dividend") and is subject to the risks or benefits of any change in the price of the security.

The supply and receipt of funds under a securities repurchase agreement, securities lending (cash collateral) or buy/sell-backs do not involve any new issuance of debt securities. Such provision of funds to institutional units other than deposit-taking corporations except the central bank is treated as loans; it is classified as a deposit if it involves liabilities of a deposit-taking corporation and is included in national measures of broad money. The features of these different operations are shown in the table below.

Feature	Securities lending		Repurchase agreements		Buy/sell-backs
	Cash collateral	Without cash collateral	Specific securities	General collateral	
Formal method of exchange	Lending of securities with an agreement by the borrower to deliver them back to the lender		Sale of securities with a commitment to repurchase them under terms of master agreement		Spot sale and forward purchase of securities
Subject of exchange	Securities for cash	Securities for other collateral (if any)	Specific securities for cash	General collateral for cash	Cash for securities
Return is paid to the supplier of	Securities		Cash		Cash
Return payable as	Fee		Repo rate		Difference between the forward and the spot prices (usually equal to the repo rate)

If a securities lending does not involve the supply of cash, that is, if there is an exchange of one security for another, or if one party supplies a security without collateral, there is no transaction in loans, deposits or securities. Margin calls in cash under a repo are classified as loans.

Gold swaps are similar to securities repurchase agreements except that the collateral is gold. They involve an exchange of gold for foreign exchange deposits with an agreement that the transaction be reversed at an agreed future date at an agreed gold price. The transaction is recorded as a collateralized loan or a deposit.

Example of a repurchase agreement

The parties to a repurchase agreement or a similar transaction agree to exchange bonds or other financial instruments for an equivalent amount of cash, with a binding agreement to reverse the transaction. Such a transaction is sometimes called a sale of bonds against cash collateral, whereas the statistical treatment is that of a loan of cash against collateral in the form of bonds. The bonds remain on the balance sheet of the original holder, who retains all the benefits and risks of owning them (including entitlement to the interest accruing on the bonds). When the repo matures, the borrower of cash will return more than he originally received, the difference reflecting interest for the use of the cash during the life of the contract. This interest should be recorded under the respective financial instrument on the balance sheets of the cash borrower and of the cash lender.

Short selling (also known as "shorting" or "going short") is the practice of selling assets, usually securities that have been borrowed from a third party, with the intention of buying back identical assets at a later date to return to the lender.[a] Short sellers hope to gain from a decline in the value of the assets, in which case they will pay a lower price to repurchase the assets than they received on selling them. Conversely, the short seller will make a loss if the price of the assets rises. Short selling may be facilitated by brokers who, for a fee, arrange the lending of a security owned by one customer (the "lender") to another (the "short seller"). The short seller then sells the security in the market (to the "purchaser"). The "lender" retains the legal and economic ownership, and may request the security at any time from the broker. The broker will then deliver an identical security, which he can usually obtain from the large pool of securities held by his customers.

When debt securities or other securities are sold short, both the security lender (the original owner of the security) and the purchaser of the security sold short are the legal and economic owners, as they are both subject to the risks and benefits of the security. To offset this double counting, a negative holding of the security should be recorded for the position of the short seller, and the transaction accounts should reflect a sale from the short seller to the purchaser, which is also the counterpart entry to the cash flow from the purchaser to the short seller. In the distribution of income account, accrued interest or other income payable by the short seller to the lender is to be treated as negative income receivable by the short seller, while the purchaser and the lender record the corresponding accrued interest or other income payments.

Example of short selling of securities and reverse repurchase agreements[a]

A trader in securities who does not own a particular security but expects its price to fall may nevertheless sell it in the expectation of buying it back more cheaply later. This is called "going short". The short seller must deliver the security to the buyer; to do so he must borrow the security, probably through a reverse repurchase agreement. Since the security will remain on the balance sheet of the original owner and appear on the balance sheet of the new owner, the short seller must record a negative holding to avoid double counting.

[a] Short selling also applies to repurchase agreements.

4.98. Examples of perpetual bonds are consols issued by the Treasury of the United Kingdom of Great Britain and Northern Ireland. Canada issued some perpetual bonds in the late 1970s. Most perpetual bonds are deeply subordinated bonds issued by banks. Most of them are callable, but the first call date is never less than five years from the date of issue – a call protection period.

(k) Stripped securities

4.99. *Stripped securities* are securities that have been transformed from a principal amount with coupon payments into a series of zero-coupon bonds with maturities matching the coupon payment date(s) and the redemption date of the principal amount(s). They are also called "STRIPS". The function of stripping is that investor preferences for particular cash flows can be met in ways different from the mix of cash flows of the original security. Stripped securities may have an issuer different from the original issuer. There are two cases of stripped securities:

(a) When no new funds are raised and the payments on the original securities are stripped and separately marketed by the issuer or through agents (such as strip dealers) acting with the issuer's consent;

(b) When a third party acquires the original securities and uses them to back the issue of the stripped securities. New funds have been raised and a new financial instrument is created.

4.100. Financial corporations purchase bonds or similar instruments, strip the coupon payments and sell the future cash flows to separate investors, that is, the principal-only claim sold to one investor and coupon-only claims sold to one or more other investors. The principal-only and coupon-only strip investors receive the cash flows from the bonds on a pass-through basis. The issuer of the strip (the financial corporation) records liabilities (classified under debt securities) for the cash flows that were stripped and sold. Financial corporations are purchasers as well as creators of principal-only and coupon-only strips.

4.101. Principal-only- and interest-only strips are also created through securitization of mortgage loan pools in a special form of CMO. The interest-only strip investors receive cash flows from the periodic interest payments received from the mortgage loan pool, and the principal-only strip investors receive the principal portions of the periodic payments. The cash flows and yields for the principal-only and interest-only strips, similar to those for other pass-through securities backed by mortgage loans, reflect the pattern of the loan payments.

4.102. When the issuer of the original security creates principal-only and coupon-only strips, he retires the original securities or leaves them in a repository (e.g. a settlement or clearing facility) on a "dormant" basis until such time when the securities are reissued or redeemed. The strip-like securities replace the original securities to avoid double counting of the issuer's liabilities.

(l) Structured debt securities

4.103. A structured debt security typically combines a debt security, or a basket of debt securities, with a financial derivative or a basket of financial derivatives. This embedded financial derivative or the basket of financial derivatives usually cannot be traded separately from the debt security. Financial instruments with embedded financial derivatives should be treated as debt securities.

4.104. Examples of structured debt securities are:

(a) Credit-linked notes (CLN), which are debt securities with embedded CDS allowing the issuers to transfer the credit risks on some other assets to investors. If one or more of the specified default events occur, the principal amount on the CLN is reduced accordingly;

(b) Structured variable-rate notes (VRNs), which are variations of standard variable-rate bonds whose interest payments are periodically reset by reference to an independent interest rate index, such as the London Interbank Offered Rate (LIBOR). The structured issue includes a derivative that allows the coupon calculation to be tailored to meet investors' interest rate expectations. For example, there may be an interest rate collar or band;

(c) VRNs, which have the standard characteristics of a variable interest rate bond, except that the spread over the reference index, instead of being fixed, varies over time with the perceived credit risk of the issue or issuer. VRNs generally have a put option for the existing holders of notes to sell the issue back to the lead manager of the issuing syndicate, at face value and on any interest payment date.

4.105. The features of structured securities can be used to specify five criteria, which are outlined as follows (table 4.9):

(a) The degree of principal at risk may be: (i) protected and returned at maturity, regardless of the performance of the reference financial instrument; (ii) exposed to losses limited to less than the full principal; (iii) fully at risk subject to a level of initial loss protection; or (iv) fully at risk;

(b) Variation in investment returns allows six different types of structured securities to be distinguished: (i) a "synthetic convertible", where the investor receives a coupon plus potential appreciation in the underlying principal; (ii) a "reverse convertible", where the investor receives a coupon and is exposed to potential depreciation in the underlying principal; (iii) a "dynamic allocation", where the investment is algorithmically or dynamically allocated between assets during the life of the investment; (iv) a "periodic capped", where the investment return is based on the sum of periodically measured returns in the underlying principal; (v) a "target return", where the investment is terminated once a certain return on the investment has been reached; and (vi) a "synthetic exposure", where there is an economically similar investment to investing directly in the underlying principal;

Table 4.9
Features of structured debt securities

		Degree of principal at risk			
		Protected	**Partly protected**	**Fully at risk subject to a level of initial loss protection**	**Fully at risk**
Investment return	Synthetic convertible Reverse convertible Dynamic allocation Periodic capped Target return Synthetic exposure				
Participation	Straight Averaging Variable Enhanced				
Type of coupon	Variable Fixed Minimum				
Type of call	Callable Auto-callable				

(c) Participation characterizes whether the return is: (i) based on the initial and the final underlying levels – it does not include averaging over more than 10 per cent of the term of the investment and the participation rate is fixed on the pricing date; (ii) based on a periodic averaging for more than 10 per cent of the term of the investment – the participation rate is fixed on the pricing date; (iii) not fixed on the pricing date, but dependent on changes in the underlying principal; or (iv) based on the change in the underlying principal with a ratio greater than one;

(d) Type of coupon might be: (i) variable, depending on the change in the underlying principal; (ii) fixed and set on the pricing date; or (iii) a minimum return in excess of the principal amount and set on the pricing date;

(e) Investment may be called from the investor: (i) at the issuer's option (callable), or (ii) if a predetermined movement in the underlying principal occurs (auto-callable).

4.106. Using the degree of principal at risk as a primary criterion, and the type of investment return and participation as secondary criteria, four types of structured debt securities can be identified. Each type is described below.

4.107. Principal-protected products are characterized by the fact that the capital initially invested is guaranteed from the investor's point of view. These products offer the full downside protection of a debt security while having the upside potential of an equity security. Investors typically give up a portion of the equity security appreciation in exchange for principal protection. As such, products that combine a debt security with one or more options should be classified as debt securities.

4.108. Yield-enhanced products are designed to achieve a maximum return on investment. Accordingly, the principal is only partially protected, buffered at risk or fully at risk. Such products offer a greater upside potential than principal-protected products but do not guarantee the full return of principal. They are partly exposed to any decline in the underlying investment below a buffer zone. Such products typically combine a debt security and a put or call option. They should be classified as debt securities.

4.109. Participation products derive their value from different types of securities. Depending on the underlying securities, these products should be classified as debt securities, equity securities, or investment fund shares or units.

4.110. Leveraged products with a large risk compared with the initial investment combine an investment in an underlying security with a future or option. Even if the initial investment is small compared with the expected risk, leverage products should be classified as debt securities.

(m) Financial assets excluded from debt securities

4.111. Non-negotiable financial instruments, such as certificates of indebtedness, should be classified as loans and not as debt securities.

4.112. CDS should be classified as financial derivatives and not as debt securities.

4. Loans

4.113. Loans (AF4) are financial assets that:

(a) Are created when creditors lend funds directly to a debtor,

(b) Are evidenced by documents that are not negotiable.

(a) Main features of loans

4.114. Loans are characterized by the following features:

(a) The conditions governing a loan are either fixed by the financial corporation granting the loan or agreed by the lender and the borrower directly or through a broker;

(b) The initiative to take out a loan usually lies with the borrower;

(c) A loan is an unconditional debt to the creditor that has to be repaid at maturity and which is interest bearing.

4.115. Loans may be financial assets or liabilities of all resident sectors and the rest of the world. By convention, deposit-taking corporations except the central bank normally record short-term liabilities as transferable deposits, not as loans.

(b) Classification of loans by original maturity, currency and purpose of lending

4.116. Loans may be divided, when relevant, by original maturity into two subcategories:

(a) Short-term loans having an original maturity of one year or less or repayable on demand (AF41);

(b) Long-term loans having an original maturity of more than one year (AF42).

4.117. It may be analytically useful to show: (a) loans denominated in domestic currency; and (b) loans denominated in foreign currencies.

(c) Types of loans

4.118. Loans cover:

(a) Overdrafts on transferable deposit accounts, where the amount overdrawn is treated as a loan and not as a negative transferable deposit;

(b) Overdrafts on other current accounts, for example intra-group balances between non-financial corporations and their subsidiaries, but excluding balances which are liabilities of deposit-taking corporations except the central bank classified in the deposit subcategories;

(c) Loans which are counterparts of bankers' acceptances;

(d) Mortgage loans;

(e) Consumer credit, such as revolving loans or instalment loans;

(f) Loans paid as a guarantee for fulfilling certain obligations;

(g) Financial claims on the IMF evidenced by loans in the General Resources Account, including lending under the GAB and NAB. These should be included in the reserve position in the IMF.

(d) Distinction between loans and deposits

4.119. As a general principle, all financial instruments that can be used for direct third-party payments should be classified as transferable deposits, regardless of the designation of the instrument, whether checking account, current account, giro account, nostro/vostro account, etc.

4.120. Classification as a loan is precluded from transferable deposits, because loans are not usable for third-party payments.

4.121. Differentiating between other deposits (i.e. non-transferable deposit) and loans can be more difficult. The classification as other deposits (AF29) or as loans (AF4) is based on the instrument characteristics specified in the documentation and the national practice for distinguishing between other deposits and loans. One distinction may be – in the case of a deposit, but not in the case of a loan – that debtors (mainly deposit-taking corporations (the central bank (S121), deposit-taking corporations except the central bank (S122)) and, in some cases, central government (S1311)) offer a standardized non-negotiable contract with the public at large as creditors allowing the placement and the subsequent withdrawal of the principal amount by the creditors.

4.122. Short-term loans granted to deposit-taking corporations except the central bank are classified, by convention, as deposits.[111] It might be analytically useful to allow for exceptions to this convention. Examples are savings deposits with general government and non-monetary gold swaps between deposit-taking corporations except the central bank.

4.123. Placements of funds between deposit-taking corporations except the central bank are always recorded as deposits.

4.124. The financial instrument should have the same classification in the accounts of the creditor (holder of the financial asset) and the debtor (issuer of the liability). When funds are provided between financial corporations, both financial corporations should use the same classification, as other deposits or loans.[112]

[111] When compiling from-whom-to-whom financial accounts and balance sheets, all loans granted to deposit-taking corporations except the central bank should be classified as deposits; data derived from monetary statistics do not allow such a split into deposits and loans.

[112] Interbank positions should always be classified as a component of transferable deposits.

(e) Distinction between loans and debt securities

4.125. The distinction between loans (AF4) and debt securities (AF3) is that loans are non-negotiable financial instruments while debt securities are negotiable financial instruments. Negotiable financial instruments are those instruments whose legal ownership is readily transferred from one unit to another by delivery or endorsement. Negotiable instruments are designed to be traded on organized or other markets.

4.126. Loans are evidenced by a single document and transactions in loans are carried out between one creditor and one debtor. (Several creditors, however, grant syndicated loans.) By contrast, debt securities issues consist of a large number of identical documents, which together form the total amount borrowed.

4.127. A secondary market in loans exists and two situations can arise:

(a) If there are frequent market quotations available, a loan is reclassified as a debt security;[113]

(b) If a loan is traded only once and if there is no evidence of a continuing market, it is not reclassified and continues to be treated as a loan.

4.128. In many cases financial corporations offer standardized loans. These are characterized by the fact that the financial corporation determines the conditions of the contract; the borrower can only accept or refuse. This is typical for household loans. The conditions applying to non-standardized loans, on the other hand, are usually the result of negotiations between the creditor and the debtor. This is an important criterion, which facilitates a distinction between non-standardized loans and debt securities. In the case of public security issues, the borrower determines the issue conditions, possibly after consulting the bank/lead manager. In the case of private security issues, however, the creditor and the debtor negotiate the issue conditions.

Worked example 4.1. Recording of the sale of loans (provided by the Banco de Portugal and the European Central Bank)

4.129. This worked example refers to the sale of loans as part of a "bailout" process. The main objective of the sale of loans is to "clean" the balance sheet of a deposit-taking corporation except the central bank. One of two options may occur with reference to the sale price of the loans:

(a) Loans are sold at "market price" (fair value);

(b) Loans are sold at a price different from the "market price" (fair value); this has an impact on net lending (+)/net borrowing (-) of both the buying institutional unit and the selling institutional unit, with opposite signs. It means that the selling institutional unit benefits from the sale in case the sale price is assumed to be above the market price.[114]

4.130. The opening balance sheets of the selling institutional unit (a deposit-taking corporation except the central bank) and of the buying institutional unit, general government through a financial defeasance structure, show the assets and liabilities involved in the envisaged operations before the sale of loans at the beginning of the period *t* (0) to *t* (1) figures. It is assumed that the nominal value of the loans is currency unit (CU) 1,300.0 and the market value (fair value) of the loans is CU 800.0.

[113] If a loan is sold several times it should be reclassified as a debt security and the valuation should change from nominal value to market value. This would create an other change in the volume of assets at the time of conversion in loans and debt securities and then a subsequent revaluation as a debt security.

[114] See also the section on financial defeasance in Eurostat (2013), Chapter IV.5.

4.131. Following the 2008 SNA, the loans are recorded at nominal value in the balance sheet of the deposit-taking corporation except the central bank as the selling institutional unit. Information on the market value (fair value) of the loans is made available from the financial accounting statements (business accounts) of the deposit-taking corporation except the central bank as the selling institutional unit.

Opening balance sheets at the beginning of period t (0) to t (1)

Deposit-taking corporation except the central bank (seller)				General government (buyer)			
Financial assets		*Liabilities and net worth*		*Financial assets*		*Liabilities and net worth*	
Currency and deposits (AF2)	X			Currency and deposits (AF2)	Y		
Loans (AF4)	1,300.0						
		600.0	Equity (AF51)			0	Equity (AF51)
		X+700.0	Net worth (B90)			Y	Net worth (B90)

Option 1: Loans are sold at "market price" (fair value)

4.132. It is assumed that the deposit-taking corporation except the central bank sells the loans to general government at "market price" (fair value), which is CU 800.0. The following table shows the transactions as accounting entries in the financial account of both institutional units.

Transactions

Deposit-taking corporation except the central bank (seller)				General government (buyer)			
Changes in financial assets		*Changes in liabilities and net worth*		*Changes in financial assets*		*Changes in liabilities and net worth*	
Currency and deposits (F2)	800.0			Currency and deposits (F2)	-800.0		
Loans (F4)	-800.0			Loans (F4)	800.0		
		0	Net lending (+) / net borrowing (-) (B9)			0	Net lending (+) / net borrowing (-) (B9)

Revaluations

4.133. The following table shows the realized holding losses of the deposit-taking corporation except the central bank as the seller of the loans (CU 500.0) and the realized holding gains of general government as the buyer of the loans (CU 500.0) as accounting entries in the revaluation account of both institutional units. It is assumed that the realized holding gains and losses are reflected directly in the equity of both institutional units.

Deposit-taking corporation except the central bank (seller)				General government (buyer)			
Changes in financial assets		*Changes in liabilities and net worth*		*Changes in financial assets*		*Changes in liabilities and net worth*	
Loans (AF4)	-500.0			Loans (AF4)	+500.0		
		-500	Equity (AF51)			500.0	Equity (AF51)
		0	Changes in net worth (B90)			0	Changes in net worth (B90)

Closing balance sheets at the end of period t (0) to t (1)

Deposit-taking corporation except the central bank (seller)				General government (buyer)			
Financial assets		*Liabilities and net worth*		*Financial assets*		*Liabilities and net worth*	
Currency and deposits (AF2)	X+800.0			Currency and deposits (AF2)	Y – 800.0		
				Loans (AF4)	1,300.0		
		100.0	Equity (AF51)			500.0	Equity (AF51)
		X+700.0	Net worth plus equity			Y	Net worth (B90)

In this case there is no impact on the net worth of both institutional units. The sale of loans leads to a relocation of assets and liabilities between the transacting institutional units.

Option 2: Loans are sold above the "market price" (fair value)

4.134. It is assumed that the deposit-taking corporation except the central bank sells the loans to general government at CU 1,000.0. This price is above the "market price" (fair value), which is CU 800. General government provides a capital transfer to the deposit-taking corporation except the central bank of CU 200.0, which is the difference between CU 1,000.0 and CU 800.0, the "market price" (fair value). The following table shows the transactions as accounting entries in the capital account and in the financial account of both institutional units.

Transactions

Deposit-taking corporation except the central bank (seller)				General government (buyer)			
Changes in assets		*Changes in liabilities and net worth*		*Changes in assets*		*Changes in liabilities and net worth*	
Capital account							
		200.0	Capital transfer receivable (D9r)			-200.0	Capital transfer payable (D9p)
	200.0		Net lending (+) / net borrowing (-) (B9)		-200.0		Net lending (+) / net borrowing (-) (B9)
Financial account							
Currency and deposits (F2)	1,000.0			Currency and deposits (F2)	-1,000.0		
Loans (F4)	-800.0			Loans (F4)	800.0		
		200.0	Net lending (+) / net borrowing (-) (B9)			-200.0	Net lending (+) / net borrowing (-) (B9)

Revaluations

4.135. The following table shows the realized holding gains and losses as accounting entries in the revaluation account of both institutional units. It is assumed that the realized holding losses and gains are reflected directly in the equity of both institutional units.

Deposit-taking corporation except the central bank (seller)				General government (buyer)			
Changes in financial assets		*Changes in liabilities and net worth*		*Changes in financial assets*		*Changes in liabilities and net worth*	
Loans (AF4)	-500.0			Loans	+500.0	+500.0	Changes in net worth plus equity
		-500.0	Equity (AF5)			+500.0	Equity (AF5)
		0	Changes in net worth			0	Changes in net worth

Closing balance sheets at the end of period t *(0) to* t *(1)*

Deposit-taking corporation except the central bank (seller)				General government (buyer)			
Financial assets		*Liabilities and net worth*		*Financial assets*		*Liabilities and net worth*	
Currency and deposits (AF2)	X+1,000.0			Currency and deposits (AF2)	Y–1,000.0		
				Loans (AF4)	1,300.0		
		100.0	Equity (AF51)			500.0	Equity (AF51)
		X+900.0	Net worth (B90)			Y+200.0	Net worth (B90)

In this case there is an impact on the net worth of both institutional units, amounting to the capital transfer from the general government to the deposit-taking corporation except the central bank. As in the previous case, the sale of loans also leads to a relocation of assets and liabilities between the transacting institutional units.

(f) Distinction between loans, trade credit and trade bills

4.136. Trade credit is credit extended directly by the suppliers of goods and services to their customers. Trade credit arises when payment for goods and services is not made at the same time as the change in ownership of a good or the provision of a service.

4.137. Trade credit is distinguished from loans to finance trade, which are classified as loans. Furthermore, trade bills drawn on a customer by the supplier of goods and services, which the supplier subsequently discounts with a financial corporation, become a claim by a third party on the customer.

(g) Financial leases

4.138. A financial lease is a contract under which a lessor, as legal owner of an asset, passes the economic ownership to a lessee who then accepts the operating risks and receives the economic benefits from using the asset in a productive activity. Under a financial lease, the lessor is deemed to make, to the lessee, a loan with which the lessee acquires the asset. Thereafter the leased asset is shown on the balance sheet of the lessee and not the lessor; the corresponding loan is shown as an asset of the lessor and a liability of the lessee.

4.139. Financial leases may be distinguished from other kinds of leases because the risks and rewards of ownership are transferred from the legal owner of the good (the lessor) to the user of the good (the lessee). Other kinds of leases are: (a) operating leases; (b) resource leases; and (c) other contracts, leases and licences.

Box 4.5
Financial leases and operating leases

There are two basic forms of lease: financial (or finance) leases and operating leases. The major differences between them are set out in international accounting standard (IAS) 17.

A financial lease is a form of financing that transfers substantially all the risks and rewards incidental to ownership of a leased asset from the lessor to the lessee. By signing the contract and delivering the leased asset, the lessor transfers economic ownership over the leased asset, while legal ownership is transferred only upon expiration of the lease, on payment of the final installment. In a financial lease, the lessee uses the leased asset for most of its life cycle, as with loans.

Features that would normally lead to a lease being classified as a financial lease include the following:

(a) Legal ownership is transferred to the lessee at the end of the lease term;

(b) The lessee has the option to acquire legal ownership at the end of the lease term at a price that is sufficiently low that the exercise of the option is reasonably certain;

(c) The lease term is for the major part of the economic life of the asset;

(d) At inception, the present value of the lease payments amount to substantially all of the value of the asset;

(e) If the lessee can cancel the lease, the lessor's losses are borne by the lessee;

(f) Gains or losses in the residual value of the residual asset accrue to the lessee;

(g) The lessee has the option to continue the lease for a secondary period for a payment substantially lower than market value.

These features may not, however, demonstrate conclusively that all of the risks have been conveyed; for example, if the asset is conveyed to the lessee at the end of the lease at its fair value at that time, then the lessor holds substantial risks of ownership. Financial leases are also called finance leases, capital leases or full-payout leases, highlighting that the motivation is to finance acquisition of the asset. Accounting practices recognize financial leases in the same way.

The treatment of financial leases is designed to move away from the legal arrangements to capture the economic reality of such arrangements, i.e. by treating assets under a financial lease as if they were purchased and owned by the user. For example, if a bank leases an aircraft to an aviation company, at the time the company is deemed to take economic ownership of the aircraft, it is shown as an asset in the balance sheet of the aviation company and the loan is recorded as a liability.

An operating lease is a lease whereby the entire risks and rewards incidental to ownership of the leased asset remain with the lessor. In this case, the lessor retains the economic and legal ownership of the leased asset, while the lessee only has right of use. Upon expiration of the contract, the leased asset is returned to the lessor. Under an operating lease, the lessee uses the leased asset for less than its useful life.

The difference between financial and operating leases is visible in their tax treatment. The financial lease provider issues an invoice to the lessee immediately upon contract activation. The invoice contains the full obligation: principal plus rent per contract (compound interest for the entire duration of the contract period) plus all value added tax (VAT) (VAT on the leased asset, invoicing VAT and VAT on the interest). Based on this, the lessee will include the leased asset, for example a piece of equipment, in its balance sheet. Accordingly, the equipment will be recorded in assets, while the long-term commitment to lease will be recorded in liabilities. The piece of equipment is subject to depreciation. If it is a fixed asset for which the user is entitled to a tax deduction, the invoice will be the basis for the deduction of the full amount of VAT.

With an operating lease, the lessee receives a monthly invoice for its lease obligation. The invoice shows the net value plus VAT. The net value includes repayment of principal plus interest for the corresponding period. In this type of lease, there is no change in the lessee's balance sheet. Monthly invoices for the lease are recorded as an expense and are reflected in the income statement. The leased asset is present in the lessor's books. If it is an item for which the user is entitled to a VAT deduction, the deduction will be made based on monthly invoices, where VAT is calculated for each monthly installment.

The following table gives an overview of the basic differences between financing and operating leases.

Table 4.5.1: Basic differences between financial and operating leases

No.	Characteristics	Financial lease	Operating lease
1.	Tax treatment	As trade of goods	As trade of services
2.	Financial aspect	Long-term loans	Long-term lease
3.	Legal ownership	Lessor	Lessor
4.	Economic ownership	Lessee	Lessor
5.	Tax savings for the user	Depreciation and interest	Rent
6.	Risks of using the good	Lessee	Lessor
7.	Lease period	Optional	Up to 75 per cent of the asset's economic life
8.	VAT invoicing	At the inception of lease transaction, on the total value of the financed asset + VAT on interest	On the individual rental, each rental being taxed, net rental + VAT
9.	Transfer of ownership after expiry of the lease contract	Upon payment of the final installment, the lessee becomes owner	Upon expiry of the contract, the lessee has a right to purchase the asset at market value
10.	Suitable form of leasing	Where the user wants to become the owner of the asset	Where the user does not want to own the leased asset, the lessor bears the entire risk

Source: International Accounting Standards Board.

(h) Credit cards

4.140. *Credit cards* are used as a convenient means of payment for purchases and as a means of financing purchases. Cardholders usually do not incur financing charges if the entire balance due for their credit card purchases is paid within each monthly billing cycle. Card holders who carry credit card balances on a month-to-month basis are charged interest on all outstanding balances, including the balances generated by new credit card purchases during the month leading up to the billing cycle.

4.141. Credit cards are not financial instruments, but rather a means of financing payment. All credit card balances should be classified as loans, as well as such payments as interest or overdue fees.

(i) Loan participation

4.142. Loan participation occurs when two or more investors (usually financial corporations) jointly fund a loan to a single borrower, either through a *loan syndication* – a loan origination by a syndicate, or group, consisting of a lead firm and one or more other creditors who jointly fund the loan – or through the purchase of portions of an outstanding loan that was originated by one creditor. Each syndicate member records the amount of the loan participation that it has funded.

4.143. Loan participation should be disaggregated by economic sector of the debtor and each creditor. Debtor/creditor relationships for loan participations are determined by the legal arrangements. If the loan participation is on an *assignment basis* (the most prevalent type), each participant has a direct creditor claim on the debtor. If the loan participation is on a *non-assignment basis*, the initial contract between a single creditor and the debtor remains intact, but the original creditor incurs a liability to each purchaser of a participation in the loan.

4.144. A financial corporation may specialize in originating loans that are to be sold (usually, shortly after origination) to another financial corporation that intends to hold the loans to maturity. It is recommended that these instruments be classified as loans.

(j) Bills of exchange and acceptances

4.145. A bill of exchange is an unconditional order written and signed by one party (drawer of the bill) requiring the party to whom it is addressed to pay on demand, or at a fixed or determinable future time, a specified sum to order or to the bearer. Bills of exchange – sometimes called *trade bills* or simply *bills* – are most often associated with foreign trade, but may also be used for domestic trade. Bills of exchange are often called *sight drafts* or *time drafts* depending on whether they are payable on demand or payable by a specified future date. A bill of exchange is an order to pay, rather than a promise to pay. When it is received and "accepted" – stamped[115] and signed – by the party on whom it is written (i.e. the drawee), the bill of exchange becomes a promissory note and is designated as an acceptance.[116]

(k) Financial assets excluded from loans

4.146. Loans do not include:

(a) Trade credit and advances (AF81) which are distinguished from loans to finance trade;

(b) Financial assets or liabilities arising from the ownership of immovable assets, such as land and structures, by non-residents. They are classified in subposition other equity (AF519).

(l) Non-performing loans

4.147. A loan is non-performing when payments of interest or principal are past due by 90 days or more; or interest payments equal to 90 days or more have been capitalized, refinanced or delayed by agreement; or payments are less than 90 days overdue but there are other good reasons (such as a debtor filing for bankruptcy) to doubt that payments will be made in full.

4.148. Loans that have not been serviced for some time are included as a memorandum item in the balance sheet of the creditor. These loans are termed "non-performing loans".

4.149. The definition of a non-performing loan depends on national convention as to when a loan is deemed to be non-performing. Once a loan is classified as non-performing, it (or any replacement loans) should remain classified as such until payments are received or the principal is written off on it or subsequent loans replacing the original.

---

[115] Traditionally, a stamp and signature were required, but modern drafts need not be stamped.

[116] An ordinary cheque written on a bank is a bill of exchange that is sometimes called a sight draft since it is payable on demand. A bank "accepts" a cheque by making the ordered payment.

Worked example 4.2. Recording of non-performing loans

4.150. The non-performing loans of the general government and financial corporations sectors need to be recorded as memorandum items. If significant, the loans to or from the rest of the world are also recorded as memorandum items.

4.151. Table 4.10 describes the positions, transactions and other flows that are recorded for non-performing loans. Other flows refer to reclassifications and write-offs.

4.152. The example shows an outstanding amount of loans at nominal value of 1000 at *t*–1, of which 500 are performing and 500 are non-performing. Loan loss provisions cover the major part, 400, of the non-performing loans, while 100 are not covered. The second part of the table provides detailed supplementary information on the market equivalent value of the non-performing loans. It is derived as the difference between the nominal value and the loan loss provisions. At *t*–1, it is assumed to be 375. During the period from *t*–1 to *t*, parts of the loans are reclassified (from performing or not yet covered to non-performing or vice versa) or written off (the latter requires specific conditions). The flows are shown in the corresponding columns of the table. For the loan loss provisions the nominal values and the market equivalent values are also presented.

4.153. The assessments on loan loss provisions have to be made in the framework of the accounting standards, the legal status and the taxation rules applicable to the units, which might lead to rather heterogeneous results in terms of amounts and duration of loan loss provisions. This makes it difficult to record non-performing loans in the main accounts and leads to their recording as a memorandum item. It is preferable instead to provide market equivalent values as memorandum items in addition to the nominal values of loans, performing and non-performing.

4.154. Two memorandum items are recommended relating to non-performing loans. The first is the nominal value of the loans so designated, including any accrued interest and service charge. The second is the market equivalent value of these loans. The closest approximation to market equivalent value is fair value, which is "the value that approximates to the value that would arise from a market transaction between two parties". Fair value can be established using transactions in comparable instruments, or using the discounted present value of cash flows, or may sometimes be available from the balance sheets of the creditor. In the absence of fair value data, the second-best approach is for the memorandum item to show nominal value less expected loan losses.

Table 4.10
Recording of non-performing loans

Positions	Stock	Transaction	Reclassification	Write-off	Stock
	t–1		period *t*–1 to *t*		*t*
	Nominal value				
Loans	1000	200	0	-90	1110
Performing loans	500	200	-50		650
Non-performing loans	500		50	-90	460
Covered by loan loss provisions	400		70	-90	380
Not yet covered by loan loss provisions	100		-20		80
	Market equivalent value				
Non-performing loans	375		24	-51	348
= Nominal value	500		50	-90	460
– Loan loss provisions	125		26	-39	112
of which not yet covered	100		-20		80

5. Equity and investment fund shares

4.155. Equity and investment fund shares (AF5) acknowledge claims on the residual value of a corporation or a quasi-corporation, after the claims of all creditors have been met.

4.156. They are divided into two subcategories: (a) equity (AF51); and (b) investment fund shares or units (AF52).

4.157. Equity and investment fund shares are grouped together in a single financial instrument category for various reasons:

(a) They represent claims by the shareholders on the net worth of the corporation;

(b) Shares, stocks, units, depository receipts, participations, or similar documents usually evidence ownership of equity and investment fund shares. Ownership does not give rise to a liability that is fixed in monetary terms and it does not always entitle the holder to a fixed or predetermined income;

(c) Investment fund shares or units are in many respects similar to equity securities from a holder's point of view.

(a) Equity

4.158. Equity (AF51) is a financial asset that acknowledges claims on the residual value of a corporation or a quasi-corporation, after the claims of all creditors have been met. It excludes investment fund shares or units (AF52).

4.159. Shares, stocks, depository receipts, participations, or similar documents usually evidence ownership of equity in legal entities. Shares and stocks have the same meaning.

4.160. Equity may be divided into: (a) listed shares (AF511); (b) unlisted shares (AF512); and (c) other equity (AF519).

(b) Equity securities

4.161. *Equity securities* are part of the financial instrument category AF5 and of the subcategory AF51. Equity securities are negotiable financial instruments: they cover *listed shares* (AF511) and *unlisted shares* (AF512) (see table 4.11).

Table 4.11
Equity and investment fund shares (AF5)

<table>
<tr><td colspan="3">Equity (AF51)</td><td colspan="2" rowspan="2">Investment fund shares/units (AF52)</td></tr>
<tr><td colspan="2">Equity securities</td><td rowspan="2">Other equity (AF519)</td></tr>
<tr><td>Listed shares (AF511)</td><td>Unlisted shares (AF512)</td><td>Money market fund shares/units (AF521)</td><td>Non-MMF investment fund shares/units (AF522)</td></tr>
</table>

(c) Listed shares

4.162. Listed shares (AF511) are equity securities listed on an exchange. Such an exchange may be a recognized stock exchange or any other form of secondary market. Listed shares are referred to as quoted shares. The existence of quoted prices of shares listed on an exchange means that current market prices are usually readily available.

4.163. *A share* may be listed but very infrequently or not at all traded, for example shares of closely held corporations. Stock exchanges are often divided into market segments: an official market, a second regulated market and a third market. Shares in some of these segments, usually the so-called "third markets", are traded less frequently; therefore, prices may not be available on a daily basis but at specific points in time when transactions take place, or when positions are valued at certain intervals, for example at the end of each month.[117]

4.164. Apart from paying regular listing fees, the corporation has to fulfil certain requirements, such as having a minimum asset base and publishing specific financial information both at the time of listing and periodically thereafter.

(d) Unlisted shares

4.165. Unlisted shares (AF512) are equity securities not listed or not registered on an exchange. They are also referred to as unquoted shares. Unlisted shares may be called private equity. Venture capital also usually takes this form. Because prices may not be observable for unlisted shares, other valuation methods may have to be applied (see chapter 5).

4.166. Unlisted shares can be distinguished as follows:

(a) Capital shares which give the holders the status of joint owners and entitle them to a share in the total distributed profits and to a share in the net assets in the event of liquidation;

(b) Redeemed shares whose capital has been repaid but which are retained by the holders who continue to be joint owners and to be entitled to a share in the profits left after dividends have been paid on the remaining registered capital and also to a share in any surplus which may be left on liquidation, that is, the net assets less the remaining registered capital;

(c) Dividend shares (sometimes called founders' shares, profit shares, dividend shares, etc.), which are not part of the registered capital. Dividend shares do not give the holders the status of joint owners – holders therefore do not have the right to a share in the repayment of the registered capital, the right to a return on this capital, the right to vote at shareholders' meetings, etc. Nevertheless, they entitle the holders to a proportion of any profits remaining after dividends have been paid on the registered capital and to a fraction of any surplus remaining on liquidation;

(d) Participating preference shares or stocks, which entitle holders to participate in the distribution of the residual value of a corporation on dissolution. The holders have also the right to participate in, or receive, additional dividends over and above the fixed percentage dividend. The additional dividends are usually paid in proportion to any ordinary dividends declared. In the event of liquidation, participating preference shareholders have the right to a share of any remaining proceeds that the ordinary shareholders receive, and receive back what they paid for their shares.

(e) Main features of shares

4.167. The main features of *shares* are: they are claims by the shareholders on the net worth of the corporation; they may be listed on a stock exchange or be unlisted; al-

[117] There are other types of trading platforms, such as OTC exchanges. Shares traded on these exchanges can be numerous and important, but may not be liquid enough to be officially listed.

though they are issued at a specific issue date and issue price, they usually do not have a stated maturity; and they are usually issued in domestic currency.

Residual claim

4.168. Shareholders own a residual claim on the assets of the institutional unit that issued the instrument.

Marketplace, listing and delisting

4.169. Listed shares are listed (or quoted) on a stock exchange. A corporation is said to be listed, quoted or have a listing if its shares can be traded in a marketplace or a stock exchange. Usually the issuing corporation applies for a listing, but in some countries the stock exchange can list a corporation, for instance because its stock is already being actively traded through informal channels.

4.170. Inclusion in the official share register is a prerequisite for trading on a stock exchange. Initial listing requirements usually include:

(a) A history of a few years of financial statements;

(b) A sufficient size of the amount being placed among the general public, both in absolute terms and as a percentage of the total outstanding stock;

(c) An approved prospectus, usually including opinions from independent assessors.

4.171. A corporation may be listed in more than one market place through *secondary listings*, or through the more complex *dual listing*.

4.172. It is common for one such listing to be a *primary listing* and the others *secondary listings*. Having *multiple listings* (multiple share registers) gives an issuer access to a wider pool of investors. Although there are mechanisms that allow multiple primary listings, these are more complex and expensive. Even if it is listed on only one share register, a corporation can still access multiple trading platforms to widen the market place of the equity security. Secondary listings may be direct listings of the equity securities concerned, or they may be listings of depository receipts.

4.173. A dual listing enables a corporation to have two equal listings in different market places. This is usually done by creating an ownership structure comprising two holding companies, each of which is listed in a different marketplace. These companies can then each own 50 per cent of the group. The main reason for a dual listing is a need to list in two different countries because of a merger of corporations listed in different countries. Alternatively, dual listing may result from a new listing to gain access to capital in a larger market.

4.174. Dual-listed corporations have specific corporate governance requirements. Equal rights of shareholders in each of the listed corporations need to be guaranteed in terms of voting rights and dividends supported by an appropriate management structure.

4.175. Dark pools are platforms for market participants who want to carry out major transactions not visible to all market participants. Such transactions are carried out off the stock exchange.

4.176. Delisting refers to the practice of removing the shares of a corporation from a stock exchange. This occurs when a corporation goes out of business, declares bankruptcy, no longer satisfies the listing rules of a stock exchange, or has become a quasi-corporation or unincorporated business, often as a result of a merger or an acquisition. Delisting can also be voluntary.

Issue date

4.177. The issue date is the date on which a corporation makes an issue of shares to the public. If it is the first such offering, it is called an initial public offering (IPO), also referred to simply as an "offering" or a "flotation"; otherwise, it is called a follow-on offering.

4.178. Where unlisted shares are issued, the issue date corresponds to the date when the corresponding capital is paid up.

4.179. In an IPO the issuer may obtain the assistance of an underwriting entity, which helps to determine what type of shares to issue, the best offering price, the time to bring it to market and to place the offering with individual and institutional investors.

4.180. An IPO is often facilitated by the issuance of allotment certificates representing the corporation's shares and which can be traded on the stock exchange.[118] These certificates expire and are converted one-to-one into shares without any additional payment when the underlying issue is registered.

4.181. The commonly used "greenshoe" (or "overallotment") option allows the issuer to sell additional shares if the demand for newly issued shares is higher than the original offering. This practice is often important to provide liquidity and to stabilize the share price after the IPO.

Issue price

4.182. A share's issue price is the price at which it is taken to market at the time of issue. It may also be called the public offering price.

4.183. When a share goes public in an IPO, the underwriter may set a price per share known as the offering price. Subsequent share offerings are also introduced at a specific price.

4.184. The issue price in an IPO is derived based on the amount of capital to be raised and the number of shares to be issued. The issue price in a new issue of shares (secondary offering) is fixed close to the prevailing market price. When the share begins to trade, its market price may be higher or lower than the issue price.

No stated maturity

4.185. Shares do not have specific maturity dates.[119] Corporations (and therefore shares) are conceptually immortal, but they can be dissolved either by statutory operation, order of court, or voluntary action on the part of shareholders. Insolvency may result in a form of a "corporate death", when creditors force the liquidation and dissolution of the corporation under court order.

Currency denomination

4.186. As shares are traded on national stock exchanges their prices are usually expressed in domestic currency, the currency of issue.[120]

[118] Allotment certificates may be issued in secondary offerings.

[119] Although *Genußscheine* (or *Genußrechte*), a type of participation certificate, sometimes have a stated maturity; they are issued mainly in European countries, such as Austria, Germany, and Switzerland.

[120] Some corporations issue equity in foreign stock exchanges (i.e. American depository shares), but they are fully indexed to the domestic currency of the country of residence of the issuing corporation, so it is not "foreign currency" (See BPM6, para. 11.50). In a few cases shares are issued in a currency other than the domestic currency, e.g. the euro in non-euro area European Union member States.

4.187. Financial investors may hold a portfolio of shares denominated in domestic currency but also in foreign currencies.

Negotiability

4.188. The characteristic feature of shares – like debt securities – is their negotiability. Negotiability relates to the legal form of the financial instrument. A financial asset is negotiable if the legal ownership is readily capable of being transferred from one unit to another unit by delivery or endorsement. Some securities may be legally negotiable, but there might be, in fact, no liquid market where they can be readily bought or sold. Therefore, negotiability can be contrasted with marketability: assets are marketable when there are ready and willing sellers and buyers.

(f) Ordinary and preferred shares

4.189. The difference between ordinary (or common) shares and preferred shares is seen in terms of the rights they carry and the terms and conditions under which they are issued. Whether shares are defined as ordinary shares or as preferred shares depends on whether the shares provide the holder with a priority claim on the corporation's assets. For example, preferred shares may have a priority over ordinary shares in the payment of dividends and on liquidation, but they are subordinated to debt securities.

Ordinary (or common) shares

4.190. *Ordinary* (or common) shares usually give holders the right to:

(a) Participate in the general policy of the corporation. They may carry the right to attend, speak and vote (voting shares) at general meetings. Holders of ordinary shares are able to vote on corporate objectives and policy, on stock splits, and to elect the corporation's board of directors;

(b) A preferential subscription in the event of a stock increase. Some holders of ordinary shares also receive pre-emptive rights, which enable them to retain their proportional ownership in a corporation should it issue another stock offering;

(c) Profit sharing. There is no fixed dividend paid out to ordinary shareholders – their returns are uncertain and contingent on earnings, corporate reinvestment and market efficiency in valuing and selling the stock.

4.191. Ordinary shares (and their certificates)[121] may be bearer shares. Subscribers of bearer shares remain anonymous and therefore the shareholder is unknown to the issuer. Subscribers of registered shares are recorded in the corporation's share register.

4.192. Priority shares are registered shares that give specific powers to the holder, such as the power to nominate candidates to the board of directors. They often also confer special rights with regard to amending the corporation's articles of association.

4.193. Deferred shares have fewer or no voting rights and, in the event of bankruptcy, holders cannot receive any payment of capital from the corporation's assets until all ordinary and preferred shareholders have been paid in full.

4.194. Ordinary shares are distinguished from preferred shares. In the event of bankruptcy, ordinary share investors receive their funds after preferred shareholders, bondholders, creditors, etc.

---

[121] Certificates of ordinary shares often have limited voting rights.

Preferred shares

4.195. *Preferred shares* (or preference shares, preferred stock or participating preferred shares) typically rank higher than ordinary shares. They may carry superior voting rights to ordinary shares (sometimes up to two votes per share) or no voting rights at all.[122]

4.196. Where the shares carry no voting rights, the shareholders do not have the right to vote at shareholders' meetings. Non-voting shares are usually offset by higher dividends or a higher share in the distribution of the residual value of a corporation on dissolution.

4.197. Preferred shares may entitle their holders to a preferential dividend, which may be higher than and paid in priority to dividends paid to ordinary shareholders. They may be convertible into ordinary shares or they may give preferential rights in the event of liquidation.

4.198. Like ordinary shares, preferred shares represent partial ownership in a corporation and often pay a fixed dividend that does not fluctuate, although the corporation does not have to pay this dividend if it lacks the financial ability to do so.

4.199. Preferred shares may be split into:

(a) Cumulative or non-cumulative preferred shares, depending on whether dividends payable are accumulated or not;

(b) Participating or non-participating preferred shares, depending on whether they carry the right to participate in the residual value of the corporation on its dissolution. Such shares are also equity securities, irrespective of whether the income is fixed or determined according to a formula. Non-participating preferred shares are to be classified as debt securities;

(c) Convertible or exchangeable preferred shares, depending on whether they can be converted into a specified amount of ordinary shares or bonds;

(d) Redeemable or retractable preferred shares, redeemed or retracted at a fixed price on a specified date or over a certain period of time, at the request of either the corporation or the holder;

(e) Straight perpetual, rate reset, fixed floating and floating rate preferred shares with different dividend payment patterns;

(f) Split and structured preferred shares, based on an underlying portfolio of ordinary shares or other financial instruments.

Shareholder rights and subscription rights

4.200. Shareholders are granted rights depending on the class of shares held. These include the rights to: (a) vote on matters such as elections to the board of directors; (b) share in distributions of the corporation's income; (c) purchase new shares issued by the corporation (subscription rights); and (d) a claim on the corporation's assets in the event of liquidation.

4.201. However, shareholders' rights to a corporation's assets are subordinated to the rights of the corporation's creditors. Moreover, ordinary shareholders' rights are subordinated to the rights of preferred shareholders.

[122] A common arrangement is for the preferred shares to carry no voting rights unless a certain number of dividend payments have been missed, in which case the preferred shareholders get superior voting rights.

4.202. Voting rights may be weighted between different shareholders but it is more common for voting rights to be proportionate to the number or nominal value of the ordinary shares held. Unless the corporation's articles of association provide otherwise, every member has one vote per ordinary share held.

4.203. Specific rights may be conferred on a particular shareholder (or class of shares) by the articles of association, by the terms of the share issue or pursuant to a shareholders' agreement. A corporation may also have separate classes of shares in the corporation's capital, to which specific rights are attached.

4.204. It is also possible to have non-voting shares; provided that a corporation has issued some voting shares, there is no limit on the percentage of capital which may be represented by non-voting shares.

4.205. Issuers of shares use subscription rights to provide existing shareholders with the opportunity to participate in new issues, so as not to have their interests diluted. To make the new shares even more attractive, the rights may also give existing shareholders the possibility to buy them below market price. Subscription rights are a special kind of warrant (BPM6, para. 5.87) and are treated as financial derivatives.

4.206. When new shares of a corporation are issued, subscription rights may be:

(a) Offered to holders of (ordinary or preference) shares that have obtained a certain amount of subscription rights at a certain date. These rights may be traded separately on the exchange during a specific period of time. Only holders of subscription rights are allowed to purchase new shares. Such tradable rights in the form of temporary listed securities are also called nil-paid letters; they give existing shareholders the opportunity to acquire shares at a favourable price in the event of a rights issue of additional shares;

(b) Excluded from holders of shares that do not carry any rights to buy new shares.

Bonus shares

4.207. Bonus shares are new shares issued to all shareholders in proportion to their existing holdings by converting the corporation's reserves into share capital (equity securities). It is merely a capitalization of the reserves of a corporation. Holders receive new shares and the number of shares increases, but the existing ownership/shareholding proportions do not change.

4.208. Issuing bonus shares does not constitute a financial transaction between the shareholders and the corporation because there is no change in the total amount of the underlying financial asset. The shareholders' claims on the corporation remain the same as before – they do not change as a result of the issuance of bonus shares.

4.209. Bonus shares are designed to improve the liquidity of the shares on the market and hence the total market value of the shares issued may rise: any such change is recorded as a holding gain. They are also a way for corporations to reward shareholders without triggering a tax event that generally takes place when cash dividends are paid.

(g) Other financial instruments included in shares

4.210. *Convertible preferred shares* are corporate fixed-income securities that give holders the possibility to convert them into equity securities of the corporation after a predetermined time period or on a specific date.

4.211. *Equity certificates* (or primary capital certificates) are shares issued by savings banks and other financial institutions that are not organized as limited liability companies or public limited companies. They can be listed (mainly equity certificates issued by saving banks) or unlisted.

4.212. *Certificates of capital development* or development capital certificates (*certificados de capital de desarrollo*) (CCDs) are used in venture capital financing. CCDs are securities in the form of unlisted shares issued by trusts to channel investment resources to equity securities of sectors and activities with potential long-term growth. The yield of these instruments depends on the results of each project; neither interest nor the repayment of principal is guaranteed. CCDs are similar to the financial instruments issued by *special purpose acquisition companies* in the United States, by *income trusts* in Canada, by *infrastructure funds* in Australia and the *specialist fund market* in the United Kingdom. Each CCD represents, for its holder, the right to collect dividends, participate in capital reductions and share redemptions, and sell or dispose of the shares.

4.213. *Dividend reinvestment plans* and *direct investment plans* are ways for shareholders to reinvest variable amounts in a corporation. These are plans offered by a corporation that allow investors to reinvest their dividends by purchasing additional shares or fractions of shares from the corporation on the dividend payment date.

(h) Stock splits and reverse splits

4.214. Stock splits are operations to split existing shares. A stock split reduces the share price and increases the number of shares available in the market with the objective of enhancing the liquidity and affordability of the share. For example, in a two-for-one stock split, every shareholder with one stock is given an additional share. So, if a corporation has 10 million shares outstanding before the split, it will have 20 million shares outstanding afterwards.

4.215. The stock's price is also affected by a stock split. After a split, the stock price will be reduced, since the number of shares outstanding has increased. In the example of a two-for-one split, the share price will be halved. Thus, although both the number of outstanding shares and the stock price change, the market capitalization remains constant.

4.216. A stock split is usually done by corporations that have seen their share price increase to levels that are either too high or exceed the price levels of similar corporations. The primary motive is to make shares more affordable to small investors, even though the underlying value of the company has not changed.

4.217. Another kind of stock split is the reverse split. This procedure is typically used by corporations with low share prices that would like to increase these prices to either gain more respectability in the market or to prevent the corporation from being delisted (many stock exchanges will delist stocks if they fall below a certain price per share). For example, in a reverse five-for-one split, 10 million outstanding shares at 0.5 CU each would become 2 million shares outstanding at 2.5 CU per share. In both cases, the company is worth 5 million CU.

4.218. Stock splits or reverse splits do not constitute transactions.

(i) Share buy-backs

4.219. Corporations may buy back their own equity in a share repurchase, also known as a stock repurchase or a share buy-back.

4.220. A share buy-back is recorded as a financial transaction, providing cash to the existing shareholders in exchange for a part of the corporation's outstanding equity. That is, cash is exchanged for a reduction in the number of shares outstanding. The corporation either retires the shares or keeps them as "treasury stock", available for reissuance.

4.221. Many listed corporations hold varying amounts of their own shares for various purposes (e.g. providing liquidity to the markets). These holdings are often subject to strict regulations and reporting obligations to financial market supervisors and/or stock exchanges. A reduction of outstanding amounts can only be recorded once the shares that have been bought back are formerly extinguished or cancelled (e.g. by the reduction of nominal or issued capital in the official balance sheet of the corporation and/or an official reduction of its market capitalization on the stock exchange). Moreover, differences between a corporation's outstanding amount of shares and its (paid-up) registered capital might be difficult to distinguish.

4.222. It should be noted that the two different ways of recording share buy-backs lead to discrepancies between securities statistics and national accounts. In securities statistics, share buy-backs are recorded gross; they are not netted as listed corporations may purchase and sell their own shares continuously.

(j) Depository receipts

4.223. Depository receipts are securities that facilitate ownership of securities listed in other economies; they are listed on one exchange but represent ownership of securities listed on another exchange. Depository receipts are widely used to enable shares to be traded in jurisdictions different from where the original shares were issued.

4.224. Depository receipts represent ownership of securities issued in other economies; ownership of the depository receipts is treated as direct ownership of the underlying financial instrument backing them (debt or equity security). Therefore, where possible, depository receipts should be recorded in such a way that "looks through" the financial institution "issuing" the receipts; that is, the holder of the receipts should be considered to have a claim on the issuer of the underlying securities.

4.225. These receipts should be allocated to the country of residence of the issuer of the original (or underlying) security and not to the residence of the financial institution that issues the receipts. For instance, American depository receipts are liabilities of the non-United States institutional unit whose securities underlie the receipt issue and not of the United States financial institution that issued the receipt.

4.226. Depository receipts exist in other countries in the form of global depository receipts, European depository receipts and international depository receipts.

4.227. Global depository receipts are securities available in one or more markets outside the corporation's home country. The basic advantage of such receipts, compared with the American depository receipts, is that they allow the issuer to raise capital on two or more markets simultaneously, which increases the shareholder base. These securities have also gained popularity because of the flexibility of their structure. A global depository receipt represents one or more shares (or part of a share) in a corporation. The shares are held in the custody of the depository bank in the home country. A global depository receipt investor has the same rights as the shareholders of ordinary shares, but typically without voting rights. Sometimes, the depository bank can execute voting rights on behalf of the global depository receipt holders. Global depository receipts are commonly listed on European stock exchanges, such as the London Stock Exchange. Both American and global depository receipts are usually denominated in United States dollars, but can also be denominated in other currencies, such as the euro.

4.228. Financial intermediaries should not report holdings of any securities issued by non-residents against which depository receipts have been issued and sold. If a depository receipt has been issued before the financial corporation arranging the issue has acquired the original (or underlying) securities, then that financial corporation should report a negative holding of the original (or underlying) securities.

4.229. Corporations have a choice of four types of depository receipt facilities:

(a) Unsponsored depository receipts, which are issued by one or more depositories in response to market demand, but without a formal agreement with the corporation. Unsponsored depository receipts are considered obsolete and, for the most part, are no longer issued owing to the corporation's lack of control and hidden costs;

(b) Sponsored depository receipts, which are issued by one depository appointed by the corporation under a deposit agreement or service contract. Sponsored depository receipts offer control over the facility, the flexibility to list on an exchange and the ability to raise capital. There are three levels of sponsored depository receipts. A *sponsored level I* depository receipt programme is the simplest method for corporations to access capital markets. Level I depository receipts are traded in the United States OTC market and on some exchanges outside the United States. The company does not have to comply with United States Generally Accepted Accounting Principles (GAAP) or full United States Securities and Exchange Commission (SEC) disclosure. Essentially, a sponsored level I depository receipt programme allows corporations to enjoy the benefits of a publicly traded security without changing its current reporting process. Corporations that wish to either list their securities on an exchange in the United States or to raise capital use *sponsored level II* or *III* depository receipts. These types of depository receipts can also be listed on some exchanges outside the United States. Each level requires different SEC registration and reporting, plus adherence to United States GAAP. The corporations must also meet the listing requirements of the United States national exchanges that they choose. Each higher level of depository receipt programme generally increases the visibility and attractiveness of the depository receipt.

4.230. In addition to the three levels of sponsored depository receipt programmes that trade publicly, a corporation can also access the United States and other markets outside the United States through a private placement of sponsored depository receipts. Through the private placement of depository receipts, a corporation can raise capital by placing depository receipts with large institutional investors in the United States, avoiding SEC registration.

(k) Borderline cases

4.231. *Participation certificates* evidence participation rights. In many countries almost no legal restrictions are placed on this type of financial instrument. Depending on their specific features, participation certificates are considered either as shares or as debt securities. A distinction can be made based on the following criteria: (a) the claims of holders of participation certificates are subordinate; (b) the remuneration of holders of participation certificates is performance related; and (c) capital is provided for an unlimited period, or at least on a long-term basis. Based on these criteria, most participation certificates are considered to be shares.[123]

---

[123] *Genußscheine* (or *Genußrechte*) are a subcategory of participation certificates. They are issued mainly in European countries, such as Austria, Germany and Switzerland. *Genußscheine* sometimes have a stated maturity.

4.232. *Private equity* consists of corporate equity that is not publicly traded on a stock exchange, such as venture capital. It is classified either as unlisted shares (AF512) or as other equity (AF519).

4.233. *Members' shares in cooperative entities* have some characteristics of equity. They also give the holder the right to request redemption for cash, although that right may be subject to certain limitations. These shares are usually classified as debt securities.

4.234. However, they are to be classified as other equity if: (a) the entity has an unconditional right to refuse redemption; or (b) local laws or regulations, or the entity's articles of association, impose prohibitions on redemption.

4.235. Shares in cooperative entities, including shares in cooperative banks and credit unions, are usually non-negotiable financial instruments and should be classified as deposits. However, there might be cases in which credit unions issue equity certificates that are classified as equity.

Box 4.6

Operations related to shares

Mergers and acquisitions

Mergers arise when two or more corporations agree to combine to form a single entity. Acquisitions involve the purchase of one corporation or group of corporations by another corporation or group of corporations (though not all the shares may be acquired by the purchaser).

Corporate restructuring through mergers and acquisitions causes financial assets and liabilities to appear and disappear. When a corporation no longer exists as an independent legal entity because one or more corporations absorb it, all the financial assets and liabilities, including shares and other equity, with regard to the corporation(s) that absorbed it disappear from the system of national accounts. This disappearance is recorded as changes in sector classification and structure in the other changes in the volume of assets and liabilities account.

However, the purchase of shares and other equity of a corporation as part of a merger or acquisition is recorded as a financial transaction between the purchasing corporation and the previous owner.

Replacements of existing shares with shares in the purchasing or new corporation are recorded as redemptions of shares accompanied by the issue of new shares. Financial assets and liabilities that existed between the absorbed corporation and third parties remain unchanged and pass to the absorbing corporation(s).

In the context of mergers and acquisitions, squeeze-outs or other restructuring operations, temporary or intermediary shares are often created for technical reasons. These intermediary shares usually exist only for a few months and are used to handle the complex exchanges and conversions of shares.

When a corporation is legally split up into two or more institutional units, new financial assets and liabilities (appearance of financial assets) are recorded as changes in sector classification and structure in the other changes in the volume of assets and liabilities account.

Privatization and nationalization

Privatization is generally the disposal to non-government owners by a government unit of the controlling equity of a public corporation or quasi-corporation. Privatization proceeds are not government revenue but a financial transaction, with no impact on the government deficit or surplus, as this event is net worth neutral and is a change in the composition of assets (equity (F51) against currency and deposits (F2)) in the government's balance sheet. Thus, privatization proceeds are to be recorded gross in the financial accounts.

Indirect privatization

Privatization may occur under more complicated institutional arrangements. For instance, assets of a public corporation may be sold by a public holding company, or another government-controlled public corporation, and all or parts of the proceeds passed to the government.

In all cases, the payment to the government of the proceeds from the sale of assets through indirect privatization is to be recorded as a financial transaction, irrespective of the way it is presented in the accounts of the government or of its subsidiary, with a simultaneous decrease in shares and other equity corresponding to the partial liquidation of assets of the holding company. Any privatization proceeds retained by the holding company are privatization receipts of the government ploughed back by way of a capital injection.

It may also happen that a public corporation acts as a "restructuring agency". In such a context, the proceeds of the sale may not be paid to the government but kept by the restructuring agency to inject capital into other enterprises.

When the restructuring unit, whatever its legal status, acts as a direct agent of the government, its main function is to restructure and change the ownership status of the public corporation and to channel funds from one unit to the other. The classification of the unit will normally be to the general government sector.

However, when the restructuring unit is a holding company controlling a group of subsidiaries, and only a minor part of its activity is dedicated to channelling funds in the way described above, on behalf of the government and for public policy purposes, the public holding company is classified in one of the corporations sectors according to its main activity, and the transactions made on behalf of the government are to be rerouted through government.

Nationalization is generally the acquisition from non-government owners by a government unit of the controlling equity of a corporation or quasi-corporation. Nationalization usually takes the form of a purchase of shares in exchange for currency or deposits or financed through a debt instrument: the government buys all or part of the shares in the corporation at market price – or at a price sufficiently close, considering usual market practices with regard to the valuation of corporations carrying out the same activity.

The transaction is by mutual agreement, even though the original owner may have little scope to refuse the offer, or to negotiate the price. The purchase of shares is a financial transaction and should be recorded in the financial account.

Exceptionally, the government may acquire ownership in a corporation through appropriation or confiscation: the change in ownership of assets is not the result of a transaction made by mutual agreement. There is no payment to the owners, or the payment does not reflect the fair value of assets. The difference between the market value of the assets acquired and any compensation provided is recorded as an uncompensated seizure in the other changes in the volume of assets account.

Equity investment

Flows between a government unit and its controlled corporation or quasi-corporation related to its equity investment are treated in the same way as flows between any corporation and its owners: equity investments from the investor into the unit controlled; distributions of earnings by the controlled unit.

It is important to distinguish between the withdrawal of equity from the corporation by an owner and the return on equity investment, notably the income earned in the form of dividends. Only regular distributions from the entrepreneurial income are recorded as dividends paid by corporations or as withdrawals of income from quasi-corporations. Large and irregular payments to the owner are recorded as a withdrawal of equity.

It is necessary to determine when payments of the government into public corporations are government expenditure or acquisition of an asset and so a financial transaction, and conversely when distributions to the government by public corporations are government revenue or a financial transaction.

Capital injection

Payments from general government to capitalize or recapitalize a beneficiary corporation and that are put at the disposal of the latter for the long term are often called "capital injections"; they are not subsidies.

Such capital injections are either capital transfers or acquisitions of equity, or a combination of both. The two cases can be distinguished as follows. A payment to cover accumulated, exceptional or future losses, or provided for public policy purposes, is recorded as a *capital transfer*. Exceptional losses are large losses recorded in one accounting period in the business accounts of a corporation, which usually arise from downward revaluations of balance sheet assets, in such a way that the corporation is under threat of financial distress (negative own funds, breach of solvency, etc.). A payment where the government is acting as a shareholder in that it has a valid expectation of earning a sufficient rate of return in the form of dividends or holding gains is an *acquisition of equity*. The corporation must enjoy a large degree of freedom in how it uses the funds provided. Where private investors' funds are part of the capital injection, this is evidence that the payment is likely to be an acquisition of equity.

In many cases, payments made by government units to public corporations are intended to compensate for losses in the past. Government payments are treated as an acquisition of equity only if there is sufficient evidence of the corporation's future profitability and its ability to pay dividends.

Given that capital injections increase the own funds of the unit invested in, it is also likely to lead to an increase of the investor's equity stake in the invested unit. This is automatically the case of those 100% owned public corporations whose equity is the value of their own funds. Such an increase in equity is not used as a criterion to judge the nature of the capital injection: instead, it leads to an entry in the revaluation account (and to an entry in the capital account) when the injection is recorded as a capital transfer and to an entry in the financial account when the injection is recorded as an addition to equity.

4.236. *Credit unions* are cooperative financial institutions owned and operated by their customer-owners. One customer-owner equals one vote at the annual general meeting. Shareholders are both customers and owners of a credit union. There is a voluntary board of directors nominated and elected by the shareholders.

4.237. Ownership is usually open to any resident organization or corporation and is based on a common share account. Shares are refundable upon ownership cancellation. They are also subject to dividends, which may be declared based on the credit union's earnings, as decided by the board of directors.

4.238. Members of a credit union can hold their savings in a variety of accounts. However, the accounts must be in the (legal) form of either a deposit account or a share account. Accordingly, shares in credit unions may be treated as deposits or as other equity.

(l) Financial assets excluded from shares

4.239. Shares do not include:

(a) Shares offered for sale but not taken up on issue. They are not recorded;

(b) Debentures and loan stock convertible into shares (convertible bonds). They are classified as debt securities (AF3) up to the time when they are converted;

(c) Equity of partners with unlimited liability (unlimited partners) in incorporated partnerships. They are classified in the subposition other equity (AF519);

(d) Investment by general government or central banks in the capital of international and supranational organizations (with the exception of the IMF quota), even if these are legally constituted financial resources of a currency union central bank (e.g. the European Central Bank) contributed by national central banks. They are conventionally classified as other equity (AF519);

(e) Issues of bonus shares; these are issues without payment of new shares to shareholders in proportion to their holdings. Such an issue, which changes neither the liability of the corporation vis-à-vis the shareholders nor the proportion of the assets that each shareholder holds in the corporation, does not constitute a financial transaction. Share split issues are also not recorded.

4.240. *Loan stocks* are classified as loans. They are loans secured using ordinary or preferred shares as collateral. The loan will earn a fixed interest rate, much like a standard loan, and can be secured or unsecured. Secured loan stocks are called convertible loan stocks if the loan stocks can be directly converted into shares under specified conditions and with a predetermined conversion rate, as with irredeemable convertible unsecured loan stocks.

4.241. *Equity-linked notes* (ELNs) – a subset of equity-linked instruments – are debt securities that differ from fixed interest rate debt securities in that the coupons or the redemption value is based on the return of a single share, a basket of shares (listed or unlisted) or an equity index (the "underlying equity"). It means that they are generally designed to return the principal of the original investment at maturity but, unlike fixed interest rate debt securities, their coupons are determined by the appreciation of the underlying equity. They also differ from structured warrants in that ELNs are usually principal-protected financial instruments.

4.242. An ELN can be constructed by packaging a call option and a zero-coupon bond. The call option provides the note buyer with exposure to the underlying equity. The zero-coupon bond provides the note buyer with principal protection. A zero-coupon bond allows for principal protection since it accretes from its discount value to its face value over a specified period of time without periodic payments of interest. The discount from the face value of the zero-coupon bond can be used to purchase the call option on the underlying equity.

4.243. The pay-off of an ELN depends on whether the stock price at maturity is above or below a specified barrier, the strike price. If the stock price exceeds this barrier, investors may receive an amount of cash based on the interest earned during the life of the equity-linked instrument; otherwise investors receive a predetermined amount of cash or quantity of the underlying stock.

4.244. An ELN holder's principal may be at risk under certain specified conditions. One such ELN structure is a reverse convertible ELN, which has a guaranteed coupon and provides full principal protection as long as the underlying corporation's share price does not drop below a certain barrier level – typically 60 to 80 per cent of the initial share price. In the event that the underlying reference stock price drops below the barrier, the reverse convertible ELN holder's principal is no longer guaranteed.

4.245. In essence, if the lower barrier is broken, the principal starts floating with the underlying share price. This is roughly equivalent to forcing the holder of the ELN to convert into the corporation's stock (hence the term *reverse convertible*), although the conversion transaction does not actually occur and the investor does not have a residual claim on the corporation. Rather, the selling unit is no longer required to pay back the investor's full principal at maturity, and the actual amount of principal returned depends on how far below the barrier the equity price has fallen.

(m) Other equity

4.246. Other equity (AF519) covers all forms of equity other than those classified in subpositions listed shares (AF511) and unlisted shares (AF512).

4.247. Other equity includes:

(a) All forms of equity in corporations which are not shares:

  (i) The equity in incorporated partnerships subscribed by unlimited partners;

  (ii) The equity in limited liability companies whose owners are partners and not shareholders;

  (iii) The capital invested in ordinary or limited partnerships recognized as independent legal entities;

  (iv) The capital invested in cooperative societies recognized as independent legal entities;

(b) Investment by general government in the capital of public corporations whose capital is not divided into shares, which by virtue of special legislation are recognized as independent legal entities;

(c) Investment by general government in the capital of the central bank;

(d) Investment by general government in the capital of international and supranational organizations (with the exception of the IMF quota), even if these are legally constituted as corporations with share capital (e.g. the European Investment Bank);

(e) The financial resources of the European Central Bank contributed by the national central banks;

(f) Capital invested in financial and non-financial quasi-corporations. The amount of such investments corresponds to new investments in cash or in kind less any capital withdrawals;

(g) The financial claims that non-resident units have against notional resident units and vice versa.

(n) Investment fund shares or units

4.248. Investment funds are collective investment undertakings through which investors pool funds for investment in financial or non-financial assets. Those units acquiring shares in the funds thus spread their risk across all the instruments in the fund.

4.249. Investment funds include mutual funds and unit trusts. Investment funds issue shares when a corporate structure is used and units when a trust structure is used. Investment fund shares refer to the shares issued by mutual funds, rather than the shares the mutual fund may hold; they may be open-ended, semi-open or closed-ended funds.

4.250. Investment fund shares or units (AF52) are issued by investment funds; they acknowledge claims on the residual value of a corporation or a quasi-corporation after the claims of all creditors have been met. Investment fund shares or units may be listed or unlisted. When they are unlisted, they are usually repayable on request, at a value corresponding to their share in the own funds of the financial corporation. These own funds are revalued regularly on the basis of the market prices of their various components.

4.251. Investment fund shares or units may be divided into: (a) money market fund (MMF) shares/units (AF521); and (b) non-MMF investment fund shares/units (AF522).

Money market fund shares or units

4.252. MMFs issue MMF shares or units. MMFs typically invest in money market instruments with a residual maturity of less than one year, are often transferable and are often regarded as close substitutes for deposits.

Non-money market fund investment fund shares or units

4.253. Non-MMF investment fund shares or units represent a claim on a portion of the value of a non-MMF investment fund. Non-MMF investment fund shares or units are issued by investment funds. They typically invest in longer-term financial assets and possibly real estate. They are not transferable and are typically not regarded as substitutes for deposits.

4.254. Unlisted non-MMF investment fund shares or units are usually repayable on request, at a value corresponding to their share in the own funds of the financial corporation.

Open-ended and closed-ended (non-money market fund) investment fund shares or units

4.255. Depending on the variability of their capital base, investment funds may also be classified as open-ended or closed-ended.

4.256. *Open-ended investment funds* can issue and redeem shares on a continuous basis, or at certain defined (short-term) time intervals (see table 4.12). An open-ended investment fund is equitably divided into shares or units, which vary in price in direct proportion to the variation of the fund's net asset value (NAV).[124]

4.257. Each time a new investment is made, new shares or units are created to match the prevailing share price. Each time, shares or units are redeemed, the assets sold match the prevailing share price. In this way, there is no supply or demand created for shares or units and they remain a direct reflection of the underlying assets.

4.258. The NAV is the value of a fund's assets less the value of its liabilities. The method for calculating the NAV varies according to the fund type and can be subject to regulation. Pricing is based on the per share NAV.

4.259. Shares or units of open-ended investment funds usually do not have a fixed maturity period. Investors generally purchase shares in the fund directly from the fund itself. By contrast, closed-ended funds typically issue all shares or units at the outset with the shares usually being listed on stock exchanges and traded between investors thereafter.

4.260. Shares or units of open-ended investment funds can have a stated maturity. They usually offer a capital guarantee to the investor on condition that he holds the shares or units until maturity.

4.261. *Shares or units of closed-ended investment funds* are limited in number and (sometimes) also have a specified maturity period, for example five to seven years (see table 4.12). They are called closed-ended funds because new shares or units are rarely issued once the fund has been launched, and because shares or units are not normally redeemable until the fund liquidates.

4.262. Closed-ended funds are open for subscription only during a specified period when the scheme is launched.[125] Investors can invest in the scheme at the time of the initial public issue. Thereafter, investors can acquire shares in a closed-ended fund by buying shares on a secondary market from a broker, market maker or other investors, as opposed to an open-ended fund, where all transactions eventually involve the fund issuing or redeeming shares or units (in exchange for cash or securities). Some closed-ended funds provide the option of selling the shares or units back to the investment fund through periodic repurchases at NAV-related prices.

Table 4.12
Features of open-ended and closed-ended investment funds

Feature	Open-ended investment funds	Closed-ended investment funds
Access to capital market	Open to new capital after it begins operating	Closed to new capital after it begins operating
Issuance and redemption	Shares or units are (typically) redeemed directly by the fund	Shares or units are (typically) traded on exchanges (securities)
Pricing	Can usually be traded only at the closing price at the end of the previous market day	Can be traded during the market day at any time
Pricing basis	Sell at their NAV (except for sales charges)	Affected by supply and demand, may have a premium or discount with reference to NAV
Assets of fund	Usually own listed securities	Can own unlisted securities
Maturity	Usually have no stated maturity	Maturity is not usually stated, but normally it is intended as the date when assets start being liquidated. Units are redeemed only when the liquidation is completed, often some years later

[124] The Classification of Financial Instruments standard (securities and related financial instruments) defines open-ended funds as those that "permanently sell new units to the public and redeem outstanding units on demand, resulting in an increase or decrease of outstanding capital".

[125] Private equity funds are closed-ended funds.

4.263. If demand for the closed-ended investment fund shares or units is high, they may trade at a premium to the NAV. If demand is low, they may trade at a discount to the NAV. The fund may make further share or unit offerings if demand is high, although this may affect the share or unit price.

4.264. There are some intermediate cases particularly hedge funds, which are neither open-ended nor closed-ended funds, and usually have monthly or quarterly subscriptions and redemptions.

Box 4.7

Types of non-money market fund investment funds

Building block data may be put together for individual sectors or subsectors, such as for the subsector non-MMF investment funds (S124). A first step should be to define the coverage of this subsector in terms of institutional units. Data on the various types of non-MMF investment funds then have to be collected, like data on real estate funds, exchange-traded funds, etc. This box provides an overview of the different categories of non-MMF investment funds from which source data can be collected.

Real estate funds

Most real estate funds are closed-ended funds. Real estate funds often use the legal form of a limited partnership, or of a private or a public limited corporation.

Specific legal structures exist for real estate funds. One example is a real estate investment trust (REIT). A REIT is a corporation that owns and, in most cases, operates real estate. Among other things, REITs invest in shopping centers, office buildings, apartment blocks, warehouses and hotels. Some REITs also engage in financing real estate. Their shares are often traded on stock exchanges.

To qualify as a REIT, a corporation must have most of its assets and income tied to real estate investment and must distribute a major amount of its taxable income to shareholders in the form of dividends. There are two main types of REITs: equity REITs, which invest in and own properties, and mortgage REITs, which invest in mortgages.

Holders can invest in REITs either by purchasing their shares directly on an open exchange or by investing in an investment fund that specializes in real estate. Many REITs are accompanied by dividend reinvestment plans. These are ways for shareholders to reinvest variable amounts in a corporation. Investors can reinvest their dividends by purchasing additional shares or fractions of shares from the corporation on the dividend payment date.

In various countries REITs are not considered to be funds and they do not always fall within the regulatory framework applying to investment funds.

Exchange-traded funds

Exchange-traded funds (ETFs) are types of index-tracking funds – they are usually actively managed to accurately mirror the performance of an index.

ETFs may be based on small-cap companies, individual industries and any combination of countries and regions. ETFs can be linked to government, corporate and high-yield debt securities and paper of varying maturities. Some ETFs are based on commodity indices and property markets; others focus on the interests of particular types of individuals or groups, e.g. the environmentally conscious or religious communities. There are leveraged ETFs, which offer a geared return on a given index, inverse ETFs, which aim to go down when a benchmark goes up (and vice versa) and, inevitably, leveraged inverse ETFs.

In contrast to closed-ended fund shares or units, the market price of an ETF trades in a narrow range very close to its NAV. This is because the structure of ETFs allows major market participants to redeem ETF shares for a "basket" of the fund's underlying assets. This feature could lead to potential arbitrage profits if the market price of the ETF were to diverge substantially from its NAV. The market price of closed-end fund shares or units is often 10 to 20 per cent higher or lower than their NAVs, while the market price of an ETF is typically within 1 per cent of its NAV.

Funds of funds

Funds of funds are investment funds investing in other funds. Their strategy consists of holding a portfolio of other investment fund shares or units, rather than investing directly in shares, bonds or other securities. There are different types of funds of funds, e.g. mutual, hedge, private equity or investment trust funds of funds.[a]

Special funds

Special (investor) funds cover all kinds of funds. They may be exempted from certain provisions regarding investment area, risk diversification, the prohibition on raising loans for the account of an investment fund and the prohibition on selling financial instruments that an investment fund does not hold (short selling).

Hedge funds

Hedge funds are unconstrained investment funds that participate in a range of assets typically involving high minimum investments, light regulation and a wide variety of investment strategies. Hedge funds are distinct from "traditional" investment funds in various ways:

(a) Hedge funds usually engage in a wider range of investment and trading activities than traditional investment funds and invest in a broader range of assets, including securities, commodities and real estate;

(b) Hedge funds speculate on future movements of the underlying assets by taking long or short positions;

(c) Most hedge fund investment strategies aim to secure a positive return on investment, regardless of overall market performance;

(d) Hedge fund managers typically invest their own money in the fund they manage, which serves to align their interests with investors in the fund;

(e) Investors in hedge funds typically pay a management fee that goes towards the operational costs of the fund, and a fee based on the fund's performance;

(f) Hedge funds are usually open for investment to a limited number of accredited or qualified investors who meet criteria set by regulators;

(g) Hedge funds may also invest, in full or in part, in other hedge funds, provided that they otherwise meet the definition.

In order to identify a hedge fund, these criteria must be assessed against the fund's public prospectus as well as its rules, articles of association, the subscription documents or investment contracts, and any marketing documents or similar statements. Obtaining data on hedge funds can be rather difficult as they are not regulated like traditional mutual funds.

Venture capital funds

A venture capital fund refers to an investment fund that primarily invests the financial capital of third-party investors in corporations that are too risky for the standard capital markets or banks.

Most venture capital funds have a fixed life of 10 years, with the possibility of a few years' extension. The investors have a fixed commitment to the fund that is initially unfunded and subsequently "called down" by the venture capital fund over time as the fund makes its investments. When all of the money has been raised, the fund is said to be closed and the 10-year lifetime begins.

Interval investment funds

Interval investment funds combine features of both open-ended and closed-ended investment funds. Holders of interval investment fund units can call for redemption of all or part of the units they hold during predetermined intervals. These intervals are usually determined on a quarterly basis. Interval investment funds are open to new capital for a defined period of time, can be traded at any time and are typically redeemed directly by the fund.

Securitization funds

Securitization funds issue securitization units classified as investment fund shares or units. Securitization units confer upon their holders the following cumulative or exclusive rights: (a) the right to payment of periodic returns; (b) the right to redeem the face value of the securitization units; and (c) the right, on termination or liquidation of the fund, to receive a quota of the total remaining value after payment of periodic returns and all other expenses and charges met by the fund in proportion to their holdings.[b]

Special purpose government funds

Given the nature of their liabilities, special purpose government funds, usually called sovereign wealth funds, are more likely to be classified as captive financial institutions than as investment funds, given the nature of their liabilities, if classified as a financial corporation (BPM6, para. 4.75).

---

[a] Funds of funds may be separated from the non-MMF investment funds subsector to measure and analyse the flow of funds vis-à-vis other sectors and financial corporation subsectors.

[b] There may be cases in which securitization funds issue bonds and not securitization units.

6. Insurance, pension and standardized guarantee schemes

4.265. Insurance, pension and standardized guarantee schemes (AF6) constitute the insurance technical reserves of insurers, pension funds and issuers of standardized guarantees.

4.266. Transactions in insurance, pension and standardized guarantee schemes involve a prepayment or a series of prepayments by the policyholder, which confer a right to receive a certain payment or a series of payments, subject to a contingent event.

4.267. Insurance, pension and standardized guarantee schemes are divided into six subcategories:

(a) Non-life insurance technical reserves (AF61);

(b) Life insurance and annuity entitlements (AF62);

(c) Pension entitlements (AF63);

(d) Claims of pension funds on pension managers (AF64);

(e) Entitlements to non-pension benefits (AF65);

(f) Provisions for calls under standardized guarantees (AF66).

(a) Non-life insurance technical reserves

4.268. Non-life insurance technical reserves (AF61) are financial claims that non-life insurance policyholders have against the technical reserves of non-life insurance corporations in respect of unearned premiums paid and claims incurred.

4.269. Transactions in non-life insurance technical reserves for unearned premiums and claims incurred relate to such risks as accidents, sickness and fire, as well as to reinsurance.

4.270. Unearned premiums are premiums paid but not yet earned. Premiums are usually paid at the beginning of the period covered by the policy. On an accrual basis, the premiums are earned throughout the policy period, so that the initial payment involves a prepayment or advance.

4.271. Claims outstanding are claims due but not yet settled, including cases where the amount is in dispute or the event leading to the claim has occurred but has not yet been reported. Claims due but not yet settled correspond to the reserves against outstanding insurance claims, which are amounts identified by insurance corporations to cover what they expect to pay out arising from events that have occurred but for which the claims are not yet settled.

4.272. Insurers may identify other technical reserves, such as equalization provisions (which give a guide to the funds that insurance corporations set aside to meet unexpectedly large claims). However, these are recognized as liabilities and corresponding assets only when there is an event giving rise to a liability. Otherwise, equalization provisions are internal accounting entries by the insurer representing saving to cover irregularly occurring catastrophes and do not represent existing claims of policyholders.

4.273. Referring to reinsurance, transactions between direct insurers and reinsurers are recorded as an entirely separate set of transactions and no consolidation takes place between the transactions of the direct insurer as issuer of policies to its clients on the one hand and the holder of a policy with the reinsurer on the other. With reinsurance specific financial transactions take place between reinsurers and direct insurers, namely transactions in reinsurance technical reserves and transactions in financial claims with ceding corporations.

4.274. Reinsurance technical reserves due to reinsurance contracts are shown as the direct insurer's financial assets in the form of claims on the reinsurer; they are not consolidated with the direct insurer's own liabilities in the form of technical reserves.

4.275. Reinsurance technical reserves are to be classified as non-life insurance technical reserves. They may be split further by type of insurance (non-life, life and pensions) or by type of reserves (unearned premiums, unpaid claims and insurance reserves).

4.276. Financial claims of reinsurers on ceding corporations are financial assets that reinsurers have with direct insurers (the ceding corporations) – as collateral provided to cover insurance liabilities that a direct insurer retains from the liquid funds which it has to pay to a reinsurer under a reinsurance contract. Such claims are established based on short-term or long-term reinsurance contracts with no significant underwriting risk transfer. They include the recognition and measurement of an asset or liability upon inception of such contracts. Such claims are usually classified as loans (AF4).

(b) Life insurance and annuity entitlements

4.277. Life insurance and annuity entitlements (AF62) are financial claims that life insurance policyholders and beneficiaries of annuities have against corporations providing life insurance.

4.278. Life insurance and annuity entitlements are used to provide benefits to policyholders upon the expiry of the policy, or to compensate beneficiaries upon the death of the policyholders, and so are kept separate from shareholders' funds. Reserves in the form of annuities are based on the actuarial calculation of the present value of the obligations to pay future income until the death of the beneficiaries.

4.279. Transactions in life insurance and annuity entitlements consist of additions less reductions, which are to be distinguished from nominal holding gains or losses on the funds invested by insurance corporations and from other changes in the volume of assets.

4.280. Additions in terms of financial transactions consist of: (a) actual premiums earned during the current accounting period; (b) premium supplements, corresponding to the income from the investment of the entitlements attributable to the policyholders after deduction of service charges; and (c) unearned premiums and benefits outstanding.

4.281. Reductions consist of: (a) amounts due to holders of endowment and similar insurance policies; and (b) payments due on policies that are surrendered before maturity.

4.282. In the case of a group insurance taken out by a corporation on behalf of its employees, the employees, but not the employer, are the beneficiaries since they are considered to be the policyholders.

(c) Pension entitlements

4.283. Pension entitlements (AF63) are financial claims that current employees (future pensioners) and former employees (current pensioners) hold against either: (a) their employers; (b) a scheme designated by the employer to pay pensions as part of a compensation agreement between the employer and the employee; or (c) a life (or a non-life) insurer.

4.284. Transactions in pension entitlements consist of additions less reductions, which are to be distinguished from nominal holding gains or losses on the funds invested by pension funds and from other changes in the volume of assets.

4.285. Additions in terms of financial transactions consist of: (a) actual contributions into pension schemes payable by employees, employers, self-employed persons or other institutional units on behalf of individuals or households with claims on the scheme, and earned during the current accounting period; (b) imputed social contributions payable by employers; and (c) contribution supplements corresponding to the income earned from the investment of the pension entitlements of the pension scheme attributable to participating households, after deduction of service charges during the period for managing the scheme.

4.286. Reductions consist of: (a) social benefits that correspond to the amounts payable to retired persons or their dependents in the form of regular payments or other benefits; and (b) social benefits which consist of any lump sums payable to persons when they retire.[126]

4.287. Pension entitlements of the various types of pension schemes are presented in a supplementary table described in the 2008 SNA. Opening and closing stocks of pension entitlements of households are shown vis-à-vis the pension obligations of all pension schemes in social insurance (including social security), and the transactions and other economic flows during the period which account for the difference between the opening and the closing positions (see para. 3.474 ff).

4.288. Pension entitlements do not include pension entitlements established by institutional units classified as unfunded government-managed defined benefit employer pension schemes (S13 except S1314) or as social security pension funds (S1314). Their transactions are not fully recorded and their stocks and other flows are not in the standard accounts, but in the supplementary table on pension schemes in social insurance. These "entitlements" are not liabilities of the central government, state government, local government or social security funds subsectors and are not financial assets of the prospective beneficiaries (households, if resident, or in the rest of the world if non-resident).

(d) Claims of pension funds on pension managers

4.289. With regard to a defined benefit fund, an employer may contract with a third party to administer the pension fund for his employees. If the employer continues to determine the terms of the pension scheme and retains the responsibility for any deficit in funding, as well as the right to retain any excess funding, the employer is described as the pension manager and the unit working under the direction of the pension manager is described as the pension administrator. If the agreement between the employer and the third party is such that the employer passes the risks and responsibilities for any deficit in funding to the third party in return for the right of the third party to retain any excess, the third party becomes the pension manager as well as the administrator.

4.290. When the pension manager is a unit different from the administrator, with the consequences that responsibility for any deficit, or claims on any excess, rest with the pension manager, the claim of the pension fund on the pension manager is shown under this heading (AF64). (The entry is negative if the pension fund makes more investment income from the pension entitlements it holds than is necessary to cover the increase in entitlements and the difference is payable to the pension manager of the scheme.)

(e) Entitlements to non-pension benefits

4.291. The excess of net contributions over benefits represents an increase in the liability of the insurance scheme towards the beneficiaries (AF65). This item is shown as an adjustment in the use of income account. As an increase in a liability, it is also shown in

[126] Additions or reductions due to transfers of pension entitlements from one pension scheme to another may also arise.

the financial account. This item is likely to occur only rarely and, for pragmatic reasons, changes in such non-pension entitlements may be included with those for pensions.

(f) Provisions for calls under standardized guarantees

4.292. Provisions for calls under standardized guarantees (AF66) are financial claims that holders of standardized guarantees have against the institutional units providing them.

4.293. Provisions relating to calls under standardized guarantees are pre-payments of net fees and provisions to meet outstanding calls under standardized guarantees. Like provisions for prepaid insurance premiums and reserves, provisions for calls under standardized guarantees include unearned fees (premiums) and calls (claims) not yet settled.

4.294. Standardized guarantees are guarantees that are issued in large numbers, usually for fairly small amounts, along identical lines. There are three parties involved in these arrangements: the borrower (debtor), the lender (creditor) and the guarantor. Either the borrower or the lender may contract with the guarantor to repay the lender if the borrower defaults. Examples are export credit guarantees and student loan guarantees.

4.295. Although it is not possible to establish the likelihood of any particular borrower defaulting, it is usual to estimate how many out of a batch of similar borrowers will default. Much like a non-life insurer, a guarantor working on commercial lines will expect all the fees paid, plus the property income earned on the fees and any reserves, to cover the expected defaults and associated costs and leave a profit. Accordingly, a similar treatment to that of non-life insurance is adopted for standardized guarantees.

4.296. Standardized guarantees cover guarantees on various financial instruments like deposits, debt securities, loans and trade credit. They are usually provided by financial corporations, including but not confined to insurance corporations, and by general government units.

4.297. When an institutional unit offers standardized guarantees, it charges fees and incurs liabilities to meet the call on the guarantee. The value of the liabilities in the accounts of the guarantor is equal to the present value of the expected calls under existing guarantees, net of any recoveries the guarantor expects to receive from the defaulting borrowers. The liability is called provisions for calls under standardized guarantees.

4.298. The counterpart sector of such provisions is that of the underlying creditor.

4.299. A guarantee may cover a multi-year period. A fee may be payable annually or upfront. In principle the fee should represent charges earned in each year the guarantee holds, with the liability decreasing, as the period gets shorter (assuming that the borrower repays in instalments). Thus recording should follow that of annuities with the fee paid reducing as the liability decreases.

4.300. The nature of a standardized guarantee scheme is that there are many guarantees of the same type, though not all for exactly the same time period nor all starting and finishing on the same dates.

4.301. Net fees are calculated as fees receivable less administrative and other costs, etc. These net fees may be payable by any sector of the economy and are receivable by the sector in which the guarantor is classified. Calls under standardized guarantee schemes are payable by the guarantor and receivable by the lender of the financial instrument under guarantee, regardless of whether the fee was paid by the lender or the borrower. Financial transactions refer to the difference between the payment of fees for new guarantees and calls made under existing guarantees.

Worked example 4.3. Accounting treatment of standardized guarantees

4.302. Provisions for calls under standardized guarantees consist of pre-payments of net fees and provisions to meet outstanding calls under standardized guarantees. The transactions for provisions for calls under standardized guarantees recorded in the sector accounts are similar to the reserves for non-life insurance; they include unearned fees and calls not yet settled.

4.303. It is assumed that a (standardized) loan (F4) of 100 is provided for five years with an interest rate of 12 per cent. The probability of the loan defaulting (on principal and interest) in each year is 5 per cent. It means that there will be one default for every 20 fees paid. It is further assumed that a guarantee is given for the whole amount of the loans.

4.304. Table 4.13 shows, in its second column, the net present value of a loan assuming an annual interest rate of 12 per cent. The net present value corresponding to the guarantee is shown in column five of the table assuming that the probability of a loan default is 5 per cent and that 20 loans are considered. The total fee charged each year is shown in column nine of the table. It covers the value of the liability at the beginning of each year and an annual financial service of 20. At the end of the fifth year, an accumulated amount of 459 has been charged covering the accumulated values of the liability of 360 and financial services of 100. The interest intervenes as part of the output, exactly as a fee supplement in the case of non-life insurance.

4.305. The accounting entries (from the granting of the loans and the provision of the guarantee to the call of the guarantee) are described below.

Table 4.13
A standardized guarantee with an annually paid fee

	Net present value (NPV) of a loan	NPV×20	Probability of default (percentage per annum)	Value of guarantee	Interest	Value of guarantee including interest	Financial service	Fee charged
1	*2*	*3*	*4*	*5*	*6*	*7*	*8*	*9*
1 Jan 01	57	1135	5	57				
Year 1		136		7	7	64	20	77
1 Jan 02	64	1271	5	64				
Year 2		153		8	8	71	20	84
1 Jan 03	71	1424	5	71				
Year 3		171		9	9	80	20	91
1 Jan 04	80	1594	5	80				
Year 4		191		10	10	89	20	99
1 Jan 05	89	1786	5	89				
Year 5		214		11	11	100	20	109
31 Dec 05	100	2000	5	100				

Table 4.14
Granting of a standardized loan

Debtors (Non-financial corporations)		Creditor (Bank)		Guarantor (Guarantee bank)	
Financial account					
Net acquisition of financial assets	Net incurrence of liabilities	Net acquisition of financial assets	Net incurrence of liabilities	Net acquisition of financial assets	Net incurrence of liabilities
F2 (+2000)	F4 (+2000)	F2 (-2000)			
		F4 (+2000)			

4.306. A creditor provides (standardized) loans to debtors for a period of five years (20×100=2000). This is recorded as financial transactions in the accounts of both the creditor and the debtors (F2 as transactions in currency and deposits).

Granting of a standardized loan

4.307. The guarantor sells a guarantee for 77 covering risks and financial services over the first year. The value of the liability is 57, the interest payable/receivable is 7 and the financial service is 20.

4.308. When a guarantee is given, a transaction in F65, a net incurrence of a liability (of the unit giving this guarantee) is recorded equal to the net present value of the expected loss. An equivalent asset is added to the balance sheet of the sector receiving the guarantee, i.e. the sector of the entity that granted the initial loan. Given that the lender is the beneficiary of the guarantee, it is deemed that the guarantee should be its asset. It is recognized that this implies an overstatement of the lender's assets and net worth. This is the case if the loan is recorded at nominal value. Some information about provisions to be applied in the books of the loan provider should be available as a memorandum item or in a set of supplementary accounts to allow analysts to assess this "overstatement" on the assets side.

4.309. The net present value of the expected loss on the guarantee is 57 at the beginning of the year and 64 at the end of the year. No claims are made in the first year; therefore actual claims minus expected claims is -64 for the loans given by the creditor to the debtors.

Granting of a standardized guarantee

(a) Cash F2 (77) with counter-entry in F65 (77);
(b) Interest (unwinding of the discount): F65 (7) and D44 (7);
(c) P1/P2 (20) with counter-entry in F65 (-20);
(d) F65 (-64) and D71 (64).

Table 4.15
Granting of a standardized guarantee – year 1

Debtors (Non-financial corporations)		Creditor (Deposit-taking corporation)		Guarantor (Guarantee bank)	
Uses	Resources	Uses	Resources	Uses	Resources
Production account					
		(c) P2 (+20)			(c) P1 (+20)
Secondary distribution of income account					
			(b) D44 (+7)	(b) D44 (+7)	
		(d) D71 (+64)			(d) D71 (+64)
Net lending (+) / net borrowing (-)					
		B9 (-77)		B9 (+77)	
Net acquisition of financial assets	Net incurrence of liabilities	Net acquisition of financial assets	Net incurrence of liabilities	Net acquisition of financial assets	Net incurrence of liabilities
Financial account					
		(a) F2 (-77)		(a) F2 (+77)	
		(a) F65(+77)			(a) F65(+77)
		(b) F65(+7)			(b) F65(+7)
		(c) F65(-20)			(c) F65(-20)
		(d) F65 (-64)			(d) F65 (-64)

Table 4.16
Granting of a standardized guarantee – year 2

Debtors (Non-financial corporations)		**Creditor (Deposit-taking corporation)**		**Guarantor (Guarantee bank)**	
Uses	**Resources**	**Uses**	**Resources**	**Uses**	**Resources**
		Production account			
		(c) P2 (+20)			(c) P1 (+20)
		Secondary distribution of income account			
			(b) D44 (+8)	(b) D44 (+8)	
			(d) D72 (+100)	(d) D72 (+100)	
		(e) D71 (+71)			(e) D71 (+71)
		Net lending (+) / net borrowing (–)			
		B9 (+17)		B9 (-17)	
Net acquisition of financial assets	Net incurrence of liabilities	Net acquisition of financial assets	Net incurrence of liabilities	Net acquisition of financial assets	Net incurrence of liabilities
		Financial account			
		(a) F2 (-84)		(a) F2 (+84)	
		(a) F65 (+84)			(a) F65 (+84)
		(b) F65 (+8)			(b) F65 (+8)
		(c) F65 (-20)			(c) F65 (-20)
		(d) F2 (+100)		(d) F2 (-100)	
		(e) F65 (-71)			(e) F65 (-71)

4.310. At the beginning of the second year, the guarantor sells a guarantee for a fee of 84 covering risks and financial services over this year. The value of the liability is 64, the interest payable/receivable is 8 and the financial service is 20. The net present value of the expected loss on the guarantee is 64 at the beginning of the year and 71 at the end of the year. A claim of 100 is paid, while the expectation for the claim is 71; therefore actual claims minus expected claims is 29 for the loans given by the creditor to the debtors. No assets are acquired when the claim is paid.

(a) Cash F2 (84) with counter-entry in F64 (84);

(b) Interest (unwinding of the discount): F65 (8) and D44 (8);

(c) P1/P2 (20) with counter-entry in F65 (-20);

(d) Actual claims: F2 and D72 (100);

(e) Expected claims: F65 (-71) and D71 (71).

Lifetime of a standardized guarantee and its expiration

4.311. It is assumed that the same transactions apply during the following three years. At the beginning of each of the following three years, the guarantor sells a guarantee for a fee of 91, 100 and 109 respectively, covering risks and financial services over each of the years. The value of the liability is 71, 80 and 89 respectively; the interest payable/receivable is 9, 10 and 11; and the financial service is 20 each year. The net present value of the expected loss on the guarantee is 71, 80 and 89 at the beginning of each year and 80, 89 and 100 at the end of each year. A claim of 100 is paid in each of the years, while the expectation for the claim is 80, 90 and 100. Therefore, actual claims minus expected claims is 20, 11 and zero for the loans given by the creditor to the debtors. No assets are acquired when the claims are paid.

Activation of a standardized guarantee

4.312. When the standardized guarantee is activated during its lifetime (in the example, during a year), the liability of the debtor is written off (or written down) by the creditor. This would not be classified as a financial transaction because it does not involve an interaction between institutional units by mutual agreement. The writing-off or writing-down of bad debts by creditors is recorded in the other changes in the volume of assets account (also for debtors). The subsequent removal by the creditor of that financial asset from its balance sheet should be accounted for, along with the removal of the counterpart liability of the debtor.

4.313. In a further step, the (remaining value of the) guarantee will have to be transferred to the guarantor in exchange for a capital (current) transfer. Finally, the creditor has to be compensated by the guarantor for the loan loss.

Standardized guarantees and one-off guarantees

4.314. Standardized guarantees should be distinguished from one-off guarantees according to two criteria: (a) standardized guarantees are characterized by often repeated transactions with similar features and pooling of risks; and (b) guarantors are able to estimate the average loss based on available statistics (see also box 4.1).

4.315. By contrast, one-off guarantees are unique (sui generis), and guarantors are not able to make a reliable estimate of the risk of calls. The granting of a one-off guarantee is a contingency and not recorded.

One-off guarantees granted by general government in certain well-defined financially distressed situations

4.316. In exceptional cases, one-off guarantees granted by general government to corporations in certain well-defined financially distressed situations (for example, where the corporation has negative own funds) and with a very high likelihood to be called are treated as if these guarantees were called at inception.

4.317. Government guarantees during a bailout are treated as one-off guarantees to entities in financial distress. An example is where the entity is not able to meet its obligations or has substantial difficulties in doing so because its cash generating abilities are limited or the tradability of its assets is severely limited due to exceptional events. This will normally lead to recording a capital transfer at inception, as if the guarantee were called, for the entirety of the granted guarantee or, if a reliable estimation is available, for the amount of the expected call, which is the expected loss of government.

4.318. The activation of a one-off guarantee is treated in the same way as a debt assumption. The original debt is liquidated and a new debt is created between the guarantor and the creditor. The debt assumption implies the recording of a capital transfer in favour of the defaulting debtor. The capital transfer is offset by a financial transaction and the financial liability transferred from the corporation to government.

4.319. The activation of a guarantee may or may not require immediate repayment of the debt. The accrual principle for time of recording suggests that the total amount of debt assumed should be recorded at the time the guarantee is activated and the debt assumed. The guarantor is the new debtor, and principal repayments by the guarantor and interest accruals on the assumed debt should be recorded when these flows occur. Thus, when calls on guarantees solely involve the settlement of the debt service due on the debt during the accounting period, as in the case of cash calls, a capital transfer is recorded for the amounts settled. However when a pattern of partial calls are observed, such as three times in succession, and is expected to continue, a debt assumption is recorded.

4.320. When the original debtor refunds the guarantor while expenditure has been recorded on past guarantee calls, the guarantor records revenue. However this revenue should be tested for super-dividends when the guarantor controls the debtor. Super-dividends are dividends that are large relative to the recent level of dividends and earnings.

4.321. The super-dividend test is used to determine whether the dividends are disproportionately large or not. For that purpose the concept of distributable income is used: the distributable income of a corporation is equal to the entrepreneurial income, plus all current transfers receivable, less all current transfers payable and less the adjustment for the change in pension entitlements relating to the pension scheme of that corporation. From this it is possible to look at the ratio of dividends to distributable income over the recent past and assess the plausibility that the current level of dividends declared is in line with past practice, accepting some degree of smoothing from year to year. If the level of dividends declared is greatly in excess of this, the excess should be treated as a financial transaction, specifically the withdrawal of owners' equity from the corporation.

7. Financial derivatives and employee stock options

4.322. Financial derivatives and employee stock options are divided into two subcategories: (a) financial derivatives other than employee stock options (AF71); and (b) employee stock options (AF72).

4.323. Financial derivatives (AF71) are financial instruments that are linked to a specific financial instrument or indicator or commodity, through which specific financial risks can be traded in financial markets in their own right. The value of a financial derivative derives from the price of the underlying item: the reference price. The reference price may relate to a commodity, a financial asset, an interest rate, an exchange rate, another derivative or a spread between two prices. The derivatives contract may also refer to an index, a basket of prices or other items, such as emissions trading and weather conditions.

4.324. Financial derivatives are used for a number of purposes, including risk management, hedging, arbitrage between markets, speculation and compensation of employees. They enable parties to trade specific financial risks, such as interest rate risk, currency, equity and commodity price risk and credit risk to other entities which are willing to take these risks – usually without trading in the primary asset. Accordingly, financial derivatives are referred to as secondary assets.

4.325. Financial derivatives other than employee stock options (AF71) cover options, forwards, swaps, forward rate agreements and credit derivatives.

4.326. In some cases, financial derivatives are classified by instrument (options, forwards and credit derivatives as a specific type of option or forward) or by market risk (currency swaps, interest rate swaps, etc.).

(a) Options

4.327. Options, tradable on organized markets and OTC, are contracts which give the holder of the option the right, but not the obligation, to purchase from (a call option) or to sell to (a put option) the issuer of the option (the option writer) a financial or non-financial asset (the underlying instrument) at a predetermined price (the strike price) within a given timespan (American option) or on a given date (European option). Many variants have been developed and are used for hedging strategies (e.g. call spreads) and speculation strategies (e.g. butterfly spreads). From these simpler options more exotic ones have been derived with complex payment structures.

Box 4.8
Recording of stocks and flows in financial derivatives

A financial derivative enables specific risks, such as changes in interest rates, foreign exchange rates, prices or credit standing, to be traded in financial markets in their own right. The 2008 SNA requires positions, transactions and other flows in financial derivatives to be recorded if they have a market value or can be offset in the market, i.e. if a party to the contract can in effect reverse it by taking out another contract with the opposite effect.

The current market price of a derivative values the claim of one party on the other. It is this value that is recorded in the balance sheet.

Whether it is recorded as an asset or as a liability depends on the market value, which may fluctuate between a positive value (an asset) and a negative value (a liability) over the life of the contract (the same derivative instrument could thus be recorded as an asset or a liability over the course of its lifetime). The market price may also be zero, as it is at the start of a swap contract.

Financial derivatives are usually recorded in balance sheets on a gross basis at market value unless business accounting rules require off-balance-sheet recording. In business accounting, they may be classified under *remaining assets* if they have a positive value for the reporting unit or *remaining liabilities* if they have a negative value, with no further details being provided.

Changes in the market value of financial derivatives contracts may also be recorded separately or derived from balance sheet positions. These changes in the market value are influenced by three main factors:

- Revaluations due to changes in the underlying instrument. When derivatives contracts are traded, their market value will typically be zero, except for options. Changes in the expectations of underlying variables of contracts at the time of valuation, away from expectations of those variables at the time of trading will generally cause the market value of a derivative to tend away from zero.
- Transactions in financial derivatives. Because the market value of a derivative is equal to the net present value of future payment streams, whenever a payment is made with respect to a contract the market valuation will be affected.
- Changes in the number of contracts held. The higher the number of contracts traded, the higher the gross market positions.

The relative importance of these factors varies depending upon market conditions. Foreign currency positions are converted to domestic currency using end-period exchange rates.

For statistical purposes, a financial derivative is treated as a financial instrument separate from the instrument on which the contract is based. Thus derivative positions recorded in balance sheets are not linked to the underlying financial instrument, nor do they reveal the nominal amount for which the contract was made.

4.328. The purchaser of the option pays a premium (the option price) for the commitment of the option writer to sell or to purchase the specified amount of the underlying instrument at the agreed price, or to pay the holder of the option the difference between the price in the contract and the current price. By convention, that commitment is treated as a financial asset of the option holder and a liability of the option writer. Sellers of options are obliged to perform when the option purchasers exercise their rights under the option contracts.

4.329. The premium can be conceptually considered to include a service charge, which is to be recorded separately. However, in the absence of detailed data, too many assumptions should not be made to identify the service element.

4.330. *Warrants* are options and should be classified as financial derivatives. They are tradable financial instruments giving the holder the right to buy, under specified terms for a specified period of time, from the issuer of the warrant (usually a corporation) a certain number of shares or debt securities (2008 SNA, para. 11.119).

4.331. Warrants include:

(a) Call or put warrants that are issued based on an underlying financial instrument (a share or an ETF), or on an index;

(b) Basket warrants as call or put warrants that are issued on a basket of two or more underlying shares;

(c) Bull equity-linked instruments that give investors the right to buy the underlying shares at a percentage discount to the prevailing underlying share price at the time of issuance. If the underlying share price exceeds the exercise price, then investors are entitled to a cash settlement at expiry of the warrant, being the exercise price multiplied by the number of warrants purchased. If the underlying share price falls below the exercise price, then the investors may receive the number of underlying shares or an equivalent cash amount;

(d) Callable bull or bear certificates which track the performance of an underlying stock without requiring investors to pay the full price necessary to own the actual stock. They are issued either as bull or bear certificates with a fixed expiry date, allowing investors to take bullish or bearish positions on the underlying stock, with the possibility of early termination before the expiry date should the underlying stock move in a direction contrary to the investor's expectations.

4.332. Warrants are frequently attached to preferred shares (or debt securities) allowing the issuer to pay lower dividends or interest rates. They can be used to enhance the yield of a bond and make them more attractive to potential buyers, as well as in private equity transactions. Warrants are often detachable and can be traded independently of the share or the debt security. In the case of warrants issued with preferred shares, shareholders may need to detach and sell the warrant before they can receive dividends.

Box 4.9
Treatment of options

(a) Characteristics of options

Options, either listed options or OTC options, are rights but not obligations to buy, within a specified period of time (American option) or at a certain point in time (European option), financial or non-financial assets like commodities (the underlying instrument) at a given price (the strike or exercise price) from the issuer of the option (call option), or to sell them to the issuer of the option (put option). For that right, the option buyer pays a premium (the option price).

Interest rate options are designed to hedge the interest rate risk. They refer to underlying instruments like debt securities in the form of fixed-income securities or promissory notes. They represent the right to buy or to sell a particular nominal amount of debt securities at a specific price. To hedge the exchange rate risk, currency options are used; they are foreign currency amounts to be valued at a specific exchange rate. Underlyings of stock options to hedge the equity risk are individual stocks or stock indices.

Four factors generally affect the price of an option: the difference between the contract price and the value of the underlying instrument; the volatility of the underlying instrument; the remaining lifetime of the contract; and the market interest rates. In the absence of an observable market price, the value can be calculated approximately using the Black-Scholes formula, which incorporates these four factors.

On completion of the contract, the option has a market value equal to the premium paid. However, its market value changes if the reference price changes and the expiry date approaches. During the lifetime of an option, the buyer of an option has always a commitment from the financial derivative, the delivery of the underlying instrument or the possibility of a payment; the seller has a corresponding claim. An option may lapse if it is not advantageous for the buyer of the option to exercise the option.

(b) Identification of the interest rate risk and of other price risks for options

The buyer of an option can actively manage its price risk. This can be done using the so-called profit/loss profile of the option period. Consider the price of a debt security. Suppose an investor buys a certain amount of this financial instrument, because he assumes that its price will increase and thus the interest rate will fall. He has purchased the debt security at a price of 100 so his securities position will move, with an increasing asset price (or a decreasing interest rate), into the profit area (figure 4.9.1(a)). If the asset price decreases (the interest rate increases), his position moves into the loss area. This investment is an unhedged position with an equal probability of profits or losses.

Avoiding the risk of interest rate fluctuations, the investor buys, in anticipation of rising asset prices, a call option (long call), which gives him the right to buy the debt security at a specified strike price (figure 4.9.1(b)). Depending on the development of the debt security's price (after deduction of the premium (=1)), the purchase will move "in the money" (profit area), while his loss is limited to the premium paid in the case of a falling asset price. The attraction of this option – compared with the unsecured position – is the limited risk if the asset price decreases and the unlimited profit opportunities if the asset price increases. The cost of the premium (=1) needs to be taken into consideration.

By contrast, the seller of the call option (short call) takes the exact opposite position of the investor (figure 4.9.1(c)). In the case of a decreasing asset price the option premium is his profit, while in the case of an increasing asset price his potential loss is unlimited.

In cases of decreasing asset prices, an investor will buy a put option (long put). The profit/loss profile as indicated in figure 4.9.1(d) shows that the holder of the option loses its premium if asset prices are rising. His profit will be unlimited if asset prices move in the expected direction. However, the seller of the option (short put) will lose if asset prices decrease, while his profit is limited to the premium paid by the holder of the option (the profit/loss profile as shown in figure 4.9.1(e)).

Figure 4.9.1: Profit and loss profiles for options

(a) Profit/loss profile of an unhedged securities position

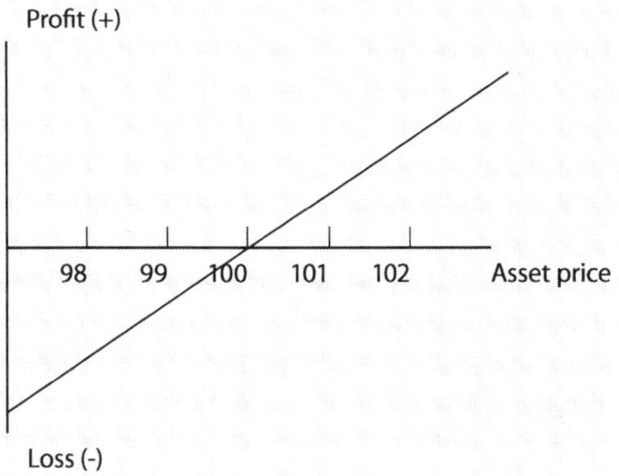

(b) Profit/loss profile of a long call securities position (purchase of call option)

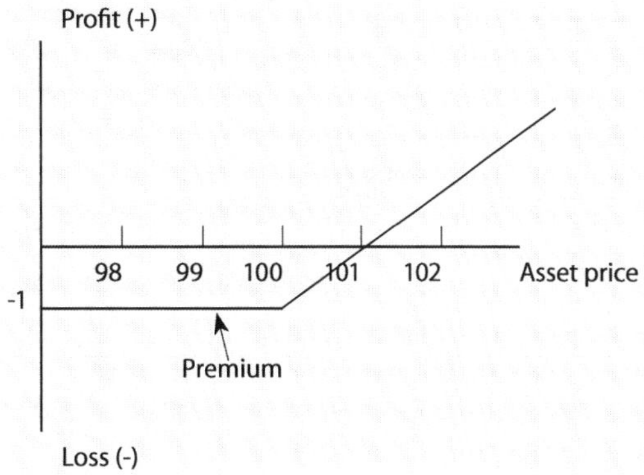

(c) Profit/loss profile of a short call (sale of call option)

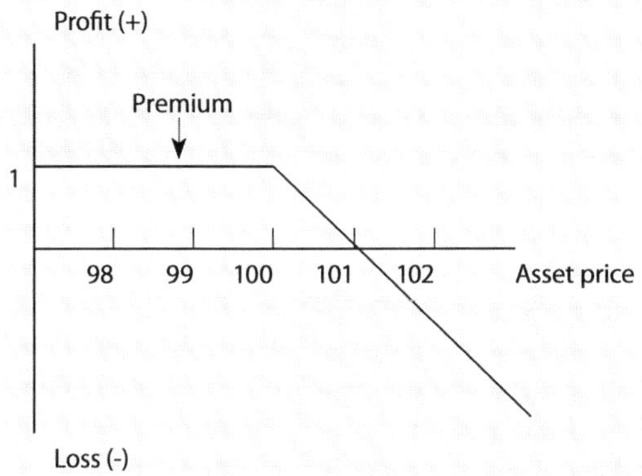

(d) Profit/loss profile of a long put (purchase of put option)

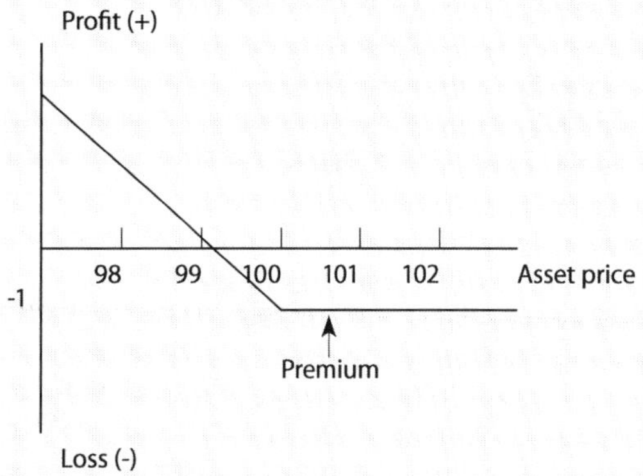

(e) Profit/loss profile of a short put (sale of a put option)

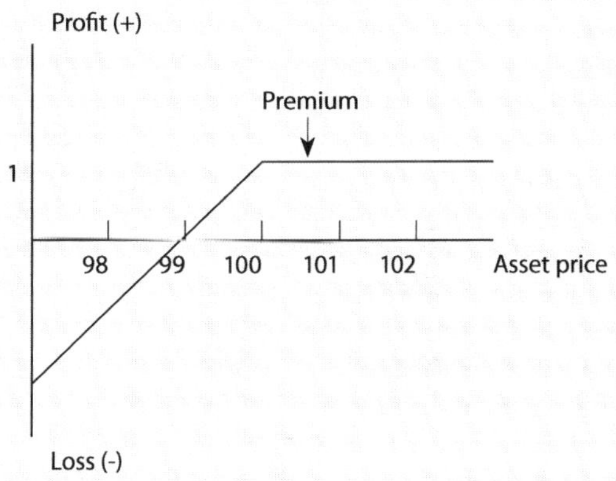

Holding gains or losses of options are limited or unlimited depending on the type of the option and the asset price (interest rate) developments. The buyer of a call is benefiting from rising asset prices, while the seller has to bear the losses. The risk of the buyer and the profit of the seller of a call, however, are limited to the premium in the case of decreasing asset prices. By contrast, the buyer of a long put makes a profit when asset prices fall, and the seller accordingly incurs losses. When assets rise, the risk of the buyer of a put and the profit of the seller are limited to the level of the premium.

Table 4.9.1: Properties of call options and put options

	Long call	Short call	Long put	Short put
Rights	Right to acquire underlying at a certain price	Receipt of the premium	Right to sell underlying at a certain price	Receipt of the premium
Obligations	Premium payment	For option being exercised delivery of the underlying at the strike price	Premium payment	For option being exercised delivery of the underlying at the strike price
Profit, if	M>(B+P)	M<(B+P)	M<(B+P)	M>(B+P)
Profit	G=M−(B+P)		G=−(M−(B+P))	
Maximum profit	Unlimited	G=P	Unlimited	G=P
Loss, if	M<(B+P)	M>(B+P)	M>(B+P)	M<(B+P)
Loss		V=M−(B+P)		V=−(M−(B+P))
Maximum loss	V=P	Unlimited	V=P	Unlimited

M = market price; B = price of the underlying instrument; P = premium; G = profit; V = loss.

The profit/loss profile can also be used to explain the exchange rate risk associated with currency options. It is assumed that a corporation has bought a specific amount of currency 2 (CU2) at a specific exchange rate (currency 1 (CU1)/CU2). In the case of an appreciation of CU2, its position moves into the profit area and vice versa. The foreign exchange transaction can be seen as an unhedged position with an equal probability of profits or losses.

Rather than be exposed to the exchange rate risk, the corporation acquires, in the expectation of a rising CU2 exchange rate, a purchase option (CU2 call). This option gives the corporation, where the exchange rate increases, the same outcome as the unhedged position, while its exposure to loss is limited to the amount of the premium (see the profit/loss profiles in figures 4.9.1(b) and 4.9.1(c) above).

If the corporation expects a falling CU2 exchange rate, it may guard against it by buying a CU2 put. The profit/loss profile in figure 4.9.1(d) shows that the corporation as holder of this option loses its premium where the CU2 exchange rate rises, but gains if the exchange rate moves in the expected direction. In comparison, the risk of a loss is considerable for the seller of the option in the event the CU2 decreases if he does not hedge its open position, as shown in figure 4.9.1(e).

As for interest rate and currency options, the advantage of stock index and stock price options is that the buyer of an option can actively manage its share price risk, by buying a call in anticipation of rising stock prices or a put with the expectation of falling share prices. For example, if a decline in the stock market is expected, it is appropriate to buy a put option to protect a stock portfolio.

(c) Treatment of the price risk for options in the *System of National Accounts 2008*

The option has a market value equal to the option price paid at the time of the contract. It determines the maximum loss of the option buyer and the maximum profit of the option seller in the event that the option is not exercised. For the evaluation of exchange-traded options, the published rates as determined on every trading day are normally used. For OTC options, available market prices may be used. Otherwise, the value of the option may be calculated by using option pricing models (such as the Black-Scholes formula mentioned above) or may be determined by a market maker.

The amount payable by the option buyer as a premium usually depends on the acquisition cost and is recorded as a liability. Similarly, the option writer has a corresponding receivable during the life of the option. An option may be forfeited with no penalty/with no financial consequences when it is disadvantageous to the buyer to exercise the option.

The accounting entries described in table 4.9.2 are based on a call option, upon the date of acquisition of the option, t (0), and time t (1), on which the option is exercised or expires. At the time of its acquisition, the option right is recorded as a financial asset (financial derivatives excluding employee stock options AF71) — as the option premium $p(0)\times q$ — to be paid by the option buyer and as a liability of the option seller (table 4.9.2). (The resulting transaction costs and other fees are not treated separately here, but should be recorded in the appropriate production and income accounts.)

Table 4.9.2: Accounting treatment of a call option

Option buyer		Option seller	
Financial account			
Changes in financial assets	*Changes in liabilities*	*Changes in financial assets*	*Changes in liabilities*
F21= $-p(0)\times q$		F21= $+p(0)\times q$	
F71= $+p(0)\times q$			F71= $+p(0)\times q$
Balance sheet			
Financial assets	*Liabilities*	*Financial assets*	*Liabilities*
AF21=A21 $-(p(0)\times q)$)		AF21=A21 $+(p(0)\times q)$)	
AF71=A71 $+(p(0)\times q)$)			AF71=L71+ $(p(0)\times q)$)

F21 and AF21=currency; F71 and AF71=financial derivatives, excluding employee stock options.

If the price of the underlying asset increases above the strike price, the option (as an American option) is exercised, because the underlying asset may be acquired at a relatively low price and sold on the spot market at a relatively high price. The owner of the call option realizes a profit equal to the difference between the prevailing market price of the underlying asset and the strike price. The premium has to be taken into account in this case. If the option buyer allows the option to expire, the option premium is derecognized from the revaluation account. There is no transaction. However, the option seller makes a holding gain and the option holder a holding loss (table 4.9.3).

Table 4.9.3: Accounting treatment of a call option

Option buyer		Option seller	
Revaluation account			
Changes in financial assets	*Changes in liabilities*	*Changes in financial assets*	*Changes in liabilities*
K.11= $-p(0)\times q$	B.10.3= $-p(0)\times q$	B.10.3= $-p(0)\times q$	K.11= $-p(0)\times q$
Balance sheet			
Financial assets	*Liabilities*	*Financial assets*	*Liabilities*
AF21=A21 $-(p(0)\times q)$	AF21=A21 $+(p(0)\times q)$		
		B10.3=BG $-(p(0)\times q)$	B10.3=BG $-(p(0)\times q)$

AF21=cash; K11=revaluation; B10.3 or BG=holding gain or holding loss.

For the liquidation (or the sale) of the option the difference between the liquidation proceeds (selling price) and the value is recorded as a holding gain of the option.

Gains and losses, which are expressed in the option price changes, are credited or charged to the buyer and seller of the option daily on a "margin" account. Although there are no payments made with the contract, there is an obligation to pay the option price. Changes in the market value of the option are recognized in the revaluation account and in the balance sheet.

The procedure is described with reference to the purchase of a call option. In addition to the time of acquisition of the option, $t(0)$, and time $t(2)$, on which the option is exercised or expires, the update is shown at $t(1)$ during the lifetime of the option.

At the acquisition of the option in $t(0)$, the option right is recorded – as an amount of the option premium to be paid $p(0)\times q$ – as an asset of the option buyer and as a liability of the option seller. This is offset by the acquisition of an advance payment (payable/receivable) of the option buyer and of the option seller (table 4.9.4).

Table 4.9.4: Accounting treatment of a call option

Option buyer		Option seller	
Financial account			
Changes in financial assets	*Changes in liabilities*	*Changes in financial assets*	*Changes in liabilities*
F71= $+p(0)\times q$			F71= $+p(0)\times q$
		F89= $+p(0)\times q$	F89= $+p(0)\times q$
Balance sheet			
Financial assets	*Liabilities*	*Financial assets*	*Liabilities*
AF71=A71 $+(p(0)\times q)$			AF71=A71 $+(p(0)\times q)$
		AF89=L71 $+(p(0)\times q)$	AF89=A71 $+(p(0)\times q)$

AF21=cash; F71 and AF71=financial derivatives excluding employee stock options; F89 and AF89=other accounts receivable/payable.

The (unrealized) gains or losses during the period $t(0)$ to $t(1)$ are reflected in the revaluation account and in $t(1)$ in the balance sheet (table 4.9.5). Therefore, holding gains arise for the buyer of a call option when prices rise and for the buyer of a put option when prices fall. The opposite is true for the option seller. In the balance sheet, the option premium is recorded, in addition to the holding gain.

Table 4.9.5: Accounting treatment of a call option

Option buyer		Option seller	
Revaluation account			
Changes in financial assets	*Changes in liabilities*	*Changes in financial assets*	*Changes in liabilities*
$K11=(p(1)-p(0))\times q$	$B10.3=(1)-p(0))\times q$	$B10.3=(p(1)-p(0))\times q$	$K11=(p(1)-p(0))\times q$
Balance sheet			
Financial assets	*Liabilities*	*Financial assets*	*Liabilities*
$AF71=A71+(p(0)\times q)+(p(1)-p(0))\times q$	$B10.3=BG+(p(1)-p(0))\times q$	$B10.3=BG+(p(1)-p(0))\times q$	$AF71=A71-(p(0)\times q)+(p(1)-p(0))\times q$
	$AF89=L89+(p(0)\times q)$	$AF89=A89+(p(0)\times q)$	

AF21=cash; F71 and AF71=financial derivatives excluding employee stock options; F89 and AF89=other accounts receivable/payable; K11=revaluations; B10.3 and BG=holding gains or losses.

If the price is above the strike price, the option will be exercised. The owner of the call option pays the premium and realizes a profit of $(p(2)-p(0))\times q$ (table 4.9.6).

Table 4.9.6: Accounting treatment of a call option

Option buyer		Option seller	
Revaluation account			
Changes in financial assets	*Changes in liabilities*	*Changes in financial assets*	*Changes in liabilities*
$K11=(p(1)-p(0))\times q$	$B10.3=(1)-p(0))\times q$	$B10.3=(p(1)-p(0))\times q$	$K11=(p(1)-p(0))\times q$
Financial account			
ΔA	ΔL	ΔA	ΔL
$F21=-p(0)\times q$	$F21=+p(0)\times q$		
	$F89=-p(0)\times q$	$F89=-p(0)\times q$	
Balance sheet			
Financial assets	*Liabilities*	*Financial assets*	*Liabilities*
$AF21=A21-(p(0)\times q)$		$AF21=A21+(p(0)\times q)$	
$AF71=A71+(p(0)\times q)+((p(2)-p(0))\times q)$	$B10.3=BG+(p(2)-p(0))\times q$	$B10.3=BG+(p(2)-p(0))\times q$	$AF71=P71+(p(0)\times q)+((p(2)-p(0))\times q)$

If the option buyer allows the option to expire, the option premium is amortized and derecognized from the revaluation account. For the liquidation (or the sale) of the option, the difference between the liquidation proceeds (selling price) and the market value of the option is recognized as a holding gain.

(d) Price risk of interest rate cap agreements (caps, floors and collars)

Properties of caps, floors and collars

Caps (to hedge against rising interest rates) are contractual agreements between a buyer and a seller where the cap purchaser may require the cap seller to pay, within a specified time period, the difference between an agreed interest rate ceiling (strike rate) and a periodically determined reference interest rate if the reference interest rate is above the strike. In return, the buyer has to pay the agreed cap premium (either pro rata or per year discounted at the beginning of the term of the cap). Since there is an independent option right within the term of the cap for each date of determining the reference interest rate, the cap is analogous to a series of individual options with an increasing lead time. The date on which the rate is determined is called the "roll-over date" and must be calculated separately from the cap premium. The total price of the cap, the premium, is then obtained as the sum of the premiums of all individual options.

The counterpart to the cap is the floor (to hedge against falling interest rates). The interest rate floor is a contractual agreement between the buyer and the seller in which the floor seller agrees to pay, within a specified time period, the difference between an agreed interest rate (strike rate) and a specified reference rate. In return, the buyer agrees to pay the premium.

The terms "cap" and "floor" are used according to whether the instrument underlying the option is a loan (hedged against rising interest rates) or a deposit (hedged against falling interest rates) – or, from the perspective of the buyer, a call or a put.

The premiums for these performance-based options are calculated on the basis of option pricing models.

It is assumed that interest rate cap agreements correspond to options with different lead times. The cap premium payable is therefore calculated by summing the premiums for the individual options. If the buyer has paid the premium to the seller, the buyer of the option has no further obligations. Rather, he simply compares, at any "roll-over date", the strike of his cap or floor at the current rate (e.g. LIBOR) and exercises the option if it is beneficial for him. Conversely, the seller of the cap or the floor receives the premium and must perform the underlying obligation, if required by the purchaser. Therefore compensation payments will take place at any agreed time for caps and floors.

Risks related to caps, floors and collars

Like options, caps and floors have an asymmetric risk profile. The interest rate risk (holding gains or losses) is thus unlimited or limited to caps and floors according to the market trend. The buyer of a cap benefits from falling interest rates (rising securities prices), while the seller has to bear the losses. When interest rates rise, the loss of the buyer is limited to the amount of the premium – as is the seller's profit.

By contrast, the buyer of a floor gains when interest rates increase (a decrease in securities prices), and the seller will lose accordingly. The profits of the buyer thus correspond to the losses of the seller, and vice versa. The loss of the buyer of the put and the profit of the seller are limited to the amount of the premium as interest rates fall (rise in securities prices).

A combination of a cap (interest rate upper limit) and a floor (interest rate floor) is called a "collar".

Treatment of the risk of price changes of caps, floors and collars in the 2008 SNA

Interest rate cap agreements are to be treated as options in the system of accounts. Accordingly, purchased or sold caps and floors, as well as other options, have to be recorded as financial assets or liabilities (financial derivatives (AF71)) at the time of the acquisition as premiums to be paid. If the premium is not paid immediately but in installments, a liability must be recorded. Conversely, the seller must record a financial asset.

The payment takes place at the end of the period in the case of caps, floors and collars. The compensation is to be recognized as a receivable from the seller of the interest rate cap agreement in addition to the premium.

The individual sub-options expire over time and so the price change risk decreases over its lifetime. For this reason, the resolution of the premium is to be made on a pro rata basis. At each fixing date (roll-over date) a portion of the interest rate cap agreement expires and is exercised by a payment in compensation. The amount attributable to share options of the total premium has to be excluded at the fixing date. Alternatively, the premium paid or received may also be recorded as a receivable or a payable.

(b) Forwards

4.333. Forwards are financial contracts under which two parties agree to exchange a specified quantity of an underlying asset (financial or non-financial) at an agreed contract price (the strike price) on a specified date.

4.334. Futures are forward contracts traded on organized exchanges.[127] Futures and other forward contracts are typically, but not always, settled by the payment of cash or the provision of some other financial asset rather than the delivery of the underlying asset, and therefore are valued and traded separately from the underlying item. Common forward-type contracts include swaps and forward rate agreements (FRAs).

4.335. Forwards can be contrasted with options in that:

(a) At inception, there is usually no upfront payment for a forward contract and the market value is zero; in the case of an option, a premium is paid when the contract is entered into and at inception the contract is valued at the amount of the premium;

(b) As market prices, interest rates or exchange rates change during the life of a forward contract, the contract may take on a positive value for one party

[127] Forwards can also be offset.

(as an asset) and a corresponding negative value (as a liability) for the other; these positions may switch between the parties, depending on market developments in the underlying financial instrument, commodity, etc. in relation to the strike price in the contract. This characteristic makes it impractical, and possibly meaningless, to identify transactions in assets separately from transactions in liabilities. Unlike other financial instruments, transactions in forwards are therefore normally reported net across assets and liabilities. In the case of an option, the buyer is always the creditor and the writer always the debtor;

(c) At maturity, redemption is mandatory for a forward, while for an option the buyer determines whether or not to redeem. Some options are redeemed automatically when they are "in the money" at maturity.

Box 4.10

Treatment of futures

Futures

Futures are forward contracts that have a market value because they are tradable or can be offset. They include a commitment to deliver a certain quantity of an underlying instrument, which may be a commodity, a currency or a security, or a basket of them, at a specific date and price. The underlying instrument may also be an index.

Futures have the following characteristics. They specify the standard underlying instrument, the amount of the contract, the due date, and the rules on safety performance and final settlement. They are traded on stock exchanges; the supply and purchase obligations are therefore vis-à-vis the clearing system of the stock exchange. For each clearing contract a cash deposit (initial margin) is to be paid as security to cover any settlement risk, which is paid back after the closing or the settlement of the contract. In addition, the buyer or the seller of a future has committed himself to participate in the margin system with daily profit and loss compensation payments (variation margins).

Futures can be used to transfer interest rate, equity price and exchange rate risks. Depending on the nature of the observed risk, a distinction is made between interest rate futures, stock index futures and currency futures.

Economic risk of futures

The economic risk in futures trading is basically unlimited and symmetric. This can be illustrated on the basis of profit/loss profiles for futures. The two possible positions in futures trading are long and short positions. The long position is the result of the purchase of a future; the short position is the result of a sale. The profit/loss profiles of the two possible futures positions are shown in figure 4.10.1.

Figure 4.10.1: Profit/loss profile of futures

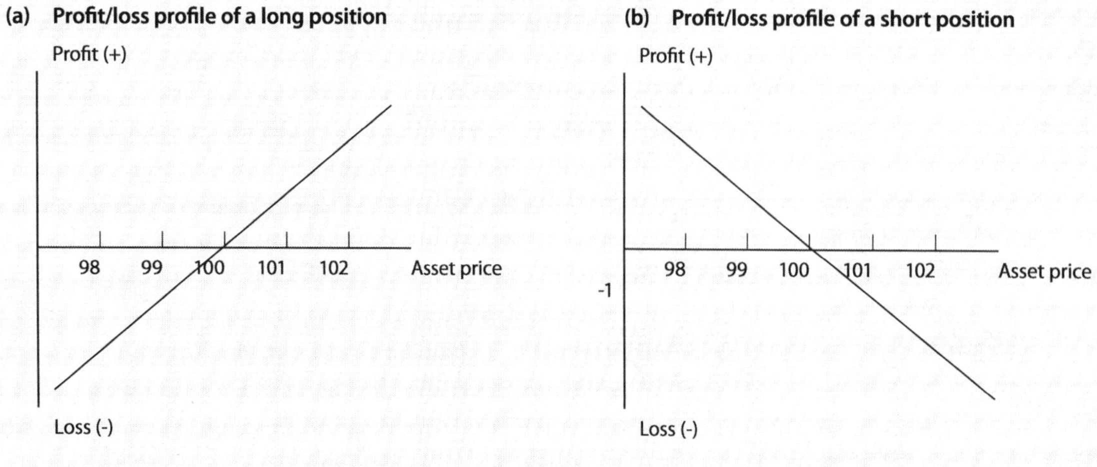

The risk of interest rate futures (holding gains or losses) can be explained as follows. The buyer of an interest rate future benefits from falling interest rates (rising securities prices), while the seller has to bear the losses. By contrast, the seller of an interest rate future gains when interest rates rise (fall in securities prices), and the buyer loses. The profits of the buyer thus correspond to the losses of the seller, and vice versa.

Holding gains in a (short) purchase arise and the interest rate future is subsequently sold if, during the lifetime of the current interest rate future, the interest rate decreases and the corresponding future price increases. According to the symmetry assumption, holding losses arise if, during the lifetime of the future, the interest rate increases. Holding gains in a (short) selling arise and the interest rate future is subsequently purchased if, during the lifetime of the current interest rate future, the interest rate increases and the corresponding future price decreases. Holding losses arise if, during the lifetime of the interest rate future, the interest rate decreases.

Holding gains and losses are calculated based on the difference between prices for futures. An example is a sale of 15 futures per CU1 1 million for three months at a future price of 92.7 per cent and a corresponding purchase three months later at a price of 91.8 per cent.

During the lifetime of the future, the price of the future decreases (owing to the increase of LIBOR) so that the subsequent (re)purchase leads to a lower price at a holding gain, which can be calculated according to the formula $G=(p(t)-p(0))\times q$). The future price at time t is derived as $p(t)=0.918\times3$ months/12 months, and at time 0, as $p(0) = 0.927\times3$ months/12 months. The quantity supplied or demanded is calculated as $q=15$ futures per CU1 1 million per futures contract.

The gain on the future is therefore:

$G=(0.2295-0.23175)\times(-\text{CU1 15 million})=\text{CU1 }33{,}750$

If the price of the future had increased during the lifetime of the future (owing to a decline of LIBOR), the repurchase at a higher price and at a later stage would have led to a holding loss. A future price of, for example, 94 per cent leads – under the same assumptions – to a loss of $G=(0.235-0.23175)\times(-\text{CU1 15 million})=-\text{CU1 }48{,}750$.

Treatment of the price risk of futures in the 2008 SNA

The market value of futures is equal to zero at the time of the contract. By contrast, price changes of the underlying instrument and the margin payments derived from them are to be recorded as transactions and in balance sheets.

Margins are broken down into refundable and non-refundable components (repayable and non-repayable margins). The refundable component is essentially the initial margin and the non-refundable component corresponds to the variation margins. The refundable component is recorded as an advance payment (F89) and the non-refundable component under financial derivatives (F71). Unless repayable margins are paid in cash, they are included in the balance sheet of the secured party (clearing house). However, if securities are pledged as collateral, no transactions are to be recorded as there is no change of ownership.

In the example (table 4.10.1), the purchase of a future in $t(0)$ is the initial margin (im) from the dealer, $im\times q$, to pay to the clearing house (F21). Since there is a refundable security payment related to the initial margin, it is recorded in the financial account as an advance payment (F89).

Table 4.10.1: Accounting treatment of a future

Dealer		Clearing house	
Financial account			
Changes in financial assets	*Changes in liabilities*	*Changes in financial assets*	*Changes in liabilities*
$F21=-im\times q$		$F21=+im\times q$	
$F89=+im\times q$			$F89=+im\times q$
Balance sheet			
Financial assets	*Liabilities*	*Financial assets*	*Liabilities*
$AF21=A21-(im\times q)$		$AF21=A21+(im\times q)$	
$AF89=A89+(im\times q)$			$AF89=L79+(im\times q)$

im=initial margin; F21 and AF21=currency; F89 and AF89=other accounts receivable/payable.

Suppose the price of the future $p(1)$ is, in $t(1)$, below the initial price $p(0)$, the difference has to be recorded as a holding loss. The clearing house has to pay a variation margin of this amount to the dealer (table 4.10.2).

Table 4.10.2: Accounting treatment of a future

Dealer		Clearing house	
Financial account			
Changes in financial assets	*Changes in liabilities*	*Changes in financial assets*	*Changes in liabilities*
$F21=-(p(1)-p(0))\times q$		$F21=+(p(1)-p(0))\times q$	
$F71=+(p(1)-p(0))\times q$			$F71=+(p(1)-p(0))\times q$
Revaluation account			
Changes in financial assets	*Changes in liabilities*	*Changes in financial assets*	*Changes in liabilities*
$K11=-(p(1)-p(0))\times q$	$B.10.3=-(p(1)-p(0))\times q$	$B.10.3=-(p(1)-p(0))\times q$	$K11=-(p(1)-p(0))\times q$
Balance sheet			
Financial assets	*Liabilities*	*Financial assets*	*Liabilities*
$AF21=A.21-(im\times q)-(p(1)-p(0))\times q$		$AF21=A.21+(im\times q)+(p(1)-p(0))\times q$	
$AF71=A71+(p(1)-p(0))\times q-(p(1)-p(0))\times q$	$B10.3=B-(p(1)-(p(0))\times q$	$B10.3=B-(p(1)-(p(0))\times q$	$AF71=L71+(p(1)-p(0))\times q-(p(1)-p(0))\times q$
$A89=A89+(im\times q)$			$AF89=A89+(im\times q)$

im=initial margin; F21 and AF21=currency; F71 and AF71=financial derivatives; AF89=other accounts receivable/payable; K11=revaluation; B103 and BG holding gain or loss.

If the future price at $t(2)$ is above the price in $t(1)$, the difference is accounted for as a holding gain, which is credited as a variation margin to the dealer of the clearing house (table 4.10.3).

Table 4.10.3: Accounting treatment of a future

Dealer		Clearing house	
Revaluation account			
Changes in financial assets	*Changes in liabilities*	*Changes in financial assets*	*Changes in liabilities*
$K11=(p(2)-p(1))\times q$	$B10.3=(p(2)-p(1))\times q$	$B10.3=(p(2)-p(1))\times q$	$K11=(p(2)-p(1))\times q$
Balance sheet			
Financial assets	*Liabilities*	*Financial assets*	*Liabilities*
$AF21=A21-(im\times q)-(p(1)-p(0))\times q$		$AF21=A21+(im\times q)+(p(1)-p(0))\times q$	
$AF71=A71+(p(1)-p(0))\times q-(p(1)-p(0))\times q+(p(2)-p(1))\times q$	$B10.3=B-(p(1)-(p(0))\times q+(p(2)-p(1))\times q$	$B10.3=B-(p(1)-(p(0))\times q+(p(2)-p(1))\times q$	$AF71=L71+(p(1)-p(0))\times q-(p(1)-p(0))\times q+(p(2)-p(1))\times q$
$AF89=A89+(im\times q)$			$AF89=A89+(im\times q)$

im=initial margin; F21 and AF21=currency; F71 and AF71=financial derivatives; AF89=other accounts receivable/payable; K11=revaluation; B103 and BG=holding gain or loss.

If the future price in $t(3)$ is above the price in $t(2)$, it results in an additional trading profit, which is credited to the margin account (table 4.10.4).

Table 4.10.4: Accounting treatment of a future

Dealer		Clearing house	
Revaluation account			
Changes in financial assets	*Changes in liabilities*	*Changes in financial assets*	*Changes in liabilities*
$K11=(p(3)-p(2))\times q$	$B10.3=(p(3)-p(2))\times q$	$B10.3=(p(3)-p(2))\times q$	$K11=(p(3)-p(2))\times q$
Balance sheet			
Financial assets	*Liabilities*	*Financial assets*	*Liabilities*
$AF21=A21-(im\times q)-(p(1)-p(0))\times q$		$AF21=A21+(im\times q)+(p(1)-p(0))\times q$	
$AF71=A71+(p(1)-p(0))\times q-(p(1)-p(0))\times q+(p(2)-p(1))\times q+(p(3)-p(2))\times q$	$B10.3=B-(p(1)-(p(0))\times q+(p(2)-p(1))\times q+(p(3)-p(2))\times q$	$B10.3=B-(p(1)-(p(0))\times q+(p(2)-p(1))\times q+(p(3)-p(2))\times q$	$AF71=L71+(p(1)-p(0))\times q-(p(1)-p(0))\times q+(p(2)-p(1))\times q+(p(3)-p(2))\times q$
$AF89=A89+(im\times q)$			$AF89=A89+(im\times q)$

im=initial margin; F21 and AF21=currency; F71 and AF71=financial derivatives; AF89=other accounts receivable/payable; K11=revaluation; B103 and BG=holding gain or loss.

In the case of the sale of the futures contract in t(3), the dealer receives a credit in the form of the initial margin and the profit (table 4.10.5).

Table 4.10.5: Accounting treatment of a future

Dealer		Clearing house	
Financial account			
Changes in financial assets	*Changes in liabilities*	*Changes in financial assets*	*Changes in liabilities*
F21=(im×q) + (p(3)–p(1))×q		F21=– (im×q) – (p(3)–p(1))×q	
F71=– (p(3)–p(1))×q		F71=+(p(3)–p(1))×q	F89=–(im×q)
F89=–(im×q)			
Balance sheet			
Financial assets	*Liabilities*	*Financial assets*	*Liabilities*
AF21=A21 + (p(3)–p(0))×q		AF21=A21+ (p(3)–p(0))×q	
	B10.3=B +(p(3)–(p(0))×q	B10.3=B –(p(3)–(p(0))×q	

im=initial margin; F21 and AF21=currency; F89 and AF89=other accounts receivable/payable; B103 and BG=holding gain or loss.

(c) Swaps

4.336. Swaps are contractual arrangements between two parties who agree to exchange, over time and according to predetermined rules, streams of payment on an agreed notional amount of principal. The most common types are interest rate swaps, foreign exchange swaps and currency swaps.

4.337. Interest rate swaps are an exchange of interest payments of different character (fixed rate or floating rate, two different floating rates, fixed rate in one currency and floating rate in another, etc.) on a notional amount of principal. Settlement is often made through net cash payments amounting to the current difference between the two interest rates stipulated in the contract applied to the agreed notional principal.

4.338. Foreign exchange swaps (including all forward contracts) are transactions in foreign currencies at the rate of exchange stated in the contract.

4.339. Currency swaps involve an exchange of cash flows related to interest payments and an exchange of principal amounts at an agreed exchange rate at the end of the contract.

Statistical treatment of swaps

Basic structure of swaps

4.340. All swaps are built around the same basic structure. Two parties, called counterparties, agree to exchange specified quantities of underlying assets, the "notionals", as distinguished from physical exchanges of cash, the "actuals". A swap may involve one exchange, two exchanges, a series of exchanges or no exchanges of notionals. Between the exchanges of notionals, the counterparties make payments to each other for the use of the underlying assets. The basic structure can be explained as follows. The first counterparty makes periodic payments at a fixed price (the swap coupon) for the use of the second counterparty's assets. At the same time, the second counterparty makes periodic payments at a floating price for the use of the first counterparty's assets.

4.341. To arrange a swap means to involve a financial intermediary (the swap dealer) that serves as counterparty to both end users. The swap dealer profits from the bid-ask spread it imposes on the swap coupon.

4.342. The cash flows associated with a typical swap are illustrated in figure 4.1.

(a) Figure 4.1(a) shows the initial exchange of notionals, which is optional in the sense that it is not required in all swaps;

(b) Figure 4.1(b) shows the periodic usage payments;

(c) Figure 4.1(c) shows the re-exchange of notionals, which, like the initial exchange of notionals, is optional in the sense that it is not required in all swaps.

Figure 4.1
Swaps

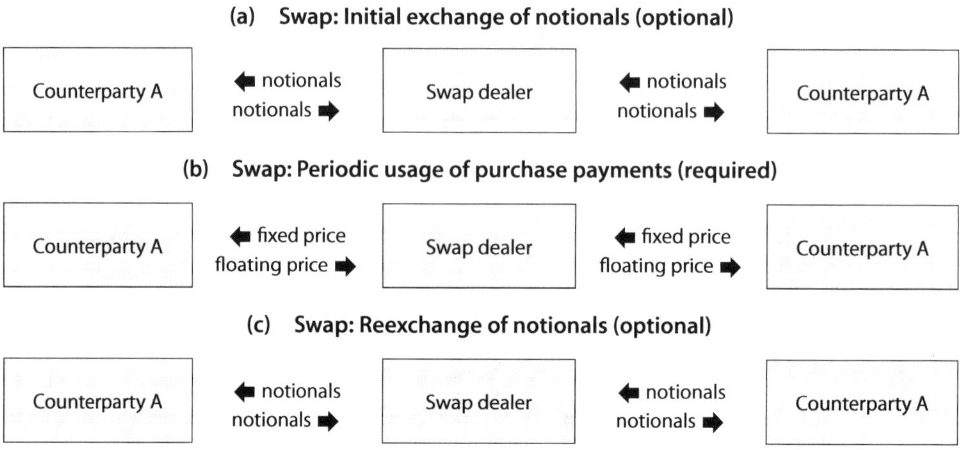

Interest rate swaps

4.343. In interest rate swaps, the exchangeable notionals take the form of quantities of money, the notional principals. The notional principals to be exchanged are identical in amount and involve the same currency. Furthermore, since the periodic usage payments, called interest, are also in the same currency, only the value differential needs to be exchanged on the periodic settlement dates.

4.344. In the most common form of interest rate swap, counterparties swap fixed interest loans for floating-rate loans. By market convention, the fixed-rate payer that has a long swap position in a fixed/floating interest rate swap is called the taker (or buyer) of the swap, while the floating-rate payer that has a short swap position in the fixed/floating interest rate swap is called the provider (or seller) of the swap.

4.345. At the date of initiation of a fixed/floating interest rate swap, the swap contract is usually executed "at the money" and the counterparties are said to have positions in a face value swap (or an "at-the-money swap" or "at-money swap") because there is no initial cash exchange between the two counterparties. Thus, at the date of contract initiation, an interest rate swap contract is neither an asset nor a liability for either counterparty. However, subsequent to that date, any market interest rate movements can cause the market value of a swap contract to become positive for one counterparty and negative for the other.

4.346. For instance, a fall in the market price of the fixed/floating interest rate swap (expressed in terms of the fixed rate of interest on a swap) will make the existing swap contract a liability to the counterparty with a long swap position (i.e. the fixed-rate payer in the swap) and an asset to the counterparty with a short swap position (i.e. the floating-rate payer in the swap). A rise in the market price of the fixed/floating interest rate swap, however, will bring a gain to the counterparty with a long swap position (the buyer) and a loss to the counterparty with a short swap position (the seller).

4.347. For example, a non-financial corporation has made a five-year, CU 50 million loan to fund part of the construction cost of a project. The loan carries a fixed interest rate of 8 per cent. Annual interest payments are therefore CU 4 million. They are made annually, and the principal will be repaid at the end of the year five.

4.348. A financial corporation wants to swap the CU 4 million, five-year annuity (the fixed interest payments) into a floating-rate annuity. The financial corporation could borrow at a 6 per cent fixed rate for five years. Therefore, the CU 4 million interest it receives could support a fixed-rate loan of CU 4 million/0.06=CU 66.67 million. This will be the notional principal amount of the swap.

4.349. The financial corporation can construct the interest rate swap as follows:

(a) It borrows CU 66.67 million at a fixed interest rate of 6 per cent for five years and simultaneously lends the same amount at LIBOR. We assume that LIBOR is now 5 per cent. The net cash flows to this strategy are shown in table 4.17;

(b) There is no net cash flow at the beginning of year 1. At the end of year 5 the principal amount of the short-term investment is used to pay off the CU 66.67 million loan;

(c) What is left? A cash flow equal to the difference between the interest earned (0.01×LIBOR×CU 66.67 million) and the CU 4 million outlay on the fixed loan. The financial corporation is also receiving CU 4 million per year from the project financing, so it has transformed that fixed payment into a floating payment keyed to LIBOR;

(d) There is an easier way to do this. The financial corporation can just call a swap dealer and agree to a five-year, fixed-to-LIBOR swap on a notional principal of CU 66.67 million.

4.350. Both strategies are equivalent to a series of forward contracts on LIBOR. The forward prices are 0.01×$LIBOR_1$×CU 66.67 million, 0.01×$LIBOR_2$×CU 66.67 million, and so on. Separately negotiated forward prices would not be CU 4 million for any one year, but the present values of the "annuities" of forward prices would be identical.

4.351. The value of the swap at year 3 and so on depends on long-term interest rates. Suppose that they move to 6 per cent, so a 6 per cent note issued by the financial corporation would trade at par. In this case, the swap has zero value. But if long rates still stay at 7 per cent, the (present) value of a three-year note would be $4/1.07+4/(1.07)^2+(4+66.67)/(1.07)^3$ = CU 64.92 million and the swap would be worth 66.67−64.92=CU 1.75 million.

Table 4.17
Cash flows of a fixed/floating interest rate swap

Year	Start 1	1	2	3	4	5
	Swap (gross and net cash flows)					
1. Borrow CU 66.67 at 6% p.a. fixed rate	+66.67	−4	−4	−4	−4	−(4+66.67)
2. Lend CU 66.67 at LIBOR floating rate (initially 5% p.a.)	−66.67	+0.05 ×66.67	+ LIBOR (2) ×66.67	+ LIBOR (3) ×66.67	+ LIBOR (4) ×66.67	+ LIBOR (5) ×66.67+66.67
Net cash flow	0	−4 +0.05 ×66.67	−4 + LIBOR (2) ×66.67	−4 + LIBOR (3) ×66.67	−4 + LIBOR (4) ×66.67	−4 + LIBOR (5) ×66.67
	Fixed/floating swap					
Net cash flow	0	−4 +0.05 ×66.67	−4 + LIBOR (2) ×66.67	−4 + LIBOR (3) ×66.67	−4 + LIBOR (4) ×66.67	−4 + LIBOR (5) ×66.67

Table 4.18
What would be the payment pattern?

1. The starting payment is based on the LIBOR rate of 5 per cent in the first year:				
FC	➡	0.08×CU 50 million = CU 4 million	➡	NFC
FC	⬅	0.05×CU 66.67 million = CU 3.33 million	⬅	NFC
FC	➡	Net = -CU 0.67 million	➡	NFC
2. The second payment is based on LIBOR at year two. Suppose it increases to 7 per cent:				
FC	➡	0.08×CU 50 million = CU 4 million	➡	NFC
FC	⬅	0.07×CU 66.67 million = CU 4.67 million	⬅	NFC
FC	⬅	Net = CU 0.67 million	⬅	NFC

Abbreviations: FC=financial corporation; NFC=non-financial corporation.

4.352. How do we know the swap is worth CU 1.75 million? Consider the following strategy:

(a) The financial corporation can enter into a new three-year swap deal in which it agrees to pay LIBOR on the same notional principal of CU 66.67 million;

(b) In return, it receives fixed payments at the 7 per cent interest rate, that is, 0.07×66.67=CU 4.67 million per year.

4.353. The new swap cancels the cash flows of the old one, but it generates an extra CU 0.67 million for three years. This extra cash flow is worth $0.67/1.07+0.67/(1.07)^2+0.67/(1.07)^3$=CU 1.75 million. Ordinary interest rate swaps have no initial cost or value (present value=0), but their value drifts away from zero as time passes and long-term interest rates change. The counterparty gains as the other loses.

Accounting treatment

4.354. The accounting treatment is demonstrated based on the notional amounts and cash flows as derived in table 4.17. Furthermore, the development of LIBOR is indicated in table 4.20 to table 4.24. There is an agreement to fix LIBOR at the beginning of each period: 5 per cent for year 1, 7 per cent for year 2, and so on and to exchange payments (netting) at the end of each year, without a swap dealer. Based on the cash flow, the net present value of transactions is calculated for each year at the beginning of the year (table 4.19).

4.355. At the date of initiation of the swap contract (long position in a fixed/floating interest rate swap with a non-financial corporation), the contract is not an asset for either counterparty.

4.356. The first payment (end-year 1) is based on the LIBOR of 5 per cent in the first year. In this case, the financial corporation, as the fixed-rate payer vis-à-vis the non-financial corporation, has a long swap position with the non-financial corporation.

Table 4.19
Transactions and net present value based on interest rate developments

Year	Start 1	1	2	3	4	5
LIBOR		0.05	0.07	0.07	0.06	0.05
Net cash flow	0	−4 +LIBOR (1) ×66.67	−4 + LIBOR (2) ×66.67	−4 + LIBOR (3) ×66.67	−4 + LIBOR (4) ×66.67	−4 + LIBOR (5) ×66.67
Transactions (net) in CU million	0	−0.67	0.67	0.67	0.67	0.67
Net present value of transactions in CU million	0	−2.89	2.26	1.75	0.00	−0.64

The cash flow to the financial corporation is CU−0.67 million, the net present value CU −2.89 million. The swap cash flow as an interest payment (D41) would lead to the following entries:

(a) For the financial corporation, there would be an outflow of cash (F21) increasing its net borrowing position (B9). In parallel, because of its negative net present value, a holding loss has to be booked in the revaluation account (F71, as financial derivatives, and B10, as changes in net worth due to nominal holding gains/losses);

(b) For the non-financial corporation as the counterparty, matching entries have to be recorded, i.e. the cash inflow in the financial account, the interest income in the current account and the holding gain in the revaluation account.

Table 4.20
Transactions at end-year 1

***Uses /* Changes in assets**				***Resources /* Changes in liabilities and net worth**			
Financial corporations (S12)		Non-financial corporations (S11)		Non-financial corporations (S11)		Financial corporations (S12)	
				Current account			
D41	0.67	B10	0.67	D41	0.67		
B10	-0.67						
				Financial account			
				B9	0.67	B9	-0.67
F21	-0.67	F21	0.67				
		F71	2.89			F71	2.89
				B10	2.89	B10	−2.89
				Revaluation account			
Total changes in assets		*Total changes in assets*		*Total changes in liabilities*		*Total changes in liabilities*	
D41	0.67			D41	0.67		
						F71	2.89
F21	-0.67	F21	0.67				
		F71	2.89	B1	2.89	B10	-2.89

4.357. Based on the LIBOR of 7 per cent for the second year, a net payment of CU 0.67 million will be made and the net present value of the swap would increase to CU 2.26 million leading to a holding gain in the books of the financial corporation. The book entries are as follows:

Table 4.21
Transactions at end-year 2

End-year 2	***Uses /* Changes in assets**		***Resources /* Changes in liabilities and net worth**		***Uses /* Changes in assets**		***Resources /* Changes in liabilities and net worth**	
	Financial corporations (S12)				Non-financial corporations (S11)			
Current account			D41	0.67	D41	0.67		
	B10	0.67			B10	-0.67		
Financial account	F21	0.67	B9	0.67	F21	-0.67	B9	-0.67
Revaluation account	F71	5.15					F71	5.15
			B10	5.15			B10	-5.15
	Total changes in assets		*Total changes in liabilities*		*Total changes in assets*		*Total changes in liabilities*	
Changes in balance sheet t=0 to 2	F71	2.26					F71	2.26
			B10	2.26			B10	-2.26

4.358. The LIBOR of 7 per cent during the third year leads again to an exchange of CU 0.67 million. Because of a reduction of the lifetime of the swap, its value is now CU 1.75 million. The book entries would be:

Table 4.22
Transactions at end-year 3

End-year 3	*Uses /* **Changes in assets**	*Resources /* **Changes in liabilities and net worth**	*Uses /* **Changes in assets**	*Resources /* **Changes in liabilities and net worth**
	Financial corporations (S12)		Non-financial corporations (S11)	
Current account		D41 0.67	D41 0.67	
	B10 0.67		B10 −0.67	
Financial account	F21 0.67	B9 0.67	F21 −0.67	B9 −0.67
Revaluation account		F71 0.51	F71 0.51	
		B10 −0.51		B10 0.51
	Total changes in assets	*Total changes in liabilities*	*Total changes in assets*	*Total changes in liabilities*
Changes in balance sheet t=0 to 3		D41 0.67	D41 0.67	
	F21 0.67		F21 −0.67	
	F71 1.75			F71 1.75
		B10 1.75		B10 −1.75

4.359. During year 4, the LIBOR of 6 per cent leads to a net exchange of zero at the end of year 4 and to the same value of the swap. There are no book entries in the current account or in the financial account. The reduction of the net present value of the swap is reflected in the revaluation account.

Table 4.23
Transactions at end-year 4

End-year 4	*Uses /* **Changes in assets**	*Resources /* **Changes in liabilities and net worth**	*Uses /* **Changes in assets**	*Resources /* **Changes in liabilities and net worth**
	Financial corporations (S12)		Non-financial corporations (S11)	
Revaluation account		F71 1.75	F71 1.75	
		B10 −1.75		B10 1.75
	Total changes in assets	*Total changes in liabilities*	*Total changes in assets*	*Total changes in liabilities*
Changes in balance sheet t=0 to 4		D41 0.67	D41 0.67	
	F21 0.67		F21 −0.67	

4.360. As at end-year 5, the further decrease of LIBOR to 5 per cent has to be taken into account which leads to a cash flow of CU−0.67 million and a net present value of CU−0.64 million (which is identical to the present value of the final payment at the end of the fifth year). It should be noted that, at the end of its lifetime, the net value of the swap would again be equal to zero.

Table 4.24
Transactions at end-year 5

End-year 5	*Uses /* **Changes in assets**	*Resources /* **Changes in liabilities and net worth**	*Uses /* **Changes in assets**	*Resources /* **Changes in liabilities and net worth**
	Financial corporations (S12)		Non-financial corporations (S11)	
Current account	D41 0.67			D41 0.67
	B10 −0.67		B10 0.67	
Financial account	F21 −0.67	B9 −0.67	F21 0.67	B9 0.67
Revaluation account		F71 0.64	F71 0.64	
		B10 −0.64		B10 0.64
	Total changes in assets	*Total changes in liabilities*	*Total changes in assets*	*Total changes in liabilities*
Changes in balance sheet t=0 to 5		F71 0.64	F71 0.64	B10 0.64
		B10 −0.64		

4.361. The treatment of swap payments as financial transactions means that the current account transaction will be classified as a financial transaction (in derivatives (F71)), leaving unchanged net lending/net borrowing of the sectors involved. The financial transactions would lead either to an exchange of financial assets (for the financial corporation) or to an enlargement of both sides of the balance sheet (for the non-financial corporation), but would not change the balancing items.

4.362. Interest movements, however, would lead to positive or negative net present values of the swap contract, which would be registered as holding gains or losses in the revaluation account.

Currency swaps

4.363. In a currency swap, the currencies in which the principals are denominated are different and, for this reason, usually (but not always) need to be exchanged. To illustrate, suppose that a financial corporation (counterparty A) can borrow currency 1 (CU1) for seven years at a fixed rate of 9 per cent and can borrow currency 2 (CU2) for seven years at a floating rate of one-year LIBOR. A non-financial corporation (counterparty B), on the other hand, can borrow seven-year floating-rate CU2 at a rate of one-year LIBOR. As it happens, the financial corporation needs floating-rate CU2 financing and the non-financial corporation needs fixed-rate CU1 financing.

4.364. Figure 4.2 shows the initial borrowings in the cash markets and the initial exchange of notional principal at the beginning of the swap.

Figure 4.2
Currency swap with cash market transactions (initial borrowings and exchanges of notional principal)

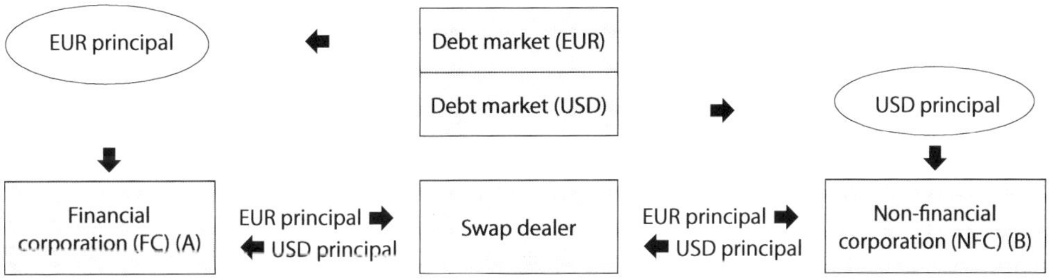

4.365. Figure 4.3 shows the debt service in the cash markets and the exchanges of interest payments on the swap. (The dealer is currently prepared to pay a fixed rate of 9.45 per cent on CU1 against CU2 LIBOR and to pay CU2 LIBOR against a fixed rate of 9.55 per cent on CU1.)

Figure 4.3
Currency swap with cash market transactions (debt service with swap payments)

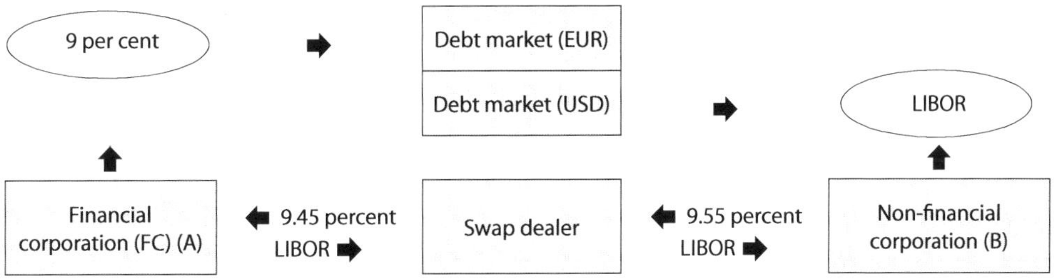

4.366. Figure 4.4 shows the re-exchange of notional principal upon termination of the swap and the repayment of the cash market borrowings.

Figure 4.4
Currency swap with cash market transactions (debt service with swap payments)

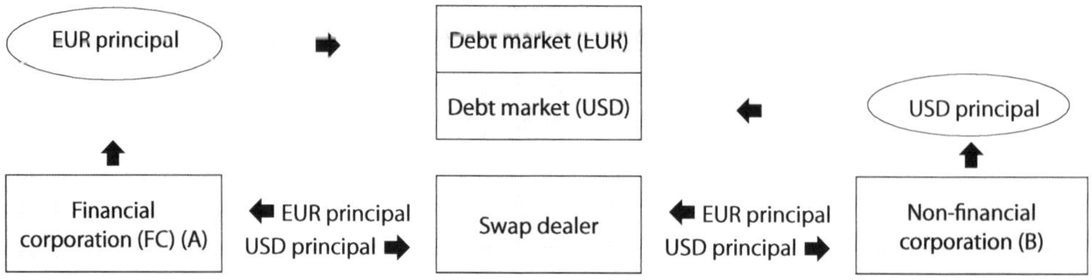

(d) Forward rate agreements

4.367. Forward rate agreements (FRAs) are contractual arrangements in which two parties, to protect themselves against interest rate changes, agree on an interest rate to be paid at a specified settlement date, on a notional amount of principal that is never exchanged. FRAs are settled by net cash payments in a similar way as interest rate swaps. The payments are related to the difference between the forward rate agreement rate and the prevailing market rate at the time of settlement.

Box 4.11
Treatment of forward rate agreements

Characteristics of forward rate agreements

Forward rate agreements are individually negotiated interest rate futures (OTC) between two parties. Unlike interest rate futures, however, FRAs are not standardized and are therefore not traded on the stock exchange. To protect themselves against interest rate risk, both parties agree on an interest rate to be paid at a settlement date based on a notional amount of principal, which is itself never exchanged in the FRA contract. The payments are related to the difference between the agreed FRA rate and the prevailing market interest rate on the settlement date.

Table 4.11.1: Comparison between forward rate agreements and interest rate futures

	FRAs	Interest rate futures
Standardized underlying instrument	No underlying	3-months FIBOR deposit or specific debt security
Amount of the contract	Above a minimum amount	Fixed
Due dates	Up to 3 years	Fixed
Collateral	No margins	Initial margin and variation margin

Economic risk of forward rate agreements

As with futures, the interest rate risk of FRAs (holding gains or losses) is theoretically unlimited and symmetric. On the settlement date (the beginning of the period) compensation for the difference between the fixed FRA rate and the agreed prevailing market rate (e.g. LIBOR) is paid. The buyer of the FRA benefits from the rising interest rates, while the seller has to bear the losses. By contrast, the seller of the FRA gains when interest rates fall, while the buyer loses. The profits of the buyer match the losses of the seller, and vice versa.

Holding gains and losses arise from the interest rate differential between the fixed FRA rate and the prevailing market interest rate on the settlement date. As interest will become payable at the end of the term, the calculated notional amount is discounted at the market interest rate on the settlement date. If the reference rate on the settlement date is higher than the FRA rate, the buyer of the FRA receives the settlement payment from the counterparty. By contrast, compensation is paid to the seller of the FRA if the market rate is below the FRA rate at settlement.

The FRA rate is determined by the length of the lead time and the total duration of the contract. For 1/7 FRA the duration of the lead time is one month and the entire duration of the contract seven months. The FRA rate of six months (time of the contract minus lead time) should be 6.73 per cent. Assuming that the LIBOR at 8 per cent is above the FRA rate after one month, the seller will pay the amount discounted at that date to the buyer. If the LIBOR was to be 6.55 per cent after one month, the buyer would have to pay an amount discounted on that date.

Treatment of the price change risk of forward rate agreements in the system of accounts

In the financial accounts, accounting entries have to be made in the revaluation account for price changes from *t*(0) to *t*(1). If there are changes in interest rates – measured by the net present value of the interest rate differential between the FRA and the reference rate – positive or negative values emerge for the FRA. They have to be recorded in the revaluation account. If the reference interest rate rises beyond the FRA, we obtain a holding gain in the present value of the interest rate differential for the buyer of a FRA and vice versa (table 4.11.2).

Table 4.11.2: Accounting treatment of a forward rate agreement

Buyer		Seller	
Revaluation account			
ΔA	ΔL	ΔA	ΔL
K11=$(p(1)–p(0))\times q$	B10.3=$(p(1)–p(0))\times q$	B10.3=$(p(1)–p(0))\times q$	K11= $(p(1)–p(0))\times q$
Balance sheet			
A	L	A	L
AF71=A71+$(p(1)-p(0))\times q$	B10.3 =$(p(1)-p(0))\times q$	B10.3 =$(p(1)-p(0))\times q$	AF71=L71+$(p(1)-p(0))\times q$

AF71=financial derivatives; K11=revaluation; B103=holding gain or loss.

After the end of the lead time, interest rates are compared and a payment made of the present value of the interest rate differential between the FRA and the reference rate. If the reference rate is higher than the FRA, the seller must pay the buyer. Conversely, if the reference rate is below the FRA, the seller must pay the buyer the present value of the interest rate differential (table 4.11.3).

Table 4.11.3: Accounting treatment of a forward rate agreements

Buyer		Seller	
Financial account			
ΔA	ΔL	ΔA	ΔL
F21=$(p(1)–p(0))\times q$		F21=$–(p(1)–p(0))\times q$	
F71=$–(p(1)–p(0))\times q$		F71=$+(p(1)–p(0))\times q$	
Balance sheet			
A	L	A	L
AF21=A21+$(p(1)–p(0))\times q$		AF21=A12–$(p(1)–p(0))\times q$	
	B10.3=$(p(1)–(p(0))\times q$	B10.3=$(p(1)–(p(0))\times q$	

F21 and AF21=currency; AF71=financial derivatives; K11=revaluation; B103=holding gain or loss.

(e) Credit derivatives

4.368. Credit derivatives are financial derivatives whose primary purpose is to trade credit risk. They are designed for trading in loan and security default risk. Credit derivatives may take the form of forward-type or option-type contracts and, like other financial derivatives, are frequently drawn up under standard legal agreements, which facilitate market valuation; they may include collateral and margining procedures. Credit risk is transferred from the risk seller (protection buyer) to the risk buyer (protection seller) in exchange for a premium.

4.369. The risk buyer pays cash to the risk seller in the event of a default. A credit derivative may also be settled by the delivery of debt securities through the unit that has defaulted.

4.370. Types of credit derivatives are credit default options, CDS and total return swaps. A CDS index as a traded credit derivative index reflects the development of CDS premiums.

4.371. CDS are credit insurance contracts. They are intended to cover losses to creditors when:

(a) A credit event occurs in relation to a reference unit, rather than being associated to a particular debt security or loan. A credit event affecting the reference unit of concern may be a default, but also a failure to make a payment on any (qualifying) liability that has become due in cases such as debt restructuring, breach of covenants, and others;

(b) A particular debt instrument, typically a debt security or a loan, goes into default. As for swap contracts, the creditor as the buyer of the CDS, the risk seller, makes a series of premium payments to the guarantor, the risk buyer.

4.372. Where there is no default on the associated unit or the debt instrument, the risk seller continues paying premiums until the end of the contract. If there is a default, the risk buyer compensates the risk seller for the loss, and the risk seller ceases to pay premiums.

(f) Financial instruments not included in financial derivatives

4.373. The category financial derivatives (other than employee stock options) (AF71) does not include:

(a) The underlying instrument upon which the financial derivative is based;

(b) Structured debt securities that combine a debt security, or a basket of debt securities, with a financial derivative, or a basket of financial derivatives, where the derivatives are inseparable from the debt security and the principal initially invested is large compared to the prospective returns from the embedded financial derivatives. Financial instruments where small principal amounts are invested relative to the prospective returns, and which are fully at risk, are classified as financial derivatives. Financial instruments where the debt security component and the financial derivative component are separable from each other are classified accordingly;

(c) Repayable margin payments related to financial derivatives are classified in other deposits (AF29) or loans (AF4) depending on the institutional units involved. However, non-repayable margin payments, reducing or eliminating the asset/liability positions which may emerge during the life of the contract, are treated as settlements under the contract, and classified as transactions in financial derivatives;

(d) Secondary instruments, which are not tradable and cannot be offset on the market;

(e) Gold swaps, which have the same nature as securities repurchase agreements.

(g) Employee stock options

4.374. An employee stock option (AF72) is an agreement made on a given date (the "grant" date) under which an employee may purchase a given number of shares of the employer's stock at a stated price (the "strike" price) either at a stated time (the "vesting" date) or within a period of time (the "exercise" period) immediately following the vesting date. The exercise date is the time at which the option is exercised. It cannot be earlier than the vesting date or later than the end of the exercise period.

4.375. Transactions in employee stock options are recorded in the financial account as the counterpart to the element of compensation of employees represented by the value of the stock option. The value of the option should be spread over the period between the grant date and vesting date; if the detailed data are lacking they are to be recorded at the vesting date. Thereafter, transactions are recorded at the exercise date or, if they are tradable and are actually traded, between the vesting date and the end of the exercise period.

Worked example 4.4. Treatment of employee stock options (provided by the Bank of Japan)

4.376. In this example, suppose that a company grants its employees employee stock options at time 0 (grant date). The options are exercisable during the period between time 2 (vesting date) and time 5 with the strike price of 30. For illustrative purposes, we assume that all of the employees will continue working for the company until time 5; satisfy any additional condition attached to the options (e.g. performance criteria); and exercise the options at the end of time 5 (exercise date).

	0	1	2	3	4	5
Time	Grant date		Vesting date	Exercise date	Exercise date	Exercise date or lapse date
		One year after grant date	Two years after	Three years after	Four years after	Five years after

4.377. The fair value of the option at time 0 is assumed to be 20 per option with the strike price of 30. The number of the employees of the company is assumed to be five, making the total value of the options 100 (20 multiplied by 5). The fair value per service period is 50, with the total divided by the number of expected service periods before the vesting date (two periods). For the sake of simplicity, the value of the option will be stable at 20 from time 0 to time 5.

4.378. The 2008 SNA captures the transactions as follows. At time 0 and 1, the company recognizes compensation of employees of 50 in the generation of income account and households record 50 in the allocation of primary income account. The compensation accrues over the two service periods.

4.379. The transaction is also recorded in the financial account. In the example, the entry is made in other accounts receivable/payable given that the vesting date has not yet been reached.[128] In the balance sheet, the amount of other accounts receivable/payable accumulates to 100 after the two service periods (at the end of time 1).

4.380. At time 2 when the options become exercisable, the amount of other accounts receivable/payable is replaced by the "employee stock options" in the financial account and in the balance sheet.

4.381. When the options are actually exercised at time 5, the stock price is expected to be 50, which is consistent with the stable option value of 20 with the strike price of 30. Households record a purchase of the company's stock of 250, by paying their own money 150 (30 times 5) and in exchange for employee stock options 100 in the financial account. The company records stock issues of 250, by deducting 100 from the employee stock options and by receiving currency and deposits 150 from households.

[128] Eurostat (2004).

Table 4.25
Recording employee stock options

	Households		Corporations	
	Uses / *Changes in financial assets /* **Financial assets**	Resources / *Changes in liabilities and net worth/* **Liabilities and net worth**	Uses / *Changes in financial assets /* **Financial assets**	Resources / *Changes in liabilities and net worth/* **Liabilities and net worth**
Time 0 Granted **Period 1 (Time 0–1)**				
Generation of income account				
Compensation of employees			50	
Allocation of primary account				
Compensation of employees		50		
Financial account				
Currency and deposits				
Employee stock options				
Equity				
Other accounts receivable/payable	*50*			*50*
Balance sheet				
Currency and deposits	**150**			
Employee stock options				
Equity				
Other accounts receivable/payable	**50**			**50**
Period 2 (Time 1–2)				
Generation of income account				
Compensation of employees			50	
Allocation of primary account				
Compensation of employees		50		
Financial account				
Currency and deposits				
Employee stock options				
Equity				
Other accounts receivable/payable	*50*			*50*
Balance sheet				
Currency and deposits	**150**			
Employee stock options				
Equity				
Other accounts receivable/payable	**100**			**100**
Time 2 Vested **Period 3 (Time 2–3)**				
Generation of income account				
Compensation of employees				
Allocation of primary account				
Compensation of employees				
Financial account				
Currency and deposits				
Employee stock options	*100*			*100*
Equity				
Other accounts receivable/payable	*-100*			*-100*
Balance sheet				
Currency and deposits	**150**			
Employee stock options	**100**			**100**
Equity				
Other accounts receivable/payable				

	Households		Corporations	
	Uses / *Changes in financial assets /* **Financial assets**	Resources / *Changes in liabilities and net worth/* **Liabilities and net worth**	Uses / *Changes in financial assets /* **Financial assets**	Resources / *Changes in liabilities and net worth/* **Liabilities and net worth**
Period 4 (Time 3–4)				
Generation of income account				
Compensation of employees				
Allocation of primary account				
Compensation of employees				
Financial account				
Currency and deposits				
Employee stock options				
Equity				
Other accounts receivable/payable				
Balance sheet				
Currency and deposits	**150**			
Employee stock options	**100**			**100**
Equity				
Other accounts receivable/payable				
Time 5 Exercised Period 5 (Time 4–5)				
Generation of income account				
Compensation of employees				
Allocation of primary account				
Compensation of employees				
Financial account				
Currency and deposits	*-150*		*150*	
Employee stock options	*-100*			*-100*
Equity	*250*			*250*
Other accounts receivable/payable				
Balance sheet				
Currency and deposits			**150**	
Employee stock options				
Equity	**250**			**250**
Other accounts receivable/payable				

Note: Non-financial transactions (uses and resources) in normal font, financial transactions in *italics (net acquisition of financial assets and net incurrence of liabilities)*, and balance sheet items in **bold (financial assets and liabilities).**

8. Other accounts receivable/payable

4.382. Other accounts receivable/payable (AF8) are financial assets and liabilities created as counterparts to financial or non-financial transactions in cases where there is a timing difference between these transactions and the corresponding payments.

4.383. Other accounts receivable/payable include transactions in financial claims, which stem from the early or late payment for transactions in goods or services, distributive transactions or financial transactions on the secondary market.

4.384. Financial transactions in other accounts receivable/payable comprise: (a) trade credits and advances (AF81); and (b) other accounts receivable/payable, excluding trade credits and advances (AF89).

(a) Trade credits and advances

4.385. Trade credits and advances (AF81) are financial claims arising from the direct extension of credit by the suppliers of goods and services to their customers, and advances for work that is in progress or is yet to be undertaken, in the form of prepayment by customers for goods and services not yet provided.

4.386. Trade credits and advances arise when payment for goods or services is not made at the same time as the change in ownership of a good or provision of a service. If a payment is made prior to the change of ownership, there is an advance.

4.387. FISIM accrued but not yet paid are included with the corresponding financial instrument, usually interest, and prepayment of insurance premiums is included in (non-life) insurance technical reserves (F61); in neither case is there an entry in F81.

4.388. This subcategory includes:

(a) Financial claims relating to the delivery of goods or services where payment has not taken place;

(b) Trade credit accepted by factoring corporations except when regarded as a loan;

(c) Rent of buildings accruing over time;

(d) Arrears concerning the payment of goods and services, when not evidenced by a loan.

4.389. Trade credits (AF81) should be distinguished from trade finance in the form of trade bills, and credit provided by third parties to finance trade.

4.390. Trade credits and advances do not include loans to finance trade credits. Any "sale" such as factoring usually leads to the reclassification of a trade credit as a loan between the new creditor and the existing debtor.

4.391. Trade credits and advances may be divided, when relevant, by original maturity into transactions in short-term and long-term trade credit and advances.

4.392. Trade credit and advances may be financial assets or liabilities of all resident sectors and of the rest of the world.

(b) Other accounts receivable/payable, excluding trade credit and advances

4.393. Other accounts receivable/payable, excluding trade credit and advances (AF89), are financial claims arising from timing differences between distributive transactions or financial transactions on the secondary market and the corresponding payments.

4.394. This subcategory includes financial claims created as a result of the timing difference between accrued transactions and payments made in respect of, for example:

(a) Wages and salaries;

(b) Taxes and social contributions;

(c) Dividends;

(d) Rent;

(e) Purchase and sale of securities;

(f) Repayable margin payments related to financial derivatives, which are liabilities of institutional units other than deposit-taking corporations except the central bank.

4.395. Interest accrued and arrears should be recorded with the financial asset or liability on which they accrue, not as other accounts receivable/payable. If the interest accrued is not recorded as being reinvested in the financial asset, it should be classified in this subcategory.

4.396. However, for securities lending and gold loan fees, which are treated as interest by convention, the corresponding entries are included under other accounts receivable/payable, rather than with the instrument to which they relate.

4.397. This subcategory does not include the following:

(a) Statistical discrepancies other than timing differences between transactions in goods and services, distributive transactions or financial transactions and the corresponding payments;

(b) Early or late payment (inclusive of arrears) in the creation of financial assets or the redemption of liabilities other than those classified in other accounts receivable/payable. They are classified in the relevant instrument category;

(c) The amount of taxes and social contributions payable to general government to be included under other accounts receivable/payable should omit the part of these taxes and social contributions which is unlikely to be collected, and which therefore represents a general government claim that has no real value.

E. Other classification schemes of financial assets and liabilities

1. Classification by negotiability

4.398. Financial claims can be distinguished according to whether they are negotiable or not. A claim is negotiable if its legal ownership is readily capable of being transferred from one unit to another unit by delivery or endorsement. While any financial instrument can potentially be traded, negotiable instruments are designed to be traded on organized and other markets. Negotiability is a matter of the legal form of the instrument. Those financial claims that are negotiable are referred to as securities. Some securities may be legally negotiable, but there is not, in fact, a liquid market where they can be readily bought or sold.

4.399. Necessary conditions of negotiability are: (a) transferability or offsetability in the case of financial derivatives; (b) standardization often evidenced by fungibility and eligibility of an international securities identification number (ISIN) code; and (c) that the holder of an asset does not retain the right of recourse against the previous holders.

4.400. Securities and financial derivatives are negotiable financial instruments. Securities include debt securities (AF3), listed shares (AF511), unlisted shares (AF512) and closed-ended investment fund shares or units. Financial derivatives are usually not classified as securities even if they are negotiable financial instruments. However, listed financial derivatives, such as warrants, are sometimes considered to be securities.

Table 4.26
Classification of financial transactions by type of income

Category, subcategory and subposition of financial transactions	Code	Type of income	Code
Monetary gold[a] and SDRs	F1	Interest[b]	D41
Currency and deposits	F2		
Currency	F21	None	
Transferable deposits	F22	Interest	D41
Other deposits	F29	Interest	D41
Debt securities	F3	Interest	D41
Loans	F4	Interest	D41
Equity and investment fund shares	F5		
Equity[b]	F51	Distributed income of corporations	D42
		Reinvested earnings on foreign direct investment[c]	D43
Listed and unlisted shares	F511 F512	Dividends	D421
		Reinvested earnings on foreign direct investment[c]	D43
Other equity	F519	Withdrawals from income of quasi-corporations	D422
		Reinvested earnings on foreign direct investment[c]	D43
Investment fund shares/units	F52	Investment income attributable to collective investment funds share holders	D443
Insurance, pension and standardized guarantee schemes	F6	Investment income attributable to insurance policyholders	D441
		Investment income payable on pension entitlements	D442
Financial derivatives and employee stock options	F7	Interest (under certain circumstances)	D41
Other accounts receivable/payable	F8	Interest (most of the accounts included here are not interest-bearing accounts)	D41

[a] Monetary gold consists of gold bullion and unallocated gold accounts. Gold bullion has no counterpart liability. However, the counterpart liability of unallocated gold accounts is in deposits, which may bear interest.

[b] By convention, lending fees on shares, gold loans and gold swaps are classified as interest.

[c] Reinvested earnings – direct investment equity only.

2. Classification by type of income

4.401. Financial transactions are to be classified by the type of income they generate. The linking of income with the corresponding financial assets and liabilities facilitates calculation of rates of return.

4.402. Table 4.26 shows the detailed classification by category, subcategory and subposition and the corresponding categories by income. While monetary gold and SDRs, deposits, debt securities, loans and other accounts receivable/payable accrue interest, equity pays predominantly dividends, reinvested earnings or withdrawals from income of quasi-corporations. Investment income is attributable to holders of investment fund shares or units and of insurance technical reserves. The remuneration related to the participation in a financial derivative is not recorded as income, because no principal amount is provided.

3. Classification by type of interest rate

4.403. Financial assets and liabilities accruing interest may be broken down by the type of interest rate: fixed, variable or mixed interest rates.

4.404. For financial instruments with a fixed interest rate, the contractual nominal interest payments are fixed in terms of the currency of denomination for the life of the financial instrument or for a certain number of years. At the date of inception, from the debtor's perspective, the timing and value of interest payments and principal repayments are therefore known.

4.405. For financial instruments with a variable interest rate, interest and/or principal payments are linked to an interest rate, a general price index for goods and services (such as the CPI) or an asset price. The reference value fluctuates in response to market conditions.

4.406. Mixed interest rate financial instruments have both a fixed and a variable interest rate over their life and are classified as variable interest rate financial instruments.

4. Classification by maturity

4.407. For the analysis of interest rates, asset yields, liquidity or debt servicing capacity, a breakdown of financial assets and liabilities by a range of maturities may be required.

4.408. A financial asset or liability with short-term maturity is repayable on demand at the request of the creditor, or in less than one year. A financial asset or liability with long-term maturity is repayable at some date in one year or beyond, or has no stated maturity.

4.409. The original maturity of financial assets or liabilities is defined as the period from the issue date until the final contractually scheduled payment date. A remaining (or residual) maturity of financial assets or of liabilities is defined as the period from the reference date until the date of the final contractually scheduled payment.

4.410. The original maturity concept is helpful in understanding debt issuance activity. Therefore, debt securities (AF3) and loans (AF4) are split by original maturity into short-term and long-term debt securities and loans.

4.411. Remaining maturity may be more relevant to the analysis of debt positions and debt servicing capabilities.

5. Classification by currency

4.412. Many of the categories, subcategories and subpositions of the financial assets and liabilities may be broken down by the currency in which they are denominated.

4.413. Denomination of a financial asset or liability in domestic currency means that it is denominated in the currency unit(s) which is (are) legal tender in the country or currency union. All other currencies are foreign currencies.

4.414. Financial assets or liabilities in foreign currency include financial assets or liabilities denominated in a currency basket, for example SDRs and financial assets or liabilities denominated in gold. A distinction between domestic currency and foreign currencies is particularly useful for the categories currency and deposits (AF2), debt securities (AF3) and loans (AF4).

4.415. The currency of settlement may be different from the currency of denomination. The currency of settlement refers to the currency into which positions and flows of financial instruments such as securities are converted each time settlement occurs.

Box 4.12

Financial assets and liabilities and financial instruments according to the International Financial Reporting Standards

The working groups and committees contributing to the process to update the 1993 SNA closely took into account the design and implementation of the International Financial Reporting Standards (IFRS). Other international initiatives to align government accounting practices and international statistical standards include the BPM6 and, in the near future, the MFSMCG and the GFSM 2014. Valuable work has also been done by the Organisation for Economic Co-operation and development (OECD)/IMF Task Force on Harmonization of Public Sector Accounting, which brought together government and national accountants. Harmonization of international accounting standards and statistical standards to the extent possible will enable the same source data to be used for several purposes, thereby improving the reliability of macroeconomic statistics and, at the same time, reducing the reporting burden for corporations.

The International Accounting Standards Board (IASB) Framework for the Preparation and Presentation of Financial Statements is relevant for statistical standards. This framework was approved by the International Accounting Standards (IAS) Committee in April 1989 for publication in July 1989, and subsequently adopted by the IASB (which took over responsibility for the standards) in April 2001. The framework sets out the concepts underlying the preparation and presentation of financial statements for external users and covers: (a) the objective of financial statements; (b) the qualitative characteristics that determine the usefulness of information in financial statements; (c) the definition, recognition and measurement of the elements from which financial statements are constructed; and (d) concepts of capital and capital maintenance. In September 2010 the IASB approved the Conceptual Framework for Financial Reporting 2010.

The elements directly related to measuring financial positions are assets, liabilities and equity. They are defined as follows: (a) an asset is a resource controlled by an entity as a result of past events and from which future economic benefits are expected to flow to the entity; (b) a liability is a present obligation of an entity arising from past events, the settlement of which is expected to result in an outflow from the entity of resources embodying economic benefits; and (c) equity is the residual interest in the assets of the entity after deducting all its liabilities.

Accounting for financial instruments under the IFRS is complex. This box focuses on the revised IAS 32, the revised IAS 39 and the IFRS 7 as they are currently applied. IAS 32 (Financial instruments: presentation) deals with the classification of financial instruments, from the perspective of the issuer, into financial assets, financial liabilities and equity instruments; the classification of related interest, dividends, losses and gains; and the circumstances in which financial assets and liabilities should be offset. The principles in this standard complement the principles for recognizing and measuring financial assets and financial liabilities in IAS 39, Financial instruments: recognition and measurement, and for disclosing information about them in IFRS 7, Financial instruments: disclosures.

Of the various financial instruments identified by the IFRS, the asset categories shown in balance sheets generally include cash and cash balances; debt instruments; loans and advances; equity instruments; derivatives; tangible (fixed) and intangible (e.g. goodwill) assets, tax assets and other assets.[a] On the liabilities side, the main categories are debt (mainly deposits in the case of banks), provisions, derivatives, tax and other liabilities and capital and reserves. Debt might be further broken down by counterpart and financial instrument, while provisions are shown separately for pensions and similar obligations. Capital and reserves are split into subscribed capital, share premium, reserves and retained earnings.

For national accounts, the balance sheet items are mainly classified by type of instrument and, to a lesser extent, by degree of liquidity. Although some obligations (e.g. provisions) are not always recognized as liabilities in the 2008 SNA, most of the national accounts instrument categories correspond to those of the balance sheet according to the IFRS.

[a] Based on the draft IAS-compliant consolidated balance sheet proposed by the Committee of European Banking Supervisors for the banking sector. The European Banking Authority was established at the beginning of 2011 and took over all the existing responsibilities and tasks of the Committee.

2008 SNA	Broad international accounts category
Monetary gold and SDRs	
Monetary gold	Other financial assets and liabilities
Gold bullion	
Unallocated gold accounts	
SDRs	Debt instruments
Currency and deposits	Debt instruments
Currency	
Deposits	
Debt securities	Debt instruments
Short-term	
Long-term	
Loans	Debt instruments
Short-term	
Long-term	
Equity and investment fund shares	Equity
Equity	
Listed shares	
Unlisted shares	
Other equity	
Investment fund shares/units	
Of which: Money market fund shares/units	
Insurance, pension and standardized guarantee schemes	Debt instruments
Non-life insurance technical reserves	
Life insurance and annuity entitlements	
Pension entitlements	
Provisions for calls under standardized schemes	
Financial derivatives and employee stock options	Other financial assets and liabilities
Financial derivatives	
Forward-type contracts	
Options	
Employee stock options	
Other accounts receivable/payable	Debt instruments
Trade credit and advances	
Other	

Chapter 5
Valuation and accrued interest

References:
2008 SNA, Chapter 12, The other changes in assets accounts, and Chapter 13, The balance sheet
BPM6, Chapter 3, Accounting principles, Chapter 7, International investment position, and Chapter 9, Other changes in financial assets and liabilities account
MFSMCG, Chapter 5, Stocks, flows, and accounting Rules
GFSM 2014, Chapter 6, Expense, and Chapter 9: Transactions in financial Assets and liabilities
HSS
ESA 2010, Chapter 6, Other flows
Eurostat, *ESA95 Manual on Government Deficit and Debt* (2002)
Eurostat, *Manual on Government Deficit and Debt: Implementation of ESA95* (2013)

A. Introduction

5.1. This chapter provides an overview of the valuation of financial assets and liabilities within the framework of the 2008 SNA. It defines and describes the various valuation principles and in which accounts to record valuation changes and other changes in the volume of assets and liabilities. The chapter also describes the treatment of accrued interest.

5.2. This chapter overlaps somewhat with chapters 3, 7 and 9 of BPM6 and chapter 5 of MFSMCG. Consistency is maintained in this Handbook with the two manuals, as well as with the 2008 SNA.

B. Balance sheets

1. Definition

5.3. A balance sheet is a statement, drawn up in respect of a particular point in time, of the values of assets owned and of the liabilities owed by an institutional unit or group of units. A balance sheet may be drawn up for institutional units, institutional sectors and the total economy.

5.4. A balance sheet shows, on its left side, non-financial and financial assets and, on its right side, liabilities. The balancing item of the balance sheet is called net worth (B90) (see table 5.1).

2. Financial balance sheets

5.5. A financial balance sheet shows, on its left side, financial assets and, on its right side, liabilities. The balancing item of the financial balance sheet is called net financial assets (NFA). The financial balance sheet of a resident sector or a subsector may be consolidated or non-consolidated. The financial balance sheet of the rest of the world is consolidated by definition.

Table 5.1
The balance sheet as a means to show assets, liabilities and net worth

Assets	Liabilities and net worth
Non-financial assets	
Produced assets	
Fixed assets	
Inventories	
Valuables	
Non-produced assets	
Natural resources	
Contracts, leases and licenses	
Goodwill and marketing assets	
Financial assets	**Liabilities**
Monetary gold and SDRs	Monetary gold and SDRs
Currency and deposits	Currency and deposits
Debt securities	Debt securities
Loans	Loans
Equity and investment fund shares or units	Equity and investment fund shares or units
Insurance, pension and standardized guarantee schemes	Insurance, pension and standardized guarantee schemes
Financial derivatives and employee stock options	Financial derivatives and employee stock options
Other accounts receivable	Other accounts payable
	Net worth

5.6. As a rule, the accounting entries in the 2008 SNA are not consolidated. Therefore, the financial balance sheet of a resident sector or subsector is to be presented on a non-consolidated basis. The non-consolidated financial balance sheet shows all the financial assets and liabilities of the institutional units classified in the sector or subsector, including those where the corresponding asset or liability is held within that sector or subsector.

5.7. The consolidated financial balance sheet eliminates the financial assets and liabilities that have counterparts in the same sector or subsector.

5.8. The from-whom-to-whom financial balance sheet (the balance sheet by debtor/creditor) is an extension of the financial balance sheet, showing in addition a breakdown of financial assets by debtor sector and a breakdown of liabilities by creditor sector. Therefore, it provides information on debtor/creditor relationships and is consistent with the financial account by debtor/creditor.

5.9. Transactions result in changes between opening and closing balance sheets. However, changes between the opening balance sheet and the closing balance sheet are also due to other flows, which are not interactions between institutional units by mutual agreement. Other flows related to assets and liabilities are broken down into revaluations in assets and liabilities, and changes in the volume of assets and liabilities not due to transactions. Revaluations are recorded in the revaluation account and changes in volume in the other changes in the volume of assets and liabilities account.

3. Balancing items of balance sheets

5.10. The balancing item of a balance sheet covering non-financial assets, financial assets and liabilities is called net worth (B90). Net worth is derived as the difference between the value of all assets – produced, non-produced and financial – and liabilities. It has to be distinguished from net financial assets, which is defined as the difference between financial assets and liabilities.

5.11. Own funds are defined as the sum of net worth plus the value of equity and investment fund shares (AF5) as liabilities in the balance sheet.

5.12. The assets and liabilities (stock) recorded in the balance sheet are valued at the appropriate price, which is usually the market price prevailing on the date to which the balance sheet relates or, for some categories, nominal value. A balance sheet is drawn up for resident institutional sectors and subsectors, the total national economy and the rest of the world. The rest of the world balance sheet is compiled in the same manner as the balance sheets of the resident institutional sectors and subsectors. It consists entirely of positions in financial assets and liabilities of non-residents vis-à-vis residents. In the BPM6 the corresponding balance sheet, drawn from the viewpoint of residents vis-à-vis non-residents, is called the international investment position (IIP).

4. Debt

5.13. Debt includes all liabilities of a sector's units (as defined in the 2008 SNA) excluding equity and investment fund shares and financial derivatives and employee stock options. The total amount of these debt liabilities is presented as the gross debt position of a sector's unit(s) for which the statistics are compiled.

5.14. Equity and investment fund shares are excluded because they do not require the payment of principal or interest (see table 5.2). Although an overdue obligation to settle a financial derivatives contract would, like any arrears, be a debt liability because a payment is required, no principal amount is advanced that must be repaid. Furthermore, no interest accrues on financial derivative or employee stock option instruments.

5.15. Debt can change without changes in net worth or net financial assets. For example, a decline in debt can be accompanied by a reduction in the stock of non-financial assets or of financial assets.

Table 5.2
Debt, net worth and own funds

Assets	Liabilities and net worth		
Non-financial assets			
Produced assets			
Fixed assets			
Inventories			
Valuables			
Non-produced assets			
Natural resources			
Contracts, leases and licences			
Goodwill and marketing assets			
		Debt (= Liabilities excluding equity and investment fund shares and financial derivatives and employee stock options)	
Financial assets			
Monetary gold and SDRs	SDRs	SDRs	
Currency and deposits	Currency and deposits	Currency and deposits	
Debt securities	Debt securities	Debt securities	
Loans	Loans	Loans	
Equity and investment fund shares	Equity and investment fund shares		
Insurance, pension and standardized guarantee schemes	Insurance, pension and standardized guarantee schemes	Insurance, pension and standardized guarantee schemes	
Financial derivatives and employee stock options	Financial derivatives and employee stock options		
Other accounts receivable	Other accounts payable	Other accounts payable	
		Financial derivatives and employee stock options	
	Net worth	Equity and investment fund shares	Own funds
		Net worth	

Box 5.1
General government debt

Definition of debt at market value and debt at nominal value

Two main general government debt measures are normally recommended for debt dissemination:

- General government debt at market value.
- General government debt at nominal value.

The two concepts of general government debt are based on the same delineation as in the general government sector. However, they differ in terms of instrument coverage, treatment of accrued interest, the valuation method applied and possibly the degree of consolidation.[a]

There is no specific definition of general government debt at market value in the 2008 SNA or the ESA 2010, but there are general provisions on institutional sectors, liabilities, and their valuation rules. The *GFSM 2001* and PSDSG propose a definition for government debt at market value. The definition covers all debt liabilities of government institutional units recorded in the core accounts (excluding equity, investment fund shares or units and financial derivatives), i.e. SDRs; currency and deposits; debt securities; loans; insurance, pension and standardized guarantee schemes; and other accounts payable.

The stock of government debt should be recorded at market value at the end of each accounting period. This market valuation method refers especially to debt securities, as nominal value is the valuation normally used for currency, deposits, loans and other debt instruments. The stock of government debt can be derived gross or net of selected financial assets, consolidated or non-consolidated. Such calculations depend mainly on the availability of appropriate balance sheet data, as well as information on the counterparties to the debt instruments (for consolidation). Government debt at market value reflects the value of the debt instruments as if they were acquired in market transactions on the balance sheet reporting date. This is equal to the value of the debt at creation plus any subsequent economic flows, such as transactions (for example, accrual of interest or repayment of principal or interest) and other changes in the volume of assets, plus exchange rate and other valuation changes, including market price changes.

Debt at nominal value is the measure of debt from the viewpoint of the debtor: at any moment in time, it is the amount that the debtor owes to the creditor, according to the terms stipulated in the contract. This is equal to the value of the debt at creation plus any subsequent economic flows, such as transactions (for example, accrual of interest or repayment of principal or interest) and other changes in the volume of assets, plus exchange rate and other valuation changes other than market price changes. When moving from a general government debt at market value to a debt at nominal value, all cumulative revaluations arising from market price changes have to be subtracted. This does not refer to revaluations of debt instruments denominated in foreign currency due to fluctuations in the exchange rate.

Extended measures of government debt

Government debt at market value and government debt at nominal value exclude two types of government liabilities. First, there are liabilities recognized by extended public sector accounting systems like provisions for expected but uncertain future payments arising from past events. Social security pension schemes are not included. Furthermore, unfunded (defined benefit) pension schemes operated by government units for their employees, paid out of government's current resources, and without special reserves, are not always included, nor are other contingent liabilities like one-off guarantees.[b] Second, liabilities of entities that are regarded as subsidiaries of government in other accounting systems but outside the general government sector boundaries in national accounts are also not covered. Both possible amendments are described in the 2008 SNA (and in the ESA 2010).

General government debt by financial instrument, creditor area or sector

The table below shows government debt by financial instrument and by creditor area or sector. Currency and deposits correspond to the value of government liabilities in coins, transferable deposits and other deposits. Transferable deposits are unlikely to be offered by government since these are deposits that can quickly and easily be converted into currency or transferred by cheque or other means. Other deposits include time deposits, savings deposits, savings books and savings certificates. Both deposit categories also include short-term liabilities in the form of repurchase agreements.

Short-term debt securities include bills and other short-term notes and bonds with an original maturity of typically one year or less, issued predominantly by the Treasury. Short-term securities are usually very liquid, of large denomination and exchanged on the money markets between banks, other financial corporations and large investors.

Other government units might also issue short-term instruments, sometimes called commercial paper or euro-commercial paper. Long-term debt securities cover all types of debt securities such as bonds, notes and treasury bills (T-bills) with an original maturity of more than one year and issued by the various government subsectors.

Loans comprise short-term and long-term borrowing by government units from deposit-taking corporations except the central bank, other financial corporations and the rest of the world. The category also includes imputed transactions in loans in respect of debt assumptions as well as imputed loans in respect of financial leases.

Government debt by financial instrument and by creditor area or sector

Component	Description
General government debt by financial instrument Currency and deposits (AF2) Short-term debt securities (AF31) Long-term debt securities (AF32) Short-term loans (AF41) Long-term loans (AF42) (Monetary gold and SDRs (AF1=, if applicable) Insurance, pension and standardized guarantee schemes (AF6) (Financial derivatives and employee stock options (AF7)) (Other accounts payable (AF8))	General government consolidated gross debt in currency and deposits (AF2), debt securities (AF3) and loans (AF4), at face value (EDP debt); short term defined as original maturity of one year or less, long term as original maturity of more than one year Government debt at nominal value extends the financial instrument coverage of EDP debt by including all debt instruments other than equity and investment fund shares or units (AF5) and financial derivatives and employee stock options (AF7); it covers accrued interest. Government debt at market value is based on a market valuation of the debt instruments.
General government debt by creditor Resident creditors the central bank (S121), deposit-taking corporations except the central bank (S122) and money market funds (S123) Other financial corporations (S124 to S129) Other non-government residents (S11, S14, S15) Non-residents (S2)	Debt held by the central bank (S121), deposit-taking corporations except the central bank (S122) and money market funds (S123), other financial corporations (S124 to S129) and other residents (resident non-financial corporations (S11), households (S14) and non-profit institutions serving households (S15) of the debt-issuing national economy) and by non-residents (S2)

Note: Paragraph 3.197 of the 2008 SNA states that "as a rule, however, the entries in the SNA are not consolidated" and "consolidation may be most relevant for financial institutions and general government". Therefore, both consolidated and unconsolidated presentations of government debt should be considered..

The breakdown of general government debt by creditor sector provides information on who is financing government. The domestic creditors are broken down into central bank and deposit-taking corporations except the central bank, other financial corporations and other (non-government) residents.

The table below refers to further breakdowns of consolidated general government debt by government subsector, by original and residual maturity and by currency.

General government debt by subsector, maturity and currency denomination

Component	Description
Government debt by subsector Central government debt State government debt Local government debt Social security funds debt	Central government (S1311), state government (S1312), local government (S1313) and social security funds (S1314) debt In each case, the subsector debt is defined as the liabilities of the subsector in financial instruments, predominantly currency and deposits, loans and debt securities, excluding any liabilities that are financial assets of units in the same subsector or of units in any other government subsector.
Government debt by original maturity Up to one year Over one year Of which variable rate instruments	Original maturity is the period between the issue and redemption of debt. Deposits are treated as having zero maturity. For long-term bonds issued in multiple tranches, all tranches are treated as having the same original maturity.
Government debt by residual maturity Up to one year Over one year	Residual maturity is the period between the reporting date and the redemption of debt. Deposits are treated as having zero residual maturity.
Government debt by currency Domestic currency Foreign currencies	Government debt in foreign currency may be subject to exchange rate changes.

[a] Referring to the methodology used in the European Union, the measurement of government debt, the so-called excessive deficit procedure EDP (excessive deficit procedure), or Maastricht debt, is at face value (although called nominal). Nominal value is not the same as face value (see paragraph para. 5.35 below). The calculation of EDP debt is based on Protocol No. 12 on the excessive deficit procedure annexed to the Treaty on the Functioning of the European Union (formerly to the Maastricht Treaty in 1992). Together with Council Regulation (EC) No. 479/2009 (OJ L 145, 10.6.2009, p. 1), it defines government, government debt and other aggregates by reference to the accounting rules as described in the ESA.

[b] The GFSM 2013GFSM 2014 and the PSDSG include these liabilities in their definitions of debt.

C. Relationship between stocks and flows

5.16. A basic accounting identity links the value of the stock of a specific type of asset in the opening balance sheet and the corresponding closing balance sheet, as shown in table 5.3.

5.17. *Stocks* or *positions* in non-financial assets, financial assets and liabilities refer to their levels at a specific point in time. *Flows* refer to the difference in positions at two consecutive points in time, and consist of *transactions* between institutional units, *revaluations* and *other changes in the volume of assets and liabilities* during the accounting period.

5.18. With reference to financial instruments, the relationship between stocks and flows can be described as follows:

$$Stock_t - Stock_{t-1} = Flows_t.$$

5.19. The term $Stock_t$ is the issuer's or holder's stock of financial instruments at the end of the accounting period t, and the term $Stock_{t-1}$ is the issuer's or holder's stock of financial instruments at the end of the accounting period t–1.

Table 5.3
Basic accounting identity

The value of the stock of a specific type of asset in the opening balance sheet		
Plus	Transactions	The total value of that asset acquired in transactions that took place during the accounting period
Minus		The total value of that asset disposed of in transactions that took place during the accounting period
Minus		Consumption of fixed capital (if applicable)
Plus	Other changes in the volume of assets	Increases in volume affecting that asset
Minus		Decreases in volume affecting that asset
Plus	Revaluations	The value of nominal holding gains accruing during the period, resulting from changes in the price of that asset
Minus		The value of nominal holding losses accruing during the period, resulting from changes in the price of that asset
Equals the value of the stock of that asset in the closing balance sheet.		

5.20. The term $Flows_t$ refers to the sum of the flows in financial instruments during the accounting period t. It comprises transactions, revaluations and other changes in the volume of assets and liabilities.

$$Flows_t = Transactions_t + Revaluations_t + Other\ changes\ in\ volume_t$$

5.21. The term $Transactions_t$ refers to net incurrences (issues less redemptions) or to net acquisitions (acquisitions less disposals) of financial instruments during the accounting period t.

$$Transactions_t = Net\ incurrences_t{}^{129} = Issues_t - Redemptions_t$$

or

$$Net\ acquisitions_t = Acquisitions_t - Disposals_t{}^{130}.$$

[129] The term "net issues" may also be used.

[130] Disposals do not refer to write-offs; write-offs should be treated as other changes in the volume of assets and liabilities and not as transactions.

5.22. The term *Revaluations*$_t$ refers to the changes in stocks due to changes in the level of prices of financial instruments during the accounting period *t*. Revaluations of assets or of liabilities arise from changes in their prices and/or from changes in exchange rates.[131]

5.23. The term *Other changes in the volume of assets and liabilities*$_t$ refers to all changes in stocks between the end of accounting period *t*–1 and the end of accounting period *t* that are due neither to transactions nor to revaluations.

D. Valuation principles

5.24. Each item in the balance sheet is valued as if it were acquired on the date to which the balance sheet relates. Assets and liabilities should be valued at prices observable on the market on the date to which the balance sheet relates.

5.25. When there are no observable market prices, which may be the case if there is a market but no assets have recently been sold on it, estimates should be made of what the price would be if the assets were acquired on the market on the date to which the balance sheet relates.

5.26. Market prices are usually available for many financial assets and liabilities, existing real estate (buildings and other structures plus the underlying land), existing transport equipment, crops and livestock, as well as for newly produced fixed assets and inventories.

5.27. Non-financial assets produced on own account should be valued at basic prices[132] or, if basic prices are not available, at the basic prices of similar goods, or, if this is not possible, at cost.

5.28. In addition to observed market prices, estimates based on observed prices or costs incurred, values of non-financial assets may be estimated by:

(a) Revaluing and accumulating acquisitions less disposals over the assets' lifetimes;

(b) The present value, that is, the discounted value, of future economic benefits.

5.29. The present value PV is calculated as

$$PV = FV/(1+\text{discount rate}/100)^n.$$

FV is the future value and n the number of periods (usually years).

Present Value

(Discounted Value)

Effect of 6% Discount Rate

Years From Now	Amount Spent or Received	Present Value (Worth Today)
0	$1000	$1000.00
1	$1000	943.40
2	$1000	890.00
3	$1000	839.62
4	$1000	792.09
5	$1000	747.26
6	$1000	704.96
7	$1000	665.06

Future Values → (Amount Spent or Received)

$PV=FV/(1+rate)^n$
where
PV is present value
FV is future value
rate is the discount rate used
n is the number of periods

[131] Changes in exchange rates apply only to holdings of equity securities denominated in foreign currencies; they are valued in the domestic currency of the country in which the issuing corporation is resident.

[132] Basic prices are defined in paragraph 2.63 of the 2008 SNA.

5.30. Market valuation is the key principle for valuing positions (and transactions) in financial instruments. The market value is that at which financial assets are acquired or disposed of, between willing parties, on the basis of commercial considerations only, excluding commissions, fees and taxes. In determining market values, trading parties also take account of accrued interest.

5.31. Nominal valuation reflects the sum of funds originally advanced, plus any subsequent advances, less any repayments, plus any accrued interest. Nominal value refers to the outstanding amount the debtor owes to the creditor, which is composed of the outstanding principal amount including any accrued interest. Nominal value is not the same as face value:

(a) The nominal value in domestic currency of a financial instrument denominated in foreign currency includes holdings gains or losses arising from movements in exchange rates. The value of financial instruments denominated in foreign currency should be converted into the domestic currency at the market exchange rate prevailing on the date to which the balance sheet relates. This rate should be the mid-point between the buying and the selling spot rates for currency transactions;

(b) For financial instruments like debt securities linked to a narrow index, the nominal value can also include holding gains or losses arising from movements in the index;[133]

(c) At any specific point in time, the market value of a financial instrument may deviate from its nominal value due to revaluations arising from market price changes. Movements in market prices arise from general market conditions, such as changes in the market rate of interest; specific circumstances, such as changes in the perceived creditworthiness of the issuer of a debt security; and changes in general market liquidity and in market liquidity specific to that debt security;

(d) Thus, the following basic equation applies to positions:

Market value = Nominal value + Cumulative revaluations arising from market price changes.

5.32. For some non-financial assets the revalued initial acquisition price reduces to zero over the asset's expected life. The value of such an asset, at any particular point of time, is given by its current acquisition price less the accumulated value of these reductions. Most fixed assets can be recorded in balance sheets at current purchasers' prices reduced for the accumulated consumption of fixed capital; this is known as the written-down replacement cost. The sum of the reduced values of all fixed assets still in use is described as the net capital stock. The gross capital stock includes the values of the accumulated consumption of fixed capital.

E. Valuation of financial assets and liabilities

1. Valuation of stocks

5.33. Financial assets and liabilities classified as negotiable financial instruments, such as debt securities or equity securities, are valued at market value. Financial instruments that are non-negotiable are usually valued at nominal value. Counterparts of financial assets and liabilities have the same valuation. The values should exclude com-

[133] Price indices based on specific assets like precious metals or oil are regarded as narrow indices. Consumer price indices are examples of broad indices: such indexation is expected to change relatively smoothly over time.

missions, fees and taxes. Commissions, fees and taxes are recorded as services provided in carrying out the transactions.

(a) Monetary gold and special drawing rights

5.34. *Monetary gold* (AF11) is to be valued at the price established in organized gold markets. As the price of *monetary gold* is usually quoted in United States dollars, the value of monetary gold is subject to nominal holding gains and losses through changes in the exchange rate as well as the price of the gold itself.

5.35. The value of special drawing rights (SDRs, AF12) is determined daily by the IMF and the rates against domestic currencies are obtainable from foreign exchange markets. As the SDRs represent a basket of currencies, its value in domestic currency terms (and consequently holding gains and losses) varies with the exchange rates of the currencies in the basket against the domestic currency.

(b) Currency and deposits

5.36. For *currency* (banknotes and coins, AF21), the valuation is the nominal value of the currency.

5.37. For *deposits* (transferable deposits, AF22, and other deposits, AF29), the values recorded in the balance sheet are nominal values.

5.38. Currency and deposits in foreign currency are converted to domestic currency at the mid-point of the bid and offer spot exchange rates prevailing on the balance sheet date.

5.39. For *structured deposits*, that is, deposits with embedded financial derivatives, nominal holding gains and losses emerge due to changes in prices as reflected in the difference between the redemption value and the initial financial investment.

5.40. The interest accruing on deposits is recorded in the financial account as being simultaneously reinvested as deposits.

(c) Debt securities

5.41. Debt securities generate accrued interest; they are recorded at market value (the "dirty price"). The "dirty price" is the price of the debt security including any interest that has accrued since the issue of the recent coupon payment. This is to be compared with the "clean price", which is the price of a debt security excluding accrued interest.[134]

5.42. Short-term debt securities (AF31) are valued at market value. Nominal holding gains and losses may accrue on short-term debt securities in the same way as for long-term debt securities. However, as short-term debt securities have much shorter times to maturity, the holding gains generated by interest rate changes are generally much smaller than on long-term debt securities with the same face values.

5.43. If market values are not available then, provided there are not conditions of high inflation or high nominal interest rates, the market value can be approximated by the nominal value for:

(a) Short-term debt securities issued at par;

(b) Short-term discounted debt securities.

---

[134] See worked example 5.5.

5.44. Long-term debt securities (AF32) are valued at market value, whether they are bonds on which interest is paid regularly or deep-discounted or zero-coupon bonds on which little or no interest is paid.

5.45. When a long-term debt security, such as a bond, is issued at premium or discount, including deep-discounted and zero-coupon bonds, the difference between its issue price and its face or redemption value when it matures measures interest that the issuer is obliged to pay over the life of the debt security. Such interest is recorded as property income payable by the issuer of the long-term debt security and receivable by the holder of the debt security, in addition to any coupon interest actually paid by the issuer at specified intervals over the life of the debt security.

5.46. The interest accruing is recorded continuously in the income account and in the financial account as being simultaneously reinvested in the debt security by the holder of the debt security. It is therefore recorded in the financial account as the acquisition of an asset, which is added to the existing asset. Thus the gradual increase in the market value of a long-term debt security that is attributable to the accumulation of accrued reinvested interest reflects a growth in the principal outstanding – that is, in the size of the asset. It is essentially a quantum or volume increase and not a price increase. It does not generate any holding gain for the holder of the long-term debt security or a holding loss for the issuer. Debt securities change qualitatively over time as they approach maturity and it is essential to recognize that increases in their values due to the accumulation of accrued interest are not price changes and do not generate holding gains.

5.47. The prices of fixed-interest long-term debt securities also change, however, when the market rates of interest change, the prices varying inversely with the interest rate movements. The impact of a given interest rate change on the price of an individual long-term debt security is lower the closer the security is to maturity. Changes in prices of long-term debt securities that are attributable to changes in market rates of interest constitute price and not quantum changes. They therefore generate nominal holding gains and losses for both the issuers and the holders of the debt securities. An increase in interest rates generates a nominal holding gain for the issuer of the debt security and an equal nominal holding loss for the holder, and vice versa in the case of a fall in interest rates.

5.48. Variable interest rate debt securities have their coupon or principal payments (or both) linked to a general price index for goods and services (such as CPI), an interest rate (such as Euribor, LIBOR or a bond yield), or an asset price:

(a) When the amounts of the coupon payments and/or the principal outstanding are linked to a general or broad price index, the change in the value of the principal outstanding between the beginning and the end of a particular accounting period due to the movement in the relevant index is treated as interest accruing in that period, in addition to any interest due for payment in that period;

(b) When indexation of the amounts to be paid at maturity includes a holding gain motive, typically indexation based on a single, narrowly defined item, any deviation of the underlying index from the originally expected path leads to holding gains or losses, which will not normally cancel out over the life of the instrument.

Worked example 5.1. Comparing market value and nominal value for debt securities as liabilities[135]

5.49. The worked example illustrates the relationship between market value and nominal value for positions in debt securities and the recording of the accrual and payment of interest for different types of debt securities, namely: (a) a fixed interest rate bond issued at par; (b) a fixed interest rate bond issued below par; (c) a zero-coupon bond; and (d) two types of index-linked bonds.

5.50. The market interest rate per annum prevailing at the start of each year (or at the end of the previous year) is derived approximately as the ratio between the (annual) accrued interest and the market value of the debt security at the start of each year (or at the end of the previous year) multiplied by 100.

(a) *A fixed interest rate bond issued at par*

5.51. A fixed interest rate bond issued at par (1,000) at the beginning of the first year is repayable at maturity in five years and pays fixed coupons of 100 at the end of each year of its life. Interest accrues on the bond throughout the year and is recorded as being reinvested in the bond, increasing its nominal value from 1,000 to 1,100 at the end of the year, before the coupon is paid. Coupon payments on the existing fixed interest rate bond will not change, although the current market interest rate may change.

5.52. At issue, the nominal value and the market value are both equal to 1,000. At the end of each year, interest of 100 has accrued and is paid by the bond issuer to the bondholder. The coupon payment of 100 by the debtor at the end of the year is treated as (partial) redemption of the bond, reducing its nominal value from 1,100 to 1,000.

5.53. To illustrate the relationship between market value and nominal value and the recording of the flows associated with each of them, the following table presents: (a) the stocks and flows (transactions and revaluations) for the first year of the life of the bond; (b) the market value and related flows during the first year of the life of the bond; and (c) the annual stocks and flows during the life of the bond.

Table 5.4
A fixed interest rate bond issued at par

Issue price: 1,000; annual coupon payments: 100; original maturity: five years; redemption price: 1,000 Stocks and flows during the life of the bond						
	Start year 1	**End year 1**	**End year 2**	**End year 3**	**End year 4**	**End year 5**
Nominal value at year-end						
before coupon payment	1,000.0	1,100.0	1,100.0	1,100.0	1,100.0	1,100.0
after coupon payment		1,000.0	1,000.0	1,000.0	1,000.0	1,000.0
Accrued interest		100.0	100.0	100.0	100.0	100.0
Coupon payment		-100.0	-100.0	-100.0	-100.0	-100.0
Market value	1,000.0	969.0	1,025.3	1,054.2	982.1	1,000.0
Interest rate (per annum)	*10.0*	*10.3*	*9.8*	*9.5*	*10.2*	*10.0*
Cumulative revaluations arising from market price changes		-31.0	25.3	54.2	-17.9	0.0

5.54. Table 5.5 shows the quadruple accounting entries of:

(a) The issuance of the bond by general government and its acquisition by a household at the start of the year 1;

[135] See also the HSS.

Table 5.5
Accounting entries for a fixed interest rate bond issued at par during year 1

Currency units

Households (S14)	General government (S13)		General government (S13)	Households (S 14)
Uses		Transactions/balancing items	Resources	
		Allocation of primary income account		
	(b) + 100	Property income (interest (D41))		(b) + 100
Change in assets			**Change in liabilities**	
		Capital account		
+100	−100	Net lending (+)/net borrowing (−)		
		Financial account		
		Net lending (+)/net borrowing (−)	−100	+100
+100	+900	Total	+1000	
(a) −1000 (c) +100	(a) +1000 (c) −100	Currency and deposits (F2)		
(a) +1000		Debt securities (F3)	(a) +1000	
(b) +100 (c) −100		Other accounts receivable/ payable (F8)	(b) +100 (c) −100	
		Revaluation account		
Holding gains			**Holding losses**	
− 31		Debt securities	−31	

(b) The accrual of interest receivable to the household and interest payable to general government during the year 1;

(c) The payment of interest (coupon payment) by general government to the household by end of the year.

5.55. The issuance of the bond and its acquisition leads – for general government – to an increase of currency and deposits by CU 1000 and of debt securities as liabilities by CU 1000. For the household, currency and deposits are reduced by CU 1000 and debt securities as financial assets by CU 1000.

5.56. The accrual of interest receivable to the household leads to an accounting entry as resources in the income account of CU 100 and to a corresponding accounting entry other accounts receivable in the financial account. For general government the accounting entries are use in the income account of CU 100 and a other accounts payable in the financial account. These transactions increase the net lending of the household by CU 100 and the net borrowing of general government also by CU 100.

5.57. The payment of interest by general government to the household is recorded as a decrease in currency and deposits and in accounts receivable by 100, while general government receives currency and deposits of CU 100 and extinguishes its accounts payable by the same amount.

5.58. The capital account and the financial account show, for households, a net lending of + CU 100 and, for general government, a net borrowing of -100. To complete the entries in the system of accumulation accounts an amount of -31 has to be recorded as a (negative) holding gain for households (a holding loss on the assets side) due to the decrease of the market value of the bond from 1000 to 969 and a corresponding holding loss of for general government (a holding gain on the liabilities side).

(b) *A fixed interest rate bond issued below par*

5.59. In this second example, a five-year fixed interest rate bond repayable at maturity is issued at a discount (below par, at 900) and pays annual fixed coupons of 73.6 during its life, which, because of the discount, corresponds to a 10 per cent rate of interest. The bond accrues annually two types of interest: (a) a coupon of 73.6; and (b) an annual discount, which is calculated as 19.2 for the first year. At the end of the first year, interest of 92.8 has accrued, but only 73.6 of this accrued interest is paid to the bondholder. This reduces the principal amount outstanding, in nominal value terms, from 992.8 to 919.2. The accrued discount of 100 is only paid at the end of the fifth year as part of the redemption price.

5.60. As in the previous example, the following table presents: (a) the stocks and flows for the first year of the life of the bond; (b) the market value and related flows during the first year of the life of the bond; and (c) the annual stocks and flows during the life of the bond.

(c) *A zero-coupon bond*

5.61. In the third example, a zero-coupon bond is issued which, by definition, pays no coupons during its life. The bond has a redemption price of 1,000 and an issue price of 620.9. The latter is the present value as at issuance of the final payment at the end of the fifth year, when discounted (on an annual basis) at the current market interest rate of 10 per cent.

5.62. The only transactions to be recorded for this kind of bond, after its issuance, are the accruals of the discount throughout its life and the payment of the principal at

Table 5.6
A fixed interest rate bond issued below par

Issue price: 900; annual coupon payments: 73.6; discount payment at redemption; original maturity: five years; redemption price: 1,000
Stocks and flows during the life of the bond

	Start year 1	End year 1	End year 2	End year 3	End year 4	End year 5
Nominal value at year-end						
before coupon payment	900.0	992.8	1,012.4	1,032.4	1,052.8	1,073.6
after coupon payment		919.2	938.7	958.7	979.1	1,000.0
Accrued interest		92.8	93.2	93.7	94.1	94.5
Coupon payment		-73.6	-73.6	-73.6	-73.6	-73.6
Market value	900.0	887.1	958.5	1,006.5	958.6	1,000.0
Interest rate (per annum)	*10.0*	*10.5*	*9.7*	*9.3*	*9.8*	*9.5*
Cumulative revaluations arising from market price changes		-32.1	19.8	47.8	-20.5	0.0

Table 5.7
A zero-coupon bond

Issue price: 620.9; implicit rate of return: 10 per cent per annum; original maturity: five years; redemption price: 1,000
Stocks and flows during the life of the bond

	Start year 1	End year 1	End year 2	End year 3	End year 4	End year 5
Nominal value	620.9	683.0	751.3	826.4	909.1	1,000.0
Accrued interest due to discount		62.1	130.4	205.5	288.2	379.1
Market value	620.9	658.7	772.2	873.4	892.9	1,000.0
Interest rate (per annum)	*10.0*	*9.4*	*8.8*	*8.6*	9.3	*9.1*
Cumulative revaluations arising from market price changes		-24.3	20.9	47.0	-16.2	0.0

maturity. Changes in market interest rates will affect the bond's market value in the same direction as in the previous two cases, but with amplified effects owing to the longer duration of the bond.

5.63. The table above presents: (a) the stocks and flows for the first year of the life of the bond; (b) the market value and related flows during the first year of the life of the bond; and (c) the annual stocks and flows during the life of the bond. At the end of the life of the bond, a transaction of 1,000 is recorded, corresponding to the repayment of 620.9 of principal and the payment of 379.1 of accrued interest.

(d) *Index-linked bonds*

(i) Linked to the consumer price index

5.64. In the fourth example, an index-linked bond, repayable at maturity in five years, with annual coupon payments of 50 (5 per cent) on a principal of 1,000, is indexed to the CPI. The inflation expected over the life of the bond is assumed to be the inflation observed during the last 12 months. Changes in the CPI will affect the market value of the security through changes in its expected redemption price, discounted at the current market interest rate. The same market interest rate and market conditions as in the previous three examples apply to the case of this index-linked bond. At the time of issuance the increase in the CPI during the previous 12 months is 5.5 per cent. The bond is issued at par, with nominal value and market value equal to 1,000.

5.65. The following table presents: (a) the stocks and flows for the first year of the life of the bond; (b) the market value and related flows during the first year of the life of the bond; and (c) the annual stocks and flows during the life of the bond. As can be seen in this table, the nominal value of the bond increases pari passu with observed inflation, while its market value also reflects expected inflation and displays the same inverse relationship with the market interest rate as in the other examples. As the bond is linked to a broad index, changes in the value of the bond due to indexation are recorded as accrued interest, that is, as a transaction and not as a revaluation, while changes in its market value are recorded as revaluations.

(ii) Linked to the gold price

5.66. The final example is a five-year bond paying an annual coupon of 100 (10 per cent) on a principal of 1,000, which is indexed to the gold price. The expected redemption price is assumed to reflect the prevailing market price of gold. Changes in the gold price will affect the market value of the security via changes in the expected redemption price of the security, discounted at the prevailing market interest rate. The same market interest rate and market conditions as in the previous four examples apply to this index-linked bond. At the time of issuance the gold price in domestic currency is 1,000 per troy ounce. The bond is issued at par, with nominal value and market value equal to 1,000.

5.67. The following table presents: (a) the stocks and flows for the first year of the life of the bond; (b) the market value and related flows during the first year of the life of the bond; and (c) the annual stocks and flows during the life of the bond. The nominal value of the bond reflects changes in the gold price and also the accrual of interest. The market value of the bond also reflects changes in the gold price and the accrual of interest. As in the other examples, the market value is inversely related to the market interest rate. Also, the difference between the nominal value and the market value stems from revaluations arising from market price changes. As the bond is linked to a narrow index, changes in the value of the bond due to changes in the gold price are recorded as revaluations and not as transactions.

Table 5.8
A bond indexed to the consumer price index

Issue price: 1,000; annual coupon payments: 50; original maturity: five years; redemption price: 1,000; indexed to the CPI Stocks and flows during the life of the bond						
	Start year 1	**End year 1**	**End year 2**	**End year 3**	**End year 4**	**End year 5**
Nominal value at year-end						
before coupon payment	1,000.0	1,120.0	1,184.2	1,240.9	1,294.5	1,344.3
after coupon payment		1,070.0	1,134.2	1,190.9	1,244.5	1,294.3
Accrued interest		120.0	184.2	240.9	294.5	344.3
due to coupon		50.0	50.0	50.0	50.0	50.0
due to indexation		70.0	134.2	190.9	244.5	294.3
Market value	1,000.0	1,079.1	1,169.7	1,237.3	1,205.8	1,294.3
Interest rate (per annum)	*10.5*	*11.1*	*9.8*	*8.6*	*8.6*	*7.7*
Cumulative revaluations arising from market price changes		9.1	35.5	46.4	-38.7	0.0
CPI (12-month change, percentages)	5.5	7.0	6.0	5.0	4.5	4.0
CPI (index with year 1 as the base year)	100.0	107.0	113.4	119.1	124.5	129.4

Table 5.9
A bond indexed to the gold price

Issue price: 1,000; annual coupon payments: 100; original maturity: five years; redemption price: 1,000, indexed to the gold price Stocks and flows during the life of the bond						
	Start year 1	**End year 1**	**End year 2**	**End year 3**	**End year 4**	**End year 5**
Nominal value at year-end						
before coupon payment	1,000.0	900.0	1,050.0	1,100.0	1,150.0	1,200.0
after coupon payment		800.0	950.0	1,000.0	1,050.0	1,100.0
Accrued interest		100.0	100.0	100.0	100.0	100.0
Coupon payment		-100.0	-100.0	-100.0	-100.0	-100.0
Market value	1,000.0	837.2	986.7	1,054.2	1,026.8	1,100.0
Interest rate (per annum)	*10.0*	*11.9*	*10.1*	*9.5*	*9.7*	*9.1*
Cumulative revaluations						
arising from changes in gold price		-200.0	-50.0	0.0	50.0	100.0
arising from market price changes		37.2	36.7	54.2	-23.2	0.0
Gold price (domestic currency per troy ounce)	1,000.0	800.0	950.0	1,000.0	1,050.0	1,100.0

(d) Loans

5.68. The values to be recorded in the balance sheets of both creditors and debtors are the nominal values irrespective of whether the loans are performing or non-performing, including interest accrued.

5.69. The interest accruing is recorded in the financial account as being simultaneously reinvested in the loan by the creditor of the loan. It is therefore recorded in the financial account as the acquisition of an asset, which is added to the existing asset. Thus the gradual increase in the value of a loan that is attributable to the accumulation of accrued interest reflects a growth in the principal outstanding – that is, in the size of the asset. It is essentially a quantum or volume increase and not a price increase. It does not generate any holding gain for the creditor of the loan or a holding loss for the debtor.

(e) Equity and investment fund shares or units

5.70. Listed shares (AF511) are valued at their current prices. The same value is adopted for both the assets side and the liabilities side, although shares and other equity are not, legally, a liability of the issuer, but an ownership right to a share in the liquidation value of a corporation, where the liquidation value is not known in advance.

5.71. The current price of listed shares is the price of the most recent trade that has been completed for the share.

Box 5.2
Share prices and share price indices

Share prices, bids, asks and spreads

Once a stock has been listed, its shares are bought and sold on organized stock markets. Such exchanges are organized systems of trading, in which the prices of any stock are set by the rule of supply and demand in an auction setting. Share prices fluctuate due to the supply and demand. However, there are many factors that influence the demand for a particular share. Fundamental and technical analyses attempt to understand market conditions that lead to price changes, or even predict future price levels. Share prices are fundamentally driven by profit expectations, but market sentiment (bullish, bearish, herd behaviour) can also affect share prices.

The current price is the price of the most recent trade that has been completed for the share. It is not necessarily the price to be paid or received for a share if an order has been placed at that moment. During the market day, share quotes are typically delayed 15 to 20 minutes, unless a real-time quote has been specifically requested. Furthermore, share prices change frequently and quickly, so the last price may no longer be very up to date. The current day's high and low prices are usually displayed, too. These are the highest and lowest prices at which shares have been bought or sold during the day.

The price quote may also include information on the bid and ask prices for the share. The bid price is the highest price any brokerage firm (a market maker) is willing to pay for a share at a particular time, just like at an auction. The ask price is the lowest price that any brokerage firm is willing to accept to sell a share at that particular time. The spread is the difference between the bid and the ask prices of a traded share.

Share price indices

Share price indices may be classified in different ways: "world" or "global" share price index (or stock market index) includes (typically large) corporations and corporate groups without regard for where they are located or carry out their business. Two examples are the MSCI World Index and S&P Global 100.

A "national" index represents the performance of the stock market of a given country – and, by proxy, reflects investor sentiment about the state of its economy. The most regularly quoted share price indices are national indices composed of the stocks of large corporations listed on the country's largest stock exchanges, such as the United States S&P 500, the Japanese Nikkei 225, the German DAX, Russian RTSI and the UK FTSE 100. The concept can be extended well beyond an exchange by representing the stock of nearly every publicly traded corporation in an economy. More specialized indices exist tracking the performance of specific sectors of the economy, corporations of a certain size or corporations being managed in a certain way.

Another distinction is between price return and total return indices (simply called "price" and "return" indices). Some indices are price indices (the UK FTSE), others are return indices (the German DAX), and others have both features (Euro Stoxx). Some indices, such as the S&P 500, have multiple versions. These versions can differ in terms of how the index components are weighted and how dividends are accounted for. For example, there are three versions of the S&P 500 index: (a) price return, which considers only the price of the components; (b) total return, which accounts for dividend reinvestment; and (c) net total return, which accounts for dividend reinvestment after the deduction of a withholding tax.

An index may also be classified according to the method used to determine its value. In a price-weighted index, the price of each component stock is the only consideration when determining the value of the index. Thus, a movement in the price of just a single security can heavily influence the value of the index irrespective of the relative size of the corporation as a whole. By contrast, a market value-weighted or capitalization-weighted index takes into account the size of the corporation. Thus, a relatively small shift in the share price of a large corporation may strongly influence the value of the index. In a market share-weighted index, the price is weighted relative to the number of shares, rather than their total value. A modified capitalization-weighted index is a hybrid between capitalization weighting and equal weighting. It is similar to a capitalization weighting with one main difference: the largest stocks are capped to a percentage of the weight of the total stock index and the excess weight is redistributed equally amongst the stocks under that cap.

5.72. The values of *unlisted shares* (AF512), which are not traded on organized markets, should be estimated with reference to either:

(a) The values of quoted shares where appropriate;

(b) The value of own funds; or

(c) Discounting forecast profits by applying an appropriate market price to earnings ratio to the smoothed recent earnings of the institutional unit.

5.73. These estimates will take into account differences between listed and unlisted shares, notably their liquidity and consider the net worth accumulated over the life of the corporation and its branch of business.

5.74. The estimation method applied depends on the basic statistics available. It may take into account, for example, data on merger activities involving unlisted shares. If the value of unlisted corporations' own funds moves similarly, on average and in proportion to their nominal capital, to that of similar corporations with listed shares, then the balance sheet value can be calculated using a ratio. This ratio compares the value of own funds of unlisted corporations to that of listed corporations: value of unlisted shares = market price of similar listed shares × (own funds of unlisted corporations) / (own funds of similar listed corporations). If the value of unlisted corporations' own funds does not move similarly or if the listed corporations are not representative of the unlisted corporations then this ratio should not be applied and the value of own funds is a superior estimate.

5.75. The ratio of share price to own funds may vary with the type of business. It is preferable to calculate the current price of unlisted shares by type. There may be other differences between listed and unlisted corporations, which can have an effect on the estimation method.

5.76. Quasi-corporations' other equity is valued as the difference between their assets and liabilities. For quasi-corporations, there is no share capital, and all equity is "other equity". Thus, their net worth is by convention equal to zero. For other units, the most appropriate valuation method should be chosen from among those described for unlisted shares.

5.77. Corporations that issue shares or units may additionally have other equity.

5.78. Investment fund shares or units (AF52) are valued at market value. The distinction between listed and unlisted investment fund shares or units is not relevant as all data have to be provided at market value.

5.79. Open-ended funds are valued using their NAV, while the use of market prices is more suitable for the valuation of closed-end investment fund shares or units.

(f) Insurance, pension and standardized guarantee schemes

5.80. The amounts recorded for non-life insurance technical reserves (AF61) cover premiums paid but not earned plus the amounts set aside to meet outstanding claims. The latter represent the present value of amounts expected to be paid out in settlement of claims, including disputed claims and an allowance for claims to cover incidents that have occurred but have not yet been reported.

5.81. The amounts recorded for life insurance and annuity entitlements (AF62) represent the reserves needed to meet all expected future claims and unearned premiums.

5.82. The amounts recorded for pension entitlements (AF63) depend on the type of pension scheme.

Box 5.3
Valuation of unlisted shares

If financial instruments are not traded in a market or only traded infrequently, a market-equivalent value should be estimated instead. This value is also referred to as fair value and is defined in the following way: "Fair value is a market-equivalent value. It is defined as the amount for which an asset could be exchanged, or a liability settled, between knowledgeable, willing parties in an arm's-length transaction" (2008 SNA, para. 3.157a. See also the BPM6, para. 3.88).

Valuation methods as recommended in international statistical standards

For unlisted shares, which are equity securities not listed on a stock exchange, various valuation methods are proposed. They can be distinguished as follows: (type a) valuation based on recent transactions; (type b) valuation based on accounting data of the corporation; and (type c) valuation based on the value of a comparable corporation or of a group of comparable corporations.[a]

The 2008 SNA and the BPM6 distinguish six different methods to value unlisted shares. These methods are based on the following:

(a) Recent transaction price (type a);

(b) Net asset value (NAV) based on accounting data (type b);

(c) Present value/price to earnings ratio by discounting the forecast future profits (P/E) (type b);

(d) Market capitalization or price to book value (P/B) method (type c);

(e) Own funds at book value (OFBV) method (type c);

(f) Apportioning the global value (type c).

Implementation of valuation methods

No single valuation method is prescribed by international statistical standards. Flexibility is encouraged in the choice of methods, and no ranking of methods has been established. The exact choice of method is left to the compilers depending on data availability and market conditions in each economy. However, some methods, e.g. price to earnings (P/E) and price to book value (P/B) are commonly used by valuation practitioners, whereas the OFBV method has been developed by statisticians in an attempt to reach a harmonized book value definition across countries and accounting standards.

To apply the price to book value (P/B) method, the following accounting data (balance sheet positions) are used. The book value of equity is compiled by: Book value = Share capital (ordinary (or common) and preferred shares) + CS (contributed surplus) + RE (retained earnings). Stock exchange data are then matched to the book value data. Price to book values are calculated by dividing the market value of an enterprise by its book value using the formula: Price to book value = Market value / Book value.

The OFBV method compares the value of own funds of unlisted corporations to that of listed corporations: Value of unlisted shares = Market price of similar[b] listed shares × (Own funds of unlisted corporations) / (Own funds of similar listed corporations). The ratio of the share price to own funds may vary with the type of business. Therefore, it is preferable to calculate the current price of unlisted shares branch by type. Other differences between listed and unlisted corporations may have an effect on the estimation method.

Liquidity, control and negative equity values

The valuation of unlisted shares compared to the valuation of listed shares may need to be further modified in terms of liquidity, control and negative equity values. Certain factors may have a significant impact on the valuation of unlisted shares:

(a) Unlisted shares are typically characterized by lower liquidity than listed shares. Lower liquidity tends to have a negative effect on the value and, if significant, should be taken into account;

(b) Unlisted corporations usually have few owners, often just one. A control premium is frequently paid when an investor obtains a controlling stake in a corporation. Since this control premium will normally be offered to all shareholders, all shares in a given corporation should be valued at the same price;

(c) The valuation methods may generate negative positions, which are not consistent with the limited liability aspect of equity. For instance, the P/E method often generates negative market value estimates, as earnings are volatile and frequently negative. The BPM6 allows the inclusion of negative foreign direct investment (FDI) equity positions in the international investment position, but individual country practices may differ.

[a] *Other equity* should be valued as equal to the value of the unit's assets less the value of its liabilities. *Unlisted investment fund shares or units* should be valued according to one of the methods described above for unlisted equity.

[b] Similar in this context means shares of listed corporations engaged in the same type of activity.

Box 5.4

Concepts of pension entitlements

There are three concepts of pension entitlements (or pension liabilities):

(a) Accrued-to-date liabilities (ADL): these pension entitlements or obligations contain the present value of pensions to be paid in the future on the basis of accrued rights. Accrued pension rights are due to already paid social contributions by current workers and remaining pension entitlements of existing pensioners. No rights accrued after the current year – neither by present nor by future workers – are considered. The time horizon of this concept is, therefore, somewhat limited;

(b) Current workers' and pensioners' liabilities (CWL): for CWL, allowance is made for the pension scheme to continue until the last current contributor dies. However, new entrants are not included. This concept covers ADL and the present value of pension entitlements that will be accrued by current contributors due to their future contributions;

(c) Open-system liabilities (OSL): in addition to CWL, this liability concept also includes the present value of pensions of new workers entering the respective pension scheme. It is assumed that the pension scheme will be continued under the same rules for a relatively long time. The present value of OSL may be compiled over an infinite time horizon. For practical reasons, however, a perspective, e.g. 200 years, is usually chosen.

Measures of pension entitlements (such as the so-called ADL) are the appropriate data to be reported in the system of national accounts. In this respect, they are useful for economic and policy analyses. They provide an estimate of the cost of a hypothetical termination of a pension scheme without reneging on accrued entitlements. As measures of household wealth (assets and contingent assets), they also give valuable statistical information to understand positions and flows in household wealth and in relation to saving and consumption. Furthermore, pension entitlements accrued to date facilitate the assessment of pension reforms of various kinds, such as establishing a new system for new contributions or new contributors, while maintaining the current system for already accrued entitlements.

However, pension entitlements accrued to date are not an appropriate indicator of fiscal sustainability. They can be interpreted as the amount of resources, which has to be set aside today in order to finance all pension rights which have been earned up to a given year. Entitlements that will accrue after that year are not included. In contrast to other liability concepts such as OSL, therefore, the time horizon of ADL is somewhat limited. The latter represent only one part of the former. Moreover, the ADL are compiled gross without including the net present value of future social contributions. To assess fiscal sustainability it is vital to compare (future) pension obligations with the corresponding future pension-related assets.

5.83. In a defined benefit pension scheme the level of pension benefits promised to participating employees is determined by a formula agreed in advance. The liability of a defined benefit pension scheme is equal to the present value of the promised benefits.

5.84. In a defined contribution scheme the benefits paid are dependent on the performance of the assets acquired by the pension scheme. The liability of a defined contribution scheme is the current market value of the funds' assets. The funds' net worth is always zero.

5.85. The value recorded for prepayments of net fees and provisions to meet outstanding calls under standardized guarantees (AF66) is the expected level of claims less the value of any expected recoveries.

(g) Financial derivatives and employee stock options

5.86. Financial derivatives (AF71) should be included in the balance sheets at their market value. If market price data are unavailable, for example in the case of over the counter (OTC) options,[136] they should be valued at either the amount required to buy out or to offset the contract or the amount of premium payable.

[136] A harmonized methodology does not exist for OTC activities. IAS/IFRS indicates several alternatives: "The best evidence of fair value is quoted prices in an active market. If the market for a financial instrument is not active, an entity establishes fair value by using a valuation technique. The objective of using a valuation technique is to establish what the transaction price would have been on the measurement date in an arm's length exchange motivated by normal business considerations. Valuation techniques include using recent arm's length market transactions between knowledgeable, willing parties, if available, reference to the current fair value of another instrument that is substantially the same, discounted cash flow analysis and option pricing models. If there is a valuation technique commonly used by market participants to price the instrument and that technique has been demonstrated to provide reliable estimates of prices obtained in actual market transactions, the entity

5.87. For options, the writer of the option is considered to have incurred a counterpart liability representing the cost of buying out the rights of the option holder, irrespective of whether the option is an option to buy or to sell.

5.88. The market value of options and forwards can switch between positive (asset) and negative (liability) positions depending on price movements in the underlying items and thus they can switch between assets and liabilities for the writers and holders. Some options and forwards operate on margin payments, where profits or losses are settled daily; in these cases the balance sheet value will be zero.

5.89. Employee stock options (AF72) are valued by reference to the fair value of the equity granted. The fair value is measured at grant date using the market value of equivalent traded options or, if unavailable, using an option-pricing model (see also worked example 4.5 on the treatment of employee stock options).

(h) Other accounts receivable/payable

5.90. Trade credits and advances (AF81) and other accounts receivable/payable (AF89), which arise due to timing differences between distributive transactions, such as taxes, social contributions, dividends, rents, wages and salaries, and financial transactions, are valued, for both creditors and debtors, at nominal value. The amounts of taxes and social contributions payable under AF89 should exclude the amounts unlikely to be collected and which therefore represent a government claim with no value.

5.91. Interest due on other accounts receivable/payable may be included here.

2. Valuation of financial transactions

5.92. Financial transactions are recorded at transaction values, that is, the values in domestic currency at which the financial assets and/or liabilities involved are created, liquidated, exchanged or assumed between resident institutional units, or between them and non-resident institutional units, on the basis of commercial considerations.

5.93. Financial transactions and their financial or non-financial counterpart transactions are recorded at the same transaction value. Three possibilities can be envisaged:

(a) The financial transaction gives rise to a payment in domestic currency: the transaction value is equal to the amount of the means of payment exchanged;

(b) The financial transaction gives rise to a payment in foreign currency and the counterpart transaction is not a transaction in (means of payment in) domestic currency: the transaction value is equal to the amount of the means of payment exchanged converted into domestic currency at the market rate prevailing when the payment takes place;

(c) Neither the financial transaction nor its counterpart transaction is a transaction in cash or through other means of payment: the transaction value is the current market value of the financial assets and/or liabilities involved.

uses that technique. The chosen valuation technique makes maximum use of market inputs and relies as little as possible on entity-specific inputs. It incorporates all factors that market participants would consider in setting a price and is consistent with accepted economic methodologies for pricing financial instruments. Periodically, an entity calibrates the valuation technique and tests it for validity using prices from any observable current market transactions in the same instrument (i.e. without modification or repackaging) or based on any available observable market data" (para. 48A, IAS 39).

5.94. The transaction value refers to a specific financial transaction and its counterpart transaction. In concept, the transaction value is to be distinguished from a value based on a price quoted in the market, a fair market price, or any price that is intended to express the generality of prices for a class of similar or even identical financial assets and/or liabilities. However, in cases where the counterpart transaction of a financial transaction is, for example, a transfer and therefore the financial transaction is undertaken other than for purely commercial considerations, the transaction value is identified with the current market value of the financial assets and/or liabilities involved.

5.95. The transaction value does not include service charges, fees, commissions and similar payments for services provided in carrying out the transactions; these are to be recorded as payments for services. Taxes on financial transactions are also excluded and should be treated as taxes on services within taxes on products. When a financial transaction involves a new issue of liabilities, the transaction value is equal to the amount of the liability incurred excluding any pre-paid interest. Similarly, when a liability is extinguished, the transaction value for both creditor and debtor must correspond to the reduction of the liability.

(a) Debt securities

5.96. Transactions in debt securities are valued at the actual price agreed upon by the institutional units involved in the transaction. Under normal conditions, the market value is the price at which debt securities are acquired or disposed of in transactions between willing parties, excluding commissions, fees and taxes.

5.97. When debt securities are marketed by issuers through underwriters or other intermediaries and then sold at higher prices to final investors, the financial assets and liabilities are to be recorded at the values paid by the investors. The differences between the amounts paid by the investors and those received by the issuers should be treated as service payments paid by the issuers to the underwriters.

5.98. Debt security issues are recorded at the issue value. When debt securities are issued at a discount or at a premium, the proceeds to the issuer at the time of sale, and not the face value, are recorded in the accounts as the actual issue value. The difference between the issue value and the redemption value is treated as interest (negative where the security is issued at a premium) that is accrued over the life of the debt security.

5.99. Deep-discounted or zero-coupon bonds should be treated as debt securities issued at a discount. The interest is accrued over the life of the bonds and treated as being reinvested in such bonds.

5.100. Indexed-linked debt securities (except those linked to a foreign currency) are treated as variable interest rate debt securities. A debt security is classified as a variable interest rate debt security if the indexation applies to the principal or coupons (or both).

5.101. Transactions in debt securities on the secondary market are recorded at the stock exchange quotation or market price.

5.102. Debt securities which have reached maturity are recorded at redemption value, which includes redemption premiums but excludes payments by lottery and savings premiums, which are recorded as interest.

5.103. The conversion of debt securities into shares should be treated as a sale of debt securities and a purchase of shares. The transaction value is to be derived from the market value of the debt securities disposed of, possibly implying a holding gain or loss on shares to be recorded in the revaluation account.

(b) Equity

5.104. Transactions in shares are valued at the actual price agreed between the institutional units involved in the transaction. Under normal conditions, the market value is the price at which these financial instruments are issued, redeemed, acquired or disposed of in transactions between independent, willing parties, excluding commissions, fees and taxes.

5.105. New shares are recorded at issue value, which normally corresponds to nominal value plus the issue premium.

5.106. Transactions in shares in circulation are to be recorded at their transaction value. When the transaction value is not known, it is approximated by the stock exchange quotation or market price for listed shares and by the market-equivalent value for unlisted shares (see also the valuation of unlisted shares described in box 5.3).

5.107. Scrip dividend shares are shares valued at the price implied by the issuer's dividend proposal and distributed in lieu of cash dividends.

5.108. Issues of bonus shares are not recorded under the 2008 SNA. They do not constitute a financial transaction between the shareholders and the corporation because there is no change in the total amount of the underlying financial asset. However, in cases where the issue of bonus shares involves changes in the total market value of the shares of a corporation, the changes in market value are to be recorded in the revaluation account.

5.109. The transaction value of equity is the amount of funds transferred by the owners to corporations or quasi-corporations. In some cases, funds can be transferred by assuming liabilities of the corporation or quasi-corporation.

(c) Investment fund shares or units

5.110. Open-ended funds are valued using NAV, while the use of market prices is more suitable for the valuation of closed-ended funds' shares.

5.111. Transactions may also be derived from the respective position data. In this case, the transaction prices will usually have to be estimated, for example by the unweighted average of the prices at the beginning and at the end of the reporting period.

5.112. Transactions in investment fund shares or units include the value of net contributions to a fund.

(d) Financial derivatives and employee stock options

5.113. Secondary trade in options and closing out options prior to delivery involve financial transactions. If an option proceeds to delivery, it may be exercised or not exercised. In cases where the option is exercised, there may be a payment from the option writer to the option holder equal to the difference between the prevailing market price of the underlying asset and the strike price, or, alternatively, there may be the acquisition or sale of the underlying financial or non-financial asset recorded at the prevailing market price and a counterpart payment between the option holder and the option writer equal to the strike price. The difference between the prevailing market price of the underlying asset and the strike price is in both cases equal to the liquidation value of the option, which is the option price on the expiry date. In cases where the option is not exercised, no transaction takes place. However, the option writer makes a holding gain and the option holder makes a holding loss (in both cases equal to the premium paid when the contract was taken out) to be recorded in the revaluation account.

5.114. The transactions recorded for financial derivatives include any trading in the contracts as well as the net value of settlements made. There may also be the need to record transactions associated with the establishment of derivatives contracts. However, in many cases, the two parties will enter into a derivatives contract without any payment by one party to the other; in these cases the value of the transaction establishing the contract is nil and nothing is recorded in the financial account.

5.115. Any explicit commissions paid or received from brokers or intermediaries for arranging options, futures, swaps, and other derivatives contracts are treated as payments for services in the appropriate accounts. The parties to a swap are not considered to be providing a service to each other, but any payment to a third party for arranging the swap should be treated as payment for a service. Under a swap arrangement, where principal amounts are exchanged the corresponding flows are to be recorded as transactions in the underlying instrument; streams of other payments (excluding commissions) are to be recorded under *financial derivatives and employee stock options* (AF7). While the premium paid to the seller of an option can conceptually be considered to include a service charge, in practice it is usually not possible to distinguish the service element. Therefore, the full price is to be recorded as an acquisition of a financial asset by the buyer and as an incurrence of a liability by the seller.

5.116. Where contracts do not involve an exchange of principal, no transaction is recorded at inception. Implicitly, a financial derivative with zero initial value is created at that point. Subsequently, the value of a swap will be equal to:

(a) For principal amounts, the current market value of the difference between the expected future market values of the amounts to be re-exchanged and the amounts specified in the contract;

(b) For other payments, the current market value of the future streams specified in the contract.

5.117. Changes in the value of the financial derivative over time are recorded in the revaluation account.

5.118. Subsequent re-exchanges of principal will be governed by the terms and conditions of the swap contract and may imply financial assets being exchanged at a price different from the prevailing market price of such assets. The counterpart payment between the parties to the swap contract will be that specified in the contract. The difference between the market price and the contract price is then equal to the liquidation value of the asset/liability as it applies on the due date and should be recorded as a transaction in category *AF7* (financial derivatives and employee stock options). In total, transactions in financial derivatives and employee stock options must match the total revaluation gain or loss throughout the duration of the swap contract. This treatment is analogous to that set out with respect to options, which proceed to delivery.

5.119. For an institutional unit, a swap or a forward rate agreement is recorded under the item financial derivatives and employee stock options on the assets side where it has a NAV. Where the swap has a net liability value, it is also recorded on the assets side by convention to avoid flipping between the assets and the liabilities side. Accordingly, negative net payments increase the net value, and vice versa.

F. Revaluations

1. Different holding gains and losses concepts

5.120. The nominal holding gain on a non-financial asset is the value of the benefit accruing to the owner of that asset as a result of a change in its price over a period of time. The nominal holding gain on a financial asset is the increase in value of the asset, other than transactions in the assets (including the accrual of interest over a period of time) and other changes in the volume of assets. The nominal holding gain on a liability is the decrease in value of the liability, other than by transactions or by other volume changes. A nominal holding gain that is negative is referred to as a holding loss. A positive holding gain, whether due to an increase in the value of a given asset or a reduction in the value of a given liability, increases the net worth of the unit in question. Conversely, a holding loss reduces the net worth of the unit in question, whether due to a reduction in the value of a given asset or an increase in the value of a given liability.

5.121. As well as the absolute change in value of an asset, it is interesting to know how the change in value compares with a general measure of inflation. When the value of an asset rises over a given period of time by more than the general price level, the asset can be exchanged for a greater volume of the goods, services and assets covered by the general price index at the end of the period than at the beginning. The increase that preserves exactly the same volume of goods and services is called a neutral holding gain. A neutral holding gain (loss) over a period is the increase (decrease) in the value of an asset that would be required, in the absence of transactions and other changes in the volume of assets, to maintain command over the same amount of goods and services as at the beginning of the period.

5.122. The difference between the nominal holding gain or loss and the neutral holding gain or loss for the same asset over the same time period is called the real holding gain or loss. If the value of the asset increases faster than the neutral holding gain, then there is a real holding gain. If the value of the asset does not increase as fast as the overall increase in prices, or does not increase at all, the owner of the asset registers a real holding loss. A real holding gain (loss) is the amount by which the value of an asset increases (decreases) over the neutral holding gain for the period, in the absence of transactions and other changes in the volume of assets.

5.123. The balancing item in the revaluation account is described as changes in net worth due to nominal holding gains or losses. It is defined as the algebraic sum of the positive or negative nominal holding gains on all the assets and liabilities of an institutional unit. Just as nominal holding gains are decomposed into neutral and real holding gains, so changes in net worth due to nominal holding gains may be decomposed into changes in net worth due to neutral holding gains or losses and changes in net worth due to real holding gains or losses. The latter is an item of considerable analytic interest.

2. Revaluations as nominal holding gains or losses

5.124. Revaluations as nominal holding gains or losses accrue during an accounting period to the owners of assets and liabilities, reflecting changes in the level and structure of their prices.

5.125. Price increases mean positive revaluations or holding gains, while price falls mean negative revaluations or holding losses on the part of the holder. Revaluations also include changes in the prices of asset holdings in foreign currency due to exchange rate changes.

5.126. The nominal holding gains and losses recorded in the revaluation account are those accruing on assets or liabilities, whether realized or not. A holding gain is said to be realized when the asset in question is sold, redeemed, used or otherwise disposed of, or the liability repaid. An unrealized gain is one accruing on an asset that is still owned or a liability that is still outstanding at the end of the accounting period. A realized gain is usually understood as the gain realized over the entire period over which the asset is owned or liability is outstanding whether this period coincides with the accounting period or not. However, as holding gains and losses are recorded on an accrual basis in the 2008 SNA, the distinction between realized and unrealized gains and losses, although useful for some purposes, does not appear in the classifications and accounts.

5.127. Four different cases are distinguished (2008 SNA 12.81):

(a) An asset is held throughout the accounting period: the revaluation accruing during the accounting period is equal to the closing balance sheet value minus the opening balance sheet value, minus transactions due to accrued interest (if any) minus any other change in volume in the accounting period. These values are the estimated values of the assets as if they were acquired at the times the balance sheets are drawn up. The revaluation (holding gain or loss) is unrealized;

(b) An asset held at the beginning of the period is sold during the period: the revaluation accruing is equal to the value at disposal minus the opening balance sheet value, minus transactions due to accrued interest (if any) minus any other change in volume in the accounting period preceding the sale. The revaluation (holding gain or loss) is realized;

(c) An asset acquired during the period is still held at the end of the period: the revaluation accruing is equal to the closing balance sheet value minus the value at acquisition, minus transactions due to accrued interest (if any) minus any other change in volume in the accounting period after the acquisition. The revaluation (holding gain or loss) is unrealized;

(d) An asset is acquired and disposed of during the accounting period: the revaluation accruing is equal to the value at disposal minus the value at acquisition, minus transactions due to accrued interest (if any) minus any other change in volume in the accounting period between acquisition and disposal. The revaluation (holding gain or loss) is realized.

5.128. Compiling revaluations in cases (b) to (d) requires the collection of transaction data. Derived transactions usually allow only for the calculation of revaluations according to case (a).

3. Asset prices as accumulated revaluations

5.129. The approach to be followed is to derive asset prices as accumulated revaluations from an integrated system of accounts.

5.130. Asset prices of financial assets and liabilities may be derived as accumulated revaluations from the revaluation account. They are of interest for evaluating the effects of price changes on specific financial assets and liabilities.

5.131. Asset prices may cover not only the prices for debt securities or equity and investment fund shares, but also prices for residential and commercial property or land. Price movements may be observed either by monitoring the single prices of specific assets like shares or residential property, or an asset price index. To monitor single asset prices, share prices or residential property prices are used. Aggregate indexes of asset prices are constructed by weighting the index of each underlying asset by its share in the assets held by households or other resident sectors.

5.132. Holding gains and losses are observable for types of (non-financial and financial) assets and liabilities with variable current values like land or shares. For financial assets and liabilities with fixed current values for which both prices, p_t and p_{t-1}, are unity by definition, nominal holding gains are always zero. This relates to financial instruments like currency and deposits, loans and other accounts receivable/payable.

5.133. Asset price movements are to be derived by isolating the revaluation component from the balance sheets. Using the basic accounting identity which links the opening and the closing balance sheet, the value of the stock of a specific type of asset in the closing balance sheet, A_t, may be derived by adding to the value of the stock of a specific type of asset in the opening balance sheet, A_{t-1}, the transactions T_t, subtracting the consumption of fixed capital, D_t, adding other volume changes O_t and revaluations R_t (in period t):

$$A_t = A_{t-1} + T_t - D_t + O_t + R_t$$

However, if A_t is known, revaluations in the period t, R_t, are derived as:

$$R_t = A_t - A_{t-1} - T_t + D_t - O_t$$

Related to the stock of assets in t-1, as:

$$100 \times R_t / A_{t-1} = 100 \times (A_t - A_{t-1}) / A_{t-1} - 100 \times (T_t + O_t - D_t) / A_{t-1.}$$

G. Other changes in the volume of assets and liabilities

5.134. Other changes in the volume of assets and liabilities are changes in the quantity or physical characteristics of assets and liabilities, or changes in classification.[137]

5.135. Changes in the quantity or physical characteristics of assets and liabilities may arise as a result of:

(a) Accidental destruction owing to natural catastrophes or political events, or destruction of evidence of ownership;

(b) Losses for reasons (such as fire, damage or theft) that are not considered catastrophic;

(c) Uncompensated seizures that occur when governments or other institutional units take possession of the assets of other institutional units, including non-resident units, without full compensation, for reasons other than the payment of taxes, fines or similar levies; and

(d) Changes in financial claims resulting from write-offs. These are not financial transactions because there is no mutual agreement between the parties. Thus a creditor may decide that a financial claim can no longer be collected, for example because of the bankruptcy or liquidation of the debtor, and remove the claim from its balance sheet. The creditor's recognition that the claim is uncollectable is recorded as other changes in the volume of assets. The corresponding liability must also be removed from the balance sheet of the debtor to maintain balance in the accounts of the total economy.[138]

5.136. Changes in classification comprise changes in sector classification and in the structure of institutional units, and changes in the classification of assets:

(a) Reclassifications of institutional units from one sector to another or changes in the structure of institutional units give rise to a reallocation and may cause the appearance and disappearance of certain financial assets, which should be recorded as other changes in volume;

[137] Other changes in the volume of assets and liabilities may also include the amounts resulting from changes in estimation methods. When a change in estimation method cannot be applied to the whole period of data series due to the limited availability of source data, the break in the data series may be reflected in "other changes."

[138] Changes in financial claims resulting from write-downs that reflect the actual market values of tradable financial claims should be accounted for in the revaluation account.

(b) When a corporation no longer exists as an independent legal entity because it is absorbed by one or more other corporations, all the financial assets in the form of debt securities with regard the corporation(s) that absorbed it disappear from the system of national accounts. Financial assets in the form of debt securities that existed between the absorbed corporation and third parties remain unchanged and pass to the absorbing corporation(s);

(c) Similarly, when a corporation is legally split up into two or more institutional units, any new financial assets that may arise in the form of debt securities (appearance of financial assets) are recorded as other changes in volume.

5.137. Changes in the classification of assets, e.g. the conversion of debt securities into shares or vice versa are recorded as two financial transactions. Cancellations of debt instruments (loans or debt securities) by mutual agreement between the debtor and the creditor (debt cancellation or debt forgiveness) are recorded as transactions between the creditor and the debtor.

Box 5.5

Debt reorganization[a]

Debt reorganization (also referred to as debt restructuring) is defined as arrangements involving both the creditor and the debtor (and sometimes third parties) that alter the terms established for servicing an existing debt. Types of debt reorganization include debt forgiveness, rescheduling, refinancing, conversion, pre-payments and assumption.

Types of debt organization

The four main types of debt reorganization are as follows.

(a) *Debt forgiveness*: a reduction in the amount of, or the extinguishing of, a debt obligation by the creditor via a contractual arrangement with the debtor;

(b) *Debt rescheduling or refinancing* (or debt exchanges): a change in the terms and conditions of the amount owed, which may or may not result in a reduction of the burden in present-value terms. Included are transactions that change the type of debt instrument owed – for example, loan for bond swaps – but not debt-forgiveness transactions;

(c) *Debt conversion*, in which the creditor exchanges the debt claim for something of economic value, other than another debt claim, on the same debtor. This includes operations such as debt-for-equity swaps, debt-for-real-estate swaps, debt-for-nature swaps,[b] and debt prepayment or debt buy-backs for cash;

(d) *Debt assumption*, in which a new debtor assumes the former debtor's outstanding liability to the creditor and is liable for repayment of the debt. Debt assumption is a trilateral agreement between a creditor, a former debtor and a new debtor. The new debtor takes the place of the former one vis-à-vis the creditor, and is liable for repayment of the debt. After it has been assumed, the debt, which was originally a liability of the former debtor, becomes a liability of the new one. This happens notably when the new debtor guarantees the debt of the former debtor and when the guarantee is called. A special case refers to a debt assumption including a transfer of non-financial assets. An example is a debt assumption organized by government involving a transfer of fixed assets from the unit benefiting from the debt assumption – typically a public corporation managing public infrastructure (e.g. railways), public transportation, etc. – to the government entity taking over the debt. This might also involve other non-financial assets, such as land.

Other types of debt reorganization refer to debt cancellations, debt repudiations and debt write-offs:

(a) A *debt cancellation* is a bilateral agreement between a creditor and a debtor to cancel (or to "forgive") part or all of a liability outstanding, incurred by the debtor to the creditor. As a consequence of the debt cancellation, the liability of the debtor and the related asset of the creditor no longer exist;

[a] See also BPM6, appendix 2, on Debt reorganization and related transactions; Inter-Agency Task Force on Finance Statistics, draft *External Debt Statistics: Guide for Compilers and Users*, chap. 8, on debt reorganization; and Eurostat (2013), chap. VII, on debt-related transactions and guarantees.

[b] Some agreements described as debt swaps are equivalent to debt forgiveness, the creditor accepts a commitment from the debtor country to undertake a number of development, environmental and other expenses. These transactions should be considered under debt forgiveness, as counterpart funds are required by, but not provided to, the creditor.

(b) *Debt repudiation* is a unilateral cancellation of a liability by a debtor. It is unlikely to happen in the case of public corporations;

(c) There is a *debt write-off* when a creditor recognizes unilaterally that a claim can no longer be collected, mainly because of bankruptcy of the debtor. The creditor removes the claim from the assets side of his balance sheet.

Accounting treatment of debt assumptions and debt cancellations

The counterpart transaction of a debt assumption and a debt cancellation made by *mutual agreement* is a capital transfer.

Thus, when government assumes a debt of a public corporation or cancels a claim it has against a public corporation, the counterpart transaction of the financial transaction recorded in the financial account is a capital transfer, more precisely another capital transfer (D99), an expenditure which has a negative impact on the net lending/net borrowing (B9) of general government.

In many cases, general government initiates the debt assumption or debt cancellation. The acceptance of this action by the public corporation, and the fact that this corporation still exists afterwards, is interpreted as mutual agreement.

Debt assumptions and debt cancellations must be recorded when the liability is actually removed from the debtor's balance sheet, and the corresponding entries made in the government balance sheet.

Moreover, the recording of a debt assumption or a debt cancellation has to be made in one time: in particular, the successive repayment dates envisaged in the context of the former debt are not relevant.

The amount to be recorded – the capital transfer expenditure – is the full amount of the outstanding debt which is assumed or cancelled. In the special case of a debt assumption including a transfer of non-financial assets, a capital transfer is recorded at the same time equal to the value of the non-financial assets transferred.

There are three exceptions to the mutual agreement treatment. In these cases, the debt assumption or the debt cancellation has no impact on government net lending/net borrowing:

(a) *Debt of quasi-corporations*

If the public enterprise is a profitable quasi-corporation, an assumption or cancellation by the general government of debts of this quasi-corporation does not give rise to the recording of a capital transfer. The counterpart transaction has to be recorded as a financial transaction (transaction in equity).

However, this is only relevant to the extent that the public quasi-corporation is not making losses requiring permanent government support. In the latter case, the general rule would apply to record the debt assumption or cancellation with a capital transfer.

(b) *Operations preceding the privatization of a public corporation*

When government cancels or assumes debts from a public corporation "as part of an ongoing process of privatization to be achieved in a short-term perspective", the counterpart transaction is not a capital transfer, but a transaction in equity. Privatization means giving up control over that public corporation by the disposal of shares and other equity.

This rule should only be applied when there is enough certainty that the privatization will occur in the short term (less than one year). In any case, the existence of a privatization plan is not in itself sufficient for considering the debt assumption/cancellation "as part of an ongoing process of privatization to be achieved in a short-term perspective".

Moreover, the flow of debt assumed or cancelled is to be recorded as a financial transaction up to the limit of the privatization proceeds. Amounts assumed or cancelled by government in excess of this limit are to be recorded according to the general rule, as a capital transfer expenditure of government.

(c) *Debt write-offs*

The only case liable to give rise to a write-off by general government of claims against a public corporation is when the cancellation of the claim is preceded by the liquidation of the corporation. The liquidation should be assessed from an economic point of view, i.e. even if the corporation legally continues to exist, it should be considered as liquidated if it has lost its financial substance and its main economic function. The write-off of bad debt is recorded as an other change in the volume of financial assets.

H. Accrued interest

5.138. Interest is a form of investment income that is receivable by the owners of certain kinds of financial assets, namely deposits, debt securities, loans, and other accounts receivable for putting the financial assets at the disposal of another institutional unit. Income on SDR holdings and SDR allocation is also included in interest. Not all financial flows associated with financial assets are interest. Some of the flows may be commissions or fees, which are charges for services and classified as financial services.

1. Recording of accrued interest

5.139. Interest is recorded on an accrual basis, i.e. interest is recorded as accruing continuously over time to the creditor on the amount of principal outstanding. Under the accrual basis, as interest accrues, the principal outstanding increases, that is, accrued interest is a part of the principal amount. What are commonly referred to as interest payments, therefore, are financial account transactions that reduce the debtor's existing liability. No entry is made in the accounts for interest not yet accrued.

Box 5.6
Arrears

Under the accrual basis of recording, *debt arrears* or *arrears* (both interest accrued and principal) arise when amounts are "past due" for payment and are unpaid. They occur when a debtor misses an interest or principal payment. The debt instrument will not normally change and debt arrears remain in the outstanding amount of the debt instrument for which payments have been missed until the liability is extinguished.

If the original contract provides for a change in the characteristics of a financial instrument when it goes into arrears, this change should be recorded as a reclassification in the other changes in the volume of assets account.

Knowing the amount of arrears can provide important information. Information on arrears is vital when assessing the liquidity or solvency of a corporation or a government unit. When feasible and important, therefore, each category of debt should be divided into those instruments that are in arrears and those not in arrears.

According to the accrual basis, repayments of debts are recorded when they are extinguished (such as when they are paid, or rescheduled or forgiven by the creditor). When arrears occur, no transactions should be imputed, but the arrears should continue to be shown in the same instrument until the liability is extinguished, and not as "other accounts receivable/payable".

In addition, the total amount of debt in arrears should be indicated as a memorandum item in the balance sheet.

If the contract provides for a change in the characteristics of a financial instrument when it goes into arrears, this change should be recorded as a reclassification in the other changes in the financial assets and liabilities account. The reclassification applies to situations where the original contract remains, but the terms within it change (for example, interest rates or repayment periods). If the contract is renegotiated or the nature of the instrument changes from one instrument category to another (for example, from bonds to equity), the consequences are to be recorded as new transactions.

Arrears can arise not only when scheduled payments on existing debt instruments are missed, but also in some cases when new liabilities are incurred. If contractually agreed payments on items such as compensation of employees, social contributions, use of goods and services, and social benefits are not made when due, a new liability (other accounts payable) should be recognized, and would be considered to be in arrears from the start.

Recording under a cash basis means that arrears are not usually recorded when they are incurred because they do not involve cash flows at the time. However, when arrears are paid, at a later date, they do involve a cash flow and are recorded at that time. In addition, arrears may not be paid but formally recognized at a certain point in time as a fixed-term contractual liability, which should also be recorded. This often applies in the case of arrears related to overdue contractual obligations other than overdue liabilities. In summary, arrears can be paid in cash or by issuing a liability in exchange, and the payment may be related to overdue liabilities or other overdue obligations. In all cases, the payment of arrears should be recorded under a cash basis.

5.140. Interest accrued on a financial instrument is the amount that the debtor becomes liable to pay over a given period of time without reducing the principal outstanding.[139] Interest accrued is income and also a financial transaction to the extent that the interest is accrued but not yet paid (as if the accrued interest were promptly reinvested in the debt). This transaction is reversed (giving rise to a repayment of debt) when interest accrued is actually paid.

2. Accrued interest by type of financial asset

(a) Deposits, loans and accounts receivable/payable

5.141. Interest receivable and payable on deposits, loans and accounts receivable/payable is determined by applying the relevant interest rate to the principal outstanding at each point of time throughout the accounting period. Most of these financial instruments have a fixed interest rate for the entire life of the instrument; some may have terms for changes in interest rates. For each period, the relevant interest rate should be used to calculate the interest accrued in that period.

5.142. Interest on deposits and loans receivable from and payable to financial institutions include an adjustment for a margin that represents an implicit payment for the services provided by the financial institutions in granting loans and accepting deposits.

5.143. Therefore, it is appropriate to divide the actual payment or receipt of interest into the service part and into the national accounts concept of interest, called *SNA interest*. The actual payments or receipts to or from financial institutions, described as *bank interest*, need to be partitioned so that SNA interest and the service charges may be recorded in the SNA separately.

5.144. The amounts of SNA interest paid by borrowers to financial institutions are less than bank interest by the estimated values of the charges payable, while the amounts of SNA interest receivable by depositors are higher than bank interest by the amount of the service charge payable. The values of the charges are recorded as sales of services in the production accounts of financial institutions and as uses in the accounts of their customers.

Worked example 5.2. Recording of accrued interest on loans

5.145. This worked example demonstrates the recording of interest accrued on different types of loans, including loans with step-up interest rates, loans with a zero interest rate and loans where interest payments are contractually deferred.

5.146. First, the worked example presents the relevant methodological principles on the recording of interest on loans in the 2008 SNA. Second, it discusses the application of the methodological principles to a number of specific cases: (a) loans with a fixed interest rate over the lifetime of the loan; (b) loans with a step-up interest rate; (c) loans with a step-up interest rate, with one of the steps being zero; and (d) loans with a deferred payment of the interest accrued.

[139] For example, a fixed interest rate bond is issued at CU 100 and pays annual fixed coupons of CU 10 during its life. Interest of CU 10 accrues, even though no coupon is actually paid. (Interest accrues up to the moment the coupon is paid, increasing the liability of the issuer. At that moment the amount due decreases.) The interest is considered as being reinvested in the bond, increasing the nominal value of the bond from CU 100 to CU 110. The coupon paid by the debtor at the end of each year is a (partial) redemption of the bond, reducing its nominal value from CU 110 to CU 100.

Methodological principles

5.147. Loans are financial assets that: (a) are created when a creditor lends funds directly to a debtor; and (b) are evidenced by a document that is not negotiable. Loans are recorded in the system of national accounts at their nominal value, that is, the outstanding amount the debtor owes to the creditor, comprising the outstanding principal amount and any accrued interest.

5.148. Interest is recorded as accruing on a continuous basis, as the financial resources (e.g. loans) are provided for use on a continuous basis. The interest accruing is recorded as a financial transaction. It represents an additional acquisition of the financial asset by the creditor and an equal incurrence of a liability by the debtor. The repayment of debt (principal amount including any accrued interest) is recorded when it is extinguished, that is, when it is paid, rescheduled or forgiven by the creditor.

5.149. To ensure a consistent and symmetric recording of accrued interest in the SNA for loans (and non-traded debt instruments), it is necessary to accrue interest using the rate(s) of interest (or sum of money) as specified in the loan contract for each individual accounting period during the lifetime of the instrument. This statistical recording shows, on a continuous basis, the actual debt that the debtor owes to the creditor. Additionally, it ensures an identical recording of accrued interest for financially and economically equivalent loan structures.

Four loans with different features

5.150. Table 5.10 shows the characteristics of four loans with a maturity of five years, a principal amount of 100 to be repaid at maturity, and an internal rate of return of 5 per cent. The loans differ with regard to the interest rates agreed for each year. Interest accrued during a year is to be paid at the end of that year.

5.151. Example 1 as described in table 5.10 shows a loan with a fixed interest rate and example 2 a loan with a step-up interest rate. Example 3 is a variant of example 2 in that the first step of the loan is a zero interest rate. A period with a zero interest rate is sometimes referred to as a *grace period* or an *interest holiday*. However, the loan contract in example 3 is specified in such a way that if the loan is redeemed during the period when the zero interest rate applies, only the principal has to be reimbursed. Example 4 is different from the other examples, as interest accrued in the first two years is paid in year 3 together with the interest accrued during year 3. In the case of an early redemption in the first two years, not only the principal but also the interest accrued but not yet paid would have to be redeemed.

Table 5.10
Four loans with different features

	Example 1	Example 2	Example 3	Example 4
	Fixed interest rate	*Step-up interest rate*	*Step-up interest rate with no interest charged in the first two years*	*Fixed interest rate with interest of the first two years paid in the third year*
Maturity (years)	5	5	5	5
Principal	100.0	100.0	100.0	100.0
Interest rate (percentage): Year 1	5.0	0.5	0 (no interest charged)	5.0 (paid in year 3)
Year 2	5.0	2.0	0 (no interest charged)	5.0 (paid in year 3)
Year 3	5.0	6.0	6.1	5.0
Year 4	5.0	7.7	8.5	5.0
Year 5	5.0	10.0	12.0	5.0
Internal rate of return (IRR)	5.0	5.0	5.0	5.0

5.152. The examples do not include an adjustment for a margin representing an implicit payment for the services provided by financial institutions (FISIM). They are shown from the debtor's perspective.

Example 1: Fixed interest rate

5.153. This is one of the most common types of loan contract. In the first year the principal amount is provided to the debtor, recorded as a transaction in loans (F4). In the same period, interest accrues at a rate of 5 per cent recorded as an interest-payable transaction (D41) and the corresponding increase of the outstanding debt is recorded in AF4 (interest accrued). Because the interest accrued is paid at the end of the year, the outstanding debt is decreased by a loan transaction (F4 – interest paid). At the end of the first year the loan closing balance (AF4) liabilities shows the same value as the principal amount (100).

		Loans (AF4)					
Year	Cash flows	Total	Principal	Interest accrued	Interest paid	Loans (AF4) (closing balance)	Interest payable (D41) (accrual basis)
1	95.0	100.0	100.0	5.0	-5.0	100.0	5.0
2	-5.0	0	0	5.0	-5.0	100.0	5.0
3	-5.0	0	0	5.0	-5.0	100.0	5.0
4	-5.0	0	0	5.0	-5.0	100.0	5.0
5	-105.0	-100.0	-100.0	5.0	-5.0	0	5.0

The same logic applies for the other years. At maturity the principal amount is repaid together with the interest accrued in that year.

Example 2: Step-up interest rate

This case implies a recording of different amounts of interest. However, the same mechanism applies as described for example 1.

		Loans (AF4)					
Year	Cash flows	Total	Principal	Interest accrued	Interest paid	Loans (AF4) (closing balance)	Interest payable (D41) (accrual basis)
1	99.5	100.0	100.0	0.5	-0.5	100.0	0.5
2	-2.0	0	0	2.0	-2.0	100.0	2.0
3	-6.0	0	0	6.0	-6.0	100.0	6.0
4	-7.7	0	0	7.7	-7.7	100.0	7.7
5	-110.0	-100.0	-100.0	10.0	-10.0	0	10.0

Example 3: Step-up interest rate (with one of the steps being zero)

5.154. This case shows a loan with step-up interest rates but where the interest rate is zero during the first two years. The recording is similar to that described in example 2, except that the accrued interest amounts to zero as a consequence of the zero interest rate during the first two years.[140]

		Loans (AF4)					
Year	Cash flows	Total	Principal	Interest accrued	Interest paid	Loans (AF4) (closing balance)	Interest payable (D41) (accrual basis)
1	100.0	100.0	100.0	0	0	100.0	0
2	0	0	0	0	0	100.0	0
3	-6.1	0	0	6.1	-6.1	100.0	6.1
4	-8.5	0	0	8.5	-8.5	100.0	8.5
5	-112.0	-100.0	-100.0	12.0	-12.0	0	12.0

140 No interest should be accrued during the grace period unless specific conditions occur. IMF (2003), para. 2.88; and Eurostat (2013).

Example 4: Postponement of the payment of accrued interest

5.155. The fourth example shows a loan on which the accrued interest in the first two years is paid together with the interest accrued in the third year, that is, the payment of interest is postponed or deferred. Transactions in interest payable (D41) are recorded each year and added to the outstanding debt to be repaid (F4 – interest accrued). As interest is not paid in the first two years the closing balance of loans (AF4) increases. Since accrued interest is calculated on the increasing debt, the interest accrued in year 2 and year 3 is higher than in year 1. In the third year the accumulated compound interest is fully paid and the outstanding debt returns to its principal value of 100. The accounting treatment during the remaining years is the same as in example 1.

Year	Cash flows	Loans (AF4)				Loans (AF4) (closing balance)	Interest payable (D41) (accrual basis)
		Total	Principal	Interest accrued	Interest paid		
1	+100.0	+105.0	+100.0	+5.0	0	+105.0	+5.0
2	0.0	+5.3	0	+5.3	0	+110.3	+5.3
3	-15.8	-10.3	00	+5.5	-15.8	+100.0	+5.5
4	-5.0	0	0	+5.0	-5.0	+100.0	+5.0
5	-105.0	-100.0	-100.0	+5.0	-5.0	0	+5.0

Fees on security lending and gold loans

5.156. Securities and monetary gold are financial instruments and the fees for securities lending without cash collateral and gold loans reflect a payment for putting a financial instrument at the disposal of another institutional unit. Fees associated with securities lending (equity securities as well as debt securities) and gold loans are treated as interest. As a simplifying convention, fees paid on loans of non-monetary gold are also treated as interest.

5.157. Although in some circumstances the fee for securities lending is payable to the custodian in the first instance (and used to defray custodial charges in whole or in part), in principle, all of the fee is payable to the owner of the security who, in turn, is deemed to pay part or all of it to the custodian in a separate transaction (representing a fee for custodial services).

Accrual of interest on impaired debt

5.158. The outstanding principal remains a legal liability of the debtor, so interest should continue to accrue unless the liability has been extinguished (for example, by repayment or as a result of a bilateral arrangement between debtor and creditor). However, for some analysis, it may be more useful to exclude, from primary income measures, interest that is not realistically expected to be paid. It would therefore be useful if the creditor provided supplementary information on accrued interest on impaired debt when it is significant and quantifiable. It is important that metadata provide information on the method adopted for defining impaired debt.

5.159. Following the accrual principle, arrears on coupons or principal repayments that are not paid on the due dates should continue to be shown in the same instrument until the liability is extinguished. For arrears arising from a debt contract, interest should accrue at the same interest rate as on the original debt, unless a different interest rate for arrears was stipulated in the original debt contract, in which case this stipulated interest rate should be used. The stipulated rate may include a penalty rate in addition to the interest rate on the original debt. If the terms and characteristics of the financial instrument automatically change when it goes into arrears, or if the classification of the loan is changed, the change should be recorded as a reclassification in the other changes in financial assets and liabilities account (see also box 5.5). If the contract is renegotiated, transactions are recorded as if a new instrument is created. If an item is purchased on credit and the debtor fails to pay within the period stated at the time the purchase was made, any extra charges incurred should be regarded as interest and accrue until the debt is extinguished.

5.160. When a one-off guarantee covering a debt that becomes impaired is activated, the guarantor assumes the liability for that debt. From the time of activation of the debt, the accrued interest becomes the liability of the guarantor. A guarantor may make payments for interest that is due on loans or other interest-bearing liabilities of other units for which it acts as the guarantor. If the guarantor has not assumed the debt, the interest that accrues is a liability of the original debtor and payments by guarantor should be classified on the basis of contractual arrangements between the guarantor and the original debtor. In most cases, such payments establish a claim by the guarantor on the original debtor, who is obliged to service the debt. In other cases, the claim on the debtor may be an increase in the existing equity participation (i.e. the activation of a guarantee made by a parent company for debt of its subsidiary will improve the balance sheet of the subsidiary and hence the parent company's equity in it). If the guarantor does not obtain a claim on the original debtor, a capital transfer from the guarantor to the debtor is recorded, particularly when the guarantor is a government unit.

Interest excluding implicitly charged financial services on deposits and loans

5.161. The rates of interest offered by financial intermediaries to their depositors are usually lower than the rates they charge to borrowers. The resulting interest margins are used by financial intermediaries to defray their expenses and to provide an operating surplus. This method of operation is an alternative to charging customers directly for services. The treatment of this margin (FISIM) and its measurement are described in chapter 3.

5.162. The calculation of FISIM is limited by convention to financial corporations and to loans and deposits. No FISIM is recorded as receivable for non-financial corporations. FISIM is a charge for services and is recorded together with explicit charges for financial services. The primary income account records *pure interest* by eliminating the implicit service charges made by financial intermediaries. *Actual interest* payable to a financial intermediary includes the service charge, which should be subtracted to give the interest as investment income.

5.163. Similarly, actual interest receivable from a financial intermediary is seen as having had a service charge already deducted, so the actual interest receivable from the financial intermediary will be increased by the value of the service received to provide interest as investment income. The pure interest is calculated using a reference interest rate that represents the pure cost of borrowing. The concept of reference interest rate and its application are described in paragraph 3.33. Actual interest charged or received by banks is useful for certain analytical purposes (such as debt sustainability analysis) and should be disseminated as a memorandum item.

5.164. Lending own funds generates a financial service and may include a service charge, despite not being financial intermediation activity. Incorporated moneylenders that provide financial services predominantly with own funds are considered financial corporations, and thus generate implicitly charged financial services. The service charge for moneylenders can be calculated as the difference between the interest rate payable by a borrower and the reference rate times the amount of the loan. Unincorporated enterprises which provide loans to a range of clients other than just family and friends as a principal activity and take on the financial risk of the debtor defaulting also generate implicitly charged financial services.

5.165. High inflation gives rise to specific issues in measuring and interpreting interest. An obvious example is that interest rates for domestic currency denominated instruments could be significantly higher than those for foreign currency denominated instruments. Thus, nominal interest for domestic currency denominated instruments includes compensation for the loss of purchasing power on the monetary value of the principal. However, conditions of high inflation have an impact on accounting that is not merely limited to the measurement of interest. Indeed the whole concept of the measurement of transactions on a current price basis is called into question when prices at the end of the period are several times greater than those at the start of the period. Annex B to chapter XIX of the 2008 SNA provides guidance on compiling and presenting data in conditions of inflation, covering the goods and services account, the income and the financial accounts, and the balance sheet.

(b) Debt securities

Defining and measuring interest for debt securities

5.166. Defining and measuring interest for traded debt securities is not straightforward. While debtors have obligations to settle according to the terms and conditions set at the inception of the debt instruments, holders of securities acquired in the secondary markets may not know or even care about the interest rate at the time of issue. There are three approaches for defining and measuring interest for traded debt instruments (BPM6 11.52):

(a) Interest is equal to the amounts the debtors will have to pay to their creditors over and above the repayment of the initial principal. Interest accrual on a debt instrument is determined for the entire life of the instrument by the conditions set at its inception. Interest accrual is determined using the original yield-to-maturity. A single effective yield, established at the time of security issuance, is used to calculate the amount of accrued interest in each period to maturity. This approach is also known as the *debtor approach*;

(b) Interest is the income that follows from applying, at any point in time, the discount rate of future receivables implicit in the instrument's market value. The accrual of interest under this approach reflects current market conditions and expectations. Interest accrual at any given time is determined using the current yield-to-maturity. The effective interest rate for calculating the accrued interest varies with period-to-period changes in the market price of the securities. This approach is also known as the *creditor approach*;

(c) Interest is the income that follows from applying the discount rate implicit in the cost at which the instrument was acquired. The accrual of interest under this approach reflects market conditions and expectations at the time of acquisition. Interest is determined using the remaining yield-to-maturity at the time the debt instrument is acquired. The effective interest rate will change only if the security is resold in the secondary market. This approach is also known as the *acquisition approach*.

The debtor approach and the creditor approach

5.167. The question of how to record accrued interest on debt securities depends on which method of accrual is used: the debtor approach or the creditor approach.[141] It reflects a long-standing inconsistency in business accounting. Book value financial accounting and reporting follow the approach that debtors should report interest due and

[141] They are also characterized as on a *historical/contractual* basis and on a *prevailing market rate* basis.

accrued on their outstanding debt. However, asset holders do not record interest alone under revenues from debt securities. Rather, they use a net yield concept that comprises interest due and accrued, including or excluding the current period amortization of the acquisition cost of the debt security asset(s). This means that across the institutional sectors of an economy, interest payments and receipts are not equal.

5.168. Institutional sector accounts based on international statistical standards address this inconsistency. As a first step, debt securities should be valued at market prices and, as a second step, accrued interest can be measured using either the debtor or the creditor approach.

5.169. In international statistical standards, including the 2008 SNA and the BPM6, interest is recorded following the debtor approach described above according to which accrued interest (and other flows, such as revaluations) is defined from the perspective of the issuer of debt securities. Interest calculated according to the market rates may be reported as a supplementary item, which is particularly important for analysing rates of return.

5.170. The rationale for using the debtor approach is that the debtor, the issuer of the security, is not liable to make the payment until the security matures and from his perspective it is appropriate to treat the total amount of interest as accruing steadily over the life of the security.

5.171. It should be noted that for debt securities the valuation and recording of transactions in the financial account and positions in the balance sheets do not depend on the method used for the calculation and recording of accrued interest. Acquisitions and disposals of debt securities are recorded at transaction prices and the positions are recorded at market prices or fair values.

5.172. Under the debtor approach, when debt securities are issued at a fixed rate, the rate of interest payable, and accruing, is fixed at the time the debt security is issued. That is to say, if the debtor issues a debt security for 100 with an original maturity of 10 years, at a fixed rate of 10 per cent, with interest payable annually, the interest payments each year are 10 for the next 10 years. The argument for this approach is that because the rate has been fixed contractually, the payment does not change when the market interest rate changes. The debt securities are issued at a fixed rate precisely because the borrower decided to finance his requirements this way, with the borrowing costs known over the life of the debt instrument. If the debtor had preferred to borrow at rates that changed with market rates, the borrowing would have been undertaken at a variable interest rate.

5.173. Under the creditor approach, the prevailing market rate during the period is used to determine the interest paid on a debt security. The argument put forward for this approach is that the rate of interest on a debt security is not fixed, but fluctuates with market conditions: as interest rates in the market change, the price of, and hence the return on, the debt security changes. There is no fixed rate of interest, since the rate is based on the observable rate of interest prevailing on the market during the period. As interest flows apply to a period of time and interest rates change almost constantly, the average of the prevailing rate applicable to the debt security over the period is used.

5.174. There are no differences between the two approaches if the value of the debt security remains unchanged throughout its life. However, as the market values of debt securities do in practice vary during their life, and as they are usually bought and sold on secondary markets, the recording of revaluations and also of realized holding gains and losses in accordance with the debtor approach deviate from the corresponding recording following the creditor approach, as illustrated in worked example 5.3.

5.175. The ability to compile accurate accounts on either the debtor or creditor basis hinges on the availability of security-by-security databases.

Worked example 5.3. The debtor approach and the creditor approach to recording accrued interest

5.176. Suppose a zero-coupon bond is issued on 1 January of year 1. The bond matures on 31 December of year 3 with a redemption value of 100. The discount (interest) rate at the time of issuance is 10 per cent. Therefore, the value of the bond at issuance is 75.13. The market interest rate remains at 10 per cent until 1 January of year 2, when it moves to 15 per cent. The change in the interest rate causes the price of the bond to fall from 82.64 (=100/1.102) to 75.61 (=100/1.152). The market interest rate then remains unchanged until the bond matures.

5.177. Table 5.11 shows the developments in the nominal value, the accrued interest due to discount, the market value and the revaluations arising from market price changes during the life of the zero-coupon bond. It also shows the accounting entries to be made in the debtor's accounts (income, financial and revaluation account and balance sheet). The creditor would record corresponding entries, but on opposite sides of the accounts.

5.178. As there is no change in the market interest rate in year 1, the same accounting entries are recorded under both the debtor approach and the creditor approach.

5.179. Under the debtor approach, interest accrues continuously, in the amount of 7.51 in year 1, 8.26 in year 2, despite the increase in the interest rate at the beginning of the year, and 9.09 in year 3. Revaluation is derived residually to ensure that the flows are equal to the changes in stocks (11.35–8.26=3.09, in year 2 and 13.04–9.09=3.95, in year 3).

Table 5.11
Debtor approach and creditor approach to recording accrued interest. Stocks and flows during the life of a zero-coupon bond

	Start year 1	End-year 1	Start year 2	End-year 2	End-year 3	Total
Characteristics of the zero-coupon bond						
Nominal value without accrued interest	75.13	75.13	75.13	75.13	75.13	
+ Accrued interest due to discount		7.51	7.51	7.51	7.51	
				+8.26	8.26	
				15.77	9.09	
					24.86	24.86
= Nominal value	75.13	82.64	82.64	90.91	100.00	
+ Revaluations arising from market price changes			-7.03	-3.95	0.00	
= Market value	75.13	82.64	75.61	86.96	100.00	
Debtor approach						
Interest payable		7.51	7.51	7.51	7.51	
				+8.26	8.26	
				15.77	9.09	
					24.86	24.86
Revaluation on liabilities in debt securities			-7.03	3.09	3.95	
Liabilities in debt securities	75.13	82.64	75.61	86.96	100	
Creditor approach						
Interest payable		7.51	7.51	7.51	7.51	
				11.34	11.34	
				18.85	13.04	
					31.89	31.89
Revaluation on liabilities in debt securities			-7.03	0	0.00	
Liabilities in debt securities	75.13	82.64	75.61	86.96	100	

5.180. Under the creditor approach, the rise in the market interest rate at the beginning of year 2 is fully reflected in the revaluation (the market value changes from 82.64 to 75.61 (=–7.03)) while interest accrues in the amount of 11.34 in year 2 (–75.61×0.15). As there is no change in the market value in year 3, no revaluation is recorded, while interest of 13.04 (86.96×0.15) accrues.

5.181. For a bond issued at a discount or a premium, the difference between the redemption price and the issue price constitutes interest that accrues period-by-period over the life of the bond, in the same way as for a bill.

5.182. Interest on bills and similar debt securities is measured by the discount on the bill, that is, the difference between the sum paid to the holder of the bill when it matures and the amount received at the time of issue.

5.183. Zero-coupon bonds do not entitle their holders to any income during the life of the security, but only to receive a stated fixed sum as repayment of principal on a specified date or dates. When zero-coupon bonds are issued, they are sold at a price that is lower than the price at which they are redeemed at maturity, reflecting the interest cost over the lifetime of the bond. The difference between the redemption value and the issue price of a zero-coupon bond represents interest accruing continuously over the life of the security until its maturity.

5.184. In line with the BPM6, it is recommended to classify all index-linked debt securities (except those linked to a foreign currency) as variable interest rate debt securities. A debt security is classified as a variable interest rate debt security if the indexation applies to both the principal and coupons.

Compiling accrued interest for debt securities as liabilities

5.185. The following section describes the compilation of accrued interest for different types of debt securities. For the purpose of defining and measuring interest, it is useful to distinguish between various categories of arrangements.

a. *Debt securities with known cash flows*

5.186. For debt securities for which the issue and redemption prices are the same (i.e. issued at par), total interest accruals over the whole life of the securities are given by the periodic coupon payments. If coupons are fixed, accrued interest can be calculated by allocating the coupon to the relevant period using daily compound formula.

5.187. Certain debt securities, like short-term bills of exchange and zero-coupon bonds, are such that the debtor is under no obligation to make any payments to the creditor until the liability matures. In effect, the debtor's liability is discharged by a single payment covering both the amount of the funds originally borrowed and the interest accrued and accumulated over the entire life of the liability. Instruments of this type are said to be discounted because the amount initially borrowed is less than the amount to be repaid. The difference between the amount to be repaid at the end of the contract and the amount originally borrowed is interest that must be allocated over the accounting periods between the beginning and end of the contract. The interest accruing in each period is recorded in the primary income account with the same amount increasing the debtor's liability for the same instrument in the financial account.

5.188. A slightly more complicated case consists of a discounted instrument that also requires periodic coupon payments. In such cases, the interest accrual is the amount of the income payable periodically plus the amount of interest accruing in each period attributable to the difference between the redemption price and the issue price. Interest accrual from the amortization of the discount (the difference between the issue and redemption prices) can be calculated by summing daily amortizations for the reporting period. Although amortization rates could be calculated on monthly or quarterly bases, amortization at a daily rate facilitates the allocation of the discount amortization to the individual reporting periods.

5.189. In some cases, debt securities are issued at a premium rather than a discount. The method of determining the interest accrual is identical to the case of a discounted instrument except that the premium (the difference between the redemption price and the issue price) is treated as negative interest accrual.

5.190. Stripped securities (separate trading of registered interest and principal securities) raise special issues for the accrual of interest. A third party without the authorization of the original issuer issues unofficial "strips" and, hence, the stripped securities are new instruments – a liability of the strip issuer. The original debt securities continue to accrue interest according to the terms specified in the contract. Interest on stripped securities accrues at the rate determined at the time of issuance of the strips. Official strips (issued with the authorization of the original issuer through a strip dealer it appoints) simply change the arrangements for holding the original instrument, and thus the strips remain the direct obligation of the original issuer. Interest on official strips, therefore, accrues at the rate on the underlying security, but not the rate prevailing at the time of stripping.

5.191. At inception, the contracting parties determine all future cash flows that the debtor must make in domestic currency. Interest for these instruments is the difference between the sum of all the debtor's payments and the principal the creditor makes available to the debtor. The information on principal outstanding and interest rates needed to calculate interest accruals is known at inception.

5.192. Three examples are described in this context, namely: (a) a fixed interest rate bond issued at par; (b) a fixed interest rate bond issued below par; and (c) a zero-coupon bond (see also worked example 5.1).

i. A fixed interest rate bond issued at par

5.193. A fixed interest rate bond issued at par (1,000) at the beginning of the first year is repayable at maturity in five years and pays fixed coupons of 100 at the end of each year of its life.

5.194. Interest accrues on the bond throughout the year and is recorded as being reinvested in the bond, increasing its nominal value from 1,000 to 1,100 at the end of the year, before the coupon is paid. Coupon payments on the existing fixed interest rate bond will not change, although the current market interest rate may change.

5.195. At issue, the nominal value and the market value are both equal to 1,000. At the end of each year, interest of 100 has accrued and is paid by the bond issuer to the bondholder. The coupon payment of 100 by the debtor at the end of the year is treated as a (partial) redemption of the bond, reducing its nominal value from 1,100 to 1,000

Table 5.12
A fixed interest rate bond issued at par

Issue price: 1,000; annual coupon payments: 100; original maturity: five years; redemption price: 1,000
Stocks and flows during the life of the bond

	Start year 1	End year 1	End year 2	End year 3	End year 4	End year 5
Nominal value at year-end						
before coupon payment	1,000.0	1,100.0	1,100.0	1,100.0	1,100.0	1,100.0
after coupon payment		1,000.0	1,000.0	1,000.0	1,000.0	1,000.0
Accrued interest		100.0	100.0	100.0	100.0	100.0
Coupon payment		-100.0	-100.0	-100.0	-100.0	-100.0

ii. A fixed interest rate bond issued below par

5.196. In this second example, a five-year fixed interest rate bond repayable at maturity is issued at a discount (below par, at 900) and pays annual fixed coupons of 73.6 during its life, which, because of the discount, corresponds to a 10 per cent rate of interest. The bond annually accrues two types of interest: (a) a coupon of 73.6; and (b) an annual discount, which is calculated as 19.2 for the first year.

5.197. At the end of the first year, interest of 92.8 has accrued, but only 73.6 of this accrued interest is paid to the bondholder. This reduces the principal amount outstanding, in nominal value terms, from 992.8 to 919.2. The accrued discount of 100 is only paid at the end of the fifth year as part of the redemption price.

iii. A zero-coupon bond

5.198. In the third example, a zero-coupon bond is issued which, by definition, pays no coupons during its life. The bond has a redemption price of 1,000 and an issue price of 620.9. The only transactions to be recorded for this kind of bond, after its issuance, are the accruals of the discount throughout its life and the payment of the principal at maturity. Changes in market interest rates will affect the bond's market value in the same direction as in the previous two cases, but with amplified effects owing to the longer duration of the bond. At the end of the life of the bond, a transaction of 1,000 is recorded, corresponding to the repayment of 620.9 of principal and the payment of 379.1 of accrued interest.

b. *Foreign currency denominated fixed-rate instruments*

5.199. At inception, future cash flows are determined in the relevant foreign currency. The recording of interest on foreign currency fixed-rate instruments is also straightforward. Interest is defined according to the formula described in (a) above, with the only difference being that, in the first instance, a foreign currency is used as the unit of account.

Table 5.13
A fixed interest rate bond issued at discount

Issue price: 900; annual coupon payments: 73.6; discount payment at redemption; original maturity: five years; redemption price: 1,000
Stocks and flows during the life of the bond

	Start year 1	End year 1	End year 2	End year 3	End year 4	End year 5
Nominal value at year-end						
before coupon payment	900.0	992.8	1,012.4	1,032.4	1,052.8	1,073.6
after coupon payment		916.3	934.3	954.2	976.0	1,000.0
Accrued interest						
due to coupon		73.6	73.6	73.6	73.6	73.6
due to discount		19.2	38.7	58.7	79.1	100.0
Coupon payment		-73.6	-73.6	-73.6	-73.6	-73.6

Table 5.14
A zero-coupon bond

Issue price: 620.9; implicit rate of return: 10 per cent per annum; original maturity: five years; redemption price: 1,000
Stocks and flows during the life of the bond

	Start year 1	End year 1	End year 2	End year 3	End year 4	End year 5
Nominal value	620.9	683.0	751.3	826.4	909.1	1,000.0
Accrued interest due to discount		62.1	130.4	205.5	288.2	379.1

5.200. Interest expressed in foreign currency is to be converted into the domestic currency units at the midpoint market exchange rate for the periods in which the interest accrues. The information on principal outstanding and interest rates needed to calculate interest accruals in the currency of denomination is known at inception. Debt instruments with both principal and coupons linked to a foreign currency are treated as though they were denominated in that foreign currency.

c. *Index-linked instruments*

5.201. An indexation mechanism links the coupon and/or principal payments to indicators agreed by the parties. The values of the indicators are not known in advance. For debt securities with indexation of principal, they may be known only at the time of redemption. As a result, interest flows before redemption are uncertain and cannot be determined. To determine interest accruals before the values of the reference indicators are known, some proxy measures will have to be used. In this regard, it is useful to distinguish the following three arrangements: (a) indexation of coupons only; (b) indexation of principal only; and (c) indexation of both coupons and principal.

5.202. When only coupon payments are index-linked, the full amount resulting from indexation is treated as interest accruing during the coupon period. It is most likely that by the time data are compiled for a reporting period, the coupon payment date will have passed and hence the value of the index is known. For some reporting periods, a part of that reporting period may cover a coupon period or part of a coupon period for which the coupon date has already passed. For that part of the reporting period covered by a coupon period, interest accrual is calculated using the daily prorated coupon after indexation. For the remaining part of the reporting period, the movement in the index during that part of the reporting period can be used to calculate the interest accrual.

5.203. When the principal is index-linked, the calculation of interest accruals becomes uncertain because the redemption value is unknown; in some cases the date of maturity may be several years in the future. Two approaches can be followed to determine the interest accrual in each accounting period:

(a) Interest accruing in an accounting period due to the indexation of principal may be calculated as the change in the value of the principal outstanding between the end and beginning of the accounting period due to the movement in the relevant index;

(b) Interest accruals may be determined by fixing the rate of accrual at the time of issue. Accordingly, interest is the difference between the issue price and the market expectation, at inception, of all payments that the debtor will have to make; this is recorded as accruing over the life of the instrument. This approach records as income the yield-to-maturity at issuance, which incorporates the results of the indexation that are foreseen at the moment the instrument was created. Any deviation of the underlying index from the originally expected path leads to holding gains or losses that will not normally cancel out over the life of the instrument.

5.204. While the first approach (using the movement in the index) has the advantage of simplicity, interest includes all changes and fluctuations in the value of the principal in each accounting period due to the movement in the relevant index. If there is a large fluctuation in the index, this approach may yield negative interest even though market interest rates at the time of issue and current period may be positive. Also, fluctuations behave like holding gains and losses. The second approach (fixing the rate at the time of issue) avoids such problems, but the actual future cash flows may differ from the initially expected cash flows unless ex ante market expectations are exactly met.

This means that interest for the life of the instrument may not be equal to the difference between the issue price and redemption value.

5.205. The first approach works well when a broad-based indexation of the principal is used (for example a CPI), as such indexation is expected to change relatively smoothly over time. However, the first approach may give counter-intuitive results when the indexation of the principal combines motives for both interest income and holding gains (for example, a commodity price, stock prices or gold prices). Therefore, when indexation includes a holding gain motive, typically indexation based on a single, narrowly defined item, the second approach is preferred, otherwise the first approach should be used for the measurement of interest accrual.

5.206. As debt instruments with both coupons and principal indexed to foreign currency are treated as though they are redenominated in that foreign currency, interest, other economic flows, and positions for these instruments should be calculated using the same principles that apply to foreign currency denominated instruments. Interest should accrue throughout the period using the foreign currency as the unit of account and converted into the domestic currency using mid-point market exchange rates. Similarly, the principal amount outstanding should be valued using the foreign currency as the unit of account with the end of period exchange rate used to determine the domestic currency value of the entire debt instrument (including any accrued interest) in the international investment position. Changes in market values of debt securities due to exchange rate movements and/or interest rate changes are treated as revaluations.

5.207. When coupons and principal are indexed to a broad-based index, interest accruals during an accounting period can be calculated by summing two elements: the amount resulting from the indexation of the coupon payment that is attributable to the accounting period and the change in the value of the principal between the end and beginning of the accounting period due to the movement in the relevant index. When coupons and principal are indexed to a narrow index, interest accruals for any accounting period can be determined by fixing the yield-to-maturity at issuance.

5.208. The indexation mechanism links the coupon and/or principal payments to indicators agreed by the parties, and the values of the indicators are not known in advance. As a result, the amount of interest cannot be known at the time of issue. For some instruments, it can only be determined at the time of redemption. Indexed instruments include those indexed to, for example, an interest rate, the CPI, a stock exchange index, a commodity price, or an exchange rate. Index-linked debt instruments are those on which payments are linked to a reference item that normally changes over time in response to market pressures. All other debt instruments should be classified as fixed rate. As noted above debt instruments with both principal and coupons linked to a foreign currency are classified and treated as though they are denominated in that foreign currency for determining interest and other economic flows. All other types of index-linked instruments, including those that are partially linked to exchange rates (for example, those for which only principal or only coupons are linked to an exchange rate), are treated as being denominated in domestic currency for the recording of interest and other economic flows.

5.209. Two examples of index-linked bonds are described in worked example 5.1:

(a) Bonds linked to the CPI: changes in the CPI affect the market value of the security through changes in its expected redemption price, discounted at the current market interest rate;

(b) Bonds linked to the gold price: changes in the gold price affect the market value of the security via changes in the expected redemption price of the security, discounted at the prevailing market interest rate.

Table 5.15
Four different types of debt securities

	Example 1	Example 2	Example 3	Example 4
	Fixed coupon	*Step-up coupon*	*Step-up coupon with zero coupon in the first two years*	*Step-up coupon with zero coupon in the first two years, but with changing market interest rate*
Maturity (years)	5	5	5	5
Principal	100.0	100	100.0	100.0
Interest rate (percentage): Year 1	5.0	0.5	0.0	0.0
Year 2	5.0	2.0	0.0	0.0
Year 3	5.0	6.0	6.1	6.1
Year 4	5.0	7.7	8.5	8.5

d. *Debt securities with embedded derivatives*

5.210. For debt securities with embedded derivatives such as call, put or equity conversion options, the accounting for accrued interest is the same as for securities that do not have such features. For all periods leading up to the exercise of the option, the interest accrual is unaffected by the presence of the option. When the embedded option is exercised, the securities are redeemed, and accrual of interest ceases.

Worked example 5.4. Accrued interest for different types of debt securities

5.211. Table 5.15 shows four different types of debt securities with a maturity of five years, a principal amount of 100 to be repaid at maturity and an original yield-to-maturity of 5 per cent. The securities differ with regard to the coupon paid at the end of each year. Example 1 shows a debt security with a fixed coupon, example 2 a loan with a step-up coupon. Example 3 is a variation of example 2 in that the first two coupons are zero.

5.212. Examples 1 to 3 implicitly assume no changes in the market interest rate during the lifetime of the security. Example 4 is a variation of example 3 in that the market interest rate does change over the lifetime of the security causing a concomitant change in the market value of the security. The statistical recordings provided in this worked example are shown from the debtor's perspective.

Example 1: Debt security with a fixed interest rate

5.213. In the first year the security is issued at nominal value, recorded as a transaction in debt securities (F3). In the same period, interest accrues at the original yield-to-maturity of 5 per cent recorded as an interest payable transaction (D41) and the corresponding increase of the outstanding debt is recorded in F3 (interest accrued). The payment of the coupon at the end of the year decreases the liability. At the end of the first year the closing balance of debt securities (AF3) liabilities shows the same value as the principal amount (100).

		Debt securities (F3)					
Year	Cash flows	Total	Principal	Interest accrued	Coupon paid	Debt securities (AF3) (closing balance)	Interest payable (D41) (accrual basis)
1	+95.0	+100.0	+100.0	+5.0	-5.0	+100.0	+5.0
2	-5.0	0.0	0.0	+5.0	-5.0	+100.0	+5.0
3	-5.0	0.0	0.0	+5.0	-5.0	+100.0	+5.0
4	-5.0	0.0	0.0	+5.0	-5.0	+100.0	+5.0
5	-105.0	-100.0	-100.0	+5.0	-5.0	0.0	+5.0

5.214. The same logic applies for the other years. At maturity the principal amount is repaid together with the coupon in that year.

Example 2: Debt security with a step-up coupon

5.215. This case implies a recording of different amounts of interest. However the same mechanism applies as in example 1. Compound interest accrues at the original yield-to-maturity of 5 per cent, recorded as an interest payable transaction (D41). The difference between the interest accrued and the coupon paid is recorded as reinvestment in/redemption of the underlying security (transaction in F3).

		Debt securities (F3)					
Year	Cash flows	Total	Principal	Interest accrued	Coupon paid	Debt securities (AF3) (closing balance)	Interest payable (D41) (accrual basis)
1	+ 99.5	104.5	+100.0	+ 5.0	-0.5	+104.5	+ 5.0
2	-2.0	3.2	0.0	+ 5.2	-2.0	+107.7	+ 5.2
3	-6.1	-0.6	0.0	+ 5.4	-6.0	+107.1	+ 5.4
4	-7.7	-2.3	0.0	+ 5.4	-7.7	+104.8	+ 5.4
5	-110.0	-104.8	-100.0	+ 5.2	-10.0	0.0	+ 5.2

Example 3: Debt security with a step-up interest coupon (with the first step equal to zero)

5.216. This case shows a debt security with a step-up coupon, but with the coupon equal to zero in the first two years. The recording is similar to that applied in example 2.

		Debt securities (F3)					
Year	Cash flows	Total	Principal	Interest accrued	Coupon paid	Debt securities (AF3) (closing balance)	Interest payable (D41) (accrual basis)
1	+100.0	+105.0	+100.0	+5.0	0.0	+105.0	+5.0
2	0.0	+5.3	0.0	+5.3	0.0	+110.3	+5.3
3	-6.1	-0.6	0.0	+5.5	-6.1	+109.7	+5.5
4	-8.5	-3.0	0.0	+5.5	-8.5	+106.7	+5.5
5	-112.0	-106.7	-100.0	+5.3	-12.0	0.0	+5.3

Example 4: Step-up interest coupon (with the first step equal to zero) and changing market interest rate

5.217. Example 4 is the same as example 3 except for the fact that the market interest rate does change in this example, leading to changes in the market value of the security. The recording of interest follows the same principles as in example 3.

		Debt securities (F3)					
Year	Cash flows	Total	Principal	Interest accrued	Coupon paid	Debt securities AF3 (closing balance at nominal value)	Interest payable (D41) (accrual basis)
1	+100.0	+105.0	+100.0	+5.0	0.0	+105.0	+5.0
2	0.0	+5.3	0.0	+5.3	0.0	+110.3	+5.3
3	-6.1	-0.6	0.0	+5.5	-6.1	+109.7	+5.5
4	-8.5	-3.0	0.0	+5.5	-8.5	+106.7	+5.5
5	-112.0	-106.7	-100.0	+5.3	-12.0	+0.0	+5.3

5.218. The changes in the market value imply other economic flows. They are calculated as the difference between the transactions in debt securities (F3) (calculated in the table above) and the change in the market value of the security during the year.

Year	Debt securities (AF3) (opening balance at market value)	Debt securities (transactions in debt securities (F3))	Other economic flows	Debt securities (AF3) (closing balance at market value)
1	+0.0	+105.0	+5.0	+110.0
2	+110.0	5.3	-12.3	+103.0
3	+103.0	-0.6	+4.6	+107.0
4	+107.0	-3.0	+2.2	+106.2
5	+106.2	-106.7	+0.5	+0.0

The effect of coupon payments: dirty and clean prices

5.219. The *clean price* does not include accrued interest due to coupon. Debt securities provide for coupon payments to be made to holders in accordance with a fixed schedule.[142] The *dirty price* of a debt security will decrease when coupons are paid, with the result that its value will follow a sawtooth pattern. This is because there will be one less future cash flow (i.e. the coupon payment just received) at that point.

5.220. To separate out the effect of the coupon payments, the accrued interest between coupon dates is subtracted from the dirty price to arrive at the clean price. The calculation of accrued interest is based on the day count convention, the coupon rate and the number of days from the preceding coupon payment date (the debtor approach).

5.221. The *day count convention* is used to calculate accrued interest on debt instruments. While interest rates are usually expressed on a per annum basis (the reference period is one year), the coupon payments are generally due over shorter intervals (monthly, quarterly, etc.).

5.222. The *day count fraction*, expressed as a number of days in the accrual period divided by the total number of days in the reference period (often 360 or 365), is used to determine the accrual payment for the period. Different conventions (or rules) determine how the numbers of days are calculated for the accrual and the reference periods. The convention to be followed generally depends on the market type, location and/or the currency in which the financial instrument is denominated.

Worked example 5.5. "Dirty prices" and "clean prices" of debt securities

5.223. To illustrate the effect of coupon payments, an example is used which is described in worked example 5.1 (example (b)). In this example, a five-year fixed interest rate bond repayable at maturity is issued at a discount (below par, at 900) and pays annual fixed coupons of 73.6 during its life, which, because of the discount, corresponds to a 10 per cent rate of interest.

5.224. The bond accrues annually two types of interest: (a) a coupon of 73.6; and (b) an annual discount, which is calculated as 19.2 for the first year. At the end of the first year, interest of 92.8 has accrued, but only 73.6 of this accrued interest is paid to the bondholder. This reduces the principal amount outstanding, in nominal value terms, from 992.8 to 919.2. The accrued discount of 100 is only paid at the end of the fifth year as part of the redemption price.

5.225. The "dirty price" is the price of the debt security including any interest that has accrued since the issue of the recent coupon payment. This is to be compared with the "clean price", which is the price of a debt security excluding accrued interest. Table 5.16 shows the market value (the dirty price) of the bond, the market price excluding the accrued interest due to coupon (the clean price), and the cumulative accrued interest

142 There are exceptions, such as zero-coupon bonds.

due to coupon. Figure 5.1 reflects the smooth path of the clean price and the saw-tooth pattern of the dirty price of the bond.

Table 5.16
The "dirty price" and the "clean price" of a five-year fixed interest rate bond

Point in time	Market value ("Dirty price")	Market value excluding accrued interest due to coupon ("Clean price")	Cumulative accrued interest due to coupon
Beginning of quarter 1	900.0	900.0	0.0
End of quarter 1	915.0	897.1	-17.9
End of quarter 2	930.0	893.8	-36.2
End of quarter 3	950.0	895.3	-54.7
Up to end of quarter 4	960.7	887.1	-73.6
End of quarter 4 = beginning of quarter 5	887.1	887.1	0.0
End of quarter 5	900.0	882.1	-17.9
End of quarter 6	920.0	883.8	-36.2
End of quarter 7	935.0	880.3	-54.7
Up to end of quarter 8	958.5	884.9	-73.6
End of quarter 8 = beginning of quarter 9	884.9	884.9	0.0
End of quarter 9	905.0	887.1	-17.9
End of quarter 10	940.0	903.8	-36.2
End of quarter 11	980.0	925.3	-54.7
Up to end of quarter 12	1006.5	932.9	-73.6
End of quarter 12 = beginning of quarter 13	932.9	932.9	0.0
End of quarter 13	937.0	919.1	-17.9
End of quarter 14	947.0	910.8	-36.2
End of quarter 15	950.0	895.3	-54.7
End of quarter 16	958.6	885.0	-73.6
End of quarter 16 = beginning of quarter 17	885.0	885.0	0.0
End of quarter 17	910.0	892.1	-17.9
End of quarter 18	937.0	900.8	-36.2
End of quarter 19	970.0	915.3	-54.7
Up to end of quarter 20	1000.0	926.4	-73.6

5.226. Accrued interest is calculated using the following formula:

Accrued interest=Principal amount×Interest rate (per annum basis) ×Day count function

100=8000×0.05×90/360

5.227. The clean price reflects more closely changes in value due to issuer risk and changes in the structure of interest rates. Its graph is smoother than that of the "dirty price". Use of the clean price also serves to distinguish interest accrued (based on the coupon rate) from revaluations.

5.228. It is market practice to quote debt securities on a clean-price basis. When a debt security is traded or redeemed, the accrued interest is added to the value based on the clean price to reflect its market value, the dirty price.

5.229. Accordingly, many users prefer clean prices for analytical purposes. However, in the context of a system of institutional sector accounts and balance sheets analysing detailed debtor/creditor relationships in terms of transactions, other flows and positions, it is appropriate to include accrued interest.

Figure 5.1
The "dirty price" and the "clean price" of a five-year fixed interest rate debt security

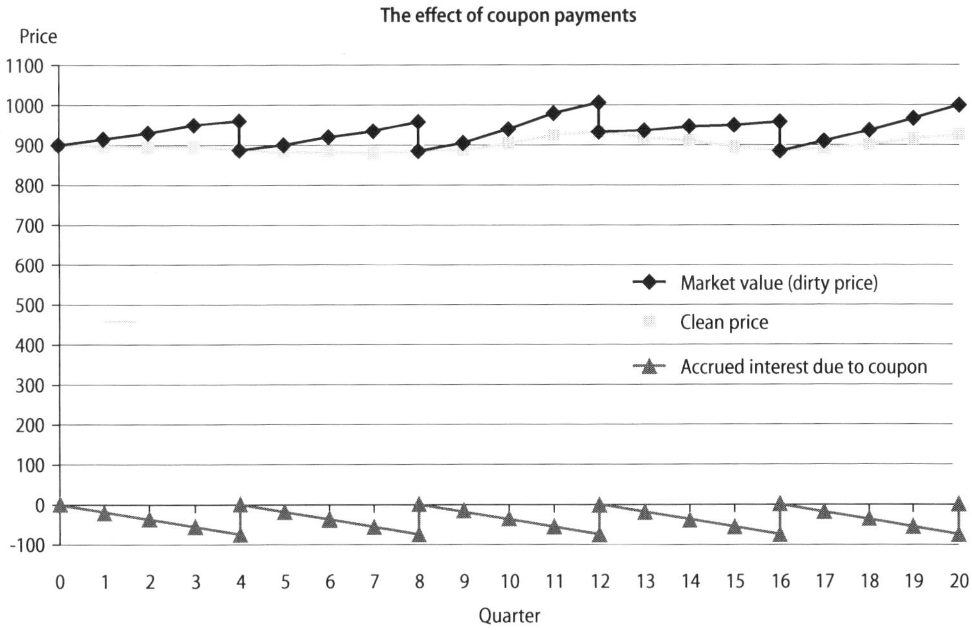

(c) Interest swaps and forward rate agreements

5.230. Payments resulting from swap arrangements (such as interest rate swaps and forward rate agreements) should be recorded as transactions in financial derivatives in the financial account and not as interest recorded under property income.

(d) Financial leases

5.231. A financial lease is an alternative to lending as a method of financing the purchase of assets. It is a contract which channels funds from a lender to a borrower: the lessor purchases the asset and the lessee contracts to pay rentals which enable the lessor, over the period of the contract, to recover all, or virtually all, of his costs, including interest.

5.232. The lessor is treated as making a loan to the lessee equal to the value of the purchaser's price paid for the asset, this loan being gradually paid off in full over the period of the lease. The rental paid each period by the lessee is therefore treated as having two components: a repayment of principal and a payment of interest. The rate of interest on the imputed loan is implicitly determined by the total amount paid in rentals over the life of the lease in relationship to the purchaser's price of the asset. The share of the rental that represents interest gradually declines over the life of the lease as the principal is repaid. The initial loan by the lessee, together with the subsequent repayments of principal, is recorded in the financial accounts of the lessor and of the lessee.

5.233. The interest payments are recorded as interest in their respective primary distribution of income accounts and in the financial account. If the lessor is not a financial corporation, the payments are split into repayments of principal and interest only; if the lessor is a financial corporation, the interest is split into SNA interest and a service charge (FISIM).

(e) Interest on other financial instruments

5.234. Interest also comprises interest charged on bank overdrafts, extra interest paid on deposits left longer than originally agreed, and lottery payments to bondholders.

(f) Interest receivable/payable by institutional sector

5.235. Financial instruments as described above are broken down into "interest-bearing financial instruments" and "other property income-bearing financial instruments". Interest-bearing financial instruments are mainly SDRs, deposits, loans, debt securities and other accounts receivable/payable.

5.236. A simplified integrated system of institutional sector accounts is presented, which is used to compile interest receivable/payable by type of financial instrument and sector. Interest is shown among resources and uses in the allocation of primary income account of the sectors and in the external account of primary income and current transfers.

5.237. Table 5.17 covers a matrix that shows, in rows, the interest receivable and payable by interest-bearing financial instruments and, in columns, the institutional sector of the economy and the rest of the world. Total interest payable of all resident sectors and of the rest of the world is equal to total interest receivable, instrument by instrument. The columns for each sector, non-financial corporations, financial corporations, general government, households including non-profit institutions serving households, and the rest of the world, show their interest expenditure and income by instrument. Net interest income is defined as the difference between interest receivable and interest payable.

5.238. The data in the shaded cells of the table sum to instrument and sector totals. These features force consistency within the table and help to minimize errors in the data.

Table 5.17

Presentation of interest receivable/payable by institutional sector and financial instrument

Uses (interest payable)									Resources (interest receivable)							
Total	Non-financial corporations	Financial corporations	General government	Households	NPISHs	Total economy	Rest of the world	Transactions	Non-financial corporations	Financial corporations	General government	Households	NPISHs	Total economy	Rest of the world	Total
								Interest payable/ interest receivable								
								SDRs								
								Transferable deposits								
								Other deposits								
								Short-term debt securities								
								Long-term debt securities								
								Short-term loans								
								Long-term loans								
								Trade credits and advances								
								Other accounts receivable / payable								
								Net interest income (=interest receivable – interest payable)								

Note: Black areas indicate cells that are in principle not applicable.

Chapter 6

From a table on financing and investment to from-whom-to-whom financial accounts and balance sheets

References:
2008 SNA
- Chapter 3, Stocks, flows and accounting rules
- Chapter 4, Institutional units and sectors
- Chapter 10, The capital account
- Chapter 11, The financial account
- Chapter 12, The other changes in assets account
- Chapter 13, The balance sheet
- Chapter 27, Links to monetary statistics and the flow of funds

BPM6
- Chapter 3, Accounting principles
- Chapter 4, Economic territory, units, institutional sectors and residence
- Chapter 5, Classifications of financial assets and liabilities
- Chapter 9, Other changes in financial assets and liabilities account

MFSMCG
GFSM 2014
HSS

A. Introduction

6.1. Chapter 6 is targeted at two broad groups of compilers. The first group comprises statistical agencies, such as national statistical offices and central banks, which do not currently compile the standard financial accounts and balance sheets by institutional sector but intend to do so. They can be considered "basic compilers". The second group comprises statistical agencies, which currently produce the standard financial accounts and balance sheets and would like to extend them to a from-whom-to-whom basis. They can be considered "advanced compilers".

6.2. For various reasons, including the lack of capacity, resources, know-how and data sources, many countries do not compile the standard financial accounts and balance sheets by institutional sector. A starting point could be to choose a limited set of financial assets and liabilities and institutional sectors depending on the available data sources. The data sources usually available are monetary and financial statistics, balance of payments and international investment position statistics and government finance statistics, supplemented by data on securities issues.

6.3. This chapter discusses the compilation of standard financial accounts and balance sheets by institutional sector. It begins with a table on financing and investment (TFI) comprising a limited set of financial asset and liability categories. From an assets point of view, financial instruments, such as deposits, loans and securities, are forms of financial investment. From a liabilities point of view, debt instruments, such as loans and debt securities, and equity securities are forms of financing. Raising equity capital through the issuance of shares is an alternative to borrowing.

6.4. The table is extended stepwise: six resident institutional "sectors" and "subsectors" and the rest of the world sector may be distinguished (see table 6.4) and all financial asset and liability categories may be included. These extensions are described in steps one to three. The distinction of six resident institutional "sectors" means that, for monetary policy purposes, the financial corporations sector (S12) is split into three financial subsectors: (a) monetary financial institutions (MFIs); (b) insurance corporations and pension funds (S128 and S129); and (c) the remaining financial corporation subsectors (S124 to S127). Moreover, three non-financial resident sectors are taken into consideration: (a) non-financial corporations (S11); (b) general government (S13); and (c) households, including non-profit institutions serving households (S14 and S15). The rest of the world is the seventh sector. This deviation from the standard presentation of five resident institutional sectors is also illustrated in table 6.4.

6.5. Step four integrates the capital accounts by institutional sector and combines them with the corresponding financial accounts. The inclusion of saving and non-financial investment allows a comprehensive description of the accumulation of assets and liabilities due to transactions.

6.6. Steps five and six describe how to move from the standard financial accounts and balance sheets by institutional sector to partial from-whom-to-whom accounts and, finally, to an integrated system of institutional sector accounts.

6.7. Expanding a system of financial accounts and balance sheets by institutional sector according to the steps mentioned above will allow compilers and users:

(a) To monitor broad money and its components, which may be complemented by the regular analysis of the investment behaviour of all non-financial sectors in an economy. In this context, money is seen as the most important component of short-term financial investment. Integration of a full sectoral breakdown of broad money and its components will permit a more comprehensive analysis;

(b) To extend financial analysis to the whole spectrum of financial assets held by non-financial sectors, of which broad money often represents a major part. Looking at the various components allows an analysis of substitution within financial investment, for instance between short and long-term or among long-term financial instruments such as debt securities, listed or unlisted shares and investment fund shares or units;

(c) To place credit provided by monetary financial institutions in the context of the overall borrowing requirements and structure of financing of non-financial sectors, and to identify financing instruments and their relative importance by non-financial sector. In particular, the balance sheets allow a detailed structural analysis of the liabilities and the indebtedness of the non-financial sectors, non-financial corporations, general government, households and non-profit institutions serving households, related to the various financial instruments and their contractual maturity;

(d) To monitor the changes in asset prices (derived from holding gains or losses) as reflected in the revaluation accounts by institutional sector for all asset categories. Asset prices are linked approximately to accumulated price changes as part of changes in stocks allowing for the evaluation of holding gains and losses of the various institutional sectors;

(e) To derive financial soundness indicators taken from the financial balance sheets or the accumulation accounts of the various non-financial sectors for purposes of financial stability analysis. Changes in their (financial) wealth and in their indebtedness may indicate mismatches between assets and liabilities, which may have important consequences for the cost and availability of financing and, in turn, an impact on investment and consumption and, eventually, on price developments;

(f) To achieve consistency in high-frequency financial data provided by monetary and financial, balance of payments, capital market and government finance statistics. It enhances the quality and consistency of data by providing more cross-checking and balancing opportunities;

(g) The flexibility provided by the 2008 SNA in terms of the level of detail of data compilation and presentation should allow its framework to be used to comply with the requirements of other analytical tools for assessing financial vulnerabilities and risks. One such tool is the IMF balance sheet approach, which provides a breakdown of counterparty positions in financial assets and liabilities by maturity and currency.

B. The table on financing and investment

1. The table on financing and investment and its data sources

6.8. The starting point in compiling sectoral financial accounts and balance sheets is to concentrate on a "reduced" set of (quarterly) data on selected financial transactions and balance sheet items – the TFI.

6.9. As indicated by the grey-shaded area in table 6.1, the TFI covers only a subset of data on financial transactions and balance sheets. These transaction data are the net acquisitions of financial assets (financial investment) or the net incurrences of liabilities (financing) in the form of main financial assets and liabilities. Balance sheet data are the corresponding stocks of the selected financial assets and liabilities.

6.10. The difference between the changes in stocks and the transactions are the "other flows" comprising revaluations and the other changes in the volume of assets and

Table 6.1

The table on financing and investment as a subset of financial account and balance sheet data within the *System of National Accounts 2008*

Transactions	Other flows[a]		Stocks	
Current account				
Production of goods and services Generation, distribution, redistribution, and use of income				
Accumulation accounts			**Balance sheet**	
Capital account	**Revaluation account**	**Other changes in the volume of assets accounts**	Non-financial assets	
Net acquisition of non-financial assets, saving and capital transfers	Holding gains and losses in non-financial assets, financial assets, and liabilities	Reclassifications and other changes in volume		
Financial account			**Financial balance sheet**	
Net acquisition of main financial assets and net incurrence of main liabilities[b]			Main financial assets	Main liabilities

[a] The two components of other flows are usually not treated separately in the TFI.

[b] The balancing items derived from these two aggregates are not equal to net lending/net borrowing under the 2008 SNA.

liabilities. It may be difficult to derive separate data for these two components at this stage, as the compilation of the TFI relies on a limited set of source data.

6.11. Source data are usually available for monetary financial institutions, the central bank (S121) and all deposit-taking corporations except the central bank (S122). Monetary financial institutions may also cover money market funds (MMFs, S123) in cases where money market fund shares or units (F521) are defined as part of broad money.[143] Financial source data may also be available for the other subsectors of financial corporations (S12), such as non-MMF investment funds (S124), insurance corporations (S128) and pension funds (S129), but not always for the remaining financial corporations subsectors, other financial intermediaries except insurance corporations and pension funds (S125), financial auxiliaries (S126) and captive financial institutions and moneylenders (S127). Source data from these institutional units are usually collected as monthly or quarterly balance sheet data. Supplementary source data are usually government finance statistics, balance of payments and international investment position statistics and securities issues statistics.

6.12. Government finance statistics data are collected and compiled based on the accounting framework of the GFSM 2014. This handbook describes a specific macroeconomic statistical system (the government finance statistics system) designed to support fiscal reporting, analysis and transparency.

6.13. The data collected in the context of balance of payments and international investment position statistics refer to the relationship between the rest of the world sector in the 2008 SNA and the international accounts as described in the BPM6. Transactions, other flows and stocks between a resident unit and the rest of the world are recorded as if the units in the rest of the world were another sector of the economy.

6.14. Securities are covered essentially by the financial instrument categories AF3 (debt securities), AF511 (listed shares) and AF512 (unlisted shares).

6.15. The methodology of collecting and compiling these statistics is described in the following related manuals and handbooks released by IMF and other international organizations described in the introduction to this Handbook:

(a) For monetary and financial statistics, MFSMCG (IMF), the *Manual on Sources and Methods for the Compilation of ESA95 Financial Accounts* (Eurostat) and the *Monetary Financial Institutions and Markets Statistics Sector Manual* (European Central Bank);

(b) For government finance statistics, GFSM 2014 and PSDSG (IMF);

(c) For balance of payments and international investment position statistics, BPM6 and the *External Debt Statistics: Guide for Compilers and Users* (IMF);

(d) HSS provides a conceptual framework for the corresponding position and flow statistics.

6.16. Source data directly collected from non-financial corporations, households and non-profit institutions serving households are not taken into consideration at this stage.

2. Components of the table on financing and investment

6.17. Based on the data sources described above, the components of the TFI essentially cover aggregated data for two groupings of resident sectors and for six financial instrument categories.

---

[143] See MFSMCG, Table 2.2.

6.18. A national economy is assumed to consist of two main groupings of sectors, namely the grouping of non-financial sectors (non-financial corporations (S11), general government (S13), households (S14), and non-profit institutions serving households (NPISHs) (S15)) and the financial corporations sector (S12) covering the groupings of monetary financial institutions (S121, S122 and S123), insurance corporations and pension funds (S128 and S129) and the remaining financial corporations (S124, S125, S126 and S127).

6.19. Focusing on the main financing and financial investment activities of the non-financial sectors, most of the liability and financial asset categories defined in the 2008 SNA are covered. These are:

(a) Currency and deposits (F2);
(b) Debt securities (F3);
(c) Loans (F4);
(d) Listed shares (F511);[144]
(e) Investment fund shares/units (F52);
(f) Certain financial instruments referred to as non-life insurance technical reserves (F61), life insurance and annuity entitlements (F62) and pension entitlements (F63).

In essence, these instruments are either mediated through financial corporations to non-financial sectors or traded on securities markets.

6.20. At the initial phase of developing a system of institutional sector accounts related to the accumulation accounts and the balance sheets, it may be difficult to obtain reliable, timely and more detailed data for individual sectors and financial corporation subsectors, as well as for financial instruments, such as unlisted shares (F512), other equity (F519), financial derivatives and employee stock options (F7) and other accounts receivable/payable (F8).

6.21. The outstanding amounts of financial assets and liabilities constitute the stocks in the framework of integrated financial accounts and balance sheets. Financial transactions reflect the financing and financial investment decisions during the quarter. Changes in outstanding amounts are the result of such transactions, but also of revaluations and other changes in the volume of assets and liabilities, such as write-offs or write-downs of loans, and reclassifications between financial asset and liability categories and institutional sectors.[145]

6.22. The components of financial investment and financing of non-financial sectors are shown in table 6.2. Currency and deposits (F2) as financial assets are split into currency (F21), transferable deposits (F22) and other deposits (F29). Transferable deposits and other deposits are further broken down into deposits with monetary financial institutions and with other institutional units, essentially central government and the rest of the world.

6.23. Other components of financial investment are debt securities (F3), listed shares (F511), investment fund shares/units (F52) and (as an of which item) money market fund shares/units (F521). Financial investment in debt securities is broken down by original maturity into short-term debt securities (F31) and long-term debt securities (F32).

[144] In many countries, including only listed shares would be misleading because a major part of equity financing (in the form of unlisted shares (F512) and other equity (F519)) would be left out.

[145] Structural breaks in time series due to the limited availability of source data may also be reflected in the changes of outstanding amounts.

Table 6.2
Table on financing and financial investment of non-financial sectors
Transactions and positions

Main financial assets (Financial investment)	2008 SNA code	Main liabilities (Financing)	2008 SNA code
Total		**Total**	
Currency and deposits	F2	Loans	F4
Currency	F21	Incurred by original maturity	
Deposits		Non-financial corporations	
Transferable deposits with	F22	Short-term	
Money-issuing corporations		Long-term	
Other institutional units		General government	
Other deposits with	F29	Short-term	
Money-issuing corporations		Long-term	
Other institutional units		Households including NPISHs	
		Short-term	
		Long-term	
		Taken from	
		Monetary financial institutions	
		Other financial corporations	
		The rest of the world	
Debt securities	F3	Debt securities	F3
Short-term		Issued by	
Long-term		General government	
		Short-term	
		Long-term	
		Non-financial corporations	
		Short-term	
		Long-term	
Listed shares	F511	Listed shares	F511
Investment fund shares/units	F52	Issued by non-financial corporations	
Of which Money market fund shares/units	F521		
Non-life insurance technical reserves	F61		
Life insurance and annuity entitlements	F62		
Pension entitlements		Pension entitlements	F63
	F63	Incurred by	
		Non-financial corporations	
		General government	
		(Other) deposits	F29
		Issued by central government[a]	
Balancing items			

Note: Loans provided by the rest of the world are also shown.
[a] Central government units may issue deposits in exceptional cases.

6.24. Investments in non-life insurance technical reserves (F61), life insurance and annuity entitlements (F62) and pension entitlements (F63) are also covered. They are mainly held by households (S14) vis-à-vis insurance corporations (S128) and pension funds (S129).

6.25. On the liabilities side, data on transactions and positions may be collected by individual non-financial sectors, that is, non-financial corporations (S11), general government (S13) and households (S14), including non-profit institutions serving households (S15).

6.26. Loans (F4) are shown as provided by monetary financial institutions (S121 to S123), other financial corporations (S124 to S129) and by the rest of the world (S2) and with breakdowns by debtor sector and by original maturity.

6.27. Debt securities (F3) are included, also with a breakdown by debtor sector (i.e. non-financial corporations (S11) and general government (S13)) and by original maturity. One additional financing instrument refers to listed shares (F511), which are issued by non-financial corporations. Finally, deposits incurred by central government and pension entitlements (F63) are also included as liabilities.

6.28. In presenting only a selected set of quarterly data on financial transactions and balance sheet items, the TFI is a compromise. However, the table is analytically useful as it provides important and timely information on the financing and the financial investment behaviour of the non-financial sectors by all major categories of financial assets and liabilities.

6.29. Net financial investment may be defined approximately by subtracting financing (liabilities or transactions in liabilities) from financial investment (financial assets or transactions in financial assets). Owing to the incomplete coverage of financial instruments as described above, the balancing items derived from the balance sheets and the financial accounts deviate from net financial assets (NFA) or net lending/net borrowing (B9) as defined in the 2008 SNA.

6.30. Therefore, it is not useful to interpret the balancing items in the same way as in the context of a complete and integrated system of sectoral accounts.

3. Presenting financial investment of non-financial sectors in relation to broad money[146]

6.31. The data on financial transactions and positions as reflected in the TFI may be used in the context of monetary policy analysis in a national economy or in a currency union. The financial investment analysis could be extended to a broader spectrum of financial assets held by the various non-financial sectors including broad money.

6.32. It may be of specific interest to compare the development of overall financial investment of the non-financial sectors with that of broad money.

6.33. Box 6.1 presents the broad money structure within the money hierarchy with respect to financial instruments and institutional sectors (see also box 6.1 of the MFSMCG).

6.34. As broad money corresponds to a major part of financial investment by non-financial sectors resident in an economy, the potential scope for substitution between financial investment included in broad money and other financial investment such as other short-term investment and long-term investment is, in principle, large (see table 6.3).

[146] See also Chapter 27 of the 2008 SNA.

Box 6.1

Broad money and its holders and issuers: benchmark sectors and liabilities[a]

Broad money holders

- Other financial corporations
- State and local government
- Non-financial corporations
- Households and non-profit institutions serving households

Broad money neutral

- Central government (domestic currency holdings are usually included in broad money)
- Non-residents (domestic currency holdings are usually included in broad money)

Broad money liabilities and broad money issuers

- **Issued by resident depository corporations**
  - Domestic currency
    - Transferable deposits[b]
      - Demand deposits (transferable by check, giro order, or similar means)
      - Cashier's cheques
      - Traveller's checks (if used for transactions with residents)
      - Deposits otherwise commonly used to make payments [c, d]
    - Other deposits
      - Non-transferable savings deposits
      - Term deposits (i.e. time or fixed deposits)
      - Deposits denominated in foreign currency (except those included in transferable deposits)
      - Other[e]
    - Money market funds' shares
    - Debt securities
      - Certificates of deposit
      - Commercial paper
      - Other[f]
- **Issued by sectors other than resident depository corporations**
  - Domestic currency issued by central government
  - Foreign currency (applies to countries in which foreign currency widely circulates as a medium of exchange)
  - Transferable deposits
    - Transferable deposits accepted by central government or the postal system
    - Traveller's cheques issued by units other than depository corporations
    - Other[g]
  - Other deposits accepted by central government or the postal system
  - Debt securities
    - Treasury bills
    - Commercial paper
    - Other[h]

---

[a] Domestic currency, transferable deposits, and other deposits shown under "issued by resident depository corporations" are included in broad money in most countries. Money market funds shares and debt securities (or specific subcategories therein) issued by resident depository corporations are included in broad money in a smaller group of countries. The currency, deposit, and debt securities categories shown under "issued by sectors other than resident depository corporations" are applicable to the broad money definitions in an even smaller group of countries.

[b] May include deposits denominated in foreign currency.

[c] May include some or all transferable deposits denominated in foreign currency.

[d] Includes shares or similar evidence of transferable deposit issued by savings and loan associations, building societies, credit unions, etc.; savings accounts that provide automatic transfer service through which savings account balances are transferred to transferable deposit accounts that would otherwise be overdrawn; electronic money issued by card or otherwise transferable; and other types not classified elsewhere.

[e] Includes shares or similar evidence of nontransferable deposit issued by savings and loan associations, building societies, credit unions, etc.; repurchase agreements included in broad money; sight deposits that are immediately redeemable, but not transferable; and other types.

[f] Any other debt securities issued by resident depository corporations that meet the definition of broad money (e.g. savings certificates or cash certificates, bankers' acceptances traded in efficient secondary markets).

[g] Includes electronic money and mobile money issued by units other than depository corporations.

[h] Includes debt securities issued by the central government such as savings certificates.

Table 6.3
The table on financing and investment of non-financial sectors by original maturity and financial instrument

Transactions and positions

Transactions and positions
(1) Short-term financial investment related to monetary liabilities (essentially broad money)
Currency vis-à-vis resident monetary financial institutions (F21)
Transferable deposits vis-à-vis resident monetary financial institutions (F22)
Part of other deposits vis-à-vis resident monetary financial institutions (F29)
Money market fund shares/units issued by resident money market funds (F521)
Debt securities (short-term at original maturity) issued by resident monetary financial institutions (F31)
(2) Other short-term financial investment
Short-term financial investment vis-à-vis non-monetary financial institutions and the rest of the world
(3) Long-term financial investment
Other deposits (F29)
Debt securities (long-term at original maturity) (F32)
Listed shares (F511)
Non-MMF investment fund shares/units (F522)
Financial investment related to insurance and pensions
Non-life insurance technical reserves (F61)
Life insurance and annuity entitlements (F62)
Pension entitlements (F63)
(4) Financing
Loans taken from monetary financial institutions (F4)
Non-financial corporations
Short-term
Long-term
General government
Short-term
Long-term
Households including non-profit institutions serving households
Short-term
Long-term
Debt securities issued by (F3)
Non-financial corporations
Short-term
Long-term
General government
Short-term
Long-term
Loans taken from other financial corporations and from the rest of the world (F4)
Listed shares issued by non-financial corporations (F511)
Deposits issued by central government (F29)
Pension entitlements (F63)
Balancing items

Note: The breakdown of financial instruments by category, subcategory and subposition may sometimes deviate from the 2008 SNA standard breakdown of financial assets and liabilities. This also applies to the concepts of short-term and long-term financial investment, which do not correspond with the concepts of "short term" and 'long term" at original maturity. For example, financial instruments, such as money market fund shares/units are classified as short-term investment, while non-MMF investment fund shares/units, listed shares, non-life insurance technical reserves, life insurance and annuity entitlements, and pension entitlements are classified as long-term financial investment.

6.35. Short-term financial investment relates predominantly to broad money, held by non-financial sectors. Broad money may cover all monetary liabilities with residents of monetary financial institutions and of some central government units.

6.36. Long-term financial investment is described as investment in other deposits, which are not part of broad money (F29), and long-term debt securities (F32), listed shares (F511), non-MMF investment fund shares/units (F522) and financial investment related to insurance and pensions (F61 to F63).[147] Other deposits (F29) are, like debt securities, interest-bearing financial instruments, but less liquid. Financial investment related to insurance and pensions is mainly with insurance corporations and pension funds. They constitute – together with listed shares and non-MMF investment fund shares/units – an important component of the long-term financial investment of households.

4. Financing and debt aggregates

6.37. Financing granted to non-financial sectors relates to their liabilities. The major components are loans and debt securities – both broken down by non-financial sector and by original maturity – and listed shares.

6.38. The TFI data allow debt aggregates to be compiled for each of the non-financial sectors, namely general government, non-financial corporations and households including non-profit institutions serving households. Debt comprises all liabilities as shown in table 6.2, excluding listed shares issued by non-financial corporations.

6.39. The TFI also places credit provided by monetary financial institutions in the context of the overall borrowing requirements and structure of financing of non-financial sectors, and identifies the main financing instruments and their relative importance by non-financial sector.

6.40. In particular, the outstanding amounts covered by the TFI allow a detailed structural analysis of the liabilities and the indebtedness of the various non-financial sectors related to the various financial instruments and their contractual maturity with a breakdown into short-term and long-term components. This also applies to financial investment as shown in table 6.3.

6.41. Various types of financing used by non-financial sectors are distinguished, such as financing through loans, debt securities and listed shares. General government debt mainly covers loans, debt securities and central government deposits as liabilities. The components of corporate debt, debt securities and loans may be used along with listed shares issued by non-financial corporations to compile leverage ratios.

6.42. The data allow the financing pattern in a national economy to be analysed across sectors, by liability category and original maturity; and show whether the financing was provided by monetary financial institutions, other financial corporations or other sectors or subsectors, and whether or not there has been a move away from borrowing from financial corporations towards securities issues.[148] However, it has to be taken into account that not all means of financing are available in a national economy in terms of financing instruments and institutional sectors.

5. Further work on the table on financing and investment of non-financial sectors

6.43. Further work may be done on the TFI to reconcile all short-term financial investment components with broad money.

6.44. This relates predominantly to a split of other deposits (F29) into deposits part and not part of broad money. The holdings of currency, money market fund shares/units

[147] Non-life insurance technical reserves (F61) are seen as long-term financial investment.

[148] It should be noted that financing as shown in the TFI may be incomplete, taking into account other types of financing through unlisted shares, other equity or intercompany loans.

and short-term debt securities by the non-financial sectors issued by monetary financial institutions need to be separated.

6.45. For debt securities, listed shares and non-MMF shares/units, data on holdings by residency and by resident sector may also be required, though are not always available.

C. Expanding the table on financing and investment in a step-by-step approach

6.46. Further developments of financial accounts and balance sheets by institutional sector may be integrated following a step-by-step approach. Based on a quarterly TFI of non-financial sectors, this table may be expanded in four directions by including:

(a) A more detailed sector breakdown;

(b) All financial asset and liability categories;

(c) Financial assets and liabilities among resident non-financial corporations and households and between non-financial corporations and households (such as trade credits and intercompany loans);

(d) A more detailed set of accumulation accounts (showing, in addition to the financial accounts by institutional sector, the capital accounts, the revaluation accounts and the other changes in the volume of assets and liabilities accounts).

6.47. The expansions form the standard financial accounts, revaluation accounts and other changes in the volume of assets and liabilities accounts in the 2008 SNA. The standard breakdown of the accounts is by five institutional sectors; however, a more detailed breakdown of the financial corporations sector or of the general government sector may be useful depending on the needs raised by users of the accounts.

6.48. Following a step-by-step approach, one key requirement may be to provide more detailed data on the financial investment and financing behaviour of the various non-financial sectors. Accordingly, the TFI may be extended by:

(a) Splitting the financial investment and financing components by resident non-financial sector, that is, non-financial corporations (S11), general government (S13) and households, including non-profit institutions serving households (S14 and S15);

(b) Including three groupings of the financial corporations subsector (monetary financial institutions (S121 to S123), insurance corporations and pension funds (S128 and S129) and other financial corporations (S124 to S127)) and of the rest of the world (S2), which expands the table to seven sectors;

(c) Adding sufficient detail on financial assets and liabilities for outstanding amounts, transactions, revaluations and other changes in the volume of assets and liabilities to move to a fully integrated and timely system of institutional sector accounts with partial from-whom-to-whom relationships between debtor and creditor sectors and between the national economy and the rest of the world.

1. Extending the table on financing and investment to seven sectors

6.49. Integrating broad money into the TFI shows the economic relationships in terms of transactions and positions between monetary financial institutions and the remaining resident sectors, that is, the non-financial sectors, insurance corporations, pension funds and other financial corporations (S124 to S127).

6.50. This requires the sector presentation to be extended beyond the standard breakdown of a national economy into five resident institutional sectors. While the financial corporations sector is split into three subsector groupings, the two sectors households and non-profit institutions serving households are shown together. Showing the two sectors separately may have analytical interest given the ongoing discussion on household distribution of income and wealth.

(a) The seven-sector approach

6.51. The seven-sector approach may be presented as follows. The national economy is assumed to consist of six resident sectors:

(a) The three non-financial sectors (non-financial corporations (S11), general government (S13) and the grouping of the two sectors households and non-profit institutions serving households (S14 and S15));

(b) Three subgroupings of the financial corporations sector (S12), namely monetary financial institutions (S121 to S123), insurance corporations and pension funds (S128 and S129) and other financial corporations (S124 to S127).

6.52. The seventh sector is the rest of the world (S2).

6.53. The sector monetary financial institutions covers the central bank (S121), deposit-taking corporations except the central bank (S122) and money market funds (S123).

6.54. The sector insurance corporations and pension funds combines insurance corporations (S128) and pension funds (S129). The other financial corporations sector comprises non-MMF investment funds (S124), other financial intermediaries except insurance corporations and pension funds (S125), financial auxiliaries (S126) and captive financial institutions and moneylenders (S127) (see table 6.4).

Table 6.4
Sectors and subsectors according to the *System of National Accounts 2008* and the recommended grouping of the financial corporations subsectors according to the seven-sector approach

Sector and subsector			2008 SNA code
Total economy			S1
Non-financial corporations			S11
Financial corporations			S12
Monetary financial institutions	Central bank		S121
	Other monetary financial institutions	Deposit-taking corporations except the central bank	S122
		Money market funds	S123
Financial corporations except monetary financial institutions and ICPF	Non-MMF investment funds		S124
	Other financial intermediaries, except insurance corporations and pension funds		S125
	Financial auxiliaries		S126
	Captive financial institutions and moneylenders		S127
Insurance corporations and pension funds (ICPF)	Insurance corporations		S128
	Pension funds		S129
General government			S13
Households and non-profit institutions serving households			S14
			S15
Rest of the world			S2

6.55. The extension of the TFI to seven sectors completes the coverage of sectoral data for broad money and also for the other main financial assets and liabilities shown in the TFI.

6.56. Extending the table in this direction allows the data to be balanced horizontally because all institutional units – aggregated in the resident sectors or included in the rest of the world sector – are covered by the approach. This balancing may be carried out for the amounts outstanding as well as for financial transactions, instrument by instrument.

6.57. Table 6.5 shows the main financial assets and liabilities as included in the TFI by sector and by financial instrument category. The totals for the economy show the total holdings and issues of each financial instrument category and the equality of the main financial asset and liability transactions and positions. The columns for each sector show financial assets held or liabilities incurred, as well as the net financial assets of the sector. The data in the respective cells of the table add up to the financial instrument and institutional sector totals.

6.58. These identities ensure consistency within the table and help to minimize errors in the data. Net figures are derived as the balancing items between stocks of financial assets and liabilities and between transactions in financial assets and liabilities. They deviate from net financial assets and net lending/net borrowing because not all financial instruments are covered at this step of expanding the TFI.

2. Including all financial asset and liability categories

6.59. Some financial instruments may have to be added which are not yet covered by the TFI. These are financial instruments for which source data are not immediately available, such as data on loans granted by non-financial sectors (F4), unlisted shares

Table 6.5
The seven-sector approach

Transactions in main financial assets Main financial assets										Transactions in main liabilities Main liabilities								
Total	Rest of the world	Total economy	Households including non-profit institutions serving households	General government	Insurance corporations and pension funds	Financial corporations except monetary financial institutions and ICPF	Monetary financial institutions	Non-financial corporations	Transactions (F) and positions (AF)	Non-financial corporations	Monetary financial institutions	Financial corporations except monetary financial institutions and ICPF	Insurance corporations and pension funds	General government	Households including non-profit institutions serving households	Total economy	Rest of the world	Total
									Currency and deposits (F2)									
									Debt securities (F3)									
									Loans (F4)									
									Listed shares (F511)									
									Investment fund shares/units (F52)									
									Insurance and pensions (F61 to F63)									
									Balancing items									

Note: Shaded areas indicate cells that are not applicable.

Monetary financial institutions cover the central bank (S121); deposit-taking corporations except the central bank (S122); and money market funds (S123). Financial corporations except monetary financial institutions and ICPF cover non-MMF investment funds (S124); other financial intermediaries, except insurance corporations and pension funds (S125); financial auxiliaries (S126); and captive financial institutions and moneylenders (S127).

(F512), other equity (F519), financial derivatives and employee stock options (F7) and other accounts receivable/payable (F8). Finally, data on monetary gold and special drawing rights (SDRs) (F1) should be included.

6.60. Additional data collection schemes may have to be set up in order to obtain such data. A complete coverage of all financial instruments according to the 2008 SNA will allow a vertical balancing of the data, following which net lending/net borrowing (B9) and financial assets (AF) by institutional sector may be derived.

(a) Monetary gold and special drawing rights

6.61. Monetary gold and SDRs (F1) are part of external assets. External assets (or reserve assets) are readily available to and controlled by a country's monetary authorities for the direct financing and regulation of international payments imbalances. Only the central bank or central government can hold these assets; they must be claims on non-residents.[149]

6.62. Monetary gold includes gold bullion held as a financial asset and as a component of reserve assets (held by the central bank or by central government). Gold bullion takes the form of coins, ingots or bars with a purity of at least 995 parts per thousand. Purchases of monetary gold are recorded as increases and sales of monetary gold are recorded as decreases in the assets of the monetary authority; the counterpart entries are decreases or increases of assets of the rest of the world.

6.63. SDRs are reserve assets created by the IMF and allocated to its members to supplement existing reserve assets. SDRs are neither currency nor a claim on the IMF. Rather, SDRs are a potential claim on the freely usable currencies of IMF members. Holders of SDRs can obtain these currencies in exchange for their SDRs in two ways:

(a) Through the arrangement of voluntary exchanges between members;

(b) Where the IMF designates members with strong external positions to purchase SDRs from members with weak external positions.

6.64. Because SDR holdings have a liability, whereas gold bullion does not, the 2008 SNA recommends that transactions and positions in monetary gold and in SDR holdings should be shown as separate transaction subcategories (F11 and F12) or position subcategories (AF11 and AF12).

6.65. Data on monetary gold and SDRs are available at the central bank or central government, as well as at the IMF.

(b) Currency, deposits and loans

6.66. Currency (F21) may be issued predominantly by general government or by the central bank. The main business of deposit-taking corporations except the central bank is to receive deposits (as transferable deposits (F22) and other deposits (F29)) and/or close substitutes for deposits from institutional units and, for their own account, to grant loans and to make investments in securities. Deposits may also be liabilities of central government units.

6.67. Most of the data may be derived from the balance sheets and cash flow statements of these institutions. They are part of the monetary and financial statistics.

6.68. Loans (F4) are in general granted by financial corporations and non-financial corporations and by the rest of the world.

---

[149] See also Chapter 4.

(c) Debt securities and equity securities

6.69. The inclusion and detailed presentation of financing and financial investment through securities (debt securities (F3) and equity securities as listed shares (F511) and unlisted shares (F512)) is a precondition for detailed analysis in the context of monetary policy and financial stability. It sheds light on the sectoral compositions of securities as financial assets and liabilities, and on potential strengths and vulnerabilities in portfolios.[150]

6.70. The complexity of a comprehensive table for securities is determined by the detail of the breakdowns chosen for these financial instruments (by subcategory, position and subposition and by residency, sector and subsector of creditor and debtor). Combining these breakdowns leads to a substantial number of time series, especially as the data may need to be shown as positions and flows. Accordingly, a selection by security subcategory, sector and subsector is essential.

6.71. A security-by-security database (SBS) may be set up to collect and compile detailed securities issues and holdings statistics.[151] An SBS is a micro database that stores information on individual securities, from which statistics can be compiled flexibly to serve diverse needs. An SBS may cover various categories of financial instruments, such as debt securities (F3), listed shares (F511), unlisted shares (F512), investment fund shares/units (F52) and financial derivatives and employee stock options (F7). Information stored on an instrument is broken down into attributes that describe its selected characteristics.

6.72. The selection of attributes may vary depending on the purpose of the database. Attributes useful for statistical applications include: the international securities identification number (ISIN); name, residence and sector or subsector of the issuer; issue date; redemption date; the type of security; currency of denomination; issue price; redemption price; the outstanding amount or the market capitalization; and the coupon payments and dates.

6.73. The production of statistics from an SBS can be presented as a three-stage process:[152]

(a) First, data on individual securities are collected and/or purchased from a range of sources, such as central banks, government agencies, commercial data providers and securities exchanges in their capacity as custodians (data input);

(b) Second, the data on individual securities collected from different sources are added to the database, merged and stored. Checks for completeness, plausibility and consistency are then performed and, where errors are detected, observations are corrected (data quality management);

(c) Third, the data on individual securities are stored according to various classification criteria.

6.74. An SBS of securities issues statistics can be linked to securities holdings statistics for resident holders (grouped by sector and subsector) and non-resident holders. For this purpose, the data provided by respondents (as holders or custodians) are linked at the individual security level to the data stored in the SBS. The link is often made using the ISIN,[153] but also referring to information on the debt securities holders and holdings:

---

150 See the HSS.

151 As an example see Giron, and others (2011).

152 See also Chapter 7, para. 7.121.

153 An ISIN code may exist for all debt equities and equity securities, as well as a single legal entity identifier for each institutional unit.

(a) The holder by residency and institutional sector and subsector, as well as by large and complex financial or non-financial group;

(b) The amount of holdings in currency.

6.75. Current reporting schemes on securities holdings are based mainly on two groups of agents having access to such information – custodians and direct reporters:

(a) In most cases, securities holdings data are collected from resident custodians (as well as centralized securities depositories) on a security-by-security basis. It is also necessary to collect data on securities holdings of residents from non-resident custodians allowing the breakdown of holdings by the residency of the issuer to be derived. However, holdings of non-resident issues placed abroad by resident sectors are normally not reported. Therefore, direct reporters should complete the resident custodians' reports by reporting their portfolios placed abroad;

(b) Direct reporters provide security-by-security data on their holdings with various breakdowns: by type of financial instrument, maturity, residence of issuer, etc. The difficulties in achieving a high response rate and regular, reliable reports have to be taken into consideration.

6.76. Establishing an integrated compilation system for securities issues and holdings statistics, that provides timely and high-frequency data with breakdowns by type of financial instrument, currency, maturity, issuing country, and sector or subsector is long-term and cost-intensive. The European System of Central Banks (ESCB) considers that several years are required before a newly established system can be used for the regular production of securities statistics, starting with financial balance sheet data.

(d) Unlisted shares and other equity

6.77. Various data sources can be used to collect data on unlisted shares (F512) and other equity (F519).[154] These data are usually included in balance sheets of financial corporations, non-financial corporations, general government and the rest of the world. However, a detailed breakdown of such stock data in unlisted shares and other equity is usually not available.

6.78. The coverage and quality of data on unlisted shares and other equity for non-financial corporations is usually insufficient. Improving these data would mean carrying out methodological and empirical work on survey methods and questionnaires to collect and compile comprehensive stock and flow data for these subcategories. Compilers could derive estimates on unlisted shares and other equity for corporations of similar size and industry class based on the surveys. However, while ultimately desirable, this work is costly and long-term (see box 6.1).

(e) Insurance, pension and standardized guarantee schemes

6.79. Supervisory authorities usually collect balance sheet data on insurance, pension and standardized guarantee schemes (F6) on an annual basis. These data refer to different types of insurance and pension business, such as non-life, life (unit-linked and non-unit-linked), reinsurance, defined benefit pensions and defined contribution pensions.

6.80. In addition, statistical agencies may set up new data collection schemes to obtain timely estimates of stock and flow data from reporting agents. Given the low

[154] With regard to unlisted shares, various data sources may have to be used for cross-checking purposes, as the corresponding data included in securities databases may not be complete.

frequency, insufficient timeliness and lack of detail and harmonization of the current supervisory data, such new data collection schemes are expected to improve the sector accounts for insurance corporations and pension funds.

(f) Financial derivatives and employee stock options

6.81. Financial derivatives (F71) and employee stock options (F72) are new financial instrument subcategories under the 2008 SNA. Financial derivatives cover options, forwards and credit derivatives.

6.82. In the context of compiling an integrated system of financial accounts and balance sheets by institutional sector, data on financial derivatives and employee stock options need to be collected. For instance, collection systems for balance of payments and international investment positions cover data on financial derivatives as a whole but not with a split into the two subcategories listed above. The same applies to monetary and financial statistics. However the coverage of data is usually incomplete owing to the accounting rules applied by banks.

6.83. The data on financial derivatives from these sources are usually available on a net basis. Data from other sources may be on a gross basis – without netting of corresponding positions or of transactions in financial assets and liabilities.

6.84. By combining accounting data from supervisory sources with data from balance of payments, monetary and financial and government finance statistics it may be possible to compile data for financial corporations. For data on transactions in financial derivatives by non-financial corporations, a main data source could be a survey or questionnaire, encompassing the transactions between resident and non-resident corporations, and information from counterpart sectors.

(g) Trade credits and advances

6.85. The collection of data on trade credits and advances (F81) is rather challenging. Most of the data may be taken from balance sheets collected for financial and non-financial corporations. Specific collection schemes may exist to obtain data on cross-border transactions and positions in trade credits and advances.

(h) The seven-sector approach with all financial assets and liabilities

6.86. Table 6.6 shows all transactions and positions in financial assets and liabilities according to the 2008 SNA. The totals for the economy show the total financial transactions and also the total holdings and issues for each financial instrument category. The columns for each sector show financial transactions and the financial assets held or liabilities incurred, as well as the net financial assets of the sector. The data in the respective cells of the table add up to the financial instrument and institutional sector totals.

6.87. This identity ensures consistency within the table and helps to minimize errors in the data. Net figures are derived as the balancing items between transactions in financial assets and liabilities and between stocks of financial assets and liabilities.

6.88. These balancing items are net lending/net borrowing (B9) and net financial assets (NFA). They are derived from the sectoral financial accounts and financial balance sheets as shown in table 6.6 because all financial instrument categories are covered in the table.

Table 6.6

The seven sector approach with all financial asset and liability categories

Transactions in financial assets Financial assets										Transactions in liabilities Liabilities								
Total	Rest of the world	Total economy	Households including non-profit institutions serving households	General government	Insurance corporations and pension funds	Financial corporations except monetary financial institutions and ICPFs	Monetary financial institutions	Non-financial corporations	**Transactions (F) and positions (AF)**	Non-financial corporations	Monetary financial institutions	Financial corporations except monetary financial institutions and ICPFs	Insurance corporations and pension funds	General government	Households including non-profit institutions serving households	Total economy	Rest of the world	Total
									Monetary gold and SDRs (F1)									
									Currency and deposits (F2)									
									Debt securities (F3)									
									Loans (F4)									
									Listed shares (F511)									
									Unlisted shares (F512)									
									Other equity (F519)									
									Investment fund shares/units (F52)									
									Insurance, pension and standardized guarantee schemes (F6)									
									Financial derivatives and employee stock options (F7)									
									Other accounts receivable/payable (F8)									
									Balancing items (B9)									

Note: Shaded areas indicate cells that are not applicable.

Monetary financial institutions cover the central bank (S121); deposit-taking corporations, except the central bank (S122); and money market funds (S123). Financial corporations except monetary financial institutions and ICPFs cover non-MMF investment funds (S124); other financial intermediaries, except insurance corporations and pension funds (S125); financial auxiliaries (S126); and captive financial institutions and moneylenders (S127).

3. Integrating saving and non-financial investment

6.89. A further extension of the TFI aims to incorporate saving and non-financial investment. This completes the coverage of investment (financial and non-financial) and financing (saving, net (B8n), capital transfers, receivable (D9r), less capital transfers, payable (D9p), and net incurrences of liabilities).

6.90. Non-financial investment covers – in addition to the current external balance (B12) – gross capital formation, changes in inventories (P52), acquisitions less disposals of valuables (P53), and acquisitions less disposals of non-produced assets (NP).

6.91. In principle, this approach means combining the financial account and the capital account (see table 6.7). There is a strict requirement in these accounts – the accumulation accounts related to transactions – that investment must equal financing for each sector and for the national economy as a whole.

Table 6.7
The seven-sector approach combining the capital and the financial account

Changes in assets										Changes in liabilities and net worth								
Total	Rest of the world	Total economy	Households including non-profit institutions serving households	General government	Insurance corporations and pension funds	Financial corporations except monetary financial institutions and ICPFs	Monetary financial institutions	Non-financial corporations	**Transactions and balancing items**	Non-financial corporations	Monetary financial institutions	Financial corporations except monetary financial institutions and ICPFs	Insurance corporations and pension funds	General government	Households including non-profit institutions serving households	Total economy	Rest of the world	Total
									Saving, net (B8n)									
									Current external balance (B12)									
									Gross capital formation (P5g)									
									Changes in inventories (P52)									
									Acquisitions less disposals of valuables (P53)									
									Acquisitions less disposals of non-produced assets (NP)									
									Capital transfers, receivable (D9r)									
									Capital transfers, payable (D9p)									
									Changes in net worth due to saving and capital transfers (B101)									
									Net lending (+) / net borrowing (-) (B9)									
									Monetary gold and SDRs (F1)									
									Currency and deposits (F2)									
									Debt securities (F3)									
									Loans (F4)									
									Equity and investment fund shares (F5)									
									Unlisted shares (F512)									
									Other equity (F519)									
									Investment fund shares/units (F52)									
									Insurance, pension and standardized guarantee schemes (F6)									
									Financial derivatives and employee stock options (F7)									
									Other accounts receivable/payable (F8)									

Note: Shaded areas indicate cells that are not applicable.

Monetary financial institutions cover the central bank (S121); deposit-taking corporations, except the central bank (S122); and money market funds (S123). Financial corporations except monetary financial institutions and ICPFs cover non-MMF investment funds (S124); other financial intermediaries, except insurance corporations and pension funds (S125); financial auxiliaries (S126); and captive financial institutions and moneylenders (S127).

6.92. Such an expansion of the accounts may depend on the availability of non-financial accounts data by institutional sector.

6.93. Investment and financing data may be further complemented by non-financial data like income, saving and consumption leading to an enhanced analysis of the link between financial and non-financial developments, which is also relevant to the monetary policy transmission process, as reflected in income and wealth effects.

Box 6.2
Statistical discrepancies

The 2008 SNA is conceptually designed in such a way that it leaves no scope for statistical discrepancies or deviations from the accounting uniformity it introduces. This applies to balancing items, such as GDP and net lending (+)/net borrowing (–).

An integrated system of national accounts has two important statistical functions: first, as a conceptual framework for ensuring the consistency of the definitions and classifications used in different, but related, fields of statistics; and, second, as an accounting framework for ensuring the numerical consistency of data drawn from different statistical sources. Given that, owing to cost considerations, the quality of primary statistics underlying national accounts will be insufficient, the presentation of national accounts needs to resolve this issue, which is reflected through statistical discrepancies. Their proper treatment is part of the regular work of national accountants.

In terms of sector accounts, the discrepancy between net lending (+)/net borrowing (–) plays a prominent role in assessing the quality of the capital and the financial accounts (data "above" and "below" the line). Net lending (+)/net borrowing (–) may be derived as non-financial investment minus the changes in net worth due to saving and capital transfers, or as net acquisitions of financial assets minus net incurrence of liabilities (B9). In theory, there should be no difference (vertical consistency) between the two balancing items derived from the capital account and from the financial account respectively.[a]

There are two main reasons for the discrepancy. The first is a lack of sufficient and sufficiently consistent primary data, and the second is a lack of coordination between the institutions involved in compiling national accounts.

Concerning primary data, resources can be invested in improving data surveys, the format of the questionnaire, sampling strategies and processing techniques, including the treatment of missing data. However, while ultimately desirable, such an approach is costly and long-term. Even with very sophisticated data collection methods, discrepancies between different estimates will persist owing to differences in coverage, valuation and lags in recording. In addition, statistical work is dependent to a greater or lesser extent on administrative sources of data and these do not always exactly meet the statistician's needs.

Equally important to improving primary statistics is the development of quality reports. Harmonized quality reports may focus on revisions, reliability marks for individual variables within the national accounts framework, or on a harmonized presentation of statistical discrepancies. While in the current national accounts practice many countries show a statistical discrepancy around net lending/net borrowing, it may be worthwhile to examine whether the statistical discrepancy would be better placed around (net) saving, the balancing item of the accumulation account or even allocated among several components of the account. This would allow the grouping of some statistically less reliable variables within the capital account (changes in inventories, acquisitions less disposals of valuables and acquisitions less disposals of non-produced non-financial assets) and the financial account (other accounts receivable and payable) in items called "remaining financing" and "remaining investment", thus contributing to a better presentation of the economic analysis of financing and investment.

The data sources considered for the compilation of national accounts usually correspond to different data-compiling agencies. In many cases the national statistical office will produce the national income and production data. The central bank will assemble, based on the monetary, securities issues and balance of payments data, the financial account and government agencies will generate the central and other government data. All of them may well compile their respective data with respect to particular statistical methods or detailed breakdowns. Nevertheless, additional coordination and cooperation among the agencies involved is desirable to discuss the presentation of discrepancies and with a view to reducing their magnitude.

There are essentially two options for dealing with statistical discrepancies. One option is to present the discrepancy separately in the accounts. When this is done, it is usual to attach it to the variable the national accountant feels is the least accurate. The aim is to give users an indication of the degree of reliability of the published data. Within the United States national accounts, a procedure is applied in which the discrepancies are explicitly identified and explained. Two sets of figures are compiled and presented for saving and investment in the flow of funds accounts as published by the Federal Reserve Board and in the national income and product accounts as disseminated by the Bureau of Economic Analysis.

The second option is to remove the discrepancy by examining the data in the light of the 2008 SNA accounting framework, making the best judgment possible about where the errors are likely to have arisen and modifying the data accordingly. The discrepancy may be distributed to specific variables within specific sectors or subsectors accompanied by a quality report explaining the adjustments. This second approach means that, as a first step, the discrepancy is moved away from the balancing item to one aggregate or is split further into various aggregates of the capital account and the financial account.

[a] Other discrepancies may be observed, such as the discrepancy between the changes of the opening and closing positions and the sum of transactions; between other changes in the volume of assets and revaluations (stock-flow inconsistency); or differences in the data reported by an accounting entry and its counterpart (counterpart inconsistency, e.g. a payable of A vis-à-vis B does not comply with the same receivable of B vis-à-vis A).

6.94. A full integration of the real and financial variables, however, would require a set of complete non-financial accounts data by institutional sector.

6.95. Net lending (+)/net borrowing (–) (B9) may be derived as non-financial investment minus the changes in net worth due to saving and capital transfers, or as net acquisitions of financial assets minus net incurrences of liabilities. There should be no difference between the two balancing items derived from the capital account and from the financial account respectively.

4. Partial from-whom-to-whom accounts

6.96. The TFI shows only partial from-whom-to-whom information, relating mainly to deposits and loans, which are not traded on markets and are, therefore, easily identifiable by counterpart sector. For example, balance sheet statistics of monetary financial institutions usually provide data on deposits acquired and loans incurred by individual sectors and subsectors resident in the national economy.

6.97. However, deposits held and loans incurred by resident sectors vis-à-vis non-resident monetary financial institutions are usually not covered by balance sheet statistics.

6.98. Only incomplete from-whom-to-whom information is currently available for other institutional sectors. Most such data are still confined to general government and the rest of the world. In future, more from-whom-to-whom data may be based on security-by-security databases.

D. Towards an integrated system of institutional sector accounts

1. Institutional sector accounts for economic, financial and monetary analysis

6.99. An integrated system of institutional sector accounts is generally seen as a significant achievement and of great assistance to economists and policymakers, who need to make a comprehensive assessment of economic and monetary developments. A key feature of such a system of accounts is that information on nearly all financial and non-financial flows and stocks is integrated within a single accounting framework. Although such a system of accounts is necessarily available somewhat later than the primary statistics on which it is based, the consistent accounting framework provides a useful basis for cross-checking the primary statistics and understanding developments in the economy as a whole.

6.100. A system of accounts provides both additional details for the analysis of macroeconomic developments by institutional sector and a comprehensive framework to complement and combine information provided by other, timelier statistics.

6.101. In particular, the accounts enhance the analysis of:

(a) The important elements of demand for households, such as consumption and residential investment, by allowing a comparison with the various sources of income (both labour and non-labor related, including dividends and interest receivable) and with the associated changes in net wealth (both financial transactions and holding gains/losses on households' assets);

(b) The production, income, investment and financing of non-financial corporations;

(c) The portfolio shifts between monetary assets and other financial instruments by institutional sector.

2. Financial flows and stocks in the context of from-whom-to-whom relationships

6.102. The 2008 SNA standard presentation of institutional sector accounts is not explicitly designed to show the intersectoral linkages, as it has traditionally focused on answering "who does what", and not "who does what with whom".

6.103. However, the 2008 SNA provides an integrated framework for developing quarterly data on financial transactions, other flows and balance sheets on a from-whom-to-whom basis because its underlying principles ensure that the linkages of the economic and financial actions of an economy and its sectors are captured.

6.104. As the 2008 SNA is the internationally accepted standard for the compilation of national accounts, the lack of prominence it gives to the from-whom-to-whom principle of data compilation and presentation may be one of the reasons why these statistics are not yet more widely available.

6.105. Promoting the implementation of the from-whom-to-whom intersectoral relationships for financial positions and flows together with the sectoral accounts of the SNA is thus an important step towards filling one of the most significant data gaps identified during the recent global financial crisis.

6.106. The integrated framework on a from-whom-to-whom basis allows certain questions to be answered, such as: who is financing whom, to what amount, and with which type of financial instrument? As regards the allocation of income, it also permits tracing who is paying income (e.g. interest) to whom and who is receiving income from whom.

6.107. The reasons to collect, compile and present from-whom-to-whom financial flows and stocks are analytical but also statistical:

(a) From-whom-to-whom statistical information considerably enriches the method of monitoring monetary transmission processes. Because price and interest changes of the various financial assets and liabilities of the various sectors play a major role in this process, the analysis may also focus on stock-flow adjustments within the various institutional sectors. In this respect, from-whom-to-whom statistical information makes it possible to analyse how financial assets, liabilities and balancing items as financial flows and stocks have changed as a consequence of policy decisions;

(b) It helps to identify data sets covered by more than one data source, by only one data source and by no data source owing to the lack of primary statistics. An example of a data set with no data source may be trade credits provided by non-financial corporations to households.

6.108. Given the complexity of from-whom-to-whom statistical information, the burden on input data providers and compilers is expected to be quite significant. In this context additional data sources need to be established, as outlined in chapter 7.

6.109. Chapter 27 of the 2008 SNA explains that detailed flow of funds accounts are based on two three-dimensional tables. One table records transactions in assets cross-classified by type of asset and by debtor sector. The second table records transactions in liabilities cross-classified by type of liability and by the creditor sector. Corresponding tables may also be designed for balance sheet items.

6.110. Similar tables are also proposed in the MFSMCG to track financial transactions between source and user sectors and the financial asset used in the transaction (chap. 8). The sectors transacting in assets are shown horizontally in the table while the type of asset, disaggregated by sector of the debtor, is presented vertically. The chapter also describes how to use such tables in various economic policy areas.

6.111. The GFSM 2014 focuses on another important reason to collect such counterpart information. Some financial assets and liabilities, most typically deposits, debt securities, loans, and other accounts receivable/payable require the debtor to pay interest. The interest accrues continuously and increases the total amount that the debtor will be required to pay. An appropriate attribution of the interest accrued to the parties requires counterpart information because the value of these assets and liabilities includes all interest that has been accrued and not yet paid.

3. The from-whom-to-whom framework

6.112. A from-whom-to-whom framework allows for a detailed presentation of financing and financial investment via financial instruments. This has a number of uses. In a broader context, it permits the analysis of relationships between institutional sectors and subsectors within an economy and also between these sectors and subsectors and non-residents (broken down even further by country and sector). Such an analysis sheds light on the sectoral composition of assets and liabilities, and on potential strengths and vulnerabilities in portfolios.

6.113. The framework provides the response to such questions as: who is financing whom, to what amount and with which type of financial instrument? It may also clarify such questions as: on which other resident sectors do the debt instruments held by, for instance, households represent claims? On which resident sectors do the financial instruments held by non-residents represent claims? Or, from the side of the issuer of financial instruments, how important are, for instance, debt securities issues of general government held by households or by financial corporations (and by which subsectors)? How significant are general government debt securities issues held by non-residents?

6.114. The presentation of financial instrument debt holdings in a from-whom-to-whom framework or by debtor/creditor[155] represents an extension of the presentation of unconsolidated financial instrument holdings without any counterpart sector or residency information, as outlined in table 6.8.

Table 6.8
From-whom-to-whom approach unconsolidated

Holder by residency and by resident sector / Issuer by residency and by resident sector		Residents						
		Non-financial corporations	Financial corporations	General government	Households and non-profit institutions serving households	Non-residents	All holders	
Residents	Non-financial corporations							Residence of issuer
	Financial corporations							
	General government							
Non-residents								
All issuers								
		Residence of holder						

[155] Chapter 27 of the 2008 SNA uses the term "flow of funds".

6.115. Table 6.8 shows a breakdown by debtor (issuing) sector of the positions (or, in the case of transactions, the net acquisitions) of a financial instrument like debt securities or equity securities (thus showing the sectors on which the securities represent claims) and a breakdown by creditor (holding) sector of positions or transactions in securities (showing the sectors acquiring securities). This presentation thus provides information on debtor/creditor relationships and is consistent with a from-whom-to-whom framework.

6.116. As a summary table, it aggregates the resident institutional units issuing and holding securities to the main institutional sectors. Table 6.8 presents the relationships between residents and non-residents as holders and issuers of these financial instruments.

6.117. Resident institutional units are grouped into sectors (non-financial corporations, financial corporations, general government, and households and non-profit institutions serving households). Depending on the purpose of the table, the resident institutional sectors as issuing and holding sectors may be further broken down into subsectors.

6.118. Table 6.8 may be designed in such a way that it shows, for a certain period, the initial positions at the beginning of the period, the transactions and other flows (revaluations and other changes in the volume of assets and liabilities) during the period, and the closing positions at the end of the period for securities issued and held by resident institutional units and by non-resident institutional units.

6.119. For residents, the presentation of unconsolidated data on securities holdings is recommended. This means that their intrasectoral positions, transactions, revaluations and other changes in the volume of assets and liabilities should be reported (cells shaded grey with diagonal lines).

6.120. Holdings of securities by non-residents (vis-à-vis resident sectors as issuers) are shown as positions in the rest of the world balance sheet (the international investment position), as financial transactions in the rest of the world financial account (part of the balance of payments), and as revaluations or other changes in the volume of assets in the rest of the world accumulation accounts (cross-hatched cells in the non-residents column of table 6.8. Issues of securities by non-residents (vis-à-vis resident sectors as holders) are reflected in the row with cross-hatched cells.

6.121. As also indicated in table 6.8, the holdings by non-residents of securities issued by non-residents are not covered (black cell). These are not relevant from a national economy's perspective. In general, households and non-profit institutions serving households do not issue such financial instruments.

6.122. For each type of security (as a position or flow), a from-whom-to-whom framework has two dimensions:

(a) The residency and sector or subsector of the debtor/issuer;

(b) The residency and sector or subsector of the creditor/holder.

6.123. A from-whom-to-whom framework requires three-dimensional tables covering the breakdowns of the security, the debtor/issuer and the creditor/holder.[156] Such tables show positions, transactions and other flows cross-classified by debtor sector and creditor sector.

6.124. As an example, table 6.9 is a from-whom-to-whom presentation of transactions in debt securities. It is the same type of table as table 6.8 and shows, for example, in its fourth column that households and non-profit institutions serving households

[156] The time series aspect of the from-whom-to-whom framework may be seen as the fourth dimension.

Table 6.9
From-whom-to-whom financial transactions in debt securities (unconsolidated)

Issuer by residency and by resident sector \ Holder by residency and by resident sector		Residents: Non-financial corporations	Residents: Financial corporations	Residents: General government	Residents: Households and non-profit institutions serving households	Residents: All residents	Non-residents	All holders
Residents	Non-financial corporations	30	23	5	65	123	24	147
	Financial corporations	11	22	2	43	78	28	106
	General government	67	25	6	124	222	54	276
	All residents	108	70	13	232	423	106	529
Non-residents		34	12	19	43	108		108
All issuers		142	82	32	275	531	106	637

acquired (net of disposals) debt securities of 275; this acquisition reflects an increase in their claims on non-financial corporations (65), financial corporations (43), general government (124) and the rest of the world (43).

6.125. Table 6.9 indicates that, for example, as a result of transactions in the reference period, non-financial corporations issued (net of redemptions) debt securities of 147, as reflected in the first row. Their liabilities in this form to other non-financial corporations increased by 30, to financial corporations by 23, to general government by 5, to households and non-profit institutions serving households by 65 and to the rest of the world by 24. Conversely, households and non-profit institutions serving households did not issue debt securities.

6.126. Table 6.9 also presents intrasectoral transactions of resident sectors in debt securities holdings (the diagonal cells). For instance, non-financial corporations issued debt securities of 30 which are being held by other institutional units of the same sector. These transactions are not covered when intrasectoral transactions are consolidated. If the transactions are consolidated for each resident sector, the table would then show only the transactions between the various resident sectors and between the latter and the rest of the world, but not the transactions within the same resident sectors.[157]

6.127. Transactions in debt securities held by residents and issued by non-residents are reflected in the "non-residents" row. The amount is 108. Transactions in debt securities held by non-residents and issued by residents are shown in the "non-residents" column. The amount is 106. Transactions in debt securities held by non-residents and issued by non-residents are not covered (black cell).

6.128. Table 6.9 also shows that, by definition, all transactions in debt securities held by residents (vis-à-vis resident and non-resident issuers) (531) and held by non-residents (vis-à-vis resident issuers) (106) are equal to all transactions in debt securities issued by residents (vis-à-vis resident and non-resident holders) (529) and in debt securities issued by non-residents (vis-à-vis resident holders) (108). The total amount is 637. Table 6.10 presents Table 6.9 in a time series format.

[157] Totals by issuer refer to issues and redemptions only; totals by holder refer to issues, redemptions and transactions in the secondary market.

Table 6.10
From-whom-to-whom financial transactions in debt securities in a time series format

Transaction		t	t+1	...	t+n
Net acquisition of debt securities by					
Non-financial corporations					
Issued by	Non-financial corporations	30			
	Financial corporations	11			
	General government	67			
	All residents	***108***			
	Non-residents	***34***			
	All issuers	**142**			
Financial corporations					
Issued by	Non-financial corporations	23			
	Financial corporations	22			
	General government	25			
	All residents	***70***			
	Non-residents	***12***			
	All issuers	**82**			
General government					
Issued by	Non-financial corporations	5			
	Financial corporations	2			
	General government	6			
	All residents	***13***			
	Non-residents	***19***			
	All issuers	**32**			
Households and non-profit institutions serving households					
Issued by	Non-financial corporations	65			
	Financial corporations	43			
	General government	124			
	All residents	***232***			
	Non-residents	***43***			
	All issuers	**275**			
All residents					
Issued by	Non-financial corporations	123			
	Financial corporations	78			
	General government	222			
	All residents	***423***			
	Non-residents	***108***			
	All issuers	**531**			
Non-residents					
Issued by	Non-financial corporations	24			
	Financial corporations	28			
	General government	54			
	All residents (=all issuers)	**106**			
All holders					
Issued by	Non-financial corporations	147			
	Financial corporations	106			
	General government	276			
	All residents	**529**			

6.129. Similar tables can be compiled for positions, revaluations and other changes in the volume of assets.

6.130. The complexity of from-whom-to-whom tables for debt securities is determined by the detail of the breakdowns chosen for debt securities (by subcategory, position and subposition) and for the creditors and debtors (by residency, sector and subsector).

6.131. Combining these breakdowns leads to a substantial number of from-whom-to-whom relationships, especially as the data may need to be shown as positions and flows. Accordingly, a selection by debt security subcategory, sector and subsector is essential.

4. From-whom-to-whom accounts

6.132. Compiling from-whom-to-whom accounts involves making use of counterpart information.[158] The basic principle is that, in any flow or stock involving two institutional units, information should be collected from the unit from which it can be most efficiently obtained. For example, information on the interest paid by deposit-taking corporations except the central bank to households can be obtained from a relatively small number of financial institutions, as opposed to a large number of households. Counterpart information is the equivalent of using commodity balances in the goods and services and production accounts to fill gaps. Counterpart information is particularly important in a quarterly context when there are more likely to be gaps.

6.133. One factor to be taken into account is that data providers may not always be able to collect data on the institutional classification of the counterparts if they do not have sufficient information or the authorization to do so.

6.134. The financial account and the financial balance sheet are usually among the more complete sector data. Balance sheet and/or transaction data are often already collected from financial corporations. If the counterparts in each transaction, asset or liability are classified by institutional sector, there is a strong basis for compiling the data for all the sectors, not only the financial corporations themselves.

6.135. In addition, balance of payments and international investment position data show transactions, assets and liabilities between non-residents and residents that are not financial corporations. Attention should also be paid to financial transactions and stocks of assets and liabilities not included in financial corporations sector and balance of payments data, such as household equity in corporations and direct financial relationships between non-financial corporations.

5. The transactor principle versus the debtor/creditor principle[159]

6.136. Two types of financial transactions in debt securities or equity securities may be distinguished. The first type, issues and redemptions of securities, typically involves only the debtor (or issuer) and one creditor (the holder). The second type, transactions on secondary markets, involves three institutional units: the two creditors exchanging the security and the institutional unit whose liability it is. Sometimes, as in the case of the assumption of a debt, the three institutional units may be two debtors and a creditor.

6.137. The involvement of three parties complicates the recording of secondary market transactions, because the positions between the issuer and the seller and between the issuer and the buyer change.

[158] It should be noted that the same compilation principles such as valuation, timing and classification should be used for both creditors and debtors, which may lead to differences in the primary statistics.

[159] Chapter 5 explains the debtor/creditor approach in recording accrued interest, which differs from the debtor/creditor principle described here in the context of from-whom-to-whom accounting.

6.138. A financial transaction between two institutional units as holders (creditors) of a security, for example a change in ownership of a security between institutional unit A, the original holder, and institutional unit B, the new holder, in a different (sub) sector from A may therefore be recorded either:

(a) As a change in ownership of a security between the two creditors with reclassification entries in the other changes in the volume of assets and liabilities account of the debtor, reflecting the fact that the creditor is now in a different sector. In this approach, the secondary market transaction is recorded in the accounts as a single transaction accompanied by a reclassification adjustment; or

(b) As the extinction of the claim (the security) of creditor A against the debtor and the creation of a claim (the security) of creditor B against the debtor. In this approach, the exchange of assets on the secondary market is recorded as two transactions.

6.139. The first approach gives prominence to the contract between the creditors (transactor principle) while the second approach emphasizes the contract between the debtor and the creditors (debtor/creditor principle) as shown in figure 6.1.

(a) The transactor principle

6.140. The transactor principle captures the change in ownership of a financial asset (or the change of debtor in the case of the assumption of a debt) in the accounts of the transactors involved, but not in the account of the debtor (or of the creditor where one institutional unit takes on the liability of another).

6.141. Thus, under the transactor principle, a change in ownership of a security is recorded without taking into consideration the involvement of the debtor.

Figure 6.1
The transactor principle and the debtor/creditor principle

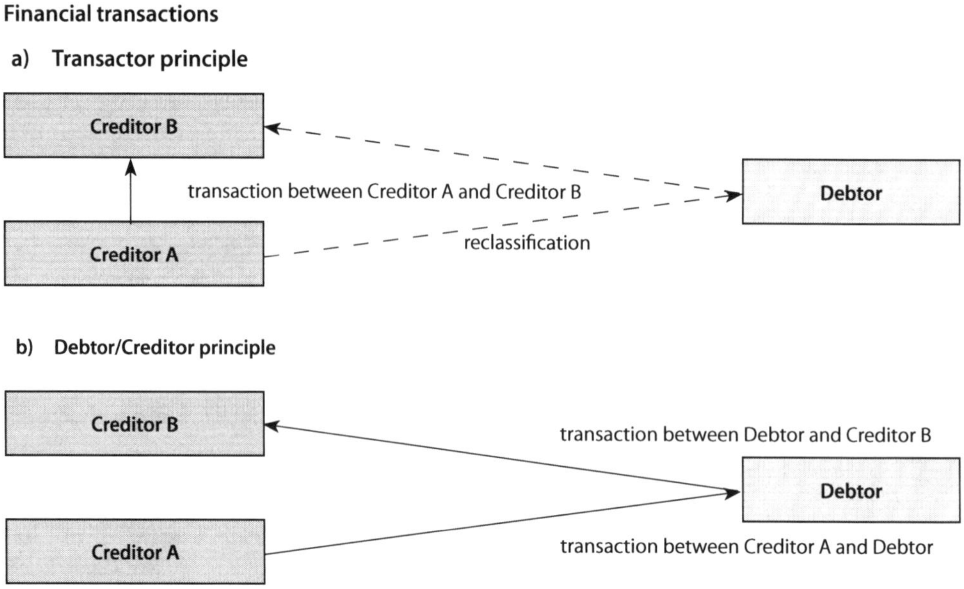

6.142. For example, when a household buys from a financial corporation a debt security issued by a non-financial corporation, following the transactor principle a single transaction in securities is recorded, as shown in table 6.11 (i.e. between a financial

Table 6.11

Recording of an acquisition of debt securities by households from financial corporations in accordance with the transactor principle

Financial assets	*Liabilities*	*Financial assets*	*Liabilities*
Households		**Non-financial corporations**	
–Currency			+ Other change in liabilities vis-à-vis households
+Debt securities			
Financial corporations			
+Currency			–Other change in liabilities vis-à-vis financial corporations
–Debt securities			

corporation and a household), without the change of ownership being reflected in the account of the debtor, as the issuer of the security (the non-financial corporation).

6.143. To reflect the change in the counterpart creditor sector in the account of the debtor, a reclassification of the creditor is recorded in the other changes in the volume of assets account of the debtor non-financial corporation. The numerous secondary market transactions in securities would necessitate many such reclassifications, which would not help analysis. Therefore, while it is appropriate for the recording of transactions and positions without taking into account the debtor/creditor relationship, the transactor principle is not recommended in the context of a from-whom-to-whom framework.

6.144. Applying the transactor principle requires data on individual transactions, including information on:

(a) The transactors (i.e. holders A and B);

(b) The type and value of the security concerned;

(c) The issuer.

6.145. The collection of data on individual transactions leads to a considerable amount of detailed statistical information, bearing in mind the volume of securities trading on any given day. Information on both transactors is available to custodians or stock exchanges.[160] If no transaction data are available, only the positions of holders of securities can be identified. Accordingly, statistical collection systems do not usually provide detailed information on transactions, relying instead on position data.[161]

(b) The debtor/creditor principle

6.146. The debtor/creditor principle captures a transaction between two institutional units in the accounts of the two transactors, and also permits the change in creditor to be recorded in the financial account of the debtor (or, in the case of the assumption of a debt, the change in debtor to be recorded in the financial account of the creditor).

6.147. Thus, when the ownership of a security changes, the debtor/creditor principle records the two links as financial transactions. When a financial corporation sells a security issued by a non-financial corporation to a household, the financial account of the non-financial corporation records an issuance of securities to a household and a corresponding repayment to a financial corporation. Financial transactions involving three institutional units are recorded as shown in table 6.12 below.

[160] However, in many cases, the transactor approach results in data on transactions with brokers and other intermediaries, not transactions with the "ultimate" owners of the securities.

[161] Some economies do capture transaction data directly, usually on a net asset or liability basis, as requested in the BPM6 for portfolio transactions. Capturing these data presents a challenge from a practical perspective.

Table 6.12
Recording of an acquisition of debt securities by households from financial corporations in accordance with the debtor/creditor principle

Financial assets	*Liabilities*	*Financial assets*	*Liabilities*
Households		**Non-financial corporations**	
–Currency		+Currency	
+Debt securities vis-à-vis non-financial corporations			+Debt securities vis-à-vis households
Financial corporations			
+Currency		–Currency	
–Debt securities vis-à-vis non-financial corporations			–Debt securities vis-à-vis financial corporations

6.148. The sale of a security issued by a resident or non-resident institutional unit (the debtor) to another institutional unit (resident or non-resident) (the two creditors) clearly conforms to the 2008 SNA definition of a transaction (the exchange of economic value between willing participants). It cannot be construed as a reclassification from either the buyer's or the seller's point of view.

6.149. Symmetry of treatment between asset holders and liability issuers would require that the issuer treat the event as a transaction (a concurrent redemption and new issue, netting to zero net issuance).

6.150. This approach is further justified by implicit or explicit conditions accepted by the issuer when creating a security. When the issue requires the debtor to record the owners of the securities in the debtors' liability register, the two creditors will inform the debtor of the change in ownership and, by recording the event, the debtor acknowledges the secondary market transaction. In the case of bearer securities (i.e. no registration requirements) the issuer will repay the bearer at maturity irrespective of how many secondary market transactions may have taken place, implicitly recognizing secondary market transactions. The secondary market transaction is re-routed via the debtor, reflecting the debtor's implicit or explicit recognition of the transaction.

Worked example 6.1. Detailed recording of debt securities following the debtor/creditor principle[162]

6.151. Position data are usually available with information on the holder (creditor B) and on the debtor of debt securities at a specific point in time, but not on the transactor from whom the debt securities were bought (creditor A).

6.152. Transactions may then be derived, residually, as the difference in positions between the beginning and the end of a period, minus any other flows:

$$Transactions_t = Position_t - Position_{t-1} - Revaluations_t - Other\ changes\ in\ volume_t$$

6.153. Based on the available information on positions, this approach complies with the debtor/creditor principle. This is demonstrated in the following table. Creditor B has positions *t*–1 in debt securities vis-à-vis debtor 1 of 10 and vis-à-vis debtor 2 of 20. These positions change to 12, vis-à-vis debtor 1, and to 10, vis-à-vis debtor 2, in *t*. It is assumed that no revaluations or other changes in volume have taken place in the period. Based on this assumption, the net acquisition of debt securities by creditor B is +2 vis-à-vis debtor 1 and -10 vis-à-vis debtor 2.

162 See also the HSS, part 2.

Table 6.13
Detailed recording following the debtor/creditor principle

		Creditor (holder)		
Debtor (issuer)		**Creditor A**	**Creditor B**	**Total**
Debtor 1	1. Position at end of previous period	5	10	15
	2. Net acquisition during current period	-2	2	0
	3. Revaluation during current period	-	-	-
	4. Other change in volume during current period	-	-	-
	5. Position at end of current period	3	12	15
Debtor 2	1. Position at end of previous period	15	20	35
	2. Net acquisition during current period	10	-10	0
	3. Revaluation during current period	-	-	-
	4. Other change in volume during current period	-	-	-
	5. Position at end of current period	25	10	35
Total	1. Position at end of previous period	20	30	50
	2. Net acquisition during current period	8	-8	0
	3. Revaluation during current period	-	-	-
	4. Other change in volume during current period	-	-	-
	5. Position at end of current period	28	22	50

6.154. Following the debtor/creditor principle, the net acquisition by creditor B of debt securities vis-à-vis debtor 1 (+2) is recorded as an acquisition of debt securities newly issued by debtor 1. Symmetrically, debtor 1 is deemed to have redeemed 2 of debt securities held by creditor A.

6.155. In parallel, the net acquisition of -10 (a disposal) has to be recorded by creditor B and a redemption of debt securities by debtor 2. A corresponding new issue of 10 of debt securities by debtor 2 is deemed to have been bought by creditor A.

6.156. Note that in reality there are no transactions in the period between the debtor and the two creditors. Rather, four transactions (one between each debtor and each of the two creditors) are imputed, and they replace the actual secondary market transactions in debt securities by the two holders. The effect is to preserve the link between the transaction data and the change in the from-whom-to-whom position data.

6.157. The transactions to be recorded for this example following the debtor/creditor principle are illustrated in figure 6.2.

6.158. The set of information required to apply the debtor/creditor principle consists of: (a) a security-by-security database that allows each issuance of a debt security to be identified (information on the debtor and the initial creditor); and (b) the link between the security-by-security database and the appropriate securities holdings statistics which keeps track of changes in the debt securities positions of creditors and includes information on the individual debtors.

Figure 6.2
Transactions according to the debtor/creditor principle

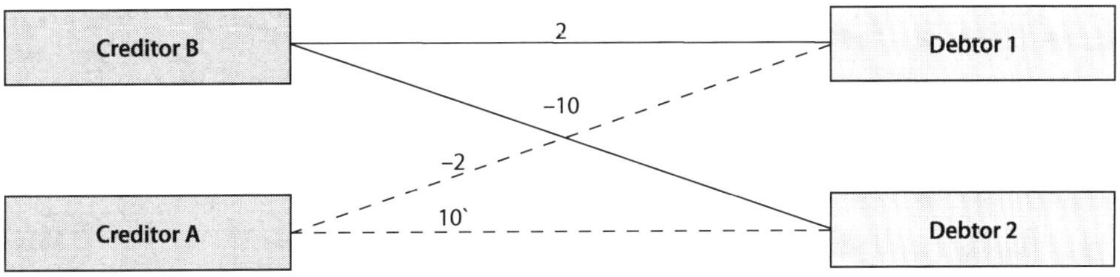

E. A multidimensional system of accumulation accounts and balance sheets

6.159. The system of accumulation accounts and balance sheets as described so far is mainly two-dimensional. The accumulation accounts and the balance sheets are limited in that they do not or only partially reveal counterpart sectors to the transactions, revaluations and the other changes in volume and the balance sheet positions. That is, although they show which sectors are acquiring financial assets, and in which financial assets they are transacting, they do not identify the sectors that issued those assets. Similarly, while they enable net borrowing sectors to be identified, and show how they borrow, the accounts do not show which sectors took up and hold the borrowing instruments. The same applies for revaluations and the other changes in the volume of assets. They accordingly do not give a complete picture of the respective flows in the economy.

6.160. For a full understanding of financial flows and stocks, it is important to know not just what types of liabilities a sector uses to finance its activities, but also which sectors are providing the financing. In addition, it is often necessary to analyse financial transactions between subsectors of a sector, such as financial corporations and general government.

6.161. Multidimensional systems of accounts include the breakdowns by financial instrument, debtor and creditor sector necessary for a detailed from-whom-to-whom presentation – either designed for the whole national economy or for specific institutional sectors.

6.162. To compile from-whom-to-whom accounts, counterpart information has to be collected for the various financial instruments held and incurred by the institutional sectors, such as deposits, loans, securities, and shares including other equity.

6.163. Following the principle that from-whom-to-whom information should be obtained from the most reliable statistical source, data derived from the various accounting systems of institutional units should be used – amended by statistical information taken from capital markets.

6.164. Usually no detailed quarterly counterpart information is available for non-financial corporations and households including non-profit institutions serving households. Partial from-whom-to-whom information can be derived from other financial statistics.

6.165. From-whom-to-whom accounts allow the debtor/creditor relationships between institutional sectors to be traced because they usually show the transactions, other flows and balance sheet positions cross-classified by debtor sector and creditor sector. Figure 6.3 illustrates the from-whom-to-whom transactions as inflows and outflows, for one financial instrument, between the five resident sectors and the rest of the world.

6.166. In order to derive from-whom-to-whom accounts, data have to be compiled based on the quadruple-entry principle. The presentation allows an analysis of who is financing whom, to what amount, and using which instrument. As regards the allocation of income, it also permits tracing who is paying (receiving) income, such as interest, to (from) whom.

6.167. The generalization of such a quadruple-entry accounting system leads to a system of from-whom-to-whom accounts. For such a system, five dimensions have to be specified: the type of account (balance sheet, transaction account, revaluation account and other changes in the volume of assets account), the instrument category, the debtor sector, the creditor sector and the specific period or point in time.

Figure 6.3
From-whom-to-whom transactions between the five resident sectors and the rest of the world sector for one financial instrument

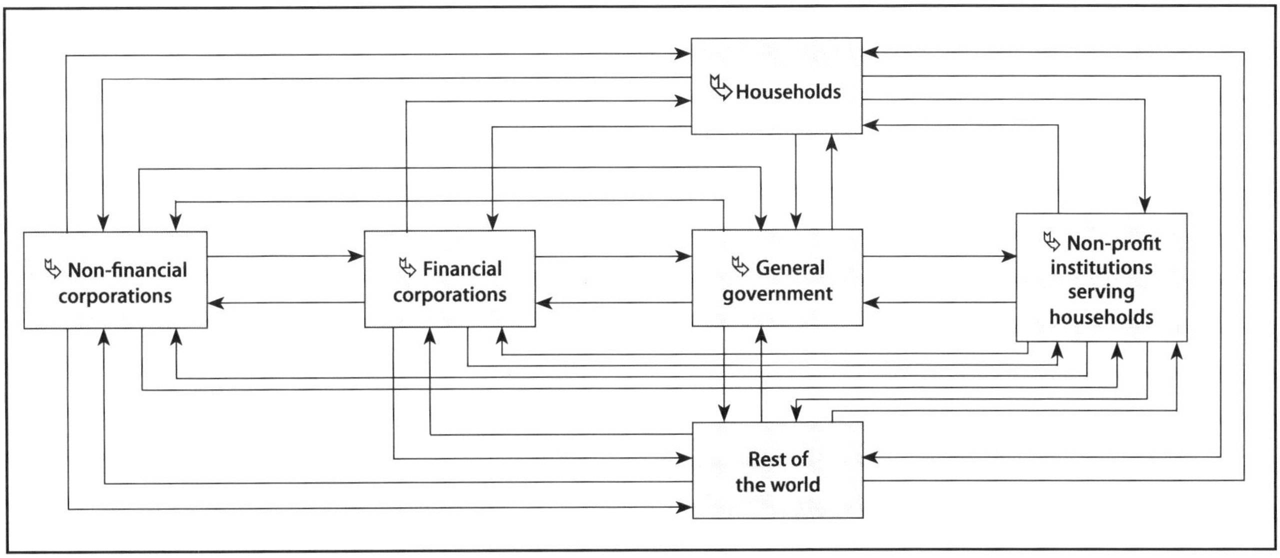

Note: The arrows drawn within the resident sectors indicate the intrasectoral transactions. Such transactions are, by definition, not shown for the rest of the world.

6.168. For a specific period or point in time, a four-dimensional system of linear equations is considered the appropriate way to present from-whom-to-whom financial accounts.

6.169. For example, looking only at one type of account, the financial account, and one period of time, a financial transaction F(i) in a period of time *t* between a debtor D(j) resident in a national economy e(k) and belonging to a sector s(l) and a creditor C(m) resident in the same national economy e(k) and belonging to a sector s(m) is described as:

$$F(i) = F(i)_t\ (D(j)_{e(k),s(l)},\ C(m)_{e(k),s(m)})$$

1. Components determining the complexity of from-whom-to-whom accounts

6.170. The complexity of the system of from-whom-to-whom accounts for a specific period or point in time is determined by the four dimensions of the system of accounts as mentioned above:

(a) The type of account;

(b) The financial instrument category or subcategory;

(c) The debtor sector or subsector;

(d) The creditor sector or subsector.

6.171. Combining the four types of accounts for stocks, transactions, revaluations and other changes in the volume of assets, the eight instrument categories and the five resident sectors and the rest of the world sector results, theoretically, in 4×8×6×6=1,152 cells to be compiled. An increase of the number of instrument categories to 16 and the number of sectors to 13 would mean that 10,816 cells would have (theoretically) to be compiled (table 6.14).

Table 6.14
Number of cells to be compiled for a complete set of from-whom-to-whom financial accounts

Number of institutional debtor and creditor sectors/subsectors	Number of financial instruments			
	2	**3**	**8**	**16**
2	32	48	128	256
3	72	108	288	576
6	288	432	1,152	2,304
8	512	768	2,048	4,096
13	1,352	2,028	5,408	10,816

2. Specific characteristics of financial instruments

6.172. A fully fledged system of from-whom-to-whom financial accounts is very complex because of all its various dimensions, even if the rest of the world sector and, eventually, some non-financial sectors are treated as consolidated sectors. However, the specific characteristics of some financial instruments imply certain restrictions which contribute to reducing somewhat the complexity of the system of financial accounts. For example, transactions in monetary gold and SDRs take place between the holder of those financial assets, the central bank or central government as the respective monetary authority, and the rest of the world.

6.173. Transactions in currency are either issuances of currency by monetary authorities or transactions between the holders of currency. The central bank usually issues currency in the form of notes, while the central government usually issues coins. Currency in circulation, either domestic or foreign, is used by all money-holding sectors as a means of transactions, financial or non-financial, but also as a store of value. Transactions in deposits usually involve credit institutions, resident and non-resident, as debtors and usually all sectors, resident or non-resident, as deposit holders. To some extent, central government may also incur deposits.

6.174. Transactions in debt securities and shares and other equity usually take place between corporations, financial or non-financial, as the issuing institutional units and the holders. Households and non-profit institutions serving households may be legally entitled to issue securities. In the case of households, debt securities can be issued to finance the purchase of dwellings. General government issues debt securities.

6.175. All sectors are usually holders of these instruments, of which debt securities, listed shares and some types of investment fund shares or units are traded on secondary markets. Finally, transactions in life insurance technical reserves are, by definition, between households as the policyholders and the insurer. The insurer can be a corporation, but also a government unit. These restrictions are shown as shaded cells in table 6.15.

6.176. Table 6.16 presents all possible financial transactions for a financial instrument F (i) within a time period between the resident sectors (S11 to S15), the national economy (S1) and the rest of the world (S2). The transactions are shown in a matrix in such a way that the cells in each row represent the flows or stocks from the debtor sectors to the creditor sectors, and the cells in each column represent the flows or stocks from the creditor sectors to the debtor sectors.

6.177. The intrasectoral financial transactions are shown in the main diagonal of the matrix. There is one restriction on the rest of the world, which is not further split

Table 6.15
Restrictions due to specific characteristics of financial instruments (*indicated as shaded cells*)

Total	S2	S1	S14/S15	S13	S12	S11	Transactions	S11	S12	S13	S14/S15	S1	S2	Total
Net acquisition of financial assets								Net incurrence of liabilities						
							Monetary gold and SDRs[a]							
							Currency and deposits							
							Debt securities							
							Loans							
							Equity and investment fund shares							
							Insurance, pension and standardized guaranteed schemes							
							Financial derivatives and employee stock options							
							Other accounts receivable/ payable							

Note: The resident institutional sectors are: S11 – non-financial corporations; S12 – financial corporations; S13 – general government; S14 – households; and S15 – non-profit institutions serving households. S1 refers to the whole economy and S2 refers to the rest of the world.

[a] Only monetary authorities normally hold these assets; monetary authorities may be the central bank or central government.

into institutional sectors in the table presented here. Moreover, the rest of the world is treated as a sector, which is by definition consolidated.

6.178. The from-whom-to-whom financial transaction account of an institutional sector or of the rest of the world is an extension of the non-consolidated financial transaction account. It shows, in addition, a breakdown of the net acquisition of financial assets by debtor sector and a breakdown of the net incurrence of liabilities by creditor sector. Therefore, it provides detailed information on the debtor/creditor relationship which is consistent with other accounts like the financial balance sheet by debtor/creditor.

6.179. In the case of financial transactions on secondary markets, however, it does not provide information on the institutional units to which financial assets are sold or from which institutional units financial assets are bought; that is to say, the financial account by debtor/creditor does not provide a complete answer to the question of who is financing whom in an accounting period.

Table 6.16
From-whom-to-whom transactions between five resident sectors and the rest of the world sector for a financial instrument F (i)

			Creditor							
Fn			S1						S2	Total
			S11	S12	S13	S14	S15	Total		
Debtor	S1	S11	S11_S11	S11_S12	S11_S13	S11_S14	S11_S15	S11_S1	S11_S2	S11_S
		S12	S12_S11	S12_S12	S12_S13	S12_S14	S12_S15	S12_S1	S12_S2	S12_S
		S13	S13_S11	S13_S12	S13_S13	S13_S14	S13_S15	S13_S1	S13_S2	S13_S
		S14	S14_S11	S14_S12	S14_S13	S14_S14	S14_S15	S14_S1	S14_S2	S14_S
		S15	S15_S11	S15_S12	S15_S13	S15_S14	S15_S15	S15_S1	S15_S2	S15_S
		Total	S1_S11	S1_S12	S1_S13	S1_S14	S1_S15	S1_S1	S1_S2	S1_S
	S2		S2_S11	S2_S12	S2_S13	S2_S14	S2_S15	S2_S1	S2_S2	S2_S
	Total		S_S11	S_S12	S_S13	S_S14	S_S15	S_S1	S_S2	S_S

6.180. The from-whom-to-whom financial balance sheet of a sector or of the rest of the world is an extension of the non-consolidated financial balance sheet. It shows, in addition, a breakdown of financial assets by debtor sector and a breakdown of liabilities by creditor sector. Therefore, it provides information on debtor/creditor relationships which is consistent with the financial transaction account by debtor/creditor.

6.181. Deriving the from-whom-to-whom financial transaction account and the financial balance sheet enables other from-whom-to-whom flow accounts to be drawn up. This information is mostly of value for revaluations, as it allows the various asset price effects measured for specific sectors vis-à-vis other sectors to be quantified.[163]

3. Financial transactions between two institutional units as debtor and creditor

6.182. For many financial transactions between two institutional units, the debtors and creditors are usually the transactors. For example, a deposit-taking corporation (the creditor, S122) grants a loan (F4) to a non-financial corporation (the debtor, S11). The transfer of deposits (F21) gives rise to a net acquisition of a financial asset by the deposit-taking corporation and to a net incurrence of a liability by the non-financial corporation.

Non-financial corporations (S11)	
Financial assets	*Liabilities*
+Transferable deposits (F21)	
	+Loans (F4)

Deposit-taking corporations (S122)	
Financial assets	*Liabilities*
−Transferable deposits (F21)	
+Loans (F4)	

6.183. The same applies if, for instance, a central government unit (as the debtor, S1311) issues a bond (F32), which is initially acquired by a household (the creditor, S14).

Central government (S1311)	
Financial assets	*Liabilities*
+Transferable deposits (F21)	
	+Long-term debt securities (F32)

Households (S14)	
Financial assets	*Liabilities*
−Transferable deposits (F21)	
+Long-term debt securities (F32)	

6.184. The transactions are recorded within the financial account of a resident institutional sector or of the rest of the world. In cases where a transaction and its counterpart are both financial transactions, they may change the relevant units' totals of both financial assets and liabilities or of the portfolio of financial assets and liabilities. Accordingly, financial transactions with financial transactions as counterpart lead to either: (a) a simultaneous rise or reduction in the financial assets and liabilities of both transactors; or (b) an exchange of financial assets between two parties (see table 6.17). The parties to the transactions can be resident institutional units or non-residents.

6.185. Another example is the buy-back of listed shares by a non-financial corporation. It is assumed that a household holds the listed shares (see table 6.18).

6.186. Transactions often involve the exchange of one financial asset for another without any exchange of currency or transferable deposits. Such operations include, for example, the conversion of unlisted shares into listed shares, of other deposits into

[163] The valuation accounting rules in the balance sheets of the different institutional units, both financial and non-financial, should be harmonized.

Table 6.17
Financial transactions with counterpart financial transactions

Simultaneous rise of financial assets and liabilities

Households (S15)	
Financial assets	*Liabilities*
+Transferable deposits (F21)	+Loans (F4)

Exchange of one financial asset for another

Deposit-taking corporations (S122)	
Financial assets	*Liabilities*
−Transferable deposits (F21)	
+Loans (F4)	

Simultaneous reduction of financial assets and liabilities

Households (S15)	
Financial assets	*Liabilities*
−Transferable deposits (F21)	−Trade credit (F9)

Exchange of one financial asset for another

Deposit-taking corporations (S122)	
Financial assets	*Liabilities*
+Transferable deposits (F21)	
−Trade credit (F9)	

Exchange of one financial asset for another

Households (S15)	
Financial assets	*Liabilities*
−Transferable deposits (F21)	−Trade credit (F9)
+Equity (F51)	

Exchange of one financial asset for another

Deposit-taking corporations (S122)	
Financial assets	*Liabilities*
+Transferable deposits (F21)	
−Equity (F51)	

Exchange of one financial asset for another

Households (S15)	
Financial assets	*Liabilities*
−Transferable deposits (F21)	−Trade credit (F9)
+Debt securities (F3)	

Simultaneous rise of financial assets and liabilities

Deposit-taking corporations (S122)	
Financial assets	*Liabilities*
+Transferable deposits (F21)	+Debt securities (F3)

Table 6.18
From-whom-to-whom financial transactions involving listed shares

Buy-back of listed shares by a non-financial corporation from a household

Households (S15)	
Financial assets	*Liabilities*
+ Transferable deposits (F21)	
−Listed shares issued by a non-financial corporation (F511)	

Non-financial corporations (S11)	
Financial assets	*Liabilities*
−Transferable deposits (F21)	−Listed shares acquired by a household (F511)

transferable deposits, or of long-term debt securities into listed shares. They raise the question of whether to treat the conversions as financial transactions or as other changes in the volume of assets. Within a system of from-whom-to-whom financial accounts, such a conversion should be treated as two financial transactions, the redemption of unlisted shares and the issuance of listed shares.

4. Financial transactions on secondary markets

6.187. From-whom-to-whom financial accounts also make it possible to show the economic activities on secondary markets and their impact. Financial transactions on secondary markets involve mainly securities (debt securities, listed shares or investment fund shares) or financial derivatives and ownership of these instruments can change without the direct involvement of the debtor. These types of transactions lead to accounting entries on the creditor side for both transactors and also on the debtor side. As an example, a household purchase of a central government bond previously held by a non-financial corporation.

Table 6.19
From-whom-to-whom financial transactions involving debt securities

Issuance of a long-term debt security by central government

Non-financial corporations (S11)	
Financial assets	***Liabilities***
−Transferable deposits (F21)	
+Debt security issued by central government (F31)	

Central government (S1311)	
Financial assets	***Liabilities***
+Transferable deposits (F21)	+Debt security acquired by a non-financial corporation (F31)

Sale of a central government long-term debt security by a non-financial corporation to a household

Non-financial corporations (S11)	
Financial assets	***Liabilities***
+Transferable deposits (F21)	
−Debt security redeemed by central government (F31)	

Central government (S1311)	
Financial assets	***Liabilities***
−Transferable deposits (F21)	−Debt security disposed of by a non-financial corporation (F31)
+Transferable deposits (F21)	+Debt security acquired by a household (F31)

Households (S15)	
Financial assets	***Liabilities***
−Transferable deposits (F21)	
+Debt security issued by central government (F31)	

6.188. The issuance of a central government long-term debt security is reflected in the financial accounts as shown in the first part of table 6.19. The sale by a non-financial corporation to a household is shown in the second part of the table.

6.189. In the from-whom-to-whom financial account framework, the corresponding transactions on the secondary market involve two transactions: the first one between the non-financial corporation (the seller of the debt security) and central government as the debtor (the redeemer of the debt security), and the second one between the household (the buyer of the debt security) and the debtor (the new issuer of the debt security) to reflect the change in ownership in the central government account.

5. Monetary variables within a three-dimensional system of accounts

6.190. A three-dimensional system of accumulation accounts and balance sheets, with a breakdown of the financial corporations sector and of the financial asset and liability categories as set out in the 2008 SNA and by counterpart, makes it possible to identify monetary aggregates in a matrix. Monetary developments can therefore be analysed in the widest possible financial framework and in a way which permits them to be related more easily to the economic developments recorded in the production and income accounts.

6.191. The monetary aggregates comprise broad money stock and changes in broad money stock. They are reflected in the developments of the so-called counterparts of broad money, derived by exploiting certain accounting identities. All countries measure monetary developments, and it is often considered that monetary growth is related to developments in economic activity and, over the longer term, in inflation, or that monetary growth contains valuable information concerning financial stability. Numerous definitions of broad money are possible; the national choice is likely to be an empirical matter, depending on what measure or measures best relate to developments in the national economy.

6.192. Such a three-dimensional system may be developed to identify the relevant holders, issuers and financial assets, and, among the holders, to distinguish between financial and non-financial sectors, since their money holdings may have different implications for economic activity and inflation. The rest of the world is assumed to be money neutral. The same may apply to central government. Financial assets as monetary variables are considered to comprise currency (issued by the central bank); liquid deposits with the central bank and other deposit-taking corporations except the central bank and marketable short-term debt instruments issued by the money-issuing sector (both with an initial maturity of up to one year); and shares or units issued by money market funds. Similarly, counterparts to money are identified in the three-dimensional framework, like domestic credit and the net external assets of money issuers.[164]

(a) The money-issuing sector vis-à-vis the money-holding sectors

6.193. The central bank (S121), deposit-taking corporations except the central bank (S122) and money market fund (S123) subsectors cover those financial intermediaries through which the central bank's monetary policy is transmitted to the other institutional units of the economy. Accordingly, this grouping of financial corporation subsectors is defined with reference to measures of broad money. It is called monetary financial institutions (the money-issuing sector), which might include or exclude MMFs depending on how broad money has been defined. Correspondingly, the money-holding sectors usually cover all resident institutional sectors excluding monetary financial institutions and central government.[165]

(b) Consolidating elements

6.194. Eliminating the aggregated financial transactions, other flows and balance sheet positions between resident monetary financial institutions results in the consolidated presentation. Owing to limitations in the recording practices, the sum of intra-monetary financial institutions flows and stocks might not necessarily be zero.

[164] See also the definitions of money-holding, issuing and neutral sectors in the MFSMCG (e.g. in para. 6.193).

[165] See also the MFSMCG, chap. 6, on the definitions of money-holding, issuing and neutral sectors.

6.195. The consolidated presentation also refers to the depository corporations survey and, in an extended form, to the financial corporations survey as developed within the context of the IMF international financial statistics based on standardized report forms. (see also chap. 9.)

6.196. The standardized report forms (SRFs) are used by most IMF members to report monetary data to the IMF. The benefits of such forms include: (a) improvement in cross-country comparability of monetary data; (b) higher quality of monetary data, given that the definitions and concepts in SRFs are based on the MFSMCG; and (c) improvement in the timeliness of monetary data. Currently, there are 137 reporting countries that use the SRFs, of which 33 extend reporting to other financial corporations data.

Chapter 7
Data sources for compiling financial accounts, other flow accounts and financial balance sheets by institutional sector

References:
2008 SNA
- Chapter 18, Elaborating and presenting the accounts
- Chapter 27, Links to monetary statistics and the flow of funds

BPM6
MFSMCG
GFSM 2014
HSS

A. Introduction

7.1. Chapter 7 provides a detailed description of the various data sources used for compiling the financial accounts, other flow accounts and the balance sheets by institutional sector. The data from these sources need to be incorporated into the accounts. As a first step, they are brought together for different institutional sectors, groupings of financial corporation subsectors and specific financial instrument categories, such as securities or loans.

7.2. To compile institutional sector accounts, various statistical sources need to be used, most of which are initially collected for other purposes (*building blocks*). These building blocks are usually high-frequency data taken from monetary and financial statistics, balance of payments and international investment position statistics, or government finance statistics. Advanced systems of accounts also integrate data on securities holdings from corporate balance sheets or from household surveys, if timely and detailed enough.

7.3. Data may be collected using questionnaires specifically designed for statistical purposes. However, most data sources are not designed for statistical purposes and or for compiling financial accounts, other flow accounts and balance sheets. They are usually collected for supervisory, regulatory or tax purposes. One example is balance sheet data of deposit-taking corporations except the central bank, which are collected by central banks or supervisory agencies in the context of their monetary policy and/or supervisory functions. The same applies to other sources, such as government finance statistics or balance of payments and international investment position statistics, which are collected to carry out fiscal or structural policy analysis within a national economy.

7.4. Financial accounts, other flow accounts and balance sheets by institutional sector may, therefore, be seen as a product of the various statistical sources used as building blocks. It is also regarded as an integrated system of accounts based on a methodological framework as reflected in the international statistical standards such as the 2008 SNA.

7.5. Using these statistical sources as building blocks for the compilation of the accounts and balance sheets implies that these accounts are regarded as a "methodological superstructure" which imparts stimuli facilitating the standardization of the various financial statistics. Examples are the changes made in monetary and financial statistics to revise the sector classification of institutional units, to improve the definitions and breakdowns of financial assets and liabilities or to adjust the valuation methods applied in the source data.

B. Collecting financial data

1. Introduction

7.6. Financial data sources are collected in three different ways:

(a) Directly from data provided for the respective institutional unit;

(b) Indirectly for an institutional unit through its counterpart;

(c) In instrument-by-instrument micro databases.

7.7. The statistical data used for the purposes of compiling institutional sector accounts are usually those collected directly from the respective institutional units or from custodians collecting data on behalf of their clients.

7.8. Financial data should ideally be taken from direct sources in a non-consolidated format. The most appropriate way would be to receive transaction, other flow and stock data sufficiently broken down by financial instrument category and by counterpart unit. This would allow, for each sector and instrument category, a split of the transaction, other flow and stock data vis-à-vis institutional units:

(a) Within the same sector or subsector;

(b) Of other resident sectors;

(c) Of the rest of the world.

7.9. Such financial data refer essentially to:

(a) Monetary and financial statistics;

(b) Balance of payments and international investment position statistics;

(c) Government finance statistics and statistics for other non-financial sectors.

(a) Monetary and financial statistics

7.10. For analytical purposes, the three main financial sectors, namely monetary financial institutions (MFIs), insurance corporations and pension funds, and the remaining financial corporations, may need to be shown separately. For the financial corporations sector, it may also be useful to distinguish non-MMF investment funds from other financial institutions.

7.11. Source data from balance sheets of monetary financial institutions are usually rather detailed in terms of deposits, loans, debt securities and shares, with corresponding breakdowns by original maturity, currency denomination and counterpart sector. These data allow the compilation of monetary aggregates and the main counterparts to broad money.

7.12. Timely balance sheet data from supervisory authorities may also be available on insurance corporations and pension funds[166] and on other financial corporations,

[166] Such data may be available annually only, with a timeliness of nine months and covering only balance sheets.

such as non-MMF investment funds. However, the data do not cover those financial corporations that are not supervised. Such data may be collected by surveys carried out by central banks or national statistical offices.

7.13. Statistical data on issues and holdings of debt securities and equity securities of various institutional sectors are sometimes derived from security-by-security databases. Moreover, data taken directly from financial corporations may be supplemented by data taken from counterpart sectors, such as those on loans granted by financial corporations to general government, to non-financial corporations or to the rest of the world.

(b) Balance of payments and international investment position statistics

7.14. The separate presentation of quarterly data for the rest of the world sector in the framework of institutional sector accounts is essential. The basic source data for this presentation are balance of payments and international investment position statistics, which should be fully consistent with the data sets available for the resident sectors. The transformation of the functional approach applied to balance of payments and international investment position data to the breakdown by financial instrument has to be taken into consideration.[167]

7.15. The balance of payments and international investment position data may be gradually enhanced by providing more breakdowns, for example, by showing debits and credits separately and by offering a geographical breakdown of major counterparts.

7.16. The international investment position mirrors the financial balance sheet of the national economy; this also refers to the breakdown of the changes in the international investment position. In addition to the balance of payments transactions, the international investment position is affected by valuation changes in financial assets and liabilities due to price and exchange rate developments, and certain other influences on the outstanding amount of external assets and liabilities.

(c) Government finance statistics and statistics for other non-financial sectors

7.17. While almost no quarterly data sources are available for non-financial corporations and households, including non-profit institutions serving households, detailed quarterly accounts may be drawn up for general government and for its subsectors.

7.18. Government accounts, mainly on a monthly or a quarterly basis, provide important information on the activities and positions of government, thus supporting fiscal and monetary policy analysis. Government accounts are a major building block of institutional sector accounts. They provide key information for the analysis of specific developments in government finance. The data are particularly useful for fiscal forecasting and monitoring and also help to improve the quality and timeliness of the government accounts in general, including the annual data.

7.19. To better understand the link between monthly government finance statistics and the quarterly government non-financial and financial accounts, the relationships between revenue, expenditure, net lending/net borrowing and their financial counterparts need to be analysed. In many cases, monthly or quarterly cash data may have to be transformed into data on an accrual basis. This also refers to the link between financial transactions, other flows and the balance sheet items for government.

[167] See also Table 7.1 (Table 26.6 of the 2008 SNA).

2. Data collected directly from institutional units

7.20. Data collected directly from institutional units are mainly balance sheet data of resident financial corporations and general government units.

7.21. Monetary and financial statistics refers to data collected monthly or quarterly from monetary financial institutions for monetary policy purposes. They are usually collected by the central bank or the supervisory agency in the context of their monetary policy and/or supervisory functions.

7.22. In order to provide comprehensive statistical coverage of the financial corporations sector as a whole, central banks or supervisory authorities may also collect data on other financial corporations, such as non-MMF investment funds, insurance corporations and pension funds and, sometimes, on specific groups of financial intermediaries, such as financial corporations engaged in the securitization of assets.

7.23. Government finance data are collected for budgetary monitoring and fiscal policy analysis. While budgetary data are usually high-frequency, other government data are not always very timely and sometimes lack good coverage, especially data on local government.

7.24. Balance of payments and international investment position statistics are collected as monthly or quarterly data either by central banks or by national statistical offices. The data are usually taken from microdatabases covering statistics on cross-border transactions and positions of resident non-financial corporations.

7.25. Only limited sets of financial data are usually available for non-financial corporations, households and non-profit institutions serving households – these are collected directly.

(a) Monetary and financial statistics

7.26. The most important direct source used to compile financial accounts, other flow accounts and balance sheets by institutional sector is monetary and financial statistics.

7.27. Monetary and financial statistics refers predominantly to balance sheet data of monetary financial institutions. These institutions are the central bank (S121), deposit-taking corporations except the central bank (S122) and money market funds (S123). They take deposits or issue securities, and grant loans and invest in securities on their own account. A complete list of monetary financial institutions is maintained and may be published by the central bank.

7.28. Monetary and financial statistics usually collected and compiled by the central bank provide detailed information on broad monetary aggregates, its components (banknotes and coins, transferable deposits and short-term marketable instruments issued by monetary financial institutions) and its counterparts (notably credit granted by monetary financial institutions and their long-term liabilities). Monetary aggregates and their counterparts are calculated from the consolidated balance sheet of monetary financial institutions.

7.29. While the source data are collected from monthly or quarterly balance sheets, transaction data are derived as differences in stocks adjusted for exchange rate variations, other revaluations, reclassifications, and any other changes in the volume of assets and liabilities.

7.30. Certain concepts in monetary and financial statistics do not always correspond with those in national accounts. The differences usually relate to accrued interest, the classification of financial instruments and the valuation of balance sheet items, especially on the liabilities side.

Worked example 7.1. Calculation of monthly transactions based on outstanding amounts

7.31. Monthly transactions are calculated from monthly differences in outstanding amounts adjusted for other flows. These are revaluations (exchange rate variations and other revaluations) and other changes in the volume of assets and liabilities.

7.32. If L_t represents the outstanding amount at the end of month t, E_t^M the exchange rate adjustment, V_t^M the other revaluation adjustments, C_t^M the reclassification adjustment and O_t^M the adjustment due to any other change in the volume of assets and liabilities in month t, the transactions F_t^M in month t are defined as:

$$F_t^M = (L_t - L_{t-1}) - E_t^M - V_t^M - C_t^M - O_t^M$$

7.33. Similarly, the quarterly transactions F_t^Q for the quarter ending in month t are defined as:

$$F_t^Q = (L_t - L_{t-1}) - E_t^Q - V_t^Q - C_t^Q - O_t^Q$$

where L_{t-3} is the amount outstanding at the end of month t–3 (the end of the previous quarter) and, for example, C_t^Q is the reclassification adjustment in the quarter ending in month t.

7.34. For those quarterly series for which monthly observations are available, the quarterly transactions can be derived as the sum of the three monthly transactions in the quarter.

Statistics on the central bank

7.35. Statistics on the central bank are based on internal accounting and reporting forms established for and used by the central bank for monetary policy analysis. Periodic statistical presentations exist – from daily and weekly statistics to quarterly and annual statements. Of particular interest for financial accounts, other flow accounts and balance sheets are the presentations of monthly and quarterly balance sheets. Quarterly balance sheets may be classified by financial instrument and institutional sector following the 2008 SNA.

7.36. Providing data on accumulated transactions (as far as they are available) at transaction values and on stocks at market prices allows changes in stocks to be divided into financial transactions and other flows, which are mainly revaluations.

Statistics on deposit-taking corporations except the central bank

7.37. Quarterly or monthly statistics for deposit-taking corporations except the central bank represent a major part of quarterly financial accounts and balance sheets. The data are usually broken down by financial instrument, original maturity, currency and partly by counterpart sector and residency. The available data sets may be well suited to compiling balance sheet positions for deposits, loans and – to some extent – for debt and equity securities issued and held by these institutions.[168]

7.38. Data on transactions are usually not directly collected but derived from changes in stocks with adjustments made to remove the impact of non-transactions from the flows. For that purpose, data on monthly or quarterly adjustments may also be collected. They may cover data on reclassifications and revaluations other than exchange rate changes.

---

[168] Collecting data on securitization is also important. Schemes for collecting monetary financial institutions' balance sheets may be adapted or new schemes set up for collecting data on financial corporations engaged in the securitization of assets (the usual counterparties of monetary financial institutions in securitization operations) in order to provide statistical information about these operations and the subsequent history of securitized loans. On securitization, see Chapter 4.

Box 7.1
Bridging national accounts, business accounts and supervisory data

The focus here is on national accounts broadly defined: the data measured and recorded following the 2008 SNA and the related manuals. Nevertheless, it may be useful to explain the difference between national accounts, business accounts and supervisory data.

International statistical standards make clear distinctions between residents and non-residents and between institutional sectors. They also strictly distinguish between transactions and other flows (revaluations and other changes) relating to assets and liabilities.

Statistical standards are observed in several dimensions of the statistical universe, including the integrated institutional sector accounts, monetary statistics and other data on financial corporations and financial markets collected and compiled principally for monetary policy purposes. Thus, for example, monetary statistics, and the monetary aggregates derived from them, cover the balance sheets, transactions and other flows of institutions classified as monetary financial institutions,[a] which are resident in the country concerned regardless of where the head office is located. These data exclude statistical information on the business of foreign branches of resident monetary financial institutions. Moreover, they exclude the business of subsidiaries of monetary financial institutions, which are not themselves monetary financial institutions, for example leasing companies or providers of consumer credit. Such entities are "other" (non-monetary) financial intermediaries, and the statistics do not merge transactions and other flows or do not combine institutional units of different sectors or residency.

Statistical data used for supervisory and financial stability purposes focus on the business of the whole supervised institution. Related to the structure of financial groups, conglomerates and multinationals, the data are accordingly consolidated across national boundaries to include also the business of foreign banking branches, and they may be consolidated across sector boundaries to include the business of financial subsidiaries which are not themselves deposit-taking corporations or monetary financial institutions.

The content of the information is also somewhat different. Although supervisors use the sectoral distinctions and the detailed financial instruments reported for statistical purposes, they are very much interested in measuring risks (such as counterparty credit or market risk). Supervisory data may consider off-balance-sheet information or data on guarantees; this may lead to different sector classifications. On valuation, loans are recorded gross in monetary statistics or national accounts, while net recording usually applies to supervisory data.

Data of the kind needed for financial stability purposes, preferably at a quarterly frequency, at least for large financial groups, may not relate very closely to the balance sheet data usually collected on monetary financial institutions and other types of financial corporations.

[a] Monetary financial institutions comprise the central bank, deposit-taking corporations except the central bank and money market funds.

Statistics on money market funds

7.39. Money market funds (MMFs) invest their proceeds primarily in money market instruments, MMF shares or units; transferable debt instruments, such as treasury bills, certificates of deposit and commercial paper; bank deposits; and instruments which pursue a rate of return that approaches the interest rates of money market instruments. They issue money market fund shares or units that are sometimes functionally close to transferable deposits.

7.40. For these entities monthly or quarterly statistics may be collected for various balance sheet positions – with some focus on MMF shares or units as financial assets and liabilities and with breakdowns by counterpart sector and residency.

7.41. Other sets of financial statistics may be available for financial corporations which are not monetary financial institutions but which are regulated or supervised, such as insurance corporations, pension funds or non-MMF investment funds. There may also be specific data collection schemes for the remaining financial corporations, like financial corporations engaged in the securitization of assets, special purpose vehicles or financial auxiliaries.[169]

[169] See corresponding regulations and guidelines adopted by the ECB.

(b) Statistics on non-money market fund investment funds

7.42. Of specific importance are non-MMF investment funds as collective investment undertakings investing capital (raised from the public by issuing shares or units) in financial and/or non-financial assets. Investment funds can be open or closed (open-ended or closed-ended investment funds). Some investment funds invest in other funds ("funds of funds"). Hedge funds as a kind of investment fund cover a heterogeneous range of collective investment schemes, typically involving high minimum investments, light regulation and a wide variety of investment strategies. Private equity funds are used for making investments in equity securities. They are typically limited partnerships with a fixed term of ten years (often with annual extensions). At inception, institutional investors make an unfunded commitment to the limited partnership, which is then drawn over the term of the fund.

7.43. Non-MMF investment funds are classified in the financial corporations subsector S124. There is a close relationship between MMFs (S123) and non-MMF investment funds and the corresponding financial instrument subcategories non-MMF investment fund shares or units and MMF shares or units. Only institutional units classified within these two financial corporations subsectors issue non-MMF investment fund shares or units and MMF shares or units, respectively. They are not issuers of shares like other financial corporations or non-financial corporations. The borderline between non-MMF investment funds and MMFs is determined by the boundaries of the MMF definition chosen. In many cases, the boundaries are set by existing definitions used for supervisory purposes or monetary policy. Funds that do not meet the criteria for an MMF, for example because they invest in rather illiquid assets, are to be recorded as a non-MMF investment fund. Therefore, international comparisons of MMFs and/or of non-MMF investment funds should take into account the possible differences in definitions.

7.44. Statistics on non-MMF investment funds refer to data collected on these entities as issuers of investment fund shares or units. Non-MMF investment funds are also called mutual funds, unit trusts, investment trusts and undertakings for collective investments in transferable securities.

7.45. Non-MMF investment funds may be constituted: (a) under the law of contract (as common funds managed by management companies); (b) under trust law (as unit trusts); (c) under a statute (as investment companies); or (d) otherwise with similar effect.

(c) Statistics on insurance corporations and pension funds

7.46. Statistics on insurance corporations and pension funds are collected either by the central bank, by the supervisory agency or by the national statistical office.

7.47. The importance of insurance corporations and pension funds is expected to increase as populations age. It is therefore essential to improve the collection and frequency of data on these institutions.

7.48. Quarterly information is often available only for the assets side of the balance sheets and, probably, a breakdown of this data into the two subsectors insurance corporations and pension funds.

7.49. In addition to the quarterly stocks (quarterly transactions may not be available), more detailed annual balance sheet data are available, or best estimates on the split of household life insurance and pension entitlements (in defined contribution, defined benefit or hybrid schemes).

7.50. Full yearly balance sheet figures containing information on the liabilities of insurance corporations may be obtained only with some delay. In addition, these data, if collected only for supervisory purposes, do not provide sufficient information by counterpart residency and institutional sector.

7.51. Transaction data can be derived only from stocks. Furthermore, certain data sets may be difficult to obtain, such as time series with maturity breakdowns (in particular for debt securities held) and the geographical and sector breakdowns of non-residents (in particular for debt securities held, unlisted shares and other equity, and life insurance entitlements).

7.52. While the main liabilities of insurance corporations and pension funds are their technical reserves or pension entitlements, their assets cover:

(a) Financial investments, typically listed securities and/or deposits;

(b) Receivables, partly comprising amounts now due from policyholders, other financial intermediaries and reinsurers. The major component is usually the reinsurers' share of the various technical reserves (which, in most jurisdictions, are shown gross of reinsurance on the liabilities side of the balance sheet);

(c) Intangibles. In addition to goodwill, insurers in some countries show a deferred acquisition cost asset. Some or all acquisition costs may be amortized over the duration of the policy. This is generally of more significance for life insurers, since acquisition costs are higher and they are amortized over a much longer period. To support the deferred acquisition cost asset, the insurer must demonstrate that sufficient future profits are expected to emerge from which the asset can be amortized. Hence, the deferred acquisition cost asset is an intangible asset, giving some credit for future profits. Some life insurers may also show the "value of business acquired". This represents the discounted value of all future profits expected to emerge from an acquired portfolio of life insurance business. It is therefore a special instance of acquired goodwill. Insurers are not normally permitted to show the value of future profits from internally generated life business on their own balance sheet, although this "embedded value" is often shown as supplementary data.

Life insurance corporations

7.53. The equivalent to the *claims equalization provision* for life insurers is the *fund for future appropriations* (in the United Kingdom) or the unallocated distributable surplus (in Germany). In years of favourable investment returns, some profits are not immediately distributed as policyholder bonuses but are retained in the fund for future appropriations. This is done so that, in future years of poor investment conditions, transfers out of the fund will not affect policyholder bonus rates, thereby providing a smoothed return for policyholders. The fund for future appropriations is therefore part of the capital of a life insurer, which is available to absorb risks arising in the corporation. However, the fund cannot be transferred to shareholders or be used to absorb risks elsewhere in the group.

7.54. Debt is normally a modest proportion of the balance sheet. Debt issued by regulated insurers is often long-term subordinated debt, since this is generally treated as regulatory capital.

7.55. The concept of earning a proportion of the *premium* in a particular year is not generally meaningful for life insurance contracts owing to their long-term nature and the fact that a significant proportion of the premium is usually invested for future years, rather than to cover the current year's risk. Consequently, life insurers do not generally report premiums as earned and unearned.

7.56. A life insurer's *income statement* shows: (a) paid claims during the year; and (b) increases in technical life reserves during the year.

Non-life insurance corporations

7.57. For a non-life insurer, the technical reserves comprise: (a) outstanding claims/loss reserves; and (b) unearned premium reserves.

7.58. Outstanding claims/loss reserves include: (a) claims whose amounts have been agreed but not yet paid; (b) known claims for which the insurer has not yet agreed the claim amount; and (c) claims incurred but not reported – a general provision for claims which have already occurred but are as yet unknown, and which the insurer expects to emerge in future years. This is often a major liability, especially in respect of "long-tail" classes of business (generally the casualty lines). Asbestos and environmental liabilities are the prime examples of very long-tailed claims from past years.

7.59. Unearned premium reserves are the proportion of premiums written in prior years which relate to a future period of risk and so have not yet been "earned". The unearned premium reserves therefore represent a provision for expected future claims in respect of premiums already received.

7.60. Some non-life insurers may have a "claims equalization provision" which acts to smooth the natural volatility of claims experienced from year to year. Amounts are transferred to the equalization provision in favorable underwriting years and transfers out are made in years of extraordinarily high claims (e.g. nuclear catastrophes or earthquakes). The claims equalization reserve is therefore a provision and not a liability. Consequently it is not permitted under the 2008 SNA.

7.61. For a non-life insurer, there are three definitions of premium income: (a) gross premiums written: the actual premiums contracted to be paid by policyholders; (b) net premiums written: gross premiums less reinsurance premiums payable by the insurer; and (c) net premiums earned: the proportion of the net written premiums relating to the amount of risk borne during the accounting year.

7.62. For example, if a new annual policy is issued on 1 December for a net written premium of currency units (CU) 1200, only one twelfth of the premium (CU 100) will be earned in that calendar year. The remaining eleven twelfths of the premium is transferred to the *unearned premium reserve*, which appears as a liability on the balance sheet. In the following accounting year, the remaining CU 1100 will be "earned". Consequently, CU 1100 is transferred from the unearned premium reserve into net earned premiums for that year.

7.63. The income statement of a non-life insurer shows "net incurred claims or losses". Gross incurred claims consist of: (a) paid claims during the year; and (b) increases in loss reserves during the year.

7.64. Net incurred claims are then derived by deducting the reinsurer's share of the gross incurred claims.

7.65. Hence, the income statement not only contains the claims occurring in the current year but may also be affected by "reserve development" in respect of previous year's claims. Loss adjustment expenses (or claims' settlement costs) for non-life insurers are generally included in the income statement along with claims, rather than with the other expenses. In countries permitting deferral of acquisition costs, the expenses in the income statement exclude the current year's deferrable acquisition costs but include the amortization of the deferred acquisition cost asset.

Reinsurance corporations

7.66. Transactions and positions between direct insurers and reinsurers are recorded as an entirely separate set of transactions. No consolidation takes place between the transactions and positions of the direct insurer as issuer of policies to its clients, on the one hand, and the holder of a policy with the reinsurer, on the other.

7.67. Specific financial transactions take place between reinsurers and direct insurers, namely transactions in reinsurance technical reserves and transactions in financial claims with ceding corporations.

7.68. Reinsurance technical reserves due to reinsurance contracts are shown as the direct insurer's financial assets in the form of claims on the reinsurer; they are not consolidated with the direct insurer's own liabilities in the form of technical reserves.

7.69. Reinsurance technical reserves are to be classified as non-life insurance technical reserves. They may be split further by type of insurance (non-life, life and pensions) or by type of reserves (unearned premiums, unpaid claims and insurance reserves).

7.70. Financial claims of reinsurers on direct insurers (ceding corporations) are financial assets that reinsurers have with direct insurers (the ceding corporations) – as collateral provided to cover insurance liabilities that a direct insurer retains from the liquid funds which it has to pay to a reinsurer under a reinsurance contract. Such claims are established based on short-term or long-term reinsurance contracts with no significant underwriting risk transfer. They include the recognition and measurement of an asset or liability upon inception of such contracts. Such claims are usually classified as loans (F4).

Pension funds

7.71. *A pension fund* is defined as a pool of assets forming an independent legal entity. The assets are bought with the contributions to the pension fund for the exclusive purpose of financing pension benefits. The fund members have a legal or beneficial right or some other contractual claim against the assets of the pension fund.

(d) Statistics on the remaining financial corporations

7.72. As the remaining financial corporations are usually not supervised or regulated, no direct data collection systems may exist for these units. They include financial corporations classified as other financial intermediaries, except insurance corporations and pension funds (subsector S125); financial auxiliaries (subsector S126); or captive financial institutions and moneylenders (subsector S127).

7.73. Some efforts have been made to clarify the classification of specific institutional units within the financial corporations sector. These units are financial corporations engaged in the securitization of assets and other institutions like special purpose entities (SPEs), conduits and brass-plate companies. The 2008 SNA classifies financial corporations engaged in the securitization of assets as part of the subsector other financial intermediaries, except insurance corporations and pension funds (S125).

7.74. For monetary policy purposes it might be important to collect data on these types of financial corporations. Financial corporations engaged in the securitization of assets as institutional units carrying out securitization transactions incur debt securities whose credit risk is transferred to the investors in these debt securities; they also acquire assets underlying the issue of debt securities. Financial corporations engaged in the securitization of assets may be constituted under contract law (as common funds managed by management companies), trust law (as unit trusts), company law (as public limited companies) or otherwise with similar effect.

7.75. Financial corporations engaged in the securitization of assets are distinguished from entities that are created solely to hold specific portfolios of financial assets and liabilities. When the entity does not bear market or credit risks, it is combined with its parent corporation, if it is resident in the same country as the parent.

7.76. When the entity is set up outside the economic territory in which the parent corporation is located, it is considered resident of the country in which the entity is incorporated, even if it has little or no physical presence there. In these cases, it is treated as a separate institutional unit of the financial corporations subsector captive financial institutions and moneylenders (S127) of the host economy.

(e) Balance of payments and international investment position statistics

7.77. Balance of payments and international investment position statistics are based on a functional approach, which distinguishes direct investment, portfolio investment, financial derivatives, other investment and reserve assets. The breakdowns by financial instrument are less detailed than those described and recommended for from-whom-to-whom accounts.

7.78. Table 7.1 provides an overview of the available data according to the functional approach applied in balance of payments and international investment position statistics and the financial instrument approach under the 2008 SNA.[170]

7.79. The table shows that data on monetary gold and SDRs are included in the reserve assets. While SDR assets are reserve assets, SDR liabilities are other investment. Data on currency and deposits are mainly part of other investment and reserve assets. Other transferable deposits and other deposits may be also included in direct investment.

7.80. Debt securities data are included in direct investment, portfolio investment and in the reserve assets, while equity and investment fund shares may be part of direct investment, portfolio investment, other investment and reserve assets.

7.81. Data on loans are included in direct investment, other investment and reserve assets, while data on other accounts receivable/payable are part of other investment and reserve assets. It may be difficult to identify the data on cross-border transactions or positions of insurance, pension and standardized guarantee schemes. They are usually part of direct investment and other investment.

7.82. Data on financial derivatives and employee stock options are collected in a specific functional category "financial derivatives" in the balance of payments and international investment position statistics; they are also included in reserve assets.

7.83. Direct investment data are broken down by equity capital and reinvested earnings and other capital, which is mostly inter-company loans. Both categories are further split by counterpart sector into monetary financial institutions and others. Portfolio investment data distinguish between figures for equity and debt instruments (bonds and notes as well as money market instruments). The breakdown by counterpart sector covers data for the central bank, deposit-taking corporations, except the central bank and money market funds, general government and other sectors. Other investment data provide figures for loans or currency and deposits, for trade credit and for other assets or liabilities with the same breakdown by counterpart sector as for the portfolio investment data.

---

170 Table 7.1 is aligned with table 26.6 of the 2008 SNA.

Table 7.1
Link between financial assets classification and functional categories

2000 SNA/MFSMCG — Financial assets and liabilities classification	Functional categories				
	Direct investment	Portfolio investment	Financial derivatives (other than reserves) and ESOs	Other investment	Reserve assets
Monetary gold					X
Special drawing rights				X[a]	X[a]
Currency and deposits					
Currency				X	X
Interbank positions				X	X
Other transferable deposits	X			X	X
Other deposits	X			X	X
Debt securities	X	X			X
Loans	X			X	X
Equity and investment fund shares					
Equity					
Listed shares	X	X			X
Unlisted shares	X	X			x
Other equity	X			X	
Investment fund shares/unit					
Money market fund shares/units	x	X			X
Other investment fund shares/units	x	X		x	X
Insurance, pension and standardized guarantee schemes					
Non-life insurance technical reserves	x			X	
Life insurance and annuity entitlements	x			X	
Pension entitlements				X	
Claims of pension funds on pension managers	X			X	
Entitlements to non-pension benefits				X	
Provisions for calls under standardized guarantees	X			X	
Financial derivatives and employee stock options					
Financial derivatives			X		X
Employee stock options			X		
Other accounts receivable/payable					
Trade credit and advances	X			X	
Other accounts receivable/payable	X			X	

[a] SDR assets are reserve assets; SDR liabilities are other investment; X shows applicable functional categories; x shows cases that are considered to be relatively uncommon.

7.84. To achieve a complete and consistent integration of balance of payments and international investment position data into the rest of the world account, recommendations have been given in the 2008 SNA and the BPM6 on the relationship between the SNA rest of the world account to the balance of payments accounts and the international investment position. See also BPM6, appendix 7, Relationship of the SNA accounts for the rest of the world to the international accounts.

7.85. Specific issues in this context relate to the available instrument breakdowns of data for the direct, portfolio and other investment categories, which seem to be insufficient for the purposes of from-whom-to-whom accounts. While some financial instruments may be easily translated into the rest of the world account, others are not. In particular, a further breakdown of direct and other investment by instrument type and original maturity might help to improve the translation process. Furthermore, some combinations of financial instruments and sectors cause major difficulties, such as loans or currency and deposits and other financial assets or liabilities. In particular, transactions in and stocks of equity by subcategory are included in direct and portfolio investment as well as in reserve assets, but are not separately specified. The same applies for the transactions in and stocks of insurance technical reserves as part of other investment.

(f) Government finance statistics

7.86. Government finance statistics are based on official public finance statistics, derived from individual budgetary documents of government units. They are usually collected from various government units on a monthly, quarterly or annual basis.

7.87. General government institutional units are classified into one of the following subsectors:

(a) Central government (usually the state budget, extrabudgetary funds and state-owned enterprises);

(b) State government;

(c) Local government;

(d) Social security funds.[171]

7.88. One shortcoming of government finance data results from the fact that accounting rules in the government accounts are somewhat different from accounting standards used in the private sector. For example, government finance data rely exclusively or to some extent on the cash principle of recording transactions and not on the accrual principle.

7.89. Ideally, government finance statistics should cover data on:

(a) Revenue and expenditure (outlays);

(b) Financial transactions (net acquisitions of financial assets and net incurrences of liabilities);

(c) Revaluations of assets and liabilities;

(d) Other changes in the volume of assets and liabilities;

(e) Balance sheets;

(f) Intragovernmental transactions and positions.

7.90. From this, rather prominent fiscal indicators may be derived, such as government revenue, expenditure (as non-financial transactions), financial transactions and the balance sheet. They are linked together as follows:

Revenue – expenditure (outlays)

= *surplus*(+)/*deficit*(-) (defined as net lending(+)/net borrowing(-) in the 2008 SNA (B9))

= *net acquisition of financial assets – net incurrence of financial liabilities* (B9F)

and

Net acquisition of financial assets

– net incurrence of financial liabilities

+ other flows

= increase in government net wealth

---

[171] Mainly social security and, in some countries, state-owned hospitals.

7.91. Revenue and expenditure data can be rather detailed (classification code with up to five digits, see GFSM 2001). This may also allow aggregates to be derived for external reporting purposes.

7.92. Data may be collected on financial transactions for all financial asset and liability categories. Sufficient statistical data are usually provided on transactions in financial assets and liabilities and on government debt. Data on government assets refer mainly to financial wealth – specifically with the central bank, deposit-taking corporations except the central bank, non-financial corporations and with the rest of the world.

7.93. Moreover, some breakdowns by subcategory may be included for currency and deposits (currency, sight deposits and other deposits); debt securities (short- and long-term at original maturity and at residual maturity); equity and investment fund shares (listed shares, unlisted shares, other equity, investment fund shares); and other accounts receivable/payable (trade credit, arrears and other accounts).

7.94. Data with the same breakdowns may also be collected for balance sheets and for revaluations and other changes in the volume of assets and liabilities. Data on intragovernmental transactions and positions may have the same breakdown as the other source data to allow a correct consolidation of the general government data.

7.95. To aggregate the source data for each institutional unit belonging to the general government sector, a register of all government entities is necessary. National statistical offices may maintain and publish a statistical register of general government units. It is important in this context that the institutional sector general government is correctly delineated according to international statistical standards. This delineation is based on specific criteria usually related to the market/non-market production test. Government units are classified as non-market producers. However, the accurate classification of small local government units can be difficult to achieve.

7.96. It is essential to update the register on a continual basis, as the status of entities can change such as through mergers and acquisitions or liquidations.

3. Data collected indirectly through counterpart units

7.97. Direct data sources are rather costly, and the reporting units may not always be willing to provide the required data, especially households. Balance sheet data of non-financial corporations may be available, but only for a subset of this sector and also with some delay. The same applies to data collected in the context of household surveys.

7.98. Therefore, direct data collection systems have to be supplemented by data taken indirectly for the counterpart sectors involved. In particular, statistics collected for monetary or fiscal policy purposes are often partially on a from-whom-to-whom basis and are accordingly a useful source.

7.99. The use of "indirect" data is generally necessary for households, non-profit institutions serving households (NPISHs), non-financial corporations, and some financial corporation subsectors for which comprehensive direct data collection systems do not always exist.

7.100. Monetary statistics are regarded as the most detailed statistical source from which data are derived for counterpart units or sectors. Data on deposits and debt securities incurred and loans granted by monetary financial institutions are usually available, along with corresponding breakdowns by counterpart sector, original maturity and currency.

7.101. Data for the rest of the world are partly derived by using counterpart information from balance sheet data of monetary financial institutions. The same applies to government finance statistics. Balance sheet data on financial assets data may be checked

Box 7.2
Quality checks on government finance data[a]

Quality checks on government finance data may be carried out at different stages:

- At the institutional unit level.
- At subsector level.
- At general government sector level.

In principle, three different sets of quality checks should be carried out covering completeness, plausibility and consistency.

The application of these quality checks may be demonstrated by an example, such as the source data set of a social security fund established by central government. For this institutional unit, different sets of source data collected by different institutions may be available: data directly collected by the institution on its revenue, expenditure and financial transactions; the balance sheet; data collected indirectly by other government units; securities issues and holdings data derived from a securities database; and financial data collected by the central bank.

Checking the completeness of the data means comparing the various data sources to find out whether data for specific items are missing and to try to derive a complete set of accounts based on the available sources.

Plausibility checks may be carried out, for example by comparing the same figure over a period of time and by detecting outliers. Other checks refer to reported data for specific categories, which may not be plausible for certain institutional units (such as the issuance of shares or the incurrence of deposits by government units other than central government or unlikely (acquisition of debt securities issued by non-government units).

There are two main consistency checks, which can be applied to source data:

- Vertical consistency means that the total of all expenditure/changes in liabilities and the total of all revenue/changes in assets entries for all transactions of an institutional unit are equal.
- Stock-flow consistency means that changes between opening and closing positions are fully accounted in transactions, other changes in the volume of assets and liabilities, and revaluations.

A full set of stock and flow data is needed in order to carry out these consistency checks.

Quality checks at a subsector level require that the source data for all social security funds be aggregated. Data on intra-social security fund transactions and positions allow a consolidated set of data for social security funds to be derived. Errors and omissions might also evolve at this stage of statistical work. Therefore, corresponding quality checks may have to be undertaken to clean the data.

A regular monthly or quarterly data quality checking procedure should be established. Such checks can be implemented by using appropriate statistical database software. An automatically integrated checking procedure indicates errors or omissions at an institutional unit level. Such errors and omissions need to be corrected and, in exceptional cases, resolved in cooperation with the institutional unit involved.

[a] Similar quality checks may be carried out for other statistical sources.

against data received from monetary statistics which also refer to government debt data as loans granted by deposit-taking corporations except the central bank.

7.102. One example is to confront government finance statistics with monetary statistics. Monetary statistics usually provide data on loans with a breakdown by counterpart debtor sector, government being one of them. At the same time, such assets of monetary financial institutions are shown as government debt in government finance statistics. Although both items should be identical, they usually do not correspond for a number of reasons, for example the counterpart entities have not been classified properly in monetary statistics or the government entities have reported incomplete data.

7.103. The timing of recording may also be an issue in relation to government deposits at banks. This item is usually available from both the banking and central government data but never equal each other owing to differences in timing.

7.104. Given the importance of maintaining consistency with monetary statistics, in particular with the associated money and respective counterparts, compilers may also use the total loans granted by monetary financial institutions as reflected in monetary statistics. This implies that the discrepancy on loans from monetary financial institutions to general government may have to be imputed to loans from monetary financial institutions to another sector. The total loans provided by monetary financial institutions would remain the same as shown in monetary statistics although not the counterpart sector breakdown, but would be consistent with government finance statistics.

7.105. This procedure depends greatly on the quality of each data source and the hierarchy of sources established by the compiler. The adjustment may be made either way.

7.106. The sector used for the adjustment could be the non-financial corporations sector, because the main reason for the discrepancy is usually a misclassification on loans granted by monetary financial institutions to general government and non-financial corporations as debtors.

4. Direct data versus indirect data for non-financial corporations and households

7.107. In the context of improving the quality of institutional sector accounts and in view of changing user needs, the focus of interest may move to areas previously less relevant and therefore insufficiently covered by the accounts, such as trade credits, intercompany loans or net acquisitions of securities in a from-whom-to-whom framework.

7.108. More specifically, data on trade credits or intercompany loans remain incomplete or of low quality because, usually, no direct data are available for non-financial corporations, households and non-profit institutions serving households.

7.109. Sector accounts of non-financial corporations – together with the accounts for households including non-profit institutions serving households – are of specific analytical interest because the investment and financing behaviour of these sectors plays an important role in explaining monetary transmission channels. Analytical and policy issues are also related to the various forms of corporate finance and to the financial stability of the sectors in the context of macroprudential analysis.

7.110. There is a strong interest in improving the collection of data and the compilation of accounts for these sectors. As yet, however, mainly survey data are available for non-financial corporations and such subgroups as like small and medium-sized enterprises and for households.

7.111. Inter-company loans, trade credits or other advances vis-à-vis resident sectors may represent a considerable part of corporate finance and financial investment. The same applies to equity not covered by security databases. Furthermore, data on other corporate financial assets and liabilities vis-à-vis households and non-profit institutions serving households, such as pension liabilities, are also not provided.

7.112. Some data may be taken from indirect sources, such as monetary, balance of payments and government finance statistics. These data include deposits held and loans taken from monetary financial institutions, trade credit vis-à-vis the rest of the world, and loans taken from general government.

(a) Data on non-financial corporations

7.113. Sources of data for non-financial corporations likely vary considerably across countries. Given this, and the fact that non-financial corporations' cover a large number of industries, it is fair to assume that data quality may also vary widely across countries.

7.114. The data sources available for non-financial corporations may be taken to compile balance sheets as well as to derive financial transactions. Deriving transactions from positions, including the required asset-liability detail, is challenging for compilers. Estimating market values from reported balance sheets is a further challenge, but the implementation of new accounting standards (IFRS) that emphasize fair values may make the task easier for statisticians in the future. With reference to these and other challenges, compilers would likely want to make use multiple data sources to the extent possible.

(b) Sources of data for compiling non-financial corporations' financial accounts and balance sheets

7.115. There are essentially four sources of data for non-financial corporations:

(a) Publicly available corporate balance sheets;

(b) Taxation statistics;

(c) Survey statistics;

(d) Counterpart (indirect) data.

Corporate balance sheet data

7.116. The most basic source is publicly available corporate balance sheets linked to annual reporting. One obstacle is that, for multinational enterprises, only globally consolidated information may be available. These balance sheet data are typically available only annually and with a lag. However, increasingly timely sub-annual balance information for large firms is becoming much more common, and the growth in private sector databases that are increasingly Internet-based makes this information more timely, organized and accessible to compilers.

7.117. However, these corporate balance sheets are usually not presented in much detail. Asset-liability information may be more detailed than that based solely on annual reports, if aggregates from industry associations are available and used.[172]

7.118. Balance sheet data are typically limited in terms of detail. Generally speaking, the asset categories may be subscribed capital still unpaid, fixed assets, current assets, and prepayments and accrued income. Fixed and current assets are further split into subcategories. Fixed assets cover intangible and tangible fixed assets and financial fixed assets. Current assets are divided into stocks, debtors, current investments, and cash at bank and in hand. Some of the financial instruments are further split by original maturity, but not by counterpart sector. Equity, for instance, is not broken down into listed and unlisted shares and other equity; however, there are other sources of data (stock exchange information) for listed corporations that can be leveraged.

7.119. On the liabilities side, the main categories are debts owing to creditors with amounts becoming due and payable within one year and more than one year (at original maturity). Further items are provisions for liabilities and charges, accruals and deferred income, and capital and reserves. The debt categories may be further broken down to varying degrees by financial instrument and by counterpart (e.g. bank loans), while provisions are shown separately for pensions and similar obligations. Capital and reserves may be split into subscribed capital, share premium account, reserves and profit.

[172] Nevertheless, there will always be data gaps. For example, corporate financial assets and liabilities vis-à-vis households and non-profit institutions serving households, such as corporate pension liabilities to households, are also not provided.

7.120. Table 7.2 provides an overview of the main items as usually presented in corporate balance sheet databases.

Table 7.2

Main items of the balance sheets and income statements in a corporate balance sheet database

Assets	Liabilities and equity
Short-term (current) assets	Liabilities
• Cash and cash equivalents	• Short-term (current) liabilities
• Stocks and other money market instruments	Loans
• Receivables	Trade credits
• Inventories	• Long-term (non-current) liabilities
Long-term (non-current) assets	Long-term debt (mortgages)
• Intangibles	Other non-current liabilities
• Tangibles	Equity
• Financial	• Capital
	Capital and reserves
	Profit

Profit and loss account
Operating income
Operating charges
Financial income

7.121. The balance sheet data may meet the needs of many users carrying out structural analyses of the corporate sector. However, it is rather cumbersome to translate the data into 2008 SNA financial instrument categories taking also into account the divergent classification and valuation criteria, which do not always comply with the statistical standards. Furthermore, the instrument, maturity and counterpart sector details are too limited for the requirements of most analysts and statisticians. Accordingly, additional breakdowns may be needed for the compilation of institutional sector accounts.

Taxation statistics

7.122. In some countries taxation statistics may be available to compilers. While only annual in frequency and available with a minimum of a one-to-two-year lag, these are domestically consolidated statements that cover the universe. As a result, they are generally a reliable source of data. They are legal-entity-based, however, meaning that there will inevitably be significant inter-company claims among domestic complex enterprises and their affiliates. In addition, the level of asset-liability detail may be similar to that of publicly available corporate balance sheets — that is, possibly not sufficiently detailed for financial accounts' purposes.

7.123. Taxation-based statistics may be used in conjunction with corporate balance sheets data (discussed above) in order to improve coverage and ensure domestic coverage only of balance sheet data in the case of complex multinational enterprises.

Enterprise surveys

7.124. Significant quality improvements of the non-financial corporate sector accounts may be feasible only if a rather detailed and timely set of accounting data is provided. This is best achieved with a structured enterprise survey, which is likely more common at centralized statistical agencies. These surveys can, by design, be as detailed, frequent (usually quarterly) and timely as compilers require. However, the need for detail would typically be balanced with firms' response burden considerations, such that the focus would be on key asset-liability information. Ideally, instrument detail would meet the requirements of the 2008 SNA. A further advantage is that these types of surveys focus on the domestic enterprises.

7.125. Enterprise surveys typically cannot be expected to collect the full universe of non-financial corporations, and they are subject to sampling and non-sampling error. They are typically stratified samples that may or may not attempt to estimate the universe. In cases where they do generate universe estimates it is not uncommon for taxation statistics to support the estimation of the universe, especially for smaller firms.

7.126. One drawback of survey data is that it can be the case that they are voluntarily collected. This can lead to bias and other problems in the sample from large non-response error. In some jurisdictions, another limitation might be differential coverage across industries of the non-financial corporations' sector. For example, there may be a lack of coverage of the services subsector, which is usually a large part of a developed economy.

Counterpart information

7.127. Either with or without an enterprise survey, some data for non-financial corporations may be taken from indirect sources, such as monetary, balance of payments and government finance statistics. Monetary or banking statistics can be important sources of information for two typically significant financial instruments on the non-financial corporations' sector: deposits held at, and loans taken from, monetary financial institutions. The balance of payments (for transactions) and the international investment position (for positions) would also typically be used as part of information on foreign loans and deposits, as well as trade credit vis-à-vis the rest of the world. More importantly, the international accounts can supply transactions and positions with foreign affiliates, in the form of inter-company loans, advances and other non-marketable debt as well as inter-company equity. In addition, counterpart data from government or government enterprises may be a source of data for these same instruments.

7.128. Securities' databases are an important source of data for non-financial corporations for two reasons: they typically cover the universe of these entities (whereas a sample survey may not include all corporations with access to capital markets); and they may be able to provide (depending on their stage of development) both transactions and positions at both book and market value and adjusted for exchange rate fluctuations where applicable. Since debt and equity issues are typically a major part of non-financial corporations' financing and liabilities, the existence of securities databases can be invaluable in constructing quality estimates for this sector.

7.129. Countries may in fact use, or plan to use, a combination of the four potential data sources above for non-financial corporations. Table 7.3 synthesizes the basic sources of data for non-financial corporations, along with their basic characteristics – frequency, timeliness, detail, consolidation and universe coverage.

(c) Compiling non-financial corporations' financial accounts and balance sheets

Data derived from the profit and loss account to compile financial transactions

7.130. In the case of an enterprise-based survey for non-financial corporations, integrated collection would likely include both an income statement and a balance sheet. The profit and loss account data is usually a significant source for completing the current

Table 7.3
Sources of data for non-financial corporations

Data source/ characteristics	Publicly available corporate balance sheets	Taxation statistics	Survey statistics	Counterpart (indirect) data
Frequency	Typically annual although with the increase in private sector databases, sub-annual information is becoming increasingly common on the Internet	Annual	Can be designed to be quarterly	Typically, quarterly
Timeliness	Varying lags, from medium to long lag (typically in excess of one year). with the increase in private sector databases, select information is becoming more timely	Long lag (often in excess of 1-2 years)	Can be designed to have an adequate lag	Typically, a short lag
Detail	Aggregated, such that only limited details may be available	Aggregated, such that only limited details may be available	Can be quite detailed, by design (taking into account response burden issues)	Instrument specific details
Consolidation	• Typically, global for complex MNEs • Domestic for others, based on legal entities	Domestic based on legal entities	• Domestically consolidated enterprises • Domestic legal entities	Reflection of domestically consolidated entities
Universe coverage	Typically, not universe coverage	Yes, for legal entities	• No, if sample survey only • Yes, if other data (e.g. tax data) are used to estimate	Typically, yes

account, which records the non-financial corporate production of goods and services and the generation, distribution, redistribution and use of income. Such components as the operating income, the value added, and the gross and the net operating profit can be drawn from the data, as shown in table 7.4. Supplementary investment and depreciation data are also available. Some of this information can also be very useful in the compilation of financial transactions.

7.131. As detailed cash flow statements typically not available, the compilation of transaction data from stocks is more challenging. As a result, the derivation of balancing items such as non-financial corporate net lending/net borrowing or net worth and its changes is rather difficult to compile and reconcile to the current account balance without using additional data sources. The profit and loss account typically offers up detail such as realized gains and losses, foreign currency revaluations and special write-ups/downs of assets and liabilities. Compilers can generally use this information to assign adjustments to the appropriate categories, given the concentration of financial instruments into a restricted number of assets and liabilities in the non-financial corporations' sector.

7.132. The accuracy and reliability of the corporate financial data are determined by various factors. One refers to the collection of the data on a sample basis, which requires that the profit and loss account data are assessed and monitored for coverage, sample error, response error and non-sampling error. Another is linked to the validation of intermediate results against other statistical information and the investigation of statistical discrepancies.

7.133. Sample data are often collected voluntarily. However, one of the major limitations of these samples is their lack of coverage of the services subsector, which is usually a large part of each developed economy. Moreover, the lack of timeliness and the sometimes annual periodicity of the publicly available corporate balance sheet data are some of the major reasons why these data are not broadly used as a source to compile institutional sector accounts. Otherwise, the annual frequency of the corporate profit

Table 7.4
Breakdown of the profit and loss account data by accounting item

Code	Description
1.	Net turnover
2.	Change in stocks of finished goods and work in progress
3.	Capitalized production
4.	Other operating income
S.*	Total operating income
5.	Costs of materials and consumables
5.a	Raw materials and consumables
5.b	Other external charges
8.	Other operating charges and taxes
T.*	Value added (S–5–8)
6.	Staff costs
6.a	Wages and salaries
6.b	Social security costs
U.*	Gross operating profit (T–6)
7.	Value adjustments on non-financial assets
7.a	Depreciation on intangible and tangible fixed assets
7.c*	Other value adjustments and provisions
V.*	Net operating profit (U–7)
9/11	Financial income
12.	Value adjustments on financial assets
13.	Interest and similar charges
13.a*	Interest paid on financial debts
13.b*	Other financial charges
W.*	Financial income net of charges (9/11–12–13)
X.*	Profit or loss on ordinary activities before taxes (V+W)
16.	Extraordinary income
17.	Extraordinary charges
Y.	Taxes on profit
21.	Profit or loss for the financial year (X+16–17–Y)

and loss account data is often considered to be sufficient for structural analyses, assuming that rather long time series are always available.

Compiling institutional sector accounts for non-financial corporations

7.134. A broad set of direct and indirect data sources should be used for the non-financial corporations sector when compiling institutional sector accounts. For example, transactions can be derived by using balance sheet data, profit and loss account data of non-financial corporations and also indirect data, as follows:

(a) Use the income statement to estimate the total (and perhaps some of the detail associated with the total) realized and unrealized holding gains or losses and extraordinary transactions that must be adjusted from the balance sheet first difference to estimate financial transactions. Some statistical agencies may be able to go further in terms of instrument accuracy for these adjustments if they have some degree of detail (e.g. on the income statement or in the form of a supplementary survey schedule) associated with holding gains or losses, write-ups or write-downs of financial assets and liabilities;

(b) The non-financial corporations' sector is a large and diverse sector with many major transactions taking place quarterly. Regardless of the sources of funds available and chosen for compilation, economic intelligence on mergers and acquisitions are invaluable. This is particularly true for measuring transactions, as mergers and acquisitions affect the assets and liabilities of the non-financial sectors but the resulting changes may not all constitute financial transactions (e.g. structural changes related to re-organization). This implies that a set of adjustments should be built in order to derive transactions in order to remove other flows (revaluations and other changes in the volume of assets and liabilities);

(c) Integrate the separate calculations of market value estimates for selected assets and liabilities and use the conversions of foreign currency denominated assets and liabilities to estimate financial transactions from balance sheet data;

(d) Use counterpart stock and flow data to the extent possible.

7.135. However, the use of a large number of data sources means that care is needed to ensure consistency of the data. The different timing in terms of the availability of the data sources also means that various recalculations will have to be carried out on the new data sets.

Box 7.3

Constructing macroeconomic estimates of non-financial corporations' financial statistics in Canada (prepared by Statistics Canada)

Background

In Canada, the quarterly *financial flow accounts* (FFA) – composed of both capital and financial accounts – were developed in the late 1960s, and the balance sheet accounts (consisting of financial assets and liabilities) were added in the early 1970s. Of note is that non-financial corporations' sector estimates were available in both of these accounts from the outset, although there have been improvements in quality over time. These gains in quality resulted primarily from improvements to enterprise survey vehicles and methodology – both directly for non-financial corporations as well as indirectly from financial institutions (for counterpart data).

The breadth and detail of the accounts have also improved over time. In the early 1980s, estimates of non-financial assets were added to the financial assets and liabilities outstanding to produce a set of *national balance sheet accounts* (NBSA) with estimates of net worth for each sector. The balance sheet data were subsequently converted to a quarterly frequency. In the early part of the millennium, relevant financial assets and liabilities were moved to a market valuation basis. The 2012 comprehensive revisions to the national accounts added new published instrument detail to all institutional sectors (e.g., listed and unlisted corporate equity). Work is under way to develop the other changes in assets account, especially given the importance of revaluations in net worth changes.

Enterprise financial survey

The major data source for the compilation for the corporate sector, including non-financial corporations (by industry), is the quarterly enterprise financial survey. This survey is linked to the centralized business register, following the practice across business surveys at Statistics Canada.

Consolidation

The statistical enterprise is the survey unit in the corporations' financial statement survey. For complex enterprises, this represents a selective consolidation of legal entities and their corresponding establishments (typically the survey unit used in business activity surveys), and this means that enterprises are usually (but not always) classified to industries, based on their major activity. For simple enterprises, the survey unit is the legal entity. The overall consolidation principle that is followed is domestically consolidated enterprises, which fits the conceptual boundary of the national and international accounts.

Coverage and basic methodology

For financial institutions/industries, the industry surveys typically achieve universe or close-to-universe coverage, with the exception of holding companies. For the non-financial corporations' industries, the survey uses a stratified sample survey approach, with *take-all, take-*

some (sampled) and *take-none* (non-sampled) segments in order to cover the universe of these enterprises. The take-all stratum covers the largest corporations (including major multinationals and/or their domestic affiliates). Non-response in this segment is imputed by using the last reported value of the missing firm and the movements in similar-sized firms in the same industry. The take-some segment covers a rotating sample of large firms (typically, complex enterprises) in the various industries. Non-response is handled in a similar fashion to the take-all stratum, and the non-sampled portion is estimated with reference to tax data. The take-none segment largely comprises small firms (legal entities) and is estimated using tax data; however, for the current period, it is estimated with reference to tax data. The enterprise survey is benchmarked to the tax data on an annual basis. Overall, this is a robust methodology.

It is important to note that, while this survey provides a key source for the universe estimate of non-financial corporations' assets and liabilities, on average it provides better-quality estimates by industry (a main use of this survey) than for the *aggregate construct* of total non-financial corporations as used in the sectoral financial accounts.

Survey content and valuation issues

The initial survey (balance sheets added to income statements in 1972) was designed to meet the needs of national accounts and financial accounts compilers and therefore continues (through periodic redesigns) to have the basic required level of instrument detail. As a result, it can be characterized as largely compatible with the requirements of the 2008 SNA. For example, the current instrument detail facilitates a split of traded and non-traded equity assets. In addition, this detail supports some degree of to-whom-from-whom instrument detail.

The valuation of assets and liabilities was, for many years, based on the standard book values/acquisition costs (for assets). This has been evolving in recent years as firms adopt the newer IFRS accounting standards that recommend current (i.e. fair) valuation of assets and liabilities. This is essentially a good development, but it is also a challenge for compilers and their compilation processes. In response, the enterprise survey vehicle adapted to this challenge in 2007 with the inclusion of a *comprehensive income variable* on the income statement. This variable both serves as a flag that a firm has adopted IFRS principles and provides a source of data for other unrealized gains/losses arising from the restating of assets-liabilities in a given period.

Survey schedules

The enterprise survey is an integrated collection of income statements and balance sheets, as well as some supplementary schedules. This makes it usable in the construction of a number of SNA components, not the least of which are the NBSA and FFA. In particular, it allows for the use of the income statement to construct adjustments in the compilation of financial transactions from the period-to-period first-difference in balance sheet accounts. An advantage for coherent sector accounts is that these adjustments also bring the financial transactions in line with the current account transactions.

An important supplementary schedule for measuring financial transactions is the *matching of income statement gains and losses with related assets and liabilities* (formerly called the *distribution of realized and unrealized gains/losses and write-ups/downs*). Unfortunately, this schedule is collected only for financial institutions, where financial holdings of marketable securities are significant.

Process and analysis

For non-financial corporations, adjustments related to realized gains/losses, unrealized gains/losses (including foreign currency) and write-ups/downs are allocated to assets and liabilities based on knowledge of large transactions and foreign currency items and, as a secondary procedure, allocated to the relevant assets-liabilities based on their weight. Universe changes arising from corporate restructuring, and sample rotations are itemized separately. Other special adjustments are also itemized. The survey area then submits a file to the financial accounts compilers with all of this information laid out in fields that include opening and closing balance sheet, change in financial position, and the various other types of categorized adjustments. This greatly facilitates the compilation of financial accounts for non-financial corporations.

Financial accounts procedures and analysis

The processed survey results are the initial step of the generation of non-financial corporations' (a) financial transactions in the FFA; and (b) stocks with relevant assets-liabilities at market value in the NBSA. The enterprise survey file is provided to financial account compilers by industry and, with access to reported microrecords, to support their further analysis. The next steps involve recourse to, and the integration of, counterpart data (including from securities' databases), economic intelligence (e.g. mergers and acquisitions), external data sources (e.g. stock exchange data, publicly available data from private sectors databases, etc.), as well as the review of the coherence of non-financial corporations' sectoral estimates in the context of the FFA and NBSA matrices.

As an example, data replacement for, say, survey methodology-based bank loan liabilities substitutes actual lending to total non-financial corporations for survey aggregate estimates of borrowing (which contain both reported and imputed and estimated records); this process improves data accuracy at the sectoral level and enhances to-whom-from-whom detail. The same point can be made for other adjustments arising from further analysis by financial accounts' compilers. Some adjustments are made at the aggregate level (e.g. bank loans), and other adjustments are made at the micro level (e.g. mergers and acquisitions). That said, it should be noted that adjustments to the survey-derived estimates are managed closely and kept to a minimum.

Analytical procedures and data replacement/adjustments are explained below (albeit not exhaustively) under the financial assets and liabilities sections, respectively.

Non-financial corporations' non-financial assets/capital acquisition; capital account

Because of significant differences from the valuation principles of the 2008 SNA, the non-financial assets from the enterprise financial survey are used for reference only. This may change as firms increasingly adapt their accounting to IFRS and convert relevant assets and liabilities to fair values.

Non-financial corporations' sector non-financial assets in the NBSA matrix are dominated by non-residential structures (building construction and engineering construction) and machinery and equipment. Other non-financial assets include land surrounding these structures, residential real estate (structures and land, separately) and research and development capital and software as well as business inventories. All produced assets are based on perpetual inventory method (PIM)-based methodology and are allocated to the sector by industry. PIM-based housing stock is allocated as part of the using the same sectoring methodology used for the household sector estimates. Land is estimated using industry-specific benchmark land-to-structure ratios (sorted by location and type) from research undertaken in the 1990s and these estimates are carried backward and forward using current real estate indicators. Business inventories are also derived from a "sum the flows" process (confronted with survey data) and are almost exclusively allocated to this sector.

The related investment flows for non-financial corporations' in the capital accounts of the FFA matrix are more aggregated – that is, they are not released in the same category detail as the stocks – but sectoring the investment components follows a similar pattern to that described above for stocks. Most of the investment flows come from surveys whose results are also fed into the PIM model, leading to consistency and reconciliation detail (e.g. price change) between the flows and stocks. Estimates of sectoral saving are derived as the balancing item in the current account, depreciation is generated from the PIM model and capital transfers are independently constructed. The capital account details of the FFA are provided by the compilers of the quarterly *income and expenditure accounts*, reflecting the integrated nature of the macroeconomic accounts in Canada.

Non-financial corporations' financial assets – stocks and flows

The initial estimates of total financial assets and the basic financial asset detail come from the enterprise survey. From here, a series of further adjustments and data substitutions are made in the construction of the FFA and NBSA. Adjustments, when they are viewed as corrections (e.g. mergers and acquisitions' adjustments in the FFA or market valuation adjustments in the NBSA) typically change the *survey-derived* financial asset totals. Substitutions from counterpart data would typically not change these financial asset totals.

Deposit assets are constructed from counterpart data from the deposit-taking institutions. These are substitutions of survey estimates for actual information from banks and other financial institutions. Counterpart data are, to some extent, of better quality for stocks than for flows. The standard practice is to maintain the total value of *survey-derived* financial assets, typically by offsetting the adjustment in the category *other financial assets*.

Inter-company investment (debt and equity) and, sometimes, other asset categories are typically adjusted for mergers and acquisitions activity, for both domestic transactions and positions and cross-border transactions and positions, the latter supplied by the international accounts compilers. While, in principle, these should be reflected in the file transmitted from the enterprise financial survey, most often these types of adjustments are missing as firms engaged in restructuring through mergers and acquisitions typically do not respond for a few quarters. These adjustments are viewed as corrections and therefore alter the *survey-derived* financial asset totals.

Inter-company investment, accounts receivable and other instruments are routinely confronted with the quarterly *Canada's balance of international payments*/quarterly *Canada's international investment position* data. This is also a reflection of the integrated nature of the macroeconomic accounts in Canada.

Other categories of financial assets (e.g. securities) are relatively smaller and are largely based on the estimated survey results (plus/minus any substitution adjustments from counterpart data) and do not have a significant impact on overall sector data quality in most quarters. Nevertheless, these assets are subject to a careful analytical review based on other sources and the process of two-way matrix balancing, and further adjustments are sometimes made. The category *other financial assets* can be subject to matrix balancing adjustments in the case of both stocks and flows.

As a result, post-analysis by financial account compilers, the major financial asset categories for non-financial corporations' are considered of good quality. That said, data accuracy and reliability is somewhat more of a concern for transactions than for positions, given the nature of the challenges in measuring transactions.

Non-financial corporations' liabilities (including equity) – stocks and flows

As with the financial assets, the initial estimates of total liabilities and equity as well as the basic underlying instrument detail come from the enterprise survey. This side of the ledger is also subject to a series of further adjustments and data substitutions in the construction of the FFA and NBSA. Following the same procedures as for financial assets (described above), data replacements are typically offset in the category *other liabilities*, while data adjustments are typically not offset.

Liabilities in the non-financial corporations' sector are derived largely from counterpart data and securities databases. Enterprise financial survey-based loan liability estimates (including capital leases) are replaced with actual loan asset details largely from financial institutions (from both survey and supplementary schedules of banks). For the transactions, these loan assets are first adjusted (to the extent possible) for allowances that were deducted in the calculation of asset positions. Nevertheless, these counterpart entries are of slightly better quality for stocks than for flows.

Bonds and short-term paper estimates from the enterprise financial survey are substituted by the relevant (a) new issues and (b) positions (both corrected for valuation) of securities. This process adds precision to the gains/losses adjustments derived from the income statement for the transactions, and it generates accurate market values for positions. The securities are sourced from security-by-security databases that cover both domestic and international issues. The International Accounts Division maintains these databases. Stocks and flows from the securities' databases are considered to be of similarly high quality.

Corporate equity is a major source of funds for non-financial enterprises and also comprises one of the significant measures of net worth in this sector. Measurement is a detailed estimation process that splits listed (traded) and unlisted (non-traded) equity:

- For transactions, there is a partial replacement of enterprise financial survey data. Net new issues of listed shares are taken from the securities' databases and unlisted equity is basically estimated as the first-difference of shares outstanding plus contributed surplus.
- For positions, the listed and unlisted shares are also segmented. The calculated market value of listed shares is taken from the securities' databases (which integrate stock market information). For unlisted equity, the larger companies are marked-to-market using industry constructed market-to-book ratios (based on listed shares). More specifically, the size cut-off threshold used rests on the assumption that large unlisted firms face the same market realities as their listed counterparts in those same industries and thus would be subject to similar valuation.

Inter-company debt and equity liabilities are confronted with the balance of payments/international investment position data. The same is true of accounts payable. Other liability categories are relatively smaller and are largely based on the survey results. Notably, these do not have a significant impact on overall sector data quality in most quarters. Nevertheless, these are subject to analytical review based on other sources and in the process of two-way matrix balancing, and further adjustments are sometimes made. Like its corresponding asset, the category *other liabilities* can be subject to matrix balancing adjustments in the case of both stocks and flows.

The analysis, estimation, adjustment and substitution procedures by financial account compilers above result in the major liability and equity categories of non-financial corporations being considered of good quality. Nevertheless, as with financial assets, data accuracy and reliability are considered lower for transactions than for positions.

Digression on data quality and completeness of the financial accounts

After a number of years of experience in the construction, expansion and improvement to the financial accounts at Statistics Canada, it is clear that a full capital and financial account (FFA) and a full balance sheet account (NBSA) not only are more useful for users but tend to significantly enhance the quality of the sectoral estimates.

The capital and financial account imposes the sector account (vertical) constraint to complement the asset-liability (horizontal) constraint. The simultaneous balancing approach often signals anomalies, such as underestimation/overestimation of asset-liability transactions in the sectors; in the case of the integrated macroeconomic accounts, it also provides a feedback mechanism to current account compilers.

Similarly, a full balance sheet account (including non-financial assets) increases the quality of the sector accounts by generating net worth estimates as a means to help confront the quality of the non-financial assets as well as the financial balances (sometimes referred to as financial net worth). NBSA matrix balancing is also substantially improved and can lead to adjustments, especially with reference to related FFA asset-liability categories. Data confrontation/analysis exercises are therefore enhanced. In addition, corporate sector net worth balances also provide a clear signal of potential data gaps (see below for reference to natural resources).

As an aside, for the NBSA, this sector generates three measures of current value net worth: (a) the *market value of corporate equities,* which is considered a liability in the economy-wide matrix, since it is held as assets by other sectors; (b) the *net asset value*, which is equal to total assets less liabilities, excluding corporate equity at market value; and (c) *residual corporate net worth* as the unallocated difference between the first two measures, which is used in the calculation of *national net worth* (i.e. the approach of the sum of the national institutional sectors' estimates of net worth). There is also a supplementary measure of equity at book value provided for certain analytical uses, and composed of survey-derived shares outstanding, plus contributed surplus plus retained earnings and reserves.

Remaining data challenges and conclusion

Compiling macroeconomic non-financial corporations' sector financial statistics remains a demanding task. Data quality has evolved over time as sources and methodology continue to improve. These improvements can be partly offset by new developments in financial markets and financial accounting that can adversely impact the compilation balance sheets and flow of funds data if not properly understood, and accounted for, by compilers.

While overall data quality is now generally considered good in the Canadian FFA and NBSA non-financial corporations' sector, there remain other data challenges. Examples include:

- *Instrument detail and quality.* There is a need to continue work on financial derivatives as well as liabilities associated with defined benefit pension plans.
- *Data gaps.* There is a project that is estimating the current value of natural resource leases in the NBSA. The inclusion of this non-financial corporations' asset should result in an improved measure of the *net asset value* of net worth that is better harmonized with the *market value of corporate equity.*
- *Component accounts.* There is a need to continue efforts on the development of the *other changes in asset account.*

(d) Data on households

Survey micro data

7.136. Statistics on households may be collected by surveys covering household financing and consumption. The survey may provide data on income and wealth for households at different income and wealth levels, and with different age profiles, family commitments, etc. Where these surveys exist, the data are usually collected with a frequency of three to five years because of the high costs of carrying them out.

Macro data

7.137. Given the high costs of carrying out such surveys, in many or most countries (even those with well-developed statistical systems) these micro data are not the primary sources in the compilation of household macroeconomic balance sheet and fi-

Box 7.4

Use of data from the survey of consumer finances and the flow of funds accounts in the United States (prepared by the Federal Reserve Board)

Households' sector balance sheets both contributed to and were dramatically affected by the recent financial crisis. The run-up in housing and stock prices in the years preceding the crisis contributed to the strong growth in consumer spending and rapid pace of debt accumulation during that period and thus helped to create a situation in which more households were more vulnerable to financial shocks. The steep declines in house values and stock prices at the onset of the crisis (along with rising unemployment and declining incomes) contributed to the substantial drop and subsequent anaemic growth in consumer spending that has dominated macroeconomic activity for the past five years. One of the usual explanations for continuing spending restraint by consumers is the desire of at least some households to avoid going back to the vulnerable balance sheet situations they faced as the crisis started.

Clearly, understanding the most recent business cycle, and the slow pace of the ongoing recovery, requires an understanding of the evolution of household balance sheets. Unfortunately, the data sets available for studying household balance sheets all have significant limitations across one or more dimensions, such as representativeness, timeliness, the level of aggregation, the degree of longitudinal information and the level of detail. These limitations impair our ability to track the evolution of household balance sheets over time in sufficient detail to identify important changes as they occur.

There are two widely used data sources available on household balance sheets, both of which are produced by the Federal Reserve Board: the flow of funds accounts (FFA), which provide quarterly estimates of the aggregate assets and liabilities held by the households sector, and the survey of consumer finances (SCF), which provides a detailed triennial snapshot of the finances and balance sheets of a representative sample of United States households.

These two data sources were developed for different purposes. The FFA provides a timely measure of the aggregate state of United States households, which is a key indicator for the macroeconomic outlook. The SCF provides a detailed look at the rich heterogeneity in household finances, which is critical for understanding the microeconomic underpinnings of macroeconomic activity. The FFA is available until the fourth quarter of 2012, but lacks micro data on household balance sheets. The SCF provides rich micro data for a point in time but, because it is costly and labour-intensive to produce, it is only available every three years, and with a two-year production lag (for example, the most recent survey is from 2010, which became available in 2012). The main idea of the project described in this paper is to combine the two data sets in an effort to create a timely data set of detailed household-level balance sheet information.

nancial transaction data. Rather, in many countries, households' sector estimates typically use counterpart data (to the extent possible) along with assets and liabilities derived residually. This implies that the construction of households sector estimates relies on both a judicious matrix balancing process (see Section 3) and a thorough analysis of the financial account in any given production period.

7.138. Households sector data quality in the financial and balance sheet accounts depends on the following: the availability of current accounts and data on non-financial assets; the availability of high-frequency stock-flow counterpart information and other indirect data; and the accuracy and reliability of other sectors' stock-flow data, given the matrix constraints that would typically derive/balance many assets and liabilities in the households sector. This takes into account the other institutional sectors' coverage and the methodologies employed to derive assets and liabilities as well as financial transactions in assets and liabilities across the other institutional sectors.

Box 7.5

Constructing macroeconomic estimates of household financial statistics in Canada (prepared by Statistics Canada)

Background

In Canada, the quarterly financial flow accounts (FFA) – both capital and financial accounts – were developed in the late 1960s, and the balance sheet accounts (consisting of financial assets and liabilities) were added in the early 1970s. It is of note that households sector estimates were available in both of these accounts from the outset, although there have been improvements in quality over time. Reflecting the households sector's dependency on the quality of other sectors' data in the financial accounts matrix framework, many of the gains in quality resulted from improvements to enterprise survey vehicles – especially for non-financial corporations as well as for financial institutions, which comprise about 20 institutional sectors in the Canadian financial accounts. In addition, the households sector estimates moved substantially in favour of the use of counterpart entries in the 1970s and 1980s, as administrative and other data improved.

The breadth and detail of the accounts have also improved over time. In the early 1980s, estimates of non-financial assets were added to the financial assets and liabilities outstanding to produce a set of national balance sheet accounts (NBSA) with estimates of net worth for each sector. The balance sheet data were subsequently converted to quarterly frequency. In the early part of the millennium, relevant assets and liabilities were moved to a market valuation basis. The pension satellite account, which provides detail on pension assets, financial transactions and income related to the households sector, was developed in 2009. The 2012 comprehensive revisions to the national accounts split the NPISH sector from the households sector and added new instrument detail to all institutional sectors (e.g. listed and unlisted corporate equity). Work is under way on developing the other changes in assets account, especially given the importance of revaluations in households sector (ultimate investor sector) net worth changes.

Households sector non-financial assets and capital acquisition

Households' sector non-financial assets are dominated by residential real estate and, to a lesser extent, consumer durables' stocks. Housing structures are based on perpetual inventory method (PIM) housing stock allocated to the households sector using type and tenure information. A similar process is followed for related capital formation flows, supplemented by sales split by singles and multiples. Land is estimated using annual historical land-to-structure ratios (sorted by location and type) from benchmark research undertaken in the 1990s. This estimate is carried backwards and forward using current real estate indicators. Related flows are also based primarily on new sales, which provide split sales including and excluding land. Household consumer durable stocks in the balance sheet accounts are also estimated using a PIM methodology. There are no corresponding flows in the capital account.

Non-financial assets also include unincorporated farms and other unincorporated business assets. Farm assets/investment that cover both capital and inventories are based on farm census data (which provide the percentage split of incorporated/unincorporated farms) as well as on higher frequency farm surveys. Non-farm unincorporated business is quite small and its share in household assets has been declining over time. Estimates of the stocks and flows of these assets are based on a variety of sources.

Households sector financial assets – stocks and flows

Estimates of financial assets rely heavily on quarterly and timely counterpart data from financial institutions (from both survey and supplementary schedules of banks). Counterpart data are, to some extent, of better quality for stocks than for flows. Deposit assets are constructed from counterpart data from the deposit-taking institutions. Life insurance asset components and pension asset components (both funded and government unfunded employer-based plans) are equivalent to the corresponding liabilities in the other institutional sectors. Investment fund assets are largely equal to investment fund liabilities, adjusted for the portions held as assets in other sectors. Government saving bonds, which are based on the corresponding government sector liabilities, dominate bonds.

Other assets are largely residually derived, but are subject to a careful analytical review based on other sources and the process of matrix balancing. As a result, the major categories are considered to be of good quality, although data quality is more of a concern for transactions than for positions. Corporate shares comprise the largest quasi-residual asset and are split into two subcomponents: listed shares, which are based on solid quality estimates of assets and liabilities across the sectoral matrix; and unlisted shares, which are dominated by large private companies and are confronted annually with related data. The remaining financial assets are relatively small in size and constitute a set where residual derivation is of lower quality. Other short-term and long-term debt securities are largely insignificant in size, such that residual derivation does not have an impact on overall sector data quality. The category other financial assets, while small in size, is of some concern, given the quality issues in this instrument across the sectoral matrix in the case of both stocks and flows.

Households sector liabilities – stocks and flows

Liabilities in the households sector are derived largely from counterpart data from financial institutions (from both survey and supplementary schedules of banks) and are considered to be of good quality. Counterpart entries are of slightly better quality for stocks than for flows. These cover, in order of size: mortgages (both residential and non-residential), which are the largest liability; consumer credit, which is also quite large; and other loans, which comprise bank loans as a counterpart entry along with other components built from other sources of information. The other components include agricultural loans and direct estimates of automobile leases. Trade payables related to unincorporated business are derived residually, but are relatively quite small.

Households sector balance sheet links to household sector surveys

Household surveys of assets and debt (the survey of financial security) are available on an occasional basis in Canada. These micro data estimates are used primarily for analysing household wealth by income and age classes. Notably, NBSA residential real estate stocks are confronted with household micro data real estate assets when these become available, as the two sets of estimates have a history of being relatively close in terms of residential real estate values. For financial assets and liabilities, the micro and macro data can be quite different for a number of assets and liabilities (mortgage liabilities being the general exception, likely reflecting the close link to survey-based residential real estate values). For this reason, NBSA households' sector estimates are only referenced to the household survey estimates of assets and debt (focusing more on trends between the two data sets) when the survey detail becomes available.

Conclusion

Compiling macroeconomic households' sector financial statistics is a demanding task. Quality continues to improve over time in the households sector as data sources and methodology continue to evolve. However, these improvements can be affected by new developments in financial markets and financial accounting that can adversely impact the balance sheets and flow of funds data, including the households' sector estimates in the financial accounts matrix, if not properly understood and accounted for by compilers. Households' sector balance sheet details and component accounts (e.g. the other changes in assets account) also continue to expand over time, allowing these accounts to meet new relevance challenges.

5. Financial data collected in micro databases

7.139. There is some impetus to collecting financial data in security-by-security databases and credit registers.[173] Security-by-security databases cover data on issues and holdings of securities, while credit registers contain detailed statistics on loans granted essentially by monetary financial institutions to non-financial sectors, such as general government, non-financial corporations, households and non-profit institutions serving households.

(a) Securities statistics

7.140. Detailed securities statistics are an important tool for improving the coverage and quality of institutional sector accounts and for developing from-whom-to-whom accounts. Securities statistics include data on issues, redemptions, secondary market transactions, amounts outstanding of securities and securities price information.

[173] There may be other micro databases available, such as of corporations' accounting data.

7.141. Securities cover debt securities and equity securities as listed and unlisted shares. Some investment fund shares or units are also considered to be securities.

Securities issues statistics

7.142. Securities issues statistics cover stock and flow data on securities issued by residents with breakdowns by subcategory and currency denomination and, for debt securities, by maturity and by type of interest rate. Data may also be collected on securities issues for non-residents in national currency.[174]

7.143. Securities issues statistics may contain time series at different levels of aggregation according to the residency of the issuer, the issuing currency and the issuing sector or subsector. Stock data on debt securities may be at market value and at nominal value.

Securities holdings statistics

7.144. Statistics on holdings of securities may be based on balance-sheet information for institutional sectors but also on depository or custodian statistics. The most straightforward way is to link existing security-by-security (SBS) databases with data on securities holdings.

Security-by-security databases

7.145. In the context of from-whom-to-whom accounts, SBS databases become rather important. An SBS database is a micro database that stores information on individual securities issues. The database can be used flexibly to compile a range of statistics to serve diverse needs.[175]

7.146. Information stored on a financial instrument is broken down into attributes that describe characteristics of the instrument. The selection of attributes may vary depending on the purpose of the database. Attributes useful for statistical applications may include: the international securities identification number (ISIN); name, residence and sector and subsector of the issuer; issue date; redemption date; type of security; currency of denomination; issue price; redemption price; the outstanding amount or the market capitalization; and the coupon payments and dates (see figure 7.1). Such information allows all the necessary features of securities to be compiled.

Figure 7.1
Example of data attributes stored in security-by-security databases for statistical usage

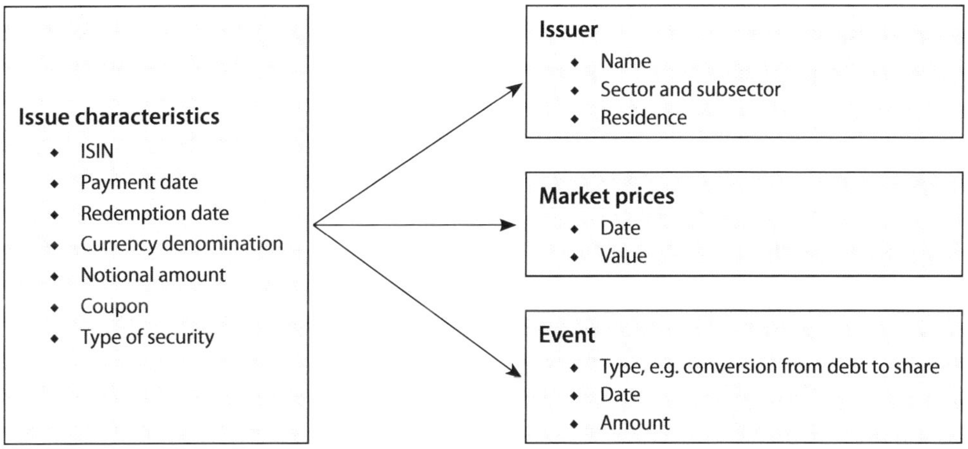

[174] Issues made abroad by residents are more difficult to trace.

[175] SBS databases may include statistics covering various categories of financial instruments – usually debt securities and equity securities. A prominent example of an SBS database is the centralized securities database set up by the European System of Central Banks.

7.147. One example of using data from SBS databases refers to the extraction of data on revaluations and other changes in the volume of assets and liabilities. The recent financial crisis has changed the focus of monetary and fiscal policy analysis in many respects. Most notably, a growing interest in balance sheets and their components, in particular whether their changes are due to transactions or other flows, has given impetus to themes like wealth effects, leverage behavior, the value of collateral and real-financial feedback loops.

7.148. The interest in understanding flows other than transactions has led compilers to start developing the statistical infrastructure for distinguishing the different subcategories of the other flows, in particular between flows due to revaluations and other volume changes.

7.149. Another example of using data from SBS databases refers to the compilation of data on debt securities broken down by remaining maturity. While balance sheets do not usually enable such data to be compiled, this could be done on the basis of security-by-security data for both issues and holdings of debt securities by institutional unit, classified by sector and subsector.

7.150. The production of statistics from an SBS database can be presented as a three-stage process (see figure 7.2). The first stage (input) typically involves collecting and/or purchasing data on individual securities from a range of sources, such as central banks, government agencies, commercial data providers and securities exchanges. The second stage covers data quality management. The data on individual securities collected from different sources are added to the database, merged and stored. Checks for completeness, plausibility and consistency are then performed and, where errors are detected, observations are corrected. The third stage involves storing data on individual securities according to various classification criteria.

7.151. Data quality management is often complicated by lack of standardization. Experience shows that different data sources frequently use different identifiers for instruments, different taxonomies for describing instrument characteristics, different data formats and different valuation criteria. Sources often lack reliable metadata and vary in terms of the quality of maintenance, that is, attributes can be outdated, but are not labelled as such. When collecting data on a large number of instruments in an SBS database, these limitations can represent a major challenge.

7.152. A fundamental quality of SBS databases is their ability to support reliable automated processing of large amounts of data for the compilation of statistical aggregates or other types of analysis. The level of standardization of the more stable reference data (identifier, key attributes and classifications) largely determines the quality and efficiency of the database and its downstream statistical and analytical processes. Standardization of the reference data, in turn, depends on the level of standardization within and among the data sources used.

7.153. The specific needs for data standardization raised by large-scale computing applications, as opposed to mere disclosure, strengthen the case for creating a standard for reference data on securities and issuers, ideally with the aim of making such data available to policymakers, regulators and the financial industry through an international public infrastructure. It is likely that such an infrastructure would reduce the costs of SBS databases, and certainly increase their value, enabling all interested parties to produce more timely analyses of increasingly complex financial markets, especially in times of turbulence.

7.154. SBS databases can be extended to include information on securities holdings for holders grouped by sector and subsector, as well as by residence. For that purpose, information provided by respondents is linked at the individual security level to

Figure 7.2
Stages in the development of security-by-security databases

Inputs	Data quality management	Outputs
Data collection Sources • Central bank • Government agencies • International sources • Commercial data providers • Securities exchanges • Numbering agencies	Data receipt, merging and storage Data consistency check and clean-up	Micro data Data aggregation Data dissemination Users • Central banks • Statistical agencies • International agencies

the data stored in the SBS database. The link is often made by using the ISIN code, but also referring to information on the debt securities' holders and holdings:

(a) The holder by residency and institutional sector and subsector and also by large and complex financial or non-financial group;

(b) The amount of holdings in currency.

7.155. At least two levels of access should be distinguished, that is, access to raw data for statisticians and access to more aggregated data for users, for instance to compile flow of funds and sectoral financial balance sheets.

7.156. Current reporting schemes on debt securities holdings are based mainly on two groups of agents having access to information on securities holdings: (a) custodians (as well as centralized securities depositories); and (b) direct reporters. In most cases, data are collected from custodians on an SBS basis. This also refers to the collection of data on the debt securities holdings of residents from non-resident custodians to allow the breakdown of holdings by the residency of the issuer to be estimated.

7.157. Direct reporters, completing the custodian report, provide SBS data on their holdings with various breakdowns: by type of instrument, maturity, residence of issuer, etc. There may also be a legal obligation in countries for residents to report their securities held in custody abroad. However, there is usually a limited coverage of data directly collected from specific sectors or subsectors, such as households and non-profit institutions serving households.

7.158. When deciding whether to construct an SBS database, the full range of benefits and costs should be considered. Most of the arguments for and against SBS databases relate to the compilers of securities statistics, although respondents and users are also affected. The benefits and costs exercise should therefore examine the process end to end. This applies especially where efforts at standardization are considered.

7.159. One of the main advantages of SBS databases is that compilers, rather than respondents, are responsible for the statistical classification of securities. This promotes accuracy and consistency of the data, and adherence to international statistical standards. For statistical purposes, particularly in cases of statistics on securities issues, government finance statistics and institutional sector accounts, individual SBS issues data are usually aggregated according to various statistical categories. SBS databases offer the flexibility to produce different aggregates based on SBS data, with no need for any further data collection. Moreover, SBS databases can be designed to allow data to be derived on positions, transactions and other flows. SBS databases also allow quality checks at a very precise level to detect outlier observations within specific statistical categories. Outliers may indicate a misclassification but can also be caused by financial innovation, which would require further investigation and potentially an amendment to the statistical aggregation categories.

7.160. SBS databases benefit respondents by reducing the amount of detailed breakdowns to be reported to compilers. Respondents no longer need to map their internal data into statistical reports and instead provide relevant information for each individual debt security in their database. A drawback for respondents, however, is the need to meet the data standards agreed with compilers, although data standardization can also benefit respondents who themselves need good-quality data to maximize efficiency and reduce operational risk in their own processes.

7.161. From the user's perspective, there may be interest in detailed disaggregated data or in combining different classifications, particularly as debt securities markets become more complex and globalized. SBS databases enable this decomposition in debt securities statistics. Sometimes, a panel of individual securities data may be set up to analyse common developments. SBS databases also permit an analysis of the financing of different sectors, the size of different market segments or the importance of different debt securities. The databases allow users to track changes in the credit ratings, prices and liquidity of individual securities and issuers.

7.162. At the same time, there are significant costs for compilers in setting up and maintaining SBS databases and adapting them to changes in users' needs.[176] To date, SBS data are sourced largely from commercial data providers. Acquiring this information is expensive and the information can often be incomplete or contradictory between sources. Information technology costs for database storage and processing are significant, especially where extensive and complex "data cleaning" is required to compensate for poor-quality data or the non-standardization of data sources.

7.163. From an operational and methodological perspective, SBS databases are characterized by their complexity, the large volumes of data and statistics stored in them and database management costs that shift from respondents to compilers. Human, financial and information technology resources need to be found. There are administrative expenses involved in setting up contracts with reporting agents for regular reporting or to conduct surveys, as well as the costs of managing procurement and delivery from commercial data sources. Furthermore, a minimum level of quality of data is needed, such as a full coverage of specific categories of securities for a given set of attributes. Some manual intervention is also needed to cross-check corresponding data received from various data providers. Finally, there can be legal and contractual obstacles preventing data exchange between central banks, statistical agencies and other authorities, as well as between different types of users within an institution.

(b) Credit registers

7.164. While such a database may be a very long-term objective, work may be done to collect and harmonize loan data across existing (central and private) credit registers.

7.165. Some central banks maintain official credit registers; there are also private registers to which monetary financial institutions and other lenders contribute data and which they may consult.

[176] Given the significant costs, there are possibilities to cooperate and share costs among compilers building up SBS databases. A high coverage of securities data has already been achieved by some SBS databases of major economies, such as the OECD countries, including the euro area, and such data sets may be exchanged at an aggregated level for statistical purposes, taking into account confidentiality rules.

7.166. There are three main uses for the information content of credit registers:

(a) To enable bank supervisors to accurately assess credit risk in supervised financial institutions, that is, to assess credit concentration and/or potential or actual default both on the lender and borrower sides;

(b) To support financial transactions by assisting credit institutions and other lenders in the evaluation of potential borrowers' risk;[177]

(c) For economic analysis. Experience has shown that, with improved data coverage and access, credit registers can support macroprudential analysis, research and statistical needs, as well as market and credit risk analysis.

7.167. Owing to legal constraints, the different operational goals pursued, and competition between private credit bureaux,[178] there has been some specialization in the various existing credit registers: positive reporting (on new and outstanding loans); negative reporting (loan default); or lending coverage (loans to non-financial corporations or loans to households for consumption or house purchase (with or without a mortgage)).

7.168. The scope and coverage of (existing) central credit registers and private credit bureaux vary considerably across countries. However, there is an increasing expectation and, indeed, some concrete experience that credit registers are evolving. Their coverage and quality may increase stepwise and they could also be used for such purposes as macroprudential analysis and research and as input to monetary and financial statistics, balance of payments statistics and institutional sector accounts.

C. Compiling institutional sector accounts

1. The building block approach

7.169. The compilation of an integrated system of institutional sector accounts follows a specific process involving the use of *building blocks*. Source data for institutional sectors, subsector groupings or even subsectors are brought together as building blocks, which are then incorporated into the standard accounts and into the from-whom-to-whom accounts. A "hierarchy of sources" applies, that is, the most reliable data source should be referred to where more than one is available for the same variable.

7.170. The building blocks comprise detailed instrument classifications and, in various degrees, from-whom-to-whom information on positions, transactions, revaluations and other changes in the volume of assets and liabilities, following 2008 SNA standards as closely as possible.

7.171. Following the seven-sector approach, the main building blocks cover the monetary financial institutions (S121 to S123), general government (S13), and the rest of the world (S2), but also insurance corporations and pension funds (S128 and S129) and non-MMF investment funds (S124) as a substantial part of the other financial corporations (S124 to S127).

7.172. Another important building block is securities statistics. While the sector building blocks may provide statistical information for all financial instruments, the

[177] Many private credit bureaux are developing value added services for their customers by modelling consumer behaviour and/or assessing default probability by types of loan or classes of borrower. Credit registers may also develop credit risk models for supervisory purposes.

[178] A private credit bureau receives data from lenders and stores that data in a common database. The data provided must be timely and accurate. Reporting lenders can then access the register to obtain consolidated information about their credit applicants.

securities statistics building block provides comprehensive data on securities issues and holdings for all resident sectors and subsectors and for the rest of the world.

7.173. Each of the building blocks has different characteristics and brings different challenges to consistency within and between the blocks in terms of valuation and accounting rules. However, given the integrated nature of the institutional sector accounts, the quality and the consistency of the building blocks are essential for the overall quality of the accounts – specifically the household and non-financial corporations sector accounts. The accounts for these two sectors are based mainly on from-whom-to-whom information provided by the various building blocks.

7.174. The building block approach is illustrated in figure 7.3. It shows the six building blocks as described above:[179]

(a) Monetary financial institutions (central bank (S121), deposit-taking corporations except the central bank (S122) and money market funds (S123));

(b) General government (central government (S1311), state government (S1312), local government (S1313) and social security funds (S1314));

(c) The rest of the world (S2);

(d) Insurance corporations (S128) and pension funds (S129):

(e) Non-MMF investment funds (S124), other financial intermediaries, except insurance corporations and pension funds (S125), financial auxiliaries (S126) and captive financial institutions and moneylenders (S127);

(f) Securities (mainly debt securities (F3), listed shares (F511) and unlisted shares (F512)).

7.175. The arrows indicate that from-whom-to-whom data are used to construct the accounts for several sectors and subsector groupings for which no direct data sources are available.

(a) The building block approach and related manuals

7.176. Various manuals exist providing guidance, in terms of methodology and definition, on how to design building blocks as the basis for compiling institutional sector accounts. The four main manuals are: the MFSMCG for building blocks as part of the financial corporations sector (S12), the GFSM 2014 for the building block general government, the BPM6 for the building block rest of the world and the HSS for the building block securities.

7.177. The MFSMCG deals essentially with the monetary financial institutions building block. It also refers to other subsectors or subsector groupings, such as non-MMF investment funds and insurance corporations and pension funds.

7.178. Nevertheless, various inconsistencies in the data may be observed within a building block and, as well as between building blocks. They may arise because, for example, the report forms cover only stock data or only transaction data, or because accounting principles deviate with regard to the time of recording or the valuation of transactions and stocks.

---

[179] The source data as covered by the six building blocks are the basis to compile institutional sector accounts according to the seven-sector approach. It means that the sector accounts for monetary financial institutions, insurance corporations and pension funds, other financial corporations, general government, and the rest of the world rely mainly on the corresponding direct source data. The accounts for non-financial corporations and for households including NPISHs are compiled based mainly on "indirect" data taken from the various building blocks and on securities statistics.

(b) Eliminating inconsistencies in data related to building blocks within the financial corporations sector

7.179. The main use of institutional sector accounts within a central bank is to enhance monetary policy analysis.

7.180. It is therefore crucial that the institutional sector accounts be consistent with monetary and financial statistics, which are the source of monthly or quarterly statistics on broad money. Because of their relevance for monetary policy analysis, these data may supersede most of the counterpart data related to monetary financial institutions (S121 to S123), specifically for loans granted and deposits incurred by these institutions. For a significant part of monetary financial institutions' assets, the market valuation principle is already used in accounting rules. The integral links between monetary and financial statistics, the financial account and the balance sheet as described in the 2008 SNA provide an overall consistency in principles and concepts, such as residence and sector classification of institutional units, classification of financial assets and liabilities, recording and valuation of financial assets and liabilities as well as transactions and other flows, and data aggregation and consolidation.

7.181. If such general consistency is not achieved, the compiler is faced with a communication challenge because the institutional sector accounts deviate from data compiled by monetary and financial statistics. This communication challenge applies eventually to valuation methods applied in monetary and financial statistics, which may follow business accounting principles but not national accounts, which are based on the market valuation principle.

7.182. Business accounting principles also apply to other building blocks within the financial corporations sector, the building blocks for non-MMF investment funds (S124) and insurance corporations and pension funds (S128 and S129).

7.183. Balance sheet data collected from financial corporations, especially from deposit-taking corporations except the central bank (S122), are often characterized by a large amount of detailed from-whom-to-whom data for deposits and loans, but sometimes also for debt securities.

7.184. Quality issues may arise occasionally:

(a) If monthly or quarterly balance sheet data are collected which are valued at nominal value or acquisition value and which do not include accrued interest;

(b) As a result of data adjustments. Because data on transactions are not directly collected but derived from changes in stocks, they are adjusted by eliminating revaluations and other changes in the volume of assets and liabilities;

(c) If major discrepancies emerge when confronting the corresponding data sets collected for different financial corporation subsectors **on a from-whom-to-whom level**.

7.185. To overcome these deficiencies, a complete set of flow data (transactions, revaluations and other changes in the volume of assets and liabilities) could be added to the balance sheet data broken down by financial instrument on a from-whom-to-whom basis. This would minimize the need for estimations and allow the overall quality of the data to be checked further.

(c) Priority rules related to data provided by the monetary financial institutions building block

7.186. The institutional sector accounts can be used to monitor the interactions of monetary financial institutions with other financial corporations, non-financial sectors and the rest of the world, revealing broader developments in financing and investment and their interactions with the real economy (thereby serving as a bridge between monetary and economic analysis).

7.187. To fulfil this role, it is crucial that the institutional sector accounts be as consistent as possible with the monetary financial institutions statistics used for regular monetary analysis. However, full consistency is not always possible owing to various deviations of these data from the institutional sector accounts.

7.188. While data on transactions are generally in line with the 2008 SNA, this is not necessarily the case for balance sheet data and, implicitly, for other flow data. For example, balance sheet data may not correctly cover (accumulated) revaluations of equity and debt securities. One option is to use the transaction data as provided by monetary financial institutions statistics (thus ensuring full consistency of the transaction data) but estimating the other flow data from other sources. This would allow for full consistency of institutional sector accounts with the monetary financial institutions statistics for transactions, but not for balance sheet positions and other flows.

7.189. Another area where monetary financial institutions statistics may not always follow the 2008 SNA is data on other accounts receivable/payable. In monetary financial institutions statistics, other accounts receivable/payable are often part of remaining assets and liabilities, which often have a completely different scope – covering also accrued interest or profit or losses of the current year.

(d) The securities statistics building block

7.190. The securities building block is an important piece of statistical information if data are collected and compiled on a security-by-security and from-whom-to-whom basis. The methodology of this building block largely follows the recommendations outlined in the HSS.

7.191. Detailed information on securities issues and holdings at an ISIN code level is used to fill the gaps as well as to support the market valuation principle throughout the institutional sector accounts.

7.192. In the absence of a security-by-security database, data on securities issues and holdings by institutional sector are combined from the different building blocks indicated in figure 7.3. The holdings of securities by households including non-profit institutions serving households or by non-financial corporations are often derived by "exploiting" identities within the accounting framework.

(e) The rest of the world building block

7.193. The rest of the world building block benefits from various direct reporting schemes. These are report forms to collect data on the balance of payments, on the international investment position or on securities issues by residents held abroad (which may also be an input to the securities statistics building block).

7.194. One strength of the rest of the world building block is its detailed financial instrument classification and from-whom-to-whom information on balance sheet positions, transactions and revaluations closely following 2008 SNA principles of recording and valuation.

Figure 7.3
Main building blocks contributing to the system of institutional sector accounts

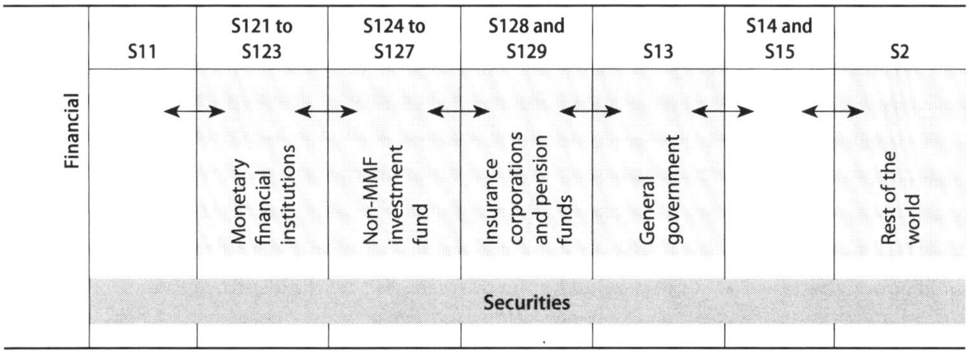

Note: The arrows ←→ indicate that from-whom-to-whom data are provided by the main building blocks. The non-MMF investment funds (S124) building block provides data for only a part of the subsectors S124 to S127. Other building blocks for financial corporations subsectors may exist, e.g. for financial auxiliaries (S126).

7.195. One of the issues related to the data available for the rest of the world is the presentation predominantly by function. This does not always allow a direct mapping to the financial instrument classification of the 2008 SNA. Moreover, in most cases a somewhat restricted breakdown exists for the rest of the world data by counterpart sector.

7.196. Vertically reconciling the rest of the world accounts as part of institutional sector accounts means eliminating all net errors and omissions. One option may be to adjust the financial account to completely remove these imbalances. However, increases in net errors and omissions may suggest a need for thorough statistical analysis.

7.197. Significant asymmetries vis-à-vis foreign countries may be identified as a major source of these discrepancies. A solution for reducing them, for example, for foreign direct investment (FDI) or portfolio investment, could be to exchange micro data among countries while still preserving data confidentiality.

(f) The general government building block

7.198. The general government building block comprises a largely consistent set of financial and non-financial data with some from-whom-to-whom information from central, state and local government and from social security funds.

7.199. The main challenge of this building block is primarily due to differences between the government finance statistics and monetary financial institutions statistics in terms of financial instrument classifications, sector delineations and netting. Work to reconcile the data, even on an institutional unit level, may be needed to improve consistency between the two blocks.

7.200. Although not as important from a monetary policy perspective, consistency of the institutional sector accounts with the government finance data is nevertheless essential owing to the political sensitivity of the data, which are often used for administrative purposes.

7.201. In this context, discrepancies between government finance data and institutional sector accounts may not be accepted because of fiscal policy considerations. Otherwise, government data are usually very carefully collected following international statistical standards and also scrutinized closely, given that they will be used for administrative purposes. This gives government finance data a level of accuracy not attainable in other statistical domains. However, administrative data normally follow the cash accounting principle, while statistical or national accounts data follow the accrual principle.

(g) Reconciliation procedures

7.202. The main strength of the building block approach is that it brings together all the data collected for various sectors, subsectors or subsector groupings into a coherent framework – the 2008 SNA. Within this framework, inconsistencies within individual data sources or between data sources are displayed and reconciled. They provide feedback to the quality checking procedures and to the longer-term improvement of individual statistical collection systems.

7.203. The compilation of institutional sector accounts is based on the main building blocks as described above but also on information from supplementary data collection schemes for sectors and subsectors not part of the building block approach. These may comprise data on the financial corporations subsectors, such as other financial intermediaries, except insurance corporations and pension funds (S125), financial auxiliaries (S126) and captive financial institutions and moneylenders (S127). In many countries, corporate balance sheet data are collected and household surveys carried out.

7.204. Each of these data sets may create the need for additional reconciliation procedures because of their individual characteristics or their late availability.

7.205. Reconciliation within institutional sector accounts should be carried out on an instrument-by-instrument basis as well as on a from-whom-to-whom basis if applicable. This is done by choosing the most relevant source data individually. In some cases, such politically important variables as broad money, household debt and government debt should not be changed to maintain coherence with the underlying statistical data source.

7.206. The reconciliation of balance sheet positions, transactions, revaluations and other changes in the volumes of assets and liabilities is carried out simultaneously. In cases of stock-flow inconsistencies after reconciliation, transactions or other flows may be adjusted. The size of and need for adjustments should be monitored closely and documented in a regular quality report.

7.207. One of the weakest areas of the reconciliation procedures refers to the confrontation of data on unlisted shares and other equity on the issuer and holder sides. Although some holder information may be available from the various building blocks, various gaps remain to be filled. Market valuation of these financial instruments is an issue of its own. Following the recommendations outlined in the 2008 SNA and in other manuals, one option is to convert own funds at book value into market values based on ratios for comparable listed corporations.

2. Compilation strategy

7.208. In the context of developing an integrated system of institutional sector accounts, work should focus on the consistency between the current accounts, the accumulation accounts and the balance sheets of the various resident institutional sectors and of the rest of the world. This work follows three principles, summarized as completeness, conformity and consistency.

7.209. Completeness means that the accounts have to be compiled by using comprehensive source data. Each institutional sector needs to be described completely. Where the coverage of source data is insufficient, additional estimates should be made to derive a meaningful total amount.

7.210. Conformity implies that the accounts comply with the definitions and accounting standards as outlined in the international statistical standards, such as the

2008 SNA, the BPM6 and other manuals. These definitions and accounting standards may differ from the concepts used in the primary data sources. Adjustments may have to be made to the input data sets to allow for these deviations. An example is the use of nominal values rather than market valuation in securities issues statistics.

7.211. Consistency takes into account the identities embedded in the accounting framework. Such identities provide the compiler with additional information, which leads to an overall improvement in the data quality. Consistency also needs to be achieved with respect to the primary data sources. Inter-temporal consistency relates to data that are published in different frequencies.

3. Data balancing

7.212. The accounts need to be integrated in three dimensions: horizontal, vertical and related to stocks and flows. Data balancing must be carried out accordingly.

(a) Horizontal balancing

7.213. Horizontal balancing refers to the maintenance of the equivalence for each transaction, revaluation and other change in volume and balance sheet item; flows and stocks balance out when summed over all resident sectors and the rest of the world.

7.214. The accounts need to be *horizontally consistent* in such a way that total uses must be equal to total resources and total (changes in) assets must be equal to total (changes in) liabilities. In this context, all transactions and positions need to be horizontally reconciled, that is, the transaction balance, expressed for any transaction or asset type as the sum across institutional sectors of uses/changes in assets, must equal the sum across institutional sectors of resources/changes in liabilities. This relationship holds at the national level for all national sectoral data sets.

7.215. Two examples are as follows:

(a) For the non-financial transaction category "compensation of employees", the sum of the amounts payable (uses) by all resident institutional sectors and by the rest of the world must be equal to the sum of the amounts receivable (resources) by all resident sectors;

(b) For the financial transaction category "debt securities", the sum of the amounts issued by all resident institutional sectors and by the rest of the world must be equal to the sum of the amount acquired by all resident sectors.

7.216. The set of horizontal accounting restrictions can be seen as a system of linear equations. Balancing in this context is a process of solving the system, for which a necessary condition is that the number of equations is at least equal to the number of unknown variables.

7.217. An example may explain this in the context of the financial accounts by sector: one equation is defined in such a way that all issues of long-term debt securities are the sum of the issues of all resident institutional sectors and of non-residents.

7.218. Such an equation for issuances (net incurrences of liabilities, I) of long-term debt securities (F32) by all sectors except households including non-profit institutions serving households is:

$$I(F32(S1+S2))=I(F32(S11))+I(F32(S121\ \dots\ S129))+I(F32(S131\ \dots\ S1314)) + I(F32(S2))$$

7.219. To solve the equation, at least n–1 variables of the n variables have to be known. If exactly n–1 variables are known, the variable n can be compiled by summation or by difference.

7.220. If less than n–1 variables are known, further statistical information needs to be collected to solve the equation. This might also be done by estimating an additional amount for a sector.

7.221. Another issue to be considered is that, in many cases, several time series are available for one variable. For example, a series for the issuance of long-term debt securities by general government can be taken either from a direct source, the government finance statistics; or from an indirect source, the sum of the various holdings of long-term debt securities by all (counterpart) sectors issued by general government; or from a third source, a security-by-security database.

7.222. In such a case, the national accountants have to decide which series to put into the equation.[180] In many instances, the direct source might be the most reliable one. Nevertheless, plausibility and consistency checks should be carried out before choosing the appropriate figure.

7.223. A related example refers to the net acquisitions or holdings (H) of long-term debt securities (F32) by all resident institutional sectors and by non-residents, which are identical to total issuances (I):

$$H(F32(S1+S2))=H(F32(S11))+H(F32(S121 \ldots S129))+H(F32(S131 \ldots S1314)) +H(F32(S14))+H(F32(S15))+H(F32(S2))$$

7.224. Compared with the previous equation on issues of debt securities, the quality of this data set may be relatively low. However, direct or indirect data on holdings of debt securities may be available. Direct data can be taken from the accounts of financial corporations and general government, but not for non-financial corporations and households. Such holdings data can only be collected from indirect sources through counterpart information.

7.225. Furthermore, SBS databases linked with securities holdings statistics can be a reliable source to fill in the required data.

7.226. Less reliable data might be compiled if some variables of the equation have to be residually compiled by subtracting the known variables from the total holdings. This might be necessary for long-term securities held by households, compiled as the difference between the total holdings and the holdings of the remaining sectors.

7.227. As indicated above, the identity implies that total issuances and total holdings of long-term debt securities are equal. Nevertheless, if the two totals differ, one of the two has to be taken. If the data on issuances are taken, then the data of holdings by one sector must be corrected.

(b) Vertical balancing

7.228. National accounts compilers also try to achieve vertical consistency for all institutional sectors. In any case, vertical consistency may be required for some key institutional sectors, such as financial corporations, general government and the rest of the world, while the remaining two sectors, households including non-profit institutions serving households and non-financial corporations, may not be fully reconciled even

[180] Here, the number of variables is reduced to meet a lower number of equations. Note that an increase in equations can also be represented in terms of a decrease in variables and the other way around.

if they are of high analytical interest. In reconciling these sectors, vertical imbalances might be substantially reduced.

7.229. In order to obtain integrated accounts, compilation work has to be extended to "vertical balancing", which refers to maintaining identities between non-financial and financial transactions within the system of accounts. This balancing is usually achieved through reconciliation exercises related to the whole and sectoral net lending/net borrowing derived from the capital account and from the financial account (B9).

7.230. The accounts also need to be *vertically consistent* so that, for each resident sector and for the rest of the world, the sum of all resources and changes in liabilities is equal to the sum of all uses and changes in assets.

7.231. This may require the elimination of asymmetries and the use of specific accounting restrictions for some sectors, for example general government, financial corporations and the rest of the world. Statistical discrepancies, similar in the amount but opposite in sign, might still remain for households and non-financial corporations.

Discrepancy between net lending/net borrowing of the capital and the financial account

7.232. In many countries, the compilation of institutional sector accounts is shared between the national statistical office and the central bank. Accordingly, error margins are predominantly shown as a discrepancy between net lending/net borrowing as compiled in the capital account and in the financial account.

7.233. Showing the statistical discrepancy in that way might be misleading if tendencies in the balancing item as derived from the two accounts suggest different directions of movement in time.

7.234. The 2008 SNA presentation of the capital and financial accounts follows a theoretical framework in which monetary and financial variables are treated separately from the "real" sector (table 7.5). This dichotomy is reflected in the two accounts. The capital account (the account above the line) comprises the "real" variables, such as saving, net capital transfers and the acquisition of non-financial assets. The "financial" components (below the line) are shown in the financial account as the net acquisition of financial assets and the net incurrence of liabilities.

7.235. The balancing item "net lending/net borrowing" is derived from both accounts as presented in the numerical example of table 7.5. If there is a difference in the capital account between saving and non-financial investment, this necessarily implies a corresponding differential between the net incurrence of liabilities and the financial investment in the financial account.

7.236. According to the prevailing current practice in countries, statistical discrepancies are shown around the balancing item net lending/net borrowing.

7.237. While usually smaller discrepancies are shown for financial corporations and general government, this is not the case for net lending/net borrowing of households and non-financial corporations.

7.238. It is difficult to give guidance on what is an acceptable level of statistical discrepancies (for example, as a percentage of gross domestic product (GDP) or gross national income (GNI)). In cases of high political sensitivity, as in the case of the balancing item net lending/net borrowing for general government (the government deficit/surplus) for European Union countries, no discrepancies are shown at all. This does not usually apply for net lending/net borrowing of other institutional sectors.

Table 7.5
Capital and financial account by sector

Changes in assets								Changes in liabilities and net worth						
Total	Rest of the world	Total economy	Non-financial corporations	Financial corporations	General government	Households and NPISHs	Transaction	Non-financial corporations	Financial corporations	General government	Households and NPISHs	Total economy	Rest of the world	Total
							III.1 Capital Account							
							Saving, gross	228	14	-35	220	427		
							Current external balance						-13	-13
							Capital transfers, receivable	33	0	6	23	62	4	66
							Capital transfers, payable	-16	-7	-34	-8	-65	-1	-66
							Changes in net worth due to saving and capital transfers	245	7	-63	235	424	-10	414
376		376	280	8	35	53	Gross fixed capital formation							
28		28	26	0	0	2	Changes in inventories							
10		10	2	0	3	5	Acquisitions less disposals of valuables							
0		0	-7	0	2	5	Acquisitions less disposals of non-produced/non-financial assets							
0	**-10**	**10**	**-56**	**-1**	**-103**	**170**	**Net lending (+)/ Net borrowing (–)**							
							III.2 Financial Account							
							Net lending (+)/ net borrowing (–)	**-56**	**-1**	**-103**	**170**	**10**	**-10**	**0**
483	47	436	83	172	-10	191	Net acquisition of financial assets							
							Net incurrence of liabilities	139	173	93	21	426	57	483

Potential causes contributing to the discrepancy

7.239. While the 2008 SNA is designed in such a way that it leaves no scope for statistical discrepancies or deviations from the accounting uniformity it introduces, statistical discrepancies and their proper treatment are part of the regular work of national accountants.

7.240. Two main reasons for the discrepancies are the lack of sufficient and sufficiently consistent source data and the lack of coordination between the institutions involved in compiling national accounts.

7.241. The data sources considered for the compilation of national accounts usually correspond to different data-compiling agencies. In many cases the national statistical office will produce the national production and income accounts. The central bank will assemble, based on monetary, securities issues and balance of payments data, the financial account, and government agencies will generate the central and other government data. All of them may well compile their respective data with respect to particular statistical methods or detailed breakdowns. Nevertheless, additional coordination and cooperation among the agencies involved is desirable to discuss the presentation of discrepancies with a view to reducing their magnitude.

Reconciling between the capital account and the financial account

7.242. It is worthwhile to elaborate on the reasons for the discrepancy in net lending/net borrowing in the capital account and the financial account.

7.243. In the euro area accounts, compiled jointly by the European Central Bank and Eurostat, all sectors and the rest of the world are fully reconciled except for the households sector and the non-financial corporations sector.

7.244. Within the United States national accounts, a procedure is followed in which the discrepancies are explicitly identified and explained. Two sets of figures are compiled and presented for net lending/net borrowing in the flow of funds accounts as published by the Federal Reserve Board and in the national income and product accounts as disseminated by the Bureau of Economic Analysis. The sources of the differences are shown in a table.

7.245. A similar approach might be to include all components of the accumulation account into the reconciliation exercise, to identify the discrepancies and to indicate, where possible, why the discrepancies emerge. This could be a starting point and the exercise could be extended by including further transaction items from the production and the income accounts, if necessary.

7.246. The national accounts cannot be better than the sum of their component parts. Further work should therefore be devoted to improving and expanding the source data used in compiling national accounts. One prominent example is the compilation of transaction and other flow data for financial corporations, which are usually derived from balance sheet information.

7.247. Similarly, the balance of payments statistics can in principle be reconciled with the 2008 SNA rest of the world account, but much work still needs to be done to achieve a mutually consistent presentation.

7.248. Equally important is the improvement of direct source data for non-financial corporations and households based on corporate balance sheet statistics and household surveys.

(c) Balancing related to stocks and flows

7.249. The accounts should also be balanced in relation to stocks and flows so that the change in the balance sheet for each asset and liability category is equal to the changes arising from non-financial transactions, financial transactions, revaluations and other changes in the volume of assets.

7.250. The consistency between the flow accounts and the balance sheet data must be maintained. This also refers to the consistency of from-whom-to-whom data through the incorporation of the counterpart sector dimension in the overall compilation process.

4. Data structure and data processing

(a) Organizing input data

7.251. To compile from-whom-to-whom accounts, source data need to be transmitted through file transfers between organizational units or even between the institutions involved. A common approach has been established to facilitate data transmission: data flows use specific facilities and messages and are supported by a transmission code, described by a data classification scheme or a data structure definition (DSD) for national accounts data and for various statistical data sources. The data flow and the data classification scheme for statistical data are closely related to the design of an institutional accounts database in a software environment and the associated compilation system.

7.252. For the transmission of source data, the structure of the data classification scheme has various dimensions, which are compatible with the keys used in several areas of statistics.[181]

7.253. For the national accounts data classification scheme, dimensions are designed to distinguish between stocks, transactions, revaluations and other changes in volume. To maintain the from-whom-to-whom framework, codes for debtor and creditor areas, sectors and subsectors need to be specified. This will allow a full presentation of the system of institutional sector accounts. Dimensions for the various activities and instruments are also required with the corresponding features, such as the breakdowns by maturity or currency denomination, or the degree of consolidation or the valuation method applied.

7.254. Table 7.6 provides an overview of the dimensions to be distinguished for a national accounts data classification scheme.

7.255. In addition to the dimensions, statistical attributes describing the transmitted time series have to be added, such as the observation status (normal value, estimation, forecast, etc.); currency code; unit (millions, billions, etc.); unit multiplier; the number of decimals; the degree of consolidation and the organization transmitting the data.

Table 7.6
An example of a national accounts data classification scheme

The national accounts data classification scheme may comprise the following dimensions:[a]

- The frequency indicates the frequency of the reported period of the series, i.e. monthly, quarterly, annual.
- The reporting area represents the supranational or international organization or the country providing the data.
- The adjustment indicator notes transformations applied to the time series, such as seasonal adjustment or working-day adjustment.
- The dimension instrument refers to the 2008 SNA breakdown into products (goods and services), income, and assets and liabilities.
- The type of account indicates the type of data, such as transactions, revaluations, and other changes in the volume of assets and liabilities and stocks.
- Two dimensions refer to the maturity (original, residual, short and long-term) and the type of interest rate of the financial instrument.
- The debtor area and the creditor area dimensions represent the respective areas – supranational or international organization or the country of residence of the institutional sector. The code list contains the standard ISO country list and some additional codes.
- Two further data fields are defined, one for the debtor sector and one for the creditor sector. For the data fields, the breakdown is based on institutional sectors and subsectors in line with the 2008 SNA. For a full identification of the debtor and the creditor sector, two area codes and two sector codes must be specified.
- The valuation method is indicated as "market valuation", or other methods, such as nominal valuation.
- The dimension indicates the statistical source, such as national accounts, monetary statistics, etc.

[a] Dimensions are those statistical concepts which are necessary to distinguish between two different time series (e.g. area, sector or instrument). Dimensions take their values from appropriate code lists. A time series is characterized (named) by its classification scheme, which is the concatenation of its corresponding dimension values. *Attributes* are statistical concepts which offer additional (usually qualitative) information about a time series or a group of series but do not need to be part of the series "key". Examples of attributes are the "units", unit multiplier, title of a series, etc.

[181] See also the section on the data structure definition of national accounts.

(b) Data transmission, key systems, metadata

7.256. Several tools are available for analysing the data included in the national accounts database. To allow data analysis, the different key families of the source data (monetary statistics, balance of payments and international investment position statistics, government finance statistics, securities statistics, etc.) are translated into national accounts keys by using bridging tables.

7.257. Additional tools need to be integrated into the compilation system to combine various subsets of financial data according to the specific dimensions or groups of dimensions of the national accounts data classification scheme. For example, one exercise would be to choose all time series available for one specific financial instrument, sector, area or various combinations of these.

7.258. In order to reduce complexity, more harmonized data sets may be compiled, such as one data set in which all time series have been converted into a common frequency. Low-frequency time series, such as stocks and transactions, may sometimes be converted into high-frequency series by using linear approximations to ensure consistency among (linear) restrictions.

Chapter 8
Presentation and dissemination of the accounts

References:
2008 SNA, Chapter 18, Elaborating and presenting the accounts
BPM6, Appendix 9, Standard components and selected other items
MFSMCG
GFSM 2014
HSS

A. Introduction

8.1. This chapter provides guidance on how national statistical offices, central banks and international organizations release and disseminate their national accounts and related methodologies through their websites and other media.

8.2. These institutions often have a policy of free access and free reuse, even commercial, with regard to their released data, although reuse is usually subject to certain conditions, for example quoting the source and not modifying the data. On the websites of national statistical offices, central banks and international organizations, statistical data and metadata can be downloaded in various formats and even by charting time series.

8.3. Users may know that figures for such aggregates as gross domestic product (GDP), private consumption, saving or debt are available from the statistical offices and central banks, but they may not be aware of the full scope and detail of national accounts data that are compiled.

8.4. This chapter refers to the development of templates for a minimum and encouraged set of internationally comparable sectoral accounts and balance sheets. The templates are described at the beginning of the chapter. They are used as tools to present and disseminate national accounts data to the public.

8.5. The tables and charts in this chapter are designed to present data on non-financial transactions and non-financial assets, but mainly on financial flows and stocks.

B. Harmonized templates of sectoral accounts and balance sheets

8.6. The Group of 20 Data Gaps Initiative outlined a number of recommendations for addressing the data gaps arising from the recent global crisis. These recommendations were presented in the IMF and Financial Stability Board Secretariat report entitled "The financial crisis and information gaps". Recommendation 15 calls for the development of a strategy to promote the compilation and dissemination of the balance sheet approach (BSA), flow of funds, and sectoral data more generally, starting with the Group of 20 economies.

8.7. The objective of recommendation 15 is to expand the dissemination and reporting of internationally comparable and detailed annual and quarterly sectoral accounts by both Group of 20 economies and non-Group of 20 advanced economies. This would involve improving the compilation of sectoral accounts in terms of details (subsectors and assets), closing data gaps, and developing financial stocks and flows on a from-whom-to-whom basis.

8.8. A Working Group on Sectoral Accounts was established under the auspices of the Inter-Agency Group on Economic and Financial Statistics. The Working Group includes the Bank for International Settlements (BIS), European Central Bank, Eurostat, IMF (Chair), Organisation for Economic Co-operation and Development (OECD), and United Nations. An important milestone in taking forward the work on implementing recommendation 15 was the development of templates for a minimum and encouraged set of internationally comparable sectoral accounts and balance sheets reached through a global consultative process led by the IMF. Through these discussions, the Working Group agreed on the following final set of templates:

(a) A framework for minimum and encouraged classifications;

(b) A data reporting template for quarterly non-financial transaction accounts;

(c) A data reporting template for quarterly stocks and transactions of financial assets and liabilities;

(d) A data reporting template for annual stocks of non-financial assets.

8.9. The framework mentioned in subparagraph (a) above provides an overview of which time series on stocks and transactions should be reported:

- Table 8.1 refers to the template mentioned in subparagraph (b) above for quarterly non-financial transactions. Such quarterly time series should be taken from the sectoral current and capital accounts.
- Table 8.2 refers to the template mentioned in subparagraph (c) above for quarterly stocks and flows of financial assets and liabilities. The time series should be taken from the sectoral financial accounts and balance sheets.
- Table 8.3 refers to the template mentioned in subparagraph (d) above for annual stocks of non-financial assets.

8.10. Cells highlighted in light grey indicate the minimum requirements, while the encouraged requirements are highlighted in dark grey.

Table 8.1

Template for quarterly non-financial transactions

Current and capital accounts: sectors and transactions (quarterly, with timeliness of one quarter)

				Total economy	Non-financial corporations	Of which: Public non-financial corporations	Financial corporations	Monetary financial institutions	Insurance corporations and pension funds	Other financial corporations	Of which: Public financial corporations	General government	Households and NPISHs	Rest of the World
				S1	S11	S11001	S12	S121 + S122 + S123	S128+ S129	S124+ S125+ S126+ S127	S12001	S13	S14+ S15	S2
P.6 (for S2)	Exports of goods and services													
P.7 (for S2)	Imports of goods and services													
B.1g	Value added, gross / Gross domestic product													
D.1	Compensation of employees													
B.2g+B.3g	Operating surplus, gross and Mixed income, gross													
D.2	Taxes on production and imports													
	Of which:													
	D.21 (for S1)	Taxes on products												
	D.29	Other taxes on production												
D.3	Subsidies													
	Of which:													
	D.31 (for S1)	−Subsidies on products												
	D.39	−Other subsidies on production												
D.4	Property income													
	Of which:													
	D.41	Interest												
	D.4N	Property income other than interest												
D.41g	Total interest before FISIM allocation													
B.5g	Balance of primary incomes, gross / National income, gross													
D.5	Current taxes on income, wealth, etc.													
D.61	Net social contributions													
D.62	Social benefits other than social transfers in kind													
D.63	Social transfers in kind													
D.7	Other current transfers													
	Of which:													
	D.71	Net non-life insurance premiums												
	D.72	Non-life insurance claims												
	D.7N	Other Current transfers, not elsewhere specified												
B.6g	Disposable income, gross													
D.8	Adjustment for the change in pension entitlements													
P.3	Final consumption expenditure													
	Of which:													
	P.31	Individual consumption expenditure												
	P.32	Collective consumption expenditure												
B.8g	Saving, gross													
D.9	Capital Transfers													
	Of which:													
	D.91	Capital Taxes												
	D.9N	Investment Grants and other capital transfers												
P.5g	Gross capital formation													
	Of which:													
	P.51g	Gross fixed capital formation												
	P.52+P53	Changes in inventories and acquisition less disposals of valuables												
P.51c	Consumption of fixed capital													
NP	Acquisitions less disposals of non-produced assets													
B.9	Net lending (+)/Net borrowing (−)													

= Minimum

= Encouraged

Note: See table 8.4 below.

Table 8.2
Template for annual stocks of non-financial assets
Stocks of non-financial assets: sectors and asset types (annual, with timeliness of nine months)

	Total Economy	Non-financial corporations		Financial corporations														General government		Households and NPISHs			Rest of the World
					Monetary financial institutions				Insurance corp. and pension funds			Other financial corporations											
		Total	Of which: Public non financial corporations	Total	Total	Central bank	Other deposit-taking corporations	Money market funds	Total	Insurance corporations	Pension funds	Total	NonMMF investment funds	Other financial intermediaries except Insurance corporations and pension funds	Financial Auxiliaries	Captive financial institutions and moneylenders	Of which: Public financial corporations	Total	Of which: Social Security Funds	Total	Households	NPISH s	
	S1	S11	S11001	S12	S121+ S122+ S123	S121	S122	S123	S128+ S129	S128	S129	S124+ S125+ S126+ S127	S124	S125	S126	S127	S12001	S13	S1314	S14+ S15	S14	S15	S2
F1 Monetary gold and SDRs																							
F11 Monetary gold																							
F12 SDRs																							
F2 Currency and deposits																							
Of which: Domestic currency																							
F21 Currency																							
F22 Transferable deposits																							
F221 Interbank positions																							
F229 Other transferable deposits																							
F29 Other deposits																							
F3 Debt securities																							
Of which: Domestic currency																							
F31 Short-term																							
F32 Long-term																							
With remaining maturity of one year or less																							
With remaining maturity of more than a year																							
F4 Loans																							
Of which: Domestic currency																							
F41 Short-term																							
F42 Long-term																							
With remaining maturity of one year or less																							
With remaining maturity of more than a year																							
F5 Equity and investment fund shares																							
F51 Equity																							
F511 Listed shares																							
F512 Unlisted shares																							
F519 Other equity																							
F52 Investment fund shares/units																							

	Total Economy	Non-financial corporations		Financial corporations													General government		Households and NPISHs			Rest of the World
					Monetary financial institutions				Insurance corp. and pension funds			Other financial corporations										
		Total	Of which: Public non financial corporations	Total	Total	Central bank	Other deposit-taking corporations	Money market funds	Total	Insurance corporations	Pension funds	Total	NonMMF investment funds	Other financial intermediaries except Insurance corporations and pension funds	Financial Auxiliaries	Captive financial institutions and moneylenders	Of which: Public financial corporations	Total	Of which: Social Security Funds	Total	Households	NPISH s	
	S1	S11	S11001	S12	S121+ S122+ S123	S121	S122	S123	S128+ S129	S128	S129	S124+ S125+ S126+ S127	S124	S125	S126	S127	S12001	S13	S1314	S14+ S15	S14	S15	S2
F521 Money market fund shares/units																							
F522 Non MMF investment fund shares/units																							
F6 Insurance, pension and standardized guarantee schemes																							
F61 Non-life insurance technical reserves																							
F62 Life insurance and annuity entitlements																							
F63+F64+F65 Retirement entitlements																							
F63 Pension entitlements																							
F64 Claim of pension fund on pension managers																							
F65 Entitlements to non-pension benefits																							
F66 Provisions for calls under standardized guarantees																							
F7 Financial derivatives and employee stock options																							
F71 Financial derivatives																							
F711 Options																							
F712 Forwards																							
F72 Employee stock options																							
F8 Other accounts receivable/payable																							
Of which: Domestic currency																							
F81 Trade credits and advances																							
F89 Other accounts receivable/payable																							

(white)	= Minimum
(shaded)	= Encouraged

Note: See table 8.5 below.

Table 8.3

Template for quarterly stocks and flows of financial assets and liabilities

Financial stocks and flows: sectors and instruments (quarterly, with timeliness of one quarter)

	Total economy	Non-financial corporations		Financial corporations					General government	Households and NPISHs	Rest of the World
			Of which: Public non-financial corporations		Monetary financial institutions	Insurance corporations and pension funds	Other financial corporations	Of which: Public financial corporations			
	S1	S11	S11001	S12	S121+ S122+ S123	S128+ S129	S124+ S125+ S126+ S127	S12001	S13	S14+ S15	S2
AN1 Produced non-financial assets											
AN11 Fixed assets of which:											
AN111 Dwellings											
AN112 Other buildings and structures											
AN12 Inventories											
AN13 Valuables											
AN2 Non-produced non-financial assets											
AN21 Natural resources											
of which:											
AN211 Land											
of which:											
AN. 2111 Land underlying buildings and structures											
AN212 Mineral and energy reserves											
AN22 Contracts, leases and licences											
AN23 Goodwill and marketing assets											

= Minimum

= Encouraged

Note: See table 8.19 below.

C. Communication of national accounts data to users[182]

8.11. It is important that the statistical information contained in national accounts data ne presented and communicated to users in an efficient and accessible way using text, tables and graphs.

8.12. To communicate national accounts data effectively, a press release, report or article should:

(a) Interpret the tables of numbers and graphs clearly;

(b) Tell a story about the data;

(c) Catch the reader's attention quickly with a headline or a graph;

(d) Be written in a clear and accessible way without (excessive) use of economic and statistical jargon;

(e) Be easily understood, interesting and entertaining;

(f) Encourage others, including the media, to use the national accounts data appropriately to add impact to what they are communicating.

8.13. Before preparing such materials, the target audience should be identified as a first step. It is also important to be aware of the available communication media, including the Internet and (rapidly evolving) social networks.

[182] The communication strategy for national accounts data generally applies to all data sets.

8.14. The communication of national accounts data needs to be based on the Fundamental Principles of Official Statistics.[183] The good practices referred to in the United Nations site cover:

(a) Relevance, impartiality and equal access;

(b) Professionalism;

(c) Accountability;

(d) Prevention of misuse;

(e) Cost-effectiveness;

(f) Confidentiality;

(g) Legislation;

(h) National coordination;

(i) International standards;

(j) International statistical cooperation.

D. Using text

8.15. Efficient written communication comprises three main elements:

(a) Structure (the way the content is laid out);

(b) Style (the way it is written);

(c) Content (what is written about).

8.16. A good structure helps to improve communication. The content and the purpose of communication should be clarified before starting the writing process. It is also essential to identify the key points and determine their logical order.

8.17. The introduction to the text should briefly describe the key message. One point per paragraph is a possible guideline, starting with the key message in the first sentence and adding supporting information using short paragraphs and sentences.

8.18. The writing style (formal or informal) should be tailored to the target audience (expert or non-expert). The author should consider how much data and detail the readers need and whether it is possible to use specific national accounts terms or other standard terminology, which might not be accessible to a wider, non-expert public.

E. Designing tables and charts

8.19. National accounts tables and charts should accompany the text. The form of the tables should be in line with the interests of the readers and will depend, of course, on the information to be communicated. Although it is possible to introduce more detail into the integrated economic accounts by adding more columns for subsectors and more rows for disaggregations of transactions, other flows and positions, this could quickly result in a very complicated and unmanageable table. For this reason, more detailed analyses of production and transactions in goods and services, financial transactions and detailed balance sheets, as well as analyses by purpose, should be presented in the annex and not in the main body of the text.

---

[183] The United Nations Statistical Commission adopted these principles in 1994. They are described in detail on the United Nations Statistics Division's website at http://unstats.un.org/unsd/methods/statorg/FP-English.htm.

8.20. There are essentially two types of tables: (a) simple tables placed within the main body of the text describing structures or specific developments of a limited number of aggregates ("text tables"); and (b) more detailed tables accompanying the text but contained in an annex ("annex tables").

8.21. Text tables may present aggregates taken from various accounts (financial or non-financial), various sectors or categories of assets and liabilities.

8.22. Annex tables may show the complete system of accounts for the national economy or for an institutional sector. One example is the presentation of the sequence of accounts in annex 2 to the 2008 SNA. One subset refers to the accumulation accounts and the balance sheets for all or selected assets and liabilities.

8.23. Charts can be used to depict national accounts data. A good chart conveys information quickly and easily to the user. Charts highlight noticeable features of the data and show relationships that are not obvious from studying a list of numbers. Charts are also a convenient way to compare different sets of data.

1. Presentation of data derived from the template of internationally comparable non-financial transactions (table 8.1)

8.24. Based on the sequence of accounts as presented in chapter 1, tables for the various accounts (the production account, the external account, the generation, distribution, redistribution and use of income accounts and the capital account) can be designed by type of transaction (table 8.4).

Table 8.4
Table presenting data on non-financial transactions by institutional sector based on the sequence of accounts

Uses / Resources	Total economy	Non-financial corporations	Financial corporations	General government	Households including NPISHs	Rest of the world
	S1	S11	S12	S13	S14+S15	S2
Production account						
Output						
Intermediate consumption						
Taxes less subsidies on products						
Gross value added (basic prices)						
Gross domestic product (market prices)						
Generation of income account						
Value added, gross/Gross domestic product						
Compensation of employees						
Taxes less subsidies on products						
Other taxes less other subsidies on production and imports						
Operating surplus, gross/Mixed income, gross						
External account						
Exports of goods and services (Ex)						
Imports of goods and services (Im)						
External balance of goods and services (-Ex +Im)						
Allocation of primary income account						
Operating surplus and mixed income (gross)						
Compensation of employees						
Taxes less subsidies on products						
Other taxes less other subsidies on production and imports						

Uses / Resources	Total economy	Non-financial corporations	Financial corporations	General government	Households including NPISHs	Rest of the world
	S1	S11	S12	S13	S14+S15	S2
Property income						
Interest						
Other property income						
National income (gross)						
Secondary distribution of income account						
National income (gross)						
Current taxes on income, wealth, etc.						
Social contributions						
Social benefits other than social transfers in kind						
Other current transfers						
Net non-life insurance premiums						
Non-life insurance claims						
Other						
Disposable income, gross						
Use of disposable income account						
Disposable income, gross						
Final consumption expenditure						
Individual consumption expenditure						
Collective consumption expenditure						
Adjustment for the change in pension entitlements						
Saving, gross						
Current external balance						
Capital account						
Saving, gross						
Current external balance						
Gross capital formation						
Gross fixed capital formation						
Changes in inventories and acquisitions less disposals of valuables						
Consumption of fixed capital						
Acquisitions less disposals of non-produced non-financial assets						
Capital transfers						
Capital taxes						
Other capital transfers						
Changes in net worth due to saving and capital transfers						
Net lending (+)/net borrowing (–)						

2. Presentation of data derived from the template of internationally comparable stocks and flows of financial assets and liabilities (table 8.2)

8.25. The following paragraphs give examples of tables presenting internationally comparable data on stocks and flows of financial assets and liabilities in different formats (table 8.2). These are:

- Tables showing, without counterpart information, either: (a) positions, net acquisitions of assets, revaluations and other changes in the volume of assets by creditor; or (b) positions, net incurrences of liabilities, revaluations and other changes in the volume of liabilities by debtor. They are so-called summary tables grouping the resident institutional units acquiring or incurring the financial instruments into the main institutional sectors. Depending on the purpose of such tables, institutional sectors may be further broken down into subsectors as shown in the templates above.

- Tables showing, with full counterpart information, either: (a) positions, net acquisitions of assets, revaluations and other changes in the volume of assets of resident creditor sectors and of non-resident creditors vis-à-vis resident debtors; or (b) positions, net incurrences of liabilities, revaluations and other changes in the volume of liabilities of resident debtor sectors and of non-resident debtors vis-à-vis resident creditors. The tables reflect the from-whom-to-whom approach as they present the relationships between resident sectors as creditors and residents and non-residents as debtors, and between non-residents as creditors and residents as debtors of financial instruments.

3. Tables without counterpart information

8.26. As an example, table 8.5 can be used to show positions, transactions or other flows (revaluations and other changes in the volume of assets and liabilities) for financial instruments held by resident and non-resident institutional units as creditors.

8.27. The resident institutional units are grouped into resident sectors (non-financial corporations, financial corporations, general government, and households and non-profit institutions serving households) having acquired financial instruments issued by all issuers, resident and non-resident, without a breakdown by residency or resident sector of issuer[184] (which is indicated by the fact that the cells of row 3 from columns 1 to 5 of table 8.5 are shaded grey).

8.28. In addition, non-residents may have acquired financial instruments issued by residents and these holdings are shown in the cell of row 1 and column 6 of table 8.5 (which is also shaded grey).

Table 8.5
Table based on the residence of the creditor, unconsolidated

Creditor / Holder → Debtor / Issuer ↓		Residents							
		Non-financial corporations	**Financial corporations**	**General government**	**Households and non-profit institutions serving households**	**Total economy**	**Rest of the world**	**Total**	
		1	2	3	4	5	6	7	
Residents	1								Residence of issuer
Non-residents	2								
Total	3								
		Residence of holder							

[184] The residency breakdown is included in Table 8.5 because the financial instruments issued by residents and acquired by non-residents need to be identified separately.

Table 8.6
Table based on the residence of the debtor, unconsolidated

Creditor / Holder \ Debtor / Issuer		Residents: Non-financial corporations	Residents: Financial corporations	Residents: General government	Residents: Households and non-profit institutions serving households	Residents: Total economy	Rest of the world	Total
		1	2	3	4	5	6	7
Residents	1							
Non-residents	2							
Total	3							

Residence of holder (rows 1–2); Residence of issuer (columns 1–6)

8.29. Table 8.6 can be used to show positions, transactions or other flows (revaluations and other changes in the volume of assets and liabilities) for financial instruments issued by resident and non-resident institutional units as debtors.

8.30. As for the holders the resident institutional units as debtors are grouped into resident sectors issuing financial instruments acquired by all holders, resident and non-resident, without a breakdown by residency or resident sector of holder[185] (which is indicated by the fact that the cells of row 3 from columns 1 to 5 of table 8.6 are shaded grey). In addition, non-residents issue financial instruments acquired by residents, and these issues are shown in the cell of row 1 and column 6 of the table (which is also shaded grey).

4. Tables based on the residence of the creditor

(a) Financial instruments held by maturity, currency and type of interest rate

8.31. Table 8.7 shows data on financial instruments held by resident sectors, resident financial corporation subsectors and non-residents broken down by maturity.

8.32. A split into short-term and long-term original maturity is recommended. The fourth row of the maturity breakdown represents financial instruments held for all maturities. A memorandum item can also be useful, if data are available, showing holdings of financial instruments with a long-term original maturity that have a remaining (residual) maturity of up to and including one year.

8.33. The financial instruments shown with a split into short-term and long-term original maturity are essentially loans and debt securities. Table 8.7 presents, as an example, data on debt securities by residency, resident sector and financial subsector of the holder, residency of the issuer and by maturity.

[185] The residency breakdown is included in Table 8.6 because the financial instruments held by residents and issued by non-residents need to be identified separately.

Table 8.7

Debt securities classified by residency, resident sector and resident financial subsector of holder, by residency of issuer and by maturity

Issuer by residency and by maturity \ Holder		Total economy											Rest of the world	Total
			Financial corporations											
		Non-financial corporations	Central bank	Deposit-taking corporations except the central bank	MMF investment funds	Non-MMF investment funds	Insurance corporations	Pension funds	Other financial corporations[a]	General government	Households and non-profit institutions serving households	Memorandum item: public corporations		
Total economy	Short-term original maturity													
	Long-term original maturity													
	Memorandum item: long-term original maturity, with a remaining maturity of up to and including one year													
	All maturities													
Rest of the world	Short-term original maturity												■	
	Long-term original maturity												■	
	Memorandum item: long-term original maturity, with a remaining maturity of up to and including one year												■	
	All maturities													
Total	Short-term original maturity													
	Long-term original maturity													
	Memorandum item: long-term original maturity, with a remaining maturity of up to and including one year													
	All maturities													

[a] These are other financial intermediaries, except insurance corporations and pension funds (S125), i.e. financial corporations engaged in the securitization of assets, security and derivative dealers, financial corporations engaged in lending, central clearing counterparties and specialized financial corporations, as outlined in the 2008 SNA (para. 4.110); financial auxiliaries (S126); and captive financial corporations and moneylenders (S127). Financial auxiliaries include head offices (of financial corporations) and captive financial institutions and moneylenders include holding corporations. It may be necessary to show them separately.

8.34. A detailed breakdown is presented for the financial corporations sector distinguishing the holdings of: (a) the central bank; (b) deposit-taking corporations except the central bank, (c) money market funds (MMFs); (d) non-MMF investment funds; (e) insurance corporations; (f) pension funds; and (g) other financial corporations.[186]

8.35. From the perspective of monetary policy and financial stability analysis, it may also be useful to show institutional investors as important holders of such financial instruments as debt securities and equity securities. Institutional investors are generally understood to comprise a subset of financial corporations, namely those classified in the subsectors: (a) investment funds (MMF and non-MMF); (b) insurance corporations; and (c) pension funds.[187]

[186] These are other financial intermediaries, except insurance corporations and pension funds (S125), i.e. financial corporations engaged in the securitization of assets, security and derivative dealers, financial corporations engaged in lending, central clearing counterparties and specialized financial corporations, as outlined in the 2008 SNA (para. 4.110); financial auxiliaries (S126); and captive financial corporations and moneylenders (S127). Financial auxiliaries include head offices (of financial corporations) and captive financial institutions and moneylenders include holding corporations. It may be necessary to show them separately.

[187] See "Institutional investors' assets" data set, OECD StatExtracts, available at the OECD website: http://stats.oecd.org.

8.36. Similar tables may present holdings of financial instruments with breakdowns by currency (domestic currency and foreign currencies) or by type of interest rate where applicable (fixed interest rate and variable interest rate).

(b) Financial instruments held as positions, transactions, revaluations and other changes in the volume of assets

8.37. Table 8.8 can be used to show the stock-flow relationship between positions, transactions, revaluations and other changes in the volume of assets for financial instruments held by resident sectors, resident financial corporation subsectors and non-residents and issued by residents and non-residents.

8.38. Expressed in terms of market value, these statistics cover the positions in financial instruments at the end of the previous period; the net acquisitions, revaluations and other changes in the volume of assets in financial instruments during the current period; and the positions at the end of the current period. Transactions are presented net (acquisitions minus disposals). They may also be presented gross (gross acquisitions and disposals).

Table 8.8
Financial instruments classified by residency, resident sector and resident financial subsector of holder and by residency of issuer positions, transactions, revaluations and other changes in the volume of assets

Holder / Issuer by residency and by positions, net acquisitions, revaluations and other changes in the volume of assets		Total economy												
			Financial corporations											
		Non-financial corporations	Central bank	Deposit-taking corporations except the central bank	MMF investment funds	Non-MMF investment funds	Insurance corporations	Pension funds	Other financial corporations[a]	General government	Households and non-profit institutions serving households	Memorandum item: public corporations	Rest of the world	Total
Total economy	Position at end of previous period													
	Net acquisitions during the current period													
	Revaluations during the current period													
	Other changes in the volume of assets in the current period													
	Position at end of the current period													
Rest of the world	Position at end of previous period													
	Net acquisitions during the current period													
	Revaluations during the current period													
	Other changes in the volume of assets in the current period													
	Position at end of the current period													
Total	Position at end of previous period													
	Net acquisitions during the current period													
	Revaluations during the current period													
	Other changes in the volume of assets in the current period													
	Position at end of the current period													

[a] These are other financial intermediaries, except insurance corporations and pension funds (S125), i.e. financial corporations engaged in the securitization of assets, security and derivative dealers, financial corporations engaged in lending, central clearing counterparties and specialized financial corporations, as outlined in the 2008 SNA (para. 4.110); financial auxiliaries (S126); and captive financial corporations and moneylenders (S127).

5. Tables based on the residence of the debtor

(a) Issuers of financial instruments by maturity, currency and type of interest rate

8.39. Four possible classifications may be distinguished to present statistics on financial instruments as liabilities: issuer, maturity, currency and type of interest rate.[188]

8.40. Table 8.9 combines classifications by issuer and maturity. It shows financial instruments with a split into short-term and long-term at original maturity, and long-term maturity broken down further into four subcategories. A memorandum item shows financial instruments issues with long-term at original maturity, with a remaining maturity of up to and including one year.

Table 8.9
Financial instruments classified by issuer/debtor and maturity

Issuer / Maturity	Total economy						
	Non-financial corporations	Financial corporation	General government	Households	NPISHs	Rest of the world	Total
Short-term at original maturity							
Long-term at original maturity							
More than one year and up to and including two years							
More than two years and up to and including five years							
More than 5 years and up to and including 10 years							
More than 10 years							
All maturities							
Memorandum item: long-term at original maturity, with a remaining maturity of up to and including one year							

(b) Financial instruments issued as positions, transactions, revaluations and other changes in the volume of assets and liabilities

8.41. Another important aspect concerning the issues of financial instruments is the presentation of positions and flows in some detail, in line with table 8.8. Table 8.10 shows the position and flow relationship for financial instruments as liabilities. Expressed in market value, these statistics cover positions at the end of the previous period, flows during the current period and positions at the end of the current period. Transactions are further split into gross (gross issues and redemptions) and net (gross issues net of redemptions).

[188] Not all financial instruments can be split by maturity. Chapter 4 of this Handbook notes that financial instruments can be classified by negotiability and income, although these classifications are not applied in the tables here.

Table 8.10
Financial instruments by issuer/debtor as positions and flows

Positions and flows \ Issuer	Total economy: Non-financial corporations	Financial corporation	General government	Households	NPISHs	Rest of the world	Total
Position at end of previous period							
Net issues (gross issues net of redemptions)							
Gross issues							
Redemptions							
Revaluations during current period							
Other changes in volume during current period							
Position at end of current period							

6. From-whom-to-whom tables

8.42. A full analysis of financing and financial (and non-financial) investment requires detailed information on the sources and destinations of a sector's funds. The flow of financial assets through the economy and the financial relationships between sectors can then be traced. For example, it is often important for policymakers to know not only what types of liabilities (and financial assets) general government is using to finance its deficit, but also which sectors (or the rest of the world) are providing the financing.

8.43. For financial corporations (and those supervising them), it is important to know not only the composition of financial assets that they have acquired, but also on which sectors these represent claims. In addition, it is often necessary to analyse financial transactions between subsectors within a sector (central government transactions with local government or social security funds, or central bank transactions with deposit-taking corporations except the central bank).

8.44. Table 8.11 reflects the from-whom-to-whom approach as it presents the relationships between resident sectors as holders and residents and non-residents as issuers, and between non-residents as holders and residents as issuers of financial instruments, for example, debt securities or equity securities.

8.45. For a national economy, it shows positions, transactions, revaluations and other changes in the volume of assets for debt securities held by residents grouped into sectors and by non-residents vis-à-vis institutional units as issuers, broken down by residency and by institutional sector (cells of table 8.11 shaded grey).

8.46. For residents, the presentation of unconsolidated data on holdings of financial instruments is recommended. This means that intrasectoral positions, transactions, revaluations and other changes in the volume of assets of financial instruments are covered (cells shaded grey with diagonal lines).

8.47. As also indicated in table 8.11, the holdings of financial instruments by non-residents issued by non-residents are not covered (black cell). These are not relevant from a national economy's perspective.

8.48. Holdings of financial instruments by non-residents (vis-à-vis resident sectors as issuers) are shown as positions in the rest of the world balance sheet (the international

Table 8.11
Table reflecting the from-whom-to-whom approach (unconsolidated)

Issuer by residency and by resident sector \ Holder by residency and by resident sector		Total economy: Non-financial corporations	Total economy: Financial corporations	Total economy: General government	Total economy: Households and non-profit institutions serving households	Rest of the world	Total
Total economy	Non-financial corporations						
	Financial corporations						
	General government						
	Households and non-profit institutions serving households						
Rest of the world							
Total							

Residence of holder (the five holder columns, Non-financial corporations to Rest of the world); Residence of issuer (the five issuer rows, Non-financial corporations to Rest of the world)

investment position); as financial transactions in the rest of the world financial account (part of the balance of payments); and as revaluations or other changes in the volume of assets in the rest of the world accumulation accounts (cross-hatched cells in the non-residents column of table 8.11).

8.49. Additional breakdowns of resident holders by financial corporation subsector and by general government subsector and of non-resident issuers by country and/or sector may be considered.

(c) Holders and issuers of financial instruments by maturity, currency and type of interest rate

8.50. Three-dimensional tables in a from-whom-to-whom framework add to the two-dimensional tables a breakdown or a combination of breakdowns of financial instruments by subcategory (currency, maturity and interest rate).[189]

(d) Financial instruments issued and held as positions, transactions, revaluations and other changes in the volume of assets

8.51. Table 8.13 shows the position and flow relationships for financial instruments held by resident sectors and by non-residents vis-à-vis resident sectors and non-residents as issuers.

8.52. Expressed in terms of market value, these statistics cover positions at the end of the previous period; transactions, revaluations and other changes in the volume of assets during the current period; and positions at the end of the current period. Transactions are presented net (acquisitions minus disposals).

[189] The classification criteria by currency and interest rate go beyond the national accounts framework and the data may have to be obtained from additional sources. They are not necessarily compiled in the framework of financial accounts.

Table 8.12
Financial instrument holdings in a from-whom-to-whom framework by residency and resident sector of holder, by currency, maturity and interest rate, and by residency and resident sector of issuer

Issuer by residency and resident sector and by currency, maturity and interest rate \ Holder by residency and resident sector			Total economy: Non-financial corporations	Total economy: Financial corporations and subsectors	Total economy: General government	Total economy: Households and non-profit institutions serving households	Rest of the world	Total
Total economy	Non-financial corporations	Currency						
		Maturity						
		Interest rate						
	Financial corporations and subsectors	Currency						
		Maturity						
		Interest rate						
	General government	Currency						
		Maturity						
		Interest rate						
	Households and non-profit institutions serving households	Currency						
		Maturity						
		Interest rate						
Rest of the world		Currency						
		Maturity						
		Interest rate						
Total		Currency						
		Maturity						
		Interest rate						

8.53. Like positions and transactions, revaluations (holding gains or losses) and other changes in volume may be presented in a three-dimensional table with breakdowns by residency and resident institutional sector of the holder and issuer. Such detailed statistical information could be provided in the future by security-by-security databases.

(e) Financial instruments issued and held by subsectors of the financial corporations sector

8.54. Presentations using three-dimensional tables may be designed for subsectors or groupings of financial corporations, such as monetary financial institutions (MFIs) or institutional investors, to show the role of financial intermediaries in providing financial resources to other sectors through maturity or asset transformation.

8.55. Positions and flows of monetary financial institutions, insurance corporations, pension funds and other financial corporations are likely to be of great interest. Such expanded presentations may also reveal a growing (or shrinking) role for other types of financial intermediaries and financial institutions, and shed light on the nature of their business in terms of the counterparties with whom they deal as well as the types of financial instruments they hold or transact in.

8.56. Table 8.14 presents a sector/subsector breakdown of holders of financial instruments in a from-whom-to-whom framework, allowing a detailed analysis of the interrelationship between issuers and holders. It shows the financial instrument holdings of five main subsectors of the financial corporations sector. The holdings are broken

Table 8.13
Holdings and issues of financial instruments in a from-whom-to-whom framework: positions and flows

Issuer by residency and resident sector and by positions, net acquisitions, revaluations and other changes in the volume of assets \ Holder by residency and resident sector			Total economy: Non-financial corporations	Total economy: Financial corporations and subsectors	Total economy: General government	Total economy: Households and non-profit institutions serving households	Rest of the world	Total
Total economy	Non-financial corporations	Position at end of previous period						
		Net acquisitions during the current period						
		Revaluations during the current period						
		Other changes in the volume of assets in the current period						
		Position at end of the current period						
	Financial corporations	Position at end of previous period						
		Net acquisitions during the current period						
		Revaluations during the current period						
		Other changes in the volume of assets in the current period						
		Position at end of the current period						
	General government	Position at end of previous period						
		Net acquisitions during the current period						
		Revaluations during the current period						
		Other changes in the volume of assets in the current period						
		Position at end of the current period						
	Households and non-profit institutions serving households	Position at end of previous period						
		Net acquisitions during the current period						
		Revaluations during the current period						
		Other changes in the volume of assets in the current period						
		Position at end of the current period						
Rest of the world		Position at end of previous period						
		Net acquisitions during the current period						
		Revaluations during the current period						
		Other changes in the volume of assets in the current period						
		Position at end of the current period						
Total		Position at end of previous period						
		Net acquisitions during the current period						
		Revaluations during the current period						
		Other changes in the volume of assets in the current period						
		Position at end of the current period						

down by (original) maturity and within each maturity category by residency and resident sector of the issuer. Depending on the availability of data, different degrees of detail could be shown, such as alternative breakdowns of holdings data by currency and type of interest rate.

8.57. For financial stability purposes, a more detailed breakdown of holdings of financial instruments is required, namely by individual issuers. As a first step, a breakdown of investors in securities of individual issuers by financial corporation subsector (e.g. monetary financial institutions, insurance corporations, pension funds and (non-MMF) investment funds) may be useful. Thereafter, issuer-by-issuer data may be required for systemically relevant investors such as large and complex financial institutions and non-financial groups consolidated on a group basis.

Table 8.14
Financial instrument holdings of financial corporations subsectors in a from-whom-to-whom framework, by residency and resident sector of issuer and by original maturity

Original maturity and issuer / Holder by resident financial corporation subsector	Central bank	Deposit-taking corporations except the central bank	MMF investment funds	Non-MMF investment funds	Financial intermediaries other than insurance corporations and pension funds	Financial auxiliaries	Captive financial institutions and moneylenders	Insurance corporations	Pension funds
Loans, debt securities									
Short-term									
Residents									
Non-financial corporations									
Financial corporations									
General government									
Households and non-profit institutions serving households									
Non-residents									
Long-term									
Residents									
Non-financial corporations									
Financial corporations									
General government									
Households and non-profit institutions serving households									
Non-residents									
Memorandum item: Long-term at original maturity, with a remaining maturity up to and including one year									
Residents									
Non-financial corporations									
...									
Non-residents									
Equity and investment fund shares or units									
Residents									
Non-financial corporations									
...									
Non-residents									
Financial derivatives and other financial instruments									
Residents									
Non-financial corporations									
...									
Non-residents									

(f) Extending the from-whom-to-whom tables

8.58. The counterpart analysis may be extended to (financial corporations) subsectors to clarify the role of financial intermediaries in mobilizing financial resources and making these resources available to other sectors in appropriate forms through maturity or asset transformation. Banking transactions and positions and those relating to insurance corporations and pension funds are likely to be of much interest.

8.59. Extending the analysis may also reveal a growing (or shrinking) role for other types of financial intermediary and financial institutions, and shed light on the nature of their business in terms of the counterparties with whom they deal as well as the instruments they transact in. Thus, the tables described above may be further expanded to show subsectors of the financial corporations sector as creditors of the resident non-financial sectors (non-financial corporations, general government and households including non-profit institutions serving households) and non-residents. A table containing all debtor/creditor relationships would contain numerous cells, many of which

Table 8.15

Detailed from-whom-to-whom table (for stocks and flows) showing the financial assets and liabilities of financial corporations by type of claim and debtor/creditor

Financial assets of financial corporations / Type of claim and debtor	Monetary financial institutions	Insurance, pension and standardized guarantee schemes	Other financial corporations
Monetary gold and special drawing rights (SDRs)			
Monetary gold			
SDRs			
Currency and deposits			
Currency			
Transferable deposits			
Residents			
Non-residents			
Other deposits …			
Debt securities			
Short-term			
Non-financial corporations			
Financial corporations			
General government			
Households and non-profit institutions serving households			
Rest of the world			
Long-term …			
Loans			
Short-term …			
Long-term …			
Equity and investment fund shares			
Equity			
Resident corporations			
Listed			
Unlisted			
Other equity			
Non-resident corporations …			
Investment fund shares/units			
Money market fund shares/units			
Residents			
Non-residents			
Non-MMF investment fund shares/units …			
Insurance, pension and standardized guarantee schemes			
Non-life insurance technical reserves			
Life insurance and annuity entitlements			
Pension entitlements			
Claim of pension fund on pension managers			
Entitlements to non-pension benefits			
Provisions for calls under standardized guarantees			
Financial derivatives and employee stock options			
Other accounts receivable/payable			
Trade credits and advances			
Other accounts receivable/payable			
Currency and deposits …			
Currency			
Domestic			
Residents			
Non-residents			
Foreign			
Residents			
Transferable deposits			
by institutional sector			
Other deposits …			

Note: Monetary financial institutions cover the central bank, deposit-taking corporations except the central bank, and money market funds.

would be blank; therefore, for the purpose of illustration, only parts of the table have been expanded here.

8.60. Table 8.15 illustrates how to show debtor and creditor counterparts (where applicable) for specific subsectors of the financial corporations sector. These counterparts are broken down by type of claim, residency and debtor or creditor sector. Depending on the availability of data, different degrees of detail can be shown, such as for currency and deposits (by creditor sector), for loans (by debtor sector) or for insurance, pension and standardized guarantee schemes (by creditor sector).

8.61. The other changes in assets accounts may also be expanded to show the holding gains or losses and the other changes in the volume of assets by institutional sector, financial asset or liability and counterpart sector. Such detailed statistical information might be provided in the future by security-by-security or corporate balance sheet databases.

7. Tables with global aggregates for financial instruments such as securities

8.62. Global aggregates covering specific financial instruments such as debt securities or equity securities, are urgently required in view of the recent financial crisis and its spread through economies and markets.

8.63. Table 8.16 shows global financial instrument holdings according to five classifications: by country (or group of countries), resident sector, currency, maturity and interest rate.

8.64. Sectors as holders of securities are non-financial corporations, financial corporations, general government and households including non-profit institutions serving households. Equity and debt securities holdings of these sectors may be broken down by currency, and debt securities holdings further by maturity and interest rate.

Table 8.16
Financial instrument holdings by country, resident sector, currency, maturity and interest rate

Financial instruments held by resident sector, currency, maturity and interest rate / Issuer resident in country	Resident holders											
	Non-financial corporations			Financial corporations			General government			Households and non-profit institutions serving households		
	Currency	Maturity	Interest rate	Currency	Maturity	Interest rate	Currency	Maturity	Interest rate	Currency	Maturity	Interest rate
Country A												
Country B												
Country C												
...												
Country Z												
All issuers (world)												

8.65. Table 8.17 is a from-whom-to-whom table for financial instrument holdings and issues with a breakdown of holders and issuers by country and by aggregated groups of countries. From-whom-to-whom tables on a country basis are of interest for international comparisons and are requested by international organizations.

8.66. Such a table with global aggregates requires national from-whom-to-whom data, which must be aggregated and reconciled. More detailed tables might show further breakdowns of financial instruments by sector, maturity, currency and interest rate.

Table 8.17
Financial instrument holdings and issues by country

Holder resident in country / Issuer resident in country	Country A	Country B	Country C	...	Country Z	All holders (world)
Country A						
Country B						
Country C						
...						
Country Z						
All issuers (world)						

8.67. Other breakdowns may show holdings of financial corporations or deposit-taking corporations except the central bank of debt securities that represent claims on specific groups of countries, for example emerging and developing countries.

8.68. Financial instrument holdings may also be presented with a breakdown by subcategory or subposition, such as original maturity (short-term or long-term) or major currency, as shown in table 8.18. The currencies are the United States dollar, euro, Japanese yen, pound sterling and all other currencies.

Table 8.18
Financial instrument holdings in major currencies

Currencies / Holdings of residents of	Currencies				
	United States dollar	Euro	Japanese yen	Pound sterling	Other currencies
United States					
Euro area					
Japan					
United Kingdom					
Other countries					
All holdings (world)					

8. Presentation of data derived from the template of internationally comparable non-financial assets (table 8.19)

8.69. A table may be designed on non-financial assets by institutional sector. Table 8.19 presents a breakdown into produced and non-produced non-financial assets. Produced assets cover mainly fixed assets (dwellings and other buildings and structures) but also inventories and valuables. Non-produced assets are split into natural resources, contracts, leases and licences, and goodwill and marketing assets.

8.70. Issues related to non-financial assets are not discussed in this Handbook.

Table 8.19
Table presenting data on non-financial assets by institutional sector

	Total economy	Non-financial corporations	Financial corporations	General government	Households including NPISHs	Rest of the world
	S1	**S11**	**S12**	**S13**	**S14+S15**	**S2**
AN1 Produced non-financial assets						
AN11 Fixed assets of which:						
AN111 Dwellings						
AN112 Other buildings and structures						
AN12 Inventories						
AN13 Valuables						
AN2 Non-produced non-financial assets						
AN21 Natural resources of which:						
AN211 Land of which:						
AN2111 Land underlying buildings and structures						
AN212 Mineral and energy reserves						
AN22 Contracts, leases and licenses						
AN23 Goodwill and marketing assets						

9. Charts

8.71. The type of data will often determine the choice of chart. The most common charts applied in national accounts are time series graphs displaying data at different points in time. The horizontal axis shows the time and the vertical axis the data values. These graphs can be used to show trends and cyclical and seasonal patterns over a time period. Other common types of charts are bar charts, pie charts and histograms or scatter plots.

8.72. From-whom-to-whom data may be presented in matrices, flow charts or networks.

8.73. The chart below (provided by the Oesterreichische Nationalbank) shows how to present sectoral accounts for use in analysing the recent financial crisis. Figure 8.1 provides "from-whom-to-whom" data on transactions in liabilities (financing) between the central bank, deposit-taking corporations except the central bank and money market funds, other financial intermediaries, insurance corporations and pension funds, non-financial corporations, general government, households including non-profit institutions serving households and the rest of the world.

8.74. Below, the Australian Bureau of Statistics shows an example of a flow chart. Figure 8.2 illustrates the net financial flows (transactions) between the resident institutional sectors and the rest of the world for Australia during the period 2010/11. The arrows show the net flows from the lenders to the borrowers.

8.75. For example, there was a 21.3 billion net flow from the households sector (including NPISHs) to financial corporations, a 48.8 billion net flow from non-financial corporations to financial corporations, and a 27.5 billion net flow from the financial corporations sector to the general government sector (all figures in Australian dollars).[190]

[190] See www.abs.gov.au/ausstats/abs@.nsf/Lookup/by%20Subject/1301.0~2012~Main%20Features~Intersectoral%20financial%20flows~265.

Figure 8.1
Sectoral accounts of Austria for an analysis of the recent financial crisis

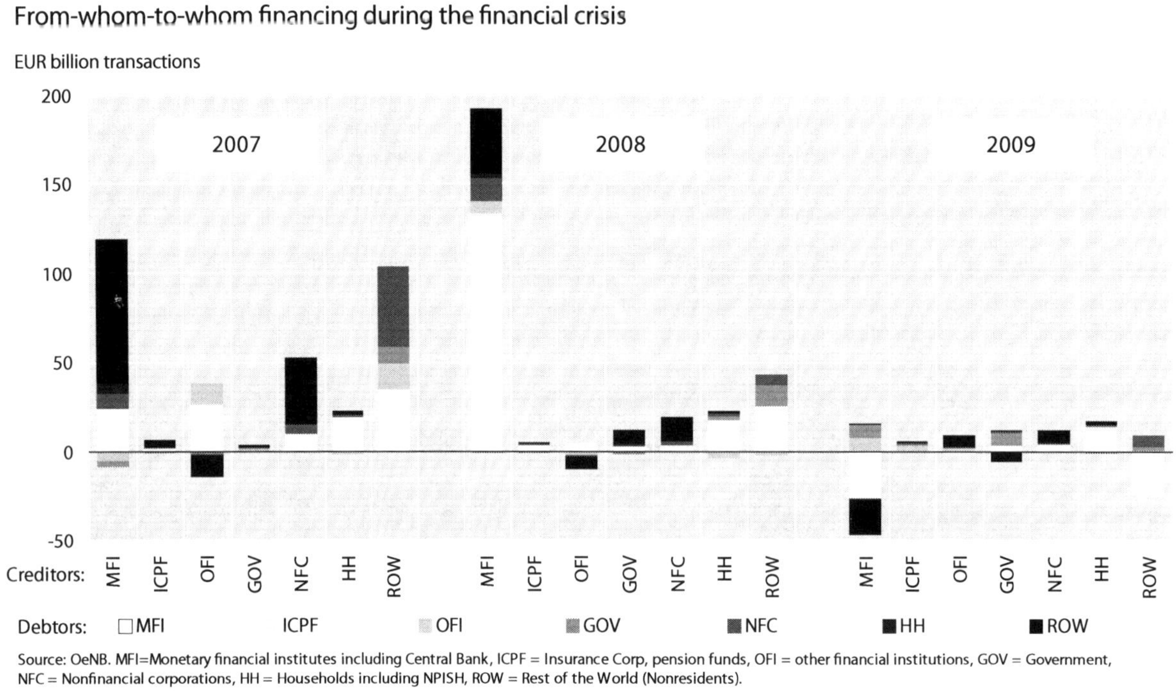

Abbreviations: Central bank, deposit-taking corporations except the central bank and money market funds, MFI; other financial intermediaries, OFI; insurance corporations and pension funds, ICPF; non-financial corporations, NFC; general government, GOV, households including non-profit institutions serving households, HH; rest of the world, RoW.

Figure 8.2
Intersectoral financial flows during the period 2010/11

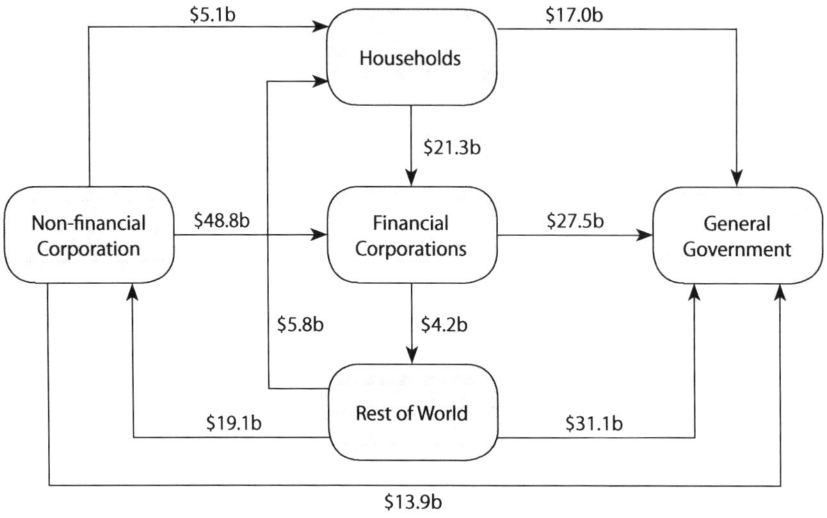

Source: Australian National Accounts: Financial Accounts (5232.0).

8.76. From-whom-to-whom data may also be presented in networks. More generally, the bilateral "exposures" among N sectors under each financial instrument category k may be presented in an NxN matrix X_k with entries x_{ij}, where x_{ij} denotes the exposure of sector i towards sector j in a financial instrument category k. The sum of the amounts in a given row corresponds to the total instrument k-specific assets $a_{i,k}$ held by a sector and issued by counterpart sectors. Accordingly, the sum of the amounts in a given column equals the total financial instrument k-specific liabilities $l_{j,k}$ of a sector claimed by counterpart sectors.

8.77. For presentations based on aggregated data, the diagonals of the matrix X_k are occupied for resident sectors because of the non-consolidated presentation of flows and positions.

8.78. Once the bilateral exposures have been compiled and presented for each financial instrument category, a network connecting all sectors can be constructed using the gross exposures, that is, assets plus liabilities connecting individual sectors in all financial instrument categories.

8.79. Figure 8.3 illustrates this network of cross-sector balance sheet exposures of euro area sectors and of the euro area rest of the world at the end of two quarters, the first quarter of 1999 and the second quarter of 2009. In this figure, the sizes of the *nodes* describe the exposures within the various sectors. The *links* show the gross bilateral cross-sector exposures, summed up across all financial instrument categories; the thickness of the link connecting two sectors corresponds to the magnitude of this gross exposure. The degree of nodes (i.e. the number of links connecting each sector) is six where all five residential sectors and the rest of the world are considered.

Figure 8.3
Cross-sector balance sheet exposures of euro area sectors and of the rest of the world
First quarter of 1999 and second quarter of 2009

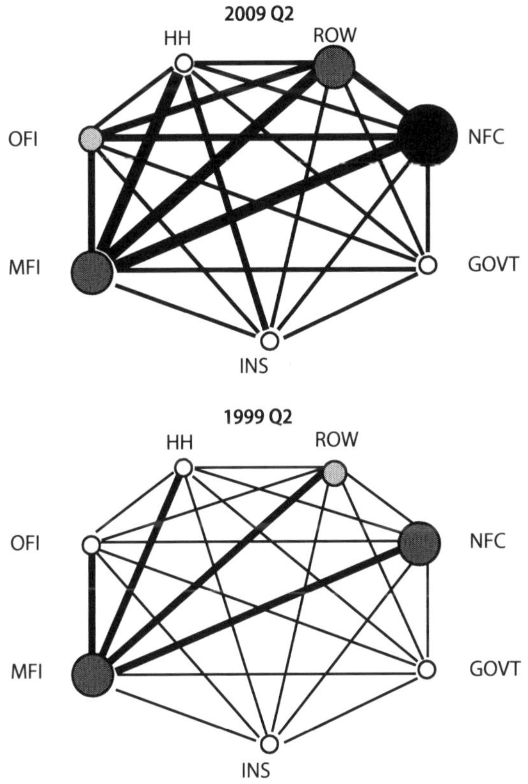

Note: The size of the node illustrates the amount of gross exposures (assets plus liabilities) within sectors. The thickness of the links shows the size of the gross exposures between two sectors.

Abbreviations: Non-financial corporations, NFC; Financial corporations, MFIs; Other financial institutions, OFIs; Insurance corporations and pension funds, INS; General government, GOVT; Households including non-profit institutions serving households HH; Euro area rest of the world, ROW.

Source: Castrén and Kavonius (2009).

8.80. Figure 8.4 highlights the degree of financial interlinkages of all sectors in the Portuguese financial accounts. The figure below illustrates the flow of funds (net) observed between the various institutional sectors, comparing the year 2007 with 2010. The diameter of the circle is proportional to the financial saving of each sector (filled in light grey if positive and dark grey if negative). The width of the links is proportional to the intersectoral relations.

Figure 8.4
Flow of funds in Portugal — 2007 and 2010

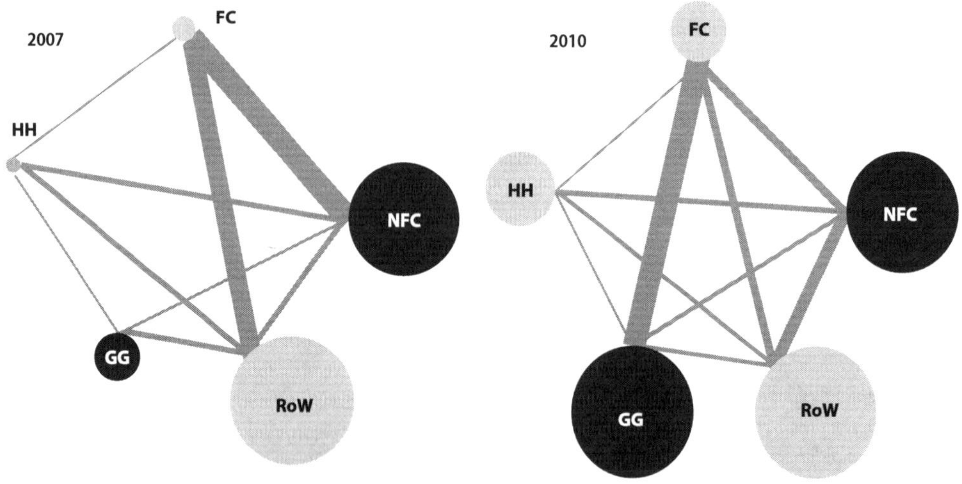

Abbreviations: NFC, non-financial corporations; FC, financial corporations; GG, general government; HH, households; RoW, rest of the world.
Source: Lima and Monteiro (2011).

F. Dissemination of national accounts data

1. Statistical information systems

8.81. Statistical information systems or data warehouses provide statistics needed for policy purposes, as well as to the interested public and to market participants.

8.82. Statistical information systems are designed to address the needs of a wide range of users, from one-time visitors searching for the most recent value of a specific statistic or single time series, to more frequent users such as market participants, journalists, analysts and researchers.

8.83. They contain robust and simple-to-use interfaces that provide access to numerous features, functions and time series, designed to make data accessible to users regardless of their knowledge of information technology systems or statistics generally.

8.84. The European Central Bank's online Statistical Data Warehouse is an example. Links to economic concepts for various statistics (such as national accounts) and to various reports (including own reports and own data groups) are shown on the left-hand side of the main (home) page.

8.85. The rest of the page gives information on selected indicators for the euro area, such as the inflation rate or the monetary aggregate M3. Other indicators are GDP in prices of the previous year, the unemployment rate or government deficit. Figure 8.5 presents, as an example, the development of general government debt (as a percentage of GDP) for the euro area.

Figure 8.5
General government debt
Reference period: November 2012

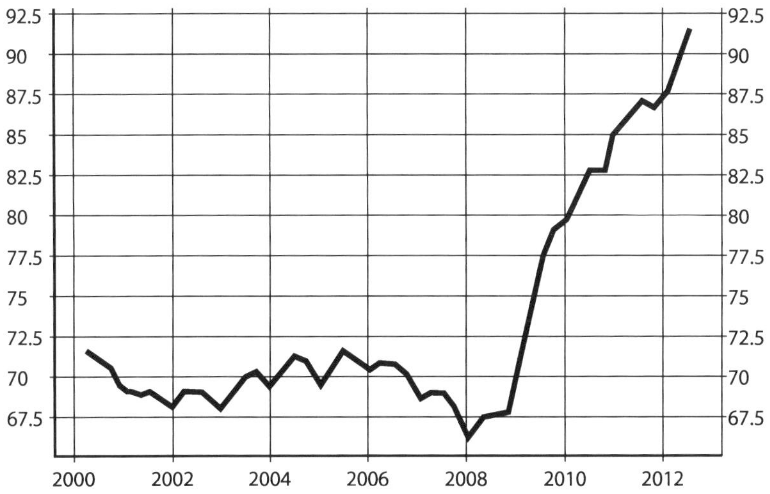

Source: European System of Central Banks, European Commission (Eurostat) and national data.

2. The Statistical Data and Metadata Exchange initiative

8.86. Seven institutions (the BIS, European Central Bank, Eurostat, IMF, OECD, United Nations and the World Bank) sponsor the Statistical Data and Metadata Exchange (SDMX) initiative to foster standards for the exchange of statistical information. The standard is an ISO standard (ISO/Technical Specification ISO 17369:2013, which revises ISO/Technical Specification 17369:2005). It offers an information model for representing statistical data and metadata, as well as several formats to represent this model (SDMX-EDI and several SDMX-ML formats). It also proposes a standard way of implementing web services, including the use of registers.

8.87. The SDMX information model covers various elements. They are listed and described as follows:

(a) *Descriptor concepts.* In order to make sense of statistical data, it is necessary to know the concepts associated with them. For example, on its own, the figure 1.2953 is pretty meaningless, but if we know that this is an exchange rate for the United States dollar against the euro on 23 November 2006, it starts to make more sense;

(b) *Packaging structure.* Statistical data can be grouped together at the following levels: the *observation level* (the measurement of a phenomenon); the *series level* (the measurement of a phenomenon over time, usually at regular intervals); the *group level* (a group of series, a well-known example being the sibling group, a set of series which are identical except for the fact that they are measured with different frequencies); and the *data set level* (comprising several groups covering, for example, a specific statistical domain). The descriptor concepts mentioned above can be attached at various levels in this hierarchy;

(c) *Dimensions and attributes.* There are two types of descriptor concepts: *dimensions*, which both identify and describe the data, and *attributes*, which are purely descriptive;

(d) *Keys.* Dimensions are grouped into keys, which allow a particular set of data (a series, for example) to be identified. The key values are attached at the series level and given in a fixed sequence. By convention, frequency is the first descriptor concept and the other concepts are assigned an order for that particular data set. Partial keys can be attached to groups;

(e) *Code lists.* Every possible value for a dimension is defined in a code list. Each value on that list is given a language-independent abbreviation (code) and a language-specific description. Attributes are represented either by codes or free-text values. Since the sole purpose of an attribute is to describe and not to identify the data, this is not a problem;

(f) *Data structure definitions.* A data structure definition (data classification scheme) specifies a set of concepts which describe and identify a set of data. It indicates which concepts are dimensions (identification and description) and which are attributes (just description), and it gives the attachment level for each of these concepts on the basis of the packaging structure (data set, group, series or observation), as well as their status (mandatory or conditional). It also specifies which code lists provide possible values for the dimensions and gives possible values for the attributes, either as code lists or free-text fields.

8.88. The SDMX-ML supports various uses and, therefore, defines several XML formats. Essentially, two formats are used:

(a) The *structure definition format.* This format will be used to define the structure (concepts, code lists, dimensions, attributes, etc.) of the key families;

(b) The *compact format.* This format will be used to define the data file. It is not a generic format (it is specific to a data structure definition), but is designed to support validation and the exchange of large data sets.

Box 8.1

The data structure definition for national accounts

Work to set up a data structure definition for national accounts started in early 2011. The European Central Bank, Eurostat and IMF, in coordination with OECD and the SDMX Secretariat, lead the project.

SDMX is a standard to foster increased efficiency in the electronic exchange of data and metadata among international organizations and national data-producing agencies. The purpose of establishing SDMX for the transmission of national accounts data is to have one standard format that can be used and avoid that the same data are transmitted in different formats to different international organizations. The IMF has worked extensively with the European Central Bank and Eurostat in preparing draft concepts and code lists for encoding 2008 SNA-based data in SDMX (the SDMX encoding structure is known as a data structure definition, or DSD).

From the start, the lead organizations agreed to construct the DSD using the core methodological concepts underlying the 2008 SNA data. These core concepts – referred to as "dimensions" in SDMX terminology – include:

1. Reference area (country or region)
2. Reference institutional sector
3. Flows and stocks entries
4. Accounting entries
5. SNA items
6. Functional classification
7. Instrument classification
8. Maturity
9. Currency of denomination of instrument
10. Counterpart area (e.g. country or region)

11. Counterpart institutional sector

Following the SDMX information model, the combination of components from the dimensions above would provide the unique "key" to identify a time series. The benefit of this is that all conceptually valid time series could be exchanged using a common approach, and not only the time series requested in a specific report form. For example, the IMF is interested in balance of payments transactions vis-à-vis the rest of the world, while the European Central Bank is interested in euro area countries' transactions defined as "extra-euro area"; these two sets of time series are distinguished by the dimension "counterpart area".

It is envisaged that the most statistically advanced countries will take advantage of the functionality offered by an SDMX web service for the dissemination of 2008 SNA-based data. The European Central Bank, IMF and OECD already provide computer-to-computer access to the data stored in their respective data warehouses through an SDMX web service. The availability of an SDMX web service eliminates the need for data reporting, as the requesting organization "pulls" the data from the "providing" organization using the web service. A number of data-producing agencies are now implementing that technology to better serve their data users.

Proposed dimensions and attributes for the 2008 SNA-based data structure definition

Dimension name	Description of the dimension
Frequency	Time series frequency (e.g. monthly)
Reference area	Reporting country code (e.g. Portugal)
Adjustment indicator	Specific adjustments or concepts for the time series (e.g. seasonal adjustment)
Flow stock entry	Flow or stock variable indicator (e.g. positions)
Balance of payments item	External statistics item classification
Accounting entry	Type of flow or stock in relation to the reporting area (e.g. assets)
Functional category	Classification by function of the financial investment (e.g. reserve assets)
Financial instrument classification	Breakdown by financial instrument (e.g. debt securities)
Resident sector	Institutional sector in the reporting area (e.g. general government)
Currency of denomination	Currency of issuance for financial items or invoicing for goods and services (e.g. euro)
Maturity	Original maturity of financial item, combined with remaining maturity (e.g. short term)
Counterpart or partner area	Country of counterpart (e.g. Japan or rest of the world)
Counterpart sector	Institutional sector of counterpart (e.g. general government)
Series unit of measure	Unit of measure used for reporting the time series (e.g. euro)

Dimensions define the time series; therefore, a valid code must be provided for each dimension in order to uniquely define the time series.

Attributes for the data structure definition

Attribute name	Description of the attribute	Reporting requirement	Attachment level
Unit multiplier	Indicates whether the unit of measure for the series represents thousands, millions ...	Mandatory	Series
Decimals	Indicates the level of precision for the series	Mandatory	Series
Observation status	Indicates whether the value is a normal value, provisional data, a forecast ...	Optional	Observation
Confidentiality status	Indicates whether an observation is freely available, restricted, confidential ...	Optional	Observation
Time format	Specifies the format used for describing the reference period	Optional	Series
Compiling organization	Identifies the organization responsible for compiling the series	Mandatory	Series
End of reporting fiscal year	Indicates whether the data are based on a fiscal year and specifies the fiscal year	Mandatory	Series

Attributes further describe time series defined by dimensions. As such, some attributes must be reported, while others are optional. In addition, attributes can be attached at various levels, such as observations, series (time series or siblings), or the data set.

Chapter 9
Use of financial accounts and balance sheets by institutional sector

References:
MFSMCG
GFSM 2014

A. Introduction

9.1. Institutional sector accounts shed greater light on economic, financial and monetary developments, which can be only partially revealed by monetary and financial statistics, balance of payments statistics or government finance statistics. In particular, the accounts provide additional information for the analysis of macroeconomic developments by institutional sector and a comprehensive framework to complement and combine data provided by other, timelier statistics. In this context, comprehensive stock-flow (transactions, revaluations and other flows) relationships, which may be derived for institutional sector accounts, are analytically useful for various purposes. Institutional sector accounts are also a means of achieving consistency in the various source data.

9.2. In this chapter, examples are given to describe how institutional sector accounts – especially the financial account and the balance sheet – can be used for policy analysis and research:

(a) Monetary and financial analysis, which includes the monitoring of monetary assets and the analysis of portfolio shifts between monetary assets and other financial instruments;

(b) The analysis of the financial structures in a national economy in terms of markets and market participants. Market participants are resident financial corporations, mainly financial intermediaries; the non-financial sectors, such as non-financial corporations, households including non-profit institutions serving households and general government – either as debtors or creditors; and the rest of the world;

(c) The analysis of internal and external financing of financial and non-financial investment of non-financial corporations, also in relation to valuation changes in the financial wealth of non-financial corporations;

(d) The analysis of households' consumption, saving, investment and wealth;

(e) Macroprudential and financial stability analysis.[191]

9.3. To illustrate their usefulness for analytical and policy purposes, some examples of institutional sector accounts are described, such as the flow of funds accounts in the United States, the institutional sector accounts as applied for the euro area, the IMF

[191] The use of institutional sector accounts for these purposes may be rather limited in comparison with other types of macroeconomic analysis owing to limited information on off-balance-sheet items and on provisions. However, the institutional sector accounts data could be used as a starting point for a network analysis.

balance sheet approach and the use of institutional sector accounts for financial stability analysis.

B. Monetary and financial analysis

9.4. The portfolio approach to analysing monetary and financial developments can be used to show money and credit with other assets within the system of institutional sector accounts. Institutional sector accounts can be used to monitor monetary variables and their components and in the analysis of portfolio shifts between monetary assets and other financial instruments. Money is seen as the most important component of short-term financial investment, and the integration of a full sectoral breakdown of broad money and its components permits a more comprehensive analysis.

9.5. Liabilities are usually arranged according to what, in usual circumstances, would be decreasing liquidity: money encompassing currency, transferable deposits, short-term debt securities and money market fund (MMF) shares or units (issues (by monetary financial institutions)). Financial assets cover credit as the sum of loans and debt securities (acquisitions (by monetary financial institutions)). Other assets include long-term debt securities, shares and other equity, and entitlements from insurance, pension and standardized guarantee schemes.

1. Integration of money in the institutional sector accounts

9.6. The framework of institutional sector accounts allows monetary aggregates to be analysed jointly with other short-term financial assets, which may represent close substitutes for money. Moreover, movements of money and credit are also presented in relation to the long-term financial investment and financing components of the resident sectors excluding the resident monetary financial institutions, especially households and non-financial corporations, but also general government and the rest of the world. As a result, it is possible to monitor the portfolio shifts within the financial wealth of these sectors and movements of their asset prices and indebtedness.

9.7. The presentation of broad money and its counterparts in the institutional sector accounts is derived from the consolidated financial transactions and balance sheets of the resident monetary financial institutions vis-à-vis the remaining resident sectors. The corresponding financial accounts and balance sheets, with a breakdown of the financial corporations sector, the financial asset and liability categories and the counterparts, permit broad money to be identified. Monetary developments can therefore be analysed in the widest possible financial framework and in such a way that they can be related more easily to the economic developments recorded in the production, income and capital accounts.

9.8. Monetary financial institutions consist of the central bank and other resident deposit-taking corporations except the central bank. Depending on the definition of broad money, resident money market funds are included as monetary financial institutions or as other deposit-taking corporations.[192] Their counterparts are the remaining resident sectors except central government. Holdings of money by monetary financial institutions themselves are netted out. Neither the liabilities of non-residents nor non-residents' holdings of broad money issued by resident money issuers are counted in broad money.[193]

[192] See Chapter 6 of the MFSMCG.

[193] The rest of the world sector holdings of any of the monetary variables are not included in broad money. Resident sectors' holdings of foreign deposits or other short-term foreign assets are not included either.

9.9. As an example, monetary variables may be considered to comprise: (a) currency (issued by the central bank); (b) transferable deposits held with monetary financial institutions; (c) deposits redeemable at a period of notice of up to and including three months (i.e. short-term savings deposits) held with monetary financial institutions; (d) deposits with an agreed maturity of up to and including two years (i.e. short-term time deposits) held with monetary financial institutions; and (e) repurchase agreements, money market fund shares or units, and debt securities with an original maturity of up to one year or less issued by monetary financial institutions.

9.10. Table 9.1 shows in italics the financial transactions in assets of resident sectors other than monetary financial institutions, which represent monetary claims on monetary financial institutions. The outstanding amount of broad money could be identified in a similar way in the financial balance sheet.

9.11. In table 9.2, the counterparts to broad money are shown in italics (components of domestic credit). The *domestic credit* counterpart reveals how changes in broad money are related to lending by monetary financial institutions to other residents in all forms, including by the acquisition of securities issued by them. This counterpart comprises part of the assets of monetary financial institutions, namely loans to, the acquisition of securities issued by, and other forms of lending to all other resident sectors, including other entities (that is, not monetary financial institutions) in the financial corporations sector.

9.12. Another part of the assets of monetary financial institutions, net of liabilities to non-residents, constitutes the *external* counterpart: the net external assets of monetary financial institutions (in balance sheet terms), or changes in them (corresponding to transactions in the financial account). The transactions and positions of the rest of the world correspond (after some rearrangements) to the balance of payments and international investment position.

Table 9.1
Broad money in the framework of institutional sector accounts

Creditor / Type of claim and debtor (monetary financial institutions)	*Non-financial corporations*	Financial corporations		*General government*	*Households and NPISH*	*Money holders (total)*	Rest of the world
		Monetary financial institutions[a]	*Other financial corporations*				
Currency and deposits							
—*short term*[b]	*50*	60	*5*	*10*	*150*	*215*	60
—long term	10	20	0	0	30		10
Debt securities							
—*short term*[c]	*10*	30	*5*	*5*	*20*	*40*	30
—long term	5	10	0	0	10		10
Money market fund shares or units	*5*	5	*2*	*0*	*20*	*27*	0
Equity and non-MMF investment fund shares	0	5	5	0	5		2
Financial derivatives and employee stock options	2	10	10	0	0		10
Other accounts receivable/payable	1	2	2	0	0		2
Money stock	***65***		***12***	***15***	***190***	***282***	
Domestic non-monetary liabilities (total)	18		17	0	45	80	
External liabilities of MFIs (total)							124

[a] Monetary financial institutions comprise the central bank, deposit-taking corporations except the central bank, and money market funds. Money-holding sectors are all resident sectors except monetary financial institutions and central government.

[b] Short-term deposits comprise transferable deposits, deposits redeemable at a period of notice of up to and including three months (i.e. short-term savings deposits) and deposits with an agreed maturity of up to and including one (or two years) (i.e. short-term time deposits) held with monetary financial institutions.

[c] Short-term debt securities comprise debt securities with an original maturity of up to one year or less issued by monetary financial institutions.

Table 9.2
Counterparts to broad money in the framework of institutional sector accounts

Debtor / Type of claim and creditor (MFI)		Financial corporations					
	Non-financial corporations	*Monetary financial institutions*[a]	*Other financial corporations*	*General government*	*House-holds and NPISH*	*Money holders (total)*	**Rest of the world**
Currency and deposits		80					30
Debt securities	*60*	40	*10*	*40*		*110*	60
Loans	*60*		*6*	*20*	*120*	*206*	45
Money market fund shares or units		5					0
Equity	*5*					*5*	
Non-MMF investment fund shares or units		5	*10*			*10*	5
Insurance, pension and standardized guarantee schemes			*3*	*0*		*3*	0
Financial derivatives and employee stock options	*2*	10	*0*	*0*	*0*	*2*	5
Other accounts receivable/payable	*0*	2	*0*	*0*	*0*	*0*	5
Domestic credit (total)	*127*		*29*	*60*	*120*	*336*	
External assets (total)							150
Net external assets (external counterpart)							26 (=150–124)

[a] Monetary financial institutions comprise the central bank, deposit-taking corporations except the central bank, and money market funds.

9.13. Net external assets of monetary financial institutions, summarizing their transactions with the rest of the world, link to broad money through the monetary financial institutions' accounting framework.

9.14. The balance of payments identity may then be used to show how the transactions of resident sectors other than monetary financial institutions with the rest of the world relate to changes in broad money. The monetary financial institutions' balance of payments transactions must equal all other resident sectors' balance of payments transactions with a reverse sign. (For this purpose it is desirable that errors and omissions in the balance of payments have been eliminated when compiling the sector accounts and balance sheets; otherwise they may be attributed to the resident sectors other than monetary financial institutions.)

9.15. Table 9.3 provides a simplified example showing this relationship.

Table 9.3
Balance of payments linked to transactions in the external counterpart of broad money

	Direct investment		*Portfolio investment*			*Other investment*				
				Liabilities						
Current and capital account	**By resident units abroad (non-MFIs[a])**	**By non-resident units in the economy**	**Assets (non-MFIs)**	**Equity**	**Debt instruments**	**Assets (non-MFIs)**	**Liabilities (non-MFIs)**	**Financial derivatives**	**Errors and omissions**	**Transactions in the external counterpart of money**
-9	-6	4	-47	32	4	-32	23	-3	6	-28

[a] All institutional units except monetary financial institutions, i.e. the central bank, deposit-taking corporations except the central bank, and money market funds.

2. Money, credit, financial investment and financing within a system of institutional sector accounts

9.16. Institutional sector accounts allow the financial analysis to be extended to the whole spectrum of financial assets held by non-financial sectors, of which broad money may represent some part.

9.17. Looking at the various components permits an analysis of substitution within financial investment, for instance between short-term and long-term or among long-term financial instruments such as debt securities, shares or investment fund shares or units. Sectoral data enable the investment behaviour of the various sectors (e.g. non-financial corporations, households including non-profit institutions serving households or general government) to be identified in detail.

9.18. This step embeds money and credit in a table showing the financial investment and financing of an economy's institutional sectors and of the rest of the world, based on data provided by the money-issuing sector, along with supplementary data on other financial instruments like securities issues and holdings (table 9.4).

Table 9.4
Broad money and credit as parts of institutional sector accounts

Financial assets (or changes in financial assets) Financial investment									Liabilities (or changes in liabilities) Financing							
Non-financial corporations	Other financial corporations	General government	Households including NPISH	Monetary financial institutions	Economy	Rest of the world	Total	Positions (or transactions)	Non-financial corporations	Other financial corporations	General government	Households including NPISH	Monetary financial institutions	Economy	Rest of the world	Total
65	**12**	**15**	**190**	**220**	**502**	**90**	**592**	Short-term[a]	**30**	**3**	**10**	**60**	**467**	**570**	**22**	**592**
50	5	10	150	60	275	60	335	Currency and deposits					335	335		335
10	5	5	20	30	70	30	100	Debt securities					100	100		100
5	2	0	20	5	32	0	32	Money market fund shares or units					32	32		32
				125	125		125	Loans	30	3	10	60		103	22	125
15	**5**	**0**	**45**	**369**	**434**	**22**	**456**	Long-term[a]	**95**	**26**	**50**	**60**	**107**	**338**	**118**	**456**
10	0	0	30	50	90	10	100	Deposits					70	70	30	100
5	0	0	10	180	195	10	205	Debt securities	60	10	40		35	145	60	205
				126	126		126	Loans	30	3	10	60		103	23	126
0	5	0	5	10	20	2	22	Equity and other investment fund shares or units	5	10			2	17	5	22
				3	3		3	Insurance, pension and standardized guarantee schemes		3	0			3	0	3
3	12	0	0	24	39	12	51	Other	2	0	0	0	39	41	10	51
2	10	0	0	17	29	10	39	Financial derivatives and employee stock options	2	0	0	0	32	24	5	39
1	2	0	0	7	10	2	12	Other accounts receivable/payable	0	0	0	0	7	7	5	12
83	29	15	235	613	975	124	1099	Total	127	29	60	120	613	949	150	1099

[a] The 2008 SNA classification of financial instruments into short-term and long-term maturity refers only to debt securities and loans. Currency and specific types of deposits and money market funds are considered to be short-term financial instruments, other financial instruments are considered to be long term.

9.19. The sources of financing (613) provided by the money-issuing sector are broken down into short-term (467), long-term (107) and other financing (39).

9.20. Broad money can be derived:

(a) By subtracting the short-term financial investment of the monetary financial institutions vis-à-vis money issuers – the intrasector transactions (in darker grey on the left-hand side: 95) – and the investment of the rest of the world in money (90); or

(b) From the non-consolidated short-term financing figure (282=467–95–90).

9.21. Money is also directly shown as the financial investment of the money-holding sectors in monetary variables. These are currency and deposits, short-term debt securities and money market fund shares/units (figures in lightest grey: 282=65+12+15+190).

9.22. Further, domestic credit (shaded in regular grey: 336) is shown as financing by the money-holding sector in the form of short-term and long-term loans granted by monetary financial institutions (206), debt securities (110), equity (15) and other financial instruments (5), as indicated in table 9.4. External assets and liabilities are derived as total financial investment (124) and financing (150) (both shaded in black) of the rest of the world vis-à-vis the money-issuing sector.

9.23. As the table provides a somewhat limited view of the financing and financial investment process within an economy, it could be expanded to include all sources of financing and uses of financial investment for all institutional sectors. For non-financial corporations, for instance, liabilities incurred vis-à-vis other non-financial corporations, non-monetary financial institutions or general government could be included as sources of financing. The same is true for the sector's financial investments, in which equity plays a rather important role. The inclusion of non-financial investment, saving and net capital transfers (the capital account) would make it possible to carry out a complete analysis of investment, financing and debt by institutional sector.

C. Analysis of financial structures

9.24. The financial structures of financial markets and of market participants aggregated in sectors or subsectors are somewhat heterogeneous across national economies despite the increasing interdependencies of financial markets worldwide. Reference is often made to a simplified distinction between bank-based and market-based financial structures observed in various national economies.

9.25. A predominantly bank-based financial structure is characterized by the fact that a major part of financial investment and financing of the non-financial sectors is provided through financial intermediaries. The corresponding financial instruments are mostly non-negotiable, such as deposits and loans or insurance products.

9.26. Market-based financial structures are characterized by financial investment and financing activities through financial markets on which negotiable financial instruments are traded. These are debt securities, equity securities or financial derivatives.

9.27. Figure 9.1 provides an overview of these two types of financial structures. Households and non-financial corporations as main lenders supply funds to borrowers, who are mainly non-financial corporations, general government or households, in two ways. The first is through financial intermediaries. These are mainly deposit-taking corporations except the central bank, insurance corporations, pension funds and other financial intermediaries such as investment funds. The second is through financial markets, that is, markets for debt or equity securities and for financial derivatives. Figure 9.1 does not take into account the lender, borrower and financial intermediation activities of the rest of the world.

Figure 9.1
Bank-based and market-based financial structures

a) Bank-based: funds channeled through financial intermediaries

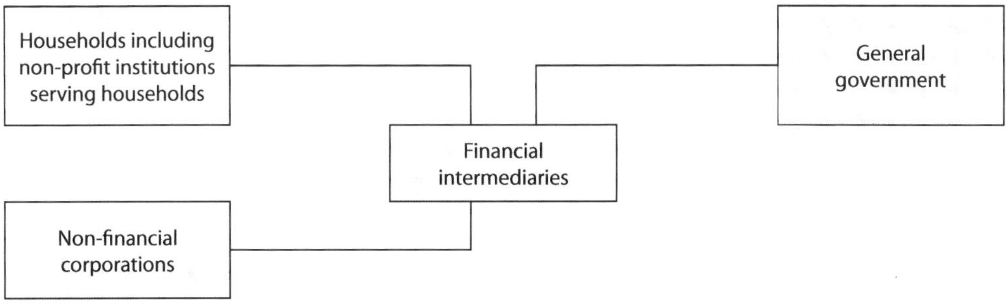

b) Market-based: funds channeled through securities and derivatives markets

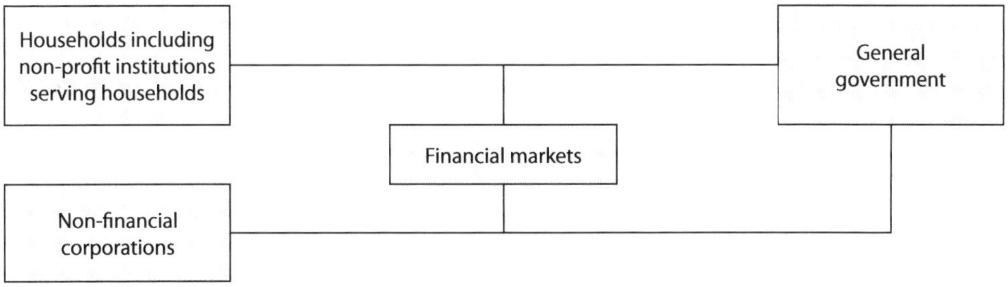

9.28. Analysing the financial structure is important in terms of measuring the efficiency of the financial system, financial stability and monetary policy transmission channels. In terms of efficiency of the financial system, analysing the financial structure enables interesting questions to be answered, such as how a financial system shares risk and who bears that risk; or what the incentives to provide and use information are. For financial stability purposes, it might be important to explore the relationship between the financial structure and such phenomena as banking crises, currency crises, asset price bubbles and crashes, contagion or financial fragility. Finally, the financial structure is important in determining monetary policy transmission channels, taking into consideration the traditional models of monetary policy and transmission – the "money view" or the "credit view" focusing on the access to finance.

9.29. Besides the view on and the comparison of bank-based and market-based financial structures, there is an interest to monitor the financial investment and financing behaviour of the various resident institutional sectors, of monetary financial institutions and institutional investors, of non-financial corporations, households and general government and of the rest of the world. It involves a detailed structural analysis of assets and liabilities and the indebtedness of these sectors related to the various financial instruments with their breakdowns by maturity, currency denomination or counterpart sector.

1. Monetary financial institutions and institutional investors

9.30. Monetary financial institutions consist mainly of the central bank, deposit-taking corporations except the central bank, and money market funds. Their main asset categories are loans and debt securities, while their liabilities cover currency and deposits, debt securities and equity. Where the financial structure of an economy is mainly "bank based", MFIs represent an important part of the financial corporations sector.

9.31. The opposite is true in a mainly market-based financial structure. In that case, institutional investors play a significant role in the financial intermediation process, as they are important holders of negotiable financial instruments such as debt and equity securities. Institutional investors are generally understood to comprise a subset of financial corporations, investment funds other than MMFs (or all investment funds if MMFs are not classified as monetary financial institutions), insurance corporations and pension funds.

9.32. The coverage of financial intermediaries may vary across countries, as it may also include financial corporations engaged in the securitization of assets, security and derivative dealers, financial corporations engaged in lending and specialized financial corporations.

2. Corporate finance

(a) Saving, investment and financing

9.33. Corporate finance refers to non-financial corporations' investment and financing in terms of transactions (activities)[194] and positions.

9.34. Analytical issues include whether or not balance sheet indicators of leverage, liquidity and creditworthiness have a significant impact on non-financial corporations' investment activities. Concerning leverage, the debt-to-equity ratio, there are two positions: first, that a corporation's financial structure plays no role in determining investment (Modigliani-Miller); and, second, with capital market imperfections, leverage matters for investment decisions. Another point is whether non-financial corporations respond to equity revaluations by increasing net acquisitions of financial assets.

9.35. A first distinction is whether investment is financed from internal funding or from external funding. Internal funding refers to the changes in net worth of non-financial corporations due to saving and capital transfers. In the example of table 9.5, internal funding amounts to 65 of which net saving is 48 and net capital transfers is 17 (=33–16). During the given period non-financial corporations have also increased their external funding by 140, the net incurrence of liabilities. Such external funding may be via debt financing (debt securities, loans and other accounts payable (=53=6+21+26));[195] equity financing (=84); or financing through financial derivatives and employee stock options (=3).

9.36. Total financing (=205) is used for investment in non-financial assets and in financial assets – non-financial investment (=134) and net acquisition of financial assets (financial investment) (=71). Most of their non-financial investment is in (net) fixed capital formation (gross fixed capital formation less consumption of fixed capital (=113 =250–137)). Net acquisition of financial assets (financial investment) comprises investment in currency and deposits (=27); debt securities (=7); loans (=19); equity and investment fund shares or units (=10); financial derivatives and employee stock options (=3); and other accounts receivable (=4).

[194] Unless financial and non-financial (transaction) accounts are fully vertically integrated, discrepancies influence the relationship between saving, investment and financing.

[195] Depending on the purpose of the analysis, the concept of debt may differ in terms of financial instruments, valuation and treatment of accrued interest.

Table 9.5
Saving, investment and financing of non-financial corporations

Changes in assets		Changes in liabilities and net worth
	Transaction	
	Financing	205
	Changes in net worth due to saving and capital transfers	65
	Saving, net	48
	Capital transfers, receivable	33
	Capital transfers, payable	-16
	Net incurrence of liabilities	140
	Debt securities	6
	Loans	21
	Equity and investment fund shares or units	84
	Financial derivatives and employee stock options	3
	Other accounts payable	26
205	*Investment*	
134	Non-financial investment	
250	**Gross fixed capital formation**	
-137	**Consumption of fixed capital (–)**	
26	**Changes in inventories**	
2	**Acquisitions less disposals of valuables**	
-7	**Acquisitions less disposals of non-produced/non-financial assets**	
71	Net acquisition of financial assets	
27	Currency and deposits	
7	Debt securities	
19	Loans	
10	Equity and investment fund shares or units	
3	Financial derivatives and employee stock options	
4	Other accounts receivable	

9.37. Not only transactions due to financing and financial investment decisions taken in a specific period of time but also revaluations of assets and liabilities and other volume changes contribute to the changes in the non-financial corporations' balance sheet positions of assets and liabilities from the beginning to the end of a period.

(b) Indicators to describe the financial structure of non-financial corporations

9.38. Indicators derived from balance sheet positions of assets and liabilities are used to describe the financial structure of non-financial corporations.[196] Such indicators are essentially *leverage*, *liquidity* and *creditworthiness*. Based on the transactions and positions data such as those shown in table 9.6, various indicators may be defined:

(a) Tobin's q: defined as the ratio of market value of the corporations and the market value of their non-financial assets (=3,482/2,407=1.45 (shaded in black));

(b) Corporate financing gap:[197] defined as investment (non-financial and financial: shaded in dark grey) minus internal funding (shaded in dark grey

[196] Any analysis of the financial structure of non-financial corporations is affected by the structure and size of the corporation, by its type of activity, its openness to financial markets and whether it is controlled by non-residents or by general government.

[197] In the United States flow of funds, the financial gap is defined as capital expenditures less the sum of internal funds and the inventory valuation adjustment.

Table 9.6
Transactions, other flows and positions of non financial corporations

Changes in assets				Positions, transactions and other flows	Changes in liabilities and net worth			
P(0)	T(1)	OF(1)	P(1)		P(0)	T(1)	OF(1)	P(1)
				Financing	3,133	205	144	3,482
				Net worth (internal funding)	-88	65	111	88
				Liabilities (external funding)	3,221	140	33	3,394
				Debt	2,182	53	20	2,255
				Equity	885	84	11	980
				Financial derivatives and ESO	154	3	2	159
3,133	205	144	3,482	Assets (investment)				
2,151	134	122	2,407	Non-financial assets				
982	71	22	1,075	Financial assets				

Note: P (0) and P (1) are positions at the beginning (0) and at the end (1) of period (1). T (1) and OF (1) are transactions and other flows during period 1.

=134 +71–65=140) as a percentage of financing or of gross domestic product (GDP);

(c) Debt-to-equity (=2,255/980=2.30 (shaded in light grey));

(d) Debt-to-assets (=2,255/3,482=0.65); or

(e) Debt-to-net worth (=2,225/88=25.3).

(c) Leverage, liquidity and creditworthiness of non-financial corporations

9.39. Leverage as a key indicator of a sound financial structure is proxied by three measures as described above: (a) the debt-to-equity ratio; (b) the debt-to-assets ratio (the market value of corporations); or (c) the debt-to-net worth ratio. The first two measures are determined by market valuations of equity in the denominator of the ratio, making it difficult to interpret the measure when equity markets show high volatility.

9.40. Liquidity problems refer to situations in which a shortage of liquid assets affects the ability of a corporation to discharge its immediate obligations. They almost always emerge in circumstances that give rise to insolvency or unwillingness to pay. The currency and interest rate composition of debt, the maturity structure of debt and the availability of assets to pay debts are important determinants of the vulnerability of non-financial corporations.

(d) Varying financial structures

9.41. Non-financial corporations' financial structures vary greatly across economies, size of corporations and industries.

9.42. Differences in the financing patterns between small and large non-financial corporations and financing constraints may suggest that monetary policy has a different impact on corporations of a different size and on the transmission mechanism itself. For instance, small non-financial corporations are often believed to face more severe financing problems than large corporations.

9.43. Innovation in financial markets may contribute to new patterns of corporate finance, where deposit-taking corporations except the central bank play new roles in terms of securitization, credit derivatives, structured finance and syndicated loans. Contributing factors to these developments are a further international integration of financial markets, regulatory developments such as the Basel II and III accords, and technological developments enhancing the quality and timeliness of information.

3. Household finance

(a) Household balance sheet and net worth

9.44. A growing interest in household balance sheets and their components, in particular whether their changes are due to transactions or other flows, has given impetus to such recurrent themes as wealth effects, leverage behaviour, the value of collateral and real-financial feedback loops. However, reference and linkage to micro data are essential for analysing the financial behaviour of households.

9.45. Monitoring the changes of household net worth based on their balance sheet is one of the strengths of an integrated system of institutional sector accounts. Such an analysis also covers not only other important indicators, such as the non-financial and financial wealth of households, but also household debt and saving.

9.46. The financial and non-financial wealth of households is affected – in its size and structure – through changes due to transactions (acquisitions or disposals of assets) and also through other flows as revaluations and other volume changes. Different arrangements in terms not only of pension schemes and social security schemes but also of housing finance and education systems may explain the different size and structure of household non-financial and financial assets in various countries.

(b) Non-financial assets as part of the household balance sheet

9.47. A challenging part of institutional sector accounts refers to the collection and compilation of balance sheet data on non-financial assets. According to the 2008 SNA, two main categories of non-financial assets are distinguished – produced and non-produced non-financial assets.

9.48. Produced non-financial assets cover fixed assets, inventories and valuables. Non-produced non-financial assets refer to natural resources and to contracts, leases and licences or goodwill.

9.49. Non-financial asset data are often available only for household housing wealth, which covers the value of all residential dwellings, including the value of the underlying land.[198]

9.50. Housing wealth, which can account for a large part of the total household wealth (depending on the structure of wealth in individual countries), is important in assessing household consumption, investment, saving and portfolio decisions.

9.51. Figure 9.2 is regularly published in the quarterly euro area accounts press release of the European Central Bank. It depicts changes to households' net worth by type of asset.[199]

---

[198] The United States considers consumer durable goods as non-financial assets. According to the 2008 SNA, consumer durable goods should be treated as consumption.

[199] In the United States flow of funds, the change in net worth for households is split into its components.

Figure 9.2
Growth of households' net worth and contributions by type of asset change

(annual percentage changes and percentage point contributions)

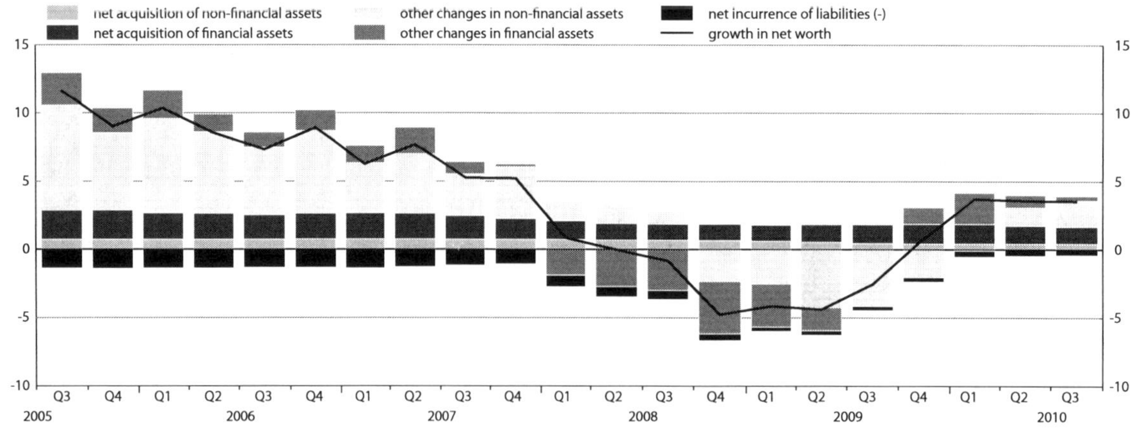

Source: European Central Bank.

c) Household asset and liability revaluations

9.52. Assets and liabilities represent the stocks within the integrated system of institutional sector accounts. Financial transactions reflect the financing and financial investment decisions during a period of time. Changes in the outstanding amounts are the result of such transactions, as well as of revaluations and other changes in the volume of assets and liabilities such as write-offs of loans or reclassifications of institutional units or financial instruments.

9.53. Institutional sector accounts allow changes in asset prices (measured as holding gains or losses) to be monitored. The basic accounting tool is the revaluation account reflecting these price changes.

9.54. Household balance sheet data display substantial holding gains or losses for the holdings of housing wealth or equity and investment fund shares or units linked to rises or falls in house prices or stock exchange prices.

9.55. The other changes of such assets, but not the other changes in liabilities, are rather important in the context of changes in household wealth or in household net worth as indicated in figure 9.2. In particular, the movement in households' financial wealth is somewhat correlated with stock market indices in countries where a large portion of household financial wealth is held in equity securities, such as in the United States and the United Kingdom.

(d) Household debt and saving

9.56. Two further indicators, household debt and saving, may be used for the analysis of household finance. Household debt should be shown non-consolidated and with market valuation. Loans and other accounts payable are usually the only financial instruments to be covered as liabilities. Nevertheless, it should be taken into consideration that, in the context of the analysis, household debt is a less relevant indicator than household net worth or net financial wealth (financial assets less liabilities) given that households often hold significant amounts of assets.

9.57. Combining the financial account with the capital account of households broadens the scope of the analysis. This leads to a relatively broad presentation covering investment as a whole (financial and non-financial investment), as well as financing (net saving, net capital transfers and net incurrence of liabilities) (table 9.7). *Household saving* may be derived from this table. It refers to gross saving which comprises net saving and consumption of fixed capital.[200] As consumption of fixed capital is not sufficiently harmonized across countries, *gross saving* should be used for comparisons instead of net saving.

9.58. It is possible to complement the investment and financing analysis by further integrating components taken from the production and the income accounts. The link with real variables allows a study of the interrelation between financial and real variables, which also refers to the monetary policy transmission process, as reflected in income and wealth effects of households but also of other institutional sectors.

Table 9.7
Saving, investment and financing of households

Changes in assets	Transaction	Changes in liabilities and net worth
	Financing	261
	Changes in net worth due to saving and capital transfers	200
	Saving, net	185
	Capital transfers, receivable	23
	Capital transfers, payable	-8
	Net incurrence of liabilities	61
261	*Investment*	
47	Non-financial investment	
80	Gross fixed capital formation	
-45	Consumption of fixed capital (-)	
2	Changes in inventories	
5	Acquisitions less disposals of valuables	
5	Acquisitions less disposals of non-produced/non-financial assets	
214	Net acquisition of financial assets	

4. Government finance

9.59. The main indicators used for fiscal policy analysis are general government deficit, expenditure, revenue and debt. The methodological differences between country data are often related to the sector delineation. Public corporations are sometimes reclassified as government units based on specific classification criteria. Moreover, at times only central government data may be available rather than general government data.

9.60. General government as a resident institutional sector must be distinguished from the public sector.[201] The general government sector comprises all institutional units which are delineated in line with their principal economic function: either the provision of goods and services to the community or to individual households at prices that are economically insignificant; or, the redistribution of income and wealth by means of

[200] The concept of "gross saving" must be distinguished from gross debt for which gross positions of the liabilities side of a balance sheet are aggregated.

[201] In the European Union the so-called "50 per cent criterion" is used together with a qualitative analysis for deciding which entities are to be classified inside general government. The "50 per cent criterion" concept does not exist explicitly in the 2008 SNA.

transfer payments. Both of these activities are financed primarily by taxes or by transfers from other government units. The public sector covers general government and all public non-financial and financial corporations.

(a) Government deficit

9.61. General government deficit (or surplus) is derived as the balancing item of general government revenue minus expenditure (outlays). It corresponds to the balancing item of the capital account or of the financial account of general government (net lending (+)/net borrowing (–), B9). In principle, there should be no discrepancy between both balancing items. However, discrepancies may be observed because of the different data sources used and the estimation methods applied to compile the accounts.[202]

9.62. A negative value of net lending/net borrowing indicates that government expenditure is higher than government revenue. This means that liabilities need to be incurred (such as selling government bonds), or financial assets need to be disposed of (such as running down bank deposits), which yield cash resources to fund an excess of expenditure over revenue. Government net lending (+)/net borrowing (-) is therefore also equal to the difference between the net acquisition of financial assets and the net incurrence of liabilities. Both are shown in the financial account, which reveals the details of how governments meet their borrowing requirements.

(b) Government debt

9.63. Government debt may be presented non-consolidated and consolidated. Reference is usually made to consolidated gross general government debt, that is, intrageneral government debt positions are consolidated and gross positions are applied. General government debt may be reported at nominal value as defined in the 2008 SNA.[203]

9.64. The following financial instruments are considered as debt: SDRs; currency and deposits; debt securities; loans; insurance, pension and standardized guarantee schemes; and other accounts payable. Equity and investment fund shares or units, financial derivatives and employee stock options are not included.

9.65. From the perspective of from-whom-to-whom accounts, a comprehensive fiscal policy analysis deals with questions such as: what are the counterpart sectors of financial investment and financing decisions of general government or of one of its subsectors? Which are the corporations (financial or non-financial, resident or non-resident) in which the government holds a stake? Or, alternatively: who is holding the government debt within the economy or abroad? General government debt data may be provided with a breakdown by holder or creditor. Such data may be split into debt held by residents and by non-residents. Holdings of debt by residents may be further divided into debt held by various institutional sectors, such as the central bank, deposit-taking corporations except the central bank, other financial institutions and other residents. Moreover, general government debt may be presented by original maturity, by residual maturity and by currency denomination.

---

[202] Often, the compilation process for the financial accounts and balance sheets is sufficiently separate from the rest of the accounts that the figures for net lending or net borrowing derived from each are different in practice even though they are conceptually the same. A discrepancy may indicate an error in the financial account or at any place in the accounts leading up to the balance in the capital account. An examination of the differences sector by sector may help identify the most likely sources of error. For example, a large discrepancy on household net borrowing may mean that some household income is not recorded; a large discrepancy in net lending for non-financial corporations may mean that some expenditure on fixed capital has not been recorded. But each discrepancy must be investigated on a case-by-case basis. See the 2008 SNA, para. 18.20.

[203] In the European Union, general government debt is reported as Maastricht debt under the excessive deficit procedure.

(c) Monitoring fiscal developments

9.66. General government indicators are used to monitor fiscal developments within an integrated system of institutional sector accounts. For that purpose, quarterly data are usually applied to assess the implementation of government expenditure, as well as the most recent developments in government revenue. This supports the ongoing monitoring of government finance within the year and allows assessments of the forecasts prepared by general government for the year as a whole. While the quarterly data are somewhat volatile, their seasonal patterns may be reasonably stable. This means that broad trends can be identified in the year-on-year comparisons and may provide reliable indicators for better assessing the forecasts.

9.67. Changes in the quarterly pattern may provide information on possible changes in the trend of government finance during the course of a year that cannot be inferred from a single figure for the year as a whole. For example, the latest annual deficit figure would not reveal whether it was increasing or decreasing during the course of the year or whether there was a turning point within the year.

9.68. The quarterly data may also help to improve the quality and timeliness of government finance statistics in general, including annual data. For example, compilation systems need to be made more automated and robust, and the treatment and recording of new types of transactions, and any potential problems, can be resolved well in advance during the course of the year.

9.69. To better understand the link between quarterly macroeconomic variables and quarterly government revenue, expenditure and financial investment and financing data within a system of institutional sector accounts, the accrual principle of accounting should be applied. This means, with respect to government revenue, that it needs to be recorded in the period in which the economic activity generating the liability to pay the tax takes place; this period may differ from the period in which the actual payment is due. While the accrual principle is generally adhered to, it cannot always be strictly applied in practice. For example, the accrual principle is difficult to apply on a quarterly basis for taxes that are levied annually. While to some extent unavoidable, deviations from the accrual principle complicate the economic analysis of the relationship between government accounts and other macroeconomic variables.

9.70. However, an integrated system of quarterly institutional sector accounts requires an analysis of the interaction between economic developments in the general government sector and the other resident sectors and the rest of the world – by exploring the quarterly profiles of government revenue, expenditure, deficit and debt.

5. Cross-border financial investment and financing

9.71. Globalization and financial integration underline the importance of reliable and timely data on cross-border transactions, other flows and positions.

9.72. Cross-border transactions, other flows and positions are reflected in the corresponding rest of the world accounts. Financial assets acquired and liabilities incurred by non-residents (vis-à-vis resident sectors) are shown as positions in the rest of the world balance sheet (the international investment position) (IIP)); as financial transactions in the rest of the world financial account (part of the balance of payments); and as revaluations or other changes in the volume of assets in the rest of the world accumulation accounts.

9.73. Indicators related to positions in the rest of the world balance sheet may refer to assets and liabilities as shown in the IMF coordinated portfolio investment survey

(CPIS) and coordinated direct investment survey (CDIS), or only to liabilities as for external debt data.

9.74. The purpose of the CPIS is to collect information on the stock of cross-border holdings of portfolio investment in securities (equity securities and short and long-term debt securities).[204] The survey has been conducted annually since 2001. It collects data from more than 75 countries on their year-end portfolio investment positions on the targeted financial instruments with a breakdown by country of issuer.

9.75. The data collected permit a from-whom-to-whom presentation at the level of each financial instrument, showing the holders of the assets vis-à-vis the issuer economies. In addition to this required set of data, the IMF also encourages the reporting of supplementary information that is considered to be useful. The CPIS identifies securities held by resident sectors with a breakdown of sectors into monetary authorities, banks, other financial institutions, general government and the non-financial sector. In addition, the currency breakdown of the securities is shown. In response to data gaps identified in the wake of the financial crisis, a number of enhancements are being made to the survey starting with end-June 2013 data collected in January 2014. These enhancements include conducting the survey on a semi-annual frequency, with data to be reported for both end-June and end-December of each year; accelerating the timeliness of data submissions to – and of data redissemination by – the IMF; and introducing additional voluntarily reported data items on the sector of foreign debtor, and on short (negative) positions. The BPM6-based classification of institutional sectors will also be introduced.

9.76. The CDIS[205] is a worldwide statistical data collection project led by the IMF, in conjunction with its inter-agency partners, including OECD, Eurostat, the European Central Bank and the United Nations Conference on Trade and Development. The survey is conducted on an annual basis starting with end-2009 data. Preliminary data are requested nine months after the end of the reference period and released in December. Revised and more comprehensive data are released in the middle of the following year (with an 18-month lag). The end-2011 survey includes revised data from 100 economies.

9.77. The CDIS collects comprehensive and harmonized data on foreign direct investment (FDI) end-year positions by economy of direct investor (for inward direct investment) and by economy of investment (for outward direct investment). It also provides a number of breakdowns, including separate data on equity and debt positions. The survey collects information on a country-to-country basis but without a breakdown by sector of investor or recipient.[206] The purpose of the survey is to improve the quality of direct investment position statistics in the IIP and by immediate counterpart economy.

9.78. Similarly to debt of other institutional sectors, the external debt of an economy is defined as gross external debt owed to non-residents by residents. It includes all liabilities recognized by the 2008 SNA as financial instruments – except for equity and investment fund shares or units and financial derivatives and employee stock options. Both financial instrument categories are excluded because they do not require the payment of principal or interest.

9.79. Indicators derived from balance of payments statistics may be taken from the accounts for goods and services (trade), income, and current transfers or capital transfers. The accounts for goods, services, income and current transfers represent the current account while capital transfers are covered by the capital account.

---

[204] Information on the CPIS and tables of results (data, metadata) are available from www.imf.org/external/np/sta/pi/cpis.htm.

[205] Information on the CDIS and tables of results (data, metadata) are available from http://cdis.imf.org/.

[206] Nevertheless, some economies report data on net debt broken down into resident financial intermediaries and resident enterprises that are not financial intermediaries.

Box 9.1
Foreign direct investment

Foreign direct investment has become a key factor in international economic integration. Accordingly, regular analysis of FDI developments is an integral part of most macroeconomic and cross-border financial analysis.

FDI positions represent an important class of investment made abroad and received from abroad. As a percentage of GDP, they give one indication of the extent of globalization and the interdependence of economies.

FDI transactions in the financial account of the balance of payments show net acquisition of financial assets and net incurrence of liabilities, including separate data on equity and debt instruments.

Direct investment income provides information on the earnings of direct investors and of direct investment enterprises. Direct investment earnings arise: (a) from distributed earnings as well as undistributed earnings, the latter being treated as if distributed and promptly reinvested in the enterprise; and (b) from interest on intercompany loans, trade credit and other forms of debt.

Further elaboration of the treatment of FDI is one of the features of the BPM6. As explained in chapter 6 of the BPM6, the direct investment relationship extends to affiliated companies with a common direct investor even in the absence of cross-shareholdings between them.

Owing to the (possible) reclassification of SPEs/holdings as part of the new financial corporations subsector captive financial institutions and moneylenders (S127), the financial activities of non-financial corporations and captive financial institutions can be affected by FDI.

9.80. It may be appropriate to focus on the broad concept and combine the current and capital account net lending (+)/net borrowing (-) to/from the rest of the world (as a percentage of GDP). This indicator corresponds to the net lending/net borrowing as derived from the financial account.

D. Macroprudential and financial stability analysis

9.81. Institutional sector accounts are used for macroprudential and financial stability analysis. This involves deriving financial soundness indicators from the financial balance sheets or the transaction accounts of resident sectors, specifically of households. Changes in households' (financial) wealth and in households' indebtedness may indicate mismatches between assets and liabilities. They may have important consequences for the cost and availability of financing and, in turn, an impact on investment and consumption and, eventually, on price developments.

9.82. The use of institutional sector accounts for macroprudential and financial stability analysis may be rather limited with regard to non-financial corporations in comparison with the other types of macroeconomic analysis as described above owing to limited information on corporate group structures, off-balance-sheet items and provisions.

9.83. Taking into account the conceptual differences that exist between the 2008 SNA and the financial stability analysis framework, national accounts data are seen as a complementary data set to consolidated data for groups of corporations. However, the institutional sector accounts data could be used as a starting point for a network analysis.

9.84. As a first step, the different concepts have to be explained and their various elements compared.

Figure 9.3
The system of national accounts approach and the corporate group approach

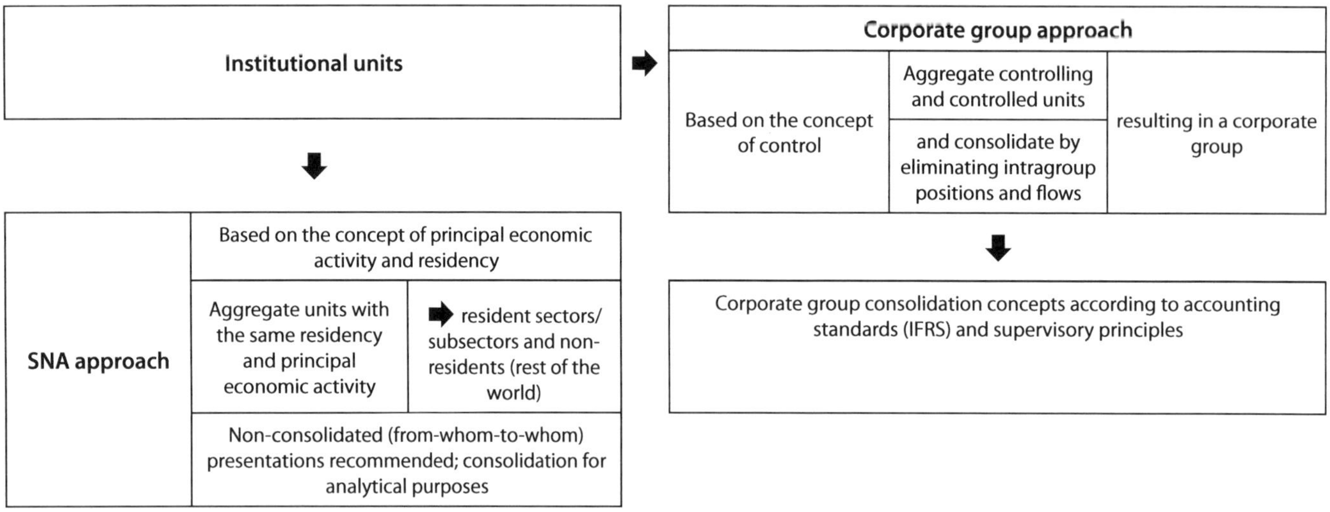

1. The system of national accounts approach and the corporate group approach

9.85. The national accounts concept based on the 2008 SNA (the "SNA approach") defines institutional units, which are aggregated in sectors and subsectors based on their residency and principal economic activity. The aggregated data are non-consolidated (from-whom-to-whom); however, consolidation by national economy, sector or subsector is applied in various cases for analytical or policy purposes.[207] Figure 9.3 illustrates this approach.

9.86. The definition of institutional units is also the starting point for explaining the corporate group approach. Based on the concept of control, controlling and controlled units are aggregated and also consolidated by eliminating intragroup positions and flows, resulting in a corporate group.

9.87. The controlling and controlled units forming a corporate group usually belong (in terms of the SNA approach) to different economies and also to different sectors or subsectors. It is therefore nearly impossible to reconcile the aggregated data based on the SNA approach and the data based on the corporate group approach. One option, however, is to truncate a corporate group into different subgroups of units with different residencies and belonging to various resident sectors.

9.88. Other modifications emerge from different consolidation concepts as they are applied according to international accounting standards (IFRS) and supervisory principles.

9.89. Based on these two concepts, different data requirements need to be specified as outlined in table 9.8. As monetary policy analysis and other types of macroeconomic policy analysis are based on international statistical standards (the SNA approach), data need to be provided according to institutional sectors. Data for financial stability purposes refer to the corporate group approach.

[207] Data on monetary financial institutions or general government, for example, are usually presented consolidated.

Table 9.8
Statistical requirements for monetary policy and for financial stability purposes

Requirement	SNA approach (international statistical standards) for monetary policy purposes	Corporate group approach for financial stability purposes
Reporting population	Monetary financial institutions, other financial corporations, non-financial sectors and rest of the world	Large corporate groups (financial corporate groups and non-financial corporate groups)
Residency	Host country approach	Primarily home country approach complemented by host country approach
Geographical consolidation	Non-consolidated	Primarily consolidated complemented by non-consolidated
Institutional consolidation	Non-consolidated[a]	Consolidated, including other financial institutions belonging to the same financial corporate group
Valuation	Market value	Market value/book value
Instrument breakdown	Basic (financial instruments according to 2008 SNA: currency and deposits (F2); debt securities (F3); loans (F4); equity and investment fund shares or units (F5); insurance, pension and standardized guarantee schemes (F6); financial derivatives and employee stock options (F7); other accounts receivable/payable (F8))	Detailed (e.g. syndicated loans, subordinated debt, e-business, etc.)
Maturity	Original maturity	Residual maturity

[a] Consolidation, however, is permitted under certain conditions within the national territory; hence, for statistical reporting purposes, an MFI can consolidate its domestic offices, but not its offices located outside the country.

9.90. International statistical standards make a clear distinction between resident and non-resident and between institutional sectors; they also treat transactions and other flows (revaluations and other volume changes) relating to assets and liabilities separately. These standards are observed in the integrated institutional sector accounts and in monetary statistics and other financial institutions and markets data compiled principally for monetary policy purposes.

9.91. Thus, for example, banking statistics, and the monetary aggregates derived from them, cover the balance sheets, transactions and other (non-transactional) flows of institutions classified as monetary financial institutions, which are resident in the country concerned, regardless of where the head office is located, and they exclude the business of foreign branches of resident monetary financial institutions. Moreover, they exclude the business of subsidiaries of monetary financial institutions which are not themselves monetary financial institutions but (for example) leasing companies or grantors of consumer credit – such entities are "other" (non-monetary) financial intermediaries. The statistics do not merge transactions and other flows or do not combine institutional units of different sectors or residency.

9.92. Statistical data used for macroprudential and financial stability purposes focus on the business of the whole corporate group. The data are accordingly consolidated across national boundaries to also include the business of foreign banking branches, and they may be consolidated across sector boundaries to include the business of financial subsidiaries, which are not banks (or monetary financial corporations). The content of the information is also somewhat different. Although supervisors use the sectoral distinctions and the detailed financial instruments reported for statistical purposes, they are very much interested in measuring risks (such as counterparty credit or market risk).

9.93. Compared with the proposed breakdown for financial stability purposes, the number of categories of financial assets and liabilities in the financial account and in the balance sheet is rather limited.

9.94. For financial stability purposes, there is some interest in collecting more detailed balance sheet data, as well as off-balance-sheet data, such as provisions and contingencies.

2. The system of national accounts approach applied to macroprudential and financial stability analysis

9.95. Institutional sector accounts in the context of the 2008 SNA are useful to ascertain:

(a) The vulnerabilities inherent in the balance sheet positions of resident sectors, such as general government, non-financial corporations, households and also of non-residents;

(b) The conditions in markets to which several of these sectors are exposed, such as the real estate markets;

(c) The financial and real sector linkages within an economy.

9.96. Institutional sector accounts provide a consistent source of constructing time series for leverage measures across the different sectors and subsectors. The analysis of balance sheets and risk networks is especially useful for macroprudential purposes; attention should be paid to the vulnerabilities arising from the interlinkages between institutional units aggregated in the various financial corporations subsectors. Sectors with high debt relative to their liquid assets tend to be vulnerable to asset price decreases.

9.97. The soundness of the financial system depends crucially on the sustainability of the level of corporate and household debt. From the financing side, corporate indebtedness and leverage are recognized as key indicators for identifying asset bubbles and financial distress.[208] In combination with credit growth, information on external (non-deposit) funding of banks and asset prices can help to detect dangerous economy-wide leverage.

9.98. Measures of fragility show an extraordinary increase in debt financing (in relation to income variables), a shift from long-term to short-term debt, an increase in speculative activities (asset markets) and a reduction in margins of safety for financial corporations. Sudden and significant rises in interest rates can lead to increases in debt write-offs, non-performing loans and debt arrears and, consequently, to systemic risk and financial crises, with contagious bank runs and a resulting inability to make payments or allocate credit.

9.99. From the non-financial side, "income-based financial fragility indicators" together with efficiency and profitability measures provide valuable information on the potential to honour commitments, that is to repay debt. Measures of the financing gap[209] supply information on the efficiency and continuity of the business, that is it provides an indication of the ability of the institution to regenerate and grow using internal cash flows (own funds). The real side also offers a rich set of information to be used in "stress testing", scenario analysis and macroeconomic modelling of the stability of the financial system, enabling a timely identification of potential instability pressures.

9.100. In summary, as indicated in figure 9.4, national accounts play a major role in the compilation of certain macroprudential indicators (MPIs) – such as debt-to-GDP ratios and the financial health of the non-financial sectors – as well as in financial structure analysis, including an assessment of the importance of the main financial instruments, the ownership structure and concentration measures for financial and non-financial corporations.

[208] See Jaeger (2003) and Teplin (2001).

[209] This is the difference between internal funds (saving) and investment.

Figure 9.4
Use of national accounts in macroprudential analysis

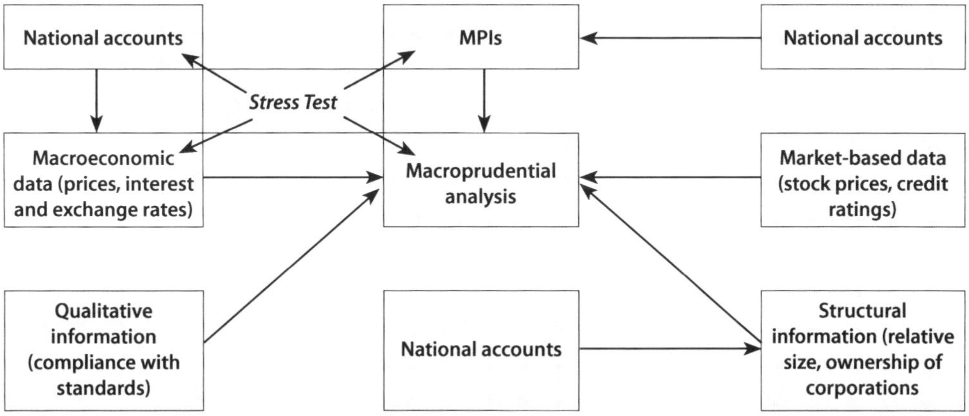

Abbreviation: MPIs, macroprudential indicators.
Source: Sundararajan and others (2002) – modified.

E. Some examples of quarterly sector accounts

1. The United States flow of funds accounts

9.101. The United States flows of funds accounts provide quarterly data on financial transactions and balance sheets by sector.[210] They combine transactions taken from the national income and product accounts (income and capital account) with the financial transactions (financial account) to show total sources and uses of funds by sector.

9.102. The history and continued interest in the United States in the flow of funds accounts suggest that they have been valued highly by policymakers at the Federal Reserve Board. But the accounts are only one set of data in a large mass of information that is used by the authorities. Moreover, the role of the flow of funds accounts in policymaking has changed over the past half-century.

9.103. Fifty years ago, the data on economic developments were less timely. National accounts were in their infancy and special reports on output, employment, prices, and financial market developments were only beginning to be developed and used. Economists were starting to build statistical models of the economy; the data needed for estimation and even the statistical techniques and computational facilities were not widely available. By today's standards, financial markets were less complicated, even if trends and cyclical changes were just as difficult to understand and predict.

9.104. Quarterly flow of funds accounts still play a role even with the increased availability of more timely detailed information on the economy. Data in the accounts may never provide headline news, but they can be important:

(a) The flow of funds accounts provide a logical framework for summarizing much of the financial information received in other forms;

(b) The accounts provide the necessary history (background) for analytical work. All economists search for precedents or "fundamental" relationships that will tell something about future developments. Even if history will not repeat itself, the accounts may provide an indication of what might be different this time;

[210] Available from www.federalreserve.gov/releases/z1/.

(c) To the extent that models are used, the data in financial accounts provide consistent time series that can be applied to derive relationships between financial sectors or between financial and real economic variables;

(d) The accounts frequently provide a perspective from which to support or refute conflicting information from other sources.

9.105. Central to monetary policy decision-making in the United States is an analysis of the current state of the economy and a detailed forecast of non-financial and financial developments, conditioned on assumptions about the path of interest rates, foreign exchange rates and fiscal policy. Obviously, the interest rate assumptions depend in part on a base case for the degree of ease or tightness of monetary policy over the forecast period. Generally, the forecasts prepared provide information to assist the Federal Open Market Committee in making decisions based on its objectives for inflation.

9.106. It is important to keep in mind that the forecast is a staff forecast: the staff determine the assumptions. Policy committee members may (and frequently do) disagree with both the assumptions and projected outcomes. Nonetheless, the overall economic forecast is a central element of the decision-making process because it provides a baseline for committee discussions.

9.107. Within this process is a flow of funds forecast, which is conditioned on the same assumptions. It is, in essence, a description of how economic activity on the real side will be financed and how the balance-sheet positions of households and corporations will change.

9.108. The flow of funds forecast provides a number of tools useful for policy analysis by staff and ultimately by the policy committee:

(a) First, it offers a standardized summary of the way the financial markets might evolve in the period ahead. But it is not limited to the growth of the monetary aggregates or to banking developments. It also contains a summary of projected activity in bond and government security markets, consumer finance, and household and business balance sheet changes. Each of these elements has been developed, or forecast, paying careful attention to the projected path of inflation and non-financial economic activity by sector;

(b) Second, the flow of funds forecast offers an opportunity to evaluate likely changes in credit conditions and the possible impediments, or lack of impediments, to growth of real activity that those conditions imply. Interest rate risk spreads, business and consumer debt default rates, and terms and standards at banks and other intermediaries must be taken into account. Credit factors can be considered without a flow of funds forecast, but the forecast provides a way of quantifying the effects on the financial side;

(c) Third, the flow of funds forecast adds a check (one of several) on the consistency of other fundamental elements of the forecast. Borrowing forecasts are made in the light of income and profit forecasts, consumption is dependent in part on balance sheet considerations, and business investment forecasts consider liquidity constraints;

(d) Fourth, the flow of funds forecast offers a basis for evaluating monthly and weekly information on financial flows as it arrives between policy committee meetings.

9.109. Some examples of relationships featured in the flow of funds forecast help illustrate:

(a) The flow of funds accounts offer an analysis of corporate financing needs over the forecast period. Corporate borrowing may certainly be of interest

Box 9.2

Forecasts, household net worth and debt growth derived from the United States flow of funds accounts (provided by the Federal Reserve Board)

Forecasts

The accounts are used for monetary policy purposes. An economic forecast that integrates the flow of funds accounts with other macroeconomic accounts provides an opportunity to quantify the effects of likely changes in credit conditions on the growth of real activity.

A flow of funds forecast also adds a check on the consistency of other elements of an economic forecast, because balance sheet conditions and access to credit and other external funds can be factors underlying the spending and production decisions of households, businesses and governments.[a]

Because the flow of funds accounts provide a logical framework for summarizing independent forecasts of financial and non-financial information, we use a simplified version of the accounts to construct the financial forecast for the Federal Open Market Committee.[b]

Forecasts are received for such items as GDP, balance of payments, bank lending and deposits, mortgages, consumer credit, bond and equity issuance, and federal government borrowing. By feeding these independently made forecasts into a flow of funds framework, we can check their consistency with each other. Another benefit of using a flow of funds framework for the projection is that it provides consistent time series for many years, allowing relationships to be derived between sectors or between financial and real economic variables.

Household net worth

The Federal Reserve has a model of the macroeconomy in which household consumption is modelled following the "life cycle" theory of consumption. According to this theory, household net worth is a critical variable in explaining and predicting consumption.

Households that are not credit constrained are assumed to smooth their consumption over time. That is, in principle, households spend 1/T per cent of their net worth each year, where T is the time remaining to their death. Of course, this is a simplistic view of the life-cycle theory, which can be altered to take into account factors such as bequest motives. Nevertheless, household net worth is a key element in this equation and is only available quarterly from the flow of funds accounts.

Debt growth

One aspect of the forecast that policymakers often focus on is the debt growth of the domestic non-financial sectors, which has averaged around 6 per cent for the past 20 years.

Figure 9.2.1

Debt growth of the domestic non-financial sectors in the United States

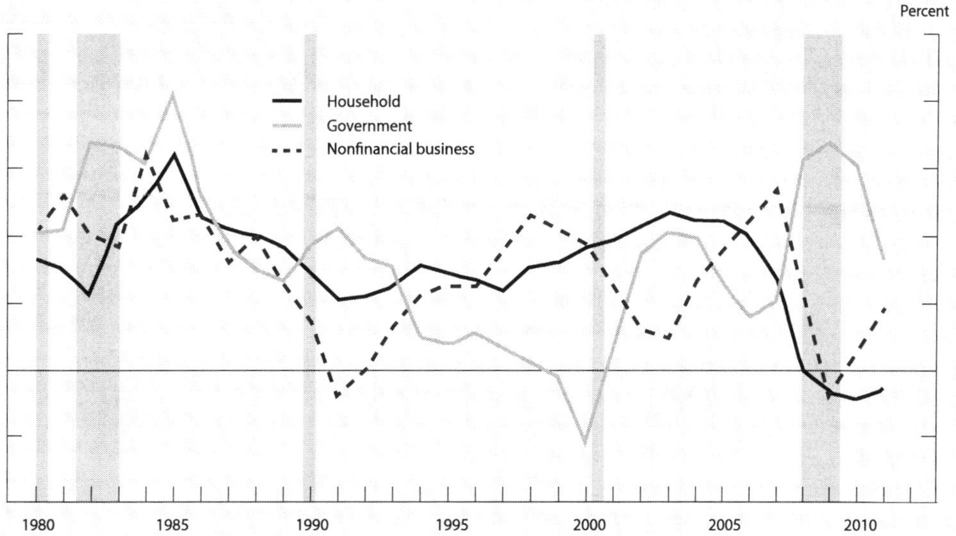

Source: Flow of Funds Accounts of the United States, June 7, 2012

However, when you decompose total debt growth by sector, as shown annually on the chart above, a much more interesting picture is revealed. For the combined government sector, both federal and state and local (grey line), debt growth accelerated before recessions (represented by the shaded bars), reaching close to 20 per cent at its peak. By contrast, non-financial business debt growth (broken line) begins to slow before recessions and actually contracts by the end of the most recent one, similar to that recorded in the early 1990s. Household debt growth (black line), on the other hand, tended to be less volatile until the last few years when household debt contracted for the first time ever recorded in the flow of funds accounts and has yet to recover.

[a] Teplin (2001).

[b] McIntosh and Ball Holmquist (2012).

in itself, but it is also a major component of domestic debt. An analysis of the factors that determine corporate borrowing can give feedback on other elements of the economic forecast;

(b) The flow of funds forecast also allows projections of household wealth to be derived. Changes in wealth have been fundamental to understanding the forces driving United States economic growth – in particular the effect that wealth has on consumption.

9.110. In recent years the Federal Reserve has worked with the Bureau of Economic Analysis in the Department of Commerce to combine information in the flow of funds accounts, the national income and product accounts, and the balance of payments accounts to produce a comprehensive set of 1993 SNA tables for the United States. These are referred to as the integrated macroeconomic accounts.

9.111. In the United States the compilation of financial accounts has proved to be of considerable value to policymakers. Over time, the particular uses of the accounts have changed along with the intensity of their use depending on the issues that are of immediate interest. Questions dealing with debt expansion have been common, however, and balance sheet effects have become particularly important of late. However, there are significant limitations to the use of the accounts. As with any other tool, the data should be interpreted with caution, and frequent recourse to supplementary material is advised.

9.112. Building and maintaining financial accounts can be seen as an investment to improve policymaking now and in the future. Compilers must monitor the need to amend the data and structure of their accounts in order to maintain them as effective tools for their primary clients.

2. Quarterly euro area accounts

9.113. The first quarterly euro area integrated economic and financial accounts by institutional sector were published in May 2007. (The first annual accounts were published a year earlier;[211] the European Central Bank had for some years published partial accounts covering the non-financial sectors in the euro area.)[212] These accounts, the result of a joint initiative with Eurostat (which produces the current and capital accounts), bring together all economic and financial transactions of the main institutional sectors in the euro area, with balance sheets recording financial assets and liabilities, and reconciliation accounts showing revaluations and other changes in the volume of assets and liabilities.

9.114. The euro area accounts provide comprehensive information not only on the economic activities of households (including NPISHs), non-financial corporations, financial corporations and general government, but also on the interactions between these sectors and the rest of the world. In addition, the euro area accounts link financial and non-financial statistics, thereby allowing for an integrated analysis of non-financial economic activities (such as gross fixed capital formation) and financial transactions (such as the issuance of debt). They also contain complete and consistent financial balance sheets, which provide, together with a largely complete description of produced non-financial assets and households' housing wealth, a good indication of the total balance sheet of the various sectors. An integral part of the accounts is the from-whom-to-whom detail currently available for deposits, loans, debt securities and equity and investment fund shares or units in both transactions and outstanding amounts.

[211] Those accounts are still compiled on the basis of the ESA 95. There is an action plan regarding the compilation and publication of data according to the ESA 2010, which is consistent with the 2008 SNA.

[212] Available from www.ecb.int/stats/acc/html/index.en.html.

9.115. The institutional sector accounts are designed in such a way that they comply with the needs centred on the monetary transmission mechanism. How does the European Central Bank monetary policy affect the euro area economy? Through which channels does the monetary policy operate?

9.116. Monetary policy is transmitted from the "monetary" sector of the euro area economy to the "real" sectors. This view focuses on the relative importance of the different links between the two groups of sectors. The theory of monetary policy, of how monetary impulses are supposed to affect income and expenditure, specifies a large number of "transmission channels", in essence, the "direct effects" and "cost-of-capital channels".

9.117. Institutional sector accounts are an analytical tool to represent the euro area economy, its sectors and transactions and the various "transmission channels" in an integrated framework. In this context, the portfolio approach analyses European Central Bank monetary policy in the context of wealth holders' decisions on expenditure. Wealth holders' decisions on expenditure are linked to corresponding flows of assets between sectors and to the changes in stocks of assets and liabilities.

9.118. The "portfolio-equilibrium approach" is the most appropriate framework in which to combine institutional sector accounts with the European Central Bank monetary policy analysis. In this approach, households, financial or non-financial corporations and government are seen as the institutional units in an economy efficiently managing their portfolios, that is, their stocks of assets and liabilities, including money (although money as the transaction medium may be considered to have specific features and importance).[213] Management comprises, besides the structure of stocks, decisions on transactions (financial and non-financial, such as the net acquisition of assets, the net incurrence of liabilities, production, income, consumption or saving) and other flows – especially changes in prices (measured as holding gains or losses). The basic accounting tools reflecting these activities are balance sheets as well as transactions and other flow accounts.

9.119. The approach focuses on the consideration of wealth holders' decisions on investment – financial or non-financial – and represents a generalization of the treatment of money, with its special characteristics, as one among the wide range of assets, which are alternative ways of holding wealth. The demand for money is seen as a decision in creating an optimal portfolio, the choice among assets being determined by a trade-off between rates of return and "liquidity services". All transactions are covered which contribute to the accumulation of assets held and liabilities incurred by sectors within a period. Saving, net capital transfers and net incurrence of liabilities (financing) are used to acquire non-financial and financial assets (investment). There is a strict requirement for each sector that its investment must be equal to its financing.

9.120. A further implication of the portfolio-equilibrium approach is to monitor the structure of interest rates and asset prices as well as the corresponding income and expenditure components resulting from assets and liabilities. Asset prices may be derived from price changes as part of changes in stocks, thus allowing the holding gains and losses of the various sectors to be determined.

9.121. While a dichotomy is evident between financial and non-financial analysis, this is neglected in the portfolio-equilibrium approach. The activities of the non-financial and the financial sectors are treated simultaneously, since sectors' portfolio decisions are considered to be interrelated. Nevertheless, assets and liabilities are broken down in relation to their economic use, liquidity and maturity, as well as their tradability and volatility, etc.

[213] Backus and others (1980).

9.122. The European Central Bank's monetary policy strategy comprises, inter alia, a two-pillar approach to the analysis of the risks to price stability: economic analysis and monetary analysis. The institutional sector accounts are designed in such a way to enhance this analysis. The accounts are a tool, which allows a cross-check of the information stemming from the short-term economic analysis with that from the monetary analysis. Such a cross-check ensures that monetary policy maintains a firm medium-term orientation beyond the conventional projection horizon, thus helping to discourage excessive policy activism and overly ambitious attempts to fine-tune economic developments.

9.123. The two-pillar structure does not partition the information set or allocate indicators rigidly to one pillar or another. Exploiting the complementarities between information variables under the two pillars is seen as the best way to ensure that all the relevant information for assessing price developments is used in a consistent and efficient manner, facilitating both the decision-making process and its communication.

9.124. Institutional sector accounts help to assess the likely impact of interest rate changes on spending decisions, allowing a deeper understanding of the monetary policy transmission process and therefore a proper calibration of monetary policy instruments.

3. The International Monetary Fund balance sheet approach

9.125. Compared with the more traditional examination of transaction data, the balance sheet approach (BSA) focuses on the analysis of stock data in an economy's sectoral balance sheets and its aggregate balance sheet, financial and non-financial assets, liabilities and net worth.

9.126. This approach to the analysis of financial stability involves an institutional sector approach as developed for various countries. It is distinctive in that the focus of attention is not solely on the activity and strength of the economy as a whole vis-à-vis the rest of the world, but also within the economy and in the interrelations between institutional sectors and subsectors. The sectors covered may be further divided into subsectors, such as the financial corporations subsectors, for example the central bank, deposit-taking corporations except the central bank and other financial corporations.

9.127. The BSA provides important insights into balance sheet mismatches that can exacerbate a sector's vulnerability to shocks, and helps identify interlinkages between sectors that may increase spillover risks. Such institutions as the IMF or the European Central Bank stress the advantages of the BSA in monitoring and supervising financial activity, alongside the analysis of financial stability, in terms of assessing the quality and diversification of each sector's and subsector's portfolio of assets and liabilities, identifying points of weaknesses in the financial system, measuring exposure to sectoral financial risks, mapping the connections between the sectors and assessing the dynamics between them in times of shocks.[214]

9.128. The framework for assessing balance sheet risks may focus on four types of balance sheet mismatches, all of which help to determine the ability of a country, sector or subsector to service debt in the face of shocks:

(a) Maturity mismatches, where a gap between liabilities due in the short term and liquid assets leaves a sector or subsector unable to honour its contrac-

[214] See, for example, the most recent issues of the IMF Global Financial Stability Report and the ECB Financial Stability Review.

Box 9.3
Compiling sectoral accounts during the recent financial crisis

The compilation of sectoral accounts during the recent financial crisis clearly illustrates their usefulness as a tool for cross-checking the consistency of statistical data sources. The accounts are compiled based on the confrontation of the various statistical sources. This process reveals the various inconsistencies in terms of coverage, valuation and accounting treatment in general and provides useful insights into the reasons behind such inconsistencies.

The financial crisis that began in mid-2007, intensified in 2008 and evolved into a recession in many economies posed a number of compilation difficulties not experienced before. The unprecedented magnitude of the financial transactions involved brought about a substantial increase in inconsistencies in the source data. Similarly, large movements in asset prices resulted in significant revaluations, which exacerbated the difficulties in balancing the data of other economic flows.

Under such circumstances, it is of utmost importance to have a broad set of metadata to improve the compilation process. The metadata should comprise information on major financial transactions, other changes in the volume of assets and liabilities, data revisions and on major balancing adjustments made on the source data.

During the financial crisis, the sheer size of some of the transactions and of other flows made it difficult to interpret specific developments, which in previous periods had been rather stable and showed a somewhat smooth pattern.

This was also the case for short selling transactions during 2008. These transactions – arising when an institutional unit sells assets of which it is not the legal owner, for example borrowed through securities lending – may be treated differently in various statistical sources. Monetary statistics may treat such short selling as an incurrence of a liability, while balance of payments statistics may treat it as a disposal of an asset (even if it is not owned, therefore giving rise to a negative stock). This difference in treatment can lead to horizontal imbalances both for the asset sold short and for the liability registered by a deposit-taking corporation.

Prior to the crisis, the amounts involved were high, but there was also a very high turnover, implying that new short positions would offset expiring short positions, resulting in a minor impact on discrepancies. However, as new short operations more or less disappeared overnight during the most severe phases of the financial crisis, the unwinding of existing positions suddenly became apparent, causing massive discrepancies. The availability of metadata proved crucial to disentangle and minimize the discrepancies.

Metadata were also useful in providing information on mergers and acquisitions or on other operations between large corporations during the financial crisis. New phenomena were observed when compiling the accounts, such as retained securitizations – securitizations fully subscribed by the originator – to gain access to repo financing. Moreover, large transactions started to unfold, such as massive government interventions in financially distressed banks. More generally, sizeable changes in financing and investment patterns emerged, notably the sharp substitution of bank financing with financing through financial markets, and large household portfolio shifts towards monetary assets, afterwards substituted with other short-term financial assets. As a result, there was a move from bank-related channels to other forms of financial intermediation.

tual commitments if the market declines to roll over debt, or creates exposure to the risk that interest rates will rise;

(b) Currency mismatches, where a change in the exchange rate leads to a capital loss;

(c) Capital structure problems, where a heavy reliance on debt rather than equity financing leaves a firm or bank less able to withstand revenue shocks;

(d) Solvency problems, where assets are insufficient to cover liabilities, including contingent liabilities.

9.129. Maturity mismatches, currency mismatches and a poor capital structure can increase the risk of a negative shock to cause liquidity problems or contribute to solvency risk. Liquidity problems are generally associated with inadequate resources to cover short-term payment requirements. Solvency risk can also arise from simply borrowing too much or from investing in low-yielding assets. Nevertheless, off-balance-sheet commitments, usually treated as contingencies in the 2008 SNA, may exist. Liquidity and solvency problems might be separate events, but can be interrelated, for example when solvency problems spill over to liquidity problems, or repeated liquidity problems raise concerns about solvency.

9.130. From this perspective, a financial crisis can occur when there is a fall in demand for financial assets of one or more sectors. Creditors may lose confidence in a country's ability to earn foreign exchange to service the external debt, in the government's ability to service its debt, in the banking system's ability to meet deposit outflows, or in the ability of households or non-financial corporations to repay loans and other debt.[215]

9.131. Table 9.9 shows a simplified version of the BSA matrix. As the liabilities in the BSA matrix are consolidated sectoral data, the matrix's diagonal (shaded boxes) of intrasectoral holdings remains empty.

Table 9.9
A simplified balance sheet approach presentation of intersectoral positions of financial assets and liabilities

Issuer of the liability (debtor)	Holder of the liability (creditor)	General government	Financial corporations (including central bank)	Non-financial corporations	Rest of the world	Total
	General government					
Domestic currency						
Total other liabilities						
short-term						
in foreign currency						
in domestic currency						
medium- and long-term						
in foreign currency						
in domestic currency						
	Financial sector (including central bank)					
Total liabilities						
deposits and other short-term						
in foreign currency						
in domestic currency						
medium- and long-term						
in foreign currency						
in domestic currency						
Equity (capital)						
	Non-financial sector					
Total liabilities						
short-term						
in foreign currency						
in domestic currency						
medium- and long-term						
in foreign currency						
in domestic currency						
Equity (capital)						
	Rest of the world					
(all in foreign currency)	**Total liabilities**					
	currency and short term					
	medium and long term					
	Equity					

Note: Short-term maturity refers to short-term original maturity; medium- and long-term refers to long-term original maturity.

[215] See Allen and others (2002); Gray, Merton and Bodie (2002); and Mink (2005).

9.132. The BSA refers to the SNA balance sheets but is limited to analysing only positions of financial assets and liabilities. It shows, for each financial instrument, the sector incurring the liability (the debtor) and the sector acquiring the counterpart asset (the creditor). In other words, it corresponds to the "detail" of the flow of funds in the SNA.

9.133. The sector breakdown of the BSA matrices consists of the general government, the financial sector and its subsectors, non-financial corporations, other resident sectors and the rest of the world. The currency denominations and the maturity (original) breakdowns of assets and liabilities play an important role in classifying assets and liabilities in the BSA framework. The classification of financial instruments by category follows the SNA, but the new breakdowns by subcategory are recommended, although data are not always available.

9.134. The main sources are data reported periodically to the IMF, including the standardized report forms for monetary statistics. As at July 2013, 33 countries report data for all the subsectors of financial corporations (central banks, other deposit-taking corporations and other financial corporations). Reports covering only the central banks and the other deposit-taking corporations are received from 137 countries (including the countries in the euro area). Other data sources for completing a BSA framework include the IIP and the CPIS, as well as the quarterly external debt statistics and the joint external debt hub.

9.135. Three different forms are used to collect data from, respectively: (a) the central banks; (b) deposit-taking corporations except the central bank; and (c) other financial corporations, if available. Data on financial assets and liabilities are collected for the main categories of financial instruments used in the SNA with a breakdown by currency (national and foreign currency) and original maturity.

9.136. The standard sectors considered are: the central bank; deposit-taking corporations except the central bank; other financial corporations; general government (separate data for central, state and local government); non-financial corporations (separate data for public and private non-financial corporations); other resident sectors (households and non-profit institutions serving households); and non-residents. These data provide satisfactory creditor/debtor positions between the financial corporations sector, the other resident sectors and the rest of the world.

Chapter 10
Compilation of financial accounts and balance sheets within monetary and economic unions

References:
2008 SNA
BPM6, Appendix 3, Regional arrangements: currency unions, economic unions, and other regional statements
MFSMCG
GFSM 2014
HSS
Handbook on quarterly financial accounts for the euro area: sources and methods

A. Introduction

10.1. This chapter describes the compilation of financial accounts and balance sheets within monetary and economic unions. It defines three different forms of regional arrangements: monetary and currency unions, economic unions, and customs unions.[216] A monetary union is defined as a situation in which there is the presence of a single monetary policy among economies, established by an intergovernmental legal agreement (e.g. a treaty). A currency union is a monetary union in which national currencies have been replaced by a common currency. Economic unions harmonize certain economic policies to foster greater economic integration. Customs unions have common tariff and other trade policies with non-member economies. Section B deals with monetary and currency unions, section C with economic unions and section D with customs arrangements.

10.2. Methodological issues related to monetary unions are discussed in section B. They raise most of the methodological issues and the essential policy need for monetary union financial accounts and balance sheets. Specific issues refer to the treatment of monetary union central banks, the arrangements for reserves management, and the definition of a domestic currency. Issues related to economic unions are largely a subset of those relevant to monetary unions.

10.3. The compilation of monetary or economic union financial accounts and balance sheets is discussed in section E. It relies on national contributions; it is therefore essential that the union member economies consistently follow internationally agreed standards for the classification of transactions and assets and liabilities and provide adequate metadata describing their methodology.[217]

[216] Appendix 3 of the BPM6, on Regional arrangements: currency unions, economic unions, and other regional statements, deals with methodological issues relevant for different types of regional cooperation. These are monetary (and currency) unions, economic unions and customs unions.

[217] See, for example, the ECB handbook on quarterly financial accounts for the euro area: sources and methods.

B. Monetary unions and currency unions

10.4. A monetary union where national currencies have been replaced with a common currency is a currency union.

1. Economic territory of a monetary or currency union

10.5. The economic territory of a monetary or currency union consists of: (a) the economic territories of the member countries of the union; and (b) the economic territories of the union's institutions.[218]

10.6. If a monetary or currency union and an economic union comprise the same member countries, the economic territories of both are the same. However, if the economic union has more member countries than the monetary union, the monetary union will cover only the economic territories of its member countries and the economic territory of the monetary union central bank.

10.7. To belong to a monetary or currency union, the economy must be a member of the central decision-making body, participate in its regular monetary policy decision-making process, and be subject to its monetary policy decisions. Participation in the monetary policy decision-making process includes representation and voting rights, possibly on a rotating basis, in the central decision-making body.

10.8. In the monetary or currency union, the monetary or currency union central bank is considered as an institutional unit in its own right, owning assets and liabilities on own account. It is non-resident of any monetary or currency union member economy but resident in the monetary or currency union. As an international or supranational financial institution, it acts as the common central bank for the member economies of the monetary or currency union. It should always be attributed to the subsector central bank (S121) of the financial corporations sector (S12). For example, a regional investment bank could be classified as a financial corporation.

10.9. If the monetary or currency union is structured such that the monetary or currency union central bank has its headquarters in one country and national offices in each member country, its headquarters are considered a separate unit resident in the region as a whole and not in any member economy. The national offices, which act as the central bank for the respective member countries, are treated as resident of the country where they are located.

10.10. Non-financial institutions, such as the parliament and other political institutions of the economic union, the court of justice and other legal entities and committees, are covered by the general budget of the economic union and may form one institutional unit, which principally provides non-market services for the benefit of the economic union. This unit should be classified in subsector economic union institutions (S1315) of the general government sector (S13).

10.11. Monetary union-wide incorporation for multi-territory enterprises might create problems in determining the residence of units and the allocation of activities across member economies in which the company has operations, and so present difficulties for national accounts. In some instances, the location of incorporation or registration may not be easily allocated to one specific economy, if the jurisdiction that allows the creation and regulates the entity is at the union level. However, the issue of attribution of residence of multi-territory enterprises also arises in other circumstances, and so the treatment described in paragraphs 4.41 to 4.44 of the BPM6 should be applied to multi-territory enterprises located in a monetary or currency union (or an economic union).

[218] The same applies to other regional arrangements, such as economic unions or customs unions.

2. Centralized and decentralized monetary or currency unions

10.12. There are two kinds of monetary or currency unions. A centralized monetary or currency union has a monetary or currency union central bank owned by the governments of the member countries. Regional branches or agencies of the central bank carry out the central bank operations in each member country. A decentralized monetary or currency union model comprises a monetary or currency union central bank and national central banks that own the monetary or currency union central bank and act as the central bank for the countries where they are located.

10.13. Examples of the centralized model are the Central Bank of West African States, the Bank of Central African States and the Eastern Caribbean Central Bank. The European Central Bank is an example of the decentralized model.

3. Reserve assets and arrangements for reserves management

10.14. Reserve assets shown in the balance of payments and the international investment position of a monetary or currency union should include only those assets that: (a) represent claims on non-residents of the monetary or currency union; and (b) meet the criteria described in chapter 6 of the BPM6. Also, the definition of the reserve assets at the monetary or currency union level and at the member economy level should be the same; in other words, with respect to national data, reserve assets should include only those assets that qualify as reserve assets at the monetary or currency union level.

10.15. Reserve assets in a decentralized monetary or currency union (such as the European Monetary Union) are held by the monetary or currency union national central banks (i.e. the assets are actually recorded on their balance sheets). Nevertheless, the institutional setting may, in certain circumstances, result in some restrictions on the effective control over these assets by the monetary or currency union national central banks. That is, monetary or currency union national central banks may be able to transact in some of the reserve assets only with the agreement of the monetary or currency union central bank, such as to ensure appropriate coordination of reserve activity among monetary or currency union national central banks. Provided that there has been no transfer of ownership to the monetary or currency union central bank and the foreign assets owned by the monetary or currency union national central banks can be mobilized by the monetary or currency union to meet balance of payments needs, that is, are reserve assets of the monetary or currency union, the monetary or currency union national central bank of the member economy should classify them as reserve assets in its national balance of payments and international investment position. This is so even though the monetary or currency union national central bank may not have complete control of their use because of operational constraints at the monetary or currency union level.

4. Definition of a domestic currency in a monetary or currency union

10.16. The currency issued in a monetary or currency union is the domestic currency of the monetary or currency union. It should always be considered a domestic currency from the viewpoint of each member economy, even though a non-resident institution (either another monetary or currency union national central bank or the monetary or currency union central bank) can issue this currency. One consequence is that, in a monetary or currency union, from a national perspective, holdings of domestic currency can be a claim on a non-resident.

Transactions and positions in banknotes

10.17. Transactions and positions in banknotes should be treated according to the same principles as for national data, with non-resident purchases recorded as an increase in external liabilities (credit) and the corresponding entry, such as travel, recorded as appropriate. From a national perspective, holdings of monetary or currency union banknotes issued by a monetary or currency union national central bank in another member economy are external assets at the same time, even though the currency is classified as a domestic currency.

10.18. If the issuer of the banknotes can be identified, such as in the African and the Caribbean currency unions at the time of writing, the methodology described in paragraph A3.42 of appendix 3 of the BPM6 can be applied in the national balance of payments and international investment position data.

10.19. However, when the issuer of the banknotes cannot be identified, such as in the European Monetary Union, where euro banknotes are collectively issued without any indication of the economy of origin, this methodology cannot be strictly applied among the monetary union members, and approximations in national data are needed.

C. Economic unions

10.20. An economic union is a union to which two or more economies belong. Economic unions are established by means of an intergovernmental legal agreement among sovereign countries or jurisdictions with the intention of fostering greater economic integration. In an economic union, some of the legal and economic characteristics associated with a national economic territory are shared among the different countries or jurisdictions.

10.21. Economic unions harmonize certain economic policies to foster greater economic integration. These include: (a) the free movement of goods and services within the economic union and a common tax regime for imports from non-economic union economies (free trade zone); (b) the free movement of finance within the economic union; and (c) the free movement of (individual and legal) persons within the economic union.

10.22. In addition, in an economic union, specific regional organizations are created to support the functioning of the economic union under points (a) to (c) above. Some form of cooperation and coordination in fiscal and monetary policy usually exists within an economic union.

10.23. For the purpose of macroeconomic coordination and cooperation, economic unions formulate specific data requirements including for national accounts or for balance of payments statistics, which help assess such aspects as the degree of integration of the economic union internal market and share of trade with economies outside the economic union.

10.24. At the economic union level, the current account, the capital account and the direct investment account are all relevant for monitoring the economic performance of the economic union. However, as different currencies continue to coexist and the respective monetary authorities set their monetary policy objectives in terms of developments of monetary variables, interest rates and exchange rates, the portfolio and other investment categories are less meaningful at the economic union level. For example, reserve assets of a union other than a monetary union are the sum of the total of the national reserves (without consolidation) – this total has no specific meaning at the union level.

10.25. The economic territory of an economic union consists of the economic territory of the member countries or jurisdictions, and the regional institutions that comprise the same, or a subset, of the same economies and are set up to manage the functioning of the economic union.

10.26. Thus, being a resident of an economy of an economic union necessarily implies being a resident of the economic union, and regional organizations that are within the definition of the economic union territory are also resident. However, regional organizations whose membership of economies is neither the same as, nor a subset of, those in the economic union should be regarded as non-residents of the economic union.

D. Customs arrangements

10.27. Regional integration can take the form of customs arrangements between several economies. In general, these customs arrangements, based on a common customs tariff vis-à-vis non-member economies, do not raise specific issues in terms of financial accounts and balance sheets. However, when customs unions generate cross-border flows, such as through a revenue-sharing formula, the recording of transactions and positions in the international accounts is affected by the institutional and administrative arrangements of the customs union.

10.28. In customs unions, such as the Southern African Customs Union, there may be a cooperative approach among members to levying, collecting and distributing customs duties. How and when these functions are undertaken is important for determining the appropriate recording approach. One or all of these functions may be assigned to one economy specifically, to all the member economies collectively, or to a designated international agency created by the members. Most importantly, economies in a customs union are encouraged to agree on common and appropriate statistical recording for the benefit of regional consistency and comparability.

E. Monetary union financial accounts and balance sheets

1. National accounts and monetary union accounts

10.29. The focus of the 2008 SNA is accounts for a national economy. Compiling accounts for a monetary union raises the question of how far (national) resident institutional sector accounts can be aggregated across a monetary union to give conceptually equivalent results across the union as a whole.

10.30. Monetary union accounts are conceptually not equal to the sum of the national accounts of the member countries after conversion to a common currency. The accounts of resident union institutions need to be added. Moreover, cross-border transactions, other flows and positions between member countries have to be withdrawn from the national rest of the world accounts.

10.31. Particular attention should be paid in monetary union accounts to the definition of resident units, to the rest of the world accounts and the netting of intra-union transactions, other flows and positions.

10.32. When the national accounts of countries A and B are aggregated, the aggregated rest of the world accounts record intra-transactions, other flows and positions between countries A and B, with other countries and with economic and monetary union institutions.

10.33. The monetary union is considered as a single economy: the accounts of the union institutions are included and only transactions, other flows and positions of resident institutional units with institutional units in third countries are recorded in the rest of the world accounts.

10.34. An important characteristic of the 2008 SNA for the purposes of monetary union aggregates is that the resident institutional sector accounts are not consolidated. This means, for example, that transactions between financial corporations are shown gross on both the resources/changes in liabilities and uses/changes in assets sides in the transaction accounts and are not netted. This makes it possible to sum sectoral accounts across the countries belonging to a union to give an aggregate which is conceptually equivalent to the national results.

2. Compilation of balance of payments and international investment position data in monetary unions

(a) Aggregating national data by taking into account intra transactions and positions

10.35. The compilation of balance of payments and international investment position data in a monetary union (and also in an economic union) has implications for the collection of data at the national level in that the issue of geographical allocation of stocks and flows, which is not essential for national data, becomes fundamental. Compiling the balance of payments and the international investment position of a monetary union from the simple aggregation of national data would not be appropriate.

10.36. There are several reasons for this. The compilation of a monetary union balance of payments and international investment position by the simple addition of gross national data would unduly inflate the gross flows and stocks of the monetary union because these would also include transactions and positions between monetary union members ("intra" transactions). The addition of only the net national transactions or positions of the monetary union members would solve this problem, but would provide only net aggregates, because only net balances could be shown, without separating out debits from credits in the current account and assets from liabilities in the financial account. In addition, it is very likely that, in practice, intra transactions would not cancel out entirely because of asymmetries in bilateral figures, which would result in erroneous aggregate data.

10.37. Therefore, the compilation of the balance of payments and the international investment position of a monetary union is typically undertaken by aggregating the national contributions for compiling the transactions and positions of the monetary union with non-residents of the monetary union, the so-called extra-monetary union data. Given the aggregation of data from different economies, it is essential that the monetary union member economies consistently follow the internationally agreed standards for classifying transactions and assets and liabilities, and provide adequate metadata describing their methodology.

10.38. Data on intra transactions and positions can also be essential. An example is with portfolio investment, where liabilities vis-à-vis non-residents of the monetary union may need to be calculated as the difference between total national securities liabilities to non-residents and the transactions and positions in these securities by residents in the other monetary union economies. The reason for this is that national balance of payments and international investment position data collection systems may not be able to identify whether non-resident purchasers and owners of domestic securities are resident of other economies of the monetary union. In such instances, asymmetries in intra data would affect the quality of the balance of payments and international investment position data of the monetary union.

10.39. For direct investment, intra-monetary union transactions between a parent company and a branch or subsidiary located within different economies of the monetary union would be classified as domestic transactions of the monetary union. Given the different treatment of entities in a direct investment relationship in the external and domestic accounts, close cooperation among compilers may be required; for example, reinvested earnings between entities in different monetary union member economies are recorded as cross-border transactions in national balance of payments, but are not recorded as transactions in monetary union national accounts.

(b) Specific intra transactions and positions

10.40. *Initial subscriptions to a monetary union central bank's capital* are to be recorded in the balance of payments and international investment position of member economies as assets, other investment, and other equity. All the member economies and the monetary union central bank must classify this transaction and position the same.

10.41. *Claims arising from a transfer of reserve assets* to the monetary union central bank are to be classified as assets, other investment, under either other equity or currency and deposits, depending on the nature of the claim. If a monetary union member does not fully meet its obligations to transfer reserve assets to the monetary union central bank, the monetary union central bank reports a claim on the member economy. Such claims on the member economy should be classified in its balance of payments and international investment position as liabilities, other investment, other accounts payable – other, central bank (or general government), short term.

10.42. *Transactions and positions corresponding to claims and liabilities among monetary union national central banks and the monetary union central bank* (including those arising from settlement and clearing arrangements) are to be recorded for the central bank under other investment, currency and deposits or loans (depending on the nature of the claim) in the balance of payments and international investment position of member economies. If changes in these intra-monetary union assets and liabilities do not arise from transactions, relevant entries are to be made under the "other adjustment" column of the international investment position. Remuneration of these claims and liabilities is to be recorded in the balance of payments of monetary union member economies as income on a gross basis under investment income, other investment.

10.43. *Seigniorage is monetary income* accruing from the issuance of currency. Reallocations of monetary income among member economies and the monetary union central bank where no underlying asset and liability positions are recognized are to be recorded as a current transfer.

10.44. *Distribution of profits* of the monetary union central bank should be classified as income on the financial asset to which member economies' subscriptions are attributed.

3. Conversion of data in different currencies

10.45. In monetary (and economic) union accounts, transactions, other flows and positions in assets and liabilities must be expressed in one single currency. For this purpose, data recorded in the different domestic currencies are converted into a single currency by either:

(a) Using the market exchange rates (or an average thereof) prevailing during the time period for which the accounts are compiled;

(b) Using fixed exchange rates over the whole time period. The fixed rate can be the one prevailing at the end of the period, in the beginning, or as an average of exchange rates over the whole time period. The exchange rate used affects the (fixed) weight of a given member country in union aggregates;

(c) Calculating an index between consecutive periods as the weighted average of the growth indices of the data of each member country expressed in domestic currency. Weights are constructed as the exchange-rate-converted share of each member country in the first period of comparison. After a reference period is chosen as a benchmark, the chain-linked index can be applied to this benchmark to generate levels for other periods of observation.

10.46. With method (a), the weights of member countries in union aggregates are updated according to the parities of their respective currencies. Union aggregates' levels are therefore up to date at any moment in time, but their changes may be affected by exchange rate fluctuations. In the case of ratios, the impact of exchange rate fluctuations on the numerator and denominator may cancel out to a large extent.

10.47. With method (b), the weights of member countries are not updated, which preserves the changes of union aggregates from exchange rate fluctuations. However, union aggregates' levels may be influenced by the choice of the (fixed) exchange rates that reflect the parities of member countries' currencies at a given moment in time.

10.48. Method (c) preserves the changes of union aggregates from exchange rate fluctuations, whereas union aggregates' levels broadly reflect the parities in force for each time period. This is at the expense of additivity and other accounting constraints. If these are required, they must be restored as a last step.

10.49. Monetary union and economic union accounts can also be compiled by converting data recorded in the different domestic currencies into purchasing power standards.[219] Methods (a), (b) or (c) described above can be used for this purpose by replacing exchange rates by the corresponding purchasing power standards.

F. Compiling aggregates for unions

10.50. One method of compiling the monetary or economic union rest of the world accounts consists of withdrawing intra-union positions and flows from the rest of the world accounts of the member countries. Although these mirror positions and flows should balance, they generally do not do so because of the asymmetrical recording of the same position or flow in the national accounts of the counterparties.

10.51. Asymmetries create mismatches in the accounts of the monetary or economic union for the whole economy and the rest of the world, which have to be reconciled. The removal of asymmetries and the subsequent balancing of the accounts may cause further discrepancies between the union aggregates and the totals of the national accounts of the member countries.

[219] The purchasing power standard is an artificial currency unit. Theoretically, one purchasing power standard can buy the same amount of goods and services in each country. However, price differences across borders mean that different amounts of domestic currency units are needed for the same goods and services depending on the country. Purchasing power standards are derived by dividing any economic aggregate of a country in domestic currency by its respective purchasing power parities. Purchasing power standard is the technical term used by Eurostat for the common currency in which national accounts aggregates are expressed when adjusted for price level differences using purchasing power parities. Thus, purchasing power parities can be interpreted as the exchange rate of the purchasing power standard against the euro.

Box 10.1

Currency in circulation in the euro area and in the individual euro area member States

Currency circulation in the euro area

Currency in circulation is the amount of euro currency issued and in circulation (i.e. not held by the European Central Bank and euro area national central banks themselves), and is the sum of amounts recorded by Eurosystem[a] central banks and the European Central Bank. In principle it also includes estimates of foreign currency banknotes and coins held by euro area residents.

Some information is available on holdings of currency. MFIs (other than central banks) and post office giro institutions report their own holdings of euro and non-euro currency monthly. MFIs distinguish between euro and other currency amounts; post office giro institutions report the two indistinguishably (presumably holdings of foreign currency are very small). Central governments report holdings of euro currency (but not holdings of other currencies) monthly. The investment fund and financial vehicle corporations statistics do not show the reporting institutions' holdings of currency; presumably they are very small. More significantly, banknote shipments by euro area commercial banks to banks located outside the euro area provide some information on holdings outside the euro area. It is assumed that such shipments account for most transactions in currency with non-residents of the euro area. Currency carried outside the euro area by travellers or movements linked to tax evasion are thought to be less important. In any case, these are difficult to measure accurately.

The European Central Bank has developed a method of estimating holdings of euro currency outside the euro area for balance of payments/international investment position and euro area accounts purposes,[b] using a weighted average of two different approaches. Estimated holdings outside the euro area are subtracted from the euro currency issuance to derive euro currency holdings by euro area residents. Guideline ECB/2011/23 (recast) formalizes the reporting of banknote shipments from March 2013.

Holdings of euro currency by entities resident in the euro area other than MFIs, post office giro institutions and central government may therefore be estimated by residual. The inevitable difficulty of estimating holdings outside the euro area and the possibility that post office giro institutions hold some foreign currency amounts introduce considerable uncertainty into estimates of the total holdings of the residual sectors (households, non-financial corporations, financial corporations other than MFIs, and governmental agencies outside central government); dividing holdings among the residual sectors is even more uncertain. Further uncertainty attaches to their holdings of foreign currency notes and coins.

Currency circulation in the individual euro area member States

Euro area financial accounts draw on national financial accounts submitted under guidelines ECB/2002/7 and ECB/2005/13. Individual member States in the euro area cannot, however, directly measure euro currency in circulation nationally, which may bear little relation to the amount actually issued by the national central bank or to the amount notionally attributed to it through the banknote allocation mechanism. Before 2009, the legal allocation according to the banknote allocation key was disregarded in compiling financial accounts, and the actual issue of currency by the national central bank was recorded on the liabilities side of the account. Intra-Eurosystem positions arising from the legal allocation of banknotes were accordingly not a feature of national financial accounts.

Since 2009, however, banknotes in circulation have been recorded in the national financial accounts of the euro area member States as a liability according to the share of the country concerned in the capital of the European Central Bank. This represents the liability of the central bank of that country in respect of euro banknotes in issue and also reflects its share in the seigniorage ("monetary income").[c] The difference between the Member State's liability in respect of currency (calculated from the capital share mechanism) and estimated holdings of euro currency by its residents (see below) will be recorded as a deposit liability to or a claim on the rest of the world.

No detailed surveys on currency holdings by residents of participating (i.e. euro area) member States are available. Some euro area member States estimate residents' holdings using explanatory variables related to the demand for currency. The variables "overnight deposits and deposits redeemable at notice" and household consumption expenditure are the most useful in tests using regression techniques to "explain" domestic holdings of currency in the form of euro banknotes and coins.

The procedure of allocating the euro currency issue among member States also uses national information available in some countries, which may reflect experience with national currency circulation before the cash changeover in 2002 (or later depending on the date of joining the euro area) and which is still considered relevant in the new circumstances. But, however national statisticians estimate currency in circulation for national financial accounts, the total must add up to the amount issued by the Eurosystem as a whole less the European Central Bank's estimate for non-resident holdings (and of course the amounts held by MFIs). Euro area member States that do not make their own national estimates share out the residual in proportion to the capital share mechanism. To ensure consistency, the allocation of currency in circulation among the member States is agreed between the European Central Bank and national statisticians.

Amounts outstanding of national currency put into circulation before the cash changeover should be recorded in other accounts payable (AF8). (This departs from the treatment in euro area monetary statistics, where they remain in currency in circulation and therefore in the monetary aggregates for a year after the cash changeover). Holdings by euro area residents of foreign currency banknotes and coins draw on national estimates.

---

[a] The Eurosystem comprises the European Central Bank and the national central banks of those European Union member States that have adopted the euro.

[b] Euro area monetary statistics, however, include total euro currency in circulation, other than holdings of MFIs in the euro area.

[c] The capital share mechanism does not cover coins, which continue to be recorded in national financial accounts as the amount issued by the national central bank. As noted earlier, coins are in fact a liability of central government but, by convention, the coin issue is recorded as a liability of the central bank to which is imputed a corresponding claim on the government. In euro area aggregates, coins are similarly deemed to be a liability of the Eurosystem, matched by an imputed claim on government.

1. Aggregated balance sheet of monetary financial institutions in a monetary union

10.52. The aggregated balance sheet of monetary financial institutions in a monetary union consists of the aggregated balance sheets of the system of monetary union central banks (i.e. the monetary union national central banks and the monetary union central bank) and of all other monetary financial institutions resident in the monetary union.

10.53. It is derived by aggregating the national balance sheets of all the monetary union national central banks and of the monetary union central bank. Similarly, the national balance sheets of all other monetary financial institutions for all countries participating in the monetary union are aggregated by summing. The aggregated balance sheets of the system of monetary union central banks and of the other monetary financial institutions are then aggregated by summing them, item by item, into the aggregated balance sheet of the monetary union money-issuing sector. It provides the basis for deriving the consolidated balance sheet. The same procedure applies to transactions.

2. Consolidated balance sheet of monetary financial institutions in a monetary union

10.54. The starting point for deriving the consolidated balance sheet is the aggregated balance sheet of the money-issuing sector in the monetary union as a whole. The consolidated balance sheet of the money-issuing sector provides statistical information on the money-issuing sector's assets and liabilities vis-à-vis residents of the monetary union outside the money-issuing sector (i.e. general government and all other monetary union residents) and vis-à-vis non-residents of the monetary union. It is obtained by netting the inter-money-issuing sector positions within the monetary union. The netting of inter-money-issuing sector positions is not confined to deposits and loans, but covers all balance sheet items where counterparty information enables the amount of the money-issuing sector liability held within the money-issuing sector to be determined.

10.55. For example, in the case of currency issued, the amounts held within the money-issuing sector are netted out. By convention, the remainder, which may be held by the monetary union money-holding sector, by central government or by the rest of the world, is allocated fully to the monetary union money-holding sector and is thus included in the monetary aggregates. Similar difficulties may arise for MMF shares or units, or debt securities issued by the money-issuing sector.

3. Data on monetary financial institutions as an input to financial accounts and balance sheets by institutional sector for a union

10.56. Balance sheet data of monetary financial institutions are an important input to compiling the financial accounts and balance sheets by institutional sector for a union. However, the data may depart in limited but important ways from the 2008 SNA definitions and accounting principles, which underlie the institutional sector accounts.

10.57. The most important departures from the 2008 SNA relate to the treatment of interest accruing on deposits and loans and the valuation of securities. It is also difficult to link some financial instruments with the corresponding 2008 SNA financial asset categories.

10.58. To enable accounting information to be used for statistical purposes, monetary financial institutions' balance sheet statistics allow discretion in the valuation of securities, whereas the 2008 SNA recommends the use of market prices for both transactions and positions.

10.59. Some balance sheet items, such as "remaining assets" and "remaining liabilities", may not coincide with the 2008 SNA financial instrument category "other accounts receivable/payable". Apart from accrued interest, these items include business in financial derivatives, in some cases current profit and loss, which properly belongs in capital and reserves.

4. Comparing different statistical data sources

10.60. Bringing together information from different sources means making choices. For example, money-issuing corporations' balance sheets may show amounts for deposits from and loans to other (non-monetary) financial intermediaries that differ from supposedly mirror data from the other (non-monetary) financial intermediaries side. Similarly, government finance data may be inconsistent with the money-issuing corporation data on positions or transactions with government entities.

10.61. Compilers may choose what they consider to be the more reliable source, making compensatory adjustments to the counterpart data as necessary, although they may be constrained in doing so, for example by a requirement to give priority to government finance data.

10.62. While much of the financial accounts data may be based on money-issuing corporations' balance sheets and other data, differences may arise for the reasons described.

10.63. There may also be certain other constraints, such as the need to balance vertically the non-financial accounts vis-à-vis the financial accounts of the financial corporations, general government and rest of the world sectors, and to balance horizontally the various financial instrument categories. All these consistency requirements may imply further deviations from the data originally provided as aggregated and consolidated data for monetary financial institutions.

5. Sectoral balance sheets

10.64. In the accounts for economic and monetary unions, sectoral balance sheets can be compiled not only for monetary financial institutions but also for all other financial corporations by subsector. Several steps must be distinguished:

(a) The sectoral balance sheets of the member countries are complemented by the balance sheets of all union institutions;

(b) Positions of financial assets of a resident of the union held by another resident ("intra positions") are withdrawn from the national rest of the world accounts;

(c) Imbalances created by the mismatch between intra-positions of financial assets and the corresponding liabilities are allocated to different sectors through balancing.

10.65. Non-financial assets as part of the sectoral balance sheets are compiled as the sum of the non-financial assets of the member countries of the economic or monetary union.

(a) From-whom-to-whom accounts

10.66. In union accounts, from whom-to-whom presentations are compiled by aggregating the national matrices and reclassifying intra transactions and intra positions as resident flows and stocks.

(b) The rest of the world accounts

10.67. The rest of the world accounts (balance of payments and international investment position data) for an economic or monetary union record the transactions and positions of financial assets and liabilities between the resident units of the union and non-resident units. Hence, the rest of the world accounts for an economic or monetary union exclude transactions and positions taking place or existing within the union. The transactions taking place within the union are called "intra transactions" and the financial positions between residents of the union are called "intra positions".

10.68. A foreign direct investment (FDI) enterprise is considered a resident of the union where an investor who is not a resident owns 10 per cent or more of the ordinary shares or voting power (for an incorporated enterprise) or the equivalent (for an unincorporated enterprise). In the national accounts of the member country, an FDI enterprise may have investors which are residents of another member country. The corresponding reinvested earnings are not recorded in the accounts.

10.69. One method of compiling the rest of the world accounts for an economic or monetary union consists of withdrawing intra transactions, on both the resources and the uses sides, from the rest of the world accounts of the member countries. Although these mirror transactions should, in theory, balance, they generally do not do so in practice because of the asymmetrical recording of the same transaction in the national accounts of the counterparties.

10.70. Asymmetries create a mismatch in union accounts between the total economy and the rest of the world accounts. Compiling union accounts therefore requires reconciliation of the accounts, achieved by methods such as the least squares criterion or proportional allocation. In the case of goods, intra-union trade statistics may be used to allocate asymmetries by expenditure category.

10.71. Removing asymmetries and the subsequent balancing of the accounts causes further differences between union aggregates and the sum of the national accounts of the member countries.

Box 10.2

Compiling European Monetary Union financial accounts and balance sheets

National financial accounts data submitted by national central banks and, in some countries, national statistical offices contribute much to the European Monetary Union financial accounts and balance sheets (euro area accounts).

However, the euro area accounts do not draw on national financial accounts alone. Substantial contributions are also made by the euro area monetary financial institutions' (MFI) balance sheet data (the main source for monetary statistics); euro area series on the assets and liabilities of investment funds, financial corporations engaged in the securitization of assets, especially in connection with securitizations, and insurance corporations and pension funds; securities issues statistics (issues, redemptions and outstandings); and the euro area balance of payments and international investment position statistics. For the institutional sector general government and its subsectors, the data compiled in accordance with a sector-specific legal framework are integrated into the euro area accounts.

Thus, the euro area accounts data are in general solidly based on the following four important areas of statistics:

- Data based on MFI balance sheets, in particular the data showing MFI business with other institutional sectors in the euro area. Although misclassifications can never be ruled out, MFI balance sheets provide reliable counterpart information on a substantial part of financial assets held by, and loan finance extended to, other sectors in the euro area.
- Securities issued by borrowers resident in the euro area. Detailed information on such (and many other) securities, including equity, is held in the European Central Bank's centralized securities database and in national securities databases. The centralized securities database includes information on the sector of the issuer, the nature of the instrument and its price, as well as information to estimate the prices of unquoted shares. The main information still lacking, however, concerns holders of securities. The development of securities holdings statistics is a high priority project for the European Central Bank. Some member States are already well advanced in collecting holder information security by security from custodians and other sources on debt and equity securities.
- The financial accounts of general government. Here European Union legislation (Regulation No. 501/2004) requires timely quarterly financial account and balance sheet information.
- The euro area balance of payments and international investment position. Some modifications are necessary to complete the rest of the world (S2) account. Nevertheless, these are well-established sources designed with euro area aggregates in mind.

For the two sectors in which European Central Bank users of the accounts take the closest interest – households and non-financial corporations – MFIs, the dominant financial intermediaries in the euro area, and the other sources mentioned above provide much or most of the financing needs and outlets for financial asset accumulation.

Source information is lacking or weak in the following areas, and estimates are usually required to compile data:

- The financing of households except through MFIs.
- The financial assets of households except in the form of claims on MFIs, investment funds and insurance corporations and pension funds.
- The financing of non-financial corporations except through MFIs and the issue of securities, including inter-company financing.
- The financial assets of non-financial corporations except in the form of claims on MFIs, including assets arising from inter-company financing.
- Financing and financial investment of financial corporations other than MFIs, investment funds, financial corporations engaged in the securitization of assets and insurance corporations and pension funds, except so far as the information is available as counterpart information from reporting financial corporations or from securities databases.

The question of a correct sectorization across the euro area and the distinction between domestic and euro area residency and residency outside the euro area need to be considered. A complication here is that the treatment in the accounts of some transactions and positions depends on whether they are internal or cross-border: the concepts of direct investment and associated income and, within the latter, the treatment of undistributed profits in the income account, are confined to cross-border business.

Thus, what is classified in French and German national statistics as a direct investment by a French enterprise in a German subsidiary must be reclassified in the euro area accounts. A further issue concerns the residence status of European Union institutions and other bodies. With the exception of the European Central Bank, which is treated statistically as an MFI resident in the euro area, although not resident in any individual Member State, such institutions are treated statistically as non-resident in both national and euro area statistics, regardless of their physical location. Financial transactions or positions between them and entities in the euro area are thus treated in euro area aggregates as transactions or positions between the euro area and the rest of the world. (For some operational purposes, the European Investment Bank is treated as resident in the euro area, but this does not affect its statistical classification as non-resident despite its location in Luxembourg).

Achieving full consistency in the euro area accounts is very difficult, given that data come from many different sources which, regardless of the principles underlying the accounts, are in practice unlikely to record transactions and balance sheet positions consistently. Even if consistency is achieved in the national data, it is unlikely to be preserved in the euro area aggregates without further adjusting the results.

The reason for this is that balance of payments transactions and the international investment position within the euro area are known to contain large discrepancies. Thus, while within national financial accounts the financial transactions of domestic sectors may be constrained to equal the financial transactions of the rest of the world (S2) – with the result that the sum of the net financial transactions of the rest of the world columns in the accounts of the euro area member States equals the sum of their domestic sectors' financial transactions – domestic sectors' financial transactions in the euro area will not sum to the financial account in the euro area balance of payments.

It is similarly difficult to achieve full consistency in domestic sectors' financial assets and liabilities outstanding and the euro area international investment position. This is because the euro area balance of payments and international investment position are compiled from extra-euro area transactions and positions and do not use the data on transactions and positions within the area which are known to be inconsistent between member States.

References

Allen, M., and others (2002). A balance sheet approach to financial crisis. IMF Working Paper, No. 02/210. Available from www.imf.org/external/pubs/cat/longres.aspx?sk=16167.0.

Australian Bureau of Statistics (1999). The measurement of non-life insurance output in the Australian national accounts. Paper presented at the OECD Meeting of National Accounts Experts, 21-24 September, Paris, France. Available from www.oecd.org/dataoecd/62/2/2681028.pdf.

Backus, D., and others (1980). A model of U.S. financial and non-financial economic behavior. *Journal of Money, Credit, and Banking*, No. 12 (2) (May), pp. 259-293.

Bank for International Settlements, International Monetary Fund and European Central Bank (forthcoming). *Handbook on Securities Statistics.* Available from www.imf.org/external/np/sta/wgsd/hbook.htm.

Bloem, A. M., C. Gorter and L. Rivas (2006). Output of central banks. Paper presented at the fourth meeting of the Advisory Expert Group on National Accounts, 30 January-8 February, Frankfurt am Main, Germany. Available from http://unstats.un.org/unsd/nationalaccount/aeg/papers/m4cb.PDF.

Cagan, P. D. (1956). The monetary dynamics of hyper-inflation. In *Studies in the Quantity Theory of Money*, Milton J. Friedman, ed. Chicago: University of Chicago Press.

Castrén, O., and I.K. Kavonius (2009). Balance sheet interlinkages and macro-financial risk analysis in the euro area. ECB Working Paper Series, No. 1124 (December). Available from www.ecb.europa.eu/pub/pdf/scpwps/ecbwp1124.pdf.

Chavoix-Mannato, M. (2011). Working party on financial statistics: Proceedings of the workshop on securitization. OECD Statistics Working Papers, No. 2011/03. OECD Publishing. Available from http://dx.doi.org/10.1787/5kg3h0jssnq6-en.

Chen, B., and D.J. Fixler (2003). Measuring the services of property-casualty insurance in the NIPAs. *Survey of Current Business* (October), pp. 10-26. Available from www.bea.gov/scb/pdf/2003/10October/1003Insurance2.pdf.

Coleman, B. E., and J. Wynne-Williams (2006). *Rural Finance in the Lao People's Democratic Republic: Demand, Supply, and Sustainability.* Manila: Asian Development Bank. Available from www.adbi.org/files/2006.rural.finance.lao.pdf.

Dippelsman, R. (2009). Recording of defined benefit pension schemes in macroeconomic statistics. Paper presented at the first European Central Bank/Eurostat workshop on pensions, 29-30 April, Frankfurt am Main, Germany. Available from www.ecb.int/pub/pdf/other/ecbeurostatworkshoponpensions201002en.pdf.

European Central Bank (2008). Regulation (EC) No. 24/2009 of the European Central Bank of 19 December 2008 concerning statistics on the assets and liabilities of financial vehicle corporations engaged in securitization transactions (ECB/2008/30) (OJ L 15, 20.1.2009, p. 1).

__________. *Financial Stability Review.* Frankfurt am Main. Available from www.ecb.europa.eu/pub/fsr/html/index.en.html.

__________. Handbook on quarterly financial accounts for the euro area: sources and methods. Frankfurt am Main. Available from www.ecb.europa.eu/stats/pdf/eaa/Handbook_on_quarterly_financial_accounts.pdf.

European Council (1996). Council Regulation (EC) No. 2223/96 of 25 June 1996 on the European system of national and regional accounts in the Community (ESA95) (OJ L 310, 30.11.96, p. 1). Available from http://eur-lex.europa.eu/LexUriServ/LexUriServ.do?uri=CELEX:31996R2223:EN:HTML.

European Parliament and Council (2013). Regulation (EU) No. 575/2013 of the European Parliament and of the Council of 26 June 2013 on prudential requirements for credit institutions and investment firms and amending Regulation (EU) No. 648/2012 (OJ L 176, 27.6.2013, p. 1).

Eurostat (2001). *Handbook on Price and Volume Measures in National Accounts*. Available from http://ec.europa.eu/eurostat/ramon/statmanuals/files/KS-41-01-543-__-N-EN.pdf.

__________ (2011). *Manual on Sources and Methods for the Compilation of ESA95 Financial Accounts*. Second edition 2011 update. Available from http://epp.eurostat.ec.europa.eu/cache/ITY_OFFPUB/KS-RA-11-004/EN/KS-RA-11-004-EN.PDF.

__________ (2013). *Manual on Government Deficit and Debt: Implementation of ESA95*. Luxembourg. Available from http://epp.eurostat.ec.europa.eu/cache/ITY_OFFPUB/KS-RA-13-001/EN/KS-RA-13-001-EN.PDF.

Eurostat and European Central Bank (2011). *Technical Compilation Guide for Pension Data in National Accounts*. Eurostat methodologies and working papers. Available from www.ecb.int/pub/pdf/other/techn_comp_gd_pens_dt_nat_accts_201201en.pdf.

Financial Stability Board and International Monetary Fund (2009). The financial crisis and information gaps: Report to the Group of 20 finance ministers and central bank governors (October). Washington, D. C. Available from www.imf.org/external/np/g20/pdf/102909.pdf.

Girón, C., and others (2011). Developing and implementing euro area accounts. Paper presented at the IMF-OECD Conference on Strengthening Sectoral Position and Flow Data in the Macroeconomic Accounts, 28 February-2 March, Washington, D.C. Available from www.imf.org/external/np/seminars/eng/2011/sta/pdf/euroarea.pdf.

Hood, K. K. (2013). Measuring the services of commercial banks in the national income and products accounts. *Survey of Current Business*, (February), pp. 8-19. Available from www.bea.gov/scb/pdf/2013/02%20February/0213_nipa-rev.pdf.

India, Ministry of Statistics and Programme Implementation (2001). Report of the National Statistical Commission (September). Available from http://mospi.nic.in/Mospi_New/site/inner.aspx?status=2&menu_id=87.

Inter-Agency Task Force on Finance Statistics (forthcoming). *External Debt Statistics: Guide for Compilers and Users*. Available from www.tffs.org/edsguide.htm.

International Accounting Standards Board (2010). The conceptual framework for financial reporting 2010 (September). Available from www.ifrs.org/News/Press-Releases/Documents/ConceptualFW2010vb.pdf.

International Accounting Standards Committee (1989). Framework for the preparation and presentation of financial statements (July).

International Monetary Fund (2000). *Monetary and Financial Statistics Manual.* Washington, D.C. Available from www.imf.org/external/pubs/ft/mfs/manual/index.htm.

__________ (2001a). *Financial Organization and Operations of the IMF.* Pamphlet Series No. 45, sixth Edition. Washington, D.C.

__________ (2001b). *Government Finance Statistics Manual.* Washington, D.C. Available from www.imf.org/external/pubs/ft/gfs/manual/pdf/all.pdf.

__________ (2002). *The Coordinated Portfolio Investment Survey Guide.* Second edition. Washington, D.C. Available from http://cpis.imf.org.

__________ (2003). *External Debt Statistics: Guide for Compilers and Users* (June). Available from www.imf.org/external/pubs/ft/eds/Eng/Guide/index.htm.

__________ (2006). *Financial Soundness Indicators: Compilation Guide* (March). Available from www.imf.org/external/pubs/ft/fsi/guide/2006/index.htm.

__________ (2008). *Monetary and Financial Statistics: Compilation Guide.* Washington, D.C. Available from www.imf.org/external/pubs/ft/cgmfs/eng/pdf/cgmfs.pdf.

__________ (2009). *Balance of Payments and International Investment Position Manual.* Sixth Edition. Available from www.imf.org/external/pubs/ft/bop/2007/pdf/bpm6.pdf.

__________ (2010). *The Coordinated Direct Investment Survey Guide.* Washington, D.C. (March). Available from www.imf.org/external/np/sta/cdis/index.htm.

__________ (2011). *Public Sector Debt Statistics : Guide for Compilers and Users.* Washington, D.C. Available from http://www.tffs.org/pdf/method/PSDS11fulltext.pdf.

__________ (2014). *Government Finance Statistics Manual 2014.* Available from www.imf.org/external/np/sta/gfsm/index.htm.

__________. Global financial stability report. Washington, D.C. Available from www.imf.org/external/pubs/ft/gfsr/.

__________ (forthcoming). *Balance of Payments and International Investment Position Compilation Guide.* Available from www.imf.org/external/pubs/ft/bop/2007/bop6comp.htm.

__________ (forthcoming). *Monetary and Financial Statistics Manual and Compilation Guide.*

Jaeger, A. (2003). Corporate balance sheet restructuring and investment in the euro area. IMF Working Paper, No. 03/117 (June). Available from www.imf.org/external/pubs/cat/longres.cfm?sk=16536.0.

Kulshreshtha, A. C. (2006). Treatment of informal sector financial activities including own moneylenders in the SNA. Paper presented at the fourth meeting of the Advisory Expert Group on National Accounts, 30 January-8 February, Frankfurt am Main, Germany. Available from http://unstats.un.org/unsd/nationalaccount/aeg/papers/m4MoneyLendersKulsh.PDF.

Lequiller, F. (2004). Recommendations on the measurement of the production of non-life insurance. Paper presented at the First Meeting of the Advisory Expert Group on National Accounts, 16-20 February, Washington, D.C. Available from http://unstats.un.org/unsd/nationalaccount/aeg/papers/m1%28p%29insurance.PDF.

Lima, F., and O. Monteiro (2011). An integrated analysis of the Portuguese economy: The financial and the real economy. Banco de Portugal, *Supplement to the Statis-*

tical Bulletin, 2/2011, pp. 37-49. Available from www.bportugal.pt/en-US/Estatisticas/PublicacoesEstatisticas/Tumbnails%20List%20Template/sup-be%202-2011-en.pdf.

McIntosh, S. H., and E. Ball Holmquist (2012). U.S. flow of funds accounts. Paper presented to the National Association of Business Economists at the Economic Measurement Seminar, Arlington, Virginia, 31 July. Available from http://nabe-web.com/ems2012/presentations/mcintosh_ems.pdf.

Mink, R. (2005). Selected key issues of financial accounts statistics. *IFC Bulletin*, No. 21 (July), pp. 6-24. Available from www.bis.org/ifc/publ/ifcb21.pdf.

Moulton, B. R., and E. P. Seskin (2003). Preview of the 2003 comprehensive revision of the national income and product accounts: Changes in definitions and classifications. *Survey of Current Business* (June), pp. 17-34. Available from www.bea.gov/scb/pdf/2003/06June/0603NIPArevs.pdf.

Nordin, A. (2006). The production of financial corporations and price/volume measurement of financial services and non-life insurance services. Paper presented at the fourth meeting of the Advisory Expert Group on National Accounts, 30 January-8 February, Frankfurt am Main, Germany. Available from http://unstats.un.org/unsd/nationalaccount/aeg/papers/m4FinancialServices.PDF.

Organisation for Economic Co-operation and Development (1998). FISIM. Paper presented at the joint OECD/ESCAP meeting on national accounts, 4-8 May, Bangkok. Available from www.oecd.org/std/na/2664768.pdf.

__________ (2009). *Measuring Capital: OECD Manual*. Second edition. Available from www.oecd.org/std/productivitystatistics/43734711.pdf.

Reinsdorf, M. B. (2009). Actuarial measures of defined benefit pension plan. Paper presented at the first European Central Bank/Eurostat workshop on pensions, 29-30 April, Frankfurt am Main, Germany. Available from www.ecb.int/pub/pdf/other/ecbeurostatworkshoponpensions201002en.pdf.

__________ (2011). Comment on the treatment of defined benefit pensions in 2008 SNA. Paper presented at the meeting of the review group for the United Nations/European Central Bank *Handbook on Financial Production, Flows and Stocks in the System of National Accounts*, 7-8 July, New York.

Reinsdorf, M. B., and D.G. Lenze (2009). Defined benefit pensions and household income and wealth. *Survey of Current Business* (August), pp. 50-62. Available from www.bea.gov/scb/pdf/2009/08%20August/0806_benefits.pdf.

Seskin, E. P., and S. Smith (2009). Preview of the 2009 comprehensive revision of the NIPAs: Changes in definitions and presentations. *Survey of Current Business* (March), pp. 10-27. Available from www.bea.gov/scb/pdf/2009/03%20March/0309_nipa_preview.pdf.

Shrestha, M. (2012). Templates for minimum and encouraged sets of internationally comparable sectoral national accounts and balance sheets. *SNA News and Notes*, No. 34 (July). Available from https://unstats.un.org/unsd/nationalaccount/sna/nn34-En.pdf.

Shrestha, M., and R. Mink (2011). An integrated framework for financial flows and positions on a from-whom-to-whom basis. Paper presented at the IMF-OECD conference on strengthening sectoral position and flow data in the macroeconomic accounts, 28 February-2 March, Washington, D.C.. Available from www.imf.org/external/np/seminars/eng/2011/sta/pdf/whom.pdf.

Sundararajan, V., and others (2002). Financial soundness indicators: analytical aspects and country practices. IMF Occasional Paper No. 212 (April). Available from www.imf.org/external/pubs/nft/op/212/.

Teplin, A. M. (2001). The U.S. flow of funds accounts and their uses. *Federal Reserve Bulletin* (July). Available from www.federalreserve.gov/pubs/bulletin/2001/0701lead.pdf.

United Nations, Eurostat, International Monetary Fund, Organisation for Economic Co-operation and Development and World Bank (1993). *System of National Accounts 1993*. Sales No. E.94.XVII.4. Available from http://unstats.un.org/unsd/nationalaccount/docs/1993sna.pdf.

United Nations, European Commission, International Monetary Fund, Organisation for Economic Co-operation and Development and World Bank (2009). *System of National Accounts 2008*. Sales No. E.08.XVII.29. Available from http://unstats.un.org/unsd/nationalaccount/docs/SNA2008.pdf.

ISBN 978-92-1-161577-7

13-48594